The Age of Terrorism

The Age of Terrorism

Walter Laqueur

LITTLE, BROWN AND COMPANY
BOSTON   TORONTO   LONDON

FIRST AMERICAN EDITION

Parts of this book first appeared in Walter Laqueur's
Terrorism, published in 1977.

Library of Congress Cataloging-in-Publication Data

Laqueur, Walter, 1921–
    The age of terrorism.

    Rev. ed. of: Terrorism. 1977.
    Bibliography: p.
    Includes index.
    1. Terrorism. I. Laqueur, Walter, 1921–
Terrorism. II. Title.
HV 6431.L36   1987   303.6′25   87-3652

ISBN 0-316-51478-0 (HC)
ISBN 0-316-51479-9 (PB)

10 9 8 7 6 5 4 3 2

RRD-VA

PRINTED IN THE UNITED STATES OF AMERICA

Contents

Introduction

1 The Origins *11*

2 The Philosophy of the Bomb *24*

3 The Sociology of Terrorism *72*

4 Interpretations of Terrorism *142*

5 The Image of the Terrorist: Literature and the Cinema *174*

6 Terrorism Today I: Nationalism and Separatism *203*

7 Terrorism Today II: Left and Right *235*

8 Terrorism Today III: International Terrorism *266*

9 Conclusions *298*

Bibliography *323*

Notes *334*

Abbreviations *361*

Index *364*

Introduction

Terrorism, one of the most widely discussed issues of our time, remains one of the least understood. Its recent manifestations have been described in countless books, monographs, articles, plays, novels and films at all possible levels of sophistication; terrorism has fascinated the metaphysicians as much as the popular novelists. This essay originally grew out of a study of guerrilla warfare, from which I concluded that urban terrorism is not a new stage in guerrilla war, but differs from it in essential respects, and that it is also heir to a different tradition. It was not my intention to deal with the problem of responses to terror, nor to describe in systematic detail various recent terrorist movements; this has been done elsewhere more or less comprehensively and competently. On the other hand, the reaction to terrorism could not be entirely ignored because the fortunes of terrorism depend largely on the response it encounters from both the public and the authorities. However, the emphasis of this study is on issues which seem to me of key importance – the doctrine of systematic terrorism, the sociology of terrorist groups, the current interpretations, the common patterns, the motives and aims, and, lastly, the efficacy of terrorism.

My original work in the middle 1970s was helped by a generous grant from the Thyssen Foundation; research and editorial assistance was provided by Kimbriel Mitchell, Aviva Golden, Janet Langmaid and Bernard Krikler. The present study, which appears almost exactly ten years later, is based on this original work, but only chapter one and two appear in this volume without change. For I had not only to record the many developments and changes during the last decade, but also to rethink the major problems in the light of these events. My work on the new book was assisted by a grant from the Earhart Foundation. I owe a debt of gratitude to Sophia Miskiewicz, Janusz Bugajski, Marek Gadzinski, Paul Saivetz, John Gutbezahl, Christopher Bussell, David Janssen, Michael Evans and Heidi Liszka, who helped me with my research. Lastly, I had to consider the observations made by critics of the first edition of this book. A short account of its reception should perhaps be my starting point. When *Terrorism* first appeared in 1977 it was on the whole well received; some reviewers thought that it was bound to become a classic, and the most comprehensive bibliography in the field, published six years later, mentioned it as perhaps the most influential work to have appeared to date.[1]

At the same time, disagreement was registered from various quarters. Some argued that I tended to belittle the importance of terrorism as a central and very dangerous political phenomenon in our time. Others maintained that I was too sceptical with regard to the potential contribution of political scientists, psychologists and other scholars towards a scientific theory of terrorism. It was said that my emphasis on the important differences between guerrilla warfare and terrorism was too rigid, or perhaps altogether artificial, and that the common features between these two forms of violence outweighed the differences. Some claimed that my study (in common with many others) was basically flawed because, instead of dealing with the all-important issue of massive state terrorism, I was preoccupied with the relatively insignificant acts of violence committed by small groups of what are known in professional language as substate actors. I shall deal with these and other arguments later on; at this point I would merely like to lay to rest one specific ghost – the argument (to paraphrase a famous saying by the late Max Horkheimer) that he who does not mention state terrorism must not speak or write about individual terrorist acts. This line of thought has unfortunately befuddled much of the writing on the subject. Thus, according to one representative of this thesis, though by no means the most extreme, the strategies and tactics of terrorism have recently become integral components in both the domestic and the foreign political realms of the modern state.[2]

No one is likely to deny that the number of victims and the amount of suffering caused by tyrannical and aggressive governments throughout history has been infinitely greater than that caused by small groups of rebels. A Hitler or a Stalin have killed in one year more people than all terrorists throughout recorded history. Violence and oppression have been an 'integral component' not just during the last few years, not just of the 'modern state', but throughout all recorded history. Massacres and arbitrary rule have figured prominently in primitive society and primitive religion, from the catacombs of the victims of ancient Mexico to the days of the Inquisition, from the days of the tyrannies to the absolutist rule in early modern history. The idea of freedom and human rights has made significant progress only during the last two centuries. To write the history of oppression and persecution is to write the history of mankind.

But there are basic differences in motive, function and effect between oppression by the state (or society, or religion) and political terrorism. To equate them, to obliterate these differences, is to spread confusion and to impede the understanding of both. The study of the Inquisition or of the Gestapo or of Stalin's Gulags is of undoubted importance, but it will shed no light whatsoever on the terrorist movements which are the subject of the present investigation.

Terrorism is a violent phenomenon and it is probably no mere coincidence that it should give rise to violent emotions, such as anger, irritation and aggression, and that this should cloud judgement. Nor is the confusion surrounding it all new. Terrorism has long exercised a great fascination, especially at a safe distance, and has always engendered greatly divergent opinions and images. The fascination it exerts (Shelley's 'tempestuous love-liness of terror'), and the difficulty of interpreting it, have the same roots; it has an unexpected, shocking and outrageous character. War, even civil war, is predictable in many ways. It occurs in the light of day and there is no mystery about the identity of the participants. Even in civil war there are certain rules, whereas the characteristic features of terrorism are anonymity and the violation of established norms. The popular image of the terrorist some ninety years ago was that of a bomb-throwing, alien anarchist, dishevelled with a black beard and a satanic (or idiotic) smile, a fanatic who was immoral, sinister and ridiculous at the same time. Dostoevski and Conrad provided more sophisticated but essentially similar descriptions. His present-day image has been streamlined but not necessarily improved; it certainly has not been explained by political scientists or psychiatrists called in for rapid consultation. Perhaps it is unfair to blame them, for there are so many different kinds of terrorists that generalizations are almost bound to be misleading.

Terrorists have found admirers and publicity agents in all ages. No words of praise have been fulsome enough for these latter-day saints and martyrs. The terrorist (we are told) is the only one who really cares, he is a totally committed fighter for freedom and justice, a gentle human being forced by cruel circumstances and an indifferent majority to play heroic yet tragic roles, the good Samaritan distributing poison, a St Francis with the bomb. Such a beatification of the terrorist is grotesque, but terrorism cannot be unconditionally rejected except on the basis of a total commitment to non-violence and non-resistance to évil. Killing, as Colonel Sexby pointed out some three hundred years ago, is not always murder, and armed resistance cannot always proceed in open battle according to some *chevaleresque* code: '*Nein, eine Grenze hat Tyrannenmacht ... zum letzten Mittel wenn kein anderes mehr verfangen will, ist ihm das Schwert gegeben*' (No, tyranny does have a limit, and, as a last resort, one has the sword if nothing else avails). Schiller's famous statement about the *ultima ratio* of free man facing intolerable persecution has been invoked by generations of rebels against tyranny. For this reason, the argument that terrorism is *always* unjustifiable is untenable.

It is true that for every Wilhelm Tell there have been many self-appointed saviours of freedom and justice; impatient men, fanatics and madmen invoking the right of self-defence in vain, using the sword (and the bomb) not as the last refuge but as a panacea for all evils, real and imaginary. Patriotism has been the last refuge for many a scoundrel, and so has been the struggle for freedom. Horse thieves in Latin America used to claim political motives for their actions as a safeguard against being hanged. The study of terrorism is not made any easier by the fact that most terrorists have been neither popular heroes in the mould of Wilhelm Tell nor plain horse thieves, but both of these things as well as many others. It is a moot point whether Burke was right when he said that one only had to scratch an ideologue to find a terrorist, but it is certainly not true that scratching a terrorist will necessarily reveal an ideologue.

The interpretation of terrorism is difficult for yet other reasons. Even over the last century, the character of terrorism has changed greatly. This goes not only for its methods, but also for the aims of the struggle, and the character of the people that were and are involved in it. Only two generations divide Sofia Perovskaya and Emma Goldman from Ulrike Meinhof and Patty Hearst (not to mention Carlos and the various Abu Nidals), yet morally and intellectually the distance between them is to be measured in light years. The other difficulty is equally fundamental. Unlike Marxism, terrorism is not an ideology but an insurrectional strategy that can be used by people of very different political convictions. For this reason, simplistic explanations should be rejected *tout court*. Contemporary terrorism is not the child of Marxism–Leninism or Muslim fundamentalism, even though regimes of these creeds have made notable contributions to the spread of terrorism. Much of the prevailing confusion on the subject of terrorism would not have occurred if those delivering sweeping statements did not suffer from partial blindness. In their anger (or enthusiasm) they have focused on one specific kind of terrorism, ignoring the fact that there are also other kinds which do not fit their preconceptions. Yet terrorism is not only a technique. Those practising it today have certain basic beliefs in common. They may belong to the left or the right; they may be nationalists or, very rarely, internationalists, but in some essential respects their mental make-up is often similar. They are closer to each other than they know, or would like to admit to themselves.* And as the technology of terrorism can be mastered by people of all creeds, so does its basic philosophy transcend the traditional dividing lines between political doctrines. It is truly all-purpose and value-free.

Terrorism is not, as is frequently believed, a subspecies of guerrilla (or 'revolutionary') warfare, and its political function today is also altogether different. 'Urban guerrilla' – a term as widespread as it is fraudulent – is indeed urban, but it is not 'guerrilla' in any meaningful sense of the term. The difference between a guerrilla and a terrorist is not one of semantics but one of quality. A guerrilla leader – to put it in the briefest possible way – aims at building up ever-growing military units and eventually an army, and establishing liberated zones in which an alternative government can be put up and propaganda openly conducted. All this is quite impossible in cities; the different environment dictates a different strategy and this has basic political consequences.† While guerrillas have quite frequently used terrorist tactics vis-à-vis their enemies, the opposite has virtually never happened, for in the urban milieu there are no opportunities for guerrilla warfare. While it is easy to think of guerrilla movements which defeated the forces opposing them, and while terrorism has been on occasion a major destabilizing force, it is difficult to think of more than one or two cases in which terrorism has brought about lasting, radical change.

My study of terrorism initially grew out of dissatisfaction with many current attempts to explain and interpret political terrorism, on both the popular and the academic levels. Writing in 1976, I listed a number of widespread but mistaken beliefs concerning the main features of contemporary terrorism. Writing ten years later, this list must be expanded.

Among these erroneous beliefs, the following should be singled out:

1. Terrorism is a new and unprecedented phenomenon. For this reason, its antecedents (if any) are of little interest. But whereas modern technology has, of course, made a great difference as far as the character of terrorist

---

* One recent illustration should suffice. Jacques Vergès has been one of the most extreme public figures on the French political scene. A diehard Stalinist, and later a Maoist, he was the star defender of the Algerian rebels, of generations of Palestinian, Armenian, German and French terrorists, including the leaders of Action Directe. In 1985 he volunteered to defend Klaus Barbie, the Gestapo 'butcher of Lyon'.
† One could think of a few cases in which 'no-go areas' in cities were established by insurrectionists, but this always happened in civil-war conditions in which terrorism played only a subordinate role. Nor did an 'equilibrium' of this kind last long; either the one side prevailed, or the other. In any case, terrorism is not a synonym for popular insurgency. On the contrary, it frequently occurs when the attempts to 'raise the masses' have not succeeded or cannot succeed.

operations are concerned, the basic issues concerning terrorism – political, moral, legal – are anything but new.

2. Terrorism is one of the most important and dangerous problems facing mankind today and it should figure uppermost on our agenda. As a noted writer has put it: 'Terrorism is the cancer of the modern world.... Its growth is inexorable until it poisons and engulfs the society on which it feeds and drags it down to destruction.'[3] Cancer is a malignant disease with, more often than not, a fatal outcome. But there has not been so far a single case of a society dragged down to destruction as a result of terrorism, nor has there been inexorable growth. More Americans were killed in terrorist attacks in 1974 (forty-two) than in 1984 (eleven), and the number of terrorist bombings has been fairly constant ever since statistics were first compiled some twenty years ago.* The killing of even a single human being – let alone mass murder – is a tragedy and a crime that should be punished. The attitude towards terrorism should certainly not be one of benign neglect. But the figures show that the medical metaphor is quite misleading with regard to both the extent of the disease and its likely course.

3. The moralists claim that terrorism is the natural response to injustice, oppression and persecution. Terrorism has indeed developed in answer to repression, more often in the nineteenth century than in the twentieth. In our time the record shows that the more severe the repression, the less terrorism occurs. This is an uncomfortable and shocking fact, and many therefore refuse to accept it. Even in democratic countries the argument frequently does not hold water; terrorism in Spain gathered strength only after Franco died, while the terrorist upswing in West Germany and Turkey took place under social democratic or left-of-centre governments. The same is true of Colombia and Peru.† More examples could easily be adduced.

4. The corollary of the moralist (terrorism-as-a-punishment) thesis is that the only known means of reducing the likelihood of terrorism is a reduction of the grievances, stresses and frustrations underlying it. There is no denying the existence of grievances, for instance on the part of national

---

* These figures are based on the US State Department's most recent statistical survey *Patterns of Global Terrorism 1984* (1985). On the problematical character of world terrorism statistics see below. But as far as US victims are concerned those figures are reliable.

† The terrorists, of course, see it differently. ETA considers PSOE, the ruling socialist party in Spain, 'Nazi–Fascist', and for good measure includes the trade unions and the Communist Party in the 'fascization of the state' (Luciano Rincon, *ETA 1974–84* (Barcelona, 1985), p. 125. Ironically, some of the characteristic features of most contemporary terrorist groups such as elitism, chauvinism, brutality, etc., are those of the Fascist movements of the second quarter of the twentieth century.

minorities. In some instances, these grievances can be put right, but frequently they cannot. In an ideal world each group of people claiming the right to full independence and statehood should receive it. In the real world, given the lack of national homogeneity, this may not be possible. An Armenian state on Turkish territory is not a practical possibility, and a Sikh state in the Punjab would not be viable, quite apart from the fact that the great majority of Sikhs do not even want it. An independent Euzkadi or Corsica would be against the wishes of the majority of the population, which is neither Basque nor Corsican. These are but a few examples. Nor is it certain that the establishment of new independent states would put an end to terrorism; on the contrary, a violent struggle for power between various terrorist groups might intensify, between 'moderates', who want to proceed with the business of statehood, and 'radicals' claiming that what has been achieved is only a beginning, and that the borders of the new state should be expanded.

5. But if the moralists are wrong, does it not follow that, as the relativists argue, 'one man's terrorist is another man's freedom fighter'? Of all the observations on terrorism this is surely one of the tritest. There is no unanimity on any subject under the sun, and it is perfectly true that terrorists do have well-wishers. But such support does not tell us anything ab the justice of their cause; in 1941 Hitler and Mussolini had many fana followers. Does it follow that they fought for a just cause?

6. Yet another argument claims that terrorists are fanatical beli driven to despair by intolerable conditions. Ideas cannot be supp by imprisonment and executions, and for this reason terrorism will unless conditions change. But the evidence does not bear this o terrorist reservoir is not unlimited. If enough terrorists are kille Khomeini's Iran) or arrested (as in Turkey, Italy and other c terrorism ceases to be an effective force. Some terroristic activity nue, but it is no more than a minor nuisance.

7. Terrorists are poor and their inspiration is deeply ideological. This was more correct fifty or a hundred years ago than it is today. Terrorists belonging to international, state-sponsored networks, linked with oil producers and narco-terrorism, are no longer poor – indeed they cannot afford to be poor given the rising cost of terrorist warfare. In the old days, a dagger was sufficient, while today millions of dollars are needed for financing a terrorist infrastructure. Only the terrorist proletariat is poor. Ideology does play a role, because without ideological motivation few people would be willing to risk their lives. But ideology alone does not explain terrorism. If it were different, then Qadhafi would not have to advertise for terrorists in newspapers from Morocco to India.

8. Terrorism is essentially a Middle Eastern problem, and most of the victims of terrorism are American. Make peace between Israel and the Arabs, give the Palestinians a homeland and terrorism will cease – or at least very much decline. Peace in the Middle East is highly desirable for a variety of reasons, and a great many people have tried to bring it about, unfortunately without much success. But since there are at present many more anti-American terrorist incidents in Latin America (369) and Western Europe (458) than in the Middle East (84), there is no good reason to suppose that peace between the Arabs and Israel would have a significant effect on anti-American terrorism.[4]

9. State-sponsored terrorism presents a new dimension and is a far more dangerous threat than any past terrorist movement. Since it is so difficult to combat, it is gradually becoming the predominant mode of warfare (by proxy) in our time. There is some truth in this argument. International state-sponsored terrorism does not offer easy and obvious targets for retaliation, innocents are bound to suffer, and the state which retaliates on a military level will find itself in the role of an aggressor. But the nature of the threat should not be overrated. It will be tolerated only as long as it is not used too frequently and if it does not cause too much damage. If it becomes more than a nuisance, the political calculus changes, and the inhibitions against retaliation no longer function as the public clamour for massive retaliation grows. A process of escalation begins which may result in full-scale military conflict. For this reason, only gross miscalculation will lead the sponsors of state terrorism beyond the point of no return, inviting retaliation which will destroy them. It may happen, but it is unlikely.

10. Terrorism can happen anywhere. This proposition is correct if suitably amended – 'except in effective dictatorial regimes'. Terrorist operations are frequently carried out by very small groups of people; it is no good enlisting sociology or mass psychology as far as the motives and actions of a few individuals are concerned. For example, the inequities of Sweden's social structure will not explain the murder of Olof Palme. It is true that terrorism is more likely to occur in some countries than in others, and this, *inter alia*, is what the present study is about.

There is a paradox involved in the study of terrorism, inasmuch as the basic issues are simple and straightforward. No prolonged training in moral philosophy, psychology or the most modern methods of social research investigation are needed to understand terrorism. Yet at the same time, terrorism is likely to remain the subject of considerable misunderstanding and misinterpretation. Political scientists will find it infertile ground for their hypotheses, and philosophers for their generalizations. The average newspaper reader and television viewer will not easily accept that there is a disproportion between the publicity given to terrorism in the media and its importance in real terms. Those who defend violence (or those who reject it under all circumstances) are bound, sooner or later, to realize that their assumptions are based not on terrorism in general but on one specific kind of terrorism. The difficulty with terrorism is that there is no terrorism *per se*, except perhaps on an abstract level, but different terrorisms. It does not follow that there is no room for objective statements on the subject, that we cannot pass judgement, and should not take action. But each situation has to be viewed in its specific, concrete context, because terrorism is dangerous ground for *simplificateurs* and *généralisateurs*. To approach it, a cool head is probably more essential than any other other intellectual quality.

The importance of terrorism should not be belittled. If the statistics do not bear out the contention that terrorism is steadily rising at an alarming rate, it is also true that there are other weighty arguments concerning the peril of terrorism. The number of victims may be small, but terrorism is designed to undermine government authority, and it may have this effect by showing that democratic governments are unable to respond effectively.

But is it realistic to expect governments which are incapable of stamping out crime, or drug peddling, or illegal immigration, to have full success in the battle against terrorism? Governments cannot protect all of the citizens all of the time against muggers and thieves; likewise, they cannot protect everyone against a terrorist attack. It may well be that, as some argue, terrorism constitutes a potentially serious domestic threat. But much experience has shown that democratic societies seldom take effective measures against *potential* threats. Something akin to a dialectical process seems to be at work: only when the threat becomes clear and present are the authorities and the public sufficiently aroused to agree on the adoption of measures likely to put an end to terrorism, or at least to cause a drastic decline in terrorist activities. A great deal of terrorism could have been prevented during the last two decades if societies had shown more understanding and governments greater determination. Instead, there was an enormous amount of talk about terrorism and little action. However, if there is a real threat in the years to come it is not so much from the domestic kind of terrorism, which is usually overcome in the end, nor from the possible use of new and more deadly weapons; it is from the danger of escalation – the possibility that terrorism may trigger off a full-scale war.

1

The Origins

The terms 'terrorism' and 'terrorist' are of relatively recent date: the meaning of terrorism was given in the 1798 supplement of the *Dictionnaire* of the Académie Française as *'système, régime de la terreur'*.[1] According to a French dictionary published in 1796, the Jacobins had on occasion used the term when speaking and writing about themselves in a positive sense; after the 9th of Thermidor, 'terrorist' became a term of abuse with criminal implications.[2] It did not take long for the term to reach Britain; Burke, in a famous passage written in 1795, wrote about 'thousands of those hell hounds called terrorist' who were let loose on the people. Terrorism at the time referred to the period in the French Revolution broadly speaking between March 1793 and July 1794 and it was more or less a synonym for 'reign of terror'. Subsequently it acquired a wider meaning in the dictionaries as a system of terror. A terrorist was anyone who attempted to further his views by a system of coercive intimidation.[3] Even more recently, the term 'terrorism' (like 'guerrilla') has been used in so many different senses as to become almost meaningless, covering almost any, and not necessarily political, act of violence. According to one of the arguments frequently used against the study of political terrorism, many more people have been killed throughout history, and more havoc has been wrought, as the result of crimes committed by governments than by terrorism from below. This is not in dispute, but the present study is concerned not with political violence in general or with the inequities of tyranny but with a more specific phenomenon.

No definition of terrorism can possibly cover all the varieties of terrorism that have appeared throughout history: peasant wars and labour disputes and brigandage have been accompanied by systematic terror, and the same is true of general wars, civil wars, revolutionary wars, wars of national liberation and resistance movements against foreign occupiers. In most of these cases, however, terrorism was no more than one of several strategies, and usually a subordinate one. My concern in the present study is with movements that have used systematic terrorism as their main weapon : others will be mentioned only in passing. It is generally believed that systematic political terrorism is a recent phenomenon dating back to the last century. This is true in the sense that the 'philosophy of the bomb' as a doctrine is indeed relatively new. Yet it hardly needs to be recalled that there have been many systematic assassinations of political enemies throughout history. Like Molière's bourgeois, who had talked prose all along, there have been terrorists (and terrorist movements) *avant la lettre*. Many countries have had their Sicilian Vespers or St Bartholomew's nights ; foes, real and imaginary, were eliminated by Roman emperors, Ottoman sultans, Russian tsars and many others.

Terrorism 'from below' has emerged in many different forms and out of such various motivations as religious protest movements, political revolts and social uprisings. One of the earliest-known examples of a terrorist movement is the *sicarii*, a highly organized religious sect consisting of men of lower orders active in the Zealot struggle in Palestine (AD 66–73). The sources telling of their activities are sparse and sometimes contradictory, but it is known from Josephus that the *sicarii* used unorthodox tactics such as attacking their enemies by daylight, preferably on holidays when crowds congregated in Jerusalem. Their favourite weapon was a short sword (*sica*) hidden under their coats. In the words of the expert in De Quincey's club who considered murder as a fine art : 'Justly considering that great crowds are in themselves a sort of darkness by means of the dense pressure, and the impossibility of finding out who it was that gave the blow, they mingled with crowds everywhere . . . and when it was asked, who was the murderer and where he was – why, then it was answered "*Non est inventus*".'[4] They destroyed the house of Ananias, the high priest, as well as the palaces of the Herodian dynasts ; they burned the public archives, eager to annihilate the bonds of money-lenders and to prevent the recovery of debts. They are also mentioned in Tacitus and in the rabbinical authorities as having burned granaries and sabotaged Jerusalem's water supplies. They were the extremist, nationalist, anti-Roman party and their victims both in Palestine and in the Egyptian diaspora were the moderates, the Jewish peace party. Some authorities claim that they had an elaborate doctrine, the so-called fourth philosophy, something in the nature of a Jewish protestantism according to whose tenets God alone was considered as the Lord ; political allegiance was refused to any earthly power ; and priests were rejected as intermediaries. Others regarded the *sicarii* as a movement of social protest intent on inciting the poor to rise against the rich. Josephus doubted their idealistic motivation and claimed that they were *listai*, robbers, out for personal gain and manipulated by outside forces, with patriotism and the demand for freedom as a mere ideological cloak.[5] But even Josephus admits that there was a frenzy of religious expectation among them, inclination to regard martyrdom as something joyful and a totally irrational belief after the fall of Jerusalem that, as the sinful regime was no longer in authority, victory over the Romans was possible and also that God would reveal Himself to His people and deliver them. Such qualities were not that common among ordinary *listai*.

A similar mixture of messianic hope and political terrorism was the prominent feature of a much better-known sect – the Assassins, an offshoot of the Ismailis who appeared in the eleventh century and were suppressed only by the Mongols in the thirteenth. The Assassins have fascinated Western authorities for a long time and this interest has grown in recent times, for some of the features of this movement remind one of contemporary terrorist movements. Based in Persia the Assassins spread to Syria, killing prefects, governors, caliphs and even Conrad of Montferrat, the Crusader King of Jerusalem. They tried twice to kill Saladin but failed. Their first leader, Hassan Sibai, seems to have realized early on that his group was too small to confront the enemy in open battle but that a planned, systematic, long-term campaign of terror carried out by a small, disciplined force could be a most effective political weapon.[6] They always operated in complete secrecy; the terrorist fighters (*fidaiin*) were disguised as strangers or even Christians.[7] The Assassins always used the dagger, never poison or missiles, and not just because the dagger was considered the safer weapon: murder was a sacramental act. Contemporary sources described the Assassins as an order of almost ascetic discipline: they courted death and martyrdom and were firm believers in a new millennium. Seen in historical perspective, the terrorist struggle of the Assassins was a fruitless attempt by a relatively small religious sect to defend its religious autonomy (and way of life) against the Seljuks who wanted to suppress them. But the means they used were certainly effective for a while, and the legends about the Old Man from the Mountain deeply impressed contemporaries and subsequent generations.

Secret societies of a different kind existed for centuries in India and the Far East. The Anglo-Indian authorities denied the existence of the Thugs until Captain (subsequently Major-General) William Sleeman studied the subject and ultimately destroyed the sect. The Thugs strangled their victims with a silk tie; Europeans were hardly ever affected, but otherwise their choice of victims was quite indiscriminate. Its devotees thought the origin of Thuggee was derived from an act of sacrifice to the goddess

Kali. It had a fatal attraction. In the words of Fresingea, a captured Thug:

> Let any man taste of that goor [sugar] of the sacrifice, and he will be a Thug, though he knows all the trades and has all the wealth in the world. ... I have been in high office myself and became so great a favourite wherever I went that I was sure of promotion. Yet I was always miserable when away from my gang and obliged to return to Thuggee.[8]

The Thugs had contempt for death. Their political aims, if any, were not easily discernible; nor did they want to terrorize the government or population.

In a survey of political terrorism this phenomenon rates no more than a footnote. The same applies to the more militant secret societies in China that existed among river pirates and the outlaws in the hills as well as among respectable city dwellers. Each society had its 'enforcer', usually a trained boxer. Some engaged in criminal extortion; there were hired killers among them selling themselves to the highest bidder. The societies ran gambling houses and smuggled salt. Some of the more important societies also had distinct political aims: they were anti-Manchu and loathed foreigners.[9] They were behind the Boxer Rebellion and helped Sun Yat-sen in the early days of his career. The 'Red Spears' of the 1920s combined politics with exercises such as deep breathing and magic formulas, rather like the counter-culture of the 1960s. But politics was only one of their many activities and in this respect they resemble more the Mafia than modern political terrorist movements.[10]

The interest of the Ku Klux Klan in politics was perhaps more pronounced, but it was still not in the mainstream of terrorist movements. It is not always remembered that there was not one Klan, but three, which did not have much in common with each other. The first Klan, a product of the Reconstruction period, was a secret, violent association, proscribing recently emancipated Negroes. The second Klan (c. 1915–44) also stood for white supremacy, but at the same time it campaigned for a great many other causes such as patriotism and attacked bootleggers, crapshooters and even wife-beaters. With all the ritual mumbo-jumbo around the Great Wizard, it became very much part of establishment politics in the South, on both the local and state levels. It also engaged in various business enterprises, such as dealing in emulsified asphalt for road construction. The second Klan was in fact an incorporated society, whose history ends in April 1944, not with a dramatic shoot-out with the police but with a federal suit for $685,000 in delinquent income tax. As a result its charter had to be surrendered and the Klan went out of business.[11]

Compared with the *sicarii* and Assassins, with Thugs, Red Spears and the Ku Klux Klan, contemporary terrorist groups seem to belong to another species altogether. For the starting point to the study of modern political terrorism one clearly has to look elsewhere and this takes one back to the Wilhelm Tell syndrome. Political assassinations of leading statesmen were relatively infrequent in the age of absolutism, once the religious conflicts had lost some of their acuteness. There was solidarity between monarchs whatever their personal differences or the clashes of interest between them; they would not normally have thought of killing one another. The idea of regicide also had temporarily gone out of fashion – with a few notable exceptions. This changed only after the French Revolution and the rise of nationalism in Europe. Outside Europe there were cases of political murder, as there had been since time immemorial, but these belonged, *grosso modo*, to the tradition of dynastic quarrels or clashes between rival groups fighting for power or of military coups or the actions of fanatics or madmen.

Systematic terrorism begins in the second half of the nineteenth century and there were several quite distinct categories of it from the very beginning. The Russian revolutionaries fought an autocratic government in 1878–81 and again in the early years of the twentieth century. Radical nationalist groups such as the Irish, Macedonians, Serbs and Armenians used terrorist methods in their struggle for autonomy or national independence. Lastly, there was the anarchist 'propaganda by deed', mainly during the 1890s in France, Italy, Spain and the United States. The few assassinations in France and Italy attracted enormous publicity, but they were not really part of a general systematic strategy. The character of terrorism in the United States and Spain was again different inasmuch as it had the support of specific sections of the population. In the United States there was working-class terrorism such as practised by the Molly Maguires and later by the Western Union of Mineworkers. In Spain there was both agrarian terrorism and industrial terrorism. Seen in historical perspective the various manifestations of terrorism, however different their aims and the political context, had a common origin: they were connected with the rise of democracy and nationalism. All the grievances had existed well before: minorities had been oppressed, nations had been denied independence, autocratic government had been the rule. But as the ideas of the enlightenment spread and as the appeal of nationalism became increasingly powerful, conditions that had been accepted for centuries became intolerable. However, the movements of armed protest had a chance of success only if the ruling classes were willing to play according to the new rules, and this precluded violent repression. In short, terrorist groups could hope to tackle only non-terrorist governments with any degree of confidence. This was the paradox facing modern terrorism, and what was true with regard to repression by old-fashioned authoritarian regimes applied, *a fortiori*, to the new-style totalitarian systems of the twentieth century.

Of all these movements the Russian Narodnaya Volya was the most important by far, even though its operations lasted only from January 1878 to March 1881. The armed struggle began when Kovalski, one of its members, resisted arrest; it continued with Vera Zasulich's shooting of the governor-general of St Petersburg and reached a first climax with the assassination of General Mezentsev, the head of the third section (the tsarist political police) in August 1878. In September 1879 Alexander II was sentenced to death by the revolutionary tribunal of the Narodnaya Volya. Even before, in April of that year, Solovev had tried to kill the tsar, but this had been a case of failed private initiative. Further attempts were no more successful; they included an attempt to blow up the train in which the tsar travelled and the explosion of a mine in the Winter Palace. Success came on 1 March 1881, paradoxically after most of the members of the group had already been apprehended by the police. This was the apogee of the terror and also its end for more than two decades.

The second major wave of terrorism in Russia was sponsored by the Social Revolutionary Party and opened with the assassination in 1902 of Sipyagin, the minister of the interior, by Balmashev. The year before, Karpovich, a young nobleman, had shot Bogolepov, minister of education. The Social Revolutionaries carried out a mere three major *attentats* in 1903 (including the killing of the governors Obolenski and Bogdanovich) and two in 1904, but the number rose to fifty-four in 1905 (the year of the war with Japan), eighty-two in 1906 and seventy-one in 1907. After that the number dwindled rapidly – three in 1908, two in 1909, one in 1910.[12] The most striking assassination was that of Plehve, minister of the interior and the strong man of the regime, in a Petersburg street in 1904. The next year Kalyayev killed the Grand Duke Serge Alexandrovich. The last spectacular assassination, that of Stolypin in the Kiev Opera House in 1911, was again the act of an individual, probably a double agent; it took place after the fighting organization of the Social Revolutionaries had ceased to exist. Some minor sporadic incidents apart, there was no individual terror after 1911. There was a third, much smaller wave of political terror after the Bolshevik coup in November 1917; it was directed partly against Communist leaders – Uritski and Volodarski were killed and Lenin wounded – but also against German diplomats and military commanders in an attempt to sabotage the peace negotiations between Russia and Germany. The Communist authorities suppressed this challenge to their rule without great difficulty.

The achievements of Irish terrorism have been much less striking, but it has continued, on and off, for a much longer period. There have been countless ups and downs ever since the emergence, partly due to agrarian unrest, of the United Irishmen in 1791. The policy of open force in the 1860s was an unmitigated failure. The activities of the Dynamiters in the 1870s and 1880s resulted in one spectacular operation, the Phoenix Park murders. After that there followed several decades of calm, with new upsurges in 1916, 1919–21, before the Second World War, and then again in the 1970s.

Armenian terrorism against Turkish oppression began in the 1890s but was shortlived and ended in disaster because the Armenians faced an enemy less patient and good-natured than did the Irish. Further terrorism occurred after 1918 in the form of assassinations of some individual Turkish leaders who had been prominently involved in the massacres of the First World War. This terrorist tradition has continued sporadically to the present day; political leaders and church dignitaries have been killed by their opponents and in 1975 there was a new upsurge of terrorism with the murder of the Turkish ambassadors in Vienna and Paris and of Turkish diplomats in other parts of the world.

At the very time that the Armenian terrorists first launched their operations, another separatist organization directed against the Turks, the Inner Macedonian Revolutionary Organization (IMRO) led by Damian Gruev, came into being. First an underground, civilian propagandist society, it turned after a few years into a military movement, preparing both for systematic terror and for a mass insurrection.[13] The mass insurrection (*Ilin Den*) was a catastrophe, yet the Macedonians were more fortunate than the Armenians, inasmuch as they did have allies and Macedonia was not part of the Turkish heartland. But Macedonia did not gain independence; in 1912–13 it was redistributed between Greece, Bulgaria and Serbia. IMRO continued its struggle from the Petrich district in Bulgaria; some of its operations were directed against Yugoslavia, but in fact it became a tool of successive Bulgarian governments. In the decade between 1924 and 1934 the number of its own members (and Bulgarian oppositionists) who perished in internecine struggles considerably exceeded the casualties it inflicted on its enemies. By the time a new Bulgarian government suppressed IMRO in the mid-1930s, it had only the name in common with the organization founded four decades earlier.

Among other nationalist terrorist groups that appeared before the First World War were the Polish socialists and some Indian groups particularly in Bengal.[14] In both cases the terrorist tradition continued well after independence had been achieved. Nehru and others had warned against terrorism and there is no doubt that the sectarian character of the terror, even though limited in scope, further poisoned the relations between the communities and contributed to the partition of India in 1947. In Poland organized terror continued for more than a decade after the First World War in the eastern territories among the Western Ukrainians, who turned against the Warsaw government when their demands for autonomy were ignored.

The high tide of terrorism in Western Europe was the anarchist 'propaganda by deed' in the 1890s. The exploits of Ravachol, Auguste Vaillant and Émile Henry between 1892 and 1894 created an enormous stir, and because the bomb throwing by individuals coincided with a turn in anarchist propaganda favouring violence, the impression of a giant international conspiracy was created, which in actual fact never existed. Ravachol was in many ways an extraordinary villain, a bandit who would have killed and robbed even if there had been no anarchist movement in France; Vaillant was a Bohemian and Émile Henry an excited young man. An analysis of the statistics of urbanization in nineteenth-century France would not add much to the understanding of their motives. The public at large was fascinated by the secret and mysterious character of the anarchist groups; anarchists, socialists, nihilists and radicals were all believed to be birds of one feather. Governments and police forces who knew better saw no reason to correct this impression.

There were a great many attempts on the lives of leading statesmen in Europe and America between the 1880s and the first decade of the twentieth century. Presidents Garfield and McKinley were among the victims; there were several unsuccessful attempts to kill Bismarck and the German emperor; French President Carnot was assassinated in 1894; Antonio Canovas, the Spanish prime minister, was murdered in 1897, Empress Elizabeth (Zita) of Austria in 1898 and King Umberto of Italy in 1900. But inasmuch as the assassins were anarchists – and quite a few were not – they all acted on their own initiative without the knowledge and support of the groups to which they belonged. It was conveniently forgotten at the time that there had been a long tradition of regicide, and attempted regicide, in Europe and that there had been countless attempts to kill Napoleon and Napoleon III. As a contemporary observer, who had little sympathy with anarchism, noted: 'It is difficult to assign to them [the anarchists] any participation in the various outrages, notably the assassination of rulers.'[15]

Psychologically interesting, the *ère des attentats* was of no great political significance. By 1905 the wave of attacks and assassinations outside Russia had abated; there were further spectacular happenings in Paris and London in the years just before the outbreak of the First World War, such as the exploits of the Bonnot gang and of groups of Poles and Latvians (Peter the Painter) in London's East End. But the motive of these groups was predominantly self-gain, and the importance of the anarchist admixture, which did exist, was usually exaggerated. There were, to summarize, no systematic terrorist campaigns in Central and Western Europe. They did exist on the fringes of Europe, in Russia, in the Balkans and, in a different form, in Spain.

Labour disputes in the United States had been more violent than in Europe almost from the beginning. The story of the Molly Maguires in the 1870s is only one of several such historical episodes; the group was identified at the time, quite wrongly, with Communism.[16] It was, of course, not a matter of Communism but of the traditional violence displayed by a group of Irishmen transplanted to a new continent and feeling itself discriminated against and exploited. But it fought not only mine owners but also fellow workers of Welsh and German extraction. There was also the Haymarket Square bombing in 1886 and many other bloody incidents involving factory police on the one hand and militant coal miners and steelworkers on the other. Again, the killing of Governor Frank Steunenberg of Idaho in 1905 was not an isolated incident; the Industrial Workers of the World (IWW) did not deny that it had been inspired by the 'Russian struggle'. There was the bombing by the MacNamara brothers of the Los Angeles Times Building in 1910 and other such incidents now remembered only by historians specializing in the byways of the American labour movement. But terrorism in the United States was limited in scope and purpose; there was no intention of overthrowing the government, killing the political leadership or changing the political system.

Spain was the other country in which systematic terrorism was a factor of some political importance. Political violence had been rampant in Spain throughout the nineteenth century, notably during the Carlist wars. The emergence of the working-class movement, very much under Bakuninist influence, was accompanied by a great deal of fighting; in the trade unions terrorism became endemic. There was also rural violence, especially in the provinces of southern Spain such as Andalusia. Like France, Spain had its *ère des attentats* in the 1890s but, unlike France, there was a resurgence in 1904–9 and again during the First World War and after. There were all sorts of anarchists, but the most militant group, the Iberian Anarchist Federation (FAI), became the dominant force. Among its leaders, Buenaventura Durruti (1896–1936) was the most outstanding ('We are not afraid of ruins').[17] This terrorism was politically quite ineffective except that it caused a great deal of internecine struggle inside the left and that it contributed to the fatal events of 1936–9. Catalonia was the main scene of terrorism up to and including the civil war. In the later stages of the Franco dictatorship the centre of gravity shifted to the Basque region, but there separatism was the main driving force, sometimes, as in Ulster, appearing under a Marxist veneer. Terrorist anarchism radiated from Spain to Latin America, especially to Argentina; Barcelona had its tragic week in 1909 and Buenos Aires' *Semana Tragica* took place a decade later.[18] Durruti shot the Archbishop of Saragossa and the indefatigable Simon Radowitsky killed the Buenos Aires chief of police.

Up to the First World War terrorism was thought to be a left-wing phenomenon, even though the highly individualistic character of terrorism somehow did not quite fit the ideological pattern. But neither the Irish nor the Macedonian freedom fighters, neither the Armenian nor the Bengali terrorists were socialist or anarchist in inspiration. The 'Black Hundred' was certainly a terrorist organization, but its main purpose was to fight the Russian revolution, engage in anti-Jewish pogroms and, generally speaking, to assassinate the leaders of the liberal–democratic opposition to tsarism. The 'Black Hundred' constituted the extreme right in Russian domestic politics and it was in fact founded with the support of the police. But as so often happened in the history of terrorist movements, the sorcerer's apprentice developed an identity of his own. Soon demands for the redistribution of land and the shortening of the working day were voiced and the members of an organization established to defend the monarchy were complaining that it would be preferable to have no government rather than the existing one. It was said that a few resolute officers, like those in Serbia, would do a world of good – a reference to Serbian regicides.

In the years after the First World War terrorist operations were mainly sponsored by right-wing and nationalist–separatist groups. Sometimes these groups were both right-wing and separatist, as in the case of the Croatian Ustasha, which received most of its support from Fascist Italy and Hungary. The Croatians wanted independence and they had no compunction about accepting support from any quarter; like the Irish they have continued their struggle to the present day. Systematic terrorism was found in the 1920s mainly on the fringes of the budding Fascist movements or among their precursors such as the Freikorps in Germany, certain French Fascist groups, in Hungary and, above all, among the Rumanian 'Iron Guard'. But by and large there was comparatively little terror, for this was the age of mass parties on both the right and left; anarchism had long outgrown its terrorist phase. There were a few spectacular political assassinations like those of Liebknecht and Luxemburg in 1919, of Rathenau in 1922 and of King Alexander of Yugoslavia and Barthou in Marseilles in April 1934. As this latter was clearly a case of international terrorism in which at least four governments were involved, the League of Nations intervened; resolutions were passed and committees were established with a view to combating terrorism on an international basis.[19] All these exercises were quite futile for the obvious reason that, although some governments were opposed to terror, others favoured it as long as it served their purposes. Three decades later the United Nations faced a similar situation.

Outside Europe too, terrorist operations were as yet infrequent. The murder of the Egyptian prime minister, Boutros Pasha, in 1910 was the action of an individual. So was the assassination in 1924 of Sir Lee Stack, commander in chief of the Egyptian army. But in the 1930s and especially in the 1940s the Muslim Brotherhood and other extreme right-wing groups such as Young Egypt were converted to systematic terrorism and killed two prime ministers and a few other leading officials. In mandatory Palestine, the Irgun Zyai Leumi and LEHI (Fighters for the Freedom of Israel) opted for individual terrorism. Irgun ceased its anti-British activities in 1939, but the more extreme LEHI continued its struggle; the murder of Lord Moyne was its most spectacular operation. Even in India, the country of non-violence, the terrorist Bhagat Singh had, in Nehru's words, a sudden and amazing popularity in the 1920s. Nehru was inclined to belittle terrorism: it represented the infancy of a revolutionary urge (he wrote); India had passed that stage and terrorism was about to die out.[20] Yet Nehru's prediction was premature; ten years later he again toured Bengal to denounce terrorism. Terrorism, he said, was the glamour of secret work and risk-taking attracting adventurous young men and women: 'It is the call of the detective story.'[21] But detective stories, for better or worse, have always found more readers than high literature. In Japan during the 1930s a group of junior army officers engaged in terror; their actions had a certain impact on the conduct of Japanese foreign policy.

Individual terrorism played a subordinate role in the European resistance movement during the Second World War. Heydrich, the governor of the Czech protectorate, was killed; so was Wilhelm Kube, the Nazi governor of White Russia, and some minor French collaborators. A few bombs were placed in Parisian cinemas. Overall there is no evidence that the German war effort or the morale of the soldiers were affected by terrorist activity. For many years after the war urban terror was overshadowed by large-scale guerrilla wars such as in China. It was only in predominantly urban regions such as mandatory Palestine and, later, Cyprus and Aden that the terrorist strategy prevailed. This is not to say that rural guerrillas would not on occasion ambush and kill enemy leaders; the assassination of Sir Henry Gurney, the British governor-general in Malaya, may have been an accident. The killing of thousands of South Vietnamese village headmen in the late 1950s and early 1960s, on the other hand, was certainly a systematic operation of the North Vietnamese and part of their general strategy.

The urban terrorist, in contrast to the rural guerrilla, could not transform small assault groups into regiments or even divisions, and the establishment of liberated zones was ruled out – except in very rare conditions when government no longer functioned. The struggles for Tel Aviv (1945–7), Nicosia (1955–8) and Aden (1964–7) lasted for three years. The attacks of Jewish and Greek Cypriot terrorists were directed against the British, but the presence of Arab and Turkish communities caused major complications. With the outbreak of the civil war in Palestine in late 1947 and the subsequent invasion of Arab armies, the terrorist groups were absorbed into the Israeli army. Ethniki Organosis Kyprion Agoniston (EOKA) activities had led to communal riots as early as 1957 and there is little doubt that their terrorism contributed to the subsequent tragic events in Cyprus. Viewed in retrospect the number of victims and the damage caused by terrorist activities in Palestine and Cyprus was very small indeed. But weakened as the result of the Second World War, Britain was about to dismantle its empire in any case and not much violence was needed to hasten the process. Aden was one of Britain's last outposts but, after India had been lost, the Crown Colony was no longer of strategic importance. The struggle for Aden began on a small scale in 1964 and culminated in the occupation of the Crater area, the oldest part of the town, in 1967. The British forces reoccupied it without much difficulty two weeks later, but the rebels had nevertheless scored a political victory which led to the British exodus in November of that year.[22]

A decade earlier the Algerian National Liberation Front (FLN) had tried to seize and hold an urban area in a far bloodier battle. By mid-1956 the slums of Algiers (the Casbah section) were securely in their hands, but the moment anti-terrorist actions were begun by the French army (January 1957) the fate of the insurgents was sealed. The FLN did not regain its position in the capital up to the very end of the war. But the tough methods used by General Massu's Paras in combating systematic terror with systematic torture provoked a worldwide outcry. The guerrilla war continued in the Algerian countryside; politically and economically it became too costly for France to combat and eventually the French forces had to withdraw.

These, then, were the major cases of urban terrorism during the two decades after the end of the Second World War. A great many guerrilla wars were going on at the time all over the world, but the main scene of action was in the countryside, as all the theoreticians from Mao to Castro and Guevara agreed it should be. Urban terrorism was regarded at best as a supplementary form of warfare, at worst as a dangerous aberration.

Castro and Guevara were firmly convinced that the city was the 'graveyard' of the revolutionary freedom fighter.[23] It was only in the middle 1960s that urban terrorism came into its own – mainly as the result of the defeat of the rural guerrillas in Latin America but also following the emergence (or in some cases the reactivation) of urban terrorist groups in Europe, North America and Japan. Thus it was only a little more than two decades ago that urban terror began to attract general attention. Seen in historical perspective it was no more than a revival of certain forms of political violence that had been used previously in many parts of the world. These methods had been widely described, analysed and debated at the time from every possible angle. But given the frailty of human memory it was perhaps not surprising that the re-emergence of terrorism should have been regarded in recent years as an altogether novel phenomenon and that its causes and the ways to cope with it should have been discussed as if nothing of the kind had ever happened before.

2

The Philosophy of the Bomb

The doctrinal origins of the philosophy of the bomb emerged in the nineteenth century but its antecedents predate the invention of modern explosives. Terrorism has always been justified as a means of resisting despotism and as such its origins are of course to be found in antiquity. Plato and Aristotle regarded tyranny as a deviation, a perversion, the worst form of government. Tyrannicides in ancient Greece were elevated to the rank of national heroes. Cicero noted in his *De Officiis* that tyrants had always found a violent end and that the Romans had usually acclaimed those who killed them. The saying was attributed to Seneca that no victim's blood was more agreeable to god than the blood of a tyrant. The civic virtues of a Brutus were praised by his fellow Romans.

The early Church fathers did not see eye to eye about regicide but there was an influential school of thought which maintained that tyranny might be resisted as it violated divine and natural law alike. As St Isidore put it, it was the task of the ruler to maintain justice and the tyrant consequently had no claim to obedience. Thomas Aquinas drew a distinction between the *tyrannus ex defectu tituli*, the usurper, who could be killed by any individual, and the *tyrannus ex parte exercitii*, who could be punished only by *publica auctoritas*. John of Salisbury in the twelfth century was the first medieval author to provide an explicit defence of tyrannicide. Referring to the legends of Jael and Sisara, of Judith and Holofernes and a great many other examples, he argued that there was a basic difference between a good king, who, in observing the law, was the guardian of the well-being of his people, and the oppressor whose rule was based merely on force: he who usurps the sword was worthy to die of the sword.[1]

Dante had banished the murderers of Caesar to the depths of his Inferno but the Renaissance rectified their place in history. The Council of Constance (1414–18) had banned tyrannicide but the concept was widely accepted in the sixteenth century by Catholic and Protestant thinkers alike:

the people had an inherent right to resist the command of the prince if it was contrary to the law of God. According to Mariana (1536–1623), the power of the king was based on a contract with the people; if the king violated his part of the contract he could and should be removed, and any private citizen was entitled to kill him, if necessary by poison. Even earlier George Buchanan (1506–82) in his *De Jure Regni apud Scotos* had argued that it was 'most just' to wage a war against a tyrant who was an enemy of all mankind; all good men should engage in perpetual warfare with such a public enemy. The author of *De droit des magistrats* (1574) noted with disdain that, among the Jews, killers of tyrants had to be specially commissioned by God (implying that the Jews should have been less fainthearted and taken the initiative without divine prodding).[2] The Monarchomachs of the sixteenth and seventeenth centuries discussed at great length the circumstances in which a king might become a tyrant. They developed a theory of popular sovereignty and this, in turn, led them into accepting the right of resistance.

The writings of these ancient and medieval authors are of more than academic interest in the context of modern terrorism for the ancient concept of justified tyrannicide provided inspiration for nineteenth-century terrorist thought. The programme of the Narodnaya Volya as drafted at their first convention (Lipetsk, June 1879) stated explicitly that 'we will fight with the means employed by Wilhelm Tell'. Very few of these young Russians knew of Buchanan, but all of them had read Schiller, so dear to successive generations of Russian progressives, and they knew the 'In Tyrannos' literature, often by heart. Nikolai Morozov, one of the first theoreticians of Russian terrorism, chose as a motto to his pamphlet quotations from Saint-Just and Robespierre to the effect that it was perfectly justifiable to execute a tyrant without any legal niceties.[3] But tyrants were usually not alone, they could not function without assistants, and the death of a tyrant was not necessarily the end of tyranny. Hence the necessity to attack the system on a broader front, first discussed in the secret societies of the late eighteenth and early nineteenth centuries. Secret societies, with their magical and religious preoccupations (but often also with very tangible social functions) and their *rites de passage*, have existed since time immemorial in many civilizations; as a result of their secrecy, the scope and importance of their activities has frequently been overrated. The eighteenth-century secret societies might debate the inequities of the world but they did not, as a rule, engage in conspiracies aimed at the violent overthrow of the existing political and social order. Alfieri, the poet of Italian liberty, discussed in the 1770s the most effective ways of doing away with tyranny *in un instante e con tutta certezza*.[4] But it was only after the Thermidor that the idea took firm root. When asked at his trial about the means he counted upon employing, Babeuf proudly declared: 'All means are legitimate against tyrants.' And later on, Buonarroti echoed him: 'No means are criminal which are employed to obtain a sacred end.' Babeuvisme was a movement without the people, and was aimed at a dictatorship; the absence of anything specifically popular was precisely what made it into terrorism.[5] Buonarroti's *History of Babeuf's Conspiracy* remained the bible of two generations of young revolutionaries all over Europe. Seen in historical perspective, it was the precursor of Blanquism, of armed insurrection rather than of individual terror. But it also influenced latter-day terrorists through its advocacy of violence, its scant regard for human life and its belief that a few determined people could make a revolution; what did the fate of a few individuals matter if the future of twenty-five millions was at stake? In the French Revolution the practice of intimidating the enemy by means of terror had gained ground, instinctive and spontaneous at first, later on bureaucratic and doctrinaire, until in the end the *sans culottes* lost faith in terror and its leading advocates were swept from the scene by the reaction triggered off by their excesses. But *terreur* was not quite synonymous with terrorism, and its proponents did not yet have a clear concept of how it should be utilized in the long term. A Jacobin tradition whose aims were vague and ill defined failed to make any notable inroads against a government which had both public support and a fairly effective police force.[6]

Elsewhere, in Spain, Piedmont and Sicily the Carbonari, their successors and similar groups succeeded in overturning governments, much to the consternation of the Holy Alliance, but this was the result of insurrections rather than systematic campaigns of terror. The critics of the Carbonari attributed to them the most terrible and sanguinary plans for revolt; the 'good cousins' through their *venditi* (branches, literally shops) were said to have fomented terror, setting fire to their enemies' houses, and helping prisoners to escape; 'several individuals, who were adverse to their maxims, were destined to the poignard', and when this was too risky, poison was used as a fitter method of liquidation.[7] The Carbonari were said to be pitiless professional revolutionaries, ready to kill anyone. Once having joined the conspiracy, their members lost all individuality, without family or fatherland, and belonged totally to their masters. At a signal they had to obey them blindly, knife in hand.[8] It is true that the language used by the Carbonari was bloodthirsty. The following passage conveys something of its flavour:

The cross should serve to crucify the tyrant who persecutes us and troubles our sacred operations. The crown of thorns should serve to pierce his head. The thread denotes the cord to lead him to the gibbet; the ladder will aid him to mount. The leaves are nails to pierce his hands and feet. The pick-axe will penetrate his breast, and shed the impure blood that flows in his veins. The axe will separate his head from his body, as the wolf who disturbs our pacific labours. The salt will prevent the corruption of his head, that it may last as a monument of the eternal infamy of despots [etc., etc.].[9]

Little is known to this day about the origins of the Carboneria other than the mere fact that the movement appeared first in Naples in 1807. Whether it drew its inspiration from earlier anti-Austrian secret societies in northern Italy or whether French republicans and freemasons had a hand in founding the movement is still a matter of contention.[10] It is certain however that terrorist acts were perpetrated but that they did not amount to a systematic campaign.

Elsewhere, I have discussed the ideas of Carlo Bianco, conte di Saint Jorioz, who was first in Europe to outline a strategy of a national war of liberation by means of guerrilla tactics; he also wrote about the necessity of imposing a revolutionary dictatorship and of applying terrorist means against the enemies of the revolution.[11] But such suggestions remained unanswered. Three decades later Orsini tried to kill Napoleon III and Cavour denounced the 'villainous doctrine of political assassination practised by the execrable sectarians'. Mazzini in an open letter wrote a withering reply: you exhumed the theory of the dagger, a theory unknown in Italy. Do you take us for villains and madmen? For whom and to what end could the death of Victor Emmanuel serve?[12] In fact, Mazzini's attitude to assassination was not that unambiguous for in letters to friends he had written that holy was the sword in the hand of Judith, the dagger of Harmodios and Brutus, the poignard of the Sicilian who had initiated the Vespers and the arrow of Wilhelm Tell – was not the finger of God to be discerned in the individual who rose against the tyrant's despotism?

In some of the secret societies of Central Europe, such as the 'League of the Just' (which later became the Communist League), the doctrine of terror was first discussed – only to be rejected. Wilhelm Weitling, a tailor and the first German Communist, suggested in letters to his friends in Paris various ways of 'founding the kingdom of heaven by unleashing the furies of hell'. They were shocked by his suggestions which also included community of women; they were positively horrified when he proposed to turn loose the 'thieving proletariat' on society. Weitling thought he could mobilize some 20,000 'smart and courageous' murderers and thieves. His correspondents thought that a desirable end could not possibly be attained by 'Jesuit tactics'.[13] It would do the cause irreparable harm if murderers and thieves were proudly to style themselves Communists. Their moral standards would not be improved by the example set by Weitling; they would not surrender their ill-gotten gains for a political movement to use; any such suggestion would be vastly amusing to them, and very likely they would kill Weitling. This exchange of letters took place in 1843, unknown to Marx and Engels who, in any event, had misgivings about Weitling's capacity as a systematic thinker. They argued that it was fraudulent to arouse the people without a sound and considered basis for action. But Weitling was not deterred by the arguments of his friends in Paris and the idea of the noble robber continued to figure in his writings in later years. In a new edition of his main opus, *Garantien der Harmonie und Freiheit*, published after the failure of the revolution of 1848, he wrote that public opinion ought to be persuaded that a robber who found his death in the fight was a martyr in a holy cause. Anyone who informed on such a man should not rest secure for a single moment from the people's vengeance, and those who sought to take revenge upon him should be given protection and cover.[14] The year of the revolution, 1848, also gave fresh impetus to the concept of terrorism, expressed most succinctly perhaps in an essay entitled 'Murder' (*Der Mord*) written by the German radical democrat Karl Heinzen (1809–80). He argued that while murder was forbidden in principle this prohibition did not apply to politics. The physical liquidation of hundreds or thousands of people could still be in the higher interests of humanity. Heinzen took tyrannicide as his starting point; he pointed out that such acts of liberation had been undertaken at all times and in all places. But it soon emerged that he was willing to justify terrorist tactics on a much more massive scale: 'If you have to blow up half a continent and pour out a sea of blood in order to destroy the party of the barbarians, have no scruples of conscience. He is no true republican who would not gladly pay with his life for the satisfaction of exterminating a million barbarians.' There could be no social and political progress unless kings and generals, the foes of liberty, were removed.

Seen in retrospect, Karl Heinzen was the first to provide a full-fledged doctrine of modern terrorism; most elements of latter-day terrorist thought can be found in the writings of this forgotten German radical democrat. It was a confused doctrine, to be sure; on one hand he argued that killing was always a crime, but on the other hand he claimed that murder might well be a 'physical necessity', that the atmosphere or the soil of the earth needed a certain quantity of blood (*Die Evolution*, 26 January 1849). He maintained that it was absolutely certain that the forces of progress would prevail over the reactionaries in any case but doubted whether the spirit of freedom and the 'good cause' would win without using dagger, poison and explosives: 'We have to become more energetic, more desperate.' This led him into speculations about the use of arms of mass destruction. For the greater strength, training and discipline of the forces of repression could be counterbalanced only by weapons that could be employed by a few people and that would cause great havoc. These weapons, Heinzen thought, could not be used by armies against a few individual fighters. Hence the great hopes attached to the potential of poison gas, to ballistic missiles (known at the time as Congreve rockets) and mines which one day 'could destroy whole cities with 100,000 inhabitants' (*Die Evolution*, 16 February 1849). Heinzen blamed the revolutionaries of 1848 for not having shown sufficient ruthlessness; the party of freedom would be defeated unless it gave the highest priority to the development of the art of murder. Heinzen, like Most after him, came to see the key to revolution in modern technology; new explosives would have to be invented, bombs planted under pavements, new means of poisoning food explored. To expedite progress he advocated prizes for research in these fields.[15] Heinzen's subsequent career was not, however, in the field of professional terrorism; he did not blow up half a continent but migrated to the United States and became an editor of various short-lived German-language newspapers, first in Louisville, Kentucky, and eventually in Boston – 'the most civilized city in America'.

The idea of the alliance between the revolutionary avant-garde and the criminal underworld was to reappear from time to time in the history of nineteenth-century terrorist movements (*pace* the Narodnaya Volya) and again among the American and West German New Left militants of the 1960s. Pavel Akselrod, one of the fathers of Russian socialism, relates in his autobiography how in 1874 he and Breshkovskaya, the future 'grandmother of the Russian revolution', went searching the forests of southern Russia, without evident success, for a famous robber who had the reputation of plundering rich landowners and Jews and distributing his booty among poor peasants.[16] Weitling's theory had been forgotten by that time but like all revolutionaries of his generation Akselrod had read Bakunin; Bakunin, in turn, had met Weitling in Zurich and had been deeply influenced by him. This meeting was one of the formative events of Bakunin's life, 'completing his transformation from a speculative philosopher into a practical revolutionary'.[17]

In his never-ending search for the main catalysts of the forthcoming Russian Revolution, Bakunin placed high hopes on the religious sectarians. But he was even more sanguine about the rebel-robbers in the tradition of Stenka Rasin and Pugachov and had nothing but contempt for the Marxists and 'Liberals' who preferred not to appeal to the so-called evil passions of the people. The robber (Bakunin wrote) was the only sincere revolutionary in Russia, a revolutionary without phraseology, without bookish rhetoric, irreconcilable and indefatigable, a revolutionary of the deed. The robber was traditionally a hero, a saviour of the people, the enemy *par excellence* of the state and its entire social order. Without an understanding of the robber one could not understand the history of the Russian people; whosoever wanted a real, popular revolution had to go to this world. It was a cruel, merciless world, but this was only the outcome of government oppression. An end to this underworld would spell either the death of the people or their final liberation. Hence Bakunin's conclusion that a truly popular revolution would emerge only if a peasants' revolt merged with a rebellion of the robbers. And the season was at hand to accomplish this task.[18] Bakunin, however, placed no emphasis on individual terror or even on guerrilla warfare. In 1848, he envisaged the emergence of a regular revolutionary army, trained with the help of former Polish officers and, perhaps, of some junior Austrian officers.[19] It was only after Bakunin's death that his anarchist followers committed themselves to 'propaganda by deed'.

Though Bakunin had been second to none in his revolutionary enthusiasm ever since he first appeared on the European scene in the 1840s, it was only two decades later, once he had met Nechaev (that 'magnificent young fanatic, that believer without God, hero without rhetoric'), that Bakunin developed a theory of destruction. In the *Principles of Revolution*, published in 1869, he wrote that 'we recognize no other action save destruction though we admit that the forms in which such action will show itself will be exceedingly varied – poison, the knife, the rope etc.'. Those intended for liquidation had already been singled out. Weeping and wailing would follow: 'society' would experience fear and remorse. The revolutionaries, however, should show indifference towards the lamentations of the doomed, and were not to enter into any compromise. Their approach might be called terroristic but this ought not to deter them. The final aim was to achieve revolution, the cause of eradicating evil was holy, Russian soil would be cleansed by sword and fire.

The demand that the revolutionary should have but one thought day and night, that is, merciless destruction, recurs in the most famous document of the period, the 'Revolutionary Catechism'.[20] The Catechism has frequently been quoted and a short summary will suffice for our purposes. It opens with a general list of rules for organization and then characterizes the attitude of the revolutionary towards himself and others. He is a lost man, without interests, belongings, personal ties of his own – not even a name. (The idea of the nameless soldier of the revolution was later to recur in many terrorist organizations as far afield as Ireland and Serbia, where members were known by number rather than by name.) He must be absorbed by a single interest, thought and passion – the revolution. He has broken with society and its laws and conventions; he must eschew doctrinairism and despise public opinion, be prepared for torture and death at any time. Hard towards himself, he must be hard towards others, leaving no place for love, friendship, gratitude or even honour – room was to be spared only for the cold passion of the revolutionary cause whose success was to give him his pleasure, gratification and reward.

Tactical advice follows: in order to effect merciless destruction, the revolutionary has to pretend to be what he is not, to infiltrate the church, the world of business, the bureaucracy and army, the secret police and even the royal palace. Bakunin divided 'society' into six categories: intelligent and energetic individuals, particularly dangerous to the revolutionary organization, were to be killed first, for their sudden and violent death would inspire fear among the government; secondly there were those, albeit no less guilty, whose lives should be temporarily spared, for their monstrous crimes objectively fomented revolution. The third category consisted of the high-ranking, the rich and powerful; they were mere 'animals', neither particularly intelligent nor dynamic, who should be duped and blackmailed. Use should be made of ambitious politicians, including the liberals among them. The revolutionaries should conspire with them, pretending to follow them blindly, but at the same time ferreting out their secrets, thereby compromising them to such a degree as would cut off their retreat from the struggle against the authorities. The fifth category, the loudmouths, those platonic advocates of revolution, should be engineered into making dangerous declarations; most would perish in the struggle but a few might become authentic revolutionaries. Finally, the women: some were useless and stupid and were to be treated like categories three and four; others were capable, passionate and devoted even though they might not yet have acquired full revolutionary consciousness. The sixth category comprised those who had completely thrown in their lot with the revolutionaries; they were the most precious possession of the revolutionary party, and their aid was absolutely essential. In its final section, the Catechism emphasizes the need for total revolution: institutions, social structures, civilization and morality were to be destroyed, root and branch. A closing reference is made to the world of brigands, the only real revolutionaries who, once united, would bring into being a terrible and invincible power.

Bakunin's Catechism was written for the benefit of a non-existent terrorist group – Nechaev's Narodnaya Rasprava; like Bakunin's 'World Revolutionary Union', it was a mere figment of imagination. The only victim of Nechaev's terrorism was a fellow conspirator, a student, Ivan Ivanovich Ivanov, who was killed in 1869 by his comrades for reasons which have remained obscure. With all his extremist rhetoric Bakunin would have lacked the ruthlessness (even if he had had the following) to practise his philosophy of pan-destructionism.

Young revolutionaries had pronounced similar ideas even before Bakunin, no doubt also without the capacity to put them into practice. Zaichnevski, the son of a landowner in the Orel district, was twenty-one years of age when he published a leaflet on behalf of 'Young Russia'. His group felt that the revolutionaries ought to be prepared for any operation, however dangerous. They ought to storm the Winter Palace, the residence of the tsar, and destroy all those who lived there. Perhaps it might be sufficient to kill only the tsar and his family? Should, however, the whole 'Tsarist Party' – the landowners, rich merchants, etc. – rise like one man in defence of the emperor, no pardon ought to be given them, just as they had given no pardon to the revolutionaries. Those who were not with the revolutionaries were against them and were enemies to be destroyed by every possible means.[21] Zaichnevski was openly contemptuous of the liberal critics of the regime, including those who lived abroad, and his critics reciprocated by dismissing his appeals as immature and un-Russian, a mixture of undigested Schiller (*Karl Moor*), Babeuf, Blanqui and Feuerbach. At the time even Bakunin attacked him for his unabashed elitism and doctrinaire scorn of the people. Zaichnevski and his few comrades were arrested soon after his appeal was published. It had had no political significance but did reflect a certain mood among the students and, as such, was a precursor of the terrorism of the 1870s.

Ishutin's 'organization' came into being two years later. It was called 'Hell' and purported to be the Russian branch of a (needless to say, nonexistent) international organization of terrorists, the 'European Revolutionary Committee'. Some of its members spoke of assassinating the tsar, and their basic ideas bore a striking resemblance to concepts developed a few years later by Bakunin and Nechaev. Their aim was to kill members of the government and big landowners. Lots were to be cast among the revolutionaries to establish who was to carry out the assassinations. The terrorist should live under an assumed name, break all ties with his family, give up his friends, and forgo marriage. He should cut himself off from his own comrades and find his friends in the underworld. On the day appointed for the assassination, he was to disfigure his face with chemicals to avoid being recognized. In his pocket he would carry a manifesto explaining his motives, and once he had carried out his attempt, he was to poison himself.[22] Not all the members of Ishutin's circle agreed with his prescriptions for revolutionary action; they preferred propaganda and the establishment of schools and co-operatives. They even thought of locking up the extremists in their ranks in lunatic asylums, and when Karakozov, a member of the group (and Ishutin's cousin), prepared for his attempt on the life of the tsar, Ishutin himself seems to have had second thoughts and tried to dissuade his cousin. Karakozov made his attempt, was apprehended and hanged. Ishutin died in prison and a period of repression followed in which organized opposition within Russia was virtually stamped out.

Only in 1878, after Vera Zasulich's shooting of General Trepov, the governor of the Russian capital, did terrorism as a doctrine, the Russian version of 'propaganda by deed', finally emerge. The tsarist authorities explained this sudden upsurge of terrorism as a result of the Narodnikis' failure to 'go to the people'; the peasants had been unresponsive, the workers had informed on the 'apostles of future happiness'. After their lack of success in mobilizing the masses, the authorities maintained, the revolutionaries had come to regard terror as the only effective means of discrediting the government and proving to society at large that a revolutionary party not only existed but was growing stronger.[23] This interpretation was not far from the truth. Plekhanov took virtually the same view when he wrote that terror was the product of the revolutionary party's weakness and followed on its realization that it could not stage a peasant uprising.[24]

Russian terrorism developed in several stages. It began with sporadic acts of armed defence in resisting arrest and as a reaction against individual police officers who had maltreated arrested revolutionaries. On a few occasions, spies who had infiltrated the revolutionary cells were executed. The very first manifesto announcing that a new era in revolutionary action had dawned was Serge Kravchinski's 'A Death for a Death', in which he explained his reasons for having taken part in the assassination of General Mezentsev, the head of the 'third section' (the tsarist political police).[25] His manifesto was full of contradictions: on the one hand, he argued that 'you, the representatives of power, are our enemies and there can be no peace between us. You should and will be destroyed.' Mezentsev, he claimed, had been sentenced to death by a revolutionary tribunal, in revenge for those who had been cruelly treated in prison. As long as the cruelty of the system continued, the revolutionary tribunal would hang over the rulers of the state like the sword of Damocles. At the moment, the movement was only of limited strength but it was growing hourly. Kravchinski, however, seemed to have had some doubts about the identity of his enemy, for in the same manifesto he contended that his real foes were the bourgeoisie and capitalists. He even suggested that the government should stay neutral in this struggle. But how was a line to be drawn between

capitalism and the state? The programme of the Narodnaya Volya specifically stated that the Russian government was a monster, that unlike Western
European states it was also the greatest capitalist exploiter, owning half
of Russia's land. Revolutionaries were permitted to confiscate state property; private property was to be inviolate as long as it was not used in
the fight against the revolutionary movement.[26]

Kravchinski's manifesto appeared in August 1878. In November that
year the first issue of the journal *Zemlya i Volya* was circulated and Kravchinski wrote its editorial in which he announced that the working masses
could not be liberated as a result of terrorist operations. Only the popular
masses could bring about a revolution and destroy the system – against
a class, only a class could rebel. The terrorists were no more than the
military vanguard of the revolutionary movement. If all their forces were
channelled into terrorist activities this would be tantamount to abandon-
ment of their chief goal. Even if they succeeded in destroying the system,
it would be a Pyrrhic victory because power would then pass into the hands
of the bourgeoisie.

These reservations about the use of terror reassured some members of
the revolutionary movement (such as Plekhanov) who all along had argued
against the concentration on terrorist acts at the expense of other activities.
Dissension on the subject of terror could not be continued for long; in
1879, when terrorist attacks multiplied, debate became more and more
heated, and ultimately led to a split. Morozov, among others, was in favour
of 'pure terror'; Zhelyabov and others aimed at a Jacobin-style coup and
felt that terror should be used only as punishment meted out to the tsar
and his hirelings for their policy of repression.[27] Aptekman, who aligned
himself with Plekhanov, wrote that political terror was recognized at the
time to be an extreme and exclusive instrument only to be employed in
special circumstances.[28]

But the general mood gradually swung towards 'armed struggle'. An
overwhelming desire to act took over and when the Central Committee
voted in March 1879 on whether or not to assassinate Drenteln, the new
head of the third section, Plekhanov found himself in a minority of one.
To some extent this swing towards terrorism was engendered by the mass
arrests, the savage sentences and the executions which continued all the
time. But perhaps even more important a factor was the belief that terrorist
operations were far more effective in promoting the revolution, if only
because of the tremendous publicity they received – very much in contrast
to illegal propaganda and organizational work, which has no visible effect.
By autumn 1879 the split was an accomplished fact. Earlier (in March
1879) the ideological justification for terrorism had already been outlined

in some detail in the *Listok Narodnoi Voli*, the organ of the radical, activist trend edited by Morozov and Tikhomirov. Political assassination was above all an act of revenge, but at the same time it was one of the best weapons of agitation. One had to strike at the centre to shake the whole system. The future belonged to mass movements but terrorism had to show the masses the way. The programme of the Narodnaya Volya Central Committee listed the liquidation of the most dangerous members of the government, the defence of the party against spies, and the punishment of those who had committed the most glaring oppression as the main tasks of the terrorist struggle. If ten to fifteen pillars of the establishment were killed at one and the same time, the government would panic and would lose its freedom of action. At the same time the masses would wake up.[29] But it was never made quite clear in what way such terror would lead to the actual conquest of power. Was the government simply to disintegrate or would there be a popular rising? If so, the party needed an organizational network to lead the masses, and a few terrorist fighting groups would not suffice. Such an organization, however, did not exist. Tikhomirov thought that two or three years of systematic terror would bring about the collapse of the government; others, Sofia Perovskaya among them, were equally optimistic. At the very least, the government would have to make far-reaching concessions and grant the basic freedoms of organization and speech. In that event the revolutionaries would cease their terrorist activities. It has been argued that not all Narodovoltsy were terrorists (and that not all terrorists were Narodovoltsy), that out of the 500-odd members who belonged to the party only a tenth actively took part in attacks and assassinations.[30]

As already noted, the mood was overwhelmingly pro-terrorist, reaching far beyond the ranks of the organization to students, the intelligentsia and other sections of society. Even the Liberals were willing to give money for bombs (though not for socialist propaganda); grand old men of the Russian emigration, such as Lavrov and Mikhailovski, gave terrorism their blessing; even Marx and Engels believed that Russia was on the eve of a revolution as a result of the actions of the Narodnaya Volya. Plekhanov, who had warned time and again against terrorism, felt he could no longer speak out against it; it would have been futile, he later wrote – the intelligentsia believed in terror 'as in God'.[31]

The most outspoken protagonists of the terrorist approach, Morozov and Romanenko, outlined their views in two pamphlets published in England and Switzerland respectively.[32] These were not official 'party documents' but they are of interest because they expressed a widespread mood and, after some initial hesitation, the party more or less accepted the reasoning on which they were based. True, the authors were as yet a little reluctant to call a spade by its real name, just as Narodnaya Volya frequently referred to 'disorganization' where terror would have been the more appropriate term. Tikhomirov wrote about 'partisan warfare', and Morozov later confessed that he did not like the term 'terror' either. Initially he had wanted to call his pamphlet 'Neo-Partisan Warfare'.[33]

Morozov described how the revolutionaries had advanced from self-defence to attack. The government with its guns, prisons, spies and millions of soldiers could easily defeat any frontal assault, but it was powerless against terrorist attacks. The only thing that the terrorists had to fear was lack of caution on the part of their own members.[34] Terrorism, according to Morozov, was an altogether new fighting method, far more 'cost-effective' than an old-fashioned revolutionary mass struggle. Despite insignificant forces, it would still be possible to concentrate every effort upon the overthrow of tyranny. Since there was no limit to human inventiveness, it was virtually impossible for the tyrants to provide safeguards against attacks. Never before were conditions so auspicious from the point of view of the revolutionary party, and once a whole series of terrorist groups came into being, they would spell the final days of the monarchy. Terrorist attempts in the past had been acts of despair and frequently of suicide. This tragic element no longer existed: the terrorists simply carried out death sentences which had been imposed by their tribunals and there was every reason to assume that the executioners would not be apprehended and would disappear without trace. Victory was inevitable sooner or later. In order to blunt the terrorist struggle and win over the bourgeoisie, the government was quite likely to grant a constitution. But the terrorist struggle could be conducted not only against tyranny but also against a constitutional oppression such as in Germany. Dictators like Napoleon or Bismarck should be liquidated at the very beginning of their rise to power '*pour décourager les autres*' and it was immaterial whether they were backed by an army or a plebiscite. In this way terror would remain a guarantee of freedom, a constant deterrent against would-be despots. In Morozov's view the principal assignments currently facing the revolutionaries were first to provide a theoretical foundation for terrorism 'which so far every one understood in his own way'; second, to apply terrorism systematically so as to achieve the demoralization, weakening and final disorganization of the government.

Romanenko's views were on similar lines: terrorism was not only effective, it was humanitarian. It cost infinitely fewer victims than a mass struggle; in a popular revolution the best were killed while the real villains looked on from the sidelines. The blows of terrorism were directed against the main culprits; a few innocent people might suffer, but this was inevitable in warfare. Terrorism, then, was the application of modern science to the revolutionary struggle. He interpreted Russian history since the days of the Decembrists as a duel between the intelligentsia and the regime. It was pointless asking the people to rise against their oppressors for the masses were insufficiently strong. It was wrong to regard systematic terror as immoral, since everything that contributed to the liberating revolution was *a priori* moral.[35] The same ideas of cost-effectiveness and, in particular, of the humanitarian character of terrorism were also voiced by Zhelyabov, the central figure of the Narodnaya Volya and, most outspokenly, in a pamphlet by Lev Sternberg (1861–1927), *Politicheski Terror v Rossii*.[36] Terrorism, in Sternberg's view, was a safety valve; if there was no terror there would be a terrible explosion from below. It was the historical mission of the intelligentsia to prevent – or, to be precise, to pre-empt – this uncontrolled explosion.

Romanenko's pamphlet was written in answer to the critique of M.P. Dragomanov (1841–95), the leading Ukrainian writer who, on the whole, was in sympathy with the Russian revolutionary movement. But Dragomanov denounced the 'Machiavellianism' of the terrorists as well as attacks against banks and post offices in which mere guards had been killed. It was one thing, Dragomanov wrote, to accept terrorism in Russia as a natural response to the terror exerted by the government. It was another to make terrorism into a system, the cardinal principle of the revolutionary struggle. For terrorism was a pathological phenomenon, and if the aim of the revolutionaries was to be unsullied it could be achieved only by purity of method. Attacks in the open, attempts to liberate revolutionaries from prison and even attacks against the secret police were all justifiable, but individual terror as a system could not be morally justified.[37]

The subsequent fate of the main protagonists of the doctrine of terrorism is of some interest: Nikolai Morozov spent more than twenty years in tsarist prisons but was released in 1905; he published poems as well as papers on chemistry, cosmogony, history and Christianity. His chemistry, according to all accounts, was sounder than his history. He became a sympathizer of the Kadets (the liberal constitutionalists) but decided to remain in Russia after 1917 and was made an honorary member of the Academy of Sciences. He died in 1946. Gerasim Romanenko (1858–1927), on the other hand, gravitated towards the extreme right, the 'Black Hundred'; some of his critics had argued from the beginning that he was a terrorist without being a socialist. Tikhomirov also solemnly renounced terrorism in later years, and became a conservative publicist. Sternberg made good use of his years in Siberian exile and became an ethnographer of world renown.

There was a striking discrepancy between the extreme means used by the Narodovoltsy and their relatively moderate political demands. In this respect they certainly did not agree with Bakunin's pan-destructionism. A letter which the Narodnaya Volya Executive Committee wrote to Alexander III, published in March 1881, ten days after the assassination of his predecessor, stated that terror was a sad necessity, that the terrorists only wanted a general amnesty and a constitution which provided elementary civil freedoms. If these demands were met, terrorist activity would cease, and a peaceful struggle of ideas would replace violence.[38] It has been said, and not without cause, that at least some of the Narodovoltsy were simply 'liberals with a bomb'. Kibalchich, the scientific genius, who produced dynamite for the Narodovoltsy, was the mildest of men in his private life as well as in his political views. If a peace-loving man like him agreed to co-operate with the terrorists, Lev Deitch later wrote, it only proved that people with a conscience saw no other way out in the given circumstances.[39] It is equally true that Nechaev (unlike Bakunin) was not a socialist but a Jacobin in the style of Robespierre, and that some of the main advocates and practitioners of Russian terrorism in the first decade of the twentieth century, such as Burtsev, Savinkov and Schweitzer, were also radical liberals rather than socialists.

The terrorist campaign conducted by Narodnaya Volya was essentially different from anarchist activities elsewhere in Europe, which were carried out (as F. Venturi has noted) by isolated individuals inspired by obscure ideals. Russian terrorism was both one aspect of the formation of a revolutionary socialist party and a symptom of a general crisis in Russian society.[40] Vera Zasulich, who had opened the terrorist campaign, was later to write that terror had been like a major storm in an enclosed space: the waves rose high but the unrest did not spread. It exhausted the moral force of the intelligentsia.[41] Kravchinski, who wrote a most moving account of the heroism of the revolutionaries, concluded that terrorism as a system had outlived its era and that it could no longer be revived. The one side no longer had its previous faith and the other side no longer feared it.[42] Kravchinski's prophecy proved premature; terror was revived only two decades later by a new generation of revolutionaries.

The tradition of the Narodnaya Volya lingered on and attempts were made to re-establish the party. From time to time its programme (in slightly modified form) and other literature was published.[43] In Russian émigré circles it had its strong defenders who disputed the strategy of the orthodox Marxists. Alexander Ulianov, Lenin's older brother, was the head of a small terrorist group of students, whose leading members were arrested and hanged in 1887. He, too, advocated 'systematic terrorism' and believed that the initiative had to come from the intelligentsia since the common people had no rights and were altogether unprepared to act.[44] The first to re-emphasize the importance of terrorist action after a long period of silence was Burtsev, a radical–democratic opponent of the regime, in a new journal, *Narodovolets* (1897), published in London.[45] In the very first number he stated unequivocally that terrorism in the tradition of the Narodnaya Volya was the only policy that held out any promise. Burtsev was arrested after intervention by the Russian government, but subsequently was released. He issued a new pamphlet in which he stressed that support for terrorism was growing fast, that all those who approved of terrorism were of one family and that they should bury, at least for the time being, all differences of opinion between them.[46] Support for terrorism came from unexpected quarters such as the moderate socialist Krichevski, who regarded the new terrorist wave after the turn of the century as a turning point of historical significance. Others who came out in its support were Grigorovich (i.e. Zhitlovski), as well as writers in various Russian- and Polish-language periodicals which began to appear at the time, such as *Nakanune*, *Przedswit*, *Revoliutsionnaya Rossiia* and *Vestnik Russkoi Revoliutsii*.

In 1900 the Social Revolutionary Party was eventually founded in Kharkov and it was this movement that became the main agent of the second wave of terror, beginning with the assassination of Sipyagin, the minister of the interior, in 1902. The leaders of the new party, which included some survivors of the old Narodnaya Volya such as Gots and Rusanov, maintained that terrorism was necessary and unavoidable. It was not intended to replace the mass struggle; on the contrary it would strengthen and supplement the revolutionization of the masses. Systematic terrorism, the party stated, in conjunction with other forms of open mass struggle such as industrial riots, agrarian risings and demonstrations, would lead to the disorganization of the enemy. 'Terrorist activity will cease only with victory over autocracy and the complete attainment of political liberty.'[47] A terrorist 'Fighting Organization' (Boevaya Organisatsia – BO) was set up and given autonomy within the party. The political purpose of terror was defined by the party leadership in a polemic against the Social Democrats.[48] The old quarrel about the use of terrorist tactics had been resolved in the light of historical experience. There were always ideological reasons against terrorism, but revolutionaries were driven to it, unable to choose the means they were forced to employ. Self-defence was necessary against the attacks of tsarist autocracy which engaged the Cossacks and their whips (*nagaikas*) to destroy the human dignity of their victims. Imprisoned revolutionaries were driven to despair and suicide. *Iskra*, the organ of the Social Democrats,

had argued that the only effects of terrorism were to isolate the revolutionary vanguard from the masses and to hamper organizational work.[49] Yet
at the same time *Iskra* demanded that the government should be made
to behave with humanity towards striking workers and political prisoners.
How could it be compelled to do so? Perhaps by speeches and articles!
The whistle of bullets was the only sound that the rulers heeded. More
and more people on the left were learning the propagandistic effect of
the terrorist act. (It should be noted in passing that many, perhaps most,
leading members of the Fighting Organization such as Kalyayev, Balmashev, Savinkov and Karpovich had initially belonged to Social Democrats,
anti-terrorist organizations.) Terror, claimed the Social Revolutionaries,
caused chaos within the establishment. Again, the statement was not exaggerated, as subsequent events were to show: Gerassimov, head of the political police at the time, later wrote that the terrorist operations had indeed
disoriented the regime: 'All ministers are human and they want to live.
. . .'[50] Durnovo, minister of the interior, used almost identical words when,
in later years, Tikhomirov spoke to him of the folly of terror – 'stupid
it may be, but it is a very poisonous idea, a very terrible one, creating
power out of impotence'.[51]

The Social Revolutionaries argued that even the actions of the Narodnaya
Volya twenty-five years earlier, despite comparatively little public support,
had had a tremendous effect, and for a while the authorities had contemplated constitutional reforms. How much greater was the impact likely
to be now that the revolutionary movement had reached more sections
of the population? Although the Social Revolutionaries regarded terror
as a psychological necessity, it was only one weapon among several; it
should not be self-perpetuating. No illusions, no exaggerated optimism
about its consequences should be entertained, and it was clear that terror
was a temporary phenomenon – the result of specific Russian conditions.
It simply strengthened other forms of the struggle. Again the Social Revolutionaries criticized the Social Democrat *Iskra* which had objected to
planned, organized, systematic terror, but accepted accidental (*'stychic'*)
terror. Unplanned terror would of necessity be indiscriminate and was
bound to entail unintended victims. The party, the organization, would
have to decide whom to attack and when. These views about the strictly
rational character of terror endorsed by party ideologists abroad were not
necessarily shared by the terrorists within Russia. The very language the
terrorists used pointed to their irrationality: the revolutionary was a hero
driven by hate, inspired by honour and a willingness to sacrifice himself –
bomb-throwing was 'holy'.[52]

The impact of terrorist operations on Russian public opinion during the early years of the century was startling. During the years 1878–81, there had been some support among the intelligentsia, whereas two decades later 'society' in its majority was sympathetic. After the assassination of Plehve, the minister of the interior, in 1903, even Plekhanov, a lifelong opponent of terrorism, was prepared to justify such operations under certain circumstances and suggested co-operating with the Social Revolutionaries. It was only after leading Social Democrats such as Akselrod and Martov threatened to leave the party that he withdrew his suggestion of co-operation.

In October 1905, when the tsar published his famous manifesto announcing the creation of a legislative assembly, the Social Revolutionaries suspended terrorist activities. They were resumed in January 1906, suspended again when the First Duma opened, and renewed when the Duma was dissolved in July 1906.[53] Meanwhile a more radical faction, the 'Maximalists', had split away and established its own fighting organization. By that time the debate about terrorism had virtually ended, for during the revolution political violence had become a daily occurrence. The Bolsheviks engaged in it on occasion, the Black Hundred organized pogroms had assassinated political opponents. The only discussions concerned terrorist tactics. The Maximalists criticized the Fighting Organization of the Social Revolutionaries for its strictly centralist, hierarchical structure: its leadership was appointed from above, and its members had no right to criticize operational plans. Such centralism had its advantages, argued the Maximalists, provided a man of genius like Gershuni was at its head, but it was bound to create dissatisfaction and frustration in the ranks, who would lose their capacity for inventiveness and improvisation. When the supreme commander was a police agent (as had been the case) it naturally led to total disaster.[54] The Maximalists were aware that far-reaching decentralization also had its disadvantages: it was likely to cost more victims, and result in operations that were badly timed from a political point of view. Decentralized terror groups could not be guaranteed against penetration by police agents either. Thus the ideal solution was to combine the advantages of centralized and decentralized terror, granting a greater measure of autonomy to local groups while retaining a strong central leadership.

It was easier, however, to discuss ideal tactics in the abstract than to carry them out in practice, and these debates, in any case, belonged to a period when terrorism had virtually petered out. There was no Maximalist fighting organization after 1907 and a similar fate had befallen the Social Revolutionaries even before Azev had been unmasked as a spy in 1909. At the Social Revolutionary Party conference of May 1909 Rubanovich had sharply denounced terrorism, which, he claimed, had become a 'business enterprise'. Everyone agreed that terrorism ought to be temporarily suspended, but what was its role in the more distant future? Chernov argued that the Azev affair had compromised the terrorists but not the system as such, whereas the critics insisted on the dissolution of the Fighting Organization. Recent events had shown that the revolutionary party in Russia no longer faced just the tsarist regime; social classes had emerged in the revolution and individual terror was of no avail in the class struggle. This in turn was rejected as a quasi-Marxist argument and the debate continued for some three more years; but while there were further sporadic terrorist actions there was no longer any 'systematic terrorism'.[55]

During and after the revolution of 1905 there was much free-wheeling terrorism in the Caucasus. Anarchist groups preached 'ruthless and total people's vengeance'. One of their sections, the Bezmotivniki (the motiveless ones), declaring 'death to the bourgeois', contemplated and occasionally committed acts of indiscriminate terror, such as throwing bombs in cafés, restaurants and theatres. Attacks took place at the Hotel Bristol in Warsaw and the Café Libman in Odessa, which, it was subsequently pointed out, was not at all a café of the rich.[56] But anarchism in Russia itself was ineffectual and its operations were on a much lesser scale than the far-reaching campaign of the Social Revolutionaries. It made no theoretical contribution to the cause of the armed struggle, except for some appeals in the style of the Futurist manifesto of 1909 which complained of the 'poisonous breath of civilization: Take the picks and hammers! Undermine the foundations of venerable towns! Everything is ours, outside us is only death. . . . All to the street! Forward! Destroy! Kill!'[57] The proper place for appeals of this kind is in the annals of expressionist literature, not in the history of terrorism.

Turkey, India and the Russian Example

The example set by the Russians had a considerable influence on terrorist movements, contemporaneous and subsequent, throughout the world. Its impact was felt all over Europe, and its methods were studied even in Ireland and America. Polish socialists came under its particular sway and also engaged in attacks on government offices, in individual assassinations and, in particular, in 'expropriations', i.e. armed robbery of banks and trains. Strong repercussions were felt in the Balkans where terrorism in various forms had been endemic for a long time. The attraction was not one-sided: Kravchinski had gone to fight in Herzegovina in the 1870s and Kalyayev once told a comrade that, while there were only a few Russian terrorists as yet, he hoped he would live to see the existence of a really popular terrorist movement such as existed in Macedonia.[58] But the Balkan terrorists were first and foremost (and usually exclusively) nationalists; if some of the southern Slavs were familiar with the writings of Bakunin and Kropotkin, the ideological inspiration of the Young Bosnians, for instance, owed much more to Mazzini than to the Narodnaya Volya. They did resemble the Narodniki in their asceticism, in the chastity they observed and in their belief that only persons of nobility of character were capable of political assassination.[59]

There is evidence to the effect that the methods of the Armenian revolutionaries of the late 1880s and 1890s were largely borrowed from the Narodnaya Volya. Their first leader in Turkey was Avetis Nazarbeck, who was converted to socialism by his fiancée. She reportedly spoke only Russian and had taken part in the Russian revolutionary movement.[60] The programme of the Dashnak Party (1892) stated that the revolutionary bands intended 'to terrorize government officials, informers, traitors, usurers and every kind of exploiter'. Organizational links with Armenians living in Russia were close: weapons were produced in a plant by workers who had gained experience in the Tula arms factory, or were bought (albeit not through official channels) from the Russian government armoury in Tiflis.[61]

The political problems facing the Armenian terrorist movement were, of course, *sui generis*: they were a minority, facing both a tyrannical government and a hostile population. Some of them advocated an immediate struggle, others warned against frittering away their forces and suggested waiting until the Ottoman government was embroiled in Arabia or Crete or with some European powers before striking.[62] The proponents of immediate action prevailed, and since they could not possibly hope to overthrow the government, their strategy had to be based on provocation. They assumed, in all probability, that their attacks on the Turks would provoke savage retaliation, and that as a result the Armenian population would be radicalized; more decisive yet, the Western powers, appalled by the massacres, would intervene on their behalf as they did for the Bulgarians two decades earlier. Lastly, they seem to have hoped that their example would lead to risings among other nationalities in the Ottoman empire, as well perhaps as inspiring disaffected Turks.[63] Their most spectacular action was the seizure of the Ottoman Bank in Constantinople in August 1896. But the results were disastrous: a three-day massacre followed in which thousands of Armenians were killed. Europe showed 'murderous indifference' and a friend of the Armenian cause, criticizing the revolutionaries, wrote that 'if our Henchakists and Drojakists continue their crazy enterprises, very few Armenians will be left in Turkey to profit one day from the application of reforms'.[64]

The Armenian example clearly showed the difficulties facing a national minority that resorted to terrorist methods. When Karakozov fired at the tsar in 1866 he was apprehended by passers-by and his shouts, 'Fools, I have done this for you,' were to no avail, for the 'masses', far from assisting him, were loyal to the tsar. (The tsar asked: Are you a Pole?) In the eyes of the Turkish population the Armenian terrorists were just foreign agents, traitors, and not much encouragement by the authorities was needed to instigate massacres against the enemies of Islam and the Turkish nation.

The Russian example gave some impetus to the revolutionary movement in India. 'Protests are of no avail,' Tilak wrote in 1906, 'days of prayer have gone.... Look to the examples of Ireland, Japan and Russia and follow their methods.'[65] There was advice of a more practical nature, too. A Russian chemical engineer gave Senapati Bapat a Russian manual for the manufacture of bombs in 1908, and a Russian student translated it for the benefit of the revolutionaries of the 'Free India Society' in North London.[66] The manual was cyclostyled and sent to India.

But the doctrine of the Narodniki contained elements quite indigestible to India; the burning idealist patriotism of Mazzini appealed much more than the polemics between various socialist factions. Savarkar, the most fiery apostle of early Indian terrorism, wrote a life of Mazzini in Marathi, a book which became the first victim of the India Press Act.

Indian terrorism was relatively infrequent and on the whole quite ineffective; more often than not Indian terrorists managed to kill some innocent bystanders rather than their intended victims. Yet the ideology of Indian terrorism is of some interest for it contained a strange mixture of Indian traditions and Western influences. In 1897 Tilak wrote that the Hindu rebel leader Shivaji had been entitled two centuries earlier to kill Afzal Khan, a Muslim general, at a peace parley: Shivaji had now become a national hero with his own festivals.[67] (Gandhi, it should be added, regarded Shivaji as a misguided patriot.) Marathi newspapers quite openly justified murder when inspired by a higher purpose. The young patriots, fired by these teachings, were orthodox Hindus and they despised the reformist politicians of the Congress Party who, they claimed, violated religious principle by partaking of biscuits, loaves, meat and spirits. In their manifestos they announced that 'we shall assuredly shed upon the earth the life-blood of the enemies who destroy religion'.[68] When ten years later the most successful of the vernacular dailies, *Yugantar*, began to appear, the same message was preached with even greater emphasis and detail. Theft and dacoity (robbery) were normally regarded as crimes, but destruction for the highest good was justified; it was work of religious merit. The murder of foreigners was no sin but *jagna*, a ceremonial sacrifice.[69] Bombs should be manufactured in secret and guns imported from abroad, for 'the people of the West will sell their own motherland for money'. Tilak, who invoked the goddess Kali in his patriotic speeches ('We are all Hindus and idolators and I am not ashamed of it'), likened the bomb to a sacred formula, to 'magic' and an 'amulet'. Savarkar and his pupils not surprisingly turned against pacifism and the universalist element (the 'mumbo jumbo') of Hindu religion; non-violence would crush 'the faculty of resisting sin' and destroy the power of national resistance. In his book on the Indian War of Independence of 1857, which became something of a classic among the extremists, Savarkar wrote that the sword of Brutus was holy and the arrow of Wilhelm Tell divine, and he cited some incidents in Indian history too – every Hiranyakashipu had his Narasimha, every Dushshasana had his Bheema, every evildoer his avenger.[70] The *Indian Sociologist* published by Krishna Varma in London also justified political assassination. The British authorities took a dim view. Like other periodicals such as *Bande Mataram* and *Talvar* it had to transfer its activities from Highgate to the continent.

There was an upsurge of terrorist activities in 1909 when Sir William Curzon Wyllie, Lord Morley's political secretary, was killed in London by one of Krishna Varma's students. But this spurt was shortlived and it was only in the 1920s that a new wave of terrorist actions took place. Indian terrorism, as preached by Savarkar and others, was directed not only against the British but also against Muslims, and, by implication, against political enemies within their own ranks. In later years Savarkar became the leader of the Hindu Mahasabha and its military–terrorist arm, the Rashtriya Swayam Sewak Sangh (RSSS). They preached that India was one and indivisible, and everyone who did not accept this precept was a traitor. The leadership of the RSSS consisted of Brahmins, mainly from Poona, Savarkar's home town and political base. One of them, Nathuram Godse, shot Gandhi in 1948. He had been Savarkar's chief aide for several years, but Savarkar's complicity could not be proven in court. He was released and died at the ripe old age of eighty-three in 1966.[71]

The inspiration of the next generation of Indian terrorists at first sight seemed altogether different. Most of them had been members of Gandhi's non-violent noncooperation movement during its early phase, and it was only after the hopes accompanying it had ebbed away that they began to turn to revolutionary ideas. The Hindustan Socialist Republican Association (HSRA) was founded in 1928. Some of its leaders, such as Bhagat Singh, had allegedly read *Das Kapital* and they were great admirers of the Soviet Union.[72] Their doctrine, as summarized in a work entitled *The Philosophy of the Bomb*, stated that they did not ask for mercy and gave no quarter: 'Ours is a war to the end – to Victory or Death.' Yet at the same time they denied that their revolution was to be identified with violence, or, more specifically, with the cult of the pistol and the bomb. In their writings they emphasized the leading role of the working class. Unfortunately, workers and peasants were as yet 'passive, dumb and voiceless' and the radical nationalist youth, idealist and restless, would have to act as the vanguard of the revolution.[73] This then was their historical mission: the youth of India, being the salt of the earth, was to conduct not just 'propaganda by deed' but propaganda by death. These glaring contradictions between doctrine and practice are not too difficult to explain. The young revolutionaries were both impatient and isolated. A Russian-style 'going to the people' was ruled out; in India – as in Latin America and Africa – manual labour has never been held in high esteem among members of the upper classes, including the revolutionaries among them. A sympathetic historian notes that the HSRA failed to do any political work among the common people, and had hardly any link or contact with them. In theory they had become totally committed to revolutionary socialism, yet the 'revolutionary consciousness' which they invoked so frequently was purely nationalist, and the young militants could be used therefore almost exclusively for nationalist action.[74]

The origins of *The Philosophy of the Bomb*, the HSRA manifesto, should be mentioned at least in passing.[75] Following the attempt of Indian terrorists to blow up the viceregal special train in 1929, Gandhi made a speech to an Indian Congress meeting (later published as an article in *Young India* under the title 'The Cult of Violence') and drafted a resolution rejecting terrorism. The terrorists were denounced as 'cowards', their actions described as 'dastardly'. Gandhi wrote that he would despair of non-violence if he was not certain that bomb-throwing was nothing but 'froth coming to the surface in an agitated liquid'. Gandhi also warned against terrorism in view of the likely internal consequences: from violence done to the foreign ruler there was only an 'easy, natural step to violence to our own people whom we may consider to be obstructing the country's progress'.[76] Prophetic words in the light of the tragic death of the Mahatma.

Gandhi had denounced terrorism, of course, on many previous occasions. History had proved, he told Calcutta students in 1915, that assassinations ('a Western institution') had done no good: 'What have they done to the Western world? We would not hesitate to rise against those who wanted to terrorize the country.'[77] The philosophers of the bomb argued on the other hand that, while terrorism was not a complete revolution, revolution was not complete without terrorism. Nor was terrorism a European product; it was home-grown.

Terrorism instils fear in the hearts of the oppressors, it brings hope of revenge and redemption to the oppressed masses. It gives courage and self-confidence to the wavering, it shatters the spell of the subject race in the eyes of the world, because it is the most convincing proof of a nation's hunger for freedom.[78]

The average Indian, the terrorists claimed, understood little about fine theological necessities of love for one's enemy. Gandhi's gospel of love would not sway the British viceroys and generals. Violence did not impede the march towards social progress and political freedom: 'Take the case of Russia and Turkey for example.'[79] Gandhi, they claimed, did not understand revolutionary psychology. A terrorist did not sacrifice his life because the crowd might shout 'bravo' in appreciation; he engaged in terrorism because reason forced him into that course and because conscience dictated it: 'It is to reason and reason alone that he bows.' There was no crime that Britain had not committed in India: 'As a race and as a people we stand dishonoured and outraged. Do people still expect us to forget and to forgive? We shall have our revenge, a people's righteous revenge on the tyrant.'[80]

The terrorists distributed *The Philosophy of the Bomb* and some other manifestos but their impact on the masses was insignificant compared with Gandhism. There were a few demonstrations of 'propaganda by deed'. A police officer was shot in Lahore in November 1928. In April 1929 Bhagat Singh and Batukeswar Datta threw two small bombs from the public gallery into the Delhi Legislative Assembly. They made no attempt to escape. Both were executed: in their statement in court they said that their sole purpose had been 'to make the deaf hear', to register a protest on behalf of those who had no other means left to give expression to their heartrending agony. They said they had been inspired by the ideals which guided Guru Govind Singh and Shivaji, Kemal Pasha and Reza Khan, Washington and Garibaldi, Lafayette and Lenin.[81]

There were some other examples of 'propaganda by deed' such as the Chittagong raid in 1930. The same year the Yugantar Party in Calcutta drew up a terrorist manifesto calling for the assassination of Europeans in hotels, clubs and cinemas, the burning of the aerodrome in Dum-Dum, the destruction of gas and electricity works.[82] But these few manifestos and actions apart, a marked decline in terrorist activities took place after 1932, coinciding with the collapse of the Civil Disobedience movement. The emergency regulations adopted by the government were quite effective, and the constitutional reforms of 1935 (in the words of one historian) blunted the edge of both the violent and non-violent methods of Indian politics.[83] Terrorism had a short-lived revival only during the Second World

War. With Partition, revolutionary violence became transformed from individual to mass terror and civil war.

Propaganda by Deed

The concept of 'propaganda by deed' has been traced back by a historian of anarchism to Carlo Pisacane, the hero of the Risorgimento who lost his life in a tragically futile expedition to Calabria in 1857. Pisacane had written that the propaganda of the idea was a chimera and that ideas result from deeds.[84] Similar thoughts, in fact, were expressed well before, but the era of 'propaganda by deed' was heralded in a statement by the Italian anarchists Malatesta and Cafiero in 1876. They made it known that their Federation believed that 'the insurrectional fact destined to affirm socialist principles by deeds is the most effective means of propaganda and the only one which, without tricking and corrupting the masses, can penetrate the deepest social layers and draw the living forces of humanity into the struggle sustained by the International'.[85] Soon after, writing in the same journal, Paul Brousse, a young French physician, coined the phrase 'propaganda by deed'.[86] Theoretical propaganda – whether mass meetings, newspapers or pamphlets – was of limited efficacy; moreover, the venal bourgeois press could always calumniate and disguise ('manipulate' in latter-day jargon) the true message and bourgeois orators could wheedle popular assemblies. Furthermore, workers who returned home, after an exhausting working day of eleven or twelve hours, had little desire to read socialist literature. Proudhon had written brilliant studies, but who had read them except a handful of people? Practical demonstrations, such as the Paris Commune, had presented the issues at stake in so dramatic a way that they could no longer be shirked. Propaganda by deed, in short, was a powerful weapon to awaken the consciousness of the people.[87] Yet Brousse did not preach political assassination in so many words; on the contrary, he expressed doubt whether political assassination could possibly change a political system. It was only two years later that Kropotkin provided the classic formulation, defining anarchist action as permanent incitement through the spoken and written word, the knife, the rifle, dynamite – everything, provided it was not legal. One single deed created more propaganda in a few days than a thousand leaflets. The government would endeavour to defend itself by intensifying its oppression, but further deeds would then be committed by one or more persons, thus driving the revolutionaries to ever more heroic acts. One deed would bring forth another, more and more people would join in the struggle and the government would lose its unity and self-confidence. Any concessions it might make would come too late, and eventually a general revolution would take place.[88]

Prince Kropotkin, the son of a high-ranking Russian officer, had served in the Corps of Pages; he joined a group of revolutionaries, was arrested in 1874, but succeeded in escaping two years later. His political career belongs to the history of the anarchist movement of which he became a leading ideologist; all that need be noted in this context is that, very much in contrast to the Nechaevs of this world, he was an almost saintly figure who, in later years, came out strongly against 'mindless terror'. But it cannot be denied that when he took over the leadership of the anarchist movement in the late 1870s he was one of the main protagonists of individual terror as a means to arouse the spirit of revolt among the masses.[89] Even in later years he was able to justify the assassination of Alexander II and attempts on the lives of leading political figures in the West in the 1880s and 1890s as acts committed by desperate men in response to unbearable conditions. The individuals responsible were not to be blamed. Society was answerable for it had taught them contempt for human life. He fully endorsed Kravchinski's view that while terror was profoundly distasteful, to submit to violence was even worse.[90]

The concept of 'propaganda by deed' figured prominently in the deliberations of the International Anarchist Congress which took place in London in July 1881. One of the delegates, Ganz, suggested that greater attention be given to the study of chemistry and technology in order to supply dreadful weapons for the struggle against the oppressors. Kropotkin thought that these were praiseworthy sentiments but noted that it was an illusion to assume that one could become a chemist or electrician in a few hours; a handful of experts could deal with these problems more competently.[91] Nor were chemistry and pyrotechnics a panacea: it was more important to understand how to mobilize the masses. The Congress nevertheless passed a resolution that as technical and chemical sciences had already rendered service to the revolutionary cause and were bound to render still greater services in the future, affiliated organizations and individuals should devote themselves to the study of these sciences.[92] These suggestions were based on the assumption – again to quote the resolution – that a general conflagration was not far distant; 'propaganda by deed' had to reinforce oral and written propaganda and arouse the spirit of the masses insofar as illusions still existed about the effectiveness of legal methods. But the conflagration did not take place, and more than a decade was to pass before certain French, Italian and Spanish anarchists engaged in 'propaganda by deed'. There were only a few bombings and assassinations throughout Western Europe during the 1880s, and most of these, such as the attempt to kill the German Emperor Wilhelm I, were not undertaken by anarchists. The original impulse for the new doctrine, of course, had been provided by the example of the Russian revolutionaries, but by the time the London resolutions were adopted the terrorist wave had abated even in Russia.

Thus the anarchist appeals had no serious consequence other than alarming the general public. There is evidence that in their endeavour to penetrate the ranks of the anarchists the police actually provided money for anarchist publications and, in some cases, apparently also for terrorist operations. One of the most bloodcurdling appeals was published in a police-sponsored French-language periodical in London: it called for blows against the left, right and centre, against religion and patriotism. Theft, murder and arson were legitimate means in the struggle and so, of course, was the great friend, the 'thunder of dynamite'.[93] In 1880 the French anarchist journal *La Révolution Sociale* began publishing instructions for the fabrication of bombs. At the time this paper was edited by Serreaux, a police spy, with money provided by Louis Andrieux, the prefect of the Paris police, who thoughtfully left us with detailed memoirs. On the other hand, the bomb, 'the last weapon of revolt', was also praised in *bona fide* anarchist publications such as Most's *Freiheit*, *La Lutte Sociale* and Swiss publications. Advice was given to place bombs or inflammable materials near storehouses where cotton or alcohol were kept. Chemical formulas for making *produits anti-bourgeois* were published. Of course, one could not be too specific: '*L'action ne se conseille, ni ne se parle, ni ne s'écrit – elle se fait.*'[94] Marie Constant, a revolutionary Paris shoemaker, composed a popular song ending

> *Maintenant la danse tragique*
> *vent une plus forte musique:*
> *Dynamitons, dynamitons.*

After the execution of Ravachol, a new verb came into being, *ravacholiser*; the 'Ravachole' was sung to the tune of the Carmagnole, 'Vive le son d'l'explosion'. A Ravachol cult caused considerable accession of strength to anarchism.[95] Among the more far-fetched suggestions was advice to domestic servants to poison their employers, advice to churchgoers to poison clerics, advice to soak rats in petrol, set them on fire and then let them loose in buildings marked for destruction.[96] Anarchist journals called on their followers to arm themselves with every weapon provided by science, to destroy the criminal institutions of a society based on the most extreme egoism: '*Pillons, brûlons, détruisons.*' The new revolutionary strategy, it was announced, was no longer based on open, frontal battles, '*mais une guerre des partisans menés de façon occulte*'.[97]

When the London congress adopted its militant resolutions, the Italian anarchists, who had wielded considerable influence in the 1870s, were already in rapid decline. After a few ineffectual insurrections the momentum petered out altogether. The murder of a Viennese shoemaker in 1882, the assassination of a police inspector the year after, of a police agent and of a money changer in 1884, also in Vienna, did nothing to bring the revolution any nearer. The fact that the small children of the money changer had also been killed in order to dispose of witnesses did not endear the terrorists to the masses either. A pharmacist was murdered in Strassbourg and a banker in Mannheim. In both these cases robbery seems to have been the motive and not political principles. A few minor incidents took place in Switzerland. This was about the sum total of 'propaganda by deed' in Central Europe. The change came only with a series of terrorist actions in France between March 1892 and June 1894. After 1894 there were still a few spectacular political assassinations usually carried out by Italians. But these actions were undertaken by individuals, and as far as can be established no organization supported them. (The only possible exception was the case of Bresci, the murderer of King Umberto of Italy in 1900, who had apparently been chosen and assisted by a group of Italian anarchists in Paterson, New Jersey.)[98] The 'great international anarchist conspiracy' existed only in the imagination of police chiefs and the press; its main importance in retrospect was to have inspired novels by Henry James, Joseph Conrad, Émile Zola and some others, just as the Russian anarchists had inspired Dostoevski. But there was no 'Anarchist Party'. When Émile Henry, who had thrown the bomb at the Café Terminus, declared at his trial that 'we ask no pity in this pitiless war which we have declared on the bourgeoisie', he was speaking for no one but himself.[99] Anarchist periodicals had virtually ceased to recommend 'propaganda by deed' several years before, noting that it was utopian to believe that individual terror could possibly be the basis of rational, active and sustained propaganda.[100] Kropotkin, once one of the most outspoken advocates of terrorism, admitted in 1891 that a mistake had been made: the revolution would not come as the result of some heroic actions. Inspired by the Russian revolutionaries in 1881, European anarchists had erroneously believed that a handful of dedicated revolutionaries armed with a few bombs could bring about a social revolution, as though a building rooted in centuries could be destroyed by a few kilograms of explosives.[101] But if the appeal of 1881 for 'propaganda by deed' had been ignored for ten years, so was the call for retreat in 1891. There was no global conspiracy, no high command, no 'party discipline'; each individual anarchist, each group, felt free to register his protest in the form and at the time he saw fit.

Arms and the Class Struggle

In Spain terrorist operations were to continue for longer than they did elsewhere. It began with the mysterious Mano Negra movement, a peasant revolt in Andalusia in the 1880s, continued mainly in Catalonia in the 1890s, and reached a climax in Barcelona, in 1904–9 and again between 1917 and 1922. Two pronounced features of Spanish terrorism were the *atentados sociales*, i.e. violence accompanying labour disputes (and conflicts between unions), and the subsequent widespread participation of criminal elements (*pistoleros*), 'thieves and gunmen who certainly would not have been accepted by any other working-class party together with idealists of the purest and most selfless kind'.[102] Behind the 'strategic terrorism' of 1905, culminating in the attempted assassination of King Alfonso, there might have been a design to trigger off a revolutionary movement. But the terror during and after the First World War, rooted according to Angel Pestana in a 'mystical and apocalyptic idealism', soon became commercialized with the *pistoleros* acting as dues collectors for the unions, terrorizing workers as well as overseers and employers.[103] Terrorism in Spain ought to be viewed in the light of Spain's long tradition of political violence, and the country's particular social conditions. The role of ideology was insignificant, nor indeed was any such doctrine needed.

Terrorist acts in the United States resembled those in Spain insofar as there was a tradition of violence and a long history of stormy, often bloody, labour disputes. This was particularly true among the miners, and continued from the days of the Molly Maguires to the Western Federation of Miners under Bill Haywood and the IWW. Following the arrival of German and later of East European proponents of 'propaganda by deed', an ideological element was infused which did not exist in Southern Europe. The anti-parliamentarian International Working People's Association, founded in Pittsburgh in 1883, was syndicalist in character and advocated violence in the form of mass strikes and sabotage rather than acts of terror. Chicago was the centre of these activities.

But as the industrial conflicts worsened and tempers rose, the *Alarm* and the *Chicagoer Arbeiterzeitung* became advocates of individual as well as mass terror. Dynamite was the great social solvent, the emancipator, and instruction was freely offered to workers on how to handle arms: 'The Weapons of the Social Revolutionist Placed within the Reach of All'. Dynamite, a reader wrote, 'of all good stuff, this is *the* stuff. . . . It is something not very ornamental but exceedingly useful. It can be used against persons and things, it is better to use it against the former than against bricks and masonry.'[104] C.S. Griffin argued that no government can exist without a head, and 'by assassinating the head just as fast as a government head appeared, the government could be destroyed, and, generally speaking, all governments be kept out of existence. Those least offensive to the people should be destroyed last.'[105] Albert Parsons, one of the accused in the Haymarket affair, editor of *Alarm* and former chief deputy collector of Internal Revenue in Austin, Texas, defended the use of dynamite even in court; it was democratic, it made everybody equal. It was a peacemaker, man's best friend. As force was the law of the universe, dynamite made all men equal and therefore free. But Parsons denied that he had anything to do with throwing the bomb.[106] Those allegedly involved in the Haymarket affair were the contemporaries and pupils of Johann Most, for many years the high priest of terrorism in America.

In the 1890s, younger and even more radical activists such as Emma Goldman and Alexander Berkman came to the fore. In July 1892, Berkman tried to shoot Henry C. Frick of the Carnegie Company, whom he regarded as responsible for the outrages committed during the Homestead strike earlier that year. Aged twenty-one at the time, Berkman had arrived in the United States five years previously. He was an enthusiast; Bazarov, Hegel, 'Liberty' and Chernishevski (apparently in this order) were his idols.[107] As he saw it, only the toilers, the producers, counted; the rest were parasites who had no right to exist. All means were justifiable, nay advisable in the fight against them: the more radical the treatment, the quicker the cure. Society was a patient, sick constitutionally and functionally; in the circumstances surgical treatment was imperative. The removal of a tyrant was an act of liberation, the highest duty of any revolutionary. As an enemy of the people, his assassination was in no way to be considered as the taking of human life.[108] Berkman's action was not only rejected by most Americans, it also caused a deep split in anarchist ranks: Most, in *Freiheit*, denounced him, while Emma Goldman in the *Anarchist* came to his defence. The fact that Most, the 'incarnation of defiance and revolt', repudiated Berkman had come to her and her circle as a bombshell.[109] It was almost as if Marx in his old age had been converted to capitalism.

Most

Johann Most, born in Germany in 1846, had had an unhappy childhood in his native country. After an apprenticeship as a bookbinder and some *Wanderjahre*, as was customary among artisans at the time, he was arrested as a radical agitator in Austria. Later he became one of the leading figures of the German Social Democrats. He was an indefatigable organizer, an effective speaker and a fluent, if erratic, strident writer. Although a member of the Reichstag, he had to flee Germany when Bismarck enacted his anti-socialist emergency laws. Most founded and edited *Freiheit*, a Social Democratic weekly, in London. In 1879 he was still a Marxist: 'As old Socialists we preach revolution not a *putsch*,' he wrote. But by temperament he was always more radical than the party leadership. At first he still covered himself by invoking the authority of others when preaching more extreme doctrines; for example, he approvingly quoted Wilhelm Liebknecht who had said that in certain circumstances, such as in a barbaric country like Russia, it might be possible to destroy the system by means of the dagger and the revolver.[110]

But why only in Russia? Most was dissatisfied with Marxist explanations, and by September 1880 he reached the conclusion that anarchist principles should be discussed in his paper. After all, they were being received with much more enthusiasm (as events in Russia showed) than social democratic gradualism. He published Bakunin's Revolutionary Catechism for the benefit of revolutionaries who (he predicted) were about to copy the Russian anarchists' tactics in Germany.[111] He hailed the Irish dynamiters: no honest social revolutionary could blame them, even if their acts of vengeance proved cruel: 'Once we are stronger, we shall act like them; a party waging war cannot tolerate traitors in its ranks. The devil take the false, weak-hearted humanitarian approach. Long live hate! Long live vengeance!' Or on another occasion: 'Let us all do our duty. Let us all work for the day when attacks will multiply against all those who bear responsibility for the servitude, exploitation and misery of the people.' After an enthusiastic editorial ('Victory, Victory'), hailing the assassination of Alexander II, Most was sent to prison by a London court.[112] In the meantime he had also been expelled from the ranks of the German Social Democrats.

Freiheit was transferred to the United States and during the next few years it became the world's most uninhibited anarchist mouthpiece, preaching 'propaganda by deed'. It was also the most influential; some issues had a circulation of 25,000 and Most's pamphlets such as *The Beast of Property* and *The Revolutionary Science of War* were widely read.

Most rejected the European socialist parties' approach. He did not believe, as they did, in patient organizational and propagandistic work; he rejected their assumption that sooner or later strong left-wing parties would emerge and that the system would collapse as a result of its own contradictions. He was convinced that the people, at all times and in every country, were mature for revolution (and the state of freedom that would follow it) but that they lacked the courage to undertake a determined effort. Thus a small minority was called upon to show the way: the mass of people had always borne a certain resemblance to something monkey-and-parrot-like, and it was quite ludicrous to wait for an initiative from the unenlightened, volatile and hesitant masses.[113] Few of those born into servitude could get rid of their chains by their own efforts, but nonetheless they should not be required to bow to the majority. Even in a future, free society there should be no tyranny by the majority. A revolutionary who really meant business had to engage in conspiracy. Once he sought his goal he could not possibly reject the means that were to lead to a realization of his aim.[114] The means were bound to be barbaric – not because the revolutionaries chose them but because the present system was essentially barbaric and could be overthrown only by its own weapons. The murderers themselves had to be killed. The road to *Humanität* led through barbarism.[115] The law of the jungle had forever prevailed in history; the victor had always been right. No Russian revolutionary of the 1880s would have accepted any such doctrine but, unlike them, Most and some of his anarchist comrades were influenced by various contemporary Social Darwinist philosophers who glorified the elite and even the superman. One of the forgotten prophets of this subculture was Ragnar Redbeard, whose writings appealed to both the extreme left and the far right, and thus should be mentioned – at least in passing.

'Blessed are the strong,' Redbeard wrote,

for they shall possess the earth; cursed are the weak, for they shall inherit the yoke. Blessed are the unmerciful, their posterity shall own the world. Human rights and wrongs are not determined by Justice but by Might. The naked sword is still kingmaker and kingbreaker as of yore – all other theories are lies and lures. Each molecule, each animal fights for its life, the workers have to fight for theirs or surrender. The survival of the strongest is the iron law of history; personal cowardice is the greatest vice of a demoralized age. Courage that delights in danger is needed, and must not know despair.[116]

Parts of Redbeard's books read in sections like a precursor of *Mein Kampf* or Alfred Rosenberg, with tirades against the non-Aryans and appeals demanding that 'we must either abandon our reason or abandon Christ'. Jesus, Peter, Paul and James were crude socialist reformers with misshapen souls, demagogues, politicians-of-the-slum. Nothing that is noble can ever emerge from the slums. Socialism, Christianity, Democracy, Equality are all the whining yelpings of base-bred mongrel-multitudes.[117]

Such reasoning was not uncommon towards the end of the nineteenth century. One of Redbeard's idols was Cecil Rhodes ('there is no cant and hypocrisy about him'). Teddy Roosevelt apparently liked the book. It was an all-purpose philosophy: the left could draw encouragement from Redbeard's thesis that not once in the whole course of human history had a subjugated people ever regained their liberty without first butchering their oppressors and then confiscating the property of their former masters. Redbeard was certainly sure of his case: he offered 50,000 ounces of pure gold to anyone who could show him one authentic example to the contrary.[118]

Traces of Redbeard's message can be detected in Most's writings. In order for the masses to be free, the rulers must be killed. Powder and lead, poison, dynamite, fire and knives were more telling than a thousand revolutionary speeches. Most did not rule out propaganda, but only 'propaganda by deed' could be regarded as effective in sowing confusion among the rulers and mobilizing the masses. He was one of the first to recognize the importance of the media: with modern means of communication, terrorist actions would immediately be known all over the globe; wherever people met they would discuss its causes. Most apprehended what became known much later as the 'echo effect': the deed would be imitated every day, even every hour.[119] He had no patience with those who argued that revolutionaries fought against a system not against individuals. There were no social systems which were not represented and, indeed, made to work, by persons. The system was defended by the forces of 'law and order'; to kill them was not murder, for policemen and spies were not human.[120] The enemies were pigs, dogs, bestial monsters, devils in human shape, reptiles, parasites, scum, the dregs of society, canaille, hellhounds. How could one exterminate them all in the most effective way? *Freiheit*, like some of the French anarchist periodicals, freely offered advice, and like them and the Russian journals saw in dynamite the tool for the destruction of society. The 'New Messiah' was hailed in editorials and even poems.

> *Zuletzt ein Hoch der Wissenschaft.*
> *Dem Dynamit, das heisst der Kraft*
> *Der Kraft in uns'ren Haenden*
> *Die Welt wird besser Tag fuer Tag.*[121]
> (At last a toast to Science
> To dynamite that is the force
> The force in our own hands;
> The world gets better day by day.)

At one time Most took a job in an explosives factory in Jersey City Heights receiving on-the-job training in the production of explosives. He stole a little dynamite and found that it was more reliable than the home-made variety.[122] He pioneered various innovations such as the letter (incendiary) bomb and in a remarkable flight of fantasy even envisaged bombing the enemy from the air. With the help of dirigible airships it would be possible one day to drop dynamite on military parades attended by tsars and emperors; neither infantry, cavalry nor artillery would be able to prevent such attacks.[123] Dynamite, in short, was an invincible weapon. Some 'innocents' (Most's quotation marks) were bound to get hurt but this did not bother him unduly: it was not their business to be in places where a bomb was likely to explode. British women and children had been injured by Irish bombs, but the British in their 'wars of extermination' had committed worse outrages in many parts of the world. (Most was not, however, an uncritical admirer of the Irish and frequently dissociated himself from the 'sectarian' character of their struggle.) The revolutionary should not be guided by considerations of chivalry; bombs should be placed quite indiscriminately wherever the upper ten thousand were likely to meet – for example, in churches and dance halls. Furthermore, a revolutionary about to commit a terrorist act was duty-bound to kill any witness likely to betray him.[124]

The question whether assassination of individual monarchs, ministers and generals would have any decisive political impact (and the arguments of his socialist opponents to the contrary) preoccupied Most throughout his life. In later years he admitted that it was illusory to believe that the removal of individual generals would lead to the defeat of an enemy army as long as the proletariat itself was not up in arms. At the same time, however, he stressed that the repressive system was highly centralized, and that a blow at the heart of tyranny would remove a not easily replaceable dangerous foe[125] (akin to the reasoning of the Russian revolutionaries about 'hitting at the centre'). Again, defending himself against charges about the inhuman character of the kind of war he preached, Most argued that governments were using the very same weapons he advocated – only theirs were a hundred times stronger and more destructive. He made it known that a pamphlet of his about the revolutionary science of war had largely been copied from a book issued under the auspices of the Austrian general staff. The revolutionary party was not a state and could not play such games as breaking off diplomatic relations. In reply to a charge that he had been ill advised to discuss the use of poison, Most replied that arsenic and strychnine had first been recommended by American newspapers to eliminate useless elements in society.[126]

Most maintained that in money – even more than in dynamite – the key to success was to be found. Money could buy more reliable and effective explosives than those made at home. A revolutionary who could somehow put his hands on a hundred million dollars would do mankind a greater service than one who killed ten monarchs; this kind of money could turn the world upside down. The few cents collected among workers were quite insufficient for any meaningful conspiratorial work. Gold would open a great many doors normally closed to the terrorist, corrupting and disarming enemy agents, and enabling the revolutionary to infiltrate 'society'. In short, funds were needed to carry out the 'deed' and these had to be 'confiscated'.[127]

It has been said that by mid-1885 Most had mellowed, and had begun to doubt the efficacy of 'propaganda by deed'.[128] In 1890, however, he still argued that it was necessary to engage in deeds, even of a bestial kind, and he continued to justify political assassinations wherever they occurred.[129] But it is quite true that there was a gradual shift in emphasis, and that in later years he put greater stress on propaganda. Most praised the Russian revolutionaries not only for throwing bombs but also for risking their lives by establishing secret printing presses. He argued that terrorist acts *per se* had little, if any, impact unless they took place at the right time and place, and that 'propaganda by deed' was no children's game.[130] Most was in favour of a dual strategy: legal or semi-legal organizations with meetings and publications, on the one hand, and on the other operations of small conspiratorial groups. The fewer people who knew about terrorist actions, the more assured would be their success. Militants usually had families and it was irresponsible to jeopardize their livelihood; intellectuals would immediately lose their jobs if it became known that they belonged to the anarchist movement.[131] There was yet another consideration which made a division of labour imperative: some revolutionaries were capable speakers and writers and might also prove good fighters in the heat of battle, but they were temperamentally incapable of planning cold-blooded assassination. This was not cowardice – such men and women were simply too good-hearted, too idealistic. Though it was desirable that every 'theoretical revolutionary' ought also to be a man of action, it was clearly unrealistic to expect this from every one of them. Out of a false sense of shame many a theoretician could not admit even to himself that he was not born to commit murder. The revolutionary movement had to accept this fact of political life which regrettably meant fewer assassinations, thereby prolonging the 'transition period', but nothing could be done about it. These then were Most's views in his later years, and it was not surprising therefore that he condemned Berkman's attack – a condemnation which made Emma Goldman so angry that she horsewhipped her former guru.

The American atmosphere was corrosive. Most's New York group with its beer evenings, excursions and amateur theatrical performances gradually came to resemble a German *Verein* rather than a Russian terrorist organization. Much of his activity was absorbed by internal dissension. His influence, by and large, was restricted to German-speaking workers; some Italians and East European Jews also came to his meetings and, on occasion, a few native Americans, but they were the exceptions. Despite all his inexhaustible energy, Most came to realize towards the end of his life that America was not to be the centre of a world revolution and that his was a voice calling in the desert. At long last he also understood that the wall dividing anarchists and the trade union movement had to be pulled down and even though he continued to oppose the American unions, he favoured the principle of worker organization.

At a distance of almost a century Most's hyper-radicalism seems both absurd and self-defeating. But in fairness his views have to be examined against the general background of time and place. It was a violent age, when public opinion freely held that workers who went on strike for higher wages and shorter working hours should be shot. A great deal of brutality accompanied labour disputes and anarchists were subjected to constant harassment by the police. On the other hand it was only in America that a newspaper such as *Freiheit* could appear for any length of time. Though the employers had the right to exploit their employees, the workers, too, could freely organize themselves and take counter-action. America, after all, was neither tsarist Russia nor Ireland. There were effective forms of political struggle other than violence. Most failed to make a convincing case as to why terrorism was necessary or likely to succeed in the United States and for this reason his influence remained restricted to a small group of newly arrived immigrants.

Marx, Engels and the Problem of Terrorism

Marx and Engels regarded Most and his supporters as semi-educated, muddleheaded men – or, alternatively, as dangerous charlatans. Nonetheless, the issue of individual terror was to occupy orthodox Marxism for a long time. Engels' common-law wife, Lizzy Burns, was a Fenian, and their house in Manchester provided a shelter for Irish militants. In a letter to Kugelmann, Engels welcomed the Fenian raid in Manchester (September 1867) in which a prison van transporting Fenians was attacked. Three months later the three main accused were hanged. Engels wrote that the only thing the Fenians had lacked were a few martyrs; he admired the violent anti-English character of their movement and thought that agrarian terror was the only effective means of protecting the Irish against extermination by the landlords. Despite their approval in principle of the Fenian approach, Marx and Engels condemned the 'foolishness which is to be found in every conspiracy'. They denounced the purposeless 'propaganda by deed' for which their party ought not to be made responsible and dissociated themselves from individual actions such as the Fenian bombing of

Clerkenwell Prison. It was one thing to call for an overthrow of Irish landlordism and to denounce Britain's truly 'Prussian behaviour' in Ireland; it was another to give unconditional support to the strictly nationalist, religious–sectarian approach of the Irish radicals who had no sympathies for Marxism and the policies of the First International.[132]

The issue of individual terror also played a certain role in the campaign of Marx and Engels against Bakunin, their main rival in the First International. In these attacks they made use of the revelations of the Nechaev trial and the brochures which Bakunin had written in 1869, in part inspired by Nechaev. Engels wrote that only a police agent could have glorified the bandit as the authentic revolutionary and identified revolution with individual and collective murder.[133] They might have taken a more tolerant view had it not been for Bakunin's Pan-Slavism and, above all, his influence in certain sections of the International. For the Marxist attitude towards the terror of the Narodnaya Volya was by no means consistent and unambiguous. Plekhanov had correctly predicted in 1879 that a terrorist campaign would end in catastrophe and setback for socialism in Russia. But Plekhanov was not yet a full-fledged Marxist at the time and his conversion certainly did not become easier when he realized that Marx and Engels who had so bitterly denounced Bakunin had encouraging words for the neo-Bakuninists in Russia and refrained from criticizing their clearly nonsensical theoretical programme. When Plekhanov published his *Nashe Raznoglasiya* (*Our Differences*) in 1884 Engels drily noted that the Narodniki were after all the only people in Russia who were doing something. And Marx's comment on the assassins of Alexander II is worth recalling: in his eyes they were sterling people through and through, simple, businesslike and heroic; they endeavoured to show Europe that their *modi operandi* were specifically Russian and historically inevitable. One could no more moralize about their action (for or against), Marx wrote, than about the earthquake of Chios.[134]

Marx and Engels exaggerated the strength of the Narodnaya Volya and overestimated the weakness of tsarist despotism. 'Russia is France of this century,' Engels told Lopatin, a Russian emigrant. And, in a letter to Vera Zasulich, he wrote that the revolution might break out any day in Russia, just a push was needed. Perhaps Blanqui and his fantasies had been right after all – with regard to Russia only, of course. Perhaps a small conspiracy could overthrow a whole society? Perhaps this was one of the few cases in which a handful of people could 'make' a revolution? Such comments were anathema to Plekhanov and he must have welcomed the fact that Engels later revised his views. In retrospect (in 1894) Engels noted that there had been an acute revolutionary situation in Russia and for this reason Marx had told the Russian revolutionaries in the late 1870s not to be in too much of a hurry to 'jump' into capitalism. There had been, in fact, two governments: on the one hand the tsar, and on the other the executive committee of the conspirators and the terrorists, whose power grew by the day. The overthrow of tsarism seemed at hand.[135] Fifteen years later these illusions had faded away and the Marxist attitude to terrorism changed. With regard to Western Europe, Marx and Engels had not been willing to make allowances for terrorism in any event: revolutions were made by classes not by a few conspirators. Hence Marx's scathing comment on Most's theoretical attempts to describe the assassination of the tsar as a panacea – this was just 'childish' (Marx in a letter dated April 1881 to his daughter Jenny). In January 1885 Engels took an even dimmer view of the activities of the Irish dynamiters and others in Western Europe who wanted to copy the terrorist struggle. This, he said, was revolution *à la Schinderhannes* (a famous German eighteenth-century robber), for it directed one's weapons not against one's real enemies but against the public at large. Such terrorists were not the friends of Russian revolutionaries but their worst enemies. Only the Russian government was interested in actions of this kind. One could possibly understand the motives of the Irish who had been driven to despair, but their effect was to stir up blind rage among British public opinion. Marx and Engels, as already noted, were highly critical of the Fenian leaders who were 'mostly asses and partly exploiters'. The Clerkenwell explosion, Marx wrote to Engels, was a very stupid act; one could not really expect the London proletarians to be blown up in honour of the Fenian emissaries: 'There is always a kind of fatality about such a secret, melodramatic conspiracy.'[136] Engels reacted even more strongly; 'cannibals', 'cowards', 'stupid fanatics' were some of the epithets used. After the Phoenix Park murders Engels wrote that such bragging, purposeless *propaganda par le fait* should be left to the Bakuninists, Mostians and those who threatened an Irish revolution which never materialized. True, on another occasion Marx wrote to his daughter that his whole family supported the Fenians. But he offered an interesting explanation: his motives were not simply humanitarian – 'To accelerate social development in Europe, you must push on the catastrophe of official England. To do so you must attack it in Ireland.'[137]

Yet with all these reservations the influence of Blanquism (which always implied an element of terrorism) on Marx and Engels, and *a fortiori* on Lenin, was stronger than they were generally prepared to admit. They rejected, of course, primitive Blanquism, the conspiracy of a handful of people who aimed at insurrection. Such attempts were invariably doomed to failure because they lacked mass support. But Marx and Engels knew, or instinctively felt, that the masses could not seize power unaided, that they needed a leadership and that in the final analysis 'Blanquism on a higher level' was essential. A conspiracy was needed that could mobilize the masses. Whether a conspiracy such as this aimed at insurrection, civil war, sabotage, a terrorist campaign or a combination of these and other elements were secondary questions. While the Marxists rejected terrorism as unsuitable for advanced Western countries, they could not possibly reject it *tout court*.

The German Social Democratic leaders were certainly more emphatic about terrorism than their teachers in London. Wilhelm Liebknecht thought Most clinically mad, Bebel took a somewhat more charitable view: Most was a gifted man but was in need of someone to discipline and guide him. The terrorist organizations, Bebel said, were deeply penetrated by police spies and agents provocateurs. Furthermore, the anarchists assisted the police in creating a public climate in which all left-wing opposition could be branded as 'terrorist'. In fact, the police considered the anarchists harmless; it was the Social Democrats they feared, and they were grateful for any pretext given to suppress them.

The debate on terrorism was resumed among the Russian Marxists when the Social Revolutionaries took up terrorist operations around the turn of the century. Lenin's attitude to individual terror was ambivalent: while paying tribute to their heroism, he rejected terrorism as practised by the Narodovoltsy. Then, it had been restricted to a group of intellectuals who were cut off from the working class and the peasants; quoting his late brother who had believed in terrorism and, at the same time, dissociating himself from him, Lenin wrote that Russian terror 'was and remains a specific kind of struggle practised by the intelligentsia'.[138] He was all the more opposed to the Social Revolutionaries practising 'old-style terror' at a time when a revolutionary mass movement had emerged. At best, it made organizational and political work among the people more complicated. According to Lenin, experience had shown anarchist terror, in the form of individual assassination, as harmful and counter-productive. He juxtaposed assassinations carried out in the name of the people (by the Socialist Revolutionaries) to revolutionary activities undertaken by the Bolsheviks 'together with the people' (whatever that may have meant in practice).[139] The long and arduous work of organization and political propaganda was preferable to a repetition of 'easy' tactics which had never proved their worth. In the final analysis Lenin's rejection of terror was tactical, not, as in Plekhanov's case, a matter of principle. He thought Plekhanov's total rejection of terror philistine and wrote in *Iskra* that he had never rejected terror in principle for the simple reason that it was a form of military operation that might be usefully applied or even be essential in certain moments of battle.[140] When Friedrich Adler shot Stürgkh, the Austrian prime minister, in October 1916, Lenin wrote that he was not opposed to political murder *per se*. In 1901, fifteen years previously, different conditions had prevailed and he thought that at that time terror was inadvisable as likely to disrupt the revolutionary forces and not the government. By contrast, in October 1905, at the height of the first Russian Revolution, he expressed real anguish that his party had merely been talking about bombs and that not a single one had been made. Terrorism was to be recommended provided that the mood of the masses and the working-class movement on the spot was taken into account.

Rosa Luxemburg and Martov thought it harmful (not only aesthetically) that ordinary bandits should collaborate with revolutionary workers. Lenin had no such scruples. In fact, several prominent Bolsheviks co-operated in terrorist enterprises: Krassin, who was an engineer, supervised the manufacture of bombs for the Maximalists: 'Kamo' (Ter Petrosian) organized some daring and successful armed robberies in the Caucasus; Litvinov and Semashko (the future minister of health) were arrested in Germany when they tried to change the money that they had 'expropriated'. The Mensheviks denounced the Bolshevik tactics, but Lenin did not even bother to reply.[141] After the suppression of the first revolution, Lenin (and also Trotsky) again argued that terror was ineffectual: the assassination of a minister would not bring the overthrow of capitalism nearer. Trotsky in 1911 wrote in the Austrian Social Democratic organ *Der Kampf* that he had grave doubts about the efficacy of terror. Even successful terrorist operations only temporarily introduced confusion into the ranks of the establishment; the capitalist state did not rest upon ministers alone and could not be destroyed with them:

> The classes whom the state serves will always find new men – the mechanism remains intact and continues to function. Far deeper is the confusion that terrorist attempts introduce into the ranks of the working masses. If it suffices to arm oneself with a revolver in order to reach our goal, then to what end are the goals of the class struggle? If a pinch of powder and a slug of lead are enough to destroy the enemy, what need is there of a class organization? If there is rhyme or reason in scaring titled personages with the noise of an explosion, what need is there for a party?[142]

These observations of Trotsky have frequently been quoted by subsequent generations of Trotskyites in their disputations with comrades who advocate a more militant line. But it is also true that Trotsky's attitude, like Lenin's, was in fact more ambiguous than would appear. He derided the 'eunuchs and pharisees' who opposed terrorism as a matter of principle. However, the account with capitalism was too great to be settled by the assassination of individual ministers – only collective action would repay the debt. On another occasion he noted that while terrorism in Russia was a thing of the past, it might have a future in what would now be called the 'Third World'; there were auspicious conditions in Bengal and Punjab; it was part of the political awakening in these countries.[143] In 1934, after the murder of Kirov, Trotsky defined individual terrorism as 'bureaucratism turned inside out' – not one of his most brilliant formulations and not even relevant to the Kirov case – indicative of his views on individual as distinct from collective terrorism, which he defended in a famous polemic with Kautsky when he was still in power.

Communist attitudes towards individual terror have shown the same ambiguity ever since. Terrorism might be rejected in principle; nonetheless on certain occasions terrorism in practice has not been ruled out (Spain after the First World War, Bulgaria in 1923, Germany in 1929–31, or Venezuela in the early 1960s). In November 1931 when the Central Committee of the German Communist Party came out against individual terror, many militants opposed this turn in the party line.[144] The official textbooks condemned individual terror in the sharpest possible terms but this did not deter the Soviet Secret police (the GPU), its predecessors and successors, from 'liquidating' political enemies such as Trotsky, who were considered particularly dangerous. More recently, individual terror has been practised on a fairly wide scale by Communist-led movements of national liberation such as that in Vietnam – less so in China. Terror is regarded, however, to quote Lenin again, as merely one form of military operation – usually not a decisive one. Communist parties have bitterly attacked rival left-wing movements for concentrating on terrorism to the detriment of other forms of political and military struggle: the history of Communism in Latin America during the last two decades offers many such examples.

Terrorism and Nationalism

The belief has gained ground in recent years that terrorism has been, and is, the monopoly of the extreme left wing. But this is true only to the extent that theoretical problems of terrorism are always much more widely discussed by the left. At least as frequently, terrorism has been employed by right-wing groups and nationalist movements. Terrorism in India in the 1890s had a distinct religious infusion (the worship of Kali and Durga and the anti-cow-killing campaign) and was frequently practised by high-caste Brahmins. Nineteenth- and early-twentieth-century Irish terrorism is a good example of empirical terrorism. While the American Clan na-Gael stood for 'bloodless terrorism' directed against buildings and similar targets, O'Donovan Rossa favoured indiscriminate attacks. The Invincibles of the the 1880s practised individual terror such as the Phoenix Park murders. The Irish proponents of terrorism were very much interested in gimmicks, whereas doctrinal issues hardly bothered them. They spent sixty thousand dollars on building three submarines in the United States which were never used; Rossa wanted to spray the House of Commons with osmic gas; and money was collected for the purchase of poison stilettoes, lucifer matches and other unlikely weapons.[145] They saw no need for elaborate theoretical justification: had Britain not behaved much worse all over the world, killing women and children in Africa, shooting into unarmed crowds, blowing Indian sepoys from cannon? The purpose of the dynamite campaign in the 1880s was to cause maximum dislocation and annoyance, to harm the tourist industry, to make travel in underground railways risky, to cause widespread 'moral panic' and the paralysis of business.[146] The Invincibles predicted that the new 'mysterious and overshadowing war of destruction' would eventually result in Britain having to adopt fiercer coercion laws at home than Ireland had known. But if the Irish leaders were not ideologists they were not ignorant men and, given the occasion, they could be quite eloquent on the subject of terrorism: 'Despotism violates the moral frontier as invasion violates the geographical frontier,' one of them wrote.

> To drive out the tyrant or to drive out the English is in either case to retake your territory. There comes an hour when protest no longer suffices. After philosophy there must be action. The strong hand finishes what the idea has planned. Prometheus Bound begins, Aristogeiton completes; the Encyclopaedists enlighten souls, the 6th of May electrifies them.

Or on mass psychology: 'The multitude has a tendency to accept a master. Their mass deposits apathy. A mob easily totalizes itself into obedience. Men must be aroused, pushed, shocked by the very benefits of their deliverance, their eyes wounded with the truth, light thrown in terrible handfuls.'[147]

Heated debates took place among the Irish leaders, but these were on tactics rather than issues of principle. John Devoy thought Rossa's dynamiters 'fools, imbeciles, insane designers', the whole show was a burlesque 'which makes us appear fools and ignoramuses'.[148] But this did not prevent Devoy from threatening in 1881 to take a British minister's life in reprisal for every Irishman killed. Thus he repeated Rossa's threat, five years earlier, that if a skirmisher was hanged, the minister who ordered the execution would be killed and the city in which the patriot was hanged would be burned down.[149] And even Parnell, who never expressed sympathy for terrorism in public, frequently conveyed in private the impression that he sympathized with the militants. His, too, was a dual strategy: constitutional means reinforced by the actions of secret organizations. No one knows to what extent he was involved in the terrorist campaign.[150] The reasons for the opposition of Devoy and most other Irish leaders to individual assassination up to the First World War was that Britain was too powerful, that Irish resources were insufficient, and that there were other, more effective means of struggle for the time being.

The Philosophy of the Bomb — The Right-wing Version

Assassinations of political opponents carried out by the Black Hundred in pre-war Russia are examples of terrorism as carried out by the extreme right. There were many more cases of assassination after the end of the First World War in other parts of Europe. Hitler had said more than once that 'heads would roll, ours, or the others' – and the Nazis would ensure that it would be those of the others. Giving evidence in the trial of four National Socialists in Berlin in 1931, he argued that this had just been a parable, a synonym for ideological confrontation, and that he had always demanded strict observance of legality. If his veto on illegality was violated, those responsible were brought to account. Acts of violence had never been contemplated by his party.[151] But if Hitler had to stick to certain legal niceties, his aides were under no such constraints. Thus Joseph Goebbels: whoever defended his own *Weltanschauung* with terror and brutality would one day gain power. The 'street', as Goebbels saw it, was the decisive place in which policy was made. Conquest of the street meant the gain of the masses: he who had the masses would conquer the state.[152] The basic Nazi strategy was to mobilize the masses in order to conquer the street, disrupt meetings of other parties, and attack their opponents' demonstrations. Occasionally they would engage in terrorism, and in defence they quoted the authority of Mussolini: 'Terror? Never. It simply is social hygiene, taking those individuals out of circulation like a doctor would take out a bacillus.'[153] Mussolini, a radical socialist in his younger years, had welcomed terrorist actions in various parts of the world: '*il proletario deve essere psicologicamente preparato all'uso della violenza liberatrice*', he once wrote.[154] His orientation towards the proletariat changed, but Mussolini's belief in 'liberating violence' remained. There was progressive, liberating violence, he said on one occasion, and stupid, reactionary violence – that used by his political enemies. The Socialists ask what is our programme? he once wrote in *Popolo d'Italia*. Our programme is to smash the heads of the Socialists.

This, too, was terror, but of a different kind – mass violence intended to intimidate opponents rather than eliminate individual enemy leaders. The Nazis always stressed that they were never the first to engage in terror. True, they were not 'bourgeois aesthetes' but only engaged in 'terror against terror' in self-defence.[155] On the other hand, no German political party appreciated better than the Nazis the tremendous uses to which political violence could be put so as to maximize publicity in the mass media. Any clash was bound to be reported on the front page of the newspapers, and a small and uninfluential group soon became nationally known. This was Goebbels' strategy in the 'conquest of Berlin' and his example was copied elsewhere.[156]

Neither the Nazis nor the Italian Fascists needed ideological justification for political violence. Theirs was the generation that had fought in the First World War, and to them it was perfectly obvious that in the struggle for power, all forms of violence were permissible. The friend–foe dichotomy was at the bottom of their politics, taking it for granted that the enemy would not be defeated by persuasion alone. The enemy was the democratic–liberal system, and radical, pseudo-socialist undertones were by no means absent in the onslaught on the 'system'. This emerged from Mussolini's early programme, also appearing in Nazi slogans during the *Kampfzeit*. The Nazis quite frankly admitted that they would cause maximum disruption, for as long as 'business was good' they would not be feared.[157] At a Berlin trial against Nazi storm troopers, Count Helldorf, their leader, argued that it was quite absurd to accuse them of having attacked Jews, for they were fighting against the capitalist system, which was represented, after all, not only by Jews. . . .[158]

On the whole, however, individual terror was comparatively rare in Germany and Italy; it was more frequently used by the smaller Fascist and proto-Fascist groups – precisely because they were small. These groups are usually labelled 'right-wing extremist', but such labels are only of limited help in understanding their motives and strategy. Certain German Free Corps, such as the Organization Consul, engaged in systematic terror in 1921–2.[159] But they were radicals, not conservatives, and the last thing they wanted was to prop up a 'doomed bourgeois society'. Some of them were pure nihilists; Ernst von Salomon later wrote about himself and his comrades that they 'killed whoever fell into our hands, we burned whatever could be burned. . . . The march into an uncertain future was for us sufficiently meaningful and suited the demands of our blood.'[160] This was gibberish, of course, but it described fairly accurately the mood prevailing in these circles. When the terrorists decided to kill Rathenau, the German foreign minister, it was not because they hated him or thought him particularly wicked; on the contrary they admired him. He had to be removed because he was more significant than mere mediocrities. They saw the struggle as a 'duel between giants' (an image that had frequently been invoked by the terrorist faction of the Narodnaya Volya). At one stage the Freikorps terrorists planned to kill Seeckt, head of the *Reichswehr*, and the Hungarian Fascists planned the assassination of the right-wing minister of the interior. The Rumanian Iron Guard assassinated two prime ministers – Duca in 1933 and Calinescu in 1939. None of these victims, or intended victims, was a man of the left, or a liberal.

The composition of 'right-wing' terrorist groups varied greatly from country to country. Many criminal elements were found among the members of the Hungarian 'Arrow Cross'; the Macedonian IMRO, once a patriotic movement, developed into a Mafia-type organization, accepting 'contracts' from the highest bidders and engaging, *inter alia*, in the traffic of narcotics.[161] The Rumanian Iron Guard on the other hand consisted largely of young idealists of sorts (the 'legionnaires') who stood for a religious revival, spiritual regeneration, sacrifice and martyrdom: 'You want programmes?' the 'Manual of the Legionnaires' asked. 'They are on everybody's lips. Better look for men. Anyone can turn out a programme in one night: that is not what the country needs.'[162] The legionnaires were in a moral quandary: as good Christians they believed in forgiveness, but as patriots they felt that the nation could be saved only by un-Christian acts. Murder had to be committed but had also to be expiated, either by surrender after the deed or at least by suffering for their sins in their hearts. Like certain anarchist groups that preceded them, the legionnaires came to believe that there was only one ideology, the Deed (Vasile Marin). Like Sorel before, and a great many minor thinkers after, they believed in 'the ethical value of force'.[163] Their terrorism comprised a mystique of death. 'Legionnaires are born to die,' it was said in their songs, and 'Death is a gladsome wedding for us.' Lombroso had first noted a suicidal impulse among anarchist groups in Western Europe and this impulse could be found among them, too. Although the Rumanian authorities claimed that the legionnaires had plans to seize power it is not certain if they ever seriously intended to do so.

A common denominator marked terrorist movements of the 'left' and the 'right' in Europe, indicating a protest against modern society, against corrupt political parties and 'plutocracy'. Patriotic and religious motivations were called in as reinforcements. This reaction was not limited to Europe. Japanese terrorism drew its inspiration from the knightly spirit of the Samurai; more surprising is the fact that some of its prominent practitioners had once been anarchists or belonged to the Tolstoyan 'School of Love for the Native Soil'.[164] Capitalism and Western civilization had to be destroyed; the members of the 'Terrorist League of Blood' were called upon to sacrifice themselves for the principle of love for the soil, to abandon their families (shades of Ishutin and Nechaev) and renounce their personal existences forever. The Japanese terrorists of the 1920s were manipulated by military leaders and right-wing adventurers, who wanted to frighten the emperor, the court and the government into accepting a more aggressive policy: peace at home, expansion abroad.[165] But the threat of assassination alone would not have sufficed in a country with traditions like those of Japan. Terrorism was also a moral force, inducing an uneasy conscience among those it threatened and intimidating the politicians who did not wish to appear disloyal to the terrorists' concept of the historical mission of the Japanese people.

Right-wing terror in Europe between the two world wars took many different forms. In France the activists of the extreme right limited their activities to the universities and the theatres, intimidating unpopular professors and playwrights. This was the terror of incitement – of speech, of the written word – which drove Roger Salengro to suicide. There was also more tangible terrorism such as that of the Comité Secret d'Action Revolutionnaire (CSAR), a small Fascist group (on which more below), leading to assassination. If the French right used journalism for its purposes, the early Austrian Nazis (and the Japanese extremists) regarded the press as one of its main enemies. 'One kills these dogs by shooting or poisoning them, every means is right,' one of the early advocates of Austrian terrorism wrote. His comrades planned to send letter bombs to leading journalists and to destroy the printing presses.[166] The Finnish Lapua movement did not kill their opponents but kidnapped them, beat them up and dropped them over the Russian border. The Italian Fascists forcibly fed castor oil to their opponents adding insult (and ridicule) to injury.

But individual terror, to repeat once again, was relatively infrequent among the Fascist mass parties; Rathenau and Erzberger were killed by small groups who had no clear political programme. Dollfuss, the Austrian chancellor, was assassinated in the course of an armed insurrection and Matteoti was murdered when the Fascists were already in power. Terrorism in Fascist, as in Communist, strategy was accredited only a minor place for reasons of effectiveness; there was nothing in Fascist doctrine which would have ruled out terrorism in principle. The thoughts of right-wing activism on the subject were expressed most succinctly by Carl Schmitt in his writings on the 'political soldier': the ethics of the Sermon on the Mount applied to the private enemy, the *inimicus*, not to the *hostis*, the public foe. Political conflicts were settled not by discussion, persuasion or barter, as the liberals mistakenly believed, but by struggle, in foreign as well as domestic policy.[167] Nazis, Fascists and other extreme right-wing groups did not need a philosopher to teach them that 'love your enemies' did not apply to politics. They knew this instinctively.

The similarities between the inspiration underlying terrorism of 'right' and 'left' have been noted: the assumption that the deed was more important than words; the belief that any change would be for the better; a contempt for liberalism and bourgeois democracy; a sense of the historical mission of the chosen few. It was no mere coincidence that Carl Schmitt, who provided the most sophisticated justification for political violence as practised by the right, should develop a 'theory of the partisan' after the Second World War in which he expressed admiration for Mao and left-wing revolutionaries – his philosophy of violence is truly value-free. On both extremes of the political spectrum terrorism was regarded as a useful weapon to discredit the 'system'. The SS too held to a perverse idealism, a belief that only they took values seriously, that they were chosen for the same quasi-religious moment of sacrifice. The Narodovoltsy killed with a bad conscience, whereas the Fascist had no such qualms of conscience. The anarchists of 'propaganda by deed' did not weep for their victims either. When Émile Henry, who had t'rown a bomb at the Café Terminus, appeared in court, he declared 'there are no innocent bourgeois'; some of his comrades went further, expressing the view that there were no innocent human beings in general. There were, of course, differences between the terror of the left and the terror of the right in other respects: the Narodovoltsy practised terror because they saw no other way to make their demands heard in a regime which had outlawed all opposition. They denounced acts of terror committed in countries in which normal political activity was possible (as in their message after the assassination of President Garfield). They genuinely believed in a free and non-violent society. The terrorists of the right did not share this belief in the essential goodness of human nature. Their ideal society was of a very different kind.

Terrorist doctrine is of considerable importance for the understanding of the terrorist phenomenon but it is only one of the motivating forces, and not always the decisive one. The Macedonian IMRO and the Croatian Ustacha began as genuine patriotic movements. By the 1930s they had become play-balls of foreign interests: the Macedonians must have known that they could not possibly attain national independence, and the Croatian separatists were aware that they would have to pay a heavy price, such as the surrender of Dalmatia to their Italian protectors. The Croatians launched indiscriminate attacks inside Yugoslavia; the Macedonian terrorists killed each other and were also used by the Bulgarian government for the liquidation of political opponents. Croats and Macedonians probably still believed that operations directed against their oppressors coupled with foreign help might one day result in a favourable international constellation in which they could attain their aims. But it is impossible to say with any degree of certainty whether they (and other groups) still predominantly comprised a political movement, or whether the key to their activities must be found in other levels of social behaviour. There was, furthermore, 'instinctive terrorism' among movements with national or social grievances that fitted into no known ideological category. It can be taken for granted that the Ukrainians in eastern Poland and the peasants of Schleswig-Holstein at the time of the Great Depression had never read terrorist tracts.[168] But they knew, even if they had not read it in books, that publicity was needed to make their protest known; it was far more likely that they would be listened to if political pressure was reinforced by terrorist action. Sometimes there was a simple division of labour: the more militant wing of a movement, dissatisfied with the lack of progress, would opt for 'direct action', whereas the more moderate would continue their non-violent activities. In short, if it has been possible since time immemorial to make love or to cook without the help of textbooks, the same applied to terrorism. In some cases the decision to adopt a terrorist strategy was taken on the basis of a detailed political analysis. But usually the mood came first, and ideological rationalization only after. On occasion this led to the emergence of a systematic strategy of terrorism and to bitter debates between proponents and opponents. But terrorism also took place without precise doctrine and systematic strategy, with only hazy notions about the direction of the struggle and its aim. Like Faust, the terrorists could truly claim *Im Anfang war die Tat* – in the beginning there was the deed.

3

The Sociology of Terrorism

Terrorism, interpreted here as the use of covert violence by a group for political ends, is usually directed against a government, but it is also used against other ethnic groups, classes or parties. The aims may vary from the redress of specific grievances to the overthrow of a government and the seizure of power, or to the liberation of a country from foreign rule. Terrorists seek to cause political, social and economic disruption, and for this purpose frequently engage in planned or indiscriminate murder.* Terrorism may appear in conjunction with a political campaign or with guerrilla war, but it also has a 'pure' form. It has been waged by national and religious groups, by the left and by the right, by nationalist as well as internationalist movements, and it has been state-sponsored. Terrorists have seldom, if ever, seized power, but they have on occasion brought about political change, such as the overthrow of democratic governments by military dictatorships. On other occasions, paradoxically, terrorism has had the opposite effect inasmuch as the terrorist challenge helped to bring about a consensus in a democratic society which did not previously exist. Terrorist movements have frequently consisted of members of the educated middle classes, but there has also been agrarian terrorism, terror by the uprooted and the rejected, and trade union and working-class terror

---

* Any definition of political terrorism which ventures beyond noting the systematic use of murder, injury and destruction, or the threat of such acts aimed at achieving political ends, is bound to lead to endless controversies. Some terrorist groups have been indiscriminate and their victims 'symbolic', others have acted differently. Some merely wanted to create a climate of fear, others aimed at the physical destruction of their opponents *tout court*. Purists will argue that one is not even entitled to stress the systematic character of terrorism because in some cases the execution of a single act did have the desired effect (Sarajevo 1914). It can be predicted with confidence that the disputes about a comprehensive, detailed definition of terrorism will continue for a long time, that they will not result in a consensus, and that they will make no notable contribution towards the understanding of terrorism. These observations, made ten years ago, still apply today.

(United States 1880–1910, Spain 1890–1936). In nationalist–separatist terrorist groups, the middle-class element has usually been weaker, and popular support stronger than in other terrorist organizations. Terror has been directed against autocratic regimes as well as democracies; sometimes there has been an obvious link with social dislocation and economic crisis, at other times there has been no such connection. Movements of national liberation and social revolution (or reaction) have turned to terrorism after political action has failed. But elsewhere, and at other times, terrorism has not been the consequence of political failure, but has been chosen by militant groups even before other options were tried. Terrorism has never occurred in modern totalitarian regimes; individual attempts at assassination have taken place, but the means of control and repression at the disposal of a totalitarian state rule out organized terrorism. It has been infrequent in modern societies where violence has not been part of the political culture, but few parts of the world have been altogether free from it, excepting only effective police states.

National oppression and social inequities are frequently mentioned as the main factors responsible for the spread of terrorism, and it is, of course, true that happy, contented people seldom, if ever, throw bombs. But this does not explain why the struggle for political freedom, for national liberation, for secession, or for other aims, sometimes has led to terrorism, but at other times has not. Furthermore, any analysis of terrorism is incomplete unless it considers those against whom terror is directed. Terrorist groups have made their appearance in our time in Britain and in France, in Spain and in West Germany. They have not been observed in Russia or China or the countries of Eastern Europe, in Libya or in Cuba. Generalizations about terrorism are exceedingly difficult for yet another reason: terrorist movements are usually small. Some are very small indeed, and while historians and sociologists can sometimes account for mass movements, the movement of small particles in politics, as in physics, often defies explanation.

Some of the most dramatic assassinations of the last hundred years were carried out by individuals without the help or knowledge of any organized body – the murders of Stolypin and President McKinley, the killings of President Carnot, Gandhi and President Kennedy.[1] Such individual actions aside, there have been groups which killed and bombed in order to express protest rather than in the hope of defeating their enemies. The anarchist propagandists of the deed clearly belong to this category. Some of them registered their protest in their novels, some in their pictures, and others threw bombs. Frequently there has been a general concept, sometimes vague, sometimes quite precise, underlying acts of terror. The advocates of 'pure terror' in Russia assumed that the assassination of a handful of leading officials and other pillars of the establishment would lead to the downfall of the regime. They were not, as a rule, concerned with what would happen beyond this point; their historical mission, as they saw it, ended with the destruction of the system (or of foreign oppression).

Yet almost inevitably, as the terrorist campaign continued, the terrorists became concerned with the seizure of power and more distant perspectives. This happened, for instance, to Narodnaya Volya, who eventually came to envisage a general insurrection, even though they must have been aware that they were too few to organize and direct a popular government. Right-wing terrorists such as the German Organization Consul or the Japanese officers of the 1930s had more modest aims – they wanted to change the policy of the government so as to prevent 'national betrayal'. It is not certain whether the Rumanian Iron Guard ever seriously intended to seize power, even though at one time it constituted a serious danger to the government. The extreme wing of the Fenians announced in 1885 that 'this dynamite work will go on till Ireland is free, or till London is laid in ashes'.[2] Again, it is unlikely that they considered this to be a realistic alternative. What they actually expected was a more complicated sequence of action and counter-action: as Captain Lomasney explained to Jim Devoy, the Irish bombings would provoke British counter-measures. But these would not succeed, for the Irish were a fighting race and their fighting spirit would be aroused by the struggle, the sympathy of the world would be won for Ireland, the English would have to make concessions and these could be used to wring further concessions, and eventually Ireland would win full freedom.[3] Similarly, in 1918 the Russian Social Revolutionaries assumed that the murder of the German ambassador in Moscow and the German governor-general of the occupied part of the Ukraine would lead to the renewal of hostilities between Russia and Germany.

This, in a nutshell, is the strategy of provocation. The Armenians in Turkey hoped that their actions would bring about the intervention of the European powers; a similar strategy, based on outside help, underlay the campaigns of Irgun, LEHI, the Palestinian Arab organizations and other groups. The Serbian Black Hundred decided to kill Archduke Franz Ferdinand not because they regarded him as particularly wicked but, on the contrary, because they were afraid that he would make political concessions, thus weakening the spirit of the nationalist movement in Bosnia.[4] For similar reasons, the Freikorps terrorists killed Rathenau, the foreign minister of the Weimar Republic, and the Italian Red Brigades abducted Aldo Moro and eventually killed him. The drawback to this strategy was that it worked only if the political constellation was auspicious. Where it was not, terrorist acts made no difference, or even led to disaster, as the Armenians discovered to their cost. Orsini's attempt on the life of Napoleon III was a political success despite the fact that it failed. Orsini was executed but he became a hero – with Napoleon's approval. His letter to the emperor ('Set my country free') was reproduced in full in the *Moniteur*. It was a success because Napoleon was already inclined to pursue an anti-Austrian policy.[5] A few years later a Pole tried to kill Napoleon III. The political effect was nil, for Poland was far away and the French emperor had no intention of antagonizing the Russians.

Where terrorism has been successful its aims have usually been limited and clearly defined. The daily wage of American iron workers (AFL) went up from $2.00 to $4.30 (for shorter hours) between 1905 and 1910, as the result of the bombing of some one hundred buildings and bridges.[6] Spanish workers, using similar methods, improved their wages during the First World War.[7]

Alternatively, terrorist actions succeeded because they were used within the framework of a wider strategy. An obvious example was the systematic killing by the Vietcong of some 10,000 village elders during the late 1950s and early 1960s, thus preparing the ground for a takeover from within.[8] They used the same tactics against opponents of the left, such as the Saigon Trotskyites, as did the Algerian FLN vis-à-vis their nationalist rivals, the Messalists. But the use of so-called 'urban guerrilla' tactics against the French was much less successful and, in any case, neither the Vietcong nor the FLN was predominantly a terrorist movement.

It is widely believed that with the growing vulnerability of modern technological society the prospects for urban terror are now greater than ever before. But so far this has not been correct. Urban terrorists have on the whole been aware of this and have recognized that, in theory, operations in cities should be linked with rural guerrilla warfare, or with attempts to win over sections of the army, or with the vision of a general insurrection, or with a people's war. But in industrialized countries the emphasis is usually on urban terror, either because the countries concerned are predominantly urbanized, or because the masses do not respond, or because the army is not inclined to co-operate with the terrorists.

While terrorist movements, including the right-wing terrorists of Central Europe, of Hungary and Rumania, attacked the police without hesitation, as did the IRA in a later age, they were mostly unwilling to take on the army, and not only because they were afraid of the outcome of an unequal contest. Thus neither the Narodnaya Volya nor the Polish terrorists in 1905–6 attacked army installations and personnel, in the hope that restraint would win over some officers; these hopes were by no means unjustified and eventually the Russians had a 'military organization' consisting entirely of officers or ex-officers. The Palestinian Arab terrorists and the IMRO preferred to direct their operations against the civilian population – this, of course, being less risky. Latin American terrorists have tried with varying success to draw army officers into their ranks: as a rule, they suffered badly whenever they clashed with soldiers.[9]

There has always been a certain discrepancy between terrorist doctrine and practice. But, even on the purely theoretical level, there was a great deal of inconsistency and some of the key questions were left unanswered. Was the terrorist struggle the prologue to revolution (or to national liberation), or was it already the revolution? Were the terrorists the avant-garde of the revolutionary (or nationalist) movement – or were they the movement? Few terrorist groups have ever claimed that radical change could be effected without the active participation of the masses, but most of them have acted as if it could be done. But for how long could they continue to act (and to speak) on behalf of the masses without losing their credibility if the population was unenthusiastic or even hostile? The position of terrorist groups acting within the framework of political movements has been less complicated; they had to carry out a mission and no one expected them to worry about long-term perspectives. This applies, for instance, to the Social Revolutionaries, the Irish terrorists, Irgun and other such groups. But the division of labour has worked more easily in theory than in practice, for the 'fighting organizations' always needed some autonomy and their political ideas usually diverged to some extent. There was always resentment against the 'politicians' who risked so little and had, therefore, no moral right to dictate a course of action to the terrorists – unless it coincided with the conviction of the 'fighters'. In short, there was almost always dissension and competition between the political and the terrorist wings of the movement, and a tendency towards full autonomy among the terrorists. Among the Palestinians, as well as among the Provisional Irish Republican Army (PIRA), the (terrorist) tail was eventually wagging the (political) dog.

The Terrorist Personality

Is there a 'terrorist personality'? Even if one assumes that the Russian terrorists of the 1880s shared with each other many common features of character – an assumption that by no means can be taken for granted – they had little in common with the Irish, and the Irish were quite different again from the Armenians, not to mention 'Abu Nidal'. Given that men and women at certain times and in various places have engaged in political violence, throwing bombs and firing pistols does not necessarily prove that they had more in common with one another than have rose growers or stamp collectors.* Generalizations are of limited validity because so much depends on the political and social conditions in which terrorism has occurred, on the historical and cultural context, on the purpose and character of the terror, and, of course, on its targets. Seen in this light no two terrorist movements were alike, and in fact few were even similar.

That their members have been young is the only feature common to all terrorist movements, and that hardly requires explanation. The latest calls to action do not usually fire the middle-aged and elderly with enthusiasm. And daring attacks also necessitate speed of movement.

Zhelyabov and Kravchinski, both aged thirty, were considered almost elderly by the members of Narodnaya Volya. Sofia Perovskaya was twenty-seven when she was sentenced to death, as was Kibalchich; Mikhailov was twenty-one. The average age of the Social Revolutionary terrorists was even lower; quite a number of them had not even left school. Sazonov, who killed Plehve, was twenty-five; Balmashev was five years younger. Émile Henry, the French anarchist, was twenty-one when he was executed. Most Latin American terrorists were, or are, of the same age group; Carlos Marighella became the leader of the Brazilian 'urban guerrillas' in his fifties, but this was a rare exception; another was Captain Lomasney who blew himself up while trying to mine London Bridge. Todor Alexandrov, who revived IMRO in the early 1920s, was forty at the time, and his chief aide, Protogerov, was in his fifties. But Alexandrov had become a member of the Central Committee of IMRO at twenty-eight and his successor Ivan Mikhailov, who took over in 1924, was not yet thirty. Many German and Italian terrorists of the 1920s were boys aged sixteen to nineteen 'envenomed by the bad luck which made the war finish too soon for them'.[10] Daniel Curley, hanged for his part in the Phoenix Park murders, was twenty years of age; Artal, who attacked the Spanish prime minister in 1904, was nineteen, as were Emelianov and Rysakov who threw the bomb at Alexander II. Gabriel Princip was twenty when he shot Franz Ferdinand in Sarajevo; his fellow conspirators, Popovic and Cabrinovic, were eighteen and seventeen respectively. None of them was executed, because they were under age. Alexander Berkman was nineteen when he tried to shoot Frick. Alexander Ulianov, Lenin's elder brother, yet another leading advocate of 'systematic' terror, was twenty-one when he was executed in 1887.

Even in our time exceptions can be found on occasion. Among the

---

* On the study of the psychological motivation of terrorist groups see also below, Chapter 4, 'Interpretations of Terrorism'.

Armenian terrorists who shot Turkish diplomats, there was a resident of California aged seventy-three. George Habash, Na'if Hawatmeh and 'Abu Nidal' were men in their middle or late fifties in the 1980s, still heads of their organizations but no longer actively involved in the detailed planning of terrorist operations – chairmen of the board rather than chief executive officers. Caetano Carpio, the best-known guerrilla leader in Central America, was sixty-two when he committed suicide in 1982; his chief rival in the struggle for the leadership was Melida Montes, aged fifty-four. Her murder at the hands of several of her comrades provoked the crisis among the El Salvador rebels from which they were not to recover for a long time.

The overwhelming majority of active terrorists are in their twenties and there has been a tendency, in particular among the Arab and Iranian groups, to use boys aged fourteen and fifteen for dangerous missions – partly perhaps because these are less likely to question instructions, but also because they are less likely to attract attention.

Apart from the fact that they belong to a certain age group, it is difficult to find other common features. Some had unhappy childhoods. Alexander Mikhailov, however, wrote that from his earliest days a happy star had shone on him – 'my childhood was one of the happiest that a man can have'.[11] Some leading West German terrorists of the 1970s grew up in fatherless families (Baader, Meinhof, Raspe, Mahler) or hated their fathers (Klein) or were the children of divorced parents (Astrid Proll), and, according to their own evidence, suffered as a result of a lack of close personal relationships.* But there were others who came from closely knit families (Gudrun Ensslin), and, in any case, what might be true for the German terrorists by no means necessarily applies to the Italians; and not enough is known about the background of other small groups. In the case of the nationalist–separatist groups, childhood and family background usually play

---

* German left-wing terrorists were more often than not students of sociology or trainee teachers. Many of them had attended the universities of West Berlin, Hamburg or Heidelberg. They shared the belief that whatever went wrong in their country was the fault of society and its institutions. There is reason to believe that, for some of them at least, armed aggression was an outlet for personal problems. See: Herbert Jaeger (ed.), *Lebenslaufanalysen* (Opladen, 1982), p. 166 *et seq.*; Hans Dieter Schwind (ed.), *Ursachen des Terrorismus* (Berlin, 1978), *passim.* Some investigators claim to have discovered that whereas right-wing German terrorists tended to love their mothers, left-wing terrorists hated them. But not too much importance should be attributed to these findings. They analysed the attitudes of *extremists* rather than *terrorists*; the samples were small and there were hardly any female right-wing German terrorists in the first place.

a minor role as far as motivation is concerned. Young people join the 'movement' because friends or neighbours belong to it.

Among the Russian terrorists, relations with their families were close, as shown by letters to the parents of terrorists about to be executed. Bakunin and Nechaev may be promising material for students of the human psyche, /but Kropotkin and Weitling are not; they were outgoing, uncomplicated people who enjoyed life – anything but sinister figures. The Russian terrorists of the 1870s were on the whole remarkably 'normal', i.e. sane and balanced human beings. So were Gershuni, who headed the Fighting Organization of the Social Revolutionaries, and Michael Collins, who led the Irish terrorists in 1919.

According to a recent Italian study, terrorists of the left have shown, by and large, fairly normal personality patterns whereas those of the extreme right were more frequently psychopathological.[12] This expressed itself in poor and defective insight, auto-destructiveness, belief in superstition and magic, and so on. In short, they reveal traits of an 'authoritarian–extremist personality'. But studies of this kind raise as many questions as they answer. From the same survey we learn that ideology played a much lesser role among terrorists of the right than among those of the left. But it was also observed that those of the right were, on the whole, from a lower educational background. This leads to the question of whether ideology, in the case of the left-wing terrorists, was a case of mere rationalization of their impulses, whereas the terrorists of the right lacked the knowledge and sophistication which would have enabled them to make a case for their behaviour in philosophical terms.

Almost a quarter of the Russian terrorists were women, whose devotion and courage are described in the work of many contemporary authors. But only in Russia were women to play such an important role at the time; there were no Judiths or Charlotte Cordays among the anarchists (Emma Goldman being a rare exception), nor in other terrorist groups of the left or right, nor in national resistance movements. Female terrorists in Ireland or Japan were quite unthinkable and there were only two or three in India. Bomb-throwing was clearly considered a man's job; the growing role played by women in Europe and America is a phenomenon of recent date. In the 1970s and 1980s women were still a small minority in the IRA and the Basque ETA, as well as among the Palestinians, the Turks, the Armenians and the Latin Americans. But they were represented in increasing numbers in many countries, including those of Western Europe and even among the Iranian Mujaheddin.*

Of the male German terrorists who had been sentenced to long prison terms, not a few dissociated themselves from terrorism, following further study and an intellectual re-examination. There are few known cases of women terrorists willing to admit that their acts of violence might have been wrong. When some of the leaders of the German Greens tried to open a dialogue with the imprisoned women terrorists, they rejected these feelers with sarcasm. Their commitment to terrorism was mainly emotional and could not be shaken by intellectual arguments. Thus it was only logical that some of the female terrorists still at large should move on to various non-German terrorist groups, once the Red Army had virtually ceased to exist.[13]

The last commander of the Japanese Red Army, Shigenobu Fusako, who eventually made her home in Beirut, was a woman, and of the fourteen most wanted West German terrorists in 1981, ten were women. The presence of so many women among the German Rote Armee Fraktion (RAF) (and also, at one time, among the US Weathermen) has given rise to various explanations. It is not merely a question of numbers, as the female members also proved to be tougher, more fanatical, more loyal, with a greater capacity for suffering. According to leading German observers of the terrorist scene, the Red Army would have ceased to exist considerably earlier but for the presence of women who showed greater perseverance than men. Women in West Germany also tended to remain as members of terrorist groups well into their thirties whereas men dropped out earlier; having cut themselves off from society, women found the way back more difficult, or had less urge to take it.

Among these female terrorists there were no working-class girls, whereas among the men there were usually at least a few working-class elements. Many have regarded the attraction of terrorism as part of a process of extreme emancipation on the part of middle-class young ladies, or alternatively as a 'break with rejected femininity'. While there may be a grain of truth in such assumptions, it is also true that the most ardent fighters for women's liberation have never opted for terrorism. Leading West German anti-terrorist experts have offered more prosaic explanations: women found it easier to disguise themselves and were, therefore, less

---

* A woman, Maria Cagol, temporarily became a leader of the Red Brigades. But after she had organized the raid on the prison where Renato Curcio, her husband, was kept, Curcio took over. (She was later killed in a shoot-out with the police.) While women are increasingly accepted as members and even fighters, there is resistance against women as commanders. A similar pattern can be found among the Irish Provisionals. Some of their members who participated in major attacks were women, but there were no female commanders.

likely to be arrested.[14]

Minorities were (and are) prominently represented in many terrorist movements. There were quite a few Jews among the Narodnaya Volya and even among the Social Revolutionaries. These included Gershuni and Azev, the two commanders of the Fighting Organization. Some of the leaders of the nineteenth-century Irish revolutionary movement were Protestants. The head of the Rumanian Iron Guard was not a Rumanian by origin, nor was Szalasi, the Führer of the Arrow Cross, a Hungarian. Dr Habash, the leader of the Popular Front for the Liberation of Palestine (PFLP), the most extreme Palestinian terrorist organization, was a Christian, like his deputy Wadi Hadad, and Na'if Hawatmeh, head of the rival Popular Democratic Front for the Liberation of Palestine (PDFLP). Among the Irgun and the Stern Gang (LEHI), there were many youngsters from the Oriental Jewish community, which was not widely represented in the non-terrorist Haganah.* In some cases these terrorists from minority groups perhaps perceived grievances even more acutely than the others; more often there may have been a psychological need to prove themselves, to show that they were as good or better patriots (or revolutionaries) than their comrades.

Lucien de la Hodde, writing in 1850, provides a most interesting analysis of the social composition of the secret societies in Paris in the first half of the last century, groups who, from time to time, engaged in terrorist acts. He listed nine categories of participants; first, and above all, were the students, for there was a rebellious tradition among students dating back to the Middle Ages. De la Hodde made it clear, however, that he did not have in mind the students who studied, but those who thought all bourgeois ideas ridiculous and who had a weakness for '*le bruit, les coups, les événements*'. The author admired the British for their political wisdom in having set up their universities outside the capital. Second, de la Hodde lists *les impuissants* – advocates without clients, physicians without patients, writers without readers, merchants without buyers, and all unsophisticated souls who saw themselves as statesmen, having studied politics in the newspapers. In short, the educated, or semi-educated, *déclassés*, who have always constituted the backbone of such groups. De la Hodde further lists '*les bohêmes, une classe de fantaisistes ayant horreur de la vie ordinaire*' mainly to be found in the capital, but hardly ever outside it.

---

* George Schoeters, the founder of the Quebec Liberation Front (FLQ), was a Belgian who arrived in Canada only in 1951. The fact that Bagrov, who in 1911 killed Stolypin, the Russian prime minister, was of Jewish origin is strongly emphasized in Solzhenitsyn's work and became the issue of a major literary controversy in the 1980s.

Furthermore, he adds *le peuple souverain*, i.e. the working class; *les gobe-mouche* – the simpletons, well meaning but naive and credulous people (and true believers); the permanently discontented; political refugees; and lastly the bandits, the criminal elements.[15]

De la Hodde was the master spy of the French police in the ranks of the revolutionary movements. While detestation made him an astute observer, his description contains no mention of idealistic motives. But even had he noted evidence of idealism, his comments on France would still be of little help for an understanding of the social background of the secret societies that were to develop soon afterwards in Ireland.

Some members of Narodnaya Volya were of humble origin: Zhelyabov's father, for instance, had been a house serf. But the sons and daughters of the aristocracy and the landed gentry were far more numerous among them. Bakunin and Kropotkin, it should be remembered, came from upper-class families, and Sofia Perovskaya's father had been governor-general of St Petersburg. A partial list of 365 revolutionaries arrested in the 1880s shows that 180 belonged to the gentry (including 32 officers), 104 were of middle-class or lower-middle-class origin, and the fathers of 46 had been priests.[16] Among the Social Revolutionary terrorists of the following generation, the middle- and lower-middle-class element was much more strongly represented, even though there were still numerous terrorists of impeccable aristocratic background. In this respect, Russian terrorism resembles the composition of terrorist groups in Latin America, in which the sons and daughters of the middle and upper-middle class have traditionally predominated. In Uruguay, as well as in other Latin American countries, available statistics tend to show that the sons and daughters of the administrative middle class were particularly strongly represented – educated persons without independent means, the academic proletariat.[17] The composition of the Argentine People's Revolutionary Army (ERP) seems to be similar, whereas among the Montoneros the lower-middle class and even, to a lesser extent, the working class appear to be more strongly represented.[18] The small West German, Japanese and US terrorist groups consisted, to a large degree, of university drop-outs, and like the early Fascist movements, of *déclassés* and *spostati* – socially uprooted elements.* The social origins of the members (and particularly the leaders) of these groups is of considerable significance. Ernst Halperin reaches an interesting quasi-

---

* It was reported in 1986 that the most recent wave of German terrorists was less well educated than their predecessors. There were fewer students of sociology and more shop assistants, apprentices and such like, which was also true of the terrorists of the right. Christopher Dobson and Ronald Payne, *War without End* (London, 1986), p. 89.

Marxist conclusion when he argues that terrorism in Latin America is 'a vigorous reaction against economic stagnation and social putrefaction by the most energetic members of the administrative class, a bid for absolute power in order to give that class the challenging task of totally transforming society'. In this way 'class interest', idealism and social consciousness neatly complement each other. But it is also true that the smaller the group, the less meaningful the search for common social patterns.

The nationalist–separatist terrorist groups almost always consist of young people of lower social background than the socialist–revolutionary groups; the IRA is an obvious example, more so than the ETA. Inasmuch as the nationalist–separatist movements have a left-wing fringe, this again consists mainly of intellectuals of middle-class background or white-collar workers; Fatah is more 'proletarian' than the more radical PFLP and PDFLP.

Close foreign observers of the Russian scene of the 1880s, such as Masaryk and George Kennan, the elder, noted that the young terrorists were men and women of the highest ethical standards. Most Russians, even their bitterest opponents, tended to agree with them. Dostoevski's villains are mere caricatures – Pyotr Verkhovenski, a buffoon, slanderer and traitor, and Shigalov with his enormous ears ('all are slaves and equal in their slavery'). Any similarity between the 'possessed' and the terrorists of the 1880s is purely accidental.[19]

The Russian terrorists anxiously asked themselves whether they had the right to kill, in contrast to many latter-day terrorists with their philosophy of killing for fun and profit. Dora Brilliant, one of the martyrs of the Social Revolutionaries, confessed that it was easier to die than to kill; Timofei Mikhailov, who was to participate in the assassination of the tsar in 1881, at the last moment felt unable to perform the deed, but he showed no weakness when he was about to be executed. Kalyayev, who set out to kill the Grand Duke Serge Alexandrovich, did not throw the bomb at his first attempt because the intended victim was accompanied by his family, and clearly it was wrong to kill children.[20] For the same reason Angiolilo, the Italian anarchist, did not shoot Canovas, the Spanish prime minister, when he first had the opportunity to do so. Police spies who had been infiltrated into the ranks of the Russian terrorists and who had been unmasked, escaped death on more than one occasion by appealing to the humanity of the terrorists, who hesitated to kill them if there was even the slightest doubt concerning their guilt.

These men and women had little in common with the IRA, the German Freikorps of the 1920s, the Japanese Red Army and other present-day terrorist groups. Killinger, the Freikorps leader who later became a Nazi *Gauleiter*, describes with evident relish how he and his comrades whipped a woman so that there was not one white spot left on her back.[21] The cruelties committed by Macedonian and Croatian terrorists are well documented, and there was also a cruel streak in Irish terrorism from an early date. John Devoy, it is true, said on one occasion that the Celtic character revolted at the mere idea of assassination. But national character changes and the practice of cutting the victim's Achilles tendon was reported in Ireland as early as 1813 – a system refined in recent years.[22] In the light of historical evidence, it would be wrong to juxtapose the 'humane' character of left-wing terrorism to the 'sadistic' terror of the nationalist and right-wing groups. Criminals have frequently shown greater humanity than terrorists; most of them are out for profit, not for psychological satisfaction. They do not normally torment their victims. Terrorists are fanatics, and fanaticism frequently makes for cruelty.

In February 1972, a United Red Army hideout was discovered in Karuizawa, a mountain spa some eighty miles from Tokyo. Fourteen mangled and tortured bodies were found; half of the group had liquidated the others for 'anti-revolutionary failings', a few had apparently been buried alive. This has been explained against the background of unfathomable Oriental traditions. It would hardly account for the comments of Bernardine Dohrn, leader of the Weather Underground, on the Sharon Tate murder: 'First they killed those pigs, then they ate dinner in the same room with them, then they even shoved a fork into a victim's stomach! Wild!' The Black September assassin of Wasfi Tal, the prime minister of Jordan, thirsted, he said, to drink his victim's blood after having fulfilled his mission.

The preoccupation with ethical problems, it has been said, was very much a nineteenth-century European phenomenon. In the twentieth century, human life became cheaper; the belief gained ground that the end justified all means, and that humanity was a bourgeois prejudice. Selfless devotion, idealism, courage and the willingness to sacrifice oneself have not disappeared, but these qualities can be found in all parts of the political spectrum. They have been demonstrated by militants of good causes as well as of the worst. Right-wing terrorism is not just gangsterism, and Brecht's *Arturo Ui* is about as helpful for an understanding of Nazism as is *The Possessed* for Russian terrorism. Horst Wessel, paradoxically, was a type out of the pages of Tolstoy or Dostoevski – the student from a middle-class home who goes to live with a prostitute in order to 'redeem her'. At another time and in another place he would have been an anarchist hero; in his life-style he belonged to the counter-culture, not to the establishment.

It has been said that the sterling qualities of the members of Narodnaya Volya deeply impressed even their political enemies. But it is also true that the fanatical devotion of some of the Nazi terrorists inspired admiration among many who were opposed to their political beliefs. For, it was asked, how could men possibly fight with such passion for a cause that was all wrong? Karl Radek wrote a famous obituary for Schlageter, the terrorist who was an early member of the Nazi Party, in which he said that this bourgeois soldier of the counter-revolution should be sincerely admired by the soldiers of the revolution. 'The fact that he risked death shows that he was determined to serve the German people. . . . We shall do everything in our power to ensure that men like Schlageter, willing to go to their deaths for an ideal, should not die in vain but be harbingers of a better world.'[23] Radek was later criticized for this indiscretion but he was, of course, right. In other circumstances Schlageter could have turned with equal ease to the left. The parents and the brothers and sisters of Fascist terrorists were as convinced as the families of Russian revolutionaries that their dear ones had died for a 'holy cause'.[24]

The mystical element has been noted in Russian terrorism, but it is also found in Ireland, in Rumania and among Japanese, Indian and Arab terrorists. Some of the Social Revolutionary terrorists were deeply religious believers. Rasputina went to church each morning, much to the consternation of the detectives shadowing her. Benevskaya, another Social Revolutionary, became a terrorist precisely because she was a believing Christian. Renato Curcio, a founder of the Red Brigades, and his wife, Maria Cagol, were not only believing but practising Catholics. There were more than a few practising Catholics among Latin American terrorists. The religious element in Shiite terrorism is, of course, a paramount factor. It is true, however, that most Russian terrorists had nothing but contempt for the religious establishment, and that most French anarchists and American terrorists were confirmed atheists. Yet their belief in their cause had a deeply religious quality. The last words of some of those about to be executed – such as Fischer (of the Haymarket trial): 'This is the happiest moment of my life' – reveal that these men and women were deeply convinced that upon them, as on Christ, rested the burden of deliverance. They were martyrs for their faith, making the supreme sacrifice for the salvation of mankind; but, in contrast to the early Christian martyrs, they no longer believed in the commandment 'Thou shalt not kill'. There is an interesting difference between nineteenth- and twentieth-century terrorists. The former accepted more or less as a matter of course that they would be executed or at least sentenced to long prison terms if apprehended. Contemporary terrorists frequently maintain that while they have the right to declare war on the state and on society, the authorities have no right to defend themselves, that any such defence is by definition inhuman and that terrorists killed or executed are, therefore, not soldiers dying on the field of battle but innocent martyrs. There are other inconsistencies. Most contemporary terrorists demand to be treated as prisoners of war, but they deny the state the right to treat them as war criminals for the indiscriminate killing of civilians. The mixture of brutality, self-pity and whining, characteristic of much of contemporary terrorism, was quite uncommon during the last century.

Most contemporary terrorists are fanatics. They, and only they, know the truth, they are the moralists, and ordinary law does not, therefore, apply to them any longer. The subject has preoccupied Western thinkers since the days of the enlightenment – above all, of course, Voltaire. Voltaire wavered between the belief that scorn and ridicule were the only remedy for fanaticism and the sad conclusion that, once fanaticism had gangrened the brain of any man, the disease should be regarded as nearly incurable. He made another observation which is true to this day, namely that the entire species of fanatics is divided into two classes, those who do nothing but pray and die and those who want to reign and massacre.[25]

Describing the spirit with which his comrades, the Russian terrorists, were imbued, Kravchinski frequently drew on illustrations from the Bible.[26] Björnsterne Björnson, the Norwegian writer, noted in his *Beyond Human Power* that it was among the anarchists that modern martyrs might be found. The idea of the martyr who has gained eternal life appears in the history of Irish terrorism from its beginnings to the present day. Writing about Russian terrorism, Masaryk detected a 'mysticism of death'; the same is true of anarchism, of some Fascist groups and, above all, of the Rumanian legionnaires, with their rite of calling the names of the dead at parades and answering 'Present'. It is true with regard to ETA and some of the Middle Eastern terrorist groups.

The political issues in nineteenth-century Russia were clear-cut; there were no constitution, no elementary rights and no legal redress against the abuse of power. Elsewhere, the issues were more complex, and terrorists had to persuade themselves that there was no alternative to violence, that democracy was dictatorship, and that radical change could be effected only if bombs were thrown and pistols fired. In these circumstances, the choice of terrorist means was less obvious, and those opting for them were usually more problematic characters.* Emma Goldman, defending the anarchists

---

* The problematical character of terrorism was, however, clear even to some of the early Russian terrorists. Thus Vera Zasulich referred to that 'particular frame of mind ... either one of great vanity, or one in which life has lost all its attractiveness'. (Jay Bergman, *Vera Zasulich* (Stanford, 1983), p. 60.)

in a famous essay, said that they were torn in a conflict between their souls and unbearable social iniquities.[27] Highly strung they certainly were, but for their motives one has to look as often as not to their private lives rather than to their political and social environment.

The early 'propaganda by deed' in Western and Southern Europe was carried out by individuals acting on their own, mostly men of little education. Some were Herostratic figures; the last words of Bonnot, the leader of a gang of anarchists and criminals in the Paris of the *belle époque*, were 'I am a celebrated man.' The same words were used by 'Carlos' when he introduced himself at the time of the terrorist attack on the OPEC headquarters in Vienna. Some were sick in mind as well as in body, which led Cesare Lombroso into his premature conclusions about the connection between bomb throwing, pellagra and avitaminosis. By the turn of the century, some terrorist groups already included adventurers and even criminal elements. In the later stages of the Russian terrorist movement, there were comments about the dictatorial behaviour on the part of some leaders, on their disregard for human life and their waste of money. Such complaints would have been unthinkable in the days of the Narodnaya Volya.[28]

The less clear the political purpose in terrorism, the greater its appeal to unbalanced persons. The motives of people fighting a cruel tyranny are quite different from those of rebels against a democratically elected government. Idealism, a social conscience or hatred of foreign oppression are powerful impulses, but so are free-floating aggression, boredom and mental confusion. Activism can give meaning to otherwise empty lives. Sofia Perovskaya and Vera Figner were the symbols of one kind of terrorism – Ulrike Meinhof and Patty Hearst of another.

The subsequent fate of some of the leading terrorists of past ages is of interest. Durruti, the fiery Spanish anarchist, was killed in the defence of Madrid, and Marighella died in a shoot-out with the Brazilian police. Johann Most and O'Donovan Rossa, two of the grand old men of violent action, mellowed a little with age. Joseph Casey, the Fenian leader, faded away in his Paris exile; he appears as Kevin Egan in Joyce's *Ulysses*: 'He prowled with Col. Richard Burke, tanist of his sept, under the walls of Clerkenwell and crouching, saw a flame of vengeance hurl them upward in the fog.' Kropotkin, Emma Goldman and Alexander Berkman advocated non-violent action in later life. Of the nineteenth-century Irish terrorists in the United States, some went into American politics and a few became congressmen or diplomats. Among those who lived to see the emergence of the Irish Free State, many were killed in the subsequent internecine struggle; the survivors constituted the political elite of the new state. Sean

MacBride, a former chief of staff of the IRA, became a distinguished international civil servant – and winner of the Nobel peace prize. The leaders of the Irgun and the Stern Gang became oppositionist members of the Knesset, the Israeli parliament, while others went into the army or into business. A Russian–Jewish terrorist of earlier vintage, Pinchas Rutenberg, reappeared in Palestine as a distinguished industrialist and founder of the local electricity company. Andrea Costa and Paul Brousse, leading anti-parliamentarians in the 1880s, were to enter parliament soon after. Brousse, who had coined the phrase 'propaganda by deed', in later years was to congratulate the king of Spain on his escape from assassination. Of the surviving Russian terrorists of the 1880s, some subsequently moved to the extreme right, and many made a name for themselves as scientists. Kropotkin had been a distinguished geographer all along. Mention has been made of Morozov and Sternberg, and one should also add to this list the biochemist A.N. Bach, a member of the Soviet Academy of Science in later years, the ethnographers Bogoraz-Tan, Yokhelson and Krol, as well as the bacteriologist Kharkin.[29]

Of the Social Revolutionary terrorists of early-twentieth-century vintage, not one joined the Bolsheviks; most emigrated from Russia, or did not return to Russia after 1917. Savinkov, who had served in the Kerenski government, actively fought the Communists, as did Maria Spiridonova; she had been given a life sentence in tsarist Russia, and in 1918 again found herself in prison, where she died twenty years later. The heroic example of the Freikorps terrorists was praised by the Nazis but, with very few exceptions, these men were kept at arm's length in the Third Reich. Pilsudski and Arciszewski, leaders of the Polish terrorist struggle in 1905–6, became chief of state and prime minister of Poland respectively. Ante Pavelic, the leader of the Ustacha, was made the Führer (Poglavnik) of an 'independent' Croatia during the Second World War. With the defeat of the Axis his career came to a sudden end, and he became one of the most wanted war criminals. It is too early to generalize about the fate of the European and North American terrorists of our time; some advocates of individual terrorism in the United States have already changed their views and life-style, so have many Italians and others.

Most of our surmises about the motives of terrorists are by necessity speculative, which is not to say that they are by necessity wrong. But few terrorists have co-operated with outsiders to undergo tests or have engaged in psychological self-analysis. Where such studies do exist, they point to certain patterns which ought to be noted even though their results are seldom clear-cut and, in any case, may not be valid in other cultures.[30] In West Germany, there was a confluence of highly idealistic motivation and revolutionary impatience with progressive radicalization ('The new order can be built only on the ruins of the old'), and an increasing loss of a sense of reality as the terrorists were cut off from society and lived in ghetto-like closed groups. Once they had become illegals they were unlikely to meet anyone who would challenge their views and with whom they could lead open discussions.[31] To members of such a small in-group everything seemed possible, provided only sufficient militancy and determination were shown. On the other hand, all those not belonging to the group were by definition enemies, mere animals ('pigs') or satanic forces towards whom no pity need be shown. The group provided love, friendship and protection, while it replaced the family, culture and politics. It had its own language, symbols and value system. Having joined the group, it became difficult to imagine an existence outside it, despite all the severe friction bound to arise between its members. The group was much more than a political party, more even than a family; hence the reluctance to leave it even after it might have become clear that its aims were wrong and its activities senseless. In earlier centuries, salvation was thought to be unattainable outside the church; now there is thought to be no meaningful life outside the group. The difficult psychological problems facing those intending to leave a Communist party in the 1930s and 1940s have frequently been described; leaving the 'terrorist party' seems to have been equally difficult.

The role of the group was probably more central in Germany than in Italy, and it may be of even lesser importance among the terrorist 'mass movements', such as the IRA and the Palestinians, where transfer from one fighting unit to another might be much easier. But to some extent, the group syndrome, the terrorist *esprit de corps*, existed everywhere.[32] It does not, however, explain why certain young militants became terrorists in the first place, whereas others did not. Did they choose violence because this seemed the rational choice in certain conditions (the 'Olson theory') or because there was an imbalance in the socio-political system? This might have been the case in some instances, but not in others. Or do biological and physiological variables play a role in the decision to opt for terrorism as some have argued? This has been violently contested by others partly for ideological reasons and partly because the evidence is not conclusive. The physiological hypothesis is not necessarily genetic in character – it does not claim that 'terrorists are born'. On the contrary, if aggression is learned behaviour, leading to arousal and certain physiological responses ('fight or flight'), it can also be unlearned.[33] But the neurophysiological model of aggression implies that terrorism cannot entirely be removed by socio-political changes such as installing a regime of freedom, justice and dignity for all. For the reality, however perfect, is always bound to fall short of the expectations of at least some people; there are no known political means to affect malfunctioning brains.

The neurophysiological model of terrorism is no more than a tentative attempt to explain the decision to engage in terrorist actions, and its proponents do not deny the interaction of physiological and socio-political variables.[34] It could well be that the decision to opt for terrorism on the part of certain individuals is a mere accident affected, up to a point, by tradition, the socio-political milieu and the presence of one or a handful of charismatic leaders. But the possibility that a non-accidental pattern exists has to be explored.* The neurophysiological variable may be of little consequence in certain circumstances – wherever political conflicts are blatant – but it may have a considerable impact in other conditions. On the basis of our present knowledge (or ignorance), it cannot be dismissed without further investigation.

The search for a 'terrorist personality' is a legitimate enterprise, but it is unlikely to result in a common denominator spanning various countries, periods, cultures and political constellations. Some terrorists were the sons of well-known revolutionaries – the Russian Balmashev, for instance, or Émile Henry, whose father was a leading communard, or Sean MacBride. But the father of young Cabrinovič, who was involved in the Sarajevo plot, was an Austrian police spy, and the large number of sons and daughters of high tsarist officials in the revolutionary movement of the 1870s and 1880s has already been noted.

Nechaev was totally devoid of moral scruples in his private life, but in this respect he was an exception among nineteenth-century revolutionaries. Most and O'Donovan Rossa were heavy drinkers, yet many of their comrades were fanatic abstentionists. Some contemporary terrorists habitually take drugs, but most do not. Some Russian and Serbian terrorists suffered from tuberculosis and died young, while others enjoyed perfect health. Ravachol, Émile Henry and a few of the Russian terrorists were mystics or believers in the occult, others had not the slightest inclination in this direction. Some contemporary observers noted a suicidal urge among

---

* Reports in recent years have indicated a relationship between aggressive behaviour and serotonin metabolism. But the study of a possible central nervous system contribution to aggression is of a relatively recent date and few scientists are willing at this stage to commit themselves one way or another. For a review of the literature see Gerald L. Brown and Frederick K. Goodwin, 'Human Aggression – A Biological Perspective', in W. H. Reid (ed.), *Unmasking the Psychopath* (New York, 1986).

terrorists; they were *todestrunken*, in the words of one observer.* But for every intellectual preoccupied with death, there were several others who enjoyed life as much as the next person. In short, there has always been a great variety in character traits, mental make-up and psychology among terrorists.

All that can be said with any degree of confidence is that terror was (and is) a pursuit of young people, and that in most other respects the differences between terrorists are more pronounced than the features they may have in common. The character of terrorism, furthermore, has undergone a profound change. Intellectuals have made the cult of violence respectable; there had been no such cult among the Russian terrorists. Vengeance did play a certain role, but not cruelty. Émile Henry, for instance, wanted to avenge Vaillant, who had thrown a bomb in the French parliament, and after Henry's execution, Caserio killed Sadi Carnot, the French president, because he had not pardoned Henry. The explosion in the Barcelona opera house (1893) was to avenge Paulino Pallas who had been executed shortly before. The bomb thrown at the Corpus Christi procession two years later, also in Barcelona, was in protest against the conditions at Monjuich prison. The particular ferocity of LEHI terrorism was no doubt connected with the desire to avenge the death of their leader, Avraham Stern. In the history of Russian terrorism, and also in Rumania and more recently in Ireland, repression frequently caused a new wave of terrorist operations.

Not all nineteenth-century terrorists were knightly (or saintly) figures; there were doubtful characters among them and some were half mad. But, by and large, these were fighters against brutal dictatorships and against hideous persecution. It was surely no coincidence that, at the time, terrorism was most widespread in tsarist Russia and Turkey – the two most oppressive regimes in Europe. Nor is there any doubt about the genuineness of the grievances of the Irish rebels, American workers and Spanish peasants. Inasmuch as there was indiscriminate terror, it was perpetrated by unstable individuals; it was not a matter of systematic policy. Atrocities were committed, but the ethical standards prevailing in Macedonia around the turn, of the century and in Mexico were not quite comparable to those of countries on a higher level of civilization.

The terror of recent decades is different in quality. The more oppressive regimes are not only free from terror, they have helped to launch it against

---

* This seems to have been true with regard to some French anarchists, and also to Orsini who wrote in his famous last letter that he had tried to kill Napoleon III in a fit of mental aberration, that he did not believe in murder, and that Italy would not be liberated by attempts to emulate his deed.

more permissive societies. The fate of the terrorist of the 1880s and 1890s, when apprehended, was not an enviable one. By contrast, no West European, North American, Japanese or Middle Eastern terrorist of the 1960s or 1970s has been executed (except in some cases by his comrades), and there is always a good chance that he will be released even before serving his term, his comrades having blackmailed the authorities into freeing him. Much of the risk has gone out of terrorism. It is no longer a daylight duel between giants in a kind of Russian *High Noon*, as the Narodovoltsy saw it. With time-bombs left in public places and the dispatch of letter-bombs, the struggle has become anonymous and much of the heroism and sacrifice have gone out of it. Sometimes terrorism has become bureaucratized and quite frequently it is manipulated from afar.

Standards and modes of behaviour have changed. The Narodnaya Volya, the French anarchists or the Irish dynamiters would not have abducted children and threatened to kill them unless ransom was paid. They would not have advertised for agents to do their own work, nor would they have given parcels with explosives to unsuspecting fiancées or tourists. They would not have sent parts of their victims' bodies with little notes to their relatives as the (right-wing) Guatemalan MANP and NOA did. They would not have expected a premium of millions of dollars from foreign governments for commissions executed, they would not have tormented, mutilated, raped and castrated their victims, nor would they have engaged in senseless wholesale slaughter of their own ranks. They would not have stolen a collection of valuable pictures (including Vermeers and Goyas) belonging to the Irish nation as the PIRA did twice; in 1974, under the leadership of an English heiress, and again in May 1986. Not all terrorist movements have made a fetish of brutality; some have behaved more humanely than others. But what was once a rare exception has become a frequent occurrence in our time.*

If a common pattern, a general trend, can be discerned at the present time, it is precisely that which has just been noted. When all allowances have been made for the primitive character and the violent traditions of certain societies, there is no escaping the fact that nineteenth-century terrorists acted according to standards very different from those prevailing at present. This is not to idealize the Narodnaya Volya or to denigrate all the terrorists of our age. Latin American or Arab terrorists may be fervent patriots or feel the injustice done to their people as acutely as the terrorists

---

* Students of Fascism are bound to discover Fascist elements in many contemporary terrorist movements whatever their professed ideological orientation. It is a Fascism which does not aim at gaining a mass basis, and brutality is one of its pronounced features.

of an earlier age, but they still belong to a different species. Whatever their motives may be, the 'ardent love of others' which Emma Goldman observed is not among them. The driving force is hate not love, ethical considerations are a matter of indifference to them and their dreams of freedom, of national and social liberation are suspect. Nineteenth-century nationalist terrorists were fighting for freedom from foreign domination. More recently, appetites have grown; the Basques have designs on Galicia, the Palestinians not only want the West Bank but also intend to destroy the Jewish state, and the IRA would like to bomb the Protestants into a united Ireland. The aims of terrorism, in brief, have changed, and so have the terrorists.

Terrorist Organization

Systematic terrorist operations involve careful planning, resembling the staff work of a minor military campaign. The intended victim has to be watched for a certain time, his habits and movements studied to establish the most promising place and time for the action. The terrorists need transportation to and from the scene of the operation; they have to have false identity papers, effective arms and, above all, money. To make the most of their operation they need a publicity department. All major terrorist movements have had a central command, sometimes highly professional and efficient, at other times rudimentary and amateurish. Important decisions among the Narodnaya Volya were taken at committee meetings, but this system has usually proved ineffective in an emergency, and since terrorist groups face emergencies much of the time, the general tendency has been towards centralization and the leadership principle. But strong leadership tends to produce rivalry and opposition, and the inevitable centralization also creates certain practical problems. Terrorism always involves an element of improvisation; even the most careful planning cannot possibly make provision for all eventualities. Elaborate planning that sacrifices the element of improvisation could redound to the disadvantage of the terrorists. A small local group, on the other hand, will usually lack the resources and the know-how for carrying out a major operation. The ideal pattern is strong, central leadership concerned with broad strategy, but with the details left to the local branches. Mao had a great deal to say about this in his writings on guerrilla warfare but, again, it is a principle easier to adhere to in terrorist theory than to observe in practice.

The central command of the terrorist movement has sometimes been located abroad; Switzerland, the United States, Lebanon, France, the Irish Republic, have been centres for movements operating elsewhere. The advantages are obvious: the terrorist leaders can move about freely without fear of arrest. But the drawbacks are equally manifest, for the more remote the headquarters from the scene of action, the less complete its knowledge of current events, and the more tenuous its contacts with its own men, even in the age of a communications revolution. While the Narodnaya Volya would never have envisaged operations outside Russia, some modern terrorist groups specialize in 'third country operations'.

The larger the terrorist movement, the greater the danger of detection. The Narodnaya Volya, at the height of its activities, had 500 members; the Fighting Organization of the Social Revolutionaries (1903–7) was considerably smaller, though there was a large periphery which it could draw upon for support. Both the Irgun and LEHI had only a few hundred members who could be enlisted for terrorist operations. The nineteenth-century Irish terrorist groups consisted of a few dozen militants. The IRA, the ETA and the Palestinian Arab terrorist organizations had many more members, but only a small number were trained for terrorist action. Terrorist groups, in contrast to guerrilla units, do not grow beyond a certain limit. The basic unit usually consists of three to ten people. Some of the recent terrorist 'armies' such as the Japanese Red Army or the Baader–Meinhof groups numbered a few dozen members at the height of their exploits. The 'Symbionese Liberation Army' had eight members. The Tupamaros started their operations with a handful of members in late 1966; five years later they had about 3,000. Yet their success was their undoing, for the very size of the movement made it easy for the security forces to track down the terrorists and eventually to arrest many of them and destroy their organization. The Argentine ERP was believed to have had 5,000 members in 1975, but again only a part engaged in fighting operations.* The Montoneros, who began with a handful of members, were in the end even more numerous, but lacked cohesion and split into several factions. The same is true of the more recent Latin American terrorist groups.

Generalizations about present-day terrorist organizations are almost impossible because of the widely different conditions prevailing. Terrorism has appeared in isolation, as well as in combination with a political movement or even in a general context of insurgency with guerrilla warfare, political action, mass demonstrations and individual terror playing their

---

* The ERP repeated some of the mistakes committed earlier by the Tupamaros and, against all the rules of urban terror, frontally attacked major army units. About seventy of them were killed in the attempt to storm the Monte Chingolo army camp in the spring of 1976. The mistake of frontal attack was also committed by the Montoneros, some of the Central American groups, the Colombian terrorists, Khomeini's Iranian opponents and others. Some learned from these defeats, others did not recover from the setbacks.

part. Some terrorist groups have found a territorial structure most useful: the Red Brigades in Italy operated in major centres such as Milan and Rome; so have the Irish Provisionals, with permanent units in West Belfast and Londonderry; and ETA with bases in Guipúzcoa, Vizcaya, Alava and a few in Navarra. In almost every case, only a few members of the territorial 'brigade' were commissioned to carry out operations. In West Germany and in France, where terrorists were fewer in number, they resembled a small circus moving from place to place, and the same is true with regard to international terrorists. Some terrorist groups have been more successful than others in adhering to the rules of strict conspiracy. The religious–separatist groups or movements like Peru's Sendero Luminoso are usually based in a small town or a refugee camp or a well-defined quarter in a big city, and it is next to impossible for outsiders to penetrate these groups.

Small groups of political militants often show certain common characteristics; the most basic being the fundamental purpose of any political organization to maintain itself.[35] They acquire certain mental attitudes, a momentum of their own, and, like elite military units, a certain cohesion, solidarity and *esprit de corps*. In many cases, they lead an existence of their own, distinct not only from the political movement which originally sponsored them but also, as time passes, quite remote from their original aims. Thus terrorist groups tend to carry on even after their purpose has been largely accomplished – such as the IRA after the establishment of the Irish Free State, LEHI after the state of Israel had come into being, and ETA after sweeping reforms had been carried out in the Basque country. In such conditions, as one observer noted, the group tends to become simultaneously more introverted and unrealistic, and the violence necessary for group maintenance cannot simply be abandoned.[36]

But the opposite is also true: in small groups as in larger ones there are in-built centrifugal tendencies and inclinations towards splits. It is difficult to think of any terrorist group which did not split at one time or another; certainly, all the major ones did. Frequently, this was the result of a confrontation between 'hardliners' and (relative) 'moderates' who thought that the time had come to declare an armistice, to change strategy, or even to cease terrorist operations altogether. But, equally often, personal ambitions play a role. There are no written rules for the election or the appointment of a leader; he emerges because he was one of the founders or because his authority was generally recognized. But his position is bound to be questioned sooner or later by others for a variety of reasons. The clash of personalities may lead not just to splits but to violence within the group. The gruesome killings of one part of the Japanese Red Army by another, the 'Snow Murders', were an extreme example. There have also been internal killings among the Irish, the ETA and, above all, among the Palestinians and the Tamils. Internal dissension is likely to take place for obvious reasons when setbacks and failure occur. But splits have also taken place in normal conditions – for instance, as the result of pressure by a younger generation of militants which does not find itself represented in the leadership. And it has occurred, as the IRA and the Palestinian–Israeli examples (of 1949) show, even with victory in sight, because for at least some terrorists the struggle is more important than the attainment of the aim. For this reason (and also because the aim may be elusive in any case) the struggle must never end.

Terrorist Finances

Modern terrorists, unlike their predecessors, do not live by enthusiasm alone; they need a great deal of money. The preparation for major operations is usually expensive; money is needed for logistic purposes, for arms, for information and, generally speaking, for paying the expenses of the militants who have no other income. Cars can be stolen, but frequently it is less risky to buy them. Safe houses cannot be stolen and money is also needed for bribes and various emergencies.

Nineteenth-century terrorism was run on a shoestring. The Narodnaya Volya got the little it needed from sympathizers inside Russia and abroad; the Social Revolutionaries relied mainly on 'expropriation' (i.e. bank robberies). The anarchists were poor and had no significant support, apart from occasional windfalls. Francisco Ferrer, the Spanish anarchist, received a million francs from a French lady he had befriended. The Irish Revolutionary Brotherhood was founded in a Dublin timber yard on St Patrick's Day 1858 with four hundred dollars received from the United States. More substantial sums were collected in later years (the Special National Fund, Rossa's Skirmishing Fund and others). Some of the money was contributed by a sympathizer who was a billiard champion. Irgun received financial support from Jews in the United States, in the early days mainly from Hollywood – owing to the personal contacts of Ben Hecht, one of the leading script writers of the time. It also engaged in 'expropriation'.

Occasionally, the political police would contribute directly or indirectly to the budget of anarchist and terrorist groups, but these gifts were hardly ever of decisive importance. In 1906–7, Indian terrorists tried to manufacture counterfeit coins and even prepared 'chemical gold'. When these attempts to raise money failed, they turned to more old-fashioned methods, namely dacoity. Some of them suggested that only government funds should be stolen, but this proved to be impractical and a resolution was passed that accurate accounts should be kept of the amounts taken from private individuals, with a view to returning these after independence had been achieved. It was also suggested that only those who had amassed wealth by dishonest means should be victimized. But, as noted by a historian of the Indian freedom movement, 'it is difficult to believe that this principle was always followed in practice'.[37] Nor could all terrorists, human nature being what it is, live up to the ideals of high moral purpose and absence of greed; dacoities were committed for personal ends, and political objectives were used as a disguise. The Ustacha forged Yugoslav 1,000-dinar notes, apparently with Italian help, and LEHI printed government bonds with the assistance of a specialist serving in the Polish army-in-exile.

After the First World War, it became the fashion among some governments to finance terrorist groups; thus the Italians and the Hungarians gave money to the Croats and Macedonian IMRO (44 million lira in 1929–33). IMRO also received funds from the Bulgarians, and the Poles allegedly at one time paid the Rumanian Iron Guard, though this has not been proven. This fashion became even more popular after the Second World War, and, with the rise of international and state-sponsored terrorism, the amounts changing hands amounted to many millions.

The European terrorists, by and large, stuck to old-fashioned methods such as bank robberies and also increasingly to abduction and ransom demands. Thus, to give but one example, the German RAF within a few months in 1971 seized DM115,000 in Kassel, DM158,000 in Munich, DM19,000 in Hanover, DM237,000 in Kiel, DM134,000 in Kaiserslautern, and DM315,000 in Berlin; altogether more than a million marks, which, given the small size of the group, must have been enough to keep them going for a year. Argentine terrorists were aiming higher – and, to be fair, conditions in their country were more conducive to thinking and acting big. The ERP collected a war fund of $30 million as the result of a number of abductions and the ransom thereby received – more than $1 million for a Ford executive in Buenos Aires, the same for a Fiat representative, $2 million for Charles Lockwood of Arrow Steel, $3 million for John Thompson of Firestone and more than $14 million for Victor Samuelson of Exxon. In addition, these and some other corporations paid the ERP protection money to prevent repeat performances. The record sum was achieved by the ERP's rivals, the Montoneros, who received some $60 million ransom for releasing Jorge and Juan Born, the sons of the owner of one of Argentina's richest corporations.

Protection money as well as voluntary contributions were collected by the IRA and the ETA. The IRA, in addition, engaged in several legitimate business ventures such as running a taxi service in Belfast, and there were substantial donations from Irish patriotic groups in America. In Catholic pubs in Northern Ireland, one penny for every glass of beer was deducted for the Provisionals.

In the United States, attacks against armoured cars have become more frequent because they seem to be less risky than bank robberies. Thus some descendants of the Weather Underground attacked a Brinks armoured car near New York in 1981, whilst a terrorist group of the extreme right stole some $3.6 million from a Brinks car in California in 1985. However, these amounts were almost dwarfed into insignificance with the rise of state-sponsored and narco-terrorism. According to the Baghdad agreement in the late 1970s, the Palestinians were to be paid $350 million annually, not counting special allocations made by Qadhafi (and to a lesser extent by the Syrians, Iraqis and Iranians) to their clients for special services rendered. Qadhafi paid not only for the accomplishment of a mission but also took out insurance policies; thus Hans Joachim Klein, a German terrorist who was wounded during the OPEC raid in Vienna in 1975, was allegedly paid $200,000. The Saudis, on the other hand, reportedly paid for terrorist operations that were threatened but not undertaken following their financial intervention. In some Arab countries direct and indirect taxes were collected from Palestinians, and also in public places of entertainment such as cinemas. Even if the promises were often greater than the funds actually delivered and even if, on occasion, forged money was used, the sums changing hands did amount to hundreds of millions of dollars.

A further boost for terrorist finances came with the expansion of the drug trade. This has played a greater role in Latin America than in the Middle East, and a greater role in the Middle East than in Western Europe. Not all terrorist groups have had windfalls like the Colombians and Peruvians. In one region in Colombia alone, the local terrorists reportedly collected $10 million protection money in a month. Many terrorist organizations of the left and the right have become to a greater or lesser degree involved in the drug trade, and this has made an enormous difference as far as their opportunities are concerned. Operations which were out of their reach in the past have now become feasible. It has also made a difference with regard to the staying power of the terrorists. No known terrorist group has had to go out of business because of insolvency or cash-flow problems. But the new affluence has also created problems for the terrorists. Nineteenth-century terrorists had been almost uniformly poor, whereas more recently there has been a 'class differentiation'. A terrorist aristocracy with rich and powerful protectors has emerged, as well as a terrorist proletariat, which does not get outside help because their aims do not coincide with the interests of foreign governments, and who have no contacts with the drug traffic either.

This development was first noted in the 1930s. 'Who are these assassins?', asked a contemporary commentator after the murder of King Alexander of Yugoslavia in Marseilles in 1934.[38]

Are they Croats, or Czechs, or Germans, or perhaps Hungarians? Everything about them is wrong – with the exception of their money and their arms. Where did the money come from, how were these poor persecuted Croats able to pay for expensive journeys through many countries? Who has armed and financed them, who has provided their false passports? In short, who has commissioned them?[39]

No one had asked questions of this kind about the Narodovoltsy or the anarchists because they had been poor and there had been no secret about their funds. But in the 1930s and, *a fortiori*, after the Second World War, terrorism became big business with multinational ramifications, and a great deal of effort was devoted to keeping the sources of income obscure. State-sponsored terrorists would use, needless to say, only carefully laundered money, and the Latin Americans would collaborate closely with respectable or semi-respectable banks on the one hand, and with the underworld on the other. Occasionally, the truth would come out, as in the case of Graiver's Banco Commercial de la Plata. David Graiver, the scion of a Buenos Aires banking family, had acted as the chief banker and investment adviser for the Montoneros; whether he did so because he sympathized with them, or because they blackmailed his family, or because he regarded it as a simple business proposition, is not clear. All we do know is that, after his executive jet crashed on a mountainside near Mexico City in 1976, his business empire collapsed. There was a shortfall of some $50 million and it also appeared that he had invested at least $17 million of the Montoneros' money in legitimate enterprises both in Argentina and abroad, paying out monthly interest to them.[40] The PLO, with its much larger holdings, used more solid banks in Amman, Kuwait, Beirut and elsewhere, with assets of many billions of dollars, so that a Graiver-like disaster was unlikely to occur.

PLO finances have been something of a riddle. The assets of the Palestine National Fund are estimated at $1.6 billion; the fund is said to spend about $300 million annually, out of which about one-third is allocated to the military wing – Al Fatah. However, according to some estimates there is a second Al Fatah fund of about $7–8 billion.[41] This sum greatly exceeds the GNP of major African countries such as Tanzania or Kenya; it is twice as large as the Jordanian GNP. The PLO is undoubtedly big business but the estimates may be exaggerated. Some of these funds have accrued from arms sales, others from drug smuggling, yet others from legitimate business activities such as running airlines in Sierra Leone and the Maldives. The Arab OPEC countries gave major sums to the PLO while the price of oil was high. As a result the PLO was in a position to give loans to Nicaragua and invest in African development projects. However, by the middle 1980s most Arab countries (including Iraq, Libya, Syria) had ceased to contribute and the Saudi allocation was down to about $80 million a year. The sums given by the Emirates and Kuwait and the PLO tax collected from Palestinians in the Gulf states provided only minor sums. Could the PLO holdings have grown to such an enormous size owing to clever speculation? This is possible but unlikely. If Fatah were as rich as is sometimes alleged, its political and military position would certainly be stronger than it is. It would certainly find it much easier to cope with its rivals in the Palestinian fold such as 'Abu Nidal' and Abu Musa. That the PLO owns several dozen big companies seems beyond doubt. But not all businesses have flourished, nor can the investment be converted on short notice into ready cash.

Allocations for state-sponsored terrorist groups have sometimes been made on account of specific actions; Black September is said to have received $7 million for the murder of the Israeli athletes at the Munich Olympic Games. In the Lebanese civil war, payments for specific operations seem to have been the rule rather than the exception.

On the other hand, this new wealth has created temptations which did not exist before. True, even among the Fenians in the 1880s and the Russian Maximalists there had been occasional accusations of misappropriation of money, about squandering funds and spending for personal use. One of the treasurers of Irgun absconded to the United States shortly after the end of the Second World War. But the sums involved in those days were insignificant in comparison with the many millions amassed by the Arab and Latin American organizations during the last two decades.

In the affluent groups, officials were paid salaries far above what they could earn in legitimate professions. Swiss bank accounts were opened, there were investments in property and other transactions, more in line with big banks than the traditional terrorist ethos of the Fenians or the Narodnaya Volya. Prolonged exposure to the *dolce vita* in luxury hotels produced a new type of terrorist, different from the lean and hungry fighters of previous generations. A member of the Berlin urban terrorist scene related that his group split on account of money: 'When there is too much money, unnecessary things are bought, first a record player and a television set, then expensive suits and cars, and in the end you look like something straight out of *Playboy*. . . .'[42] The German terrorists had a weakness for expensive BMW cars to make their getaway, but then they could always justify this predilection for they obviously needed fast cars. In Irish terrorism as well, there continue to be accusations of misuse of money and embezzlement. A fairly typical one concerned Hughes, a Provisional IRA man from County Tyrone who fled to the US with about £100,000 seized in a bank raid in County Meath in 1975. A spokesman for the organization said that a certain decision was taken regarding Hughes and it did not include military honours at his funeral.[43]

Modern terrorism, it was initially said, involves a great deal of money, and most organizations have disposed of considerable sums. In some cases, the income of the terrorists has clearly been in excess of their needs. The funds accruing from co-operation with drug dealers are sufficient to finance not just sustained terrorist campaigns but also military insurgencies and, in certain Third World countries, political leaders and parties, and also if need be to pervert elections. In these circumstances, the wealth of the terrorists has paradoxical consequences. The rich terrorists have enough money to hire others to do their work.* This new wealth may lead to a perpetuation of terrorism; why should one give up a profitable business? On the other hand, by co-operating with the drug dealers, terrorists may become part of the corrupt system which they originally wanted to destroy.

Terrorist Arms

The dagger and the pistol were the traditional terrorist weapons up to the dawning of the age of dynamite. The invention of the first time-bomb is attributed to a M.Chevalier, a resident of Paris; he produced a cask filled with powder and missiles to which a musket barrel with trigger was attached. A similar machine was used by one Saint Regent, a former naval officer, who tried to blow up Napoleon when he was still first consul. The barrel was placed on a cart at the corner of the Rue Niçaise, on the road from the Tuileries to the Rue Richelieu. A time fuse was used, but either Saint Regent had miscalculated or Napoleon's driver was in a hurry – the explosion took place a little too late.[44]

---

* A fairly typical case of subcontracting was that of Habib Ma'amar, a twenty-four-year-old Tunisian arrested by the French police in early 1986. He had placed bombs in the Marks and Spencer stores in Paris and London and engaged in other terrorist operations. There was no evidence that Ma'amar had deep feelings about the Palestinians or Israel, but he had close contacts with the criminal underworld and was paid by the PFLP a monthly salary of 20,000 francs – in dollars. He was caught because he beat too frequently and brutally his accomplice, an Algerian woman who gave him away to the police. No secret is made of the fact that terrorists are employed on a mercenary basis. The Libyan government advertised in the press for volunteers from Morocco to India, at the rate of ten times the salary of an Indian industrial worker.

Terrorist Budget[a]

Year	Terrorist group	Country	Income in 1980 US$	Sources
1880	Narodnaya Volya	Russia	insignificant	donations from well-wishers
1880	Irish dynamiters	Ireland	50,000	Irish sympathizers in US
1896	Anarchists	France, Italy	insignificant	donations
1906	Social Revolutionaries and other groups	Russia	5–10 million	robberies, some voluntary donations
1932	IMRO	Bulgaria	2–3 million	extortion, Bulgaria, Italy
1933	Ustasha	Yugoslavia	1–2 million	Italy, Hungary
1947	IZL–Stern Gang	Palestine	1–2 million	donations from well-wishers, robbery
1970	Tupamaros	Uruguay	5–10 million	abductions, robbery
1970	ALN	Brazil	5–10 million	abductions, bank robbery
1974	ERP–Montoneros[b]	Argentina	50 million	abductions, robbery
1975	Fatah[c]	Middle East	150–200 million	mainly from Arab oil-producing countries
1975	PFLP, PDFLP, Saiqa	Middle East	20–30 million	donations from Libya, Iraq and Syria

Notes

[a] The figures are based on estimates; terrorist movements have not, as a rule, kept accounts to be examined by outsiders or tax inspectors. However, enough facts and figurers are known to give a general idea of their income. The estimates are calculated on the basis of 1976 dollars; the sums that were at the disposal of terrorist groups before the Second World War were, of course, in absolute terms much smaller. But prices were much lower too; the Irish paid five to six dollars for a rifle in 1914; the Russian A K-47 assault rifle sold for 110 dollars in the 1970s and may cost now several times as much.

[b] 1974 and 1975 were exceptionally profitable years for the Argentinian terrorists.

[c] Estimates of the income of Palestinian terrorist organizations vary greatly. According to Israeli sources, Fatah had an income of $150–200 million in 1976; figures mentioned in the press of the 'Rejection Front' and by Syrian spokesmen ($240 million) were higher.

Terrorist Budget[a] *(contd.)*

Year	Terrorist group	Country	Income in 1980 US$	Sources
1975	IRA, Provisionals and Officials	Ireland, Ulster	1–3 million	donations and robberies, protection rackets and income from legitimate business
1975	UDA, UVF	Ulster	?	same
1980	ETA	Spain	1–2 million	donations, robbery
1980	Turkish terrorists	Turkey	10–15 million	donations from outside sponsors, robbery[d]
1980	Red Brigades	Italy	5–10 million	bank robbery, ransom
1982	FMNL	El Salvador	30 million	abductions, bank robberies
1985	Abu Musa (Fatah opposition)	Middle East	10–20 million	state-sponsored (Libya and Syria)
1985	Abu Nidal	Middle East	30–40 million	state-sponsored (Libya and Syria)
1985	FARC	Colombia	50–150 million	narco-terrorism
1985	M 19	Colombia	50–150 million	narco-terrorism
1985	Sendero Luminoso	Peru		narco-terrorism

If expenses for political work and donations in kind rather than cash (arms, equipment, training camps, etc.) are included, the higher figures may well be closer to the truth.

There were enormous discrepancies even in 1986 with regard to estimates of the income and the property of the PLO. *Forbes* magazine wrote in May 1986 that, while the PLO's income had declined to about $150 million, it was spending at the rate of $300 million; that it was, in other words, on the verge of bankrupcy. James Adams on the other hand stated that the PLO was 'one of the most successful businesses in the world' with an income of (US dollars) '750 m', 'a billion', 'more than 1.25 billion' and between 1.25 and 5 billions annually – figures which are probably greatly exaggerated (*The Financing of Terror: The PLO, IRA, Red Brigades, M 19, and Their Money Supply* (New York, 1986); and *Sunday Times Magazine*, 13 July 1986).

[d] According to official Turkish sources no more than 1 per cent of the income of the Turkish terrorists – left and right – was from bank robberies; the rest must have come from abroad.

Explosives such as gunpowder and fulminate of mercury had been used before Alfred Nobel made his invention, and occasionally with great effect. Twelve persons were killed and 120 injured when the Fenians blew up Clerkenwell Prison in December 1867 – 500 pounds of black powder were used on that occasion. A decade earlier, in Paris, Orsini's bombs left eight dead and 156 wounded. The quantities of explosives needed were considerable; it was difficult to transport them without arousing suspicion and it was only with the invention of nitroglycerine and later of nitrocellulose (gelignite) in the 1860s and 1870s that bombing and mining became much easier. It was widely believed at the time that dynamite was the ultimate weapon. The American and French anarchists based their whole strategy on its use and Patrick Rallihan of Brooklyn published a paper with the title *Ireland's Liberator and Dynamite Monthly*.[45]

Narodnaya Volya was the first to use dynamite on a wide scale. One of their members, Serge Kibalchich, was an accomplished scientist who introduced important innovations such as mixing nitroglycerine with other materials and using fulminate of mercury as a detonator.[46] But if the new explosives were highly effective they were also extremely dangerous. Quite a few Russian revolutionaries were killed while producing or transporting dynamite. Grinevetski was blown up by the very bomb which killed the tsar in 1881; Rokotilov was fatally injured while preparing bombs; Dembov lost his life while experimenting with dynamite, as did Schweitzer, one of the leaders of the Social Revolutionaries and their main weapons expert. Similar mishaps were frequent in the history of Irish terrorism, from the time of Captain Lomasney to present-day operations in Ulster. Since the early, exaggerated hopes connected with dynamite were not fulfilled, the revolver, the rifle and even the dagger remained often-used terrorist weapons – President Carnot was knifed, as was Empress Elizabeth of Austria in 1898.

Dynamite was far more destructive than all previous explosives, but the quantities needed were still substantial. The average mine prepared by the Narodnaya Volya weighed sixty pounds or more and, even then, it did not always have the desired effect. Khalturin, who had access to the Winter Palace and placed a bomb there, asked his comrades for a mine of about two hundred pounds. They gave him only seventy pounds of dynamite which, as it emerged, was not enough for his purpose. The mines used by the Irish dynamiters of the 1880s were smaller and, on the whole, not very effective. In his handbook, Most had solemnly predicted that a ten-pound bomb would totally destroy any warship; the terrorists were learning by trial and error that this was just not so.[47]

The great technical problem that faced the terrorist during the last third of the nineteenth century was the miniaturization of bombs, the production of a hand grenade no bigger than an apple which could be easily hidden and thrown a considerable distance, while having as much explosive power as an old-fashioned mine. The Russian terrorists of the 1880s experimented with metal boxes containing some five pounds of dynamite. But workable grenades of this weight were produced only by the Social Revolutionaries and were used in the killing of Plehve and the Grand Duke Alexei.

The bomb clearly was not the all-destructive weapon it had been thought to be, but it had become a symbol which replaced the barricade, and it certainly made a great deal of noise. Ivan Dragomiroff, the head of the Assassination Bureau in Jack London's novel, while giving a cut-rate to anarchists, regretted their enthusiasm for dynamite and other extremely hazardous materials used to ensure that their executions were sensational and spectacular ('our killings must be red . . .'). Dragomiroff charged them ten thousand dollars for the killing of a police chief of a great city, half a million for a major king or emperor, seventy-five to a hundred thousand for second- or third-rate kings.[48]

The American Irish made many suggestions for improving terrorist technology. These included an early version of the Molotov cocktail – a zinc vessel filled with a pint and a half of benzine and regulated by a clock connected to it to light and burn for a certain time.[49] Rossa's plan for using osmic gas in the British Houses of Parliament has been mentioned. The British government was worried, unnecessarily as it emerged, by the reports concerning submarines built in New York. Sixty thousand dollars were spent on building three such vessels, but it appears that only one was actually constructed, by Messrs Delamater & Co. of New York. The 'Torpedo Boat' was said to have 'most wonderful powers as a destructive machine, more so than any boat yet invented'.[50] But the ship never saw action. Captain McCafferty pioneered the idea of using a railway train and a steamer in a terrorist operation in the 1860s, but the raid did not materialize.

The idea of preparing letter-bombs seems to have first occurred to the Russian terrorists of the 1880s. They discussed the dispatch of small quantities of explosives to the tsar in little parcels purporting to contain drugs against rheumatism and asthma.[51] But this plan was apparently not carried out. Johann Most, in his journal and in his other writings, recommended incendiary devices contained in letters and small parcels, but again the technical difficulties were apparently insurmountable at the time. *

---

* The first recorded actual use of a letter-bomb (or to be precise, a parcel-bomb weighing some twenty-five pounds) was in June 1895, when a package that was leaking was opened in a Berlin Post Office. It had been prepared and dispatched by Paul Koschemann, a mechanic,

Footnote continued on next page

One of the first successful cases of assassination by means of a letter-bomb was the killing of the Hungarian (Uniate) vicar-general in Transylvania by a group of Rumanian terrorists just before the First World War. In 1908, Indian terrorists first used (unsuccessfully) a primitive book-bomb. The Irgun used the technique on a few occasions and it was widely used by Arab terrorists and others in the early 1970s. Azev, the head of the Social Revolutionaries Fighting Organization, acutely feeling the need for innovation, told his comrades that new methods were needed since the police were familiar with all the old tricks. He intended to buy an auto-mobile, and, when he heard in 1906 that Buchalo, an anarchist engineer, was constructing a new type of aeroplane in Munich, he gave him 20,000 rubles in the hope of using the plane in a future operation.[52] But Buchalo's plane was never completed. It was not until some seventy years later, in January 1974, that an aircraft was used for the first time in a terrorist operation, when the IRA dropped two bombs from a stolen helicopter. Motorcars were first used for terrorist purposes by the Bonnot gang in Paris in 1913 to facilitate their escape following bank raids. The modern submachine-gun was first used, so far as can be established, by the IRA shortly after the First World War; Irish sympathizers had just delivered a few specimens of Colonel Thompson's new gun.[53]

If the terrorists did not find the miracle weapon, they had no great difficulties in obtaining firearms and explosives; there was usually ample opportunity for buying or stealing them. Arms for the Irish terrorists were smuggled in ships from the United States; revolvers for the Indian terrorists came from Britain. The Armenians smuggled some of their weapons from Russia, and the Balkan terrorists received theirs from their protectors abroad. Army arsenals were always a potential source of supply, either because individual officers or soldiers sympathized with the terrorists or because the terrorists found some venal official. Following major wars, weapons and explosives were in ample supply all over the world. The Western Federation of Mine Workers in the United States certainly had no difficulties in getting explosives for their operations in the early years of the century, and in the 1960s, with the emergence of multinational terrorism, plastic bombs and

---

Footnote continued from p. 105

twenty-one years of age, with anarchist leanings. It was addressed to a senior police officer. But the addressee was not at all connected with the political police, nor did Koschemann have the backing of any organized group; the motive for the action did not become any clearer in court. The design was primitive: Koschemann used gunpowder and bottles filled with ligroin; a little revolver activated by an alarm clock was to serve as the detonator. (H. Friedlaender, *Interessante Kriminalprozesse* (Berlin, 1922), II, p. 156.) A few years later, more sophisticated parcel-bombs were used by criminals in the United States (Roy A. Giles in *Scientific American*, April 1923, p. 226).

even missile launchers were transported from country to country under the seal of diplomatic baggage. Since the Second World War, explosives have been made even more effective and the new developments were taken up by the terrorists with only a few years' delay.* TNT and picric acid, which had been the main military explosives in the First World War, have been replaced by the more powerful and durable RDX and PTN.

The plastic explosives, known in the US as C 3-4, PE 2-4, Semtex-4, and so on, come in wrapped blocks and are used for various purposes; the orange-coloured Semtex, for instance, has been used for most terrorist letter-bombs. Contemporary terrorists have drawn for a long time on the experience of the special forces in the Second World War. The various components of explosive devices were packaged and separate from one another and assembled when the device was to be used. The plastic explosive came in four- or eight-ounce sticks, and five-pound slabs, but also in ready-to-use special packages.[54] Mercury fulminate, which served several generations of terrorists as both primary and secondary explosives, has gone out of fashion and great progress has been made with igniters (blasting caps). Pencil time fuses were followed by various EED (Electro Explosive Devices), including microwave, passive infrared and ultrasonic detonators. Lastly, the group of environmental fusing systems ought to be mentioned – changes in temperature or atmospheric pressure are used to ignite an explosive device, for instance in an ascending or descending aircraft. With the progress in batteries, and their miniaturization, which has made some of them difficult or impossible to detect even with x-ray equipment, further advances were made in bombing technique.

The terrorist's standard weapon has, however, remained the pistol and the automatic rifle. The AK-47 (Kalashnikov) is the symbol of both the Palestinian groups, the African National Congress (ANC) and many others, whereas the US Armalite rifle is the symbol of the IRA. In the resistance movement in Western Europe during the Second World War, the Colt

---

* The first booby-trapped bombs appeared well before the First World War. The public was warned that it was dangerous to tear out a burning fuse and then freely handle the bomb, for 'many dynamiters are ingenious enough to attach the fuses to the more dangerous bombs of the liquid type, in order to mislead the finder' ('Studying the Anarchists' Bombs Scientifically', *Scientific American* (July 1911), p. 100; the article had originally been published in a German periodical, *Reclam's Universum*). The great technical difficulties involved in the construction of home-made bombs were amply described in the professional literature (see, for instance, Jules Bebie, *Manual of Explosives* (New York, 1943), p. 156). Some of these complications vanished with the appearance of plastic explosives, such as Nexit, which were apparently used for the first time in the assassination of Heydrich, the head of the Gestapo, in Prague on 29 May 1942. The bomb which exploded in Hitler's bunker on 20 July 1944 consisted of a similar material, presumably cycloite mixed with a plasticizing medium.

automatic and the Webley Mark IV revolver were status symbols, whereas the Germans had the 9 mm Parabellum. They were succeeded by the Browning 9 mm, with which Agca shot the Pope. The Makarow, the Czech Skorpion (used in the murder of Aldo Moro) and other arms of short range were mainly for self-defence, whereas the standard rifles used by the East European partisans had greater range and accuracy, but not much firepower. As a rule, they have not been used for terrorist attacks in cities, since they could not be hidden.

During the last two decades, automatic and semi-automatic weapons have replaced the old army rifle. The two most frequently used early automatic weapons were the Thompson (Tommy) gun of 1921, frequently remodelled, and the Sten gun. Both were technological breakthroughs: the Sten gun was simple and cheap; the Tommy gun was heavy and costly but reliable. They were also sturdy and used standard ammunition, but the Sten was not accurate except at close range, and the Tommy gun was impossible to conceal, while the firing rate was so great that aiming was very difficult.

These, in turn, were replaced by newer generations of small arms. Revolvers are still widely used at close range, but they cannot be used with silencers. Pistols, which nowadays are usually semi-automatic, have much greater firepower, but their ammunition is less effective. Shotguns, using small lead or steel balls, have frequently been used by terrorists. They are most effective at a range of 25–40 yards, but most can only fire five shots at a time which reduces their usefulness. This leaves machine-guns, which come in many makes from many countries. Terrorists have most frequently used submachine-guns and assault rifles (such as the Russian AK-47), whereas the heavier machine-guns are of use only in guerrilla warfare. Submachine-guns weigh between four and nine pounds; the average magazine contains thirty cartridges and they take pistol ammunition.[55]

Technologically advanced weapons, such as anti-tank rockets which are usually shoulder-fired and rocket-propelled, have also entered the terrorist armoury. They are of use mainly against cars and buildings, as their average range is little more than 100 yards, but the Soviet RPG-7 (rocket-propelled grenade, first fired at Orly airport in 1975) has a range of 350 yards. On at least one occasion (Rome 1973), Palestinian terrorists have used SA-7 heat-seaking anti-aircraft rockets. These weapons are relatively small; the anti-tank rockets are two to three feet in length and some of them can be fired from a van or a lorry.

The most effective new weapon used by terrorists in the 1970s and 1980s was the car-bomb; it was also the one which took the highest toll in human life. The basic principle was, of course, anything but novel; Saint Regent's barrel on a cart, with which he intended to kill Napoleon, was an early version of the vehicle-bomb. The car-bomb was perfected in the prohibition era, especially by Al Capone and his Chicago gangsters. These 'bombs' consisted of a few sticks of dynamite – from a dozen ounces to five pounds – which, if correctly placed on the petrol line, the petrol tank, or on the wheelwells, functioned with devastating effect.[56] The more primitive car-bombs were ignited when the driver started the engine. But since terrorists do not always have access to the car for any length of time, in order to install them in the right place, limpet mines of various sorts (originally used in the Second World War for affixing to naval craft) have been stuck to the vehicle and detonated by remote control. This was the case, for instance, in the assassination in Washington DC in 1976 of Letelier, the former Chilean ambassador to the US.

The car as a super torpedo was first used in Northern Ireland, in Palestine and, above all, in Lebanon. In a few cases, such as in the bombing of the French embassy in Beirut, a sizeable quantity of explosives was put into the car of an unwitting embassy employee. In other cases, trucks and lorries were used for delivering substantial quantities. It is estimated that, in the bombing of the US embassy in Beirut (April 1983), one ton of explosives was used, two tons for the US embassy in Kuwait in December 1983, and possibly six tons (12,000 pounds) when the US Marine Head-quarters in Beirut were attacked in October 1983. In the two Beirut explosions, the lorries were crashed into the wall of the buildings and the loss of life was very heavy. In Kuwait, and on some other occasions, the vehicle was stopped at some distance from the building, or only part of the explosives were detonated, and there was less damage. Since this time, car-bombs have been less frequently used – except indiscriminately against civilians. For, while the Americans, French and Israelis were initially unprepared for attacks of this kind, defensive measures were quickly introduced ranging from physical barriers to banning motor transport altogether in the vicinity of buildings believed to be possible targets.* These simple and obvious measures have proved effective.

Intelligence

The success of terrorist operations depends on reliable information about the targets to be attacked and the movements of the victims to be killed

---

* In the meantime, inventive constructors have produced a Cadillac selling at $250,000 with dozens of defensive gadgets which makes abduction difficult. Gadgets which start cars from a distance have become commonplace. There can be no defence against landmines on country roads or against indiscriminate bombings in a big city, but selective attacks on cars and by cars have become more difficult.

or abducted. The Social Revolutionaries disguised themselves as coachmen and street traders in order to patrol unobtrusively in the neighbourhood chosen for an attack.* Other terrorist groups used sympathizers, such as repair workers, postmen or street cleaners, for intelligence gathering. Government employees were of great help and sources inside the police were invaluable, since they could warn the terrorists about impending raids and help to unmask spies in their ranks. Narodnaya Volya owned some of their successes to the information received from Nikolai Kletochnikov, who had found employment in the 'third section' – the tsarist political police. From perusing police files, he established that there was a spy (Reinstein) among the Narodovoltsy – who was promptly killed. The Social Revolutionaries also had a sympathizer in the police who helped them on several occasions, and it is doubtful whether Azev would ever have been unmasked but for the information they received from leading police officials.[57] Michael Collins' attack against British intelligence headquarters in Dublin in November 1920 effectively paralysed British operations during the critical period of the insurrection, since vital documents were destroyed and undercover agents were discovered and killed. The IRA regarded the 'G' Division of the Dublin Metropolitan Police as its main target; the British could always send new soldiers to Ireland, but the number of knowledgeable intelligence officers was limited and they could not easily be replaced.

Nationalist terrorist groups such as the Irgun had sources of information in the police, who collaborated with them either because they were sympathizers or because they were paid. Schulze and Tillesen, the murderers of Erzberger, the leading Catholic politician, were tipped off by the German police and succeeded in escaping abroad. The Nazis boasted, on occasion, that they received copies of the secret communications of the police and of the ministry of the interior almost as soon as they had been dispatched from headquarters.[58] Latin American terrorists had well-wishers in key positions, and the multinational terrorist groups of the 1960s and 1970s, with almost unlimited funds at their disposal, had no difficulty in getting information, presumably including Interpol bulletins.

Some of the major terrorist operations of the 1970s and 1980s were carried out with military precision which revealed not only excellent planning but also superior intelligence. This is true, for instance, of the Aldo Moro abduction, the assassination of Carrero Blanco and the Schleyer

---

* When Bhagwati Charan and his friends of the Hindustan Socialist Revolutionary Army planned to blow up the viceroy's train near Delhi in 1929, one of the group disguised himself as a fakir so as to study the locality without arousing suspicion (Yashpal, *Singhavalokan II* (Lucknow, 1951), p. 93, quoted in Vajpeyi, *The Extremist Movement in India* (Allahabad, 1947), p. 247).

ambush. In some cases, if the victim was not guarded or took no special precautions (such as Olof Palme), or if the murder was carried out by insiders (as in the case of Indira Gandhi), simple observation by a person or two for a few days would be sufficient to find out all that was necessary.

In other cases, far more elaborate staff work was needed. It was not sufficient to establish the likely pattern of the victim's movements; the approaches to a building or the site of an ambush had to be carefully studied and, of course, also the various possibilities of a getaway. Much of this could be done by old-fashioned methods such as inspecting the site on foot, repeatedly if possible, without, of course, attracting attention. But electronic communication aids also played an important role: if the police and the army had their walkie-talkies, the terrorists sometimes had equipment of even better quality.

Above all, human intelligence sources remained of crucial importance – the men and women who watched the trains and cars go by, the airport employees who knew all the details about the arrival and departure of aircraft, the transfer of passengers and luggage, and who could, if necessary, smuggle arms on board a plane for the benefit of the hijackers. For the kind of operations which the Abu Nidal group and other international terrorist groups carried out, the presence of friendly (and reasonably well-paid) agents among the ground personnel was essential. Turkish terrorists of the left received useful tips from well-wishers among the police, and those of the right got information from sympathizers of the right – the Turkish police being deeply divided along political lines. The German terrorists used the good services of some of their lawyers; in Italy there were judges of the extreme left who were not averse to giving terrorists a helping hand. In France and Spain, on the other hand, some former police officials with good connections inside the force tended to veer towards the far right; they supported terrorist groups of the same persuasion, and probably even took part in certain operations. The fact that the police (the 'pigs') were often singled out as victims by the terrorists of the left was no doubt an additional inducement. In all, most terrorist groups suffered no shortage of human sources, and received information from fellow travellers, from unwilling persons, through blackmail, and also from paid informers. *

---

* The Argentine Montoneros reportedly had an excellent intelligence service, the Servicio de Informaciones Montonero, which rested on the unpaid collaboration of individuals in many spheres of public life: 'Primarily through the *agrupaciones*, data were channelled to it concerning the security forces, "traitors", employers, the lay-out of barracks and police stations, and the operation of public services' (Richard Gillespie, *Soldiers of Perón: Argentina's Montoneros* (Oxford, 1982), p. 179).

Varieties of Terrorist Tactics

The assassination of leading representatives of the 'system' is the oldest method and has been frequently adopted by terrorists.[59] Indiscriminate terror has become widespread only in recent times with the invention of more effective explosives and the emergence of the modern mass media. The case for indiscriminate murder is, of course, well known: it dramatizes the demands of the terrorists; it spreads a climate of fear and discredits the government incapable of suppressing it; and, if frequently repeated, it disrupts the normal functioning of society. At the same time, from the terrorist point of view, it is far less risky than attempts against the lives of leading personalities, who may be well guarded. The drawbacks of indiscriminate terror are equally obvious – 'intimidation by deed' will not gain political support, and it is, therefore, mostly used against foreigners or by very small terrorist groups lacking both a clear political aim and a consistent strategy.

If the 'death penalty' is the rule, other punishment has occasionally been meted out by terrorist groups. The Tupamaros set up 'people's prisons' where the inmates were usually hostages to be released upon receipt of money. Irish terrorists have occasionally inflicted injuries on suspected minor spies or 'collaborationists', and this has also been the practice of the Ku Klux Klan and similar organizations – ranging from beating up the victim, tarring and feathering, to permanently depriving him of the use of a limb.

The other most frequent kind of terrorist operation has been 'expropriation', i.e. bank robbery or the robbery of mail trains or of vans transferring large sums of money. The Russian terrorists first attacked a bank in 1879 and the practice spread rapidly during the first Russian Revolution (1905–6). In October 1906 alone, there were some 362 'expropriations'. The most notable was the robbery (by the Maximalists) of a bank in Fonarny Pereulok in Moscow when some twenty assailants seized nearly a million rubles. Polish terrorists were even more successful in 1908, attacking the St Petersburg–Warsaw mail train and getting away with more than two million rubles. The Bolsheviks netted more than 300,000 rubles when 'Kamo' and his Caucasian comrades robbed a convoy in Tiflis in June 1907. Banks were occasionally robbed by the Irgun and the Stern Gang and also by small European and North American terrorist groups. Robberies became almost a daily occurrence in Latin America in the late 1960s. It was generally considered the easiest kind of operation, in which new recruits could be tested. Well-established terrorist groups also collected contributions from supporters or extracted money by threats. This was the practice among the Macedonian IMRO and the Palestinian terrorists before they received regular major allocations from the oil states.

The liberation of captured comrades from prison has always been a top priority for terrorists. The Fenians equipped and dispatched a ship (the *Catalpa*) to Australia to help in the escape of six of their members who had been exiled there. Their attempts to liberate Fenian prisoners in Clerkenwell and Manchester failed, with tragic consequences. Narodnaya Volya had to shelve a project to liberate Nechaev, because Schluesselburg was too well guarded. But there were individual and mass escapes, usually with some help from outside, in tsarist Russia, mandatory Palestine (Latrun and Acre), Ulster, West Germany, Uruguay and Argentina. In recent years, attacks on prisons have become rare because they involve too many risks. On the other hand, 'swapping' has increased – the release of hostages in exchange for the release of imprisoned terrorists.

Kidnapping for political purposes and the extortion of ransoms has been practised since time immemorial. In 1819, Guglielmo Pepe, Neapolitan general and Italian patriot, planned to capture Emperor Franz I and Metternich. But this plot proved to be as unrealistic as the Fenians' scheme in the 1860s to abduct the Prince of Wales. In 1920, the IRA kidnapped a British general while he was fishing. In the United States, following the arrest of socialist militants and their extradition across state lines in the early years of the century, Eugene Debs threatened retaliation in kind: if kidnapping was a legitimate practice 'we all have a perfect right to engage in it . . .'.[60] He proposed that for every working man kidnapped a capitalist should be seized and held for ransom; the kidnapping of the first capitalist would convulse the nation. Even earlier, in a pamphlet published in London in 1903, Vladimir Burtsev had recommended kidnapping as one of the tactics to be used in the terrorist struggle, but his advice was not heeded by the Social Revolutionaries. In 1947, the Irgun kidnapped and later hanged two British sergeants in a futile attempt to prevent the execution of two of their members under sentence of death. Abduction became exceedingly fashionable in the late 1960s and continued throughout the 1970s. Among those kidnapped, to mention but a few of the outstanding cases, were the United States ambassadors to Guatemala and Brazil; the West German ambassadors to Guatemala, Haiti and Brazil; Aramburu, the former president of Argentina (May 1970); Pierre Laporte, Quebec labour minister (October 1970); the Swiss ambassador to Brazil; the British ambassador to Uruguay (kidnapped in January 1971, released in September); the leader of the West Berlin Christian Democrats, as well as the whole OPEC executive in Vienna (December 1975) and countless consuls, public figures, businessmen, officers, racing drivers, football stars and men and women who could not be considered public figures by any stretch of the imagination.[61] In some cases, no ransom terms were demanded and the victims were killed after a few hours or days; more often the release was made conditional on the release of political prisoners, payment of ransom and, of course, safe passage. In yet other cases, such as the OPEC hijacking, no clear demands were made by the kidnappers. After 1973, the number of kidnappings decreased, with the exception of Lebanon. For while guerrillas can always take their hostages to a 'liberated area', terrorists have much greater difficulty in hiding their victims. The Moro, Schleyer and Dozier cases remained exceptions.

This list of the varieties of terrorist activities is far from complete. Agrarian terror was practised in Andalusia in the early 1890s by a mysterious organization called the Mano Negra.[62] Agrarian terrorism also took place in Ireland, in eastern Poland and in North Germany (in 1920) against big landowners, tax collectors or government representatives. Industrialists and trade union leaders have been threatened and occasionally killed in labour disputes, and systematic intimidation has been used against judges and journalists. A Berlin chief justice, Drenkmann, was killed by terrorists in West Berlin in the autumn of 1974. A fairly typical incident which took place before 1933 was described by a Nazi publication after Hitler had come to power. It was directed against a 'disgusting scribbler' called Paeschke who edited a left-wing newspaper in the city of Reichenbach. Every day the storm troopers were subjected to poisonous comment and, as a result, a 'few courageous men' decided to give the villain the deserts he had so amply deserved. Paeschke was to be killed on his way home from his office; unfortunately, the artillery shell which was to serve as a landmine exploded in the hands of the SA man who carried it.[63] Similar methods were used in various parts of the world by left-wing and right-wing terrorists against public figures, sometimes to intimidate, at other times to kill. In February 1971, the Tupamaros kidnapped Homero Farina, editor of *Accion*, because (in their own words) 'we wanted to make clear the role played by the media at that time, namely, the role of being part of the repressive forces.... We do ask them not to tell too many lies; we understand we cannot ask them not to lie at all because the lie is essential to bourgeois journalism.'[64] Farina was released after eighteen days, having been given a stern warning.

Perhaps the most dramatic new technique used by terrorists has been the hijacking of aeroplanes. One of the first recorded cases was the taking of a Peruvian plane in 1931 during a military coup in that country. Between 1945 and 1950, some twenty-five hijackings took place; in most cases refugees from Iron Curtain countries used aircraft to escape to the

West. During the 1960s, a great many American planes were compelled to fly to Cuba, not always by political terrorists – there were twenty-two such cases in 1968 and forty the following year. But, following an agreement between the United States and Cuba in 1969, the number fell rapidly. In July 1968, Palestinian terrorist organizations first hijacked an El Al plane which was subsequently flown to Algeria; the last passengers were released only after some eighteen arrested Arab terrorists had been freed in Israel. Following the introduction of stringent security measures, no further Israeli planes were successfully seized after that date. But the hijacking of third-country aircraft increased rapidly, culminating in the Dawson Field incident in 1970 when several jumbo jets were compelled to land on an airfield in Jordan and were subsequently destroyed.

These operations attracted enormous attention at the time, and great apprehension was expressed with regard to the future of civil aviation. But the fears were exaggerated – after 1972 there was a steady decrease, partly due to more effective security measures at airports, and partly because of the growing reluctance of governments, even those of Libya, Syria and Iran, to provide shelter for hijackers. Moreover, it was a case of diminishing returns, for there were few tangible achievements and even the publicity value of hijacking decreased with repetition.[65] Although sixty-four planes had been hijacked in 1971, this figure was down to thirteen by 1979, and seventeen the year after. On the other hand, there was a rise in attacks against travellers at airports, sometimes against specific airlines, on other occasions quite indiscriminately and even without threats or claims for credit.

If the hijacking of planes declined, there was temporarily a sharp increase in attacks against embassies, culminating in the seizure of forty-two embassies in 1980, twenty of which were in Latin America, and during the course of which fifty-three men and women were killed. The most famous was the 444 days' occupation of the US embassy in Tehran which began in November 1979; while not originally state-sponsored – Iran was experiencing conditions of semi-anarchy in 1979 – the Iranian government certainly supported it later on.

Mention has been made of the use of car-bombs especially in Lebanon, but the same weapon was also used elsewhere, including South Africa, Syria and Iraq. In other respects, only minor innovations have taken place on the terrorist scene: the various terrorist groups continued their favourite tactics – the use of the culvert bomb by the PIRA, the shooting of the victims at traffic lights by the Armenian Secret Army for the Liberation of Armenia (ASALA), and the placing of bombs in Israeli buses and supermarkets by Palestinian groups. South African and Latin American terrorist groups frequently selected targets of economic importance. There were striking resemblances in the execution of the kidnapping of Aldo Moro in Rome and that of Hans Martin Schleyer in Cologne. In each case, the cars in which the victims were driving were forced to a halt, the drivers and guards were shot, and the victim bundled into a getaway car. The whole operation took less than a minute.

There were two instances in which senior NATO officers were attacked, both by German terrorists. In Brussels in June 1979, General Haig escaped injury because the driver who stood in for his regular chauffeur was driving faster than usual and the culvert bomb, detonated from a distance of 150 yards, exploded too late. An attack near Heidelberg in September 1981, against General Kroesen, commander of the US Army in Europe, was staged by means of an RPG from a distance of more than 100 yards, followed by small-arms fire.[66]

On some occasions, more exotic approaches or targets were used, but they usually did not succeed. This refers, for instance, to the hijacking of the *Achille Lauro* in the eastern Mediterranean, the anti-tourism campaign by ETA and the attempt by a Palestinian group to poison Israeli oranges destined for export. Quite often there would be minor or major mishaps among the terrorists, usually while handling bombs. To provide but one example, some thirty people were killed in August 1984 at Madras airport in southern India, when bombs meant to be loaded on a Sri Lanka flight exploded with two hours' delay. On other occasions, a charade would be put on, as in December 1984 when a Kuwaiti airliner, which had been hijacked by Iranian agents, was 'stormed' and liberated by other Iranian agents at Tehran airport, but only after two US citizens had been killed.

There is an infinite variety of terrorist acts, but, while weapons have greatly improved over the last 100 years, there have been few basic changes in the aims of terrorist operations.

Popular Support

Terrorist groups always hope for public support. Extreme nationalists operating against foreigners can usually count on some sympathy among their fellow countrymen. The misguided actions of a few hotheads will be condemned, but, at the same time, extenuating circumstances will be found to explain, if not altogether to excuse, their behaviour. This goes for Irish, Basque and Palestinian terrorists, whereas public support for Armenian, Indian and Jewish (Irgun and LEHI) terrorism was less wholehearted because their activities were considered politically harmful.

Nationalist terrorists can, at the very least, expect not to be betrayed by their compatriots. In Palestine, co-operation between the Haganah and the British mandatory government against the 'dissidents' (i.e. terrorists) was a rare exception and took place while the Second World War was still in progress. The same applies to the (limited) co-operation between Whitehall and Dublin in the 1970s and 1980s; but then the Provisionals were almost as much opposed to the Irish government as they were to the British. The support mustered by terrorists fighting their own government depends very much on the plausibility of their cause. The operations of Narodnaya Volya had not the slightest impact on the peasantry and very little on the working class. But the intelligentsia was overwhelmingly sympathetic, and the same was true for the next generation of Russian revolutionaries. The two major Russian writers, Leskov and Dostoevski, who in their novels depicted terrorists in a negative light, were never forgiven by the Russian intelligentsia even though they made amends in their later works – for example, in Dostoevski's Pushkin anniversary speech. In intellectual circles such criticism was anathema; it was believed – as in Latin America or in the Arab world today – that even if terrorists tended to make mistakes, they were motivated by a deep humanism and the desire to build a better world, and for this reason even their outrages were forgiven.

In Western Europe, support was limited, by and large, to fairly small sections of the intelligentsia. Quite a few French writers and artists toyed with anarchism in the 1880s and 1890s, among them Zola, Paul Adam, Octave Mirbeau, Mallarmé, Pissarro, Seurat, Signac and Steinlen. They could understand the motives of a Vaillant and an Émile Henry, even a Ravachol; they would sign petitions on behalf of Vaillant since no one had been killed by the bomb he had thrown. 'We were all anarchists without throwing bombs,' Kees van Donghen wrote in later years, 'we had those kinds of ideas.'[67] Mallarmé appeared as a character witness on behalf of his anarchist friend Fénelon. Clemenceau, watching the execution of Émile Henry, was deeply disturbed; he saw a man (he wrote) with the face of the tormented Christ, terribly pale, implacable in expression, 'trying to impose his intellectual pride upon his child's body'. There was some sympathy even from the extreme right which hated the Third Republic and everything it stood for, and on the part of aesthetes like Laurent Tailhade whose *petite phrase* became immortal: '*Qu'importe les victimes si le geste est beau.*' Tailhade, who lost an eye in a subsequent terrorist attack, was not exactly a man of the left, looking forward (as he once wrote) to the 'happy days when the plebs would kiss the poets' footprints'. But this was purely platonic support; in the last resort even the French intellectuals of the left were horrified by the senseless violence perpetrated by the anarchists. There was even less sympathy for terrorism in Britain and the United States. There was some support for the victims of the Haymarket trial, but chiefly because those executed were almost certainly innocent of the crime.

The working-class terrorism of later years, such as the McNamara brothers' bombing of the Los Angeles Times building, was attacked even by the left; such acts, it was argued, were commercial, not idealistic. Enthusiasm for the terrorism of the 1960s was limited in extent and, like most fashions in America, shortlived.

Right-wing terrorists in Weimar Germany could almost always count on lenient judges and on support, hidden or open, from the nationalist parties. The murderers of Erzberger and Rathenau became heroes in these circles, for, to paraphrase a famous slogan of the period, there were 'no enemies on the right'. The Baader–Meinhof gang and the 2 June Movement had some sympathizers among left-wing intellectuals; there was no attempt to justify their actions, but they were understood; it was society which was mainly to blame and not the terrorists. Thus after Ulrike Meinhof's suicide in May 1976, a group of French intellectuals (including Sartre, Simone de Beauvoir, Claude Bourdet, Claude Mauriac) published an appeal deploring Meinhof's 'inhuman sufferings' and stating that the practices of the federal German government reminded them of Nazism.[68] Yet members of the Baader–Meinhof group and of the 2 June Movement had been kept in prison in conditions of almost unparalleled permissiveness, and, while in prison, had in fact continued to direct the terrorist operations of those members of their group who were still at liberty.

Sartre had visited the RAF in their Stammheim prison, and, after Baader's suicide, Jean Genet – not known as a leading advocate of progressive thought and humanism – published a paean on German terrorism. It is only fair to add that such sympathies were sentimental rather than ideological. There was an identification with the anti-bourgeois stance of the terrorists rather than with their views, on the part of some writers both on the French left and on the extreme right.[69] Furthermore, such sympathies were limited to terrorism outside France – in West Germany, to a lesser degree in Italy, and, of course, in the Third World, with Sartre's endorsement of Frantz Fanon's advocacy of violence as the best-known example.

In Italy, intellectual support for the Red Brigades hardly existed, but more than a few well-known writers, including Alberto Moravia, Umberto

Eco and Leonardo Scascia,[70] proclaimed their equidistance from the Italian state and the terrorists – the state was considered to be hopeless and not worth defending. Furthermore, there was in Italy a longstanding tradition of regarding many robbers (and occasionally even leading mafiosi) as Robin Hoods in disguise ('social bandits') and, for all one knew, the Red Brigades belonged to the same species. However, many other intellectuals sharply attacked attitudes of this kind which, they maintained, were based on a mixture of deep cynicism and profound ignorance. After the Moro killing the ambiguities about the Red Brigades ceased.

In West Germany, the crucial question was not whether one should actively help the terrorists – no one of repute suggested this much – but whether one had the moral right to give them away. What if a terrorist knocked on one's door at night in search of shelter? Böll had no sympathy with the Baader–Meinhof, but he had even less with their detractors from the right. He was enraged by the accusations of right-wing politicians and the media, according to which Adorno, Marcuse and the left-wing intelligentsia in general, had somehow paved the way for the murderous attacks of the RAF by creating the spiritual and moral climate in which German terrorism had grown roots. This led Böll and also Günter Grass, at that time politically still a moderate, to bitter and extreme attacks which in later years they probably regretted. While there was more than a little demagogy in charging certain thinkers and writers with responsibility for the RAF, it is also true that German terrorism did not develop in an intellectual vacuum. Was there no connection at all between the philosophical arguments in favour of 'progressive violence' and the practice of violence? Had no one listened to the intellectual mentors?

Walter Jens, a frequent spokesman for German intellectuals, asserted that they had always been the sceptics, rejecting violence and preaching tolerance, but he exaggerated the spirit of tolerance that had prevailed in West Germany at the time among the *hommes des lettres*. Habermas was probably closer to the point when he noted that the terrorists had picked and chosen whatever ideas fitted their preconceptions from the teachings of their gurus. But just as Nietzsche could not be made responsible for the crimes of Nazism, the intellectuals of the left were not responsible for the actions of the terrorists. Should they have kept altogether silent just because there was always the danger that someone would borrow certain of their ideas, exaggerate or distort them? There had been in some of these circles a tendency to justify violence – on the abstract level, needless to say – and this had been taken literally by a handful of extremists. It is, of course, impossible to say how important this inspiration was as a motive; extremists have frequently thrown bombs in the contemporary world without the encouragement of philosophers, poets and playwrights.[71]

The nationalist–separatist terrorist movements have never shown much interest in intellectuals. Individual intellectuals – not many, on the whole – were active in their ranks, and others supported them in speech or writing, but neither the IRA nor the Palestine Liberation Organization paid much attention to ideological debates, and if ETA showed a little more sophistication this applied more to the students than to the professors. In fact, in some of these groups an anti-intellectual sentiment, reminiscent of the anti-intellectualism of Fascism, and occasionally of Communism, could be detected. The true hero was the fighter, not the man or woman of ideas.

In Latin America, as in pre-revolutionary Russia, there has traditionally been a reservoir of good will for what the terrorists stand for. True, the Tupamaros and the Brazilian ALN, as well as the Colombian and Peruvian terrorists, were bitterly criticized by the left for their misguided and counter-productive actions. But in an emergency they could usually rely on the support of some intellectuals, churchmen and sections of the middle class to defend them against the harsher forms of government repression.

On the other hand, terrorist groups have seldom done well in parliamentary elections. When in the 1960s the Tupamaros participated in elections, as did the Colombian FARC in 1986, the results were exceedingly meagre. Sinn Fein and ETA had their regional strongholds, but nationwide – or region-wide – they never polled more than 10–12 per cent. (ETA improved its position in the elections of 1986.) Irgun emerged as a major political party in Israel, but it took some thirty years of living down their past before they became the government. At the time of the kidnapping of General Dozier in 1981, almost 10 per cent of the Italian public expressed sympathies with the Red Brigades, and 30 per cent said that the terrorists were using mistaken means to pursue the right ends. And yet it is doubtful whether a terrorist party would have received even one percentage point in free elections. The PLO had, no doubt, wide sympathies in the Israeli-occupied territories, but it is by no means certain that they would have emerged as the strongest political force in free elections competing with the Muslim Brotherhood, the Communists and other parties.

Terrorist groups have transformed themselves into political parties or movements, of both a democratic and a non-democratic kind. But, in contrast to guerrilla movements, they have seldom been successful.* By their

---

* The Tupamaros were one of the few exceptions. They eventually became a political party after a false start in the late 1960s. They collaborated with the Communists and various left-wing forces in the Frente Amplio and scored 20 per cent in national elections in the 1980s. Their first (legal) national convention took place in December 1985.

very structure they could not reach the masses, and while propaganda played a certain part in their operations it was usually 'propaganda by deed'. The commanders they produced had their qualities, but, with rare exceptions (such as Begin), they were not of the kind needed by popular leaders with fiery oratory and charismatic appeal. Thus the reluctance of terrorist groups to turn (or return) to politics is understandable. Their experience was not in the political field, and they had grave misgivings whether political means would bring about the changes they wanted. They were not temperamentally democrats and they lacked the rabble-rousing qualifications of the non-democratic popular leaders.

Terrorism and the Media

If terrorism is propaganda by deed, the success of a terrorist campaign depends decisively on the amount of publicity it receives. Seen in this perspective, the journalist and the television camera are the terrorists' best friends.[72] This is not to say that journalists have greater sympathies for terrorism than any other professional group in society; in fact, more journalists were hurt, abducted or even killed by terrorists on purpose, to intimidate or punish them (even inadvertently), than members of any other group.* But, in the final analysis, there is a close symbiotic relationship between the two, because violence is news, and peace and harmony are not. The terrorists need the media, and the media find in terrorism almost all the ingredients for an exciting story. Terrorism, to put it bluntly if inelegantly, sells newspapers and is good for television ratings. The attitude of television to terrorism has spanned the whole gamut from exaggerated respect to sycophancy. Media coverage has supplied constant grist to the mills of terrorists, it has magnified the importance of terrorism out of all proportion, it has served their propaganda, it has been indirectly responsible for the murder of innocents, and sometimes prevented or complicated rescue missions. However, not all terrorists have benefited equally from media support, but only those whose operations could be filmed, whose leaders could be interviewed, and whose victims and hostages could be photographed.

Despite a great deal of criticism, spokesmen for the media have argued that the public has the right to know and that it is the journalists' duty

---

* José Maria Portell, editor of *Hoja del Lunes* in Bilbao, was killed by the ETA *militar* because he published a manifesto by Basque intellectuals critical of terrorism. Foreign correspondents in Beirut in the 1970s were more or less systematically threatened by terrorist groups if their dispatches were unfriendly. Several were abducted, a few were killed and others had to leave.

to report without fear or favour – that these considerations override all others. These arguments have not, however, been found very convincing. Much of the time the contemporary media (television admittedly much more than the press) act as the purveyors not so much of information as of entertainment, and there are no provisions in law or the constitution concerning an inalienable right to be entertained. Even if it were always a question of providing accurate information, this does not convey absolute privileges overriding all others. Just as freedom of speech does not include the right to shout 'fire' in a crowded cinema in order to test the public's reactions, the defence of the democratic order (without which there would be no free press in the first place) takes precedence over freedom for the media, and the duty to save human lives is of a higher moral and legal order than the journalist's duty to scoop the competition. The record of the media in dealing with terrorism has been bad, with television again as the main offender by far, and this has caused heart-searching within the profession. But it has not caused a change in basic attitudes. Various codes of behaviour for the media have been prepared, but they have had little effect.

Terrorists recognized early on the importance of skilful manipulation of the media. The British War Office noted in 1922 that Sinn Fein mastery of publicity was unrivalled. Its publicity department was 'energetic, subtle and exceptionally skilful in mixing truth, falsehood and exaggeration . . .'.[73] The Irgun and the Stern Gang had excellent contacts with the foreign press in mandatory Palestine, which greatly magnified their strength and thus helped their cause.

The shift in Latin America from rural guerrilla to urban terror was caused, at least in part, by the media, for in the cities the terrorists could always count on the presence of journalists and TV cameras and so obtain a large audience. In the words of a Latin American terrorist:

> If we put even a small bomb in a building in town we could be certain of making the headlines in the press. But if the rural guerrilleros liquidated some thirty soldiers there was just a small news item on the last page. The city is exceedingly important both for the political struggle and for propaganda.[74]

The lesson was quickly learned by North African and Arab terrorists; thus an Algerian leader said: 'Is it better for our cause to kill ten of our enemies in a remote village where this will cause no comment, or to kill one man in Algiers where the American press will get hold of the story the next day?'[75] Abdul Fatah Ismail, one of the leaders of the anti-British struggle in the Aden protectorate, reached similar conclusions: the struggle in the countryside was not worthwhile, because no attention was paid to it.[76]

Guerrilla warfare can exist without media coverage, but for terrorism publicity is absolutely essential, and the smaller the terrorist gang the more it depends on publicity. This is one of the reasons – admittedly not the only one – why terrorism occurs in some countries but not in others. Under a totalitarian regime, or any effective dictatorship, a terrorist group will find it exceedingly difficult to get organized in the first place. Even if, against all odds, it should succeed in doing so, its exploits would not normally be reported in the media and this, of course, would defeat the whole purpose of the exercise – the deed would pass unheralded and unrecognized. In democratic societies, on the other hand, journalists have almost unrestricted access and they will, therefore, concentrate their efforts on events in these countries. Inside Israel in 1985, twelve people fell victim to terrorist attacks; in 1982, seven Americans were assassinated by terrorists; and in Northern Ireland in 1985 only two British soldiers were killed. But the concentration of correspondents and television cameras stationed in these places was massive, and they could not be kept idle. There was constant, detailed coverage, however unimportant the events, and thus the impression was created that internal security was breaking down, that terrorism was a tremendous force, and that a major political explosion was about to take place. At the very same time, tens of thousands of soldiers lost their lives in the war between Iran and Iraq; hundreds of thousands of civilians were killed in Cambodia and in the Ugandan civil war; there were major insurgencies in Afghanistan and in southern Sudan; and many thousands were killed in two Syrian cities alone (Homs and Hama). But, since the television crews were not allowed to cover these events, they remained non-events as far as TV was concerned – which is like the man who lost a coin in the darkness of the night and went searching not where the loss had occurred but close to the nearest streetlight. Such denial of access to where the real action took place was, of course, not the fault of the media,[77] but it still resulted in a radical distortion in the coverage of international affairs.

The 1985 Beirut hostage crisis was a striking example. For a long time, all three major US networks devoted two-thirds or more of their early evening news to this story. On four nights ABC spent less than two minutes on all non-hostage news.[78] This could be explained as a mere error of judgement, but, in other respects, the symbiotic relationship between terrorism and the media was more direct and manifest. This refers, for instance, to the in-built inclination towards exaggeration in media coverage – in part the result of the wish to scoop the other papers and networks. Since small earthquakes are not newsworthy a tiny group of people becomes an 'army', their handouts a 'communiqué', lunatics and assassins are promoted to 'martyrs' and 'revengers', and the killing of a child or an old lady is described as a 'military operation'.[79] Journalism takes over the language of terrorism and its exaggerations, including reports on purely imaginary operations. Spokesmen for the media have frequently referred to their 'obligation to the public', to the need to be 'impartial in order to retain their credibility'. These are lofty ideals, but the actual motives were probably more prosaic and less public-spirited; above all there was the desire to get a story first. As a result, some Western journalists have stooped to practices which were not only aesthetically displeasing but morally indefensible, just to obtain a story from the spokesman of a gang of cut-throats. If a photographer in Algeria wanted a picture, he had to know when an assassination was going to take place; many of the most startling pictures in Algeria were obtained in that fashion. There is a very fine line between reporting and instigating murder.[80]

It might be unfair to blame journalists for not trying to help hostages, even though on occasion they might have done so. But there were many instances in which media coverage either directly helped terrorism or contributed to the prolongation of a crisis. This was true of the Bogota siege in 1977, which lasted sixty days, and probably also for the 444 days' detention of the US diplomats in Tehran. Only after the last ounce of publicity had been squeezed out by the captors were the hostages released.

While terrorist groups have been built up and their leaders glorified, there has not been much interest in their victims – those shot in cold blood or left to die in agony. Those permanently maimed are no commercial asset, whereas flattering terrorist leaders hold open the promise of further interviews. In some instances, terrorists seem to have been paid by the media. In the Beirut crisis of 1985 – the hijacking of TWA 847 – US networks allegedly paid over $1 million a week to assure their monopoly over access to the hostage spectacular. ABC reportedly paid Amal $30,000 for sole access to a hostage interview session and $50,000 for the 'farewell banquet'.*[81]

What did the media get in return for this investment? They received

---

* The manipulation of the media did not of course begin with Beirut. A West German television executive wrote after the abduction of Peter Lorenz in 1972. 'For 72 hours we just lost control of the media. It was theirs, not ours.' The Italian Brigate Rosse usually chose Wednesdays and Saturdays for their communiqués, for on the following days Italian newspapers were always thicker. For other examples see Alex P.Schmid, *Political Terrorism* (Amsterdam, 1983).

tapes from hostages in which they reported feeling fine, that the captors were nice people, and massive doses of propaganda. Only later was it revealed – as after the Tehran embassy siege – that the hostages had by no means felt good and that some had been severely mistreated. The same commentators who would not let a single statement by senior US officials pass without critical examination and comment had neither seen nor heard evil in the circumstances in which the interviews with the hostages had taken place. The terrorists were aware of the competition between the American networks in which a few additional points in ratings meant huge increases in advertising revenues; they put their knowledge to good use. As a British correspondent noted at the time: 'It was done quite consciously. There were graduates of media studies from American colleges at meetings at Nabih Berri's house in West Beirut while tactics were being worked out ... non-American and non-television journalists were not considered during the whole affair as I ruefully discovered.'[82] Some of the hostages bitterly resented the activities of the networks in Beirut, referring to ABC as the 'Amal Broadcasting Corporation' and NBC as the 'Nabih Berri Corporation'.

At a previous siege, a decade earlier, the expression 'Stockholm syndrome' had first been coined, namely the tendency of hostages to identify with their captors and to form bonds with them. Whether such a syndrome really exists is a moot point; more than likely it is just the tendency on the part of frightened and confused people not to annoy their gaolers, but to hope for better treatment as the result of obeying and flattering them. Following the events at Beirut airport, the term 'Beirut syndrome' entered the language, referring to the tendency of the media, in particular television, to become apologists for those providing access to interesting news stories.*

The frequent repetition of terrorist propaganda, on this as on other occasions, had a diminishing effect, and it could be argued that all that mattered

---

* This is also true with regard to background coverage. A British correspondent described the filming of a seemingly fanatical crowd in total agreement with Colonel Qadhafi outside the Aziza barracks, the Libyan leader's residence. In actual fact, the cries of the well-rehearsed children were conducted by their scout masters. The cameras recorded scenes of passionate fanaticism whereas in reality the drafted youngsters looked bored as long as they were not on camera. 'But such things do not make good television pictures.' The show culminated in a group of militiamen killing a bullock which had been ceremoniously daubed in English with the name of the American president. 'Crazed they thrust their arms and guns into the animal's throat. They jumped on its thrashing body. But all the while they turned to the camera and as they jabbed their bloody hands towards the ever open lenses there was no doubt that this was a performance too.' Paul Vallely, 'Gadaffi's Command Performance', *The Times* (London), 28 March 1986.

was that in the end the hostages were released. But there were also cases in which hostages were killed because of journalistic scoops. This refers, for instance, to the killing of a German businessman in November 1974 in a British Airways plane on its way from Dubai to Libya, and the murder of Jürgen Schumann, the captain of a Lufthansa jet in Mogadishu. In both cases, the hijackers had learned from the media that their demands were not to be fulfilled and that the authorities were just playing for time to prepare a rescue mission. In Northern Ireland, several assassinations took place following BBC television broadcasts containing allegations of torture in British prisons, which, for all one knows, might have been untrue.[83] There were more such cases, and this leads to the broader issue of 'contagion' and imitative acts – in other words, the responsibility of the media for the diffusion of terrorism. Most investigations have shown that there is some correlation between coverage by the media (above all television) and the spread of terrorism, specifically hijackings and assassinations. The most serious effect of media reporting on terrorism is the likely increase of terroristic activities:

The media can provide the potential terrorist with all the ingredients that are necessary to engage in this type of violence. They can reduce inhibitions against the use of violence, they can offer models and know-how to potential terrorists and they can motivate them in various ways.[84]

The overall effect of the symbiotic relationship between the media and terrorism has been the exaggeration of the importance of terrorism, and its embellishment. This stems from the inclination towards sensationalism by the media and their bias towards violence.* They have also contributed to the spread of terrorism, though it is difficult to assess with any certainty to what degree they have done so. These observations apply far more to television than to the printed media, and these trends have been more pronounced in American television than in that of any other country. There has been no decline in foreign tourism among Europeans comparable to that among Americans, and this has been mainly the result of saturation television coverage:

---

* On some occasions, the media have been accused of identifying themselves unduly with the interests of the state in its fight against terrorism, and for exercising self-censorship. Two British authors have complained that the 'propaganda war' waged against the enemies of the state in Italy by the Italian press has 'made no contribution to a permanent solution of the problem' (Bob Kumley and Philip Schlesinger, 'The Press, the State and its Enemies: The Italian Case', *Sociological Review*, 30 (1982), p. 603 *et seq.*). However the 'propaganda war' did have a certain effect and it is doubtful, in any case, whether the authors would have protested if the 'enemies of the state' had been of the extreme right rather than the left.

Terrorism has manipulated the media, but not much persuasion was needed. In quantitative terms, terrorism has been a huge success; an enormous amount of prime time and space has been devoted to this subject. But this has seldom led to tangible political achievements and in more than a few cases publicity has even been counter-productive. If American television has devoted more time to the coverage of terrorist operations than television in other countries, this has by no means caused more favourable attitudes towards terrorism among the US government and public opinion. While the terrorists' spokesmen are often people with a certain intellectual polish and at least a veneer of moderation, they still have to voice extreme demands by fanatical groups, and in the end they have at least to imply that the enemy has to be destroyed. Such an attitude does not normally generate sympathy. Neither does an obsequious approach by the media towards people who kill add to the media's prestige and credibility. Furthermore, television, like other forms of entertainment, needs variety, but terrorist operations are essentially repetitive; another siege, yet another hijacking or assassination, the same though always slightly different. To sustain media exposure, terrorists have to think of new exploits, yet the number of possibilities is limited. Lastly, there is the fact of life that while a media event may be an impressive show it is not necessarily a real world event.

The fact that an individual or a group of people receive a great deal of media exposure certainly gives their cause welcome publicity. But, as the late Senator Joe McCarthy and many others have since found to their detriment, it does not necessarily bring them any nearer to the realization of their aims.[85] The media are a fickle ally and exposure can work both ways. Mao's long march and the battles of Tito's partisans were not covered by film or television crews, and yet they were more successful in the end than the contemporary terrorists.

Terrorists, Penitents and Informers

The most dangerous external threat to terrorists is the promise of a reward for information leading to their capture. This weapon has, of course, been widely used. After the Phoenix Park murders an almost unprecedented reward of £10,000 was promised. Gershuni, the head of the Fighting Organization of the Social Revolutionaries, had a price of 15,000 rubles on his head. The Weimar government promised a reward of one million marks for information leading to the capture of Rathenau's murderers. In the same way, Nazi security forces caught Heydrich's assassin and effectively smashed most of the Allied underground in occupied France. A terrorist, unlike a guerrilla, cannot hide in forests, jungles or desolate mountain ranges; he has to find cover among people, many of whom will feel no sympathy for him. He needs a roof over his head, food and other supplies. He is never alone in the big city; some people will know of his whereabouts and many more will have their suspicions. He is exceedingly vulnerable, and the greed of an informer or the ill-will of an enemy can overcome the fear of vengeance – especially if the reward is high enough.[86] But police forces in democratic societies have never been at liberty to use this weapon to full effect; informing has never been considered an occupation for gentlemen and there has almost always been opposition to encouraging the practice. After the Irish dynamiters' attempt to blow up London Bridge in the 1880s, a reward of £5,000 was first promised – and then withdrawn.

When Prime Minister Palme of Sweden was killed in March 1986, the Swedish government decided to offer a reward of $70,000 for clues leading to the apprehension of his murderers. This, according to media comment, was a 'substantial' reward. In actual fact, the sum was risible in comparison with the sums paid by the sponsors of state terrorism or the major drug dealers. The rewards given by the British security forces in Northern Ireland are yet another example. The range of payment given to the informers was $80–150 per week as well as rent-free accommodation, and even the 'super-grasses' (both IRA and Loyalists) were offered no more than $60,000. According to the British Attorney-General, the total sum paid to informers in Northern Ireland up to November 1983 was just over $600,000. Even the largest sums offered – in the cases of the German RAF or the attackers of the US marines and diplomats in Lebanon – did not exceed $500,000.

There is a curious disproportion between the rhetoric of the politicians who claim that terrorism is the greatest danger facing mankind and their unwillingness or inability to allocate funds for preventing and combating it.* There is no certainty, needless to say, that much higher rewards would always bring results. But there is every reason to assume that in many cases it would. In societies in which many millions can be won in football and other pools and lotteries, the sums to be earned for the capture of the greatest threats to man are not very impressive. Not many people will

---

* In the case of the US, it has not been possible for legal–administrative reasons to offer higher rewards. This is because of the 1984 Act to Combat International Terrorism that authorizes payment of up to $500,000 for information in cases of national and international terrorism. And, while the Vice-President's Task Force suggested in its report of 1986 that the ceiling be raised to $1 million, the State Department's fund for this purpose amounts to only $3 million. The German government does not offer more than $25,000 in each individual case, and the French government, which decided to give cash rewards for information on terrorist acts in May 1986, will offer between a few hundred and a few thousand dollars.

even know about such rewards, and those who do know may think twice in view of the risks involved. Bureaucracies will demand and receive billions for armies, navies and air forces, but they are quite incapable of coping with challenges for which they are psychologically unprepared.

A nineteenth-century police chief in Britain, France or Russia could dispose of relatively large sums with no questions asked. Sir Robert Anderson, from whom Joseph Conrad drew some of his inspiration for *The Secret Agent*, related with some pride that his idea of secrecy was not to tell the secretary of state:

The first Fenian who ever gave me information was murdered on his arrival in New York. I had given his name to no one but Lord Mayo; and he assured me that he had mentioned it only to the Lord Lieutenant, when sitting alone with him after dinner at the vice-regal lodge. But there happened to be a servant behind the screen, and through him it was, as the Dublin police ascertained, that the information reached the Fenians. Never again would I give an informant's name to anyone and no man who afterwards gave me information was ever betrayed.[87]

Rewards remain the most effective weapon by far, and when, in 1975, Ross McWhirter was killed in London by the IRA, it was precisely because he had announced a substantial reward to be given for the collection of information.

Many captured terrorists have behaved with great dignity and even heroism. Leonid Andreyev (*The Seven Who Were Hanged*, 1909) described the whole gamut of emotions among a group of Russian revolutionaries sentenced to death: 'Werner totally sure of himself, young Tanya caring like a mother for her comrades, Vasily absorbed in a frightful struggle "between the intolerable terror of death and the desperate desire to subdue his fear and conceal it from his judges".'

But not all men and women are heroes (or have suicidal impulses), and quite a few terrorists have broken down during interrogation, though they were neither tortured nor even threatened with violence. Some have not even been promised that their sentence would be reduced. Every case has been different; some realized that what they had done was wrong. Ivan Okladski proudly declared at his trial in October 1880 that he would be deeply offended if he did not receive a death sentence. Soon afterwards he became a police agent on a monthly salary of 200 rubles. Merkulov also became a police official. Mirski, Goldenberg and Rysakov quite unnecessarily implicated their comrades in their depositions; they were young, inexperienced and confused. Rysakov was executed anyway, and Goldenberg committed suicide in prison after he had realized the enormity of his betrayal. Some became police agents, others merely pretended to serve the police, having no intention of working for their new masters, and there were all possible variations in between. Some acted as double agents, with the knowledge of their comrades. As a result of Degayev's betrayal in 1883, the whole existing apparatus of the Narodnaya Volya was destroyed. The police engineered his escape from prison, but Degayev deeply regretted his betrayal; to expiate his crime, he killed Sudykin, a high official of the 'third section'. Degayev later voluntarily submitted to a trial by a revolutionary tribunal in Paris which expelled him. He went to the United States, changed his name to 'Dr Pell', graduated in mathematics from Johns Hopkins University, became a professor at the Armour Institute of Technology, and died at Bryn Mawr in 1921.[88]

Solomon Ryss ('Mortimer'), one of the leaders of the Maximalists, also collaborated with the police after his arrest; he too was helped to escape, but he returned to terrorist work, was again captured, and this time was hanged. His case, like that of Bagrov, the police agent who killed Stolypin, has remained a mystery to this day.[89] Among the anarchists, there were few such startling intrigues and double games simply because most of them had acted alone, without the knowledge and help of an organization.

In Ireland, too, co-operation with the police was by no means infrequent; Carey, one of the chief accused in the Phoenix Park murder trial, turned Queen's evidence. He was acquitted and left Britain, but was killed on board a ship sailing between Cape Town and Port Elizabeth, allegedly by an 'avenger' in circumstances that have remained obscure.

Many terrorist groups have attracted criminal elements at one time or another. Some originally *bona fide* political terrorists later turned to crime, other terrorists were predominantly criminal from the very beginning but also had political interests. The dividing line between politics and crime was by no means always clear-cut; criminals were quite often good patriots or instinctive revolutionaries (or reactionaries) and they certainly could teach the terrorists more than a few tricks of the trade. But they would not accept discipline and their presence caused friction, corruption and eventually demoralization. The temptation to use the loot for private gain or to settle personal accounts was overwhelming. The Bonnot gang (the *bande tragique*), operating in Paris in 1912, kept 90 per cent of their booty for personal use and only the remainder was allocated to the cause. Sometimes former terrorists engaged in blackmail or entered the protection racket. There was the famous case of Juan Rull who prepared bombs which were deposited by his old mother in the streets of Barcelona. As long as he was paid a monthly retainer by the authorities there were no bombs. Of great psychological interest are the terrorist groups which gradually changed their character. The lofty ideals of IMRO were movingly described in the diary of a young member:

We know that the revolutionary is something of an ascetic who has given up the idea of enjoyment and personal happiness. Not one of us will marry and settle down. No one will leave Macedonia or think of studying. Whoever marries or leaves Macedonia or enrols in a university is a villain, a traitor. Macedonia cannot wait. . . . There can be no other love.[90]

This was written on 1 January 1902; three decades later IMRO still existed, but it had become a group of hired assassins.

Criminal elements joined the ranks of terrorist groups in times of general unrest, when there were good opportunities for looting, as in the Russian Revolution of 1905 and on many subsequent occasions. The 'Symbionese Liberation Army', like some early terrorist sects, but unlike the Narodniki, deliberately enlisted criminals; they did not go to the people but to the underworld. Other terrorist groups such as the Italian Red Brigades also tried to convert imprisoned criminals to their cause, but the results were usually negligible, and sometimes positively harmful.

Contemporary security forces in democratic societies are frequently unable to penetrate terrorist groups. Since they are also hamstrung in other respects, the rate of capture was considerably lower in the 1970s than before the First World War; and terrorist movements now have a longer life-span. While terrorists became more professional, the police seemed to become more amateurish. But the security forces still have certain weapons that can be used with considerable effect. The Italian Red Brigades were smashed largely because, having been promised that their sentences would be halved, many of their leaders and rank-and-file made full confessions about their activities. Up to February 1980, the Italian terrorists had refused to collaborate with the police, but following the arrest of Fabrico Peci of the Turin Brigade this situation began to change. Luigi Scrichio told the police about the Rome Brigades. Other *pentiti* (penitents) included Antonio Savasto, who had been in charge of kidnapping General Dozier; Valerio Morucci and his girlfriend Adriana Feranda revealed the details about the Moro kidnapping, arrest and murder.* These and others provided details about terrorist arms supplies and foreign contacts; there were about

---

* The major Italian newspapers reported in great detail the revelations of the *pentiti* in their trials. See also Giorgio Bocca, *Noi Terroristi* (Milan, 1980); Daniela Salvioni and Anders Stephanson, 'Reflections on the Red Brigades', *Orbis* (Fall 1985), p. 489 *et seq*.; and Richard Drake, 'The Red Brigades and the Italian Political Tradition', in Y. Alexander and K. Myers (eds), *Terrorism in Europe* (London, 1982), *passim*.

300 arrests and even more recantations. This change of mind among the Italian terrorists was brought about not only by promises, but also as a result of internal dissent. The promises therefore came at the right time, when many terrorists had begun to have doubts whether their operations were having any major effect.

The situation in Northern Ireland was very similar. As the Chief Constable of the Royal Ulster Constabulary, and also an Irish commentator, put it: up to about 1978–9, the Provisionals were certain that they would win the struggle within a few months or years; and that if arrested they would soon be set free and acclaimed as heroes. But as victory seemed more and more elusive, there was a growing readiness to buy freedom by co-operating with the authorities. The informers became a major threat to the existence of the Provisionals, who, after 1981, repeatedly declared an 'amnesty' for those who would reveal their guilt. Informers were the undoing of the Tupamaros. Following the defection of one leader (Hector Amodio Perez), thirty safe houses were discovered by the Uruguayan police, including the 'people's prison' and the terrorists' field hospital. The downfall of the Montoneros began with the information provided in 1975.[91] Even the closely knit ETA had more than thirty militants who subsequently co-operated with the police.

This leads back to the main internal threat facing terrorists, namely conflict in their own ranks. True, not every conflict leads to fighting. The terrorists' fighting potential was not always reduced; despite their disagreements they did not necessarily strike at one another. The Social Revolutionaries did not attack the Maximalists, Irgun and LEHI kept a truce, and there has been an understanding of sorts between the ERP and the Montoneros. In some ways these divisions made the task of the police even more difficult, for its resources had to be spread even more thinly. But in many cases, rivalry between terrorist groups led to bloody clashes, as in the Irish troubles in the early 1920s, the killing of IRA officials by Provisionals and vice versa, and the feud between Mikhailovists and Protogerovists in Bulgaria (forty of the former and 220 of the latter were killed between 1924 and 1934). Besides interfactional strife, there was always the tendency in an underground movement to liquidate those who challenged the authority of the leader, as happened among the Iron Guard in Rumania and in various Latin American terrorist movements. Sometimes a leading member would be shot because he was considered a liability to the whole group – the case of 'Shaul' in LEHI. In other cases, mere suspicion of treason (*Verräter verfallen der Fehme* – the Freikorps) would be sufficient cause for murder. Dr Patrick Cronin, the American–Irish patriot, was killed in May 1889 simply because he had accused another leader of misappropriating funds.

This case profoundly shocked the whole movement; 12,000 men and women walked past his bier.* History, as Albert Camus has noted, offers few examples of fanatics suffering from scruples. The Russian terrorists of 1881 and of 1905 were an exception, but from that time on a general decline set in and there have been few of which it could be said, as Savinkov said about Dora Brilliant, that terror weighed on them like a cross. Killing without hesitation, often without thought and reason, has become the rule, and, at least to some of the murderers, the act of killing has been a source of thrills and enjoyment.

Counter-terrorism

Police forces in democratic societies, applying traditional methods, have found it exceedingly difficult to cope with terrorist activities. There are not enough policemen to deal with an enemy likely to strike at any time against almost any target. Even in a totalitarian regime, the police force cannot always guarantee the life of the dictator against attempted assassination by one man acting entirely on his own. Terrorists do sometimes fail through sheer incompetence, either because they do not adhere to their own timetable, which happened often in the case of nineteenth-century Irish terrorists, or because too many people know about the plot. Sometimes their weapons are not in good working order, and sometimes they are simply unlucky. But they have the great advantage that, unlike the security forces in a democratic society, they do not have to act within the law. The police, on the other hand, must not use illegal methods to repress terrorism – in theory, if not always in practice. They cannot engage in indiscriminate arrests, nor can they torture captured terrorists to extract information. The forces of law and order have not always been able to hold those already arrested and sentenced; one need only recall the mass escapes from prison and internment camps of Irish terrorists or of members of the Irgun and the Stern Gang. Russian revolutionaries (including Bakunin, Kropotkin, Deitch, Savinkov, Trotsky and many others) escaped from prison or from Siberia. In the 1970s, mass escapes of terrorists occurred in Northern Ireland, Italy and Spain, and, with only a few exceptions,

---

* Like the Palestinians, the Central American guerrilla and terrorist groups have also traditionally been plagued by internal dissension. The best-known case was the conflict between Caetano Carpio and Melida Montes in 1982 which ended in the murder of the one and the suicide of the other. These had been the leading figures of the FMNL, the El Salvador armed resistance. The Tamil and Sikh terrorists killed their own kinsmen with as much enthusiasm as they did their enemies.

international terrorists were released from prison after a short time following the abduction of some Europeans in the Middle East.

The nineteenth century was the classical age of the police informer, who played a crucial role in the suppression of terrorism. The success of the British police in repressing Irish terrorism through the nineteenth century was largely due to the presence of a few agents in the ranks of the terrorists (Leonard MacNally, Nagle, Corydon, Richard Pigott, 'Red' Jim Mac-Dermott, 'Nero' and Massey). The 'Prince of spies' was Major Le Caron (1841–94) who first informed his father in 1865 that he had been contacted by an Irish revolutionary organization; the father told the police, and Le Caron supplied important information for the next two decades. His cover in the United States was that of an agent for drug manufacturers and he was thus able to travel constantly. Le Caron later wrote that he had done his duty as a man who loved his country and who saw it threatened by a deadly and unscrupulous foe: 'I consider myself a military spy and my conduct justifiable under the same ethical considerations which justify all military spies.'[92] The French police were served by Lucien de la Hodde, the master spy and provocateur of the 1830s and 1840s, who later published an interesting if somewhat subjective history of the secret societies.[93] Even earlier, Babeuf's conspiracy had been betrayed by Grisel, who, in the words of Buonarroti, had pretended to be the 'most outrageous patriot'; the Decembrist plot in Russia was denounced by Sherwood.

Andrieux, prefect of the Paris police, had his agents among the anarchists; he provided money for anarchist newspapers and later wrote that, though he fought anarchism, he preferred the spread of their doctrine by the press rather than by other means and saw 'no reason for depriving myself longer of their gratitude'.[94] The German and Austrian anarchist movements were riddled with police spies, who included some of Most's closest collaborators. When Most was in a British prison, *Freiheit* was published by Schroeder, a police agent in Schaffhausen. But these police agents were inclined, as Bismarck once put it in a letter to his wife, to 'lie and exaggerate in a most inexcusable manner'. For want of material, when there was nothing to report, they and their superiors began to play politics and to instigate acts of violence. Some of the heads of the Okhrana were past masters in this game; they had had their agents among the revolutionaries since the late 1880s, with Harting-Landesen the most prominent among them.

By 1912, in addition to a permanent staff of some 50,000, the Okhrana had some 26,000 paid agents, most of them part-time informers. Informers were paid between twenty and fifty rubles a month, but Azev had a monthly salary of five hundred by 1902 and in later years presumably got even more.[95] Azev, a young Jewish engineer, had offered his services to the political police while studying in Germany, with the approval and help of his bosses. He worked his way up in the Fighting Organization of the Social Revolutionaries until he became its commander. His was a complex personality, for he was neither a petty provocateur out for a few rubles nor an admirer of the tsarist system. He played a very intricate double game, and, while betraying many of his comrades, he also misled the Okhrana by withholding from them essential information about forthcoming terrorist operations. He was involved in the assassinations of Plehve, of the Grand Duke Serge Alexeievich and of other leading personalities. He was eventually unmasked in 1908 and the Social Revolutionary Fighting Organization never recovered from the blow. While he was active, much of the time and energy of the Okhrana had to be invested in combating acts of terror they had themselves instigated. Azev's protectors in the Okhrana were driven by personal ambitions and rivalries, but they were also convinced that they had to demonstrate to the government (and public opinion) that there was a major terrorist menace which had to be fought. For this purpose they needed occasional demonstrations such as the assassination of highly placed personalities.[96]

Mention has been made of the fact that a considerable proportion of the terrorist journals of the 1880s and 1890s were in fact founded or maintained by secret-police money. The tendency of the secret police was usually to discredit the terrorists by sheer exaggeration. One such Russian émigré paper called not only for the killing of all landowners, but also for the destruction of all their cattle.[97] Terrorist journals would accuse each other of co-operating with the police – and on occasion both were right. There was enormous confusion; those who had provided the funds obviously got value for money. In Russia, special units were established to combat terrorism. These units acted separately from, and often in competition with and in opposition to, the general police forces. This approach prevailed in most countries. When Brackenbury was appointed under-secretary for police by Gladstone after the Phoenix Park murders in 1881, he argued from the very beginning that the police were quite incapable of coping with secret societies and that for this purpose a (secret and separate) organization was needed with a budget of its own (£20,000 at the time) to infiltrate the terrorists and 'break their nerve'.[98] But the British officials, unlike the heads of the Okhrana, did not believe in a mammoth counter-organization – nor would they have obtained a sufficiently high budget to keep such an apparatus going. Unless the terrorist movement was very strong and/or highly decentralized, a few police agents, strategically placed, were quite sufficient to paralyse the whole organization. Thus one single agent, James

McParlan, acting on behalf of the Pinkerton Agency, caused the downfall of the Molly Maguires in the 1870s.

Present-day police forces have much less freedom of manoeuvre in democratic societies. The penetration of terrorist gangs has become much more difficult; members of the police forces cannot normally infiltrate such gangs for they would almost certainly become involved in criminal activities. This could not be kept secret; they would be put on disciplinary trial; they might even lose their pension rights. Police administrators, as well as public opinion, were less scrupulous in bygone ages. But the use of agents has also become much more intricate; once upon a time the police chief would deal directly with his main informers and pay them from his slush fund. Today's security forces are much bigger and more bureaucratically structured. Payments have to be accounted for in many copies, they have to be authorized and checked, administrators and accountants have to be involved, and the chances of keeping secrets in these conditions are very much reduced.

Up to the Second World War, the secrecy of the post and telephone was less than fully safeguarded in most democratic countries; today the interception of communications between persons suspected of terrorism has to be authorized.*

If the security forces have nevertheless succeeded in fighting terrorism, this has to do in part with sophisticated computer technology, such as in West Germany where terrorists on the run have been relatively quickly identified. But on the whole, the miracle gadgets of modern intelligence services, the sensors and satellites, have not been of much help in confronting small groups of terrorists. If they were caught it was usually *in flagrante* or escaping from the scene of action. Furthermore, the collaboration of the population has been of great importance for the police. The same applies to international co-operation. There have been many resolutions to this effect, but results have been meagre. Exchange of information has improved between the West European countries and the United States, but actual co-operation has been rare for political reasons; only a very few terrorists have been extradited and this is unlikely to change in the future – unless, of course, there is a major upsurge in terrorist activity.

---

* François Le Mouel, the head of the French anti-terrorist co-ordination unit, stated in December 1985 that the French police had virtually no informers among the terrorists and that during the preceding year it had very seldom been permitted to use wire taps. It is difficult to imagine how Commissaire Maigret would have functioned in such conditions.

Is Terrorism Effective?

That the murder of political opponents has altered, or could have altered, the course of history in certain circumstances goes without saying. If Piche-gru or Cadoudal had killed Napoleon, if Lenin had met with an accident on the road to the Finland Station, if Hitler had been shot in front of the Munich Feldherrnhalle in 1923, the map of Europe would look different today. But these are the exceptions; in democratic and many undemocratic societies, statesmen are usually expendable.

Since the end of the Second World War, some fifty prime ministers and heads of state have been killed, yet it would be difficult to think of a single case in which the policy of the country in question has radically changed as a result of the assassination. Indira Gandhi's son continued her policy; Olof Palme's murder did not affect Swedish policy, and even the killing of Anwar Sadat had no major impact on Egyptian domestic or foreign policy. It has been said that Orsini's attempt on the life of Napoleon III contributed to the unification of Italy. But Napoleon was, in any case, inclined to intervene in Italy. The Sarajevo assassination triggered off the First World War, but, given the tensions and military preparations in Europe at the time, a war would probably have broken out anyway – if not in 1914, then perhaps a year or two later. It has been maintained that, as a result of the murder of Canovas in 1897 and of King Umberto I in 1900, the treatment of political prisoners in Spain and Italy improved somewhat. But even if this were true, these were hardly results of world-shaking importance.[99] In a similar way, it has been argued that Sazonov's bomb which killed Plehve, the Russian minister of the interior, intimidated the tsarist regime and inaugurated a more liberal course. Sazonov, to be sure, was not sentenced to death; he died soon afterwards in prison. But the shortlived era of liberality was overtaken by the first Russian Revolution, which was caused not so much by the bombs of the Social Revolutionaries as by the Russian defeat in the war against Japan.

These examples refer to individual assassinations, but the results of systematic terrorist campaigns have not been very different. If there was an impact at all, it was usually negative; unlike King Midas, everything that was touched by the propagandists of the deed turned to ashes. Their actions usually produced violent repression and a polarization which precluded political progress. Anarchist activities bedevilled political life in Spain for decades, culminating in the civil war of 1936–9 and its fateful consequences. The activities of the Portuguese terrorists of the early 1920s had similar results: the murder of the right-wing dictator Major Sidonio Pais in December 1920 led to the butchery of the liberal government headed by

Antonio Granjo in 1921. Left-wing and right-wing terrorist groups, the Red Legion (Legião Vermelha), the Scorpions (Os Lacraus), The Thirteen (O Grupo des Treze), so proliferated in Portugal that one left-wing historian (A.H. de Oliveira Marques) later wrote of them that it was difficult to draw a clear line dividing political aims from criminal purposes. These and other groups decisively contributed to the fatal weakening of the democratic republic and the emergence of the dictatorship which ruled Portugal for the next four decades. While it is unlikely that tsarism would have been able to change from within, whatever small hope there was for compromise and peaceful development was destroyed by the terrorists.

The prospects for democracy in Central and South-eastern Europe were not promising after the First World War. But again, right-wing and, to a lesser extent, left-wing terrorism further reduced these chances. Following the Second World War, the strategy of provocation practised by the 'urban guerrillas' has had similar results. The Uruguayan experience is a striking example. The Tupamaros were one of the more attractive Latin American terrorist groups, reminiscent in some ways of the early Russian terrorists. They did not, on the whole, engage in indiscriminate murder and they wept when they killed (but they killed). They were genuine idealists; some of the best of the young generation belonged to them. Their activities were initially quite successful, proving that civilian government could easily be disrupted. Moreover, they provided striking headlines for the world press. But, in the end, the only result of their campaign was the destruction of freedom in a country which, alone in Latin America, had had an unbroken democratic tradition of many decades and which had been the first Latin American welfare state. True, the Uruguay of the 1960s was far from perfect and was faced with serious economic and social problems, but it is in any case doubtful whether the Tupamaros had a better answer to these problems than the government of the day. The Tupamaros' campaign resulted in the emergence of a right-wing military dictatorship; in destroying the democratic system, they also destroyed their own movement. By the 1970s, they and their sympathizers were reduced to bitter protests in exile against the crimes of a repressive regime which, but for their own action, would not have come into existence. The grave-diggers of liberal Uruguay, as Regis Debray later wrote, also dug their own grave. There were many other such cases of sorcerer's apprentices bewailing the cruelties of the demons they themselves had released. Terrorism from below produced massive and infinitely more effective terror from above.

Terrorist groups that were more successful in attaining their objectives can be divided, broadly speaking, into three groups. First of all, there were some that had narrow, clearly defined aims, for instance in an industrial dispute. Second, there were those with powerful outside protectors. The Palestinian Arab groups succeeded in keeping the Palestinian problem alive; so did the Croat Ustasha, who, for a while, got their own state. Left to their own resources they would have been no more successful than the South Moluccans. Lastly, there were the terrorist groups facing imperial powers that were no longer able or willing to hold on to their colonies or protectorates. Thus Britain gave up Ireland after the First World War, and the Palestine mandate and Cyprus after the Second World War; the terrorism of the IRA, the Irgun and LEHI, and EOKA certainly played a part in these decisions. But terrorism was not the decisive factor in any of these countries, where the British retreat was, after all, part of a general historical process. Political resistance in Ireland, as in Palestine, while less dramatic and less widely publicized, was, in the long run, more effective. Historical experience shows that the nationalist–sectarians stand a better chance of success than other types of terrorists. But even their achievements are problematical. By aggravating the crisis, they make the solution of the problems more difficult or even impossible. National and religious minorities are dispersed in such a way in today's world that resolving one grievance usually creates a new one. Given the complexity of the modern world, not every minority can have a state of its own. Seemingly successful terrorist operations (such as in Cyprus) have, in fact, ended in disaster insofar as they have poisoned relations between the communities and made peaceful coexistence impossible.

A balance sheet of two decades shows that in some countries terrorism has been virtually wiped out; this refers to the major Latin American countries such as Brazil and Argentina, as well as to Canada, Iran and Turkey. In comparison with the state of affairs ten or fifteen years ago, there has been a decline in terrorism in Northern Ireland, in the Basque country and in Israel. Terrorism is stronger now in Colombia and Peru, and it has appeared (or reappeared) in the context of popular insurgencies in Central America, India and Sri Lanka. But international airlines continue to fly despite occasional attacks on airports, and international banks operate despite occasional robberies. Not a single government has been overthrown as a result of terrorist action. It is frequently argued that contemporary society is so vulnerable that the activities of a few individuals suffice to paralyse it. This may occur one day, but it has not happened yet. So far, the damage caused by terrorists has been repaired without much delay and with relatively little cost.

Terrorism did play a certain part in the overthrow of the Somoza government in Nicaragua, and it has been a factor of some importance in El Salvador and Guatemala. But the Sandinista example shows that an insurgency will succeed only if it is based on much wider support than a terrorist gang can provide – a political movement, guerrilla groups, the middle class, unions and sections of the army which cross over to the insurgents. If the Tamils of Sri Lanka one day obtain autonomy, or if the African National Congress achieves some or all of its aims in South Africa, it will not be as the result of the occasional car-bomb or ambush, but in consequence of political and military activities on a wide scale which create a climate of insecurity.

The terror of the Provisional IRA, and the counter-terror of the Protestant militants, may one day cause a British government to retire from Northern Ireland under some face-saving formula. This would be a terrorist success, one of the few which can be envisaged at the present time. But it is by no means certain that either side will like the outcome. The Armenians and Palestinians have used terrorism so that their problem is not forgotten, and to this extent they have succeeded. But under no possible circumstances will an Armenian state be established on Turkish soil. The dilemma of the Palestinians is similar, though in some respects they are in a more favourable position. For there is always the chance that their operations will trigger off a new war between Israel and the Arab countries. But since the signs in the Middle East do not point to peace in any case, these operations may well be irrelevant. The assassinations of individual 'collaborators', such as the Arab mayor of Nablus, Zafer al Masri, in 1986 is probably the closest to a terrorist success one can find in recent times in that area, for it will deter other potential 'collaborators' from accepting such posts. But since the prospects for a lasting reconciliation between Israelis and Palestinians are non-existent at the present time, the overall effect of such actions is less than is commonly assumed.

The case of Israel is a good example of the paradoxical benefits of terrorism, as far as the internal cohesion of a country or a society facing a terrorist onslaught is concerned. Israeli society is deeply divided between left and right, between North Africans and Jews of European origins, and between secularists and those who stand for a Jewish theocracy. These internal conflicts would no doubt be infinitely more acute and divisive but for the outside threat. The outside threat helps to restore a consensus which otherwise might not exist, because the survival of the country takes precedence. The Israeli case is not unique. If Italy is more united in 1987 than it was ten years earlier, this is largely due to the Red Brigades. Similar trends can be detected in other countries; for example, the terrorism of Sendero Luminoso succeeded in uniting the Peruvian far left and the right. Terrorist campaigns may cause major destabilization in certain circumstances if they are broadly based and face a weak enemy, but far more often they simply provoke counter-violence and strengthen the forces of 'law and order'.

The car-bomb attacks against US marines in the Lebanon were a terrorist success, inasmuch as they resulted in the withdrawal of American forces from Lebanon, and highlighted, as it were, the impotence of a global power facing a handful of fanatical terrorists. But the dispatch of these forces had not been part of a grand strategy and it would not, in any case, have put an end to the Lebanese civil war; in fact, it would probably have made no difference at all. By forcing the US marines to withdraw, the terrorists may have actually saved the Americans from both deeper involvement in the war and a more humiliating defeat. To put it differently, terrorist operations of this kind may have an effect as long as they concern marginal issues; the moment they impinge on the core interests of a great power – or indeed any modern state in working order – they are bound to fail.

Seen in historical perspective, terrorism has been effective only in very specific circumstances. It has not succeeded against effective dictatorships, let alone modern totalitarian regimes. In democratic societies or against ineffective authoritarian regimes, it has on occasion been more successful, but it is doubtful whether the Tupamaros have felt altogether happy, in retrospect, about their victory over the liberal system. There have been, broadly speaking, three kinds of results of terrorist action. In most cases, terrorism, in the longer run, made no political difference one way or another – in some, it caused the exact opposite of what the terrorists hoped and intended to achieve. And in a few cases terrorism was successful. These exceptions have usually occurred whenever terrorism appears as part of a wider political strategy – for instance, against Machado in Cuba in 1933.[100] The systematic assassinations of village headmen by the Vietcong in the early 1960s also served a purpose within a wider strategy. Past experience shows that terrorism frequently occurs where there are other, non-violent, political alternatives. Where terrorism might be justified as the *ultima ratio*, such as against totalitarian rule, it has no chance, and where it seemingly succeeds, the political results are in the long run often self-defeating. Terrorism always attracts great publicity, but its political impact is usually inversely proportional to the attention it receives in the media. Terrorists are usually driven by thirst for action rather than by the rational consideration of consequences; past failures will not in any way act, therefore, as a deterrent in the future.

4

Interpretations of Terrorism

Ideally, all discussions of terrorism, its motives and inspiration, its specific character and mode of operation, its political orientation and long-term consequences, should start with a clear, exact and comprehensive definition of the subject. For unless there is broad agreement on the definition of the subject, there is the risk that everyone will interpret it in a different way. There will be no agreement on whether terrorism is violence in general or some specific form of violence; on whether stress should be put on its political character, on its methods of combat, or on the extra-normal character of its strategy; on whether one should single out its purposive, systematic character, or its unpredictability and symbolic aspects, or perhaps the fact that many of its victims are innocents. One could point to other questions which ought to be clarified before research on terrorism gets underway.

Unfortunately, such a comprehensive and universally accepted definition does not exist for reasons which have already been discussed in our study. This is not altogether surprising. Even now, four decades after the end of the Fascist era, the controversies about its character continue and there is no generally accepted definition. But its contemporaries had to confront Fascism in any case, on both the theoretical and practical level. There is no agreement to this day about what socialism is, and the same is true with regard to most other movements of the nineteenth and twentieth centuries. Historians do not agree to this day about the French Revolution, Napoleon, imperialism or the outbreak of the First World War – let alone about more recent events.

However, even if there is no agreed definition of socialism or Fascism, it would be absurd to argue that the subject cannot be studied, for much progress has been made in these fields – as in the study of terrorism. It is, in many ways, the time-honoured debate between historians, on the one hand, and sociologists and political scientists on the other. Historians tend to focus on the unique features of events and instinctively shy away from generalizations, whereas sociologists and political scientists are forever searching for common patterns and characteristics. If they cannot discover laws, as is so often the case, they at least want probabilities. This is a laudable aim which ought to be pursued, and if there is no agreement on definitions and concepts, this is not to say that we do not know more about the substance of terrorism than we did ten or twenty years ago.

The author of a recent excellent research guide to the concepts, theories and literature on political terrorism has collected 109 different definitions provided by various writers between 1936 and 1981, and there is every reason to assume that there have been more since.[1] Most authors agree that terrorism is the use or the threat of the use of violence, a method of combat, or a strategy to achieve certain targets, that it aims to induce a state of fear in the victim, that it is ruthless and does not conform with humanitarian rules, and that publicity is an essential factor in the terrorist strategy. Beyond this point definitions diverge, often sharply. Some maintain that terror is a symbolic act designed to modify the political behaviour of the enemy.[2] This is undoubtedly true in some cases, but not in others. When the Vietcong engaged in a systematic campaign to eliminate the heads of villages who did not support them, this was more than a symbolic act, nor did they merely want to intimidate them. When right-wing terrorists in West Germany or in France bombed homes of Turkish or Algerian guest workers, they did not just want them to modify their behaviour – they wanted them to leave.

Many definitions equate terrorism with revolutionary terrorism (be it anarchist or Marxist–Leninist in inspiration) aimed at the overthrow of the existing social order and the state. But other terrorist groups have by no means been inspired by left-wing ideas, however broadly defined. The existence of right-wing terrorism in Europe and in other parts of the world should not be ignored; neither does the revolutionary label fit most of the separatist–nationalist groups. Other authors have favoured a relativist conception: one man's terrorist is another man's freedom fighter; what is terrorism to some is heroism to others.[3] Such observations are correct – to the same extent as it is true to say that both Adolf Hitler and Mother Theresa had many admirers, as if barbarism and humanism were a matter of culinary or sartorial taste. Yet other writers on this topic have emphasized the arbitrary and utterly unpredictable character of terrorism, which allegedly distinguishes it from other forms of political violence. It is perfectly true that the terrorist action must come as a surprise, otherwise the forces of law and order would prevent it. It is also correct that many terrorist groups have been quite indiscriminate in the choice of their victims, for they assume that the slaughter of innocents would sow panic, give them publicity and help to destabilize the state and society. However, elsewhere terrorist operations have been quite selective. It can hardly be argued that President Sadat, the Pope, Aldo Moro or Indira Gandhi were arbitrary targets. Therefore, the argument that terrorist violence is by its nature random, and that innocence is the quintessential condition for the choice of victims, cannot be accepted as a general proposition; this would imply that there is a conscious selection process on the part of the terrorists, that they give immunity to the 'guilty' and choose only the innocents.[4]

Some definitions focus on the desire of terrorists to harm or radically alter the policy of the government. The left- and right-wing terrorists in Turkey saw each other rather than the state as the main enemy, and in Lebanon, where the state had virtually ceased to exist, it was of course not the main target of terrorist attacks.

Some experts have stressed that terrorist attacks are always, or nearly always, directed against civilians, but this is clearly not so when, in the case of the occupation of a country, military personnel are the main or only target. Others have put the stress on the 'extra-normal' violence applied by terrorists; however, there are no universally recognized norms. What was believed to be perfectly normal in the Lebanese civil war is not considered normal in Scandinavia.

According to the definition of a US task force in the 1960s, terrorists engage in a 'certain type of criminal activity'. Subsequent definitions by various branches of the US government were slightly more cautious, but they all mention the 'unlawful use of force' (Departments of Defense, State and Justice, and FBI). This is certainly true inasmuch as terrorism violates both international and domestic law. The application of legal norms is of little help in establishing the political character of a terrorist movement; the plotters against Hitler also tried to use force unlawfully, and the same is true of the rebels in Afghanistan and many other such groups. A 1983 Department of Defense definition emphasizes the use of force or violence by a 'revolutionary organization', and the State Department mentioned in 1984 'noncombatant targets' – both were controversial statements. The Vice-President's Task Force on combating terrorism (Bush Committee, 1986) used a definition which is a mixture of those previously used by other government departments. It reads as follows: 'The unlawful use or threat of violence against persons or property to further political or social objectives. It is usually intended to intimidate or coerce a government, individuals, or groups, or to modify their behavior or politics.' Terrorism, of course, is in contravention of the laws of the land and also of international law. But the application of legal norms presents certain difficulties, for seen in this light legitimate resistance (legitimate according to natural law) against tyrants is also criminal.

All specific definitions of terrorism have their shortcomings simply because reality is always richer (or more complicated) than any generalization. Unlike some chemical elements, there is no such thing as pure, unalloyed, unchanging terrorism, but there are many forms of terrorism. In the circumstances, a case can be made for broader and, of necessity, vaguer definitions, such as the one which appears in the British Prevention of Terrorism Act of 1974. This act states that, for the purpose of legislation, terrorism is the 'use of violence for political ends, and includes any use of violence for the purpose of putting the public or any section of the public in fear'. One cannot find fault with a statement of this kind, but, at the same time, it also applies to a great many other manifestations of violence – for instance, mass violence in the form of riots, violent demonstrations, street battles or civil war.

The issue of state terrorism ought to be mentioned in this context, even though it goes well beyond the question of definition. This refers to acts of terror carried out by governments against their own population, including systematic intimidation, arrests, killings and other means of coercion. This is usually directed against political opponents, but it can also affect sections of the population considered 'objectively' harmful, and it has been, on occasion, altogether indiscriminate. Nazi Germany and the Soviet Union under Stalin, and more recently Cambodia under Pol Pot, were extreme manifestations of such regimes of terror, but it would be easy to point to many others both past and present. Some of these regimes have also engaged in individual terror outside their borders – the assassination of King Alexander of Yugoslavia in Marseilles in 1934 was sponsored by Fascist Italy and the murder of Trotsky in Mexico was instigated by the Soviet Union. More recently, Colonel Qadhafi has sent murder squads to various parts of the world in order to 'liquidate' Libyan émigrés.

It has been argued in various quarters that the study of terrorism must include state terrorism, and that the exclusion of this subspecies is tantamount to an attempt to whitewash tyrannical governments. This kind of criticism usually comes from the Soviet Union, Cuba and Libya, but there have also been Western authors arguing in a similar vein. Frequently, the underlying assumptions are political in character. If it is claimed that 'Washington has become the torture and political murder capital of the world', the statement is clearly not meant to be a contribution to the scholarly investigation of terrorism.[5] But the demand for the inclusion of state terrorism in the present framework is by no means always due to political motivation; ironically, the CIA has also included state terrorism in its attempt to 'refine' the concept of terrorism.[6]

Acts of terror carried out by police states and tyrannical governments, in general, have been responsible for a thousand times more victims and more misery than all actions of individual terrorism taken together. A good case, no doubt, can be made in favour of the proposition that too little attention has been paid to state terrorism by historians, sociologists and political scientists, and too much to individual terrorism. But the case in favour of *obliterating* the basic differences between a regime of terror exerted by a state and terrorist activities by 'non-state actors' is a very weak one indeed. Both kinds aim at inducing a state of fear among the 'enemy'. But beyond this there are no important similarities, as they fulfil different functions and manifest themselves in different ways, such as mass arrests, concentration camps and mass executions in the case of state terrorism. A study of the functions and the techniques of the Gestapo is important, but it will be of no more help in understanding the Baader–Meinhof gang than the study of Auschwitz or of Pol Pot would be for comprehending the IRA or Abu Nidal. It is always important to bear in mind that individual, substate terrorism is only one form of violence and not necessarily the most murderous one. There have been in the history of mankind a great many manifestations of violence and oppression, frequently by the state, sometimes by organized religion (the Inquisition) or other authorities. Nothing is to be gained by ignoring the specifics of violence, be it out of political bias or ignorance. It will certainly not make for a better understanding of the various manifestations of violence, but will only spread confusion.

Another frequent source of confusion is the lack of precision in terminology. The following example should suffice. When reporting the bomb attacks at Rome and Vienna airports on 28 December 1985 by members of the Abu Nidal group, the London *Financial Times* used on its title page the terms 'terrorists' and 'gunmen', whereas on the second page reference was made to 'guerrillas' (or 'urban guerrillas'). The London *Guardian* used mainly the term 'terrorists' on the front page, but later referred to 'gunmen' and 'guerrilla'. The practice of other newspapers was similar.

Unfortunately, the state of affairs is not much better as far as official statements, and some of the professional literature, are concerned. The unsuspecting reader is bound to reach the conclusion that 'terrorist', 'guerrilla', 'commando', 'raider', 'urban guerrilla', 'gunman', 'partisan', 'urban terrorist' and other even more fanciful terms are synonyms and can be used interchangeably.*

Several writers on terrorism, such as Paul Wilkinson and the present writer, and including, incidentally, some in the Soviet Union, have repeatedly pointed out certain essential differences between terrorism and guerrilla warfare, but without much apparent success. The essence of guerrilla warfare is to establish *foci*, or liberated areas, in the countryside and to set up small military units which will gradually grow in strength, number and equipment – from squads to companies and regiments, eventually to divisions and armies, as in Yugoslavia and China during the Second World War – in order to fight battles against government troops. In the liberated areas, the guerrillas establish their own institutions, conduct propaganda and engage in other open political activities.†

None of this applies to terrorists, whose base of operation is in the cities, and who have to operate clandestinely in small units. Any major concentration would immediately expose them to retaliation by the government. The terrorists may be part of a political movement that engages in propaganda and other political activities (such as the IRA and the Basque ETA), but there is a strict division of labour between the legal and the military arms of the movement. Terrorists no more engage in political

---

* According to newspaper reports a 'Palestinian commando' named Hassan Nasser Ali was arrested in Madrid in June 1986 (*Washington Post*, 28 June 1986). A 'commando' according to Webster's Dictionary is a military unit or command of the Boers or a raiding expedition or a 'military unit trained or organized as shock troops especially for hit and run raids in enemy territory'. However, the story about Hassan Ali revealed that he was not a Boer nor had he engaged as a shock troop in a hit-and-run raid. Instead, he had hired a petty crook named Manuel Jalafe to smuggle a suitcase on a plane to Israel, which, according to Ali, contained heroin, but in reality was a hidden time-bomb. Such incidents occur daily and show the power of the media to correct the dictionaries.

† Some writers have called terrorism 'the main weapon of the guerrillas', others have gone so far as to call the difference between terrorism and guerrilla 'purely semantic' (G. Langguth). The main culprits responsible for this kind of obfuscation are the *terribles simplificateurs* in the media. But certain military writers have also tended to subsume *all* violence below the level of conventional warfare under one heading, be it guerrilla or terrorism. The theoreticians of guerrilla warfare have never been oblivious to the basic difference between the kind of strategy they advocated and terrorism. Mao wrote about this; Che Guevara said that terrorism was a 'method of little efficacy' which could have fateful consequences. Regis Debray also noted that urban terrorism could not play a decisive role, and furthermore that it involved political dangers. (For a detailed discussion see Herfried Münkler, 'Guerillakrieg und Terrorismus', *Neue Politische Literatur*, 3 (1980), pp. 299–326.)

The Colombian and the Peruvian terrorists of recent date have been active both in the countryside and in the cities. For this reason, a writer on the subject noted that the distinction between guerrilla and terrorism in Latin America had become complicated. (Michael S. Radu, 'Terror, Terrorism and Insurgency in Latin America', *Orbis* (Spring 1984), p. 36.) But even in these instances the main action was in the countryside rather than in the cities.

propaganda than spies, as their chief assignment is to remain under deep cover.

Despite these fundamental differences, the term 'urban guerrilla' (a contradiction in terms) is frequently used in the media, as are some of the other terms mentioned earlier. How can one explain the disinclination to call a spade by its rightful name? In some cases, to be sure, the dividing line between guerrilla and terrorist warfare tends to become blurred. The IRA cannot retreat to (non-existent) jungles or mountain forests on their native island in order to organize major guerrilla units. But it has come close at one time to establishing no-go areas for the British police and army, and its political activities are conducted more or less openly, as they were in the Basque provinces of Spain. But their operations were still strictly terrorist in character; they went out of their way not to clash with the army.

In Lebanon, such well-defined zones emerged during the civil war, and, within these borders, private armies came into existence possessing tanks and medium and even heavy weapons not normally used by terrorists. However, such situations are exceptional. In Lebanon a civil war of all against all took place, in which terrorist acts were frequently committed, but these did not play the most crucial role in the military confrontations between rival militias.

Generally speaking, guerrilla forces have used terrorist techniques on many occasions. This was the case, for instance, in Algeria and Vietnam, but the opposite has virtually never been the case. The urban milieu is not suitable for guerrilla warfare.

If, nevertheless, so much obfuscation has occurred, this is partly rooted in ignorance of the difference between guerrilla warfare and other forms of substate violence. On other occasions, the indiscriminate use of terms was probably deliberate: 'guerrilla' has acquired over the ages a positive, attractive image, whereas 'terrorist' has not. Most terrorist groups have used such names as 'Red Army' or 'Liberation Army' (even if they numbered only five or ten members), 'Revenge Brigade', 'Red Brigade', 'Thunder Commando', 'Liberation Movement', 'Direct Action', 'Proletarian Army Group', 'Armed Cells' or, at the least, 'Party of God' or 'suicide squads'. Only in a very few instances (such as in Brazil under Carlos Marighella) have terrorists openly accepted the terrorist label. The preference for the guerrilla label should be considered, therefore, a public relations exercise, and, in their endeavour to be fair to the 'gunmen', the media have frequently accepted their self-styled designations, sometimes with comic results. The British or Italian media reporting a bomb explosion in a London or Rome hotel will never refer to IRA or Red Brigades as 'urban guerrillas', 'commandos', let alone 'freedom fighters'. But they will not hesitate to do so when reporting events in other countries. The same is true with regard to virtually every country; for the Soviet press there are only bandits in Afghanistan and only resistance fighters in Africa and the Middle East. Furthermore, if terrorists engage in a particularly gruesome operation, they are likely to be labelled terrorists, but if their attack fails or if only relatively few victims are involved, the chances are that they will revert back to their 'commando' or 'urban guerrilla' status.

It will have been noted that no provision has been made for moral judgements in a definition of terrorism.[7] Terrorism is, above all, a technique of political warfare, and it is not difficult to think of circumstances in which a terrorist act is not only permissible, but almost a categorical imperative – for instance, in defence against a tyrant responsible for imposing a state of terror on his people. The assassination of a Hitler or a Stalin in good time would have saved many human lives. One could think of similar cases in our time and in past ages. The nature of the terrorist targets is of decisive significance, because there is a qualitative difference between the terrorism directed against a democratic regime and one which is not. True, there will always be some who maintain that freedom is servitude, and vice versa, but such arguments should not seriously preoccupy us. There are other, more weighty, considerations. In between murderous tyrannies and near-perfect democracies, there is a fairly wide grey zone of regimes which are neither quite free nor slave. Who is, therefore, entitled to decide whether terrorism is permissible in these circumstances or not? It can be said, broadly speaking, that terrorism is always reprehensible whenever other means of political struggle exist, and where injustice can be put right by democratic means, or through mass pressure. But even against the worst oppression there is no absolute licence; it is clearly wrong to kill a million people in order to get at a super-villain. Any sensible interpretation of terrorism must be based on political values. Neither means nor ends can be absolute criteria, as each case is different and has to be judged on its merits.

Our starting point was the observation that a comprehensive, generally accepted definition of terrorism does not exist and is unlikely to come into existence, if only because terrorists and their victims will not agree on the matter. But a working definition is certainly not beyond our reach; in any case, political decision-makers will not wait for a consensus to emerge among political scientists before they take the measures they deem necessary to combat terrorism.[8] Physicians use many drugs, even though their exact physiological effects remain a mystery. What applies to medicine should be acceptable in the study of terrorism. Even if there were an objective, value-free definition of terrorism, covering all its important aspects and features, it would still be rejected by some for ideological reasons, just as a generally accepted definition of Fascism is beyond our reach. Those who sympathize with terrorists will continue to do so whatever the definition. Seen in this light, the fact that no more progress has been made so far is of no crucial importance.

The question of terrorist motivation is far from new, and has received an enormous variety of answers. This is hardly surprising, for terrorism has assumed widely differing characteristics from age to age and from country to country. Any explanation that attempts to account for all of its many manifestations is bound to be either exceedingly vague or alto-gether wrong. It has been said that highly idealistic and deeply motivated young people have opted for terrorism when they faced unresolved grie-vances, and when there was no other way of registering protest and effecting change. Dostoevski and many others would hardly have agreed. It has also been said that terrorists are criminals, moral imbeciles, mentally der-anged people or sadists (or sado-masochists), but sweeping definitions of this kind are bound to provoke scepticism. Terrorist movements are usually some kind of youth movement, but to dwell upon the idealistic character of youth movements is only stressing the obvious. They are not out for personal gain and they always oppose the *status quo*. But political goals are not necessarily wholly altruistic, as idealism and interest may coincide. Neither are personal ambitions absent; terrorists have also been driven by impatience and a kind of *machismo* (or, more recently, its female equiva-lent). Terrorism has occurred with increasing frequency in societies in which peaceful change is possible. Grievances always exist, but in certain cases oppression has been borne without protest, whereas elsewhere and at other times relatively minor grievances have resulted in violent reaction. Nor is the choice of terrorism as a weapon altogether obvious, for frequently there are other ways of resistance, both political and military.

In short, the problem of terrorism is complicated, and what can be said without fear of contradiction about a terrorist group in one country is by no means true for other groups at other times and in other societies. Love of liberty, as well as the ardent love of others, were invoked by sympathetic observers trying to explain the motives of terrorists in the last third of the nineteenth century – 'the last, desperate struggle of outraged and exas-perated human nature for breathing space and life'. Emma Goldman noted that the anarchist terrorists were impelled to violence not by the teachings of anarchism, but by the tremendous pressure of conditions which made life unbearable to their sensitive natures. Compared to the wholesale vio-lence of capital and government, political acts of violence were but a drop in the ocean: 'High strung like a violin string, the anarchists weep and moan for life, so relentless, so cruel, so terribly inhuman. In a desperate moment the string breaks.'[9]

Other contemporary observers interpreted terrorism in a less complimentary light. It was considered altogether evil, and even a form of madness with perhaps an underlying physical disorder. It was noted that quite a few terrorists of the period suffered from epilepsy, tuberculosis and other diseases. Lombroso saw a connection between bomb throwing and pellagra and other vitamin deficiencies among the maize-eating peoples of Southern Europe. Others detected a link with the general nervous overexcitement of the period, which also manifested itself in an exaggerated individualism and the spread of decadent literature. The connection between terrorism and barometric pressure, moon phases, alcoholism and droughts was investigated, and cranial measurements of terrorists were very much in fashion.[10]

It is not true, however, that early interpretations of terrorism were merely hysterical and that there were no genuine attempts to understand deeper motives. Many contemporary observers took a remarkably detached view, arguing *inter alia* that the importance of anarchist terrorism should not be exaggerated, that repression was less important than prevention, and that capital punishment was not called for.[11] Lombroso had doubts from the beginning about the efficiency of international co-operation against anarchist terrorism, and he also opposed capital punishment. He argued that punishment was no antidote to fanaticism. If, as he maintained, terrorism was an indirect form of suicide, then capital punishment, leading to the desired end, would merely act as a spur.[12] Zenker, one of the earliest historians of anarchism, suggested that all exceptional ('emergency') legislation against anarchism should be avoided; it would be far more helpful if the state made an effort to redress social inequalities. But Zenker was too close and objective an observer to be satisfied with facile explanations and solutions; he stated *expressis verbis* that anarchist terrorism could by no means be explained by pauperism alone.[13]

By the turn of the century, anarchism had outgrown its terrorist phase, but terrorist actions did not cease. Compared with other manifestations of political violence, they seemed to be of minor importance and this is perhaps one of the reasons why no serious attempt was made to study the phenomenon. There were other reasons as well, such as its fundamentally shocking and disturbing character, which may have inhibited serious study.[14] It is also true that from an early stage terrorism was perceived as a very complex phenomenon, varying from country to country as the result of cultural traditions, social structures, political relationships, and many other factors which made generalization very difficult indeed. One of the few attempts to give a definition and explanation was Hardman's entry in the *Encyclopaedia of the Social Sciences*, published in the 1930s. The author defined terrorism as the method (or the theory behind the method) whereby an organized group or party sought to achieve its avowed aims chiefly through the systematic use of violence. Thus, terrorism was different in substance not only from governmental terror, but also from mob violence and mass insurrection. Hardman regarded the publicity value of terrorist acts as a cardinal point, he noted that the inspiration for terrorism could be left-wing as well as rightist, and he realized that terrorism has never attained real success as a complete revolutionary tactic. Some of his other observations, although perhaps correct at the time, clearly show the changes that terrorism has undergone more recently. Thus the doctrine of indiscriminate terror did not yet exist in the 1930s: 'Terrorist acts are directed against persons who, as individuals, agents, or representatives of authority, interfere with the consummation of the objectives of such a group.'[15] Nor is it likely that any observer of the terrorist movements of the 1960s and the 1970s would still subscribe to the view that 'the terrorist does not threaten; death and destruction are not intended to produce revenue or to terrorize the persons attacked'. Books on terrorism continued to appear, but these were usually either historical monographs on recent Russian or Irish history, or journalistic accounts of exotic movements such as the Macedonian IMRO, or studies of the legal implications of terrorist operations.

It was only in the 1960s that the social scientists became interested in political violence. Some had believed that it was a relatively rare phenomenon; others may have neglected it for different reasons.[16]

The theory of political crisis, instability, legitimacy and revolutionary situations became an attractive field of study. By 1968, some 650 political scientists listed 'revolutions and political violence' as their field of specialization. Among the more influential concepts used was that of Samuel Huntington, according to which revolutions were an aspect of modernization peculiar to Western societies. In most other parts of the globe, according to Huntington, it was too late for agrarian revolutions but probably too early for urban industrial revolutions.[17] Other authors pointed to the historical role of the peasantry and its political mobilization, the existence of basic conflicts of interest within the ruling class, the function of the revolution from above, and the apparent connection between revolution and war.[18] The 'J curve' hypothesis propagated by Davies found some supporters. It was based on certain insights formulated earlier by de Tocqueville and Marx – that a revolution was most likely when, after a long period of rising expectations (and their satisfaction), there was a setback, in which the distance between expectations and their fulfilment was rapidly growing. Many, though not all, of these studies were cross-national and quantitative.

Within the context of macro cross-national research, Rummel investigated the dimensions of conflict behaviour within and between nations (1946–59), and Raymond Tanter did the same for a shorter period (1958–60). This led them to examine the relationship between domestic and foreign conflict behaviour, and they found, perhaps to their surprise, that apparently there was none. Perhaps there was a third factor that had been ignored, such as the personality characteristics of the national decision-makers, or perhaps there was a causal relationship after all which was still obscured by some unknown phenomenon. Douglas Bwy examined political instability in Latin America, in many ways a more propitious topic, precisely because the author was dealing with societies having roughly similar traditions. But the search did not lead very far, because it was established that there was no obvious correlation between the legitimacy ascribed to a political system and the intensity or frequency of violence. Riots broke out as frequently in highly legitimate as they did in less legitimate systems.[19]

Some economists and political scientists have suggested that economic methods and 'rational actor' models be applied to the study of terrorism. But it is doubtful whether the economics of (organized) crime can shed much light on terrorist motives, let alone predict terrorist behaviour. The main difficulty is not that the rational model is useless with regard to people engaging in suicide missions (of which there are only very few), but that it also tends to ignore factors such as frustration, anger, fanaticism, aggression, etc., which are very frequent in terrorism. Above all, economic man is a rational being wishing to maximize beneficial returns; few people would go into a business in which the chances of success are as dim as they are in terrorism. This approach may still be of some limited interest to those engaging in counter-terrorism, for instance in connection with the negotiation process concerning the release of hostages.[20]

Some researchers saw the decisive factor in the break-up of traditional society; others concentrated on the unequal distribution of property or land; and a third group took the social consequences of rapid economic development as their starting point. According to some investigators, the most modern and the most backward societies were the most stable, whereas those in the middle displayed a high degree of instability. Sometimes the results were a little unexpected, showing in one case that the citizens of the United States (including blacks) were more content than those of other countries. Perhaps misery and frustration were insufficient to explain riots and anarchy; perhaps the need to prove *machismo* had to be taken into account, as well as the desire to raise hell out of sheer exhilaration and the habit of lawlessness.[21]

A study of violence in eighty-four countries reached the conclusion that a little repression increases instability whereas a great deal of it has the opposite effect; or to put it more obscurely:

Political instability is curvilinearly related to the level of the coerciveness of the political regime; the probability of a high level of political instability increases with mid-levels of coerciveness, insufficient to be a deterrent to aggression, but sufficient to increase the level of systemic frustration.

Change leads to unrest; modern countries are more stable because they can satisfy the wants of their citizens; the less advanced countries are characterized by greater instability because of the aggressive responses to systemic frustration among the populace. But because there has been dissatisfaction in advanced societies as well as in backward ones, the investigators wisely hedged their bets: the satisfaction of wants may have a feedback effect and may increase the drive for more satisfaction, thus adding to the sense of systemic frustration. It is only when a high enough level of satisfaction has been reached (on the Patty Hearst level, malevolent critics would add) that a country will tend towards stability rather than instability.[22]

The cross-national studies were usually based on the index of the *New York Times* or similar sources. Assassinations committed by madmen and terrorist groups were listed side by side. The victims of the Nazi purge of June 1934 were enumerated, but not those who had died as the result of the Soviet purge of 1936–8. The authors of a study on assassination found it directly related to, among other things, external aggression and minority hostility. In these calculations, some of which had a distinctly Alice-in-Wonderland quality, East Germany, Jordan and Guatemala were defined as belonging to the 'high external aggression' category; Bulgaria, Czechoslovakia, Afghanistan and Panama (to provide some random examples) were rated 'low external aggression'. Turkey, Peru, Tunisia and Switzerland were countries with 'high minority hostility'; Yugoslavia, the Philippines, Syria and the United Kingdom appear under 'low minority hostility'.[23]

Other investigators had meanwhile reached the conclusion that their scales were not truly applicable to political violence in Communist nations because these countries were not 'scalable', and that the models of modernization and its effects did not apply to these countries either.[24] But leaving aside questions of general principle, such as the application of quantification, it was by no means certain whether Third World countries were 'scalable' either, if only due to the difficulty in obtaining reliable data. The researchers were not unaware of the weaknesses of their concepts and conclusions, which are all too often based on shotgun statistical marriages. 'Factor analysis' has been used to give the appearance of statistical order to what remains conceptual chaos.[25] Yet at the same time, until about 1972, the general feeling was one of great optimism. Thus the Feierabend study in 1966 stated: 'Although exploratory in nature, the findings are sufficiently striking and persuasive to argue for continuing with additional designs.'[26] Ted Gurr, writing in 1972, believed that the study of civil conflict was on the eve of a major breakthrough:

the accomplishments of these studies to date seem to have more than justified their doing. It is problematic but entirely possible, on the basis of results so far, that civil conflict will become one of the first fields of social science outside of psychology and economics in which parameter, etiology and processes are understood well enough to constitute a cohesive scientific field in the narrow sense of that term.[27]

This optimism was not shared by all political scientists, let alone by historians. Harry Eckstein, writing in 1964 and again in 1969, expressed scepticism about the conclusions reached up until that time. Erich Weede, surveying the work of a whole decade, doubted whether there had been any progress at all.[28] Eventually, the authors of the studies of the 1960s, who had emphasized the psychological origins of strife, themselves became dissatisfied with the results achieved. New investigations were launched with the emphasis on tension and strain rather than on relative deprivation as in the older studies. Social tensions were now interpreted as the result of persistent strain or short-term stress. These strains were said to be particularly strong where a social system had a long tradition of conflict.

Internal conflict, according to this argument, occurs when injustice and inequality persist, and when domestic rule is based on constraints rather than on consensus.[29] This model tries to take into account economic and political discrimination, the presence of religious and nationalist–separatist trends, and also economic dependence on other countries. Another hypothesis was based on the assumption that protests escalate into internal war as a result of negative sanctions on the part of the government.[30] Protest provokes government repression, which itself helps to produce a fresh and more intense wave of protest and violence. Increased coerciveness offers no likelihood or guarantee of enhancing public order; on the contrary, it tends to undermine it. Thus, in the final analysis, government coerciveness is positively related to political instability. Such findings may have applied perhaps to a few countries, but they were obviously wrong with regard

to many others. Meanwhile, again from within the profession, some searching studies were challenging the conventional wisdom underlying most of
the work that had been done. Was it really true that hardship was always
the cause of collective violence, and that there was a close correspondence
between urbanization, crime and collective violence? Tilly and his colleagues, from studies of nineteenth- and twentieth-century France, reached
the conclusion that it was quite wrong to assume that urban growth – by
dissolving ties, disrupting existing controls or disorienting newcomers to
the city – had a strong and consistent tendency to increase the level of
crime, violence and disorder. More important yet, their research showed
that there was no general connection between collective violence and hardship 'such that an observer could predict one from another ... and we
suppose that the principle, immediate causes of collective violence are political'.[31] A monograph on Africa showed that social mobilization on that
continent, contrary to expectations, did not generally lead to frustration
and violence.

Other studies of some relevance in this context were those of George
Rude, dealing with collective violence in eighteenth-century France and
Britain, and Calvert's investigation into 363 revolutionary events between
1901 and 1960, which also included all kinds of *coups d'état* and wars of
succession and independence.[32]

Radical students of political terrorism have sharply criticized their non-
radical colleagues on many counts, but as far as their starting point is concerned, and also their methods, there was a striking similarity. The scope
of the radicals' work was conditioned by the liberal–democratic political
regime in which they lived and operated; what Marx said about the condi-
tioning of human political consciousness was certainly applicable to these
radicals.

A recent assessment of revolutionary warfare (including political terrorism) by radical political scientists may serve as an example.[33] According
to this school of thought, such warfare has acquired unprecedented popularity; it is a 'moral explosion' among the disenchanted masses in underdeveloped countries. It does not break out where there are institutions
and mechanisms through which one can hope to influence and change the
existing system. The question of legitimacy is crucial: legitimacy comes
to governments when citizens actively and meaningfully participate in the
process of government, that is when there is a maximum of self-government.
There is little to quarrel with in the sentiments expressed: that there should
be a maximum of self-government in society, that government should have
legitimacy, and that there should be free institutions, goes without saying.
It may even be true that this concept is historically true with regard to

one or two countries, for such is the variety of history that few theories are altogether wrong. But with the occurrence and success of terrorism on a worldwide basis, such general propositions have no more relevance than the correlation between the number of storks and the birthrate in Sweden. There have been few moral explosions among the disenchanted masses in underdeveloped countries of late, because their new rulers have abandoned the moral inhibitions of the former colonial masters. As far as self-government is concerned, it is unfortunately true that, by and large, the less there has been of it in a country, the more immune the country has been from terrorism. True, the Shah of Iran was overthrown by a popular movement not by terrorists, and so was Marcos's rule in the Philippines. But in both cases this happened when, for a variety of reasons, the rulers were losing their self-confidence and were about to introduce half-hearted liberal reforms. Wherever the means of repression have been most complete and perfected, there has been no terrorism at all. These facts are not in dispute, but there is psychological resistance to accepting the obvious. Seldom has it been admitted that virtue in politics is not always rewarded. As Romero Maura noted, writing on anarchism in Spain:

> The safety-valve metaphor is popular but based on a misrepresentation of Spanish modern history, while failing to take into account the plain fact that anarchism and other revolutionary movements have only been strong in conditions where other, more moderate political alternatives were available.[34]

It has been argued that even if there existed a valid theory of political instability, collective violence or revolution, it would still be a long way from a theory of terrorism.[35] For terrorism is something far more specific than instability and violence in general. It is not a mass movement, but usually resorted to by small groups of people whose motives may not necessarily be connected with observable 'objective' political, economic, social or psychological trends. What of the theories and models which not only addressed themselves to violence in general, but were thought to have a direct bearing on terrorism and therefore enjoyed a certain vogue among students of this subject? Much of the research took place in the United States in the 1960s, and it was only natural that there should be a direct connection with America's own internal turmoil and, of course, the Vietnam war.

The fact that there has always been a great deal of violence had somehow not quite registered. With the experience of American suburbs in mind, it was widely believed that political life all over the globe was steadily becoming more civilized and that stability could be regarded as the norm and political violence as a regrettable aberration. When it was suddenly realized that this appraisal may have been over-optimistic, the pendulum began to swing to the other extreme, and the conviction gained ground that the frequency of violence must somehow reflect the inequities of society – the 'system', low income, bad housing, insufficient education and so on. The shock of recognition was apparently so great as to make comment quite incoherent on occasion: 'If there is a streak of violence in the national character, then it is precisely that streak which sets itself in opposition to change.'[36]

The implied assumption was that a healthy society faced no such problems, and that a government which could count on the loyalty of its citizens had no reason to fear terrorist outrages and other perils. These assumptions were at the bottom of the new departures in conflict studies, which, in turn, were mainly based on the work done by Dollard and his collaborators, concerning frustration and aggression, just before the outbreak of the Second World War.[37] They had stated that aggression is *always* a consequence of frustration, an assumption which was by no means universally shared. It came under attack, for instance, from ethologists who maintained that aggressive behaviour was spontaneous, an inner drive. But most psychologists also found this theory wanting: 'War occurs because fighting is a fundamental tendency in human beings,' one of them wrote.[38] Anthony Storr noted that the frustration–aggression concept was widely accepted among Americans. Perhaps it was true that perennial optimism made it hard for them to believe that there was anything unpleasant either in the physical world or in human nature which could not be 'fixed'.*

The Dollard concept was widely accepted for a while by students of conflict, who regarded protest and violence as the result of discontent caused by frustration. They saw social discontent as the discrepancy between demand and fulfilment; in more scientific language, the higher the social-want formation and the lower the social-want satisfaction, the greater the systemic frustration. Violence, seen in this light, is the result of socialization patterns which either encourage or discourage aggression, and of cultural traditions sanctioning collective responses to various kinds of deprivation.[39] Students of conflict had a rich armoury at their disposal to

---

* The frustration–aggression hypothesis was refined in the 1960s by Leonard Berkowitz. Frustration, as he saw it, produces an emotional state – anger – which heightens the probability of the occurrence of aggression. Berkowitz was more aware than his predecessors of outside stimuli. Even if there was frustration and anger, the probability that aggression will take place still depends on the presence (or absence) of factors restraining aggression. Stated in this more cautious form, the hypothesis seemed to be of greater validity, but as a tool of empirical research it is still of limited use, especially with regard to larger social groups. Leonard Berkowitz, *Aggression* (New York, 1962), and Reed Lawson (ed.), *Frustration, the Development of a Scientific Concept* (New York, 1965).

explain protest and violence-causal models, such as factor analysis and multiple regression (a way of predicting the dependent variable from one or two independent variables). Over the following years, many dozens of papers and books were published investigating correlations between violence, on the one hand, and such variables as literacy, urbanization, caloric intake, GNP and the number of newspapers and physicians on the other hand. This was the so-called frustration index. Its composition was, of course, bound to be highly arbitrary, for it could not be taken for granted that the circulation of newspapers inevitably makes for happiness. Nor was it at all clear whether a lack of schooling made for greater discontent than the existence of schools and universities taken together with an absence of sufficient jobs for graduates.

The frustration–aggression thesis had much to recommend it, if only because it was a relatively simple model and seemed in accordance with common sense. Clearly, people would not rebel and engage in either collective or individual violence if they were not frustrated, but were reasonably happy. But the more the thesis was applied and submitted to further thought, the more doubts arose. Some pointed to the fact that the status of the thesis was still shaky in psychology; others stressed that much research had shown that frustration did not invariably lead to aggression, which could occur without frustration, that threat and insult could evoke more aggression than frustration, and so on.[40] Yet another student of terrorism, who had attempted to test this thesis, reached the conclusion that relative deprivation was elusive as a measurement. As for the causes of terrorism, they were obscure, for terrorism had occurred among both rich and poor, oppressive and relatively unoppressive societies. It has been used to promote causes with no popular support, as well as causes endorsed by a large majority.[41]

Ted Gurr, who had pioneered the frustration–aggression thesis in its sociological application, seems to have modified and restricted it in his subsequent work, noting that 'the typical terrorist campaign was conducted by tiny groups and was short-lived'. Their public motives were not notably different from those of groups using other unconventional methods of political action. More specifically, the perpetrators of terrorist activities seemed more often motivated by hostility towards particular policies and political figures than by revolutionary aspirations.[42] Whether the observations are correct with regard to the more important terrorist groups of the 1970s, such as the PLO, the IRA or the ETA, is a moot point; in any case it is a far cry from the original frustration–aggression thesis and the relative-deprivation concept.

That there must be some connection between terrorism and aggression has never been seriously questioned. Other things being equal (such as the perception of injustice and oppression), how can one explain that some men and women turn to terrorist action, whereas others opt for political action, and still others find alternative social outlets for their aggression – such as becoming, for instance, 'aggressive' lawyers or businessmen? The issue of aggression, and its origins, has been a matter of dispute for several decades. There were heated controversies centred around Konrad Lorenz's theories of instinctive behaviour, which were based on the systematic study of primates.[43] His views were sharply criticized by some, who denied that an independent, innate fighting instinct existed, and by others, because they thought it hazardous to draw analogies between chimpanzees or baboons observed in the wild and human beings.[44] However, Lorenz also found many supporters. Furthermore, much could be found in the teachings of Freud and of certain geneticists which attributed importance to aggression as a drive or instinct, in contrast to those who had sought to explain it exclusively with reference to societal factors, such as the character of an aggressive, competitive society.

As far back as 1876, Cesare Lombroso had written about the 'born criminal'; he also saw the terrorists of his time as genetical misfits.[45] Such seemingly far-fetched speculation was ridiculed by subsequent generations of criminologists, but more recent genetic research, especially that concerning the XYY syndrome among males, pointed to certain connections between chromosome aberrations, on the one hand, and aggressive behaviour and mental subnormality, on the other.[46] Some writers immediately drew sweeping conclusions about 'born criminals', who in many ways were not responsible for their actions because of their constitution or because of the way they were genetically programmed. Others, without denying the importance of chromosome aberrations, were reluctant to accept that heredity played a greater (perhaps exclusive) role in social behaviour than outside influences.

Research in this field is only in its early stages, and the personality of terrorists has not yet been studied in any systematic way, if only because they have seldom submitted themselves to psychological tests, which would either prove or disprove the theses which have been put forward about a predisposition towards terrorism. There is no denying that aggression has played a role, sometimes an important role, in the psychological make-up of terrorists. Ulrike Meinhof wrote from Stammheim prison about 'the horrible [*rasend*] aggression' which she felt, and for which there was no safety valve. Generally speaking, there was much free-floating aggression among that generation of German terrorists, just as there was a great deal of drug taking. In the end, this aggression was turned against themselves

– hence, the collective suicide in prison. However, it is not at all clear whether this aggression was indeed spontaneous and natural or whether, like the drug taking and the use of foul language, it was part of general counter-culture and was 'willed' and even cultivated, especially among the women, for whom it seemed a part of their sexual liberation. In these respects, the psychological profile of the Red Army Brigade and the 2 June Movement seems to have resembled that of the shortlived Weathermen. But the Italian Red Brigade terrorists were less affected by the counter-culture, and drug taking was apparently more common among terrorists of the right than of the left. From what we know of Turkish and Armenian terrorists, their psychological make-up was quite different from that of West European student rebels. It is also known that the IRA, as well as the ETA and, of course, the Arab terrorist organizations took a dim view of the permissive life-style, sexual and otherwise, of their German comrades.

Among the German terrorists of the 1960s and 1970s, a fairly high incidence of abnormal psychological behaviour and even mental disease could apparently be found. It seems to have been no accident that the second generation of German terrorists was constituted to a certain extent of members of the Heidelberg psychiatric patients collective. Baader, who emerged as the leader of the RAF, had shown asocial tendencies even as a boy. These became more pronounced in later years; the lack of inhibitions was part of his charisma as a leader. A fairly high percentage of the German terrorists (including Baader and Meinhof) grew up without a father or without both parents. But there were others who came from perfectly 'normal' parental homes; and there was a pronounced number of practising Protestants or clergymen among them. No abnormal tendencies can be found among the (far more numerous) Italian terrorists of the same period, and the state of the art being what it is one cannot be too careful when applying generalizations.

The author of a critical review of the literature on the psychology of political terrorism has reached the conclusion that it is uneven and sparsely developed.[47] This is true, not because there is no generally accepted definition of terrorism, but because the differences in the real world between terrorist groups are so wide. Psychology should, in principle, help us to understand why individuals become terrorists, to what extent they are influenced by subconscious psychological motives, the importance of groups and of leadership, the question of attraction by violence, the psychological effects of terrorist actions, and so on. The motives of a German terrorist who joined the RAF were altogether different from the recruits of Sendero Luminoso, and the motives of Sendero were again quite different from those of the Tupamaros, even though both were Spanish-speaking and belonged to the same cultural orbit. Young Catholics in Belfast or London-derry slums join the PIRA because everyone in the neighbourhood does it, and the same is true with regard to Palestinian camps in Lebanon. Else-where the motives may be quite different. The small group plays a very important role in the marginal terrorist movements such as the RAF, but it is of much less significance in the national separatist movements.

Some terrorists may be neurotically hostile or paranoid or 'stress seekers' and unstable, while elsewhere there may be no evidence of major mental aberrations. It goes without saying that the psychological consequences of terrorism are bound to be different in a society like America where the loss of one single human life comes as a great shock, compared with most Asian, African and Latin American societies where different attitudes towards life and death prevail. In short, the question is not whether great caution should prevail with regard to generalizations; the real issue is to what extent generalizations are at all possible. We shall know the answer once there are more systematic studies of specific terrorist groups, which at present are virtually non-existent.

What can be said without fear of contradiction is that individual terrorism frequently appeared where there had been a long, historical tradition, and a popular culture, of individual violence, as in Ireland and the Middle East. But, on the other hand, terrorism did not appear in countries with an equally high incidence – such as Mexico – and this alone clearly does not suffice to explain the emergence of terrorism in recent decades. Even if it could be shown that there is something akin to a 'terrorist personality', or a tradition of violence in a country, this is not sufficient to explain terror-ism, just as the 'authoritarian personality' cannot explain modern dictator-ships.

The same applies to other psychological and social factors which have been singled out in the search for 'preconditions' and 'precipitants': includ-ing the domestic causes of terrorism, the international environment and the subcultural environment such as the universities in the late 1960s and early 1970s.[48]

Various ingenious hypotheses have been adduced to explain the occur-rence of terrorism. They help to explain, at best, the situation in one country but not in others. Thus it has frequently been argued that the 'blocked character' of Italian society, the lack of social and political change in Italy, with the Christian Democrats as the dominant force since the end of the Second World War, has been the main reason for unrest among the young; on the other hand, the appointment of the Socialist Craxi as prime minister, and the reforms which were carried out under his leadership, greatly restricted the appeal of terrorism in Italy. It is doubtful whether this is a satisfactory theory for the rise and decline of Italian terrorism, because Craxi's reforms were not that radical and extensive ; the revulsion following the murder of Aldo Moro played a considerable role, as did the arrest of leading members of the Red Brigades and their willingness to co-operate with the authorities. But even if the 'blocked system' explanation were correct, it would not help to explain the situation in West Germany, where the terrorist upsurge took place precisely at the time when there was a shift in political power from the Christian Democrats to the left.

Yet others have pointed to historical explanations. Seen in this light, the upsurge of terrorism in Italy and West Germany was a belated after-effect of Fascism, a revolt against the parents' generation, in which the ruling stratum had first collaborated with these loathsome dictatorships, and later refused to confront the past. If this assumption were true, there ought to have been a great deal of terrorist activity in Austria, where Nazism at one time had been genuinely popular, and where, in contrast to Germany, there had been no attempt at all even to admit to the Nazi heritage. The seven years had simply been blotted out from the collective memory. Yet Austria was remarkably free of native terrorism, whereas a great deal of terrorism occurred in the countries which had been part of the anti-Nazi coalition during the war, and also in the neutral countries (Turkey, Spain).

Nowhere has the terrorist scene been investigated in greater detail than in West Germany. An ambitious research project into the causes and conditions of terrorism was undertaken between 1977 and 1983; it brought together a sizeable group of political scientists, sociologists, philosophers and psychologists, as well as criminologists and jurists – on the correct assumption that terrorism could not be monocausally explained.[49] While devoted to German terrorism, the study sensibly also dealt with, for the sake of comparison, conditions in France, Italy and the Netherlands, noting national differences, such as the fact that in France left-wing radicalism had been integrated to a higher degree, and that in Italy there was, traditionally, greater readiness to live with disorder. The experts examined the ideologies and strategies of terrorism, including the crucial question whether ideology had led the extremists into terrorist action, or whether it served as a post-factum justification for latent aggression, which found its outlet in violent actions. A detailed investigation of the biographies of left-wing and right-wing terrorists was undertaken, as well as an analysis of group structures and processes, and the social conditions in which terrorism developed. Lastly, the relationship between the terrorists and society and the state was explored. Some authors pointed to shortcomings in the state and society, which might have contributed to the emergence of terrorism.

These investigations include much that is of great value to the micro-history of various groups and *groupuscules*, out of which the Baader–Mein-hof and the 2 June group developed. There is much of interest on the specific counter-culture in which the process was embedded, and genera-tional processes were not neglected. Of particular interest is the description of the Berlin scene and the specific demographic situation of the former German capital. It is not, however, readily obvious why the fact that rela-tively many residents of Berlin live in roomy apartments, or that communi-cations in the city are good, should have a direct bearing on the genesis of terrorism. It is certainly true that Berlin was more open to the world before than after the Second World War, but whether it was also more tolerant, as claimed in this study, is more doubtful. A similar process of decline could be observed in Vienna, once the capital of a great empire; and yet there has been no terrorism in Austria.

The basic problem facing those who see in terrorism the result of the shortcomings of society is not that their observations are basically incorrect, but that, with all its shortcomings, German society is freer than at any time in its past – in Wilhelmian Germany, in the Third Reich and even in the Weimar Republic – and yet, in the past, there was no terrorism. Left-wing terrorism emerged in West Germany not in a time of intensified right-wing repression, but, on the contrary, when Social Democrats had entered the government for the first time. Thus it could be argued with equal justice that the terrorism of the 1970s was not the outcome of the failures of democracy, but the reaction of a generation which suffered from too much freedom, and which needed guidance and leadership – and could not find it.

But such generalizations would still be of questionable value, for the simple reason that there were very few terrorists, so that concepts borrowed from group psychology would rest on a tiny factual basis. Similarly, refer-ences to 'objective' factors are frequently doubtful, for these trends cannot possibly explain the behaviour of very small groups. Terrorism in the con-temporary world has occurred in all kinds of conditions – in times of econo-mic prosperity and decline; it has occurred in big cities and in small towns; and it has affected people of various social classes. True, there may still be good reasons why German terrorism sprouted in West Berlin and not in Ingolstadt or Passau, and Italian terrorism appeared in Milan, Turin and Rome, and not in Venice or Bari. But these reasons are obvious, and no great investment in social science theory is needed to come up with explanations. On the other hand, accidents were frequently of crucial importance. If the presence, or absence, of one leader played a crucial role in the Russian Revolution of 1917, in the Cuban Revolution, or in the rise of Fascism, how much greater is the role of accident as far as the behaviour of tiny groups of people is concerned. This fact was noticed by the authors of the West German study, who correctly noted that 'accident probably played a great role in the drift of young people into the diabolical circle of terrorism.[50] Many others could have joined, but did not. The objective conditions – the 'scene', the housing conditions, the specific character of Berlin – continue to exist, but terrorism has all but disappeared. All of which shows that there are certain probabilities in the development of terrorism, but there is also the realm of accident, and for this reason generalization remains so difficult.

No truly scientific (that is predictive and explanatory) theory with regard to terrorism has emerged, nor has there been any significant progress in this direction over the last decade. Several reasons come to mind. A quantitative index cannot possibly reflect variables such as a loss of confidence or relative deprivation, which defy objective measurement. Most of the research undertaken was ahistorical; it ignored the fact that political violence has occurred in ages of rapid social change, as well as in periods of stagnation. It has happened in countries that were ethnically homogeneous, as well as heterogeneous. Terrorism has been sponsored by the left as well as by the right. There have been basic differences between 'internal' terrorism, Italian- or Turkish-style, and nationalist–separatist terrorism. Frequently, terrorism has been just one weapon among others used by the 'military' arm of a political movement. The very character of terrorism has been subject to change.

A good case can be made for the comparative study of terrorism, provided that certain elementary facts are remembered. Above all, it should be kept in mind that not everything can be compared with everything else. The student of political terrorism has various empirical tools at his disposal, such as data banks, the CIA ITERATE project (International Terrorism: Attributes of Terrorist Events) being perhaps the most ambitious and wideranging. In principle, all such data-gathering efforts should be warmly welcomed. However, an analysis of how data are arrived at shows the problematic character of these undertakings, especially if they aim at cross-national research, as most of them do. There are certain terrorist operations which cannot be hidden irrespective of where they occur. This refers, for instance, to the hijacking of planes, the seizing of foreign embassies or the kidnapping of diplomats. However, the statistics on terrorism include many other categories, such as bombings, letter-bombs, thefts, break-ins, sabotage, arms categories, conspiracy or simple 'threats' and 'hoaxes'. These are vague categories, differently defined in various countries, or not reported at all in most countries outside North America and Western Europe.[51]

This means that truly representative and reliable statistical comparisons of terrorism are *a priori* impossible. While in Western societies even the smallest incidents are recorded, this is not so in other parts of the world, and assertions based mainly or exclusively on statistics that terrorism on a global base has gone up or down are in need of further verification. According to the annual CIA reports based on their own databank, 1978 was the year of the largest number of recorded incidents during the 1970s; a new record high was reached in 1983–4. But 1978 was the year of Iran, and 1983–4 of the deployment of US marines in Lebanon; the sudden increase in the number of terrorist acts can be explained almost entirely with reference to the Iranian revolution and the Lebanese civil war. Terrorism certainly played a notable part in these events, but in the final analysis mass action was decisive for the outcome of changes in both countries. It is an open question whether the attacks against US diplomats and military personnel in these two countries were terrorist operations, or acts of war in a civil war in which normal rules of belligerency no longer applied.

Accident plays an enormous role. If the bomb on a Japanese airliner in 1984 had exploded not at Tokyo airport, but an hour earlier, the annual statistics on victims of international terrorism would have had to be rewritten, as well as the conclusions; Japanese citizens would have figured as the main target.

Generally speaking, the statistics on terrorist events have changed retrospectively every year, as the CIA has expanded the sources from which the data were drawn.* But it is still doubtful how reliable these data are for all but a handful of countries. A great 'data battle' took place in 1981–2, when the Reagan administration put great emphasis on international terrorism and the need to combat it. The number of those killed in previous years did not change, of course, but the number of terrorist incidents increased. If the figures have to be carefully scrutinized, the conclusions have to be placed in their proper perspective. Thus the CIA report for 1980 states that in the year under review, US and Canadian nationals were the most victimized. Yet a careful reading shows that altogether four Americans were killed that year as the result of international terrorist operations, not counting another six who perished in the civil war in El Salvador.

The problems of terrorism statistics point to a wider issue. Much of the analysis of political violence has not only been one-dimensional in time, synchronic rather than diachronic, and exclusively preoccupied with the

---

* See note on terrorist statistics, *Notes*, pp. 334–5.

present age, but it has also implicitly assumed that democratic societies are the norm, and ignored other forms of political power in the modern world. This is at a time when a relatively small part of humanity has the good fortune to live in democratic, or quasi-democratic, societies. This curious parochialism has resulted in assertions that regimes resorting to coercion tend to defeat themselves, which cannot be seriously maintained in the light of historical experience. History may sometimes reward the virtuous, but unfortunately this is not a historical law. Meriam's dictum that 'power is not strongest where it uses violence, but weakest' may or may not apply to certain cases in the past; it is certainly not valid in the twentieth century. The use of the notion of legitimacy has frequently served to obscure some patent facts about the modern world. What is one to say about a quantitative study analysis of 114 countries which indicates that as the legitimacy of governments decreases, internal violence decreases, or about a State Department conference (in the late 1960s) which reached the conclusion that recourse to repression is a self-defeating tendency because the regime thereby loses the appearance of legitimacy? Can it be seriously maintained that the governments of Algeria, Albania and Czechoslovakia (to choose at random from the statistical tables a few countries which experienced no terrorism, except from above) were or are more legitimate than those of England, West Germany, Canada, France, Italy or Spain, which have been the targets of terrorist operations?

It is by no means always clear whether, as is often claimed, instability breeds terrorism or whether, on the contrary, terrorism causes instability. Terrorism is almost always resorted to by small groups of people, whose motives may or may not be connected with observable objective political, economic, social or psychological trends. If it could be shown that the state of affairs in a given country has become altogether intolerable and that the feeling of relative deprivation, oppression and injustice is widespread, it would be only logical to conclude that tens or hundreds of thousands of young people would join the ranks of the terrorists. But this has never been the case; if we talk about a terrorist 'movement', we mean at most a few hundred people among many millions. Nor does it follow that the handful of active terrorists are those most acutely suffering from oppression and injustice. Even physicists find it difficult to account for the behaviour of very small particles in the cosmos. Political scientists may (or may not) explain the rise and decline of mass movements, but they cannot possibly predict the behaviour of a handful of people.

True, there are some general theories of terrorism, but they are of no help to the student of terrorism in the modern world, because they deal with primitive societies, and are furthermore concerned with the rule of terror exercised by the holders of power and exclude movements attempting to overthrow established systems of power.[52] Other hypotheses about terrorism have been helpful in some instances, but not in others. Mention has been made of the concept which regards terror as a symbolic act in an internal war, designed to influence political behaviour. To this, one ought to add the advertising function of terrorism as one of its most important functions. As Bowyer Bell puts it, 'terrorists want a lot of people watching and a lot of people listening, and not a lot of people dead'. The first part of the proposition seems to be truer than the second, because the amount of publicity usually depends on the number of victims. The basic idea goes back to the anarchist philosophy of 'propaganda by deed', but the fact that terrorism is not only violence but also propaganda ought to be restated from time to time.

A historian (Z. Ivianski) has explained the anarchist terrorism of the 1890s with reference to urbanization, cultural crisis, the breakdown of traditional society and mass migration. The same points could be made with regard to Italian and Turkish terrorism in our time. But these factors were of no consequence with regard to Russian terrorism in the nineteenth century, and most of the ethnic–nationalist–religious terrorism in our time. Crozier and Thornton wrote in the 1960s that terrorism is associated with the initial phase of guerrilla warfare, and this was certainly true in a few cases. But in other instances, terrorism came *after* guerrilla warfare had failed (Latin American, the PLO), and in any case guerrilla wars have become very rare in the 1980s.

Hannah Arendt, in her writings about the totalitarian state, has noted a connection between terrorism and protests against the anonymous character of modern society. *Obiter dicta* of this kind sometimes contain a grain of truth; Zenker, the historian of anarchism, made the same point many decades ago. But the anonymity of society does not explain the activities of the IRA, the Basque ETA or the Palestinians; their complaints have a different motive and character. One of the early writers on terrorism, Feliks Gross, made a number of points still valid today – that a terrorist response frequently occurs as a result of foreign oppressive rule or domestic systems perceived as oppressive, but that objective circumstances *per se* are not a sufficient, perhaps not even a necessary condition – for oppression must be perceived as such by a particular group. Gross stressed the importance of ethnic and ideological–political tensions, rather than economic and social conditions, and noted that terror in these conditions may be long-lasting and become institutionalized.[53] There can be no doubt that ethnic terrorism (Irish, Basque, Palestinian) has had considerably broader support, and has been much longer lasting, than the internal terrorism which is not directed against a 'foreign enemy'. Sometimes there is, in addition, a religious element – for instance Catholicism *vs* Protestantism in Ireland, the Catholicism of the Croat opposition in Yugoslavia, the Islamic element in the Palestinian resistance. But the Basques are no less Catholic than the Spaniards against whom they fight; in fact, Catholic priests were the forefathers of Basque nationalism. Some have argued that the conflict in Ulster is not really ethnic or religious in character, but has a strong social component inasmuch as the Catholics are among the poorer sections of the population. However, the strongest resistance to the IRA comes not from the Protestant upper-middle class, but from the Protestant working and lower-middle class. As far as other separatist movements are concerned, the hypothesis of poverty and social backwardness is altogether inapplicable. Euzkadi, the Basque country, was among the richest and most developed in Spain, and the same is true with regard to Croatia in the Yugoslav context, while economic grievances certainly play no role whatsoever in Armenian terrorism.

Two more concepts of terrorism ought to be mentioned, at least in passing. One is the terrorists' own view and that of some of their supporters, that terrorism appears whenever some grave injustice has been done. Therefore, if the injustice is removed, the terrorism will vanish. This sounds plausible enough; happy and contented people are unlikely to commit savage acts of violence. But while this may be true as a general proposition in the abstract, it is seldom true in the real world.* There will always be some people in a society who are bored or aggressive, and who will persuade themselves that the 'system' is intolerable, that any change would be for the better, and that the only possible change is by violent means. West Germany in the 1970s was not a perfect state, but it was certainly freer than it had ever been in the past; this did not prevent a small minority from reaching the conclusion that the situation was altogether intolerable and ought to be destroyed.

Ethnic terrorists may have a good case in their fight for autonomy – though some, admittedly, have a better case than others. But given the mixture of populations, and the migration of recent times, justice for one group would almost automatically mean injustice for another. The Basques and the Corsicans want autonomy, but there are more people in these

---

* It ought to be said to the credit of Soviet authors that this argument, which has found a few advocates in the West, has always been rejected by the Russians: 'The idea that without uprooting the causes of terrorism it cannot be defeated inescapably leads towards giving up the struggle against terrorism' (S.A.Efirov, *Pokushenie na Budushe* (Moscow, 1984), p. 203).

regions who are neither Basque nor Corsican, and who would find themselves minorities in a Basque or Corsican state, if it ever came into being. Justice for the Tamils in Sri Lanka may well mean oppression for the Singhalese; the Protestants in Ulster, for better or worse, do not want to be part of a united Ireland, and neither do the Cypriot Turks want to live in a united Cyprus. If the Palestinian Arab state came into being, this would certainly not put an end to terror in the Arab world. Ethnic groups, with their own national identity, should get as much autonomy as is compatible with the rights of other groups; conflicts should be defused and a spirit of compromise prevail. But there should be no illusions regarding the fact that genuine conflicts do exist and absolute justice cannot be implemented. Not every ethnic conflict has led to guerrilla warfare or terrorism; frequently, problems can be settled on the political level, and in some cases terrorist campaigns have faded – for instance, in Quebec and in Alto Adige (South Tyrol).

At the other extreme is the belief that, without the help of certain sponsors who have a vital stake in fomenting and supporting the terrorists, there would be much less violence. There is no denying that international conspiracies do exist, that considerable sums of money, weapons and logistic help have been provided by a handful of countries. This is a subject to which we shall return in some detail. Though outside help has played an important, and sometimes a decisive, role, it would have been ineffective in most cases unless a terrorist potential existed in the first place. A terrorist movement entirely based on foreign support will have no appeal and is unlikely to last. Mercenaries can be used for individual assassinations, but not for a sustained terrorist campaign.

How important are assassinations? There is no universally valid answer. World history would not have taken a different turn, even if Trotsky had been permitted to live five or ten more years in Mexico; the killing of King Alexander and Prime Minister Barthou in Marseilles in 1934, or of Indira Gandhi in 1985, had no lasting political consequences. It is not even certain whether recent American history would have been radically different if John F. Kennedy had lived. There are exceptions; if Adolf Hitler had been killed in Munich in 1923 there might never have been a second world war. But it is one of the ironies of world history that assassinations seldom, if ever, take place where they would have made a difference. The Hitlers and Stalins are too well guarded.

All of this tends to show that, after two decades of theorizing on terrorism, there are analytical frameworks and general checklists which have a certain value. But there is no comprehensive theory, and quantitative research into the origins and character of political violence has not contributed much to the understanding of terrorism. The more ambitious the project and the wider its scope, the more sweeping are the hypotheses, the more reckless is the quantification of data, and the more disappointing are the results. But this is not to say that the study of terrorist movements is *a priori* unfeasible, and that it should not be undertaken. There is an accidental element in the emergence of terrorism, and for this reason a truly scientific, predictive study is impossible. But it is also true that terrorism is more likely to occur in certain social and political conditions than in others, and that there are interesting parallels between the aetiology and the properties of terrorist movements which have been insufficiently investigated. To compare the Narodovoltsy of the 1870s with the Symbionese Liberation Army or the Baader–Meinhof gang would be a waste of time, but a comparative study of 'urban guerrilla' groups in Latin America or a juxtaposition of past and present national terrorist groups, such as the IRA, the Basque ETA and perhaps the Macedonian IMRO and the Croat Ustasha, could be of considerable interest.

It is possible that the record would have been a little less negative if an idea first suggested in the 1960s had been followed up and expanded. H. Eckstein noted at the time that aetiologies of internal wars were chaotic and unproductive because, among other things, they concentrated on insurgents and ignored incumbents. In real life, internal war results from the interplay of forces and counter-forces, from a balance of possibilities. There are forces pushing towards internal war, but there are also prerequisites for it and obstacles to it.[54] The idea that revolutions were as much due to the incapacity of elites as to the vigour and skill of those challenging the system had, of course, been expressed before; but it had not served as a point of departure for the study of terrorism. Such an investigation, covering the last hundred years, would, at the very least, have saved considerable time and effort and prevented a great many projects that were doomed to failure from the very beginning. It would have shown that terrorism, however justified the grievances of its proponents, has under no circumstances succeeded against an effective dictatorship; it has not managed to weaken it, modify its policies or affect its course of action in any way. If terrorism has had any success at all, it has been against democratic governments and ineffective, obsolete or half-hearted dictatorships. It has been relatively frequent among separatist–nationalist minorities. It was predominantly 'right-wing' in character between the two world wars, and it has more often than not been left-wing, with important exceptions, since the 1950s.

The indiscriminate use of terms such as 'left-wing' and 'right-wing', and the inclination to take political ideology at face value, have made an understanding of the issues involved all the more difficult. Slogans apart, 'left-wing' and 'right-wing' terrorism have more in common than is usually acknowledged. Terrorism always assumes the protective colouring of certain features of the *Zeitgeist*, which was Fascist in the 1920s and 1930s, but took a different direction in the 1960s and 1970s. However, there is usually a free-floating activism underlying both 'left-wing' and 'right-wing' terrorism – it is populist, frequently nationalist, intensive in character, but also vague and confused. Writing well before the recent wave of terrorism, the late G.D.H.Cole, a man of impeccable left-wing credentials, noted that in a later age the anarchist terrorists of the 1890s would probably have been Fascists. Such a generalization may well be unfair towards the anarchists of the 1890s, but it provides food for thought with regard to terrorist politics of a later age. Many Latin American terrorists of the 1960s and 1970s, for instance, would almost certainly have been Fascist had they been born twenty years earlier.

Accepting the disturbing fact that effective dictatorships are immune to terror, but that even the most just and permissive democratic countries are not, it would still be of interest to know why certain democratic societies (Scandinavia, Australia, New Zealand, Switzerland, Belgium, Holland and a few others) have witnessed relatively little terrorism. It will be noted that the population of these countries is small, that these states are predominantly Protestant in character, and that their political culture in recent history has been generally peaceful. As for the non-Communist dictatorships, some have managed with comparatively little repression to subdue or prevent opposition, whereas others have had to invest much greater efforts; this is altogether irrespective of how far the grievances of the opposition were justified. It would be interesting to know why certain national minorities have accepted their fate *qua* minorities, while others have launched into bitter and protracted warfare. In certain cases, separatist terrorism may be explained with reference to outside support, but this is not always true, and in the last resort the outcome of such confrontation depends upon the determination of the terrorists, and that of their opponents. It is doubtful whether studying the impact of economic development on the spread of terrorism will provide many new clues for understanding the phenomenon. The relationship seems to be tenuous in the extreme. Economic stagnation certainly is not a cause of terrorism; industrial development in Ulster was faster than in England in the 1960s, and the same applies to the Basque region in comparison to Spain as a whole. Terrorism in Latin America has occurred in the countries with the highest per-capita income, such as Cuba and Venezuela, and it has been more rampant in developed Uruguay and Argentina than in backward Paraguay or Ecuador.

However, it would not be difficult to think of prolonged and bloody periods of *violencia*, Colombian style, in poor and stagnant societies. To unravel the mysterious character of terrorist movements with reference to general economic trends is like using a giant nutcracker to crush a very tiny object, which might not even be a nut. There should be no illusions concerning what can be discovered about the origins and character of terrorism. All that can be established is that terrorism is more likely to occur in certain circumstances than in others, and that in some conditions it cannot take root at all.

5

The Image of the Terrorist: Literature and the Cinema

Fiction holds some promise for the understanding of the terrorist phenomenon but some words of caution are nevertheless called for. Terrorism has figured prominently in works of modern literature, but the novels, plays, poems and films are of unequal value in providing historical evidence and psychological explanation – some are of no value at all, at least for our purpose.

It is easy to point to certain common patterns in the study of terrorism as practised by political scientists, for there are only a few basic schools of thought, with only minor variations within each trend. The conclusions may not be true, but they are certainly stated in an orderly, unequivocal fashion as befitting a scientific discipline. With the transition from the sciences to the arts we move from the level of relative certainties to the realm of impression. To provide a coherent framework of orderly and lucid argument, to single out common patterns becomes well high impossible. It can be done, but only by singling out certain themes in certain books (or plays or films) at the expense of others. Literature as a source for the study of terrorism is still virtually *terra incognita*. A survey of a hitherto uncharted field may be more profitable at this stage than the attempt to impose a single clear pattern on the stories of individual heroes and villains.

The Outsiders

For the student of terrorism, as distinct from the lover of literature, Ropshin (Savinkov), the Russian ex-terrorist turned writer, is of as much interest as Dostoevski, and Liam O'Flaherty is more revealing than Henry James. O'Flaherty's preoccupation is not with the art of the novel, but with the authenticity of the account. O'Flaherty served with the IRA, whereas the author of *Princess Casamassima* later wrote that his novel 'proceeded quite directly from the habit and the interest of walking the streets of London'. ('Hyacinth Robinson sprung at me out of the London

174

pavement.')[1] The streets of London have a great deal to offer, but there are obvious limits to what they can teach about terrorists, their motives, thoughts and actions. Henry James and Joseph Conrad were attracted by certain specific facets of terrorism, the most dramatic, grotesque or fascinating ones for the student of the human soul. They also used it, as did Dostoevski, to juxtapose destructive terrorism and their own philosophy. Among the most dramatic (and politically most interesting) aspects of terrorism is of course the Judas motive. It has been noted that Mr Leopold Bloom thinks on not less than three occasions of Carey, the small-time building contractor and the chief organizer of the Phoenix Park murders, who became a witness for the prosecution; and this in a book (*Ulysses*) written more than two decades after the event.[2] Terrorism inspired Borges to outline a plot on the theme of the traitor and the hero 'which I shall perhaps write someday'.[3] Betrayal is the main motive in Joseph Conrad's *Secret Agent* and *Under Western Eyes* and countless other novels. It is of course true that few, if any, terrorist groups escaped defectors and traitors in their ranks. However, the heavy emphasis on treason to the detriment of other motives is bound to distort the general picture. It may result in a brilliant work of fiction, but then the novelist is preoccupied with the fate of the individual, whereas the historian pays more attention to social and political movements. Robert Louis Stevenson and G.K.Chesterton were attracted by the grotesque element in terrorism. The hero in Stevenson's *The Dynamiters* is the redoubtable Zero, who wants to bomb Shakespeare's statue in Leicester Square, but instead blows up the home of an inoffensive lady, believing that this will shake England to the heart and that 'Gladstone, the truculent old man, will quail before the pointing finger of revenge'.[4] Gabriel Syme, the writer–hero of Chesterton's *The Man who was Thursday*, is involved in the exploits of a group of anarchists, all of whom are police agents spying on each other. One of the high points of the novel is a chase through London on the back of an elephant.[5] Joseph Conrad made his views on Russia quite clear in his introduction to *Under Western Eyes*. His heroes are the 'apes of a sinister jungle'; one of them, Nikita, is the 'perfect flower of the terrorist wilderness'. Conrad noted of his character: 'What troubled me most in dealing with him was not his monstrosity, but his banality.' The behaviour of the terrorists reflects the moral and emotional reactions of the Russian temperament to the pressure of tyrannical lawlessness, 'which, in general human terms, could be reduced to the formula of senseless desperation provoked by senseless tyranny'. Mr Conrad clearly did not love Russians; nor did he like anarchists, who, without exception, are depicted as degenerates of ludicrous physique or madmen like the 'Professor' in *The Secret Agent*, who always left home with a bomb in his pocket so that at a moment's notice he could blow himself up as well as the policeman trying to arrest him.

Anarchism was a riddle as far as Western European public opinion at the time was concerned. The newspapers reported the existence of a mysterious society of ruthless men, who had as their watchword the murder of monarchs and the overthrow of governments.[6] About the origin of these wild men there was, at best, speculation. Were they socialists or nihilists (whatever that meant), misguided idealists, criminals or madmen? Henry James could not make up his mind. In *Princess Casamassima*, Hyacinth Robinson is a young skilled worker who joins the anarchists because of vague social sympathy (the same motive broadly speaking applies to the princess herself). He commits suicide when asked to murder on behalf of a cause in which he no longer believes. Hyacinth is a mere fellow traveller, 'divided to the point of torture' by sympathies pulling him in different directions. In the same novel a few real revolutionaries such as Muniment and Hoffendall make their appearance and so far as they are concerned it is not at all clear what causes them to act as they do. It has been said that there is no political event in the novel which is not confirmed by multitudinous records (Lionel Trilling). But although Henry James read about Fenians and anarchists, he was, of course, dealing with a world with which he lacked intimate contact. Ricarda Huch, a German neo-Romantic writer, knew, if possible, even less at first hand about terrorists than Henry James and her novel *Der letzte Sommer* (*The Last Summer*), written in 1910, seemed at the time altogether unreal. It is the story of Lju, a young teacher who joins the household of a high tsarist official, one of his functions being the protection of Jegor, the governor. He comes to like and respect the family, but this does not prevent him from carrying out his mission, which is to kill his employer. A most ingenious method is used: the letter 'J' in the official's typewriter is the fuse for a bomb which explodes the moment Jegor signs the letter he has written to his children. This, needless to say, is also the end of the novel.*

A fairly realistic picture of 'propaganda of the deed' emerges from several semi-documentary novels of varying literary quality published around the beginning of the century. Zola's *Paris* (1898) is not one of his outstanding

---

* Sixty-six years later Ana Maria Gonzalez, aged eighteen, worked her way into the family of General Cardozo, chief of the Buenos Aires police, and became a close friend of his eldest daughter, Graciela. The general was warned by his own informants about Miss Gonzalez but disregarded these warnings. She often slept in their flat and eventually planted a bomb under the general's bed. Cardozo was killed; the corpse of Miss Gonzalez, a member of the ERP, was found a few days later in the streets of Buenos Aires. (*New York Herald Tribune*, 22 June 1976.)

works, but it conveys interesting impressions of the age of spectacular assassinations. The reader is subjected to a lecture on explosives, pursues the anarchist through the Bois de Boulogne, and watches his trial and execution.[7] London is the scene of Mackay's *The Anarchists*, which is mainly devoted to disputes between advocates of physical violence (Trupp) and those (Auban) who argue that the terrorists simply play into the hands of the authorities.[8] Mackay, born in Britain, grew up in Germany and wrote in German. His subsequent literary and political career led him far away from the anarchist ideals of his youth. Mackay's novel is now virtually unreadable, but this is by no means true of two other novels, one in Spanish, the other in Czech, which have unfortunately remained quite unknown outside their own countries. Pio Baroja's *Aurora Roja*, which takes place in Paris and Madrid around the turn of the century, is full of discussions about socialism and anarchism, the future of Spain and the use of dynamite. It is a far more vivid novel than Mackay's work, not only because a great many historical figures make their appearance. [9] The hero, Juan Alcazar, is a young painter and sculptor who reaches the conclusion that he must fight for women and children and for all weak and defenceless people. For their sake society must be destroyed and the social fabric brutally cauterized. All ways, all means are good if they lead to revolution, *un Aurora de un nuevo dia*. But the idealistic young hero fails in a world in which base egotism prevails; a comrade says at his graveside that he became a rebel because he wanted to be just (*fue un rebelde porque quiso ser un justo*).*[10]

Even closer to historical events is a Czech novel, Marie Majerova's *Namesti Republiky*.[11] This is the story of a young Polish–Jewish tailor, Jakub Goldshmid ('Luka Vershinin'), who moves to Paris and joins the Libertad terrorist group. Disappointed by the false freedom of French republicanism on the one hand and repelled by the cynical attitude of Libertad on the other, he decides to do something that (he hopes) will trigger off a revolutionary rising. On 1 May 1905, he shoots three officers on the Place de la République. But, far from rising, the masses want to lynch him, and he is saved only by the arrival of the police.[12] Frank Harris's *The Bomb* (1908) is also based on a well-known historical incident – the

---

* The Spanish anarchists of the 1930s in Ramon Sender's novel *Siete Domingos Rojos* (*Seven Red Sundays*) are Tolstoyans and vegetarians, but they have no hesitation about throwing bombs; furthermore, there is a substantial dose of egocentrism in their *Weltanschauung*. Thus, Samar, the anarchist, calls to the 'naked crowds': 'I hate you all! The unhappy and the happy! I hate you and despise you! For the imbecility of your outlook, for the feebleness of your passions.' He dies when the prison is stormed, shouting, 'Freedom or death', for death, 'metaphysically and actually, is the only possible freedom'.

Haymarket bombing in Chicago in 1886. Harris, who lived in America for several years, tells the story of Louis Lingg, one of the main defendants in the subsequent trial, through the device of the recollections of one Rudolf Schnaubelt, who, for the purposes of the novel, is the man who threw the bomb. Schnaubelt, a recent immigrant, joins Lingg's anarchist circle, having been shocked by the exploitation of foreign workers. Lingg says that he believes in force, the supreme arbiter of human affairs: 'One cannot meet bludgeons with words, nor blows by turning the other cheek. Violence must be met by violence.' Much of the material used by Harris is drawn from contemporary newspaper accounts; the anarchists are depicted in a sympathetic light and *The Bomb* has been considered by later critics to be a small masterpiece. It has been given high marks by left-wing reviewers, despite the somewhat unstable convictions of the author.

In the 1890s there was already a vision of terror and counter-terror leading to universal disaster. In Ignatius Donnelly's *Caesar's Column*, New York is burned to the ground in the Brotherhood of Destruction's rebellion against a small oligarchy, which maintains itself in power with a fleet of dirigibles armed with gas bombs. This is a remarkable piece of science fiction considering that the novel was written in 1891. In Part Two of Björnson's *Over Aevne* (*Beyond Human Powers*), Elias Sang, the leader of the striking workers, confronts the brutal and arrogant Holger, representing the interest of 'grand capital'. He too decides to use dynamite as his *ultima ratio*; Sang is killed in the process and Holger crippled, but the last act witnesses a not altogether convincing reconciliation. Björnson did not like anarchists, but he noted that they were the modern martyrs, welcoming death with a smile because they believed like Christ that their martyrdom would redeem humanity.[13]

Terrorism as a moral problem continued to preoccupy some of the leading writers of the 1930s and 1940s. Brecht, as so often, was an exception; he was fascinated by violence and wanted to shock the public. The young comrade (in *Die Massnahme*) has to be killed, because, out of foolish pity and a misplaced sense of honour and justice, he had revealed his own identity and so endangered the whole conspiratorial group: 'Hence we decided to cut off our own foot from the body.' True, the Communists are unhappy ('it is horrible to kill') and before committing the deed they ask the victim's permission.[14]

The dilemma of terrorism reappears in Sartre's *Les Mains sales* (*Dirty Hands*), and Camus' *Les Justes*. The action in Sartre's play takes place in a South European country. Hugo decides to kill Hoederer, the party secretary. Although there are political reasons, his real motives are personal: he wants to be recognized by his comrades not only as a journalist but also as a doer. In the end, after many hesitations, he does kill Hoederer, but only after finding his wife in Hoederer's arms. Hugo knows full well that he too will now be liquidated and that this has given meaning to his action. Though dramatically effective, *Les Mains sales* is confusing; like Brecht's play it was sharply attacked by the Communists, much to Sartre's dismay, but it has remained one of his great popular successes.

Moral issues are more clear-cut in Camus' play which takes Kalyayev's assassination of the Grand Duke Serge as its starting point.[15] The first attempt has failed because Kalyayev did not want to kill the Grand Duke's children who were with him. There is a bitter quarrel among the terrorists: Dora, Annenkov and Voinov justify his action because the new and better world should not be inaugurated by the murder of children. On the other hand, Stepan, the iron Jacobin, argues that in the scale of the fate of humanity the lives of two children weigh lightly when measured against the thousands who will die every year of starvation – unless the system is destroyed. But Kalyayev does not accept the argument: certainly the Grand Duke has to die and he has to do the deed. But murder is wrong; all life is sacred and the crime has to be expiated by the death of the murderer. And so, after the assassination, Kalyayev does not ask for the pardon which he might have been given. When the news of his execution arrives, Dora, his mistress, announces that she will be the next to throw a bomb.

Terrorism in Russian Literature

Dostoevski's *Besy* (*The Possessed*), written in 1871–2, is the best known 'terrorist' novel in world literature and is largely based on the Bakunin–Nechaev affair. Pyotr Verkhovenski, possessed by the idea of destruction, kills the student Shatov, a fellow conspirator, allegedly because he represents a threat of denunciation. In fact, he kills him out of pure boredom. In Ivan Leskov's *Nekuda* (*Nowhere to Go*) (1864), the nihilists, with one exception, are all either infantile characters or degenerates, and in *Na Nozhakh* (*At Daggers Drawn*) (1870–1), they act as 'contract killers', murdering a rich husband to enable his widow to inherit. They promote murder, theft and corruption in every possible way. Leskov was accused by his more progressive contemporaries of having been commissioned to write this novel by the secret police. Leskov claimed that he had simply provided a 'photographic rendering of reality'.[16]

The terrorist motive fascinated many Russian writers of the second half of the nineteenth century: the avant-garde defended the 'nihilists', but, in view of tsarist censorship, this had to be done in Aesopian language.

In contrast the anti-nihilist novels and plays (of Klyushnikov, Markevich, Ustryalov, Prince Meshcherski) were more outspoken. This entire literature is now deservedly forgotten with the exception of the works of Turgenev, whose nihilists were not, however, terrorists.

More intriguing are the books published outside Russia and in Russia after 1905, when censorship was considerably relaxed. Serge Stepniak-Kravchinski, a leading Narodovolets, was the author of several indifferent novels, but he also wrote the classic account of the terrorist movement of the late 1870s.[17] *Underground Russia* was clearly a labour of love; his heroes, the leading members of the Narodnaya Volya, are without exception idealists of the highest moral standards.* Stefanovich was an atheist, but his closest relationship was with his father, an old village priest. Lisogub is described as a 'saint', Vera Zasulich as a woman of 'great moments and great decisions', and Sofia Perovskaya as a revolutionary of 'iron will, iron self-discipline who always went first into the fire'. True, there are passing references to Ossinski's feverish excitement and to the fact that he loved women and was loved by them. It is also made clear that Klements was a charismatic leader but quite unsuited for work in a small conspiratorial group. On the whole, however, there were few shadows in this story of heroic and virtuous people, and there is reason to assume that the picture is true to life: the men and women of the Narodnaya Volya were indeed most attractive human beings. This also emerges from other contemporary accounts. Young Vera Barantzova, in Sophia Kovalevsky's novel, follows her terrorist husband to his Siberian exile: 'Are you weeping for me?' she said with a cheerful smile. 'If only you knew how I pity those who are left behind.'[18] There is always the motive of sacrifice by the chosen few and the belief in final victory. For example, one novel by Stepniak closes with a declaration that though the hero, Andrei Kozhukhov, has perished, the cause for which he died still lives: 'It goes forward from defeat to defeat towards the final victory, which in this sad world of ours cannot be obtained save by the sufferings and the sacrifice of the chosen few.'[19] The Narodovoltsy appear in a similar light in Leopold Stanislav Brzozowski's *Plomienie* (*Flames*), which has remained almost totally unknown in the West.[20]

Where Conrad saw nothing but an 'imbecile and atrocious answer of a purely Utopian revolutionism', Brzozowski invoked high moral pathos

---

* *Underground Russia* was basically an autobiographical account, the first of a great many. The recollections of Morozov, Frolenko, Vera Figner, Gershuni, Savinkov and others are one of the most important sources for the study of Russian terrorism. This is also true of some other terrorist groups; the autobiographical accounts of Natan Yalin-Mor and Geula Cohen are of greater interest than the novels written about Irgun and LEHI.

when describing the thoughts and actions of the handful of young heroes who challenged the overwhelming power of the tsarist regime. Where Conrad saw a strange conviction, that a fundamental change of heart must follow the downfall of any given human institution ('these people are unable to see that all they can effect is merely a change of names'), his fellow Pole was dazzled by the vision of the emergence of a new man and a new society. Brzozowski's novel is in the form of a diary kept by a young Polish nobleman, Michael Kaniowski, who throws in his lot with the revolutionaries of the 1870s. Nechaev, Mikhailov, Zhelyabov, Goldenberg and many others make their appearance, sometimes under hardly veiled *noms de clef* (Tichonravov = Tikhomirov), and the author, on the whole, sticks fairly closely to the historical record. The reader follows the hero on his revolutionary grand tour to the Paris Commune, to the workers of the Swiss Jura and to Italy. But above all it is the political, cultural and social life of Russia of the period which constitutes the canvas of the great epic, which ends with the release of Kaniowski from the Schlusselburg fortress where he has been a prisoner for many years. *Flames* was clearly a labour of love: the Narodovoltsy are seen, as in so many other accounts of the period, as knights engaged in a hopeless struggle on behalf of a cause that will triumph only at some future date: the blood of the martyrs is the seed of the church. The religious elements of the novel are reflected in chapter headings such as *Dies Illa* or *Dolori et Amori Sacrum*. Despite certain literary weaknesses, *Flames* is one of the most vivid accounts of the Narodovoltsy ever written and perhaps the most inspiring, yet the book never had the success it deserved. Written in Polish it remained a work of marginal interest in Brzozowski's native country, because it dealt with the revolutionary tradition of the oppressor nation. The Russians were reluctant to look for inspiration to an author whose own credentials were not above suspicion; some years after the novel was written, Burtsev, the indefatigable sleuth of the Russian revolutionary movement, declared that the novelist had been a tsarist police spy. But Burtsev, though the first to make it publicly known that Azev had been a police agent, was not infallible: Brzozowski's friends all stood by him and defended him against the accusations.[21] Burtsev's informant was Bakaj, an official of the Okhrana in Warsaw with conceivable personal motive for denouncing Brzozowski. Could *Flames* have been written by a police informant? The affair continued to preoccupy Polish literary circles throughout the 1920s and 1930s, and although the evidence is perhaps not conclusive, there is some reason to assume that Brzozowski (who died in Florence in 1910) may have acted at one time as a police informer.

All this refers to the heroes of the 1870s and 1880s. The Russian terrorist movement of the early twentieth century was less fortunate in its authors – but it is also true that reality had become more complex and that the motives of terrorists were often less obvious. True, there were admirers of the movement from Gorky to Leonid Andreyev, but those with more intimate knowledge provided less flattering pictures. Boris Savinkov (Ropshin), the one-time leader of the terrorist organization of the Social Revolutionaries, is a good example. When planning assassinations in 1905, he was not plagued by doubts about the rightness of his cause; the terrorist–hero of his novel four years later is a very different character, describing himself as bored by his own thoughts and desires: 'People and their lives bore me. There is a wall between them and myself. Let love save the world. I need no love. I am alone. Damned be the world. . . .'[22] Yet at the same time there is a preoccupation with moral issues: the choice, says the hero, is either to kill all the time or never to kill at all. Why should he be eulogized for having killed the police chief, and why should the colonel be a villain for hanging the revolutionaries? Did not he too act out of conviction and not for material gain? And, if so, who made these rules? Marx, Engels and Kant, who had never killed a man in their lives?

In Savinkov's *Pale Horse*, a story in diary form, each of the five heroes is driven by different motives: Vanya is a religious fanatic; Genrich is a socialist; and Fyodor is an 'emotional terrorist' who opted for revolutionary violence, having seen a woman killed by the Cossacks during a riot; Erna participates because she loves George, the main hero, who does not believe in anything or anyone. *The Pale Horse* created a minor storm in Russian left-wing circles and was severely condemned by Savinkov's erstwhile comrades. The storm became a major scandal in 1913 with the publication of Ropshin–Savinkov's second novel *To chevo ne bylo*.[23] Now the moral chaos is absolute; beneath a Nietzschean veneer there is only emptiness, crime and betrayal. The leader of the group, Dr Berg (Azev?), a police agent, is killed by Abram, a Jewish terrorist.[24] The whole atmosphere is one of hopelessness: the struggle cannot possibly be won, the government is bound to prevail. Savinkov's subsequent fate is of some interest. He served in the French army during the First World War, was for a short time governor-general of Petrograd under Kerensky in 1917 and committed suicide or was killed in a Soviet prison in 1924, after allegedly having organized terrorist operations against the Bolsheviks.

The Insiders

Savinkov was a unique case among the Russian writers of his day: French and English literature on anarchism, with some notable exceptions, reveals more about those who wrote it than about those who engaged in it. Irish literature is far more rewarding in this respect.

In Irish plays, novels and short stories one is never far from the bomb and the sniper – and this applies to Yeats and Joyce, as well as to Brendan Behan, who at sixteen arrived in Britain on the eve of the Second World War with a few bombs.[25] It appears in Yeats' 'Easter 1916' and his 'Rose Tree', that needs but to be watered to make the green come out again, or in the 'Sixteen Dead Men' loitering there to stir the boiling pot. What Auden said about Yeats ('Mad Ireland hurt you into poetry') is perhaps even more true for the writers of the following generation. Sometimes the allusions are obscure (as in Yeats' 'Second Coming') and the experts are still hard at work interpreting them. Nor are they always complimentary; in *Ulysses* and *Finnegans Wake* the heroes of a past age usually appear in a lurid light, but then Joyce was never the paradigm of an Irish patriot. The 'terrible beauty' is in any case balanced by a great many ugly things. But Yeats too was irked by the fact that the 'Young Irelanders' treated literature as subservient to political doctrine, as an instrument for politics. And it has been noted that when Yeats justified the Easter Rising he did so on other than moral grounds – 'A terrible beauty is born', not a terrible virtue.[26] There is Sean O'Casey's moving epitaph to the heroes of 1916:

> They had helped God to rouse up Ireland: let the people answer for them now! For them now, tired and worn, there was but a long, long sleep; a thin ribbon of flame from a line of levelled muskets, and then a long sleep. . . . But Cathleen, the daughter of Houlihan, walks from now, a flush on her haughty cheek. She hears the murmur in the people's hearts. Her lovers are gathering around her, for things are changed, changed utterly:

A terrible beauty is born, poor, dear deadmen; poor W. B. Yeats.[27]

But there is little of that pathos in O'Casey's plays: the women are fanatics; the men fight because they are afraid to admit their fear or, worse, in order to plunder.[28] Above all, almost everyone is given to boasting. In *The Shadow of a Gunman* Minnie, the admiring young woman, asks Davoren ('poet and poltroon'): 'Do you never be afraid?' Davoren: 'I'll admit one does be a little nervous, at first, but a fellow gets used to it after a bit till, at last, a gunman throws a bomb as carelessly as a schoolboy throws a snowball.' But eventually Minnie gets out in the streets, shouts 'Up the Republic' at the top of her voice and is killed, while Davoren goes on hiding.[29]

The case of Jack Cliteroe in *The Plough and the Stars* (1926) is also quite revealing: 'Why doesn't Cliteroe have anything to do with the Citizens Army?' 'Just because he wasn't made a Captain of. He wasn't goin' to be in anything where he couldn't be conspicuous. He was so cocksure of being made one that he bought a Sam Browne belt an' was always puttin' it on an' standing' at th' door showing it off in.' There was a public scandal at the first performance and O'Casey had to leave Dublin for London. In *Juno and the Paycock* (which also became a film in 1930), young neurotic Johnny Boyle is executed by IRA fanatics for having betrayed his neighbour to the police. The Irish writers, playwrights and poets were awkward witnesses, perhaps doubly so because they knew the terrorists so well. Most of them came to agree with what O'Leary had said on an earlier occasion about the dynamiters: 'There are things no man should do, even to save a nation.' Yeats' *Cathleen ni Houlihan* includes the old woman's promise to those who die for Ireland: 'They shall be remembered for ever.' In this play Ireland appears in the guise of an old woman but in the end she is transformed into her true likeness: 'Did you see an old woman going down the path?' 'I saw no old woman, but a young girl and she had the walk of a queen.' When in 1939 Yeats lay dying he remembered these words with a certain horror and asked himself the question, 'Did that play of mine send out certain men the English shot?'[30]

The real heroes in Sean O'Casey's plays and in O'Flaherty's novels are (non-combatant) women; the men are dubious types more often than not. Sean O'Faolain's Leo O'Donnell is an anti-hero and Commander Dan Gallagher in Liam O'Flaherty's *The Informer* tells his girlfriend that 'they talk at headquarters about romanticism and leftism and all sort of freak notions. What do they know about the peculiar type of hog mind that constitutes an Irish peasant?' Yet O'Flaherty, Frank O'Connor and Sean O'Faolain all fought in the ranks of the IRA (the last-mentioned was its director of publications) and O'Casey was a Communist of sorts. Whatever their professed politics, most terrorists are really mystics and the idea of martyrdom obsesses them. It is the central theme in one of Liam O'Flaherty's novels. Crosbie, the martyr, is a strange mixture of mystic and Nietzschean, recalling some of Savinkov's heroes. He is, in his own words, 'a light shining in the darkness', he needs no guide to heaven:

I'm waiting on the mountains in Europe and the whole of Christendom is waiting for the resurrection when the brazen gods of money and sensual pleasure shall be burned in the dust and Christ, our Saviour, again enthroned as the King of Kings. There will be peace between all men. There will be no hunger, no disease and the only suffering will be the craving of souls for union with God.[31]

All this from a terrorist engaged in indiscriminate killing after the war against the foreign occupier has already been won.

The question of motive reappears time and again in the books written by insiders. There are the conventional explanations: to serve people, to save the nation, to redeem mankind. But there is also the bad conscience of the intellectual as described by Regis Debray. Frank, his hero, never finds real identity with the guerrillas; he joined them because he had pangs of conscience.

Où étais-je le jour où des paysans en sandales donnèrent l'assaut à Dien Bien Phu? Le jour ou Frank Pais s'écroula, criblé par les flics de Batista sur un trottoir de Santiago de Cuba? ... Tout occupé à siroter un vin de pays, à caresser les seins d'une brune un peu fugace. ...

There is much talk about Gramsci and Lukacs, but in the end: '*Peu m'importe en effet la destination – socialisme ou autre – voire même le sort des autres voyageurs. Pourvu que ça roule.*'[32]

When the Macedonian revolt broke out around the turn of the century, Pejo Javorov was a young Bulgarian poet groping for the meaning of life. 'All my interior world is in ruins,' he wrote to a friend; 'I am lost if I do not find a new religion to inspire me.'[33] He found it in the ranks of the IMRO and saw action on Ilin Den; he wrote some fine poems as a result. The enthusiasm lasted for a year or two, and then he was back to depression, hopelessness – and symbolist poetry in the French style.

The motive of the intellectual who vainly yearns to be a terrorist appears also in Arthur Koestler's *Thieves in the Night.** Joseph is told by the terrorist commander that he has that intellectual squint which makes him see both sides of a medal – 'a luxury we cannot longer afford. We have to use violence and deception, to save others from violence and deception.' But despite his moral scruples, Joseph asks permission to take part in an action – 'even if only one'. It is so much easier for the young boy who, when asked what made him join the Freedom Fighters, answers: Exodus twenty, one, Deuteronomy nineteen, one, 'Block out the remembrance of Amalek from under heaven.' 'Thine eye shall not pity.' 'I will make mine arrows drunk with blood.' Koestler's Joseph is a democratic socialist who turns to terrorism because he has realized that a nation of conscientious objectors cannot survive and that 'if we left it to them we shall share the fate that befell their comrades in Germany, Austria, Italy and so on'. Hence the necessity to speak 'the only language universally understood from Shanghai

---

* Koestler was not, of course, an 'insider'. But he knew and admired Jabotinsky, who had been until his death in 1940 the supreme authority of Irgun. He also met some of the Irgun and LEHI commanders.

to Madrid, the new Esperanto that is so easy to learn – the gun under the leather jacket'.

The Bible provided constant inspiration to Avraham Stern ('Yair'): God himself is a warrior (*Ish milkhama Adonai zvaot*), armed struggle and bomb throwing are acts of praise to God (*Halleluya be Kravot ubepezazot*). The kingdom of Israel, the central and somewhat vague concept in Yair's thought, will be reached only by way of the valley of the shadow of death. The theme of death appears in almost every one of Stern's poems, including the anthem of LEHI: 'Unknown soldiers without uniform, we have joined for our whole life – around us only horror and the shadow of death.'[34]

Joseph, Koestler's hero, graduates from democratic socialism to terrorism. Gyorgy Kardos, another novelist of Hungarian origin, wrote a novel showing what made one terrorist give up the armed struggle – not weakness, but because he found fulfilment in another way of life. The action takes place in mandatory Palestine in 1946 or 1947. David is on the run: the British chase him as a terrorist; Irgun is after him for failing to carry out an assignment. He hides on the farm of one Avraham Bogatyr, and his contempt for those who have opted for non-violent resistance gradually turns into admiration.[35]

The Irish, Irgun, LEHI and Debray's hero Frank were bothered by a great many problems, but the question of purpose was not among them. The struggle against oppression was their overriding concern; right and wrong were certainties, they were fighting for a sacred cause. They would have been incapable of understanding the (mainly platonic) advocates of terrorism in America of a later generation, who saw their heroes in Bonnie and Clyde; indeed, any such argument would have appeared blasphemous. The very concept of destruction as instant theatre would have been demeaning if not altogether incomprehensible.* This was the language of pseudo-terrorists. Yet in a strange way the nihilistic syndrome was by no means new and it appeared on the right as well as among the left. Chen, the terrorist in Malraux's *Condition humaine*, has ceased to believe in humanity long ago: 'I do not like mankind to be so indifferent towards all the suffering.' Yet in the end he throws himself with his bomb in front of the car in which he mistakenly believes Chiang Kai-shek is driving.

The question of purpose never bothered Ernst von Salomon and his comrades who assassinated Rathenau.[36] 'What do you want?' they were asked. 'We could not even understand the question. We did not act accord-

---

* 'When in doubt, burn. Fire is the revolutionary's god. Fire is instant theatre. No words can match fire. Burn the flag, burn the churches. Burn, burn, burn.' Barely five years later, Cleaver and Rubin were changed men, burning the gods of violence they had once worshipped.

ing to plans and well-defined aims.' They were certainly not fighting 'so that the people should be happy'; they were propelled into action by some inner force. From one excitement they went on to the next. Kern, the leader of the group, told them that he had been dead since 9 November 1918 – Armistice Day, the day of national disgrace. All that remained was the work of destruction: 'We want the revolution. Our task is the "push" not the seizure of power.'[37] When asked what kind of motives they should admit to if caught by the police after the assassination, Kern answered, half bored, half amused: 'Oh, God, how little does it matter. Say that he was one of the Elders of Zion or that he let his sister marry Radek – who cares. . . .' They feared one thing only – that the dead Rathenau would suddenly appear as a witness in their trial. . . .

The nihilistic mood pervades much of the right-wing literature of the early 1920s. Schlageter, in Hanns Johst's play of the same name (dedicated to Adolf Hitler in 'loving admiration') is not troubled by metaphysical questions; since the French are occupying the Ruhr, it is the duty of every German patriot to resist them in every possible way – ethical problems do not bother the former soldier. If he has doubts at first, they concern the effect of terror:

SCHLAGETER: Politics can't be created with one bundle of Ekrasit, that's just playing at terror; every action must have a purpose. . . . Twenty-five pounds of dynamite won't free so much as a square yard of German soil. Individual *Sturm und Drang* without mass support is nonsense.
ÜBERNITZ: No, our utter desperation should sweep away the slave mentality, the profit motive, and all petty bureaucracy.
SCHLAGETER: If so, all Germany will be a cemetery.
ÜBERNITZ: Better a decent cemetery than a fifth-rate old clothes shop.
SCHLAGETER: That's a matter of opinion.

But eventually he joins his friends in terrorist operations:

What does it matter whether I die of a bullet at twenty, or of cancer at forty, or of apoplexy at sixty. The people need priests who have the courage to sacrifice the best – priests who slaughter. . . .[38]

Arnolt Bronnen's heroes, the Freikorps fighters in Upper Silesia, are cut from the same cloth. Bronnen, once a friend of Brecht and, like him, attracted by violent action, moved sharply to the right. To the Nazis, however, he always remained somewhat suspect and, while using him, they kept him at arm's length. The same is true of Hans Fallada, who wrote a semi-documentary account of the bomb-throwing peasants of Schleswig-Holstein and who hoped that their violent actions would draw attention to their plight.[39]

In Salomon's story, which has been mentioned earlier, Otto, the leader of a Communist fighting group, makes an appearance. He is a sympathetic young man, a fighter like the right-wingers to whom he shows a natural affinity: 'Soon we were friends.' Such apparently incongruous friendships were by no means rare; activists, after all, have a great deal in common. In his autobiography Milovan Djilas relates that in prison the Communists soon found a common language with the Croat Ustacha, 'national revolutionaries and fanatical believers'. They had a common enemy – the government – and they despised the democratic opposition for its lack of daring. The Communists certainly did not approve of the links of the Ustacha with Fascist Italy and with Hungary, but neither did they condemn them.[40] Theirs was a 'conditional friendship'.

For the Narodnaya Volya, the Irish or the Macedonians, sexual problems did not exist or, if they did, there was general agreement not to discuss them in public. Underground life in theory, if not always in practice, involved members of the group refraining from any close relationship; some even preached asceticism: everything that would deflect the terrorist from his main assignment was reprehensible. Whether this was repression, sublimation or simply the reaction of a generation with different values and standards is a question would could no doubt be discussed at great length. Sexual problems have indeed figured very prominently in the writings of contemporary terrorists, mainly in the United States and in Germany, and the explosion of a bomb has come to be regarded as something like an ersatz orgasm. Michael Baumann, a former member of a terrorist group, has even maintained that the choice or rejection of terrorism was 'programmed' – the individual's unavoidable reaction to the presence or absence of a fear of love: most terrorists, if not all, escaped from that fear into total violence. From his own experience, as well as from the writings of Malatesta and Fromm, he reached the conclusion that revolutionary (meaning terrorist) practice and love could not coincide.[41] He may well have been right with regard to the European and North American terrorism of the 1960s and 1970s; whether one can draw more far-reaching conclusions from statements of this kind is less certain.*

---

* Some of the novels and plays mentioned above inspired the film-makers. Among the fruits were *Under Western Eyes* (*Sous les yeux de l'Occident*), with Jean-Louis Barrault (France, 1936); *The Secret Agent* (directed by Hitchcock, 1936); Sartre's *Les Mains sales* (1951). The most impressive film was without doubt John Ford's *The Informer*, based on Liam O'Flaherty's novel, with Victor McLaglen in the role of Gypo Nolan, who betrays his comrades. There had been a silent version of *The Informer* directed by Arthur Robinson in 1929. John Ford made yet another film with an IRA background, *The Plough and the Stars* (1937), based

on Sean O'Casey's play, but this was much less successful than *The Informer*. Other memorable films with an Irish civil war background were Carol Reed's powerful *Odd Man Out* (1947), starring James Mason; *Ourselves Alone* (1936), shown under the title *River of Unrest* in the United States; and *Shake Hands with the Devil* (1959), with James Cagney. During the Second World War two films on the Irish underground were produced in Nazi Germany, *Der Fuchs von Glenarvon* (1940), and *Mein Leben für Irland* (1941). More recently Gillo Pontecorvo's *The Battle of Algiers* and Costa Gavras' *State of Siege* offer much of interest to the student of terrorism. The former, a very impressive film, 'offers a blueprint for other struggles and revolutions', teaching 'urban guerrilla warfare' (Piernico Solinas, *Gillo Ponte-corvo's 'The Battle of Algiers'* (New York, 1973), IX). This film of 'rare ideological consistency' can be shown in France but not in Algeria, for street demonstrations and the shouts 'Free Ben Bella' might well be misunderstood in view of the fact that Ben Bella was in Algerian prisons for twelve years. The latter film is a quasi-documentary study of the Tupamaros which, however, takes considerable liberties with the historical record – a countrywide vote is taken before the execution of the American hostage (Dan Mitrione). The very first 'terrorist' feature film I have been able to discover was Protazanov's *Andrei Kozhukhov* in 1917, with Ivan Moshukhin, known in Hollywood in later years as Ivan Mosjoukine, as the chief hero. This is based on Stepniak-Kravchinski's novel *The Road of a Nihilist* of 1889, of which more below. There was an even earlier short American film *Queen of the Nihilists* (c. 1910), but it dealt with escape from prison rather than with terrorist operations. A bowdlerized version of Dostoevski's *Possessed* was produced in 1915 in Russia; also directed by Protazanov with Moshukhin in the title role (Protazanov was the first Russian producer of distinction). Andreyev's *Story of Seven Who Were Hanged* was produced in Russia in 1920, and there was a film on Stepan Khalturin in 1925. A film on Nechaev was envisaged in the 1920s but the idea had to be dropped for ideological reasons. This is almost the sum total of films on nineteenth-century Russian terrorism, which both during and after Stalin's regime has remained a very delicate subject – very much in contrast to the Russian military tradition from Alexander Nevski to Kutuzov which has provided Soviet film-makers with a wealth of material. Terrorist operations were the subject of many films with a Second World War background, most dramatically perhaps Andrzej Wajda's *Kanal* (1957) and *Popiol i Diament* (*Ashes and Diamonds*) (1958). The setting of *Kanal*, the fate of a unit of the Armia Krajowa forced into the sewers of Warsaw, was used in Aleksander Ford's *Piatka z ulicy Barskiej* (*The Five from Barska Street*). Fritz Lang's *Hangmen Also Die*, on the assassination of Heydrich, also might be mentioned in this context. *The Molly Maguires* (1969), with Richard Harris and Sean Connery, was shot on location in Eckley, Pennsylvania, to give it greater authenticity; Eckley was said to be the ugliest town in America. Some critics complained that they found it impossible to identify with either warring side. This may be an excellent testimony for the historical accuracy of the film but it did not make it a box office success. There was a renewed interest in terrorism in the late 1960s and early 1970s, as manifested, for instance, in Chabrol's *Nada* or in Alan Resnais' *La Guerre est finie* with Yves Montand, the story of an old Spanish revolutionary who finds it difficult to accept the changing world: *Trente ans sont passés et les anciens m'emmerdent.* ... The same motif, the inability of the anarchist released from prison in the 1880s to adapt to the new political mood, recurs in Taviani's *San Michele* (1971). There was a recent Swiss film on Nechaev in which the hero, contrary to historical evidence, has an affair with Natalie Herzen; a French film on the exploits of the Bonnot gang in pre-First World War Paris; the Taviani brothers in Italy produced films on various nineteenth- and twentieth-century terrorist groups and Brazilian film-makers operating in Chile (under Allende) and in Mexico chose similar topics. Some of these films were not widely shown and there are by now, in any case, far too many of them for enumeration. Some are listed in Guy Hennebelle, *Cinéma Militant* (Paris, n.d.) and in *Guide des films anti-impérialistes* (Paris, n.d.).

Terrorism and Propaganda

There is a literature on terrorism that sees its sole function in uplifting morale. The fight is total, the aim the destruction of the enemy; seen in this light, literature is also a weapon in the sacred struggle. A Bulgarian novel, critical of IMRO, would have been sacrilege about the turn of the century;* an Arab novel or play showering less than fulsome praise on Fatah or the PFLP would be treason. However deserving the cause, books inspired by such terrorist groups can seldom or never be called literature, nor will they tell us much about the terrorists themselves. For, if there are no inner conflicts, no troubled consciences, if the heroes have no private lives and no weaknesses, if, in short, everyone does his duty, the only remaining problems are technical in character and more effectively tackled by military experts than by novelists or playwrights. This is true even with regard to the most accomplished novels produced by Palestinian writers such as Ghassen Khanafani, the editor of *Al Hadaf*, a periodical sponsored by the PFLP, who was killed by a booby trap in his car. His main theme is that 'there is nothing to say. ... This matter can be settled only by war' (*Return to Haifa*, 1970).[42] That Palestinian authors show no detachment in their novels is perhaps only natural; what makes their novels less than credible is the absence of a wish to understand the enemy. The Palestinians are described as fearless patriots and handsome paragons of every manly and womanly virtue; the Jews more often than not are pimps and ugly prostitutes making love in mosques and graveyards when they are not engaged in killing Arab civilians as sadistically as possible.[43] Moen Basisu provided an up-to-date version of Samson and Delilah, with Samson as a brutal Israeli officer defeated by Delilah, the self-sacrificing Arab patriot. In another novel (*Sahra min Dam*) even the Arab informer realizes the wickedness of his ways and joins the resistance. True, there is frequent criticism of non-Palestinians who show little sympathy for the cause and visit the refugee camps as a tourist's curiosity (A. Sharqawi). Just as the villains in these novels and plays are unconvincing, so are the heroes, and some Arab critics have asked: if all Israelis were pimps and prostitutes, how could they have defeated us? The only Jews appearing in a somewhat better light are those of Oriental ('Arab') origin, which is a little ironic because it is precisely among these circles that goodwill towards Arabs

---

* There were anti-IMRO novels, including one or two good ones, but they were written by Turks or Greeks. *Bomba*, a classic of modern Turkish literature, describes the misfortunes that befell the family of a Bulgarian freedom fighter who decided the time had come to give up the armed struggle. (See Omar Seyfeddin, *Bomba* (Constantinople, 1913); Ion Dragumis, *Martiron Ke iroon ema* (Athens, 1907).)

is strictly limited, whereas the attitude of 'European' Jews has traditionally been one of indifference rather than hate.*

What has been said about Arab literature on Palestinian terrorism refers, *mutatis mutandis*, to much of Third World writing on terrorism. There were some exceptions in India, no doubt because public opinion was divided on whether terrorism was the most effective means in the struggle against the British, and also among some French-speaking North African writers who live in France.

In Latin America there is a long-established tradition of revolutionary songs, the *cancones de protesta*, to which guerrilla and terrorist groups have made a significant contribution in recent decades.[44] There was a similar tradition in pre-revolutionary Russia; some of the members of Narodnaya Volya, such as Morozov and Klements, wrote and composed songs which became quite popular. They ranged from ironic comment on Drenteln, the head of the tsarist political police, to funeral songs for comrades who fell in the struggle for freedom, expressing the conviction that one day an avenger would arise – variations on Virgil's *Exoriare aliquis*....[45] At this point the literature of and on terrorism begins to merge with its folklore, an intriguing topic but not the subject of the present study.

It has been shown how the terrorists of the nineteenth and twentieth centuries made their way into world literature just as Brutus and Wilhelm Tell, Judith, and Charlotte Corday had attracted writers of earlier generations and for similar reasons. Sometimes it was the liberating deed rather than the ethical dilemma which fascinated the writers: Judith and Wilhelm Tell were in no danger of moral censure. With Caesar we move on to more uncertain and psychologically more interesting ground: the admiration for the great statesman is tempered by criticism for the man who destroyed the tradition of freedom, and the tragedy of Caesar is also the tragedy of Brutus. Charlotte Corday is the first truly modern terrorist heroine; a vile reactionary in the eyes of the Jacobins, she is a figure of great

---

* Hebrew literature on the terrorist groups of the 1930s and 1940s is not of outstanding interest. The most ambitious novel from a literary point of view is Haim Hazaz's *Bekolar ehad* (freely translated: *Together* (Tel Aviv, 1962)), a *roman à clef* describing the last days in prison of two young terrorists, Feinstein and Barsani, who blow themselves up on the eve of their execution. Yigal Mossenson's *Derekh Gever* (*The Way of a Man* (Tel Aviv, 1950)) has the early post-war period as its background and the ambivalent attitudes of members of the Haganah towards the 'dissidents' (i.e. terrorists). Some interesting and psychologically revealing novels by writers of a younger generation have appeared recently – for instance, Yizhak Ben Ner's *Mischakim bechoref* (*Games in Winter* (Tel Aviv, 1976)).

courage and angelic purity for all those who dreaded and despised the extremists. Her personality expressed itself in a political act, but politics do not explain her personality; Jeanne d'Arc had acted on what her voices told her, but what had inspired Charlotte Corday? The great German writer Jean Paul, writing less than a decade after Marat's assassination, saw the roots of her behaviour partly in her education and reading: the heroes of ancient Rome had been her great example. But intellectual adventures alone were clearly insufficient as an explanation: a great many young people had read Plutarch, but she had killed Marat. Perhaps it was because as a woman she was not free to develop her strong personality, or because she was not distracted by (or had not found fulfilment in) love or marriage. Jean Paul's *Halbgespräche* appeared in 1801: it would be a long time before nineteenth- and twentieth-century terrorists were treated with similar perception. Novels and plays are not an ideal vehicle for long ideological discussions, as various abysmal failures demonstrated (Mackay). But literature was ideally suited to deal precisely with those vital issues for which there was no room in the learned treatises on the history of anarchism and kindred political movements: the question of motive, the analysis of character.

This proved to be exceedingly difficult in the case of the anarchists, for they constituted a subculture (as it would now be called) on the fringes of society, far removed from the circles in which writers usually moved. Those who wrote about them drew, like everyone else, on newspaper reports rather than on personal experience. The anarchist figures in the novels of the period are usually unconvincing, strange or sick people, marginal characters, outsiders, eccentric or perverse. All this may have been true, but it was not very satisfactory, nor did it make for a clearer understanding of why these people had banded together and engaged in actions which shocked society so profoundly. Was it only their tortured inner life and some Herostratic impulse which impelled them to go out and knife kings and presidents and throw bombs in cafés and parliaments? They were clearly dissatisfied with society and wanted to take a kind of revenge. But at this point personal and political motives somehow merged, and the how and why usually remained a mystery. Furthermore, some of our anarchist heroes and villains had not been mistreated by society: their childhood had been reasonably happy; they were by no means disadvantaged, so that personal revenge was certainly not their central motive. Nor were they particularly unbalanced or wicked or ambitious – which made it all the more difficult to understand them.

With a few exceptions the anarchists appeared as sinister or pathetic miscreants in the literature of the period – fascinating, perhaps, but hardly ever true to life, and in the last resort inexplicable. A decade or two were to pass until anarchists became more credible: the initial shock had passed (and so had the anarchists–terrorists), a younger generation of writers had appeared, more familiar with their habits and ideas, more inclined to regard them as well-meaning but misguided failures rather than as *hostes humani generis.*

It was easier for the Russians to understand their own terrorists. True, there was the same generation gap, the same consternation as young people began to adopt a strange life-style, propagate incomprehensible ideas and finally engage in dastardly actions such as killing the tsar. But they were flesh of their own flesh, the generation gap was not vast. And if Dostoevski found terrorism in 1871 a sinister enigma, this was at least in part due to forgetfulness; two decades earlier he would have found it much easier to understand the Narodovoltsy. The interpretation of terrorism in the Russian novel varied, of course, with the politics of the writer. Hence the total rejection in the works of Dostoevski and Leskov, for whom it was nothing less than the anti-Christ, the incarnation of all evil, the negation of all values. Hence, on the other hand, the boundless admiration of the progressive intelligentsia; in this climate of adulation a psychological analysis of the personal motives of these heroes and martyrs would have been as much out of place as an investigation into the sex life of a saint in an official church history. Again, some time was to pass before the initial excitement died away and a calmer approach made it easier to rethink and refeel the motives which had induced young people to engage in desperate actions.

These were no déclassé Bohemians or outcasts of society, but, quite often, the offspring of the elite; clearly their idealism could not be denied, they had no personal accounts to settle with society. On the other hand some specifically Russian features were evident: this, after all, was not the first generation of rebellious young intellectuals. But whereas their predecessors had talked revolution for nights on end, they were the first to act and did so with a frenzy quite un-Russian: Oblomov had passed away. But this had not come easily to them, nor were they really 'nihilists'. On the contrary, they were very much preoccupied with moral questions and had an ethical code of behaviour stricter in many ways than that of established society with its dual standards. Only a few among them were strong and resolute characters and even they wavered and quarrelled; sometimes they were unhappy and occasionally they gave up or even betrayed the cause. In short, they emerge as credible human beings from Russian literature.

Savinkov's books shocked his left-wing contemporaries not merely because these were the novels of a man just about to renege on the cause. The critics could not possibly accept the unflattering accounts of men and women who had daily risked their lives in the struggle against tsarist despotism. Many of them had, in fact, made the ultimate sacrifice. Perhaps the critics were right, perhaps the heavy emphasis on personal passion and prejudice distorted his descriptions, perhaps one who had lost hope could not do justice to those who had not. But Savinkov had really been a leading terrorist, whereas his critics – were critics. They had never made a bomb, let alone killed anyone, and the most important decision facing them was the topic of their next essay.

Eventually the critics realized that though there were wonderful young men and women among the terrorists, the new generation was not quite comparable to that of 1880. Among the Narodovoltsy there had been Hamlet-like figures and some foolish young men who thought they could outwit the police while collaborating with them. But there had been no Azev. After the arch-traitor had been unmasked, the old innocence of terrorism had gone, it was no longer a subject on which one could write with ease. But the personality of Azev, too, remained an impenetrable mystery. It would have been easy to solve the enigma had he just been a police spy out to get the maximum of money from the chiefs of the Okhrana. But he was an agent on the greatest scale, he took their money and frequently delivered. Yet he was not their tool; he had political aims and ambitions of his own which by no means always coincided with the views of the Okhrana. He played a double role so complex that its threads could never again be unravelled once the game was over.

The books on the Russian terrorists of 1905 were the first to raise some of the issues that were to recur ever after. They showed how difficult it was to separate real heroism and the lust for adventure, steadfastness and routine, how in certain conditions the borderline between loyalty to the cause and betrayal becomes almost invisible. They showed that most terrorists were bound to ask themselves sooner or later whether the game was worth the candle, and not merely because of the many losses in their ranks. Above all, they raised the moral question of the right to kill.

This dilemma did not trouble many later writers on nationalist terrorism. There were exceptions, above all in Irish literature with its ambivalence about terrorism. 'No people hate as we do,' wrote Yeats. But he also said that everything he loved had come to him through the English language. For a while, towards the end of the last century, the political and the literary movements in Ireland coincided or ran concurrently, but later there was a parting of ways – the philistine character of Irish society and the hostile reception of their works drove some of the writers from Ireland

and deeply wounded others. Most of them were to rally to the cause in 1916 and again in 1919, but with the establishment of the Free State there came a new wave of introspective criticism. Examples have been given of the spirit of candour with which former terrorists wrote about their past, their friends and their comrades-in-arms; it made the Irish literature of the 1920s and 1930s uniquely revealing for the comprehension of patriot and reformer alike.

The uses of fiction as a source for the understanding of terrorism are not unlimited. A witness recently advised a US congressional committee that Joseph Conrad's *Secret Agent* should be made mandatory reading for every police officer in the United States: 'Conrad tried to get into the human mind of an anarchist living in London in the early 1900s. If a police officer could read this, he could start understanding how much a revolutionary is really motivated by political ideology and how much by individual needs.'[46] Such recommendations, though well meant, are, of course, a little naive. Police officers (and not only they) will benefit from reading a book that has become a classic of world literature. It is equally clear that they will not draw any immediate profit for coping with the problems facing them in their work. Conrad's hero, Adolf Verloc, it will be recalled, is a police agent; after his death Winnie, his widow, looks for help. Ossipon, the anarchist and womanizer to whom she turns in utter despair, disappears with her savings and drives her to suicide. There have been Verlocs and Ossipons at all times and in all countries, but an analysis of their thoughts and actions, however intrinsically interesting, is of no help in understanding why a young man or woman may join a Latin American terrorist group, the IRA or Abu Nidal. Nor does it explain what makes them commit acts of heroism and betrayal, what induces them to continue a hopeless struggle or to surrender. The writer, it must be emphasized once more, deals with the individual and his motives, putting the stress on boredom or ambition or selfless devotion as he sees fit. He cannot possibly provide an identikit picture of the 'typical' terrorist. There are, in any case, infinite varieties, and as terrorism has changed during the last century, so have those practising it. Everyone is impelled by considerations transcending the self as well as by motives of a personal character. Fiction cannot offer a master key to the soul of the terrorist; the most one can hope for is to detect certain common patterns in the character and mental make-up of the *dramatis personae*, who acted as a group at a certain time and place. To accomplish even this modest task a great deal of empathy, psychological understanding and creative mastery is needed. Once this has been accepted a great deal can be learned about terrorism from contemporary fiction, provided these books, plays and films are not regarded as manuals for the study of terrorism, aspiring to photographic exactitude and universal applicability.*

The Last Decade

The almost constant preoccupation with terrorism throughout the 1970s and the 1980s brought about a spate of novels on the subject, nowhere more than in the English reading world. For reasons which are not entirely clear, popular writers in other countries, at least as much affected by terrorism as England and the United States, were less fascinated by the topic. This refers to Western Europe, the Arab countries, and Israel, as well as to Latin America. The reason was perhaps that England and America had been the cradle of detective stories and thrillers; thriller writers were always on the lookout for new twists and angles. The underworld of terrorism contained all the ingredients needed for a good read: conspiracy, tragedy, treason and above all sustained tension. Many well-known writers of our time, from Graham Greene to Heinrich Böll, from Mary McCarthy to Doris Lessing, have dealt with the subject at one time or another.[47] These novels usually tell us more about the authors than about the psychology or the deeds of the terrorists, but this had also been true with regard to Dostoevski and Conrad. Lessing's ironical description about how members of a London left-wing commune gradually slide into violence is the most negative, whereas Böll, at least in two of his novels, detected redeeming factors in the violent men and women.† Most of them had probably never met a real-life terrorist, or witnessed a terrorist attack. While experience and factual knowledge is not necessarily a precondition for a great work of art, terrorists who are the product of a fertile imagination

---

* There are, of course, many more novels, plays and films of interest to the student of terrorism than have been mentioned here. Some have been inaccessible to the author; for instance, Ramon Sempau's *Los victimarios* (1906), an important document for the history of Spanish anarchism around the turn of the century. Sempau was an active terrorist; sentenced to death by a military tribunal, he was later acquitted by a civil court. Others were written in languages with which I am not familiar – novels on Bengali terrorism, for instance, or on the Rumanian Iron Guard. Of late a great many novels have been published dealing with the most recent phase of terrorism; Klaus Rainer Röhl's *Die Genossin* (Munich, 1975) is an unflattering portrait of the late Ulrike Meinhof by her ex-husband. Another interesting documentary novel dealing with the kidnapping of the FLQ is Brian Moore's *The Revolution Script* (London, 1972).

† Böll and other Western writers such as Grass, Sartre, Simone de Beauvoir and Moravia were criticized not only in their native countries but also in Russia for 'foolish sentimentalism' in view of their attitude towards the terrorists for whom they found mitigating circumstances. Soviet writers also criticized German academics such as Iring Fetscher and M. Greifenhagen, and, of course, some of the theologians, for being unduly lenient towards terrorism. See for instance S. A. Efirov, *Pokushenie na Budushe* (Moscow, 1984), pp. 51–2.

alone are of greater interest to the student of literature than to the student of terrorism. Böll dealt primarily neither with the Meinhofs and Baaders nor with the innocent bystanders, but with the vague sympathizers, those affected by the anti-terrorist backlash, brutal police practices and a yellow press operating without inhibitions and conscience. Lessing, on the other hand, sees mainly the negative sides in her description of the gradual involvement of members of an (anarchist) group, well meaning and not at all bloodthirsty, in the sinister machinations of outside wire pullers, and the transformation of innocents into militants who are no longer masters of their own fate.

Böll's opinions were predictable in view of his general attitude towards contemporary German society. Fritz Tolm, the owner of a newspaper empire stalked by terror, is forced to admit that his sons who opposed the 'system' were right, whereas he, who tried to fool it, was wrong, and had failed.[48] Lessing is less predictable; she was herself a committed member of the left, but her book, triggered off by a real happening, is a bitter attack against the pseudo-revolutionaries:

who like the idea of violence, brutality, murder, torture, get a thrill from it, spend a great deal of time thinking about these things, imagining themselves in various extreme situations. ... Generations after generations of young people (I was for a time one of them) put their imaginations at the service not of the actual problems facing their country, but of dramas derived from elsewhere. ... It was they who delighted in the excesses of the Cultural Revolution; who will greet the news of any extreme political action with satisfaction, regardless of how often these excesses are proved to be disasters for the countries they occur in.[49]

Lessing concludes that such people judged political events by the emotions they felt about them, which made them easy prey for demagogues, and from which they could easily drift into terrorism.

But, above all, terrorism came into its own in mass literature. It had figured in popular novels from time to time even before 1970, but after that date it became a veritable avalanche. Many hundreds of such books were written on every level of sophistication, from the quasi-highbrow psychology of a Le Carré to the primitive actionism of the pulp novel.[50] Indeed, so much was written about so little that in the early 1980s a certain decline could be observed. All the dramatic possibilities had been exhausted. The number of basic situations was limited; they could be counted, broadly speaking, on the fingers of two hands. Most popular was the nuclear theme: a group of terrorists – Arab, Israeli or other – searching for the ultimate weapon, by theft (James Rowe) or frontal attack on a nuclear arsenal, or by abducting a scientist or a group of scientists who could build a weapon of this sort (Nicholas Freeling). Alternatively, the terrorists already have the weapon (twenty-four of them in Lawrence Delaney's case), and they are about to detonate it in London (G. Household, Anthony Trew) or in New York (Larry Collins and Dominique Lapierre, Ian Todd). Fortunately, it is only a question of time before they are caught, or until one of them feels some last-minute pangs of conscience. There are several variations on the means of delivery used. It can be an oil tanker (William Katz), or the Good Year television blimp over the Super Bowl (Tom Harris, *The Black Sunday*).

The perpetrators are frequently Third World crazies or cold-blooded freelancers operating on behalf of a state which sponsors terrorism. In some cases, the terrorists are right-wing super-patriots who aim at the Olympic Games (Robert P. Parker, *The Judas Goat*, and Joseph di Mona, *The Benedict Arnold Connection*). In Ted Allbeury's *The Only Good German*, a right-wing terrorist group is run from a Hamburg brothel. Quite often it is not made clear what the terrorists want, except that they are a sinister group of people – for instance, in Helen MacInnes, *The Hidden Target*. But one should not be too hard on the authors, since in fact terrorists do not always know what they want. In another novel, a group of schoolboys produce their bombs in a cellar (James Mills, *The Seventh Power*).[51] In some cases, the weapon of mass destruction is not nuclear, but a deadly toxin (Alastair MacLean, and botulism in Peter Way's *Belshazzar's Feast*), or a chemical substance.[52] Arab extremists usually prepare an attack against Tel Aviv (Eric Ambler; Gerald Seymour, *Red Fox*; Anthony Price, *The Alamut Ambush*) or another Western target. The United Nations General Assembly is a favourite target among the novelists (Sandor Frankel and Webster Mews), but even more popular is the US secretary of state (Robert Katz, M. Albert) or his wife (Marvin Kalb and Ted Koppel).[53] Frequently, the political intentions of the terrorists are sweeping but obscure, and in at least one case they want to kill all the world's leading statesmen (Ludlum's *The Matarese Circle*), but are prevented by the CIA and KGB who, for once, co-operate. In Brock Yates' *Dead in the Water*, the target is the Canadian prime minister, in Lionel Black's *Arafat Is Next*, the head of the PLO, and in Aricha-Landau's *Phoenix*, it is the late Moshe Dayan. More often than not the terrorists belong to the extreme left, but in a few cases they are of the extreme right (Forsyth's *Day of the Jackal*, Jack Higgins' *Wrath of the Lion*, Colin Forbes' *The Stone Leopard* and Douglas Fairbarn's *Street 8*, which takes place among anti-Castro militants). In some cases, the terrorists are modelled after the famous Carlos, but since obviously not one of the authors (including Ludlum, *The Bourne Identity*, 1980) ever interviewed Carlos or his colleagues, this kind of literature owes everything to imagination.[54]

Irish terrorism has traditionally been much nearer to the experience of English authors than the Middle East, and many of the novels with an IRA–Belfast background are more realistic than those dealing with Arabs or unnamed 'international terrorists'.* This applies to Gerald Seymour's *Harry's Game*, as well as Bill Granger's *November Man* (with the Mountbatten murder as the background), N.Stahl's *The Assault on Mavis A* (a mass prison escape), J.Higgins' *The Savage Day* (on how the IRA gets its arms supplies), James Reid's *The Offering* (with a priest as its hero), as well as some others and most recently M.Power's *The Killing of Yesterday's Children* (1986).[55] A few novels were written from a far-left point of view, such as Dominic McCartan's *Operation Emerald* (London, 1985).

Other countries, except only those in the Middle East, have not attracted the same measure of interest, though there is hardly a single one which has escaped attention altogether. In Michael Wolfe's *Panama Paradox*, the Panama canal is attacked. Black terrorists want to take over America in a thriller which also offers an early description of involvement in the drug trade (Richard Condon's *The Whisper of the Axe*).[56] The Argentine death squads appear in Warren Kiefer's *The Kidnappers*, while the Tupamaros kidnappings are described in David Chandler's *The Casablanca Opening*. Philip Atlas's *The Underground Cities Contract* takes place in Turkey, and there are several novels describing terror in the Soviet Union (Derek Lambert, Oliver Jacks and Kenneth Royce, David Lippincott).[57] Some of the operations are more far-fetched than others. In David Lippincott's novel, Lenin's corpse is taken hostage; in Peter Ritner's *The Passion of Richard Thyme*, Harvard's Widener Library is the target; and in William Marshall's *Gelignite*, it is a Hong Kong cemetery. Considering the fact that the Montoneros at one stage stole the corpse of General Aramburu, one should not be quick to dismiss grave robbing for lack of verisimilitude.

Combined operations involving several terrorist groups are the subject of Seymour's *The Glory Boys*, in which the IRA and the PLO try to kill an Israeli scientist in London. Other terrorist operations described in some detail are the storming of a hotel (Norman Hartley), the hijacking of a plane (Adam Hall, Gerald Seymour), the hijacking of a supertanker (Frederick Forsyth, *The Devil's Alternative*), and many others.[58]

This genre is mainly of a certain interest not for its realistic content, but because the popular image of terrorism is largely shaped by writings of this kind, which have a far wider circle of readers than non-fiction. But there are also books which reveal real background knowledge. In

---

* One of the best examples is Gerald Seymour's *Field of Blood* (London, 1985), which describes how Sean Pius McAnally, PIRA militant, turns into a super-grass.

addition to the books on the IRA already mentioned, one could add Alan Burn's *The Angry Brigade*, based on conversations with members of this shortlived anarchist group in London. The South African Broederbond never tried to kill Prime Minister Vorster, but the author of *Rogue Eagle*, James McClive, shows familiarity with the South African background in sharp contrast to many writers who try to compensate with a wealth of technical detail about pistols, bombs or logistics for the inherent psychological implausibility of their stories.[59]

Among the realistic novels on terrorism, several Spanish books ought to be singled out, such as Angel Amigo's *Operacion Poncho*, based on a real occurrence, the mass escape from Segovia prison, while Martin Ugalde in *Las Brujas de Sorjin* deals convincingly with the perennial theme of the traitor when an ETA cell suspects that an informer is among its ranks.[60]

There are few German and French novels dealing with terrorism, whereas an American publishing house has provided terrorist stories for young readers (from 'twelve and upwards'), such as K.C.Tessendorf's *Kill the Tsar* (Pantheon, 1986), based apparently on the assumption that one cannot tell youngsters the violent facts of life soon enough.[61]

One of the most interesting novels (*Terroristerna*) takes place in Sweden. Written by two well-known thriller writers, Maj Sjöwall and Per Wahlöö, it deals with the attempted assassination of a visiting US senator – apparently Barry Goldwater – by an eighteen-year-old girl. She shoots, instead, the Swedish minister of justice. The authors, who were members of the Communist Party, show understanding for her action. Her fiancé, a Vietnam war deserter, had committed suicide after his return to America. As for Rebecca, the murderer, her lawyer claims that her act was politically motivated, though she did not belong to any political party – it was a protest against the general corruption of capitalist society. The victim – the minister of justice – bore an unmistakable resemblance to Olof Palme, who was shot and killed in Stockholm twelve years later. Elsewhere, we have drawn attention to a scurrilous book (by Scascia), which anticipated the murder of Aldo Moro by a few years, and in Eric Ambler's *The Levanter* there is an uncanny resemblance between a Christian Lebanese owner of a boutique, who belongs to a radical pro-terrorist group, and a real-life owner of a boutique, who in 1986 was suspected of having smuggled a bomb aboard an American plane in either Cairo or Athens.

Compared with the enormous literary output, there have been relatively few films with a terrorist background. Several novels have been adapted for the screen, such as *The Day of the Jackal* (Fred Zinnemann, 1973), dealing with the OAS attempt to assassinate De Gaulle; others have been less successful, such as Le Carré's *Little Drummer Girl*, which is too complex and convoluted for a mere two hours' showing. Other films based on novels include *The Kidnapping of the President* (Canada, 1980) by Ch. Tempelton, in which the president is kidnapped during a visit to Ottawa and held in an armoured car loaded with explosives. Mention has been made of *Black Sunday*, where a mad pilot collaborates with terrorists trying to kill the Super Bowl spectators, only to be frustrated by an Israeli agent. The semi-documentaries include *Under Siege* (US, 1986), in which a small group of terrorists throw America into confusion and the head of the CIA is under pressure to declare that the terror is Iranian-sponsored. He is not certain, however, and resists the pressure. American film-makers have not given high priority to terrorism, on the assumption that viewers wish to see such films only in moderation. Political considerations may also have played a certain role in this context, and this is also true with regard to European films. Several Italian terrorist movies were envisaged or even started, but had to be suspended (among others, those by Franco Solinas, Salvatore Samperi and Giuliano Montaldo). The story of *Ogro*, directed by Gillo Pontecorvo, is typical case. It deals with the assassination of Carrero Blanco; and since Blanco was Franco's successor, the political issues seemed straightforward and the murder apppeared altogether justified. Yet by the time work on this film was in progress, Aldo Moro had been kidnapped and subsequently killed; this had an indirect impact on the making of the film. Thus the message of *Ogro* became more involved; Txabi, a former priest and one of the main Basque plotters, kills two Spanish policemen who are both clumsy and innocent, and as a punishment he himself is mortally wounded.[62]

Other Italian terrorist films include Dino Rigi's *Caro Papa*, in which the millionaire father is gravely injured as the result of a terrorist operation carried out by his son, and *Il Belpaese*, in which an Italian returning to his native country after many years is utterly baffled by the general chaos. Among the German films on this topic *Germany in Autumn* is the most famous. Some of the leading directors of the day co-operated on this picture, such as Schlöndorff, Fassbinder and Kluge. But there is no clear message. The producers were obviously saddened by the suicide of the heads of the RAF, but at the same time had only limited enthusiasm for their cause – they were anti-anti-terrorists rather than sympathizers. This is also true with regard to Volker Schlöndorff's *The Lost Honour of Katherine Blum*. Fassbinder had on another occasion provided a fairly devastating critique of the false values and the radical chic of the terrorists (*The Third Generation*). *Stammheim*, produced in 1985, was a semi-documentary about the trial and the suicide of the leaders of the RAF. While showing sympathy towards the accused, it angered the radicals for not being sympathetic enough.

A Spanish film shown in the US under the title *Black Brood* is about a right-wing terrorist group masquerading as a church choir; in it a young man has to kill a woman he likes as part of his rite of initiation. While television has frequently discovered mitigating circumstances for terrorists, this has not been true with regard to feature films. 'Terrorism', said Émile de Antonio, 'simply isn't a popular subject for Hollywood, because they don't have the brains to understand the complexity that might make it interesting.'[63] But Antonio, whose *Underground* (1970) took a sympathetic view of the Weather Underground, and who presumably did have the brains to understand the complexities, did not succeed any more than Hollywood. All in all, terrorism has attracted film-makers less than disasters, science fiction, horror or even espionage, and this is true not only of Hollywood but also of film industries in other countries. One could speculate endlessly about the reasons. While terrorists certainly make a great deal of noise, the human element involved is not particularly interesting. On the whole, terrorists are neither very attractive nor are they monsters; most of them seem to be bored and boring people. True, there are the classic situations of stalking the victim and of betrayal. But there are not many possible variations on these themes; had Hitchcock lived he might have thought of some fresh angle. Without a new Hitchcock, the terrorist genre does not seem to have much of a future.*

---

* One of the reasons for the relatively small number of terrorist films was probably the fact that most of those made were both artistic and commercial failures, thus deterring film-makers and sponsors. They include, in addition to those already mentioned, *The Day of the Dolphin* (1973), *The Enforcer* (1976, with Clint Eastwood), *Exposed* (1983, in which Nastassia Kinski falls in love with a screwball violinist played by Rudolf Nureyev), *The Human Factor* (1975), *The Killer Elite* (1975, in which Japanese terrorists want to assassinate Chinese leaders), and *Rollercoaster* (1979, with George Segal), which has an original non-political idea – the blackmailing of amusement-park owners.

6

Terrorism Today I:
Nationalism and Separatism

The post-war wave of urban terrorism began in the late 1960s and has now continued, on and off, for two decades. It has occurred in many countries and taken many different forms but, broadly speaking, it can be divided into three or four different subspecies, depending on whether we regard state-sponsored terrorism as a separate category. First, there is separatist–nationalist terrorism, such as in Ulster and the Middle East, Canada and Spain, an old acquaintance from past ages in new clothes. Second, Latin American terrorism, once the trendsetter and, in many respects, a phenomenon *sui generis*. The continent has seen more civil wars, *coups d'état* and assassinations than anywhere else, but systematic urban terror was an innovation. There was urban terrorism in North America, Western Europe and Japan, which grew out of the New Left or, to be precise, the failure of the New Left in West Germany, Italy, America and Japan. The terrorists of the New Left mistakenly assumed that methods used in Latin America would work elsewhere, or that Latin American conditions could be created artificially in the more developed countries, and this at a time when these methods had not even been too effective south of the Rio Grande. Lastly, there has been in various parts of the world terrorism of the extreme right, or semi-Fascist in character. These groups, in contrast to those of the left, seldom co-operated with each other nor did they have, with a few exceptions, international sponsors.

It was perhaps accidental that the emergence (or re-emergence) of these strands of terrorism coincided in time, for basically they had little in common. Neither the IRA nor Fatah owed anything to the New Left; Latin American terrorism certainly developed quite independently. As the terrorist wave gathered momentum, there was a certain amount of co-operation between terrorist movements (on which more below) and also some cross-fertilization: West German terrorists, for instance, freely admitted that they had been influenced by the example of the Tupamaros and learned from their experience.[1] Other groups took the battle for Algiers as their model, even though it had ended in failure for the insurgents.

There were important differences between contemporary terrorism and previous terrorist waves. Above all, there was the fact that most of the terrorist groups of the 1960s were left-wing in orientation or, in any case, used left-wing phraseology in their appeals and manifestos.

The use of certain slogans is admittedly not sufficient evidence of the real character of the political group. This is not to imply that left-wing slogans were always used to deceive the public; most 'left-wing' terrorists no doubt genuinely believed that they were the heirs of the French Revolution, of Marx and Lenin. But it is also true that their policies differed in essential aspects from those of the traditional left. They were certainly radical in the sense that they opposed the 'system', the 'establishment', that they wanted violent change. But their belief in the historical mission of a small group of people had more in common with voluntarist and idealist traditions than with Marx; they were not radical democrats, and the cult of violence propagated by them resembled Fascism rather than socialism.

Another major difference was the intervention of foreign powers, directly or discreetly, who provided help for terrorist movements. There had been some precedents before the Second World War, with Italy and some Balkan countries as the main wire-pullers. But this had been the exception; it was only in the 1960s that this new form of warfare by proxy really came into its own, thus opening entirely new possibilities for terrorism. Operations in third countries became far more frequent; in past ages it had been the rule that Russian terrorists would limit their attacks to Russia, and the Irish to Ireland (or England). In the 1960s, on the other hand, Palestinians would operate in Paraguay or France; Japanese terrorists in Kuwait, Israel and Holland; Germans in Sweden or Uganda. This new multinational terrorism was bound to create occasional confusion with regard to the identity of the attackers and the purpose of their action. Last, mention has to be made of the new weapons and techniques which had not existed before.

While political violence became intellectually respectable in the 1960s in some circles, the ability of the authorities to counteract terrorism was more restricted than in the past. Up to the Second World War, terrorists who had been apprehended by the authorities faced, at best, lengthy prison terms. With the dawning of the permissive age, it became far less risky to engage in terrorism, except in less enlightened countries. Where terrorism would have been dangerous, it was rare. If the judiciary was reluctant to impose draconian penalties on its own citizens, the foreign terrorist could expect to get away with light sentences if his case reached trial at

all, for his imprisonment would have exposed the 'host' country to retaliation, to fresh terrorist attacks, to the seizing of hostages and to blackmail.
Few Western leaders were willing to accept this risk even if their own
nationals had been killed; the outcome of the contest between the philosophy of the bomb and the philosophy of the permissive society was predictable. Thus the general climate seemed more auspicious from the
terrorists' point of view than ever before: if there were no mass support
and no prospect of gaining it in the foreseeable future, there were other
factors that seemed to work in favour of terrorism. But to some extent
these advantages were deceptive, as the terrorists found out to their cost.
It was relatively easy to provoke a Latin American government and to
discredit it, but it was far more difficult to survive the backlash of a military
dictatorship. Even in Western countries terrorism became distinctly unpopular the moment it ceased to be a nuisance and caused real inconvenience
to society. Once this point had been reached, governments had no difficulty
in introducing more stringent laws to combat terrorism. These laws did
not always have the expected results because there were fairly narrow limits
to the measures that could be applied by the security services in a democratic
society, even in an emergency. Above all, the international character of
the new terrorism provided backing and reassurance, both moral and material, so that terrorist groups would continue their campaigns where in the
past they would have given up the struggle.

These generalizations apply to most terrorist movements but not to all;
conditions, as stressed more than once in this study, varied from country
to country. To establish these distinctions one has to look more closely
at the main varieties of terrorism.

Any classification of terrorist groups is bound to simplify a complex reality. It is impossible to provide for terrorism the kind of typology Cuvier
and Linné gave to biology in the nineteenth century. Terrorism knows
no eternal fixity of species. Some groups which began on the extreme right
(for instance the Palestinian PFLP, the Montoneros, and the Colombian
M 19) ended up on the far left at least as far as their phraseology was
concerned. Others which used and continue to use Marxist–Leninist slogans
contain in fact nihilist, anarchist or even Fascist elements.

Our typology, like all others, is bound to be deficient because it does
not mention terrorist trends which played a considerable part in the past
(such as the anarchist or anarcho-syndicalist groups), nor does it consider
certain religious elements in contemporary terrorism. The problem facing
the student of terrorism is that these religious–fanatical elements seldom,
if ever, appear in a pure state; they are usually intermingled with nationalist
motives and social protest. One wishes that the borderlines between the

various terrorist groups were better defined than they are, but frequently they are vague, and sometimes even non-existent; to bring artificial order into chaos does not contribute to our understanding.*

On a deeper level of analysis, one could perhaps after all find an explanation for the simultaneous re-emergence of terrorism in various parts of the world in the late 1960s. The very same impulses which gave rise to the New Left provided fresh impetus, albeit indirectly, to the activities of various national minorities, particularly in Europe and North America. To some extent it was, of course, also a generational issue: the impatience and greater militancy of new generations which made their appearance on the political scene during that period, and whose members were dissatisfied with the caution and moderation of their predecessors, whose main formative experience had been the Second World War.

The nationalist–separatist groups engaging in terrorism have shown on the whole considerably greater staying power in recent decades than all others. The Baader–Meinhof gang, the Italian Red Brigades, most of the Latin American groups, even the Turkish terrorist movements which were so strong at one time, have come and gone whereas those expressing nationalist aims have stayed the course. True, a few such as the Quebec FLQ or the South Moluccans in Holland have vanished. On the other hand some new groups have joined the ranks of the fighters for 'national liberation', including the Tamils in Sri Lanka, the Sikh extremist groups and the Armenian ASALA. True, even they have suffered setbacks and were subject to internal divisions. But in contrast to the 'internal' terrorists of the 'left' and 'right', they had a broader base of support, a distinct national or religious group, on whose help they could count for recruitment, money and other kinds of assistance. The nationalist terrorist groups are usually the 'military' arm of a radical political movement. But the division of labour is kept secret, which makes it possible for the 'politicians' to dissociate themselves from

---

* Wolfgang Mommsen differentiates between terrorist groups of social protest, neo- and pseudo-Marxists and anarchists on the left, and also between national emancipation movements and movements of integral nationalism (W. Mommsen and G. Hirschfeld, *Social Protest, Violence and Terror* (London, 1982), p. 394 *et seq.*). As far as ideology is concerned, these differences no doubt exist, but in actual political (and terrorist) practice it is often impossible to discover them with the naked eye. The ideological proclamations of terrorist groups (especially when they concern their internationalist democratic, 'progressive', non-sectarian character) are more often than not deliberately misleading, or the result of self-deception. Some groups, such as the Shiite extremists or the Israeli zealots, have made no secret of their true inspiration but such frankness is by no means the rule.

certain terrorist actions which failed, or which were particularly gruesome, or which killed the 'wrong' victims.

Certain general observations apply to most nationalist terrorists. They frequently adopt radical programmes and slogans, sometimes Marxist–Leninist in style. To be a nationalist *tout court*, to call a spade a spade, is no longer quite fashionable.[2] This trend is more pronounced in some cases than in others; it applies, for instance, less to the mainline Palestinian groups than to the Basques. But it is important to bear in mind that even where Marxism–Leninism is most pronounced, this is usually a synonym for anti-Americanism or anti-Westernism or a general populistic mood. The *basic* motivation is almost always nationalist–sectarian: slogans of 'proletarian internationalism' are merely a matter of paying lip-service. Not much scratching is usually needed to establish this fact, for the Leninist veneer is thin. The colour of skin, or national identity, or religion are the decisive factors, not the 'class origin' of the opponent. The nationalist terrorists will seldom admit this much, just as they always reject the terrorist label: they are engaged in conducting a people's (or people's liberation) war and not a terrorist campaign.

Beyond this point generalizations become difficult.

The insurrections in the Philippines and Sri Lanka have been predominantly guerrilla in character and they ought to be mentioned only in passing in the present context. The ANC has engaged in terrorist operations, but only after decades of political work and it is so far of relatively little importance compared with the other manifestations of insurgency. The blacks constitute the majority of the population in South Africa, whereas ASALA is fighting on behalf of an Armenian state in Turkey which has never existed. This demographic fact is bound to dictate the form in which the struggle is conducted. The great majority of IRA operations have taken place inside Ulster, whereas the Palestinians have been active more often than not outside Israel and the West Bank territories; civil war conditions did not prevail in Israel, and the Palestinians could not hope to establish in Israel the infrastructure necessary for a sustained terrorist campaign. On the other hand, the Palestinians have been doing much better politically than most other such groups, simply because they have had considerable support throughout the Arab world. Some terrorist groups have been strictly selective in the choice of targets; thus the Armenians, for a number of years, attacked only Turkish government representatives, mainly diplomats, whereas most of the victims of Palestinian groups such as Abu Nidal have been neither Israeli nor Jewish. Considerably more Arab leaders than Israelis have been killed by Arab militants. Differences in the constitution, motivation, milieu and purpose of the various terrorist groups are so wide that they must be considered separately in order to point to their specific character.

Northern Ireland

The history of the struggle for Irish independence is well known and need not be retold in detail. As some Irish nationalists saw it, it did not end with the establishment of the Free State in 1921. It had to go on until the six counties of Northern Ireland were reunited with the rest. There was a resurgence of terrorism just before the outbreak of the Second World War, and again in the 1950s and 1960s. These were mainly guerrilla raids across the border, or attempts to seize weapons from army camps or police stations, and more often than not they were unsuccessful. But it is interesting to note that even operations which failed had a morale-boosting effect: they showed that the struggle went on. The same is true with regard to the development of other terrorist movements. The battle of Karame became a symbol for Fatah heroism because the Palestinians at long last resisted an Israeli raid and inflicted casualties on them, even though they were defeated in the end.

The terrorist struggle developed gradually out of a civil rights campaign in Northern Ireland. The Catholic population was politically and socially underprivileged, many of the key jobs in industry, banking and other fields went to Protestants; there was blatant discrimination in housing, and as a result of elaborate gerrymandering, Catholic political representation was well below what it should have been. More or less peaceful Catholic demonstrations in 1968–9 turned violent, largely as the result of Protestant counter-demonstrations and attacks. Inside the Protestant camp the leaders who favoured modest reforms such as Prime Ministers O'Neill and Chichester-Clark were outflanked by the more radical, demagogic elements such as the Reverend Ian Paisley.

Rioting and widespread communal violence broke out in both Belfast and Londonderry, and British troops were first brought over in August 1969. Ironically, the main purpose of their arrival was to protect the Catholics, by whom they were, on the whole, welcomed. Even the IRA had some good words for them at the time. The clashes took place at first between the army and the Protestant paramilitary forces; the Reverend Ian Paisley was to compare the British troops with the SS.

The situation deteriorated during the following two years, mainly as the result of sectarian clashes between mobs in Belfast. Protestant gangs attacked the Shortstrand area – much of the fighting centred around St Mathews, a local Catholic church. Catholic mobs took on the army, which was carrying out a search for arms in the Falls Road sector, which led to shooting, the killing of civilians and the imposition of a curfew.

In the meantime, important changes occurred inside the IRA which had been taken more or less unawares by the outbreak of the troubles. The leadership of the IRA was at the time in the hands of Communist fellow travellers who stuck to the relatively moderate 'three-stage theory'. The first stage was to work for unity – which meant, in practical terms, democratic reforms rather than taking up arms which would inevitably lead to a further deepening of the chasm between Catholics and Protestants; the struggle for independence was to be postponed until the second stage.

If the official IRA had had its way much bloodshed would have been prevented, but it did not take account of the militant mood of the Belfast Catholics under siege who did not receive the IRA protection they had hoped for against Protestant attacks. There was also a demand for more action among the younger IRA members and some of the old-timers who had always believed in direct, 'military' (that is terrorist) action. Thus a split took place in December 1969; the dissenters were headed by Sean MacStiofain, a former Royal Air Force corporal, who was to become first chief of staff of the Provisional IRA, as the new group came to be called. At first they comprised only thirty to forty militants, but during the summer of 1970 most of the new recruits, as well as most of the money and arms, went to them rather than to the Officials; the more militant wing of the IRA held greater attraction for the Northern Irish Catholics. The Officials also engaged in some fighting in Northern Ireland and in bomb attacks in Britain, as well as in armed robberies in Eire and killings between the various nationalist groups. But by and large the Officials suspended their activities in May 1972. While they kept some of their influence in Eire even after that date, the history of the civil war in Northern Ireland after 1972 is largely the story of the Provisionals (PIRA), and (to a much smaller degree) of the Irish National Liberation Army (INLA), a subsequent breakaway from the Officials.

According to their programme (*Eura Nuva*), adopted in 1972, the Provisionals and their political wing stood for a democratic, socialist republic and a federal system of government; later on, in 1982, the idea of federalism was dropped; Northern Ireland was to take its place in a united Ireland. There was to be extensive nationalization, and the economy was to be based on a system of co-operatives. Elements of Marxism–Leninism could be discerned in this programme, but also of Third World ideology and anti-industrialist, anti-modernist ideas resembling the concepts of the

Greens and the ecological parties. Eire, as the Provisionals saw it, was an unfree state; the new Ireland was to come into existence as the result of a revolution in both South and North, just as the radical wing of the PLO claimed for many years that the road to Tel Aviv was by way of revolution in Amman, Beirut, Riyadh and other Arab capitals. Contradictions and omissions could be detected in this programme. A movement such as the Provisional IRA should have been strongly anti-American, but in fact anti-Americanism was very muted until the early 1980s; partly, no doubt, because of the traditional ties between Ireland and the United States. As Libyan financial aid and arms supplies grew, PIRA anti-Americanism became more strident, but probably more as a *quid pro quo* rather than out of deep conviction.

More important yet, in theory the Provisionals were only fighting the 'oppressors', not their fellow citizens who happened to be Protestants. In actual fact, the great majority of their victims were Protestant civilians, whereas in 1985 only two soldiers of the 'occupation army' were killed. In past ages, the fight for Irish freedom always had the support of at least some leading Protestants. Under the Provisionals the movement became exclusively sectarian, while emphatically denying their sectarian character and their sectarian murders. Even the extreme left among the Republicans was forced to admit that the aim of uniting the Protestant and Catholic 'working masses' was elusive. The sectarian character of their attacks was the source of the Provisionals' strength in the Catholic community, and the same was true, *mutatis mutandis*, with regard to Protestant terrorism.

The Irish troubles reached their highest point in 1972 when 467 people were killed, including 103 army officers and soldiers. By that time the Provisionals had trained many new recruits, their arsenal had greatly increased and, above all, there had been considerable Protestant provocations, such as the blowing up of a bar in Belfast in December 1971 when fifteen people were killed. Even more significant as a watershed was 'Bloody Sunday' in Londonderry on 30 January 1972 when, following a Catholic protest march, thirteen Catholic civilians were shot by members of the Parachute Regiment. As subsequent investigations were to show, the soldiers – having been fired upon and acting under great provocation – had mishandled the situation; the army was to learn from this sad experience in later years. But the immediate result was a great escalation of the conflict. Hundreds of bomb attacks, mainly by Catholics, led to mass arrests, but frequently the wrong people were seized because the old leadership of the IRA was better known to the authorities than those who succeeded them. This made it possible for younger and more militant elements to come to the fore.

The violence led to a Protestant backlash and to the imposition of direct rule, putting aside Stormont – the Ulster parliament dominated by the Protestants. While the British forces had in some respects overreacted, they now showed weakness, such as when they tacitly permitted for a while no-go areas in the heavily Catholic districts of Londonderry and Belfast, in which the Provisionals could freely organize. Most of these areas were removed during Operation Motorman later in 1972.

The intensity of violence abated somewhat after 1972; the death-toll statistics tell the story. They fell from 467 to 250 in 1973 and to 216 the year after. There was a small rise in 1975–6 with 247 and 297 deaths respectively. In 1977 the total declined to 112; in 1984 it was 64 (with 187 people killed in traffic accidents in Ulster that year), and only 49 in 1985.

Some of the specifics of terrorism in Northern Ireland ought to be singled out. The Provisionals, like the old IRA, were headed by an 'Army Council' and divided into 'Companies', 'Battalions' and even 'Brigades' – based on Belfast, Londonderry and the border area. These relatively large units were a heritage of the troubles of 1919–22 when much of the military action had been carried out by flying columns of thirty to forty men in the country-side. As the Provisionals absorbed many new recruits in 1971–2 – perhaps as many as 2,000 – the paramilitary tradition of a past age reasserted itself. But the Provos soon found out that this structure was not suitable for terrorist warfare in cities. It exposed them to army and police action and it also made it much easier for enemy agents to infiltrate their ranks. Such infiltration had been the bane of Irish terrorism in the nineteenth century and vitiated most of their operations.

The IRA suffered many setbacks during 1973–4, partly because of their unwieldy organization and lack of experience with the new and more deadly weapons; not a few militants managed to blow up themselves rather than their enemies. But the security forces also improved their techniques and thus the Provisionals, whose number considerably declined after 1972, decided on a basic reorganization, establishing smaller units – squads of three to five people.

To a certain extent they also modified their strategy; the idea of obtaining a quick victory was more or less abandoned. The new concept was to make the British presence too costly. Economic targets became more frequent; shopping centres were burned, managers abducted and factories sabotaged. This strategy was at first quite successful but security measures gradually improved. It appeared that what had been quickly destroyed could frequently be built again equally quickly. Furthermore, Catholics were as likely to be affected as Protestants by these operations. It should be noted in passing that the Provos were never afraid of a Protestant backlash. They assumed that if they made the British leave, the Protestants would also leave without British protection or submit to the Provisionals' demands. They clearly underrated the resilience and prowess of the Protestant militants. Having realized this in the 1980s, IRA strategy underwent yet another change; from that date onwards members of the RUC (the Royal Ulster Constabulary – predominantly Protestant in composition) were singled out for assassination. In 1985, twenty-five policemen were killed in IRA attacks compared with two soldiers, even though there were more soldiers than policemen stationed in Northern Ireland.

Two other peculiarities of Northern Irish terrorism ought to be mentioned. At times the terrorist campaign was carried to England, notably in 1972–3 and again in the 1980s, culminating in the attempted murder of Prime Minister Margaret Thatcher and other members of the Tory leadership at their annual convention in Brighton. These campaigns usually lasted only a few months; out of their native Northern Ireland milieu the bombers' squads were bound to be apprehended sooner or later. But equally the indiscriminate murder of British civilians, often working class, as in the bombing of a Birmingham pub in which nineteen people were killed, had negative political effects from the Provos' point of view.[3]

In the mid-1970s the security situation in Northern Ireland began to improve and negotiations got under way between Britain and the Irish Republic, and also directly with the PIRA leadership. While the talks with Dublin made considerable progress, culminating in the Hillborough agreement of 1985, giving Eire a say in any future solution, chances for a settlement between Catholics and Protestants in Ulster remained elusive. All the proposals for power-sharing made by London did not go remotely far enough as far as the PIRA was concerned. At the same time they caused deep resentment among the Protestants. Terrorism has continued since the middle 1970s almost without interruption, though on a decreasing level. Among the more striking exploits was the murder of Lord Mountbatten while on an angling excursion in the Irish Republic, and the mortar attacks against police stations in Northern Ireland in 1984 and 1985.

Protestant terrorism, with a few exceptions, has been reactive during the last decade. After a PIRA attack the paramilitary Protestant gangs would retaliate by killing some Catholics, usually civilians, and in a few cases political activists. The toll in human lives and injuries was still appalling, but Northern Ireland was no longer on the brink of a civil war, and in the absence of a political solution many came to regard the violence as regrettable but acceptable.

In view of the fact that the Provisionals did not make much headway after 1972–3, it is remarkable that they were still capable of a sustained terrorist effort. Their strongholds were relatively few – the border area with the Irish Republic, above all County Armagh and certain parts of Belfast (Ardoyne, Falls and Ballymurphy) as well as Londonderry (Bogside). Their political influence was also limited. In the Republic they virtually had no support; in Northern Ireland they never polled more than 10–12 per cent of the vote, except in a few strongholds such as West Belfast. If the British government had been able to carry out a limited population transfer within Northern Ireland or if, as after the Turkish army coup in 1980, those suspected of terrorism had been rounded up, and if at the same time a far-reaching political settlement had been imposed granting substantial concessions to the Catholics, terrorism might have ceased altogether. But such drastic measures were, of course, ruled out, given the democratic rules of the game. The British forces (unlike the Turks) had to consult their little book of instructions which told them what they could and could not do. The diehard Protestants were unyielding, feeling threatened by the terrorists and betrayed by the British.

Thus terrorism continued, partly owing to the professionalism of the PIRA, its conspiratorial experience dating back several generations, and its deep social roots. The PIRA arsenal, which had originally consisted of a few submachine-guns, rifles and revolvers, grew considerably as great quantities of modern arms reached Northern Ireland. The US Armalite rifle became the standard weapon; the Provisionals also had mine-throwers and apparently unlimited quantities of explosives. Bombs of up to one ton of TNT have been used; on occasion these were detonated from across the Irish border.

The Provisionals received financial support from a variety of sources. Above all there were the appeals made in the US, ostensibly for humanitarian purposes (NORAID). But the IRA also ran more or less legitimate businesses, such as a fleet of 200 taxis in Belfast, the profits of which were channelled into its war chest. An unofficial tax was imposed on drink in pubs in Catholic areas, and protection money came from 'guarding' building sites and other installations. Contributions were made voluntarily by Catholic supporters, and sometimes under pressure. However, despite the experience which had been gained during the many years of the 'armed struggle', despite the enthusiasm and the help from abroad, the terror would not have lasted if the PIRA (and the Protestant groups) had faced an antagonist more ruthless than the British forces.

Terrorism in Northern Ireland during the last two decades has been more indiscriminate and more cruel than in the past. Bars, stores and public transport were among the favourite targets, though the police and army patrols have also frequently come under attack. The ambushes have been relatively easy, especially in areas bordering the Republic because the frontier could be crossed without difficulty. It was probably because these operations were so easy to carry out that the PIRA has not engaged in more exotic operations such as the hijacking of aircraft.[4]

Inside the Republic, where the IRA is banned, its operations have been limited to occasional bank robberies, the liberation of prisoners and the assassination of some prominent Englishmen. The PIRA has also abducted hostages for ransom, and in one case even a champion race horse. But these have been the exceptions rather than the rule. What distinguishes Irish terrorism from other such movements is its social composition, which has been predominantly working class and lower middle class. The same is also true of the Protestant paramilitary units. There has been a pronounced anti-intellectual bias on both sides, even though the PIRA has conducted a vigorous propaganda campaign.

Relations between the Provisionals and the Catholic Church have been less close than in earlier times, which makes the intensity of the sectarian warfare even more puzzling. But there have been quite a few examples in history when enmity continued to exist (and even to grow) between two sections of the population long after the original causes had weakened or vanished. Ulster terrorism has its roots in the nationalist mystique of the anti-British struggle, on the one hand, and in religious fears on the other. Furthermore, free-floating aggression has been a frequent phenomenon in Irish history. The nineteenth-century 'faction fighters' were in the tradition of the old warrior clans of Ulster. They fought each other savagely: 'I never saw fellows more determined on the destruction of each other,' wrote a British army lieutenant stationed in County Limerick in 1824, having watched one of these faction fights which had no other visible purpose than the desire to fight; neither politics, religion nor social factors were involved.[5]

Fighting, in one way or another, has been part of the Northern Irish way of life for a long time and the tradition of prisoners fasting to death (though abhorrent to the Catholic church) also goes back several generations.[6] Martyrs such as Bobby Sands, who starved to death in May 1981, have certainly helped to keep the flame of the PIRA cause burning. At the same time, Irish terrorism has always been in jeopardy following the penetration of their ranks by 'enemy agents'. The super-grasses of 1983–5 caused the arrest and the conviction of many militants.

The Irish National Liberation Army (INLA) has been more radical than the Provisional IRA; however, though wedded to 'scientific socialist' and 'anti-imperialist' doctrine, the discrepancy between their theory and their practice could not have been greater. The leaders and members of the

INLA were long regarded as the wild men in Northern Ireland's terrorist struggle. Their tactics included the kidnapping of children for ransom as well as organized and systematic racketeering and extortion. Costello, the leader of the INLA, was shot by members of the IRA Officials in Dublin soon after the split. Ten years later, Martin McGuinness, head of Sinn Fein (the political wing of the IRA) called the INLA tactics 'anti-social gangsterism for which there was no part in Ireland's liberation war'. This provoked the comment on the part of the (anti-terrorist) Irish Social Democrats that there was not much to choose between INLA and IRA kidnappings.[7]

By the middle 1980s there were clear signs that terrorism was down, though not out. But there was also growing pessimism in the Protestant camp and increasing restlessness in Britain. The momentum of Provisional IRA terrorism was kept going by the belief that perhaps one last push would lead them to victory.

The Palestinians

There is a certain, limited resemblance between the situations in Northern Ireland, Euzkadi and the West Bank. The IRA, the ETA and the Palestinian terrorist groups can all point to injustices suffered and the desire of their members to have a state of their own, or, in the case of the IRA and the Palestinians, to destroy the present structures. They intend to liberate countries against the desire of the majority of their inhabitants. Catholics are a minority in Ulster, just as the Basques are in Euzkadi and the Palestinians in Israel. But they can argue that once upon a time the situation was different, that they have been reduced to minority status and that they have to fight by political and military (i.e. terrorist) means to put right this injustice. Comparisons, needless to say, should not be carried too far because the differences between one country and another are usually more pronounced than the common patterns.

The history of the Palestinian resistance can be briefly recapitulated. Palestinian militants did not accept the foundation of the Jewish state in 1948, nor did they make use of the opportunity to establish a state of their own. There were small-scale hit-and-run operations against Israel in the 1950s; in 1964, before the Israeli occupation of the Left Bank, the PLO came into being and acted as a political roof for Fatah and the smaller terrorist organizations. Aside from Fatah, which was the largest group by far, the historical constituents of the PLO were Dr Habash's PFLP, Na'if Hawatmeh's PDFLP, (both ideologically well to the left of Fatah), as well as PFLP–General Command and As-Saiqa – both under Syrian influence. As a result of the long Lebanese civil war, the balance of power between these groups has changed, further splits have occurred and new groups have emerged.

A fundamental difference between the Palestinians on the one hand, and the IRA and ETA on the other, has already been mentioned: the former had their bases outside regions they wanted to liberate, and most of their operations also took place in countries other than Israel, even though they had, of course, members and sympathizers in the Jewish state.

Attempts to set up a rural guerrilla movement shortly after the Six Day War (1967) failed; the terrain was unsuitable, and the Israeli security forces were too watchful. Since then the Palestinian organizations have engaged, roughly speaking, in three kinds of operations: hit-and-run attacks from across the border, usually by small units against Israeli transport or settlements, the planting of bombs, and the shelling of Israeli settlements. Such infiltration and shelling almost always provoked Israeli retaliation, and the neighbouring Arab states therefore severely limited these activities. Another reason for the decline in the number of hit-and-run attacks was the Lebanese civil war and the resulting misfortunes of Fatah. On the other hand, there was an increase in attacks against Jewish and Israeli individuals and institutions in third countries, and also against targets which were neither Jewish nor Israeli. These operations were in pursuance of other aims, such as the release of Palestinians arrested in Europe, support for non-Arab terrorist gangs, and, of course, the desire to attract publicity for the Palestinian cause.

While Fatah, and *a fortiori* PFLP and PDFLP, doctrine stressed the participation of the masses in the armed struggle, in practice this was not feasible. The masses could occasionally demonstrate against Israeli rule on the West Bank, but they could quite obviously not participate in operations such as the hijacking of planes or the attack at the Munich Olympic Village in 1972.

There are certain features which distinguish Fatah from other groups, above all its sheer size: in 1980 it had four brigades (20,000 men) under arms; by 1986 their number had declined to 14,000. Its equipment included T-34 tanks, Saladin armoured cars and SA-7 missiles. However, as subsequent events were to show, while such equipment was of certain importance in the context of the Lebanese civil war, it was of no use in the struggle against Israel. The PLO was far better financed than other such movements; according to the Baghdad agreement of 1978, the Arab states were to contribute $400 million to its budget.[8] Even more important, the PLO had stronger political support than any other such movement. It was recognized by more than 100 member states of the United Nations even though, for a variety of reasons, it had decided not to establish for the time being a government-in-exile. The PLO had observer status at the UN and its leader

Yasser Arafat was triumphantly received when he appeared at East River in New York.

Seen in this perspective the story of the PLO and Fatah was one of tremendous success, even though Palestinian terrorist operations were neither frequent nor effective. The number of Israeli victims was not remotely as high as the number of victims in Northern Ireland, Turkey or Italy, let alone in Latin America. There was a striking disproportion between the actual amount of terrorism and the political achievements of the PLO, which were considerable while the going was good.

Why did the Palestinians succeed where others failed? That the Palestinians had legitimate grievances against Israel was not the decisive issue; many millions of people lost their homes and their independence after the Second World War. But whereas the Lithuanians, the Germans expelled from the east, the Kurds, the South Moluccans or the Biafrans looked in vain for international support, the Palestinians were backed by the whole Arab and Islamic world, including some of the world's leading oil producers. The military and terrorist activities were of certain significance in keeping the Palestinian demands in the limelight. But it may well be true that the PLO would have had the same political achievements even if its supporters had never fired a single shot in anger. The 'armed struggle' was perhaps a psychological necessity, but in reality the PLO was swept to political success on a wave not of blood but of oil. However, as subsequent events were to show, these political achievements had narrow limits and were not irreversible. While the PLO were received as honoured guests in many capitals, this did not bring about the liberation of a single inch of Palestinian soil, a fact which in the course of time was to cause much dissent and infighting in the ranks of the PLO.

While the Palestinian organizations were not the first to hijack planes, they carried out some of the most spectacular early hijackings culminating in events at Dawson's Field (Jordan) when several jumbo jets were blown up on the ground in September 1970. In later years, the practice was only infrequently employed. Dawson's Field led to 'Black September', the bloody suppression and expulsion of Fatah from Jordan. Summarizing the experience of almost a decade of hijacking, a leading Arab journalist wrote that far from harming Israel, these hijackings strengthened her and aroused hostility against the perpetrators and against Arabs in general.[9] It would be perhaps more correct to conclude that while hijackings and similar operations were certainly not popular in democratic Western countries, they were always newsworthy. The figure of the hijacker–kidnapper was usually one of fascination rather than horror (Leila Khaled, Carlos *et al.*). There was frequently some sympathy for him, on the assumption that if people commit such desperate acts they must surely have good reason for doing so; people willing to die for a cause must have pure hearts and lofty ideals.

One of the main drawbacks of these spectaculars was that frequent repetition reduced their publicity value. For this reason Fatah, but also some of the smaller radical organizations, decided to discontinue hijacking. As Dr Habash said, these attacks 'hampered rather than helped the building of a socialist, proletarian organization'. Other terrorist groups, such as Abu Nidal, continued to hijack planes, and on some occasions the bigger groups, under a 'false flag', would do the same.

The move of the Palestinian organizations to Lebanon gave them enormous opportunities; they became virtually a state within a state (*Fatah Land*) and an important factor in Lebanese politics. They could provide terrorist training to visitors from all over the globe and they had a base from which they could operate more or less freely against Israel. But their massive presence in Lebanon helped to trigger off a long and bloody civil war, and as a result the Palestinians were to suffer terrible blows – at the hands not so much of the Zionists as of their fellow Arabs.

They would argue that they had learned only too well the lessons of Jordan; never again would they be drawn into the internal affairs of Arab countries. But in fact they became involved in the Lebanese fighting from an early date on the side of the Lebanese 'left', meaning the Druze and some of the Sunnis. One of their units tried to kill Maronite leaders in January 1976; they stormed Damour, a town in southern Lebanon, in the course of which some 600 civilians, mainly Maronites, were killed. It is possible that even if they had kept scrupulously neutral, which they certainly did not, their mere physical presence would have upset the delicate demographic and political balance in Lebanon and thus acted as a provocation, just as their attacks against Israel (Ma'alot, Kiryat Shmona and Naharia, all in 1974) triggered off counter-blows, culminating in the two Israeli invasions of southern Lebanon.

Fatah's fight against the Israelis, though resulting in their evacuation from Beirut, was not the worst thing that happened to the Palestinians, for they could argue that for three months they had offered courageous resistance. The real blows came from other quarters, which unlike the Israelis were not subject to restraints, rules of war or American pressure. In the siege of Tel al Za'atar, a Fatah base in the middle of a major refugee camp, some 1,500 Palestinians were killed by the Falange and the Syrians. The Syrians, who wanted to impose their own leadership on the Palestinians, hammered Fatah relentlessly in the Tripoli area after they had been evacuated from Beirut. Even before, many hundreds had died in the camps of Sabra and Shatila again at the hands of the Falange, who earlier had suffered grievously from the Palestinians. And when the civil war seemed almost over in 1984–5, the Shiites turned against Fatah and inflicted hundreds more losses in the camps near Beirut. When Fatah had withdrawn from Beirut in 1982 its morale was still high, but one year later the movement was weaker and more deeply divided than ever before. Yasser Arafat was fighting for political and physical survival, both Dr Habash's and Hawatmeh's groups had declined, and the headquarters of the movement were transferred to Tunis, far away from the main scene of the struggle.

For an understanding of the ups and downs of the Palestinians one has to refer to their internal divisions, and these can be explained to a large extent as a result of the rivalries between the Arab governments. There was, and is, a feeling of solidarity between the Arab countries as far as the Palestinian cause is concerned, but there is also a great deal of mutual resentment which has accumulated over the years. Each Arab government has been trying above all to promote the interests of its own favourite group among the Palestinians and to harm the others. Inevitably perhaps, like the Macedonian terrorists in the 1920s, sections of the Palestinian movement ceased to be free agents and virtually became proxies of Arab governments fighting each other as bitterly as – or even more so than – the Israeli enemy. The murder of Wasfi Tal, the Jordanian prime minister in Cairo, the assassination of leading Fatah members, such as Said Hamami in 1978 and Isham Sartawi in 1983, the killing of Abu Abbas and his whole staff (who had split away from the 'General Command' group in 1978), are only a few of the hundreds of murders that were committed inside the Palestinian camp.

In 1974 the Rejection Front was created in opposition to Arafat's 'moderate' leadership, despite the fact that Fatah had steadfastly refused to recognize Israel. After the Camp David agreement the Rejectionists temporarily returned to the fold. The Iranian revolution seemed to give a new uplift to the cause of the Palestinians, but as so often it proved to be a false dawn. There was fresh dissent, part of the Fatah military command rebelled against Arafat's autocratic leadership in May 1983. This was followed by a new agreement among several components of the PLO in June 1984. The whole history of the Palestinians will one day be written in terms of an unending chain of splits and temporary reconciliations.

Like most Latin American terrorist movements, but in contrast to the smaller PFLP and PDFLP, Fatah has kept its programme deliberately vague. For this it was sharply criticized, especially by the left, but the strategy had much to recommend itself. Helped by the inherent vagueness of the Arab political language, the leaders of Fatah stated their aims in a way that could appeal to the left as well as to the right, to Pan-Arabists and

Palestine-firsters, to those who were orthodox Muslims as well as to those who were not, both domestically and on the international scene. The fact that PFLP and PDFLP were more outspoken in their ideological pronouncements hardly mattered in practice. They would invoke death and damnation on the heads of the 'reactionary circles' in the Arab world, yet in practice they would do little or nothing to annoy or provoke them. Thus the PFLP proposes in its programme a 'popular war of liberation by arming and mobilizing the people in popular militias so that the war can be fought on the widest possible front . . . . protracted war waged by a mobilized, self-reliant people, armed with proletarian ideology, is the sole road for national socialism. . . .'[10] And as late as 1985, Dr Habash stuck to his attacks against the 'bourgeois' or 'petty bourgeois' Palestinian leadership,[11] even though as far as social background was concerned, Fatah derived its membership from socially lower sections of the population than the elitist PFLP and the PDFLP, which at the beginning had been Fascist in inspiration.

If the PFLP and the PDFLP had stuck to their programme, their place would not be in the present study, the subject of which is terrorism rather than 'war on the widest possible front'. But in fact their main operations were the hijacking and derouting of planes, the attack at Lod airport (May 1972) carried out by members of the Japanese Red Army rather than Palestinians, the OPEC kidnapping (December 1975), and the Entebbe hijacking. Most of these actions were carried out by foreigners or by mixed Arab–German, Japanese or Latin American teams, not by popular militias fighting a war of national liberation. A new 'international brigade' came into being, able and willing to co-operate on both the strategic and tactical level all over the globe, provided the terrorist campaigns happened to be of interest and profit.

The fact that the Palestinian resistance was split hindered its operations, and to a large extent thwarted the whole struggle. For it was no longer clear who was speaking on behalf of the Palestinians, and it seemed futile to negotiate with Arafat and to try to reach an agreement. The governments of Italy, Austria, Greece and others had working arrangements with Fatah according to which no terrorist acts would be carried out on their territory. But other Palestinian groups ignored such agreements, and this in turn undermined Arafat's international authority.

But the constant divisions had certain advantages. It made it possible to establish false-flag *ad hoc* organizations for carrying out operations which involved international complications. This technique was used on many occasions not only in the West, but also in the Arab world. Thus the murder of Wasfi Tal, prime minister of Jordan, and the murders at the Saudi embassy in Khartoum (March 1973) were carried out by an organization

called 'Black September', even though the Jordanian and Sudanese governments published ample evidence that no such organization had ever existed
as an independent entity and that the actions were supported by Libya.
A leading member of 'Black September' confirmed this in an interview
on Jordanian television. The attack against a train carrying Jewish immigrants from the Soviet Union to Vienna was executed by a group calling
itself 'Eagles of the Palestinian revolution', whilst five Saudi Arabian diplomats were kidnapped in Paris by a group which called itself 'Al Iqab',
of which no one had heard before or since. Such a division of labour had
undoubted advantages, but since the whole Palestinian movement was so
riddled by internal divisions, there was always the danger that the sorcerer's
apprentice would become truly independent, and this is what happened
not infrequently throughout the 1970s (the defections of Abu Mahmoud
to Libya, of Abu Nidal to Iraq and later to Libya, and of an entire Fatah
group to Syria).

The historical leadership of Fatah had survived the Lebanese war more
or less intact, except for some of the commanders in the field who had
been hunted down by the Israelis for their part in various massacres, and
others who had been gunned down as traitors by their fellow Arabs. The
PFLP emerged rather badly; its main leader Dr Habash had been incapaci-
tated by a stroke, and his chief aide Wadi Hadad had died. This faction
became more and more doctrinaire: in its manifestos there was ever more
talk about 'class struggle', 'proletarian organization' and other categories
quite inapplicable to the intrigues and in-fighting of inter-Arab relations.
Ideologically, this was the faction closest to the Soviet Union, but because
it was small and declining it was of only limited interest to Moscow. Thus
the weakening of Arafat's authority benefited not the PFLP and Hawatmeh's
group, but all kinds of shadowy factions which emerged in Baghdad (ALF
– an offshoot of the Iraqi Ba'ath), Damascus and Tripoli. Neither the Egyp-
tians nor the Jordanians wanted to become too closely involved in Palestinian affairs. But the Iraqis, Qadhafi and above all the Syrians were very
active in this field. It was for this reason that the Syrians wanted to remove
Arafat, not so much because he was a 'moderate' (as they claimed) but
because he was too independent for their liking.

The establishment of a government-in-exile would have been the most
obvious step to strengthen their independence, but with the exception of
one group (Hawatmeh's PDFLP) all PLO leaders were opposed to the idea.
A provisional government, they argued, should be formed only if there
was some reason to assume that it would not forever remain provisional.
And so the Palestinian leaders were torn for over a decade in various
directions between optimism – that the end of the 'Zionist entity' was just

around the corner – and deep pessimism – that time was working against them and that they would be well advised to accept a Palestinian state, however small. They wanted to continue the struggle, but they understood only too well that they could and should not rely on Arab leaders, however sympathetic to their cause.

The fight against the 'Zionists' continued but on a reduced scale. There was some terrorist activity inside Israel, especially on the West Bank, but this was as much home-grown as instigated from abroad. Some new tactics were tried, such as reaching Israel by sea and by air (by means of gliders), and the poisoning of Israeli oranges destined for export. Neither approach proved to be of much success. What remained were the usual attacks against airports in Europe, Jewish restaurants and synagogues, or the hijacking of the *Achille Lauro* in the eastern Mediterranean in 1985. Some of the operations were carried out by Fatah and the two smaller left-wing groups, despite the fact that they were officially wedded to the principle of launching attacks only inside Israel and the occupied territories. But Israel was a difficult target, whereas it was much easier to attack buildings and people in third countries. Very often the small units carrying out these missions were trained or even manned by the secret police of Iraq, Syria and Libya, and the purpose of these actions was often as unclear as the identity of the perpetrators. The attempt to kill Shlomo Argov, the Israeli ambassador in London (June 1982), was obviously part of a wider strategy, and the attacks against Jordanian and Egyptian planes and airline offices in Spain, Cyprus, Greece, Italy and Germany by the Abu Nidal gunmen probably was a settlement of old scores. But the attack on British tourists in Athens (the capital of a country well disposed to the Palestinians), or similar attacks in Rome's Via Veneto and at Frankfurt airport were without apparent purpose and no terrorist group even claimed responsibility.

Seen in the perspective of two decades, the Palestinian groups have undergone significant changes; they have grown well beyond the size of other terrorist groups. In fact, the PLO cannot be regarded only as a terrorist group, because almost from the beginning it has combined political and 'military' action. Perhaps it was the only possible strategy, but it has not worked too well. As a result of their dependence on the Arab states, the Palestinian groups have become a football in inter-Arab conflicts, and some of these groups are now no more than sub-agencies of the secret services of Syria and Libya. The purpose of the Palestinian struggle was either to create a situation in which war between Israel and the Arab countries would become inevitable, or to weaken Israel so much that it would eventually become amenable to concessions and a political solution. First, the consequences of 1967 were to be liquidated – and, at a later stage, the

consequences of 1948. But the internal divisions in the Palestinian movement made a political solution virtually impossible. Even if the mainstream
groups such as Fatah would have been willing to envisage the recognition
of Israel, if only temporarily, the 'rejectionists' and the Arab governments
supporting them would have prevented this. Arafat and Fatah were rightly
criticized for having missed opportunities in the political struggle, yet given
the fragmented character of the Palestinian camp this was in all probability
inevitable.[12]

ETA

Of all the European terrorist groups, ETA is one of the strangest, as much
sui generis as the Basque language its members fight to preserve. Parallels
have occasionally been drawn with the IRA, and it is true that there are
certain similarities in the struggle against a central government that does
not want to fulfil all the political demands of minorities. There is also
the fact that ETA has sustained a terrorist campaign longer than any other
major terrorist group in Europe – except the IRA. However, the differences
between the two are even more striking. There is no underlying religious
strife in Spain as there is in Northern Ireland; in fact, the clergy played
a notable role in the revival of Basque nationalism in the nineteenth century.
While Ulster was among the poorest and most depressed areas of the United
Kingdom, the historical Basque provinces have traditionally been among
the richest and most developed parts of Spain, and if the north-west has
declined during the last decade, this is at least in part the fault of the
insurgency waged by the ETA. The Basque radicals have frequently complained about its colonial status vis-à-vis Madrid, whereas the Spaniards have
argued that if indeed the Basque region is a colony, it is an almost unique
case of the colony exploiting the metropolis. For Basque (and Catalan) industry could develop only owing to protectionism – the cost of which, for a
long time, had to be carried by the Spanish taxpayer. Since medieval days
the Basques have had their special privileges, extending to self-administ-
ration and, particularly, cultural autonomy. Under Franco the last of these
rights were abolished; the suppression of the Basque language and customs
was more acute and widespread than repression in other parts of Spain.

The birth of ETA (Euzkadi ta Azkazatuna) in the 1950s was the reaction
to the policy of the dictatorship. Its basic demands were the creation of
an independent Basque state with Basque as its official language; the character of the state was to be part Third World populist and part Marxist–
Leninist. While ETA has been afflicted by many splits during the last thirty
years, including the secession of the 'Culturists' and the 'Trotskyites', its

basic demands have not radically changed; nor has the idea that these aims could be achieved only through the use of violence. As the IRA is part of a political movement, Sinn Fein, so ETA has its political outlet, Herri Batasuna, which is, in fact, a coalition of various factions.

The main problem facing ETA since the beginning of its activities has been a lack of mass support. It has claimed to speak on behalf of the whole Basque nation, yet in fact no more than 10–15 per cent of the Basques have supported its strategy. This has not, however, dampened ETA enthusiasm.* The situation is further complicated by the fact that even in the four Basque provinces where about three million people live, only about half of the residents are, in fact, of Basque origin (less than half in the case of the manual working class), and the Spanish people living in the region have no wish to become second-class citizens in a Basque state – or assimilated Basques. In one of the four provinces, Alava, there is little support for ETA; in Navarra, the biggest of them, there is hardly any at all. Strong ETA support is restricted to Guipúzcoa and Vizcaya, or, to be precise, to the southern parts of these two districts.

However, quite irrespective of the wishes of the people of Navarra, the Basque radicals insist on including them in their state. Some observers of the Spanish scene have argued that the radicalism and extreme character of ETA must be viewed against the background of the fear that demographic trends are working against them, and that this race will be lost unless their demands are fulfilled in the near future.[13]

As for the radical socialist doctrine of ETA, it would be uncharitable to dismiss it as mere mimicry, concessions to the *Zeitgeist*; it has certainly made it easier for ETA to establish useful international connections. But neither should it be taken too seriously for in its deeds, as distinct from its doctrine, ETA has acted, by and large, as a typical separatist group – with nationalism rather than the class struggle playing the central role.

A historical review of ETA militancy shows that there were relatively few attacks while Franco was still in power (the first attack, the derailment of a train, took place in 1961). There were altogether thirty-four assassina-

---

* A list of estimates is given in Robert R. Clark, *The Basque Insurgents* (Madison, Wisconsin, 1984), by far the most detailed history and analysis of ETA. It is written with a great deal of understanding and even sympathy for the Basque radicals. Mr Clark subscribes to the notion that ETA has not killed innocent bystanders indiscriminately, and should not be, therefore, regarded as terrorist. Other important sources are Jose Maia Garmendia, *Historia de ETA*, 2 vols. (San Sebastian, 1980), and Luciano Rincon, *ETA* (Barcelona, 1985). See also Gerhard Brunn, 'Nationalist Violence and Terror in the Spanish Border Provinces', in W. J. Mommsen and C. Hirschfeld, *op. cit.*, pp. 112–30. Herri Batasuna strengthened its position in the elections of 1986, but it was still far from attaining majority status. It had 300,000 votes out of a population of three million in the Basque country and Navarra.

tions between 1968 and 1975. The campaign escalated following the liberalization of the regime, with the murder of Prime Minister Carrero Blanco as its most famous exploit during the interim period. ETA terrorism reached its climax in 1978–80, precisely at a time when a democratic government in Madrid had made far-reaching concessions to the Basques. In 1979, there were seventy-two murders, and eighty-eight the year after. However, the paradox was more apparent than real, for repression under Franco had been brutal and fairly effective, whereas the democratic government seemed to be willing to negotiate with the ETA. By 1978, virtually all Basque terrorists had been released from prison – which made it so much easier for ETA to resume its campaign later that year.

ETA claimed that the concessions did not go far enough and were given grudgingly ; but ETA demands were such that no democratic Spanish government, even one dominated by the left, could possibly accede to them. Nor was it in the power of the government to reverse demographic trends. If the Basque language is losing out, this is not the result of a conscious policy of repression on the part of the democratic central government – but the consequence of industrialization, migration, the impact of the mass media and so on. No Spanish government can turn the wheel back and undo the history of the last 150 years. Many ETA attacks were directed against policemen and the Guardia Civil ; among the victims were more than a few senior officers, or former senior officers, including the military governors of Madrid and Guipúzcoa. But it has also killed journalists and others believed to be 'traitors' or people inimical to its cause.

Several businessmen were murdered for not paying protection money, and in some cases sympathizers of rival Basque nationalist parties were abducted. This caused considerable ill-will towards the ETA in the very places which should have been its main bulwarks. On two occasions, in 1980 and 1985–6, ETA engaged in anti-tourism campaigns in various parts of Spain, in the hope of contributing to general destabilization and weakening the central government. During the early 1980s, ETA was itself weakened partly as the result of new arrests – 300 members were in jail by late 1981 – partly as the result of an anti-ETA terrorist group named GAL which, probably with the help of the Spanish police or the army, carried the war to France where ETA had operated almost freely. Some ETA leaders were killed in ambushes and this caused disarray in the ranks of this relatively small organization. While ETA sympathizers could be numbered in the thousands, there were no more than 50–200 fighters at any time. An analysis of the composition and the social origins of ETA shows some interesting peculiarities. Like the IRA (and unlike the Red Brigades and Baader–Meinhof), ETA believes that the woman's place is at home,[14] and that in any case 'they talk too much'. There have been few, if any, women in the ranks of the ETA, which came into being as a students' group of middle-class, or lower-middle-class, origin, impatient with the too cautious line taken by the traditional Basque parties. Almost half of the *eteras* have a university education; there are workers in the ranks of the organization but virtually no farmers. Ideology and ideological quarrels have played a greater role in ETA than in the IRA, and it is also true that ETA, unlike the IRA, has tried not to antagonize their Spanish neighbours in Euzkadi, unless these belonged to the security forces. While ETA membership comes mainly from areas in which the Basque language is still widely spoken, it is by no means certain that most of its members have a perfect knowledge of the language, or that they use it as the language of conversation among themselves.

The ETA has not found it difficult to collect the funds needed for its operations and for sustaining its full-time members. Some have come from voluntary contributions, some from extortion and ransom paid for kidnapping, as well as from bank robberies. It is not known whether substantial contributions have been made by foreign powers, though the ETA has certainly received other assistance such as training in Algeria, Libya, Cuba, Nicaragua and Middle Eastern and Soviet bloc countries. These international ties have been important but probably not decisive, whereas the relative freedom which the ETA enjoyed in France was of crucial importance. Under Franco, and for years afterwards, the French authorities refused to extradite political émigrés, even if they were accused of having committed murder, much to the chagrin of successive Spanish governments. This tolerant attitude gradually changed after 1982, as the French authorities realized that they would not be able to contain the violence; they began to impose stricter control over ETA members in France; some were arrested and the French even co-operated to a certain degree with the Spanish authorities. In retaliation, ETA opened a second front and in 1984 began to attack targets in France, albeit on a small scale.

The ETA is a fascinating phenomenon to the outside observer: the mixture of conservative–romantic motives and progressive doctrine, of democratic theory and authoritarian practice, its belief that a Basque mini-state would be viable and its general anti-modern, anti-industrialist orientation, again point to certain similarities with the IRA or the various Green parties. Unlike Northern Ireland, the Basque country has no tradition of pronounced political violence. What, therefore, keeps the ETA hankering after ideals, at least some of which are clearly absurd or impossible to carry out? There is not one simple answer. Spanish retaliation helps to perpetuate the terrorist campaign; a considerable section of the Basque population, while not in agreement with the *eteras*, still believes them to be misguided idealists

and patriots who may ultimately play a positive role, insofar as they induce
the central government to make concessions to the Basques which otherwise
might have come only much later – or not at all.[15] But it is also true that
many, perhaps most of the militants (as Robert R. Clark has written), have
been engaged in terrorism since they were adolescents and they probably
cannot envisage another kind of life, in which violence no longer plays
a central role. They have become alienated from normal society or may
fear for their lives; this is also true of some other terrorist groups, but
perhaps nowhere is it more pronounced. All the *eteras* can reasonably
hope for has been achieved in Euzkadi, yet they continue their attacks
as if Franco had been replaced by another even fiercer tyrant. Seen in
this light, the ETA question is not so much one of political change but
of the problem of a generation. It will disappear only as this generation
ages and is succeeded by a new one with different values and aspirations.

The Armenians

Armenian terrorism, which surfaced in the 1970s, has its origins in the
Armenian massacres which took place in the eastern provinces of Turkey
during the First World War. As an Armenian historian has put it:

> At the end of July 1915, there were no more Armenians in the Eastern provinces.
> A few months earlier 1,200,000 Armenians had been living there, of whom some
> 300,000 had managed to seek refuge in Russia. Fewer than 100,000 were continuing
> the exodus. The rest were dead.[16]

The horrible story of the killings and deportations has been told in one
of the great novels of world literature, Franz Werfel's *40 Days of Musa
Dagh*. These massacres were the great trauma in Armenian history, so
much so that American historians who question the number of victims,
and cast doubt on the circumstances, have been physically threatened in
recent years.

There can be no doubt that the massacres took place, and the refusal
of most Turks to accept the fact has greatly contributed to the terrorist
resurgence sixty years after the event. Yet it is also true – a fact seldom
mentioned in Armenian writings – that the massacres did not come as
a bolt from the blue. There had been in Turkey, beginning in the 1890s,
a separatist–revolutionary movement with a terrorist wing which fought
for the secession of Armenia from Turkey and the establishment of an
independent Armenian state. The relevant point is not whether the demand
was justified or feasible, but that, as so often in the Middle East and in
other parts of the world, legitimate claims of a minority collided with the

interests of the state – and of other minorities living in their midst and surrounding them.

There had been an Armenian diaspora even before the massacres, with its main communities in what is now the Soviet Union (where an Armenian Republic came into being after 1918), Iran, Lebanon, France and the United States, and it was among these diaspora Armenians that the demand for retribution and putting right the injustice always found many supporters. This led to the resurgence of terrorism after 1975 and the killing of some thirty Turks, mainly diplomats, in various parts of the United States, in France, Italy, Spain, Portugal, Australia, Yugoslavia, Bulgaria and in one case even inside Turkey. The technique used was frequently the same: a Turkish diplomat was shot in his car usually while stopping at traffic lights. Of twenty-one Turkish diplomats killed between 1975 and 1982, fourteen were killed while slowing down in their cars at street corners – almost always they were shot with the same kind of weapon – a 9 mm revolver. In a few cases, attempts were made to seize Turkish embassies or other offices.

Some of these attacks were carried out by JCAG, the Justice Command for the Armenian Genocide, which was a branch of Dashnaq, one of the historical Armenian parties, more moderate on the whole (it chose as its targets only Turkish officials) and pro-American in orientation. But most of the assassinations were executed by ASALA. This was a group of younger people, impatient with the caution of the historical leadership. ASALA proclaimed its doctrine alternatively as Marxist–Leninist and Third Worldish, and considered itself part of the world revolutionary movement. It was also less discriminating in the choice of targets.

The killing of Turkish representatives did not come as a total surprise. In 1921 Talaat, one of the leaders of the Young Turks who had been instrumental in the massacres, had been slain in Berlin. But there had never been a systematic campaign, and if the militant elements of a subsequent generation opted for terrorism, this was mainly because they believed that without gaining publicity they would never receive a fair hearing. As one of them wrote: 'In our world it is not enough to have a cause, one also has to be noteworthy. . . .' There is no denying the truth of this statement, but what was the purpose of the terrorist campaign other than to give vent to feelings of frustration and vengeance? One such demand was to obtain recognition from the world and an apology from the Turks, who, with rare exceptions, have preferred to ignore the whole issue to this day.

But the more extreme elements, those organized in ASALA, went well beyond this. They also demanded the liberation of the occupied Armenian lands, and reunification with Soviet Armenia in a democratic and socialist state. For them, Soviet Armenia served, for the time being, as the revolutionary base.* This demand was, of course, unrealistic because these lands are no longer inhabited by Armenians and it is unthinkable that the Armenians would, in fact, return to these territories if they were 'liberated' and emptied of their present inhabitants. True, the militant Armenians have tried to establish a common anti-Turkish front with the Kurds. But they cannot have nursed many illusions about the value of this alliance; while Armenians and Kurds lived together in eastern Turkey, relations between the two peoples were less than cordial. It is obvious that an alliance of this kind would not survive the establishment of an independent Armenian state, if it should ever come to that.

Armenian terrorism was discriminating in the beginning; it did not hijack aeroplanes or place bombs in supermarkets. But as it became involved in the intrigues of the international terrorist scene – many ASALA militants were trained in Palestinian camps in Syria and Lebanon – it lost its erstwhile terrorist virtue and also, apparently, some of its independence. Bomb attacks were carried out against the offices not only of Turkish airlines, but also of various Western airlines; the reason given was that these countries were somehow involved with Turkey. There were indiscriminate killings at Orly airport in 1981, and when the Swiss arrested two Armenian terrorists who had been caught *in flagrante*, they were threatened by ASALA with dire consequences – even though no one in his right mind could possibly make the Swiss responsible for the Armenian massacres. Worse still, the Orly shootings provoked much criticism and eventually a split inside the Armenian community which previously had given overwhelming support to the young militants. Instead of admitting their mistakes, those guilty now began to threaten their critics inside the Armenian community. The evolving pattern was not, of course, new; there was an escalation of terrorism which became more indiscriminate. This provoked criticism, which meant the opening of a second front inside the community. At the same time, lacking both resources and a firm social basis, the terrorist group turned to various outside allies and sponsors. As a result, it became entangled in intrigues which had nothing to do with its original national aspirations, and exposed itself to manipulation for purposes alien to its cause. These dangers were recognized in the Armenian community; they caused further splits and a marked decline in ASALA terrorist activity during 1984

---

* Soviet attitudes towards the ASALA demands have been ambivalent. On one hand, they sympathized with the idea of expanding their influence along their southern borders; in 1946 they had demanded the surrender of Turkey's eastern provinces. On the other hand, they had no wish to make Turkey into a deadly enemy, and they traditionally suspected all pan-movements, fearing a negative impact on the Armenians living in the Soviet Union.

and 1985.[17]

Shiite Terrorism

In the early 1980s a new player appeared on the Middle Eastern political scene, overshadowing for a while all other actors. As one expert put it at the time: 'The message from Tehran is in my opinion the single most impressive political ideology which has been proposed in the 20th century since the Bolshevik revolution.'[118] There have always been certain elements in the Shia branch of Islam which made it different from the rest. In recent generations, Shiite theology has become more militant. Imam Husayn, its idol and founder, was for a long time a symbol of self-sacrifice, a subject of pity. Of late he has become an active hero; the 'spirit of the Kerbela' (after the name of the battle in which he lost his life) has changed its significance and meaning. Seen in this light, Khomeini is not a conservative, as frequently claimed, but an innovator; so was 'Abu Nidal' (not a Shiite by origin) who referred to himself as acting in the 'Karmati spirit'.* But this was never the mainstream of Islam, and Muslim theologians almost from the beginning stressed the need to stamp out *muharriba* (terrorism). It would therefore be misleading to explain the recent upsurge of Shiite terrorism mainly by reference to the distant past. Religious fanaticism did, of course, play a role but this can be found in many other parts of the globe; the specific political–social situation in Iran and Lebanon was of at least equal significance. Since some of the most important terrorist operations were carried out by young men or women allegedly bent on suicide, some observers of the terrorist scene, and above all the media, persuaded themselves that there was some deep connection between suicide and the Shiite faith. Some went so far as to argue that contemporary terrorism, not just in the Middle East but all over the world, had entered a new phase and that it might have become invincible. For what defence was there against people anxious to sacrifice their own lives? However, subsequent developments have shown that the element of suicide was grossly exaggerated, that in the attacks of Al Jihad al Islami (the most militant of the terrorist sects) only five or six were carried out by people bent on committing suicide (three or four in Beirut, one or two in Kuwait), that of the perpetrators some were not Shiites, some were mentally dis-

---

* The Karmatis were a ninth-century terrorist sect, in some respects a successor to the fanatical Azarika (684–700) who believed not only in the killing of their male enemies, but also of their women and children (*istirad*). Paradoxically they were more liberal than other Islamic sects towards Christians and Jews.

turbed, and the others were apparently under the influence of drugs. Since 1984 there have been no more suicide operations.

Some individuals can almost always be found to engage in suicide missions. A dozen IRA militants and half a dozen leaders of Baader–Meinhof, none of them Shiites by persuasion, also committed suicide by refusing food – a decision far more difficult to sustain mentally than a minute of glory.[19] Furthermore, the Japanese authorities in the Second World War found thousands of volunteers for Kamikaze missions.* Ariel Merari has noted that more Irish Catholic terrorists have thus far committed suicide than Shiites, although Catholic belief unequivocally opposes suicide. Shiite terrorism has acquired publicity as a result of three elements, none of them new: the use of suicide, the use of car-bombs, and the use of very large quantities of explosives – six tons in the case of the attack against the US marine headquarters in Beirut. Hence the conclusion that the 'more significant feature of Shi'ite terrorism is the degree of state-sponsorship, rather than the suicidal aspect'.[20]

The socio-political background of Shiite terrorism can be summarized as follows. Khomeini's rise had a considerable impact in countries with a significant Shiite minority, such as Lebanon. Even before, in the mid-1970s, a Shiite militia had been founded in Lebanon by Musa Sadr, a populist preacher who turned against both the traditional establishment in his community and the extreme left. His movement was originally called Harakat al Mahrumim – the movement of the oppressed – and not by accident, for the Shiites, while numerous and fast growing, were by and large poor and under-represented in the echelons of power.[21] Musa Sadr disappeared in 1978 while on a mission to Libya; he was most probably killed by Qadhafi's minions for reasons not entirely clear to this day. This caused a great deal of friction and Libya's embassy in Lebanon was sacked by the Lebanese Shiites, who might have been Qadhafi's natural allies. Under its new leader, Nabih Berri, Al Amal gathered strength, mainly in South Lebanon and West Beirut. It fought in the Lebanese civil war both with and against the Palestinians and the Druze. It was at first neutral vis-à-vis Israel, but following the Israeli invasion of South Lebanon it turned against the invaders.

Several radical groups split away from Al Amal in 1982 and became known under the name Islamic Amal, Al Jihad al Islami and Hizb Allah – the party of God. Al Amal received considerable assistance from Iran

---

* Some 4,600 actually gave their lives, mainly army and naval aviators. See Richard O'Neill, *Suicide Squads* (New York, 1981), *passim*, and Denis Warner and Peggy Warner, *The Suicide Warriors* (New York, 1984), *passim*.

and Syria, but by and large preserved its autonomy. The smaller, radical groups, on the other hand, seem to have been almost from the beginning under the control of the Tehran and Damascus governments, with Ali Akhbar Mohtashami, the Iranian ambassador in Syria, acting as chief co-ordinator. The identity of several leading figures of these groups became known, including Husain Mussawi and Sheikh Fadlallah ; their headquarters were in Baalbek and Zabdani, their training bases at Ras al Ain and Yanta. They showed much professionalism concerning both the effectiveness of their operations and their conspiratorial character. Thus it was never satis-factorily established whether the Islamic Amal and the Jihad were one and the same group or only closely associated. What emerged from the beginning was the fact that they both had considerable quantities of modern arms and a great deal of technical sophistication. Whether they were only trained by regular Iranian army officers (part of the Iranian volunteer corps in the Lebanese civil war), or whether these experts actually participated in person is not known. Al Jihad al Islami first became known in March 1983, as the result of attacks against the US and French embassies in Beirut, the attack against the marines compound in the Lebanese capital, the explo-sion at the Israeli military government building in Tyre, and a series of attacks in Kuwait in November and December 1983. These attacks were very destructive; the bombing of the marines compound caused more casualties than any other terrorist attack, except the explosion in an Air India jumbo jet in 1985. From a publicity point of view, even more successful (because of its long duration) was the hijacking of a TWA plane and its detention for several weeks at Beirut airport. Nabih Berri, who had mean-while become minister of justice, played the role of mediator between the US and the terrorist groups. But it soon appeared that he had only limited influence on the extremists, and even less on their Tehran and Damascus sponsors. Following the withdrawal of the US marines, major Shiite terrorist operations ceased, and the attacks in Kuwait and Baghdad also declined in frequency, partly, no doubt, because counter-measures had become more effective, and partly because terrorist attacks outside Beirut had not brought any palpable political success. Shiite terror was not carried to America, Western Europe or Israel, as had been threatened at one time.[22]

Thus the universal attraction of the 'message from Tehran' should not be overrated, and it is more than likely that one day Khomeini will be regarded as a curious aberration at home as well as abroad.[23] The fervour of religious fanaticism cannot be kept up indefinitely, and in the modern world it tends to decrease even more quickly than in past ages. But while it lasts it is a major danger and the end is not yet in sight.

Conclusion

This review of nationalist–separatist terrorist groups is, of necessity, far from complete. The search for motives and common denominators is essential, but it ought to be clear from the very beginning that seldom, if ever, will answers emerge which are altogether conclusive. There are a great many nationalities in India with resentments against the central government, and yet an organized terrorist movement has emerged recently mainly among the Sikhs. Students of the Sikh religion will point to elements of fanaticism and martyrdom. Marxists will stress the fact that the radical anti-government elements among the Sikhs belong to the small Punjab cultivators who have suffered from India's green revolution. But the same applies to other small cultivators in India, who have not risen in revolt, nor does it explain the deep divisions between Sikhs and Indians (and also within the Sikh community) in England and Canada, where Sikhs do not engage in agriculture. Historians report that there is a tradition of violence among the Sikhs: 'The Sikh Jar indulged in violence without motive or provocation.'[24] Similar observations have been made with regard to the Irish, but such a violent tradition has not existed among the Basques. Could it be that the Sikh, like the Basque, feels himself to be an endangered species, living in mixed regions, surrounded by far more numerous populations of different origin, fearful of losing his national identity?[25]

There is room for many interesting hypotheses, and some of them will, no doubt, help our understanding. But it is also true that throughout history cultural and ethnic assimilation has taken place, and the idea that it should be resisted at almost any price is a relatively new one. In some cases armed resistance has not come as a surprise. It was predictable that Palestinians would fight the Israelis, not just because they felt wronged, but because they had reason to expect the support of the Arab and Muslim world, much superior in numbers and resources to the Israelis, to reverse the decisions of 1948. But in many other instances it is by no means clear, and probably never will be, why some national and religious minorities took up arms and others did not, why some who had become active in terrorist activities desisted after a while (such as the Canadian FLQ and the South Tyroleans), why some accepted the verdict of history – however brutal and unjust – or, at any rate, forgot it, and others did not, such as the Armenians.

It has been the fashion to attribute to all (or almost all) national movements fighting for full political autonomy a progressive character, even though the consequences of Balkanization on a global scale should have had a sobering effect. But there is no doubt that the staying power of nationalism was vastly underrated by our ancestors, and Marx and Engels were no exceptions. If additional proof were needed for its continuing vitality, the relative strength of nationalist–separatist terrorism, in comparison with other species, would be obvious evidence.

7

Terrorism Today II:
Left and Right

Neither the IRA nor the Palestinians nor the Basques needed outside intellectual inspiration for their terrorist campaigns. But the upsurge of 'internal' revolutionary or quasi-revolutionary terrorism in West Germany and Italy has had a great deal to do with the rise and decline of the New Left, which became a leading force on the university campuses in the late 1960s. The number of students had grown considerably in the post-war period, and since these millions of students were among the most politically active members of society, their radicalization was bound to have political consequences. This was the force which helped to defeat an American president and almost overthrew the Gaullist regime in France. Although it was basically a European and North American phenomenon, it also had some indirect impact on the radical movements in the Third World and, of course, in Japan.

The New Left was of mixed parentage. On the one hand, there was genuine idealism, anti-militarism and revulsion against the inequities of modern industrial societies, poverty, hunger and exploitation in the Third World. No one could fairly dispute that the ossification of the structures of society in a country such as Italy was a fact, not a figment of the imagination of the extreme left.

But there was also boredom, as well as the free-floating extremism and aggression which can be found in many young generations. Seen in retrospect, the New Left produced much interesting material for the student of social and cultural trends. Politically it was not innovative. The ideas it advocated had been floating around for many years: deriving from Gramsci, Lukacs and the unorthodox German Marxists of the 1920s. There was little that was not known to the student of left-wing ideology. Perhaps the only significant new admixture was Frantz Fanon's concept of the 'liberating influence of violence'. Fanon had written for Africans, but he found most of his admirers in Europe and North America. He argued not only that violence unified the people, but that it was a cleansing force, freeing the native from his inferiority complex and from despair and inaction: 'It makes him fearless and restores his self-respect. ... When the people have taken violent part in national liberation they will allow no one to set themselves up as "liberators".'*[1]

This was a paraphrase of Morozov's vision of systematic terror as a guard against would-be dictators after liberation, and it was about as prescient for Africa as for Russia: 'The beggars have changed places but the lash goes on' (Yeats). True, it was now a native lash, but the predictions about the 'curative properties' of liberating violence make melancholic reading in retrospect.

The New Left lasted several years, after which time some of its proponents found their way back to mainstream socialism, Communism or anarchism. A few turned to *Situationisme* and other small sects. Many more, while retaining a vaguely liberal or even radical orientation, lost interest in politics. This was the case above all in the United States. In West Germany depoliticization took longer and did not go that far: the Green Party was in some ways a reincarnation of the New Left.

With the decline of the New Left a few of its members turned to terrorism. Thus more or less at the same time the United Red Army developed in Japan out of the student organization Zenga Kuren, the American Students for a Democratic Society (SDS) gave birth to the Weathermen, and some of the German students of the far left founded the Rote Armee Fraktion (RAF) and the Bewegung 2. Juni. There were other such groups in Italy (Brigate Rosse) and on a much smaller scale in Britain (Angry Brigade), France (Action Directe), Belgium (Cellules Communistes Combattants – CCC) and Turkey.

West Germany

There has been an unending stream of publications on the major groups, on their views, moods, beliefs, motives and aims. Seldom in history has so much been written about so few – as in the case of West Germany. Their doctrine has been minutely analysed, although this did them a grave injustice, for they were not really an ideological movement but eclecticists borrowing certain concepts from various doctrines, including the Leninist

---

* Fanon's concept was not original: Patrick Pearse, leader of the Irish Easter Rising (1916), had written: 'Bloodshed is a cleansing and satisfactory thing, and the nation which regards it as the final horror has lost its manhood.' Similar motifs can be found in Mazzini's writings. A generation lacking interest in history had to rediscover well-trodden paths in the history of radical ideas.

theory of imperialism. Above all they believed in the 'primacy of action'. As the RAF put it, only the practice of terror would show whether an armed opposition could be built up. This voluntarist concept had been borrowed from Mao and Castro, even though in other respects the life-style of the New Left terrorists was the negation of everything which the Chinese stood for.

'Armed action' in West Germany began with an attempt to burn down a Frankfurt department store in 1968. It continued with various bomb-laying activities against state institutions as well as private citizens, a newspaper office and several banks, and the murder of the president of a Berlin court, Drenkmann, who was a Social Democrat and had nothing to do with the cases brought against the RAF. Other victims included the general prosecutor of the Federal Republic as well as several industrialists and bankers who were not particularly prominent and who, for all one knows, might have been picked at random from a telephone directory. A 'traitor' in the RAF's own ranks was executed, the West German embassy in Stockholm was burned and destroyed, and there were a few more such operations – not a very impressive balance sheet for eight years of terrorist operations.

By 1976 the leadership of the RAF was under arrest, as were most of its members.[2] The 2 June Movement and the 'Red Cells' continued their attacks, sometimes in co-operation with terrorists from other countries. By the middle 1980s the identity of the perpetrators of sporadic attacks – against a US military base, at Frankfurt airport, the murder of the Munich industrialist Zimmermann and the scientist Beckurts – was no longer entirely clear, nor were their aims and general orientation. All one knew was that a number of terrorists, perhaps a dozen or two, were still active. Even those who at one time sympathized with the terrorists now argued that far from weakening the state and the other 'enemies', the terrorist approach actually strengthened them and it was therefore counter-productive in a country such as Germany.

The first and most important phase of West German terrorism ended with the suicides in 1976–7 of Ulrike Meinhof, Holger Meins, Andreas Baader, Gudrun Ensslin and two others. The leaders of the RAF were concentrated in a special prison at Stammheim, a Stuttgart suburb. Those under arrest and their lawyers complained about the inhuman torture of isolation, but in actual fact the terrorists were given larger cells than other inmates; they had frequent letters and visitors, including Jean-Paul Sartre; they had television and substantial libraries; and the defence lawyers also smuggled in a Minox camera, hashish, an internal communication system, several revolvers, ammunition and explosives. Thus the isolation, about which they constantly complained, was not quite complete. The real tragedy of the arrested was that they understood only too well that they had failed and that they were incapable of turning the court proceedings into an indictment of the system, as Rosa Luxemburg, Dimitrov and other revolutionaries of former generations had done. Instead there was name-calling. The judge was usually addressed as a 'fascist arsehole' or, alternatively, 'old swine' or 'old monkey'.[3] Instead of a powerful condemnation there was only verbal abuse, which had no political impact. The terrorists wanted to say something, but they found themselves incapable of doing so – perhaps they had nothing to say and this made them all the more angry.

Their isolation was of their own making. They had never been able to establish contact with the masses; the frequent use of four-letter words was not a substitute for a proletarian background. The terrorist groups consisted almost exclusively of students or ex-students from impeccable middle-class families. Some showed signs of mental instability. Andreas Baader asked for and received dozens of drugs every day. As in the US, terrorist groups had more women in their ranks than men, and the women were usually the more fanatical. The parents of Ulrike Meinhof were art historians, and she was brought up by another well-known historian and leader of the peace movement. Gudrun Ensslin's father was a theologian. Holger Meins' father was a wealthy Hamburg merchant. The parents of others were university professors, writers and professional people. Their children were radical idealists – and utterly confused. Their policy was not to fight for the 'oppressed and exploited' in their own country but to destroy the 'islands of wealth in Western Europe', to act as agents of a Third World which existed only in their imagination; hence their collaboration with terrorists from Latin America and the Middle East.

Horst Mahler and a few others had second thoughts in later years about whether this was the correct way to make friends and influence people. But most of his former comrades stuck to this hodge-podge of ill-digested Marxism and manifest nonsense up to the bitter end. Their frequently invoked 'concept of the urban guerrilla' was, as they knew, of Latin American origin: 'the revolutionary method to be used by weak revolutionary forces'. It was their firm belief that this method could be used at all times and in all places; in actual fact the concept had failed in Latin America and was bound to fail, *a fortiori*, in West Germany.[4]

There was a second and third generation of German terrorists after 1977, but whereas the Baaders and the Meinhofs had at least tried to provide some ideological justification for their operations, the new terror was 'actionism' pure and simple. To the extent that acts of terror continued to the middle 1980s, they were directed more against NATO military installations on German soil and seemed to be no longer specifically German but remote-operations, part of a concerted campaign extending to several countries.

Italy

If West German terrorism had never been a serious threat, terror in Italy was on a much wider and more dangerous scale. The Brigate Rosse came into existence in 1970. Together with several smaller groups, they were responsible for a systematic campaign of violence which shook Italy and caused many outside observers to believe that the days of democratic order in Italy were about to end. Whereas there were never more than a few dozen German terrorists, more than 1,300 terrorists of the left and 238 of the right were in Italian prisons by the end of 1982. (There were some 300 more arrests of the left and 140 of the right during the subsequent two years.) They were responsible for some 14,000 acts of terrorism since 1968, including murder – 40 in 1973, 27 in 1974 and 120 in 1980. After 1980 there was a gradual decline in terrorist activities, and by 1985 most of the militants of both left and right were either in prison or – about 300 of them – in French and Latin American exile. These figures do not, however, convey a full picture. While some parts of Italy were relatively free of terrorism all along, in some key regions such as Rome and the industrial centres of the north it was very strong indeed. The terrorist threat seemed to paralyse the judicial systems: jurors were too threatened to fulfil their duty and the police were unprepared to cope with the challenge.

The Brigate Rosse thought of themselves as a Marxist–Leninist organization, which, in contrast to the 'reformist' Communist Party, had the courage of its convictions and therefore engaged in 'armed struggle'. Though Italy was a democratic republic, it was (as they saw it) an oppressive capitalist machine: in fact, a dictatorship of the bourgeoisie over the proletariat. The only language which the 'servants of imperialism' understood was the language of arms; the historical task of the Red Brigades was to establish proletarian power with its own system of justice – to pass judgement on and punish the enemies of the proletariat.[5]

The original inspiration for Italian terrorism came not so much from the New Left, which was less influential in Italy than in Germany, as from the various other groups of the left: the Communist youth organization (FGCI) and left-wing Catholic students of the sociology departments of some northern Italian universities. The militants were predominantly in their twenties at the time, and there were considerably more males than females (the ratio seems to have been 4:1 or even 5:1); they came predominantly from middle-class homes. There were some working-class cadres, but on the other hand there was also a strong element of radical chic, personified by the figure of Feltrinelli, the famous publisher and scion of one of Italy's richest families. Psychological tests, to the extent that they were at all possible, did not show any specific pattern of mental instability – as they did in West Germany. Organizationally, the Brigate were divided into small units of four to five members, though on occasion, as in the abduction and murder of Aldo Moro, the former prime minister, several cells would collaborate.

To explain the great upsurge of terrorism in the 1970s reference has been made to the rigid and unchanging structures of Italian society; to the fact that one party had been in power since the end of the war; and to the dismal conditions on university campuses, where the number of students had grown tenfold. But much of this could also be found in other European countries, where these conditions led to political rather than terroristic action. There was substantial support for the terrorists among the public up to the time of the Moro murder, which was universally condemned.

Even before, the Brigate had managed to alienate many of their well-wishers with their attacks against journalists and union officials. Aldo Moro was the most liberal of the Christian Democratic leaders, and the reasons which induced the terrorists to kill him were too Machiavellian to make sense among the Italian left. If the Brigate received logistic and financial support from Czechoslovakia and later also from Bulgaria, then it is also true that the Italian Communist Party showed no sympathy at all.

Through the 1970s almost all of the victims of the Red Brigades had been Italians, whereas in later years there was, as in West Germany, a pronounced swing against US and NATO targets. The abduction of Brigadier-General James Dozier in Verona in November 1981, and the murder of Leamon Hunt, a US diplomat, were the best-known such cases. True, individual acts of terror continued on a small scale; in June 1982 a professor of labour law at the University of Rome was ambushed and shot for no apparent reason. (Giogni was the architect of pro-labour legislation in contemporary Italy.) But such operations became rare after 1981: the Brigate Rosse were weakened by internal dissent, and the police and judiciary showed greater sophistication. There were many more arrests than previously and more than a few of the arrested militants (including some of their leaders, such as the head of the Brigate in Rome, Morucci) began to 'sing': these were the so-called *pentiti*.

The revelations in the trials, including references to links with foreign governments, added to the division in the ranks of the terrorists. By late 1984 only one member of the command of the Brigate had not been apprehended. True, there were always a few to take the places of those who had been arrested, but the erstwhile enthusiasm had clearly gone out of the Brigate. They had thought that after one major push the Christian Democrats, their main enemy, would fall apart, and that the parliamentary left, above all the Communists, would be revolutionized.

After more than a decade and countless terrorist attacks, they realized that far from weakening their enemies, they had actually helped to strengthen them: facing a major terrorist onslaught, all the democratic parties had rallied, leaving the terrorists in isolation.[6]

Turkey

Terrorism spread on Turkish university campuses in the late 1960s partly under the influence of the events in Western Europe. The initiative was mainly in the hands of extreme left-wing groups inspired by the ideas of Lenin and Mao – and the actions of Guevara and Carlos Marighella. Their victims were Americans, Israelis and opponents from the right. They also engaged in bank robberies to finance their operations. As in many Latin American countries police did not enter the university campuses, which thus served for a time as inviolate bases in which considerable arsenals were stored. In 1973 the Turkish government prepared a White Book identifying the sources of the terrorists' arms supply. In the end it was not published; since it named foreign governments, it would have caused diplomatic complications.

Due to a further increase in terrorism, martial law was imposed in April 1971, and by 1974 the rule of law had more or less been restored and a general amnesty declared. However, the situation was not intrinsically as stable as the authorities had thought; seen in retrospect, the amnesty was a mistake, because it enabled many militants to resume their violent activities. There were more than a hundred political murders in 1976, including those committed by the extreme right who had now entered the scene. (The first wave of terrorist operations was almost entirely sponsored by the extreme left.) There was a rapid acceleration in attacks in the year that followed, with 2,400 murders in 1978 and 1979. There was a distinct danger that terrorism would turn into open warfare in the streets. Then on 12 October 1980 the army took over and terrorism was stamped out within a matter of days: 730,000 weapons were seized and 75,000 suspects were arrested during the year after the army coup; 24,000 were charged with terrorist offences.

Prior to the army coup the Turkish scene had become almost a free-for-all not only between extreme left and right (and both against the government), but also all kinds of communal and ethnic riots occurred, such as the events in 1978 in the provincial capital, Kahramanmaras, in which more than a hundred people were killed. Religious factors also played a certain role in these attacks and counter-attacks.[7] But the major actors were the terrorist groups of the left, such as the Turkish Liberation Army (TPLA) and the armed groups on the extreme right inspired by Colonel Türkes' (legal) party, the Commandos of the National Action Party. Students and teachers were prominently involved on both sides, and the situation was further complicated by the struggle between left- and right-wing labour union organizers, and by a resurgence of violence on the part of Turkey's dissatisfied minorities, above all the Kurds,

The main battles were fought in the big cities; once the army had clamped down and restored order, there was a great soul-searching about the deeper reasons for the upsurge of terrorism. According to one school of thought, the reasons were largely social in origin. In Turkey (as in Italy) rapid urbanization and internal migration had caused much dislocation and internal tension. The emergence of shanty towns around the industrial centres seemed to provide a big reservoir of uprooted and dissatisfied elements for the extremist and terrorist movements.

However, as closer investigations were to show, the great majority of terrorists were not recruited in this milieu. Some analysts pointed to the emergence of doctrines preaching violence on both the extreme left and the right (Pan-Turkism and the re-Islamization of Turkey). This was bound to cause conflict in a society which in the past had been distinguished by its respect for authority. Lastly, there were those who looked, not without justice, to foreign instigation – certain countries had an interest in the destabilization of Turkey. They pointed to the fact that the value of the weapons seized was at least $250 million, whereas the war chest of the various terrorist groups was less than 2 per cent of that sum, following various robberies. Who were the philanthropists who had paid for these arms? Turkish terrorists had been trained in Syria, weapons had come from Bulgaria and probably other Soviet-bloc countries. On one occasion in 1977, a whole shipload of arms was intercepted (on the *Vasoula*), and while the arms had Western (Argentine) serial numbers, it soon appeared that these had been faked, and that they had originated from Bulgaria, which served as a safe haven for Turkish terrorists. In later years Soviet and East-bloc authors were to write with great indignation about the 'Fascist provocateur' Agca, who had tried to assassinate the Pope. The fact that Agca and his colleagues had used Sofia as their headquarters was conveniently forgotten.

True, even massive foreign help would not have been sufficient to trigger off violence on such a level of intensity. But for the presence of a considerable terrorist potential, the situation in Turkey would never have deteriorated so much. It could well have been that democracy and Western civilization in Turkey had made less progress than Ataturk and his colleagues had wanted; that the country still needed a strong government, and that the democratic experiment of the 1970s had not been a complete success. The collapse of terrorism after the military took over tends to bear this out; terrorism was eliminated within a few weeks, even though the amount of violence applied by the authorities and the number of those executed was insignificant in comparison with those killed by Khomeini's henchmen in Iran or by the Argentine junta.

Japan and the United States

The organizational antecedents of the Japanese Red Army were similar to those of the German, but there were also native traditions at work.[8] They derived from, on the one hand, the ideological disputations of the student left of the 1960s, and, on the other hand, the traditional spirit of Bushido. It was perhaps no coincidence that in their very first major action, the hijacking of a Japanese aircraft in March 1970, the attackers used Samurai swords and daggers. Subsequently there were a few murders and acts of sabotage inside Japan, but on the whole it was, as in West Germany, a self-perpetuating cycle of arrests, new attacks, new arrests and so forth. Thus in January 1974 the United Red Army attacked a Shell refinery in Singapore; those involved were captured by the police. Ten days later, to effect the release of the prisoners in Singapore, the URA struck at the Japanese embassy in Kuwait. In September 1974 they attacked the French embassy in The Hague, demanding freedom for one of their comrades who had been arrested in France. The Japanese terrorists, even more than the West Germans, took a prominent part in 'transnational terrorism', frequently in collaboration with Palestinians, but also with the 'Carlos' gang (Yutaka Furaya) and other such groups.

Compared with the extent of terrorist operations in Italy and Turkey, terrorism in the United States was of short duration and almost negligible in quantity. It is probably more rewarding to ask why there was so little of it rather than why isolated attacks did occur. By 1980 terrorism had virtually disappeared; former American militants had aged and entered professional careers as they grew older. True, a handful continued to make the headlines at ever longer intervals, but no ideological statements were published and for all one knew their motivation was no longer political.

Organizationally, American terrorism developed out of radical white and black groups. On one hand there was the SDS, the extreme wing of which – the Weathermen – went underground after a 'war council' in Flint,

Michigan, in December 1969.[9] Three years earlier the Black Panther party had been formed in California by Huey Newton (subsequently its 'minister of defence') and Bobby Seale. It was later joined by Eldridge Cleaver whose *Soul on Ice* had sold two million copies and who became its 'minister of information'. Black Panther thinking was inspired, in its own words, by Che Guevara, Malcom X, Lumumba, Ho Chi Minh and Mao. But undue importance should not be attributed to such pronouncements; it was not as if the works of Mao had been carefully studied; all that their proponents knew of Mao was that power grew out of the barrel of a gun. They saw the *Lumpenproletariat* as the main revolutionary force, although they had little success in mobilizing it, and they rejected collaboration with the Weathermen, whose members came from a very different social milieu and whose preoccupations with ego trips, women's lib and various manifestations of the counter-culture were not to their liking. On the other hand, the Black Panthers put strong emphasis on cultural nationalism. In the beginning it was not a terrorist group; urban terrorism was first advocated by Cleaver from his Algerian exile and by George Jackson, who was killed in August 1971 while trying to escape from San Quentin. Jackson thought of himself as a Communist, had widely read terrorist literature in prison ('I no longer adhere to all of Nechaev's revolutionary catechism'), and stated that the objective was the destruction of the city-based industrial establishment by creating perfect disorder and by disrupting the manufacture and distribution of goods.[10] There were a few shoot-outs between members of the Black Panthers and the police and some bomb attacks, but the Black Panthers succumbed to 'perfect disorder' well before American society. Cleaver, who had been the first to advocate the armed struggle, became disillusioned following his painful experiences, first in Cuba and later in Algeria. Huey Newton and his friends opted for community action from within the system, and Stokely Carmichael, who had retreated with his wife, a well-known singer, to a comfortable existence in Africa, advocated political struggle.

There was no direct link between the Black Panthers and the Symbionese Liberation Army, which also originated in Berkeley. Consisting of a few students and criminals, it committed some murders of white and black people, robbed a few banks and, following the involvement of Patty Hearst, attained worldwide notoriety. Counting about a dozen members, it was one of the smallest and most bizarre terrorist groups. Like the Manson family, it can perhaps be understood against that specific Californian background which has remained a riddle to most foreigners. The name 'Symbionese' was defined as 'body of harmony of dissimilar bodies and organisms living in deep and loving harmony and partnership in the best interest of within the body'. Its emblem was a seven-headed cobra, a 170,000-year-old sign signifying God and life.

The motives that induced young blacks to join a terrorist group were, of course, altogether different from the motives which had driven white middle-class youngsters underground. On one side, there was the despair of the black ghetto, unemployment, poverty and the misery of broken families; on the other, the crisis of identity, suburban boredom, the desire for excitement and action, a certain romantic streak – in short terrorism as a cure for personality problems. All this was enmeshed in immense intellectual confusion, an absence of values, the conviction that everything was permitted; all the bitter things the Weathermen said and wrote about American society and American culture were *a fortiori* true of themselves. For in their violent opposition to this society and culture, they remained its offspring, embodying its negative features. It was not just their style which set them apart from previous generations of terrorists – the obscenity of their language and their cruelty – the style in this case was the man, or the woman: a very inferior species of revolutionary indeed.

While the black youngster could point to very real social problems, the white suffered mainly from personal hangups. Yet any attempt to engage in generalizations about the behaviour of a handful of young men and women is of doubtful value, since the overwhelming majority of their con-temporaries, whether they perceived their surroundings in a similar light or not, did not turn to terrorism. And so the Weathermen, even more than the Black Panthers, remained a marginal phenomenon; whatever they did in the underground, it did not affect American life. The statistics still showed a great number of bombings and attacks during the years after 1970 and some of these were undoubtedly the work of the Weathermen. But most of them were perpetrated by lunatics or criminals – a few oper-ations more or less made no difference.

Latin America

In the 1950s and the early 1960s terrorism seemed all but forgotten, although there was no shortage of guerrilla warfare in Asia, Africa and Latin Amer-ica. The latter proceeded, however, according to a very different pattern. Underlying the guerrilla warfare were the assumptions that a revolutionary movement would develop in some distant province of the country and gradually gather strength, and that eventually, as happened in China, the 'countryside' would envelop the cities. The prevailing idea was that a contest of this kind ought to be based on mass participation. The concept that a small group of people could and should be the main agent of political change was rejected for both doctrinal and practical reasons. This then was the rule, and if there were a few exceptions, they could easily be explained as a result of unique local conditions: Cyprus was a small island, easy to control by the rulers – it was impossible to establish a 'National Liberation Army' in the countryside and, in these circumstances, the use of urban terror was quite natural. But tactics used on an island of half a million inhabitants were not thought to be applicable elsewhere. Equally, the incidence of urban terror in the struggle for Algeria was explained as part of the political mobilization of the masses in the capital of the country; demonstrations and propaganda were part of it, but bombs also had much to recommend them. The city of Algiers, in any case, was not really considered the main battlefront; the defeat of the ALN in the capital did not, in the event, affect the outcome of the struggle.

The transition from rural guerrilla warfare to urban terror came after disaster overtook Che Guevara in Bolivia; it was also connected with the radicalization of sections of the New Left in industrialized countries, and reached its climax in the years 1969–72. If this was the general trend on a global scale, the situation in individual countries did, of course, vary. In a few places urban terror had been launched well before 1967, and it had already petered out by the time it reached its climax elsewhere. In other places, the fashion arrived after some delay, and in some countries urban terror continues to the present day.

The earliest and, in some ways, most interesting manifestation of urban terror on a substantial scale was in Venezuela in 1962–3 – well before the wave had spread elsewhere. Venezuela seemed in some way predestined: about two-thirds of the population lived in urban centres and urban terror had the support of the activist wing of the local Communist Party, which had persuaded itself that an 'objective revolutionary situation' existed and that only a little push was needed to topple the regime. The cadres were mainly students with a sprinkling of the urban working class or, to put it less charitably, the *Lumpenproletariat* of the *barrios* (slums) of Caracas. True, urban terror was considered only one of three approaches to be tried simultaneously: the rebels also endeavoured to win over sections of the army in an attempt to stage a military coup; they also contemplated rural guerrilla warfare.

The Venezuelan urban terrorists had no specific doctrine to guide them – they acted by instinct – but their repertoire was nevertheless a wide one, ranging from bank robberies to hijacking planes and ships to the kidnapping of prominent personalities (including the Argentine soccer star di Stefano). They understood perfectly well the paramount importance of gaining publicity for their struggle.

It has been said that the whole arsenal of the urban guerrilla operations, later used in many other countries, was in fact developed with much imagination in Caracas.[11] But it was the misfortune of the MIR 'urban guerrillas' that they faced, not an inefficient dictatorship such as Batista's in Cuba, but a regime that had come to power in free elections; it was headed by Betancourt, leader of the Acción Democrática.

Betancourt's counter-measures against the terrorists seemed half-hearted; there was no massive police repression or army counter-attack. He acted decisively only when the terrorists became more and more of a nuisance to the general public, causing disruption to daily life in the capital, and after a popular groundswell against the terrorists had developed. With insufficient support from the middle class and even less from workers, the terrorists found themselves isolated, only to be told by the older Communist cadres that this was the inevitable result of their adventurist tactics. Following a particularly senseless and counter-productive attack against an excursion train, forceful action was at last taken by the government and this finally broke the terrorists' will to continue the struggle in the city; rural guerrilla fighting continued for a number of years.

Events in Venezuela seemed to confirm what Castro and Guevara had taught the revolutionaries all along – that in underdeveloped Latin America the countryside was the basic area for armed fighting. They had to establish rural *foci*, which could not overthrow the system but would act as a detonator. The countryside, according to the Cubans, had much to recommend itself, from a political point of view – with its enormous untapped revolutionary potential – and also militarily, because access to the rural areas was much more difficult for the government troops. Fidel's slogan had been, 'All guns, all bullets, all reserves to the Sierra'; the idea of leading a guerrilla movement from the city seemed altogether absurd, for an urban terrorist group could not develop into a revolutionary force. It could not transform itself into a people's army and ultimately seize power. The 'urban guerrilla' (the Cubans, in fact, frequently used the derogatory term 'urban terrorism') was at best an instrument for agitation, a tool for political manoeuvre and negotiation. But, lacking any central command in the cities, the guerrillas were forced to disperse and this was bound to weaken the insurgents far more than the governmental forces.

Moreover, there were sound political and psychological reasons militating against the 'urban guerrilla'. The Cubans and, following them, Regis Debray, regarded the urban working class (not excluding the Communist parties) as an essentially conservative element. The city, as Castro put it, was 'the grave of the guerrilla'. Debray was even more outspoken:

life in town was tantamount to an 'objective betrayal' for 'the mountain proletarianizes the bourgeois and peasant elements, whereas the city makes bourgeois of the proletarians'.[12] Living conditions in the towns were fundamentally different from those prevailing in the countryside; even the best comrades were corrupted in the cities and affected by alien patterns of thought. This sounded more like Rousseau and the twentieth-century *Kulturkritiker* than Marx and Lenin, but from a military point of view it seemed to make sense, at least for a while.

It was only after 1967 that guerrilla doctrine was adjusted: the Venezuelans and the guerrillas in Peru and Colombia had been defeated; the death of Guevara in Bolivia in 1967 and the arrest of Debray highlighted the failure of rural guerrilla practice. The age of urban terror dawned with Uruguay, Brazil and Argentina as the main scene.

The Uruguayan MLN (Movimento de Liberacion Nacional – the Tupamaros) was founded in the early 1960s; in the beginning they displayed only sporadic activity. Their very first operation was an attack against a Swiss rifle club in July 1963. Their activities reached a peak in 1970–1; the following year they were decisively defeated.

In Brazil there were several urban terrorist groups – the ALN (Acao Libertadora Nacional), the VAR (Vanguarda Armada Revolucionaria) and the VAR-Palmares, all considerably smaller than the Tupamaros. They launched an urban terrorist campaign in 1968 which was to last for three years. In Argentina, too, the urban terrorists were split into several factions; the ERP started its activities in 1970, as did the left-wing Peronist FAR (Fuerzas Armadas Revolucionarias) and the Montoneros, whose first publicized operation was the kidnapping and murder of ex-President Aramburu, also in 1970.

In addition there were a great many other small groups in various Latin American countries. From time to time there would be reports about bank robberies, kidnappings and assassinations in Mexico, Guatemala, Colombia, the Dominican Republic and other places; a detailed analysis of these countries' terrorist groups is of importance for the student of Latin American politics, but on the whole they were politically ineffective and a detailed review of their activities would not add much to the understanding of the general phenomenon of terrorism.[13] For, in the present contexts, Latin American terrorism is of interest mainly insofar as it throws some new light on the possibilities and limitations of terror as a political weapon in modern conditions.

The upsurge of terrorism in Uruguay occurred against the background of a deep economic structural crisis and the same is true, *mutatis mutandis*, with regard to Argentina; in Brazil, on the other hand, it took place precisely at the time of a major boom. The Tupamaros confronted a liberal government; they suspended their activities during the elections of 1971. The Brazilians faced an army dictatorship, and their terrorism, in some ways, was 'defensive'. In Argentina, urban terror developed in the period preceding Peron's second coming, after years of inefficient military rule. But the return of the popular leader by no means induced the ERP to cease their activities, whereas their main rivals, the Montoneros, stopped operations for a while. Tupamaros terrorism was far more discriminating and sophisticated than the operations carried out by their Brazilian counterparts. No doubt this reflected the less violent political culture in their country. Cold-blooded murder was not approved by public opinion in Uruguay and the Tupamaros were well aware of this fact. They mainly raided banks, businesses, offices and arms stores; on occasion they distributed stolen goods and published documents they had seized revealing corruption in high places. In February 1970 they raided a leading gambling house and stole a quarter of a million dollars, but later distributed the money among workers and employees. After 1970 their operations became more violent. Foreign diplomats and local officials were kidnapped and Dan Mitrione, an American police adviser, was killed.[14]

Further escalation in violence took place in 1972, when the Tupamaros decided to launch a 'direct and systematic attack against the repressive forces'. An army officer and several police officials engaged in counter-subversion were killed in hit-and-run attacks against army personnel. It quickly appeared that the attempt of the Tupamaros to establish a real 'alternative power'(people's courts and people's prisons) to the government had less support than they had thought. 'The Tupamaros are the people and the people are the Tupamaros' was a fine slogan, but the Frente Amplio, which the Tupamaros supported in the elections of November 1971 (and which was also backed by the non-terrorist left), polled less than 20 per cent.

Terrorist operations in Argentina likewise were at first on a modest scale (bank raids, kidnappings), but by 1970 the first assassinations had occurred.[15] The ERP and the Montoneros claimed that this was in retaliation for the Rawson jail escape (in Patagonia), when sixteen out of nineteen recaptured prisoners were shot while allegedly trying to escape for a second time. But this massacre did not take place until August 1972, whereas the killing (by the ERP) of Dr Sallustro, general manager of Fiat, had been committed five months earlier, and the Montoneros had killed ex-President Aramburu in May 1970. Later murder became quite indiscriminate; the victims included moderate trade union officials, who were accused of having betrayed the working class. True, the ERP stopped their assassinations for a short time when, in December 1974, some of their militants had murdered the small daughter of an army captain together with her father. But there is reason to believe that they were more concerned with the impact on public opinion than with the purity of their souls.

Meanwhile, Santucho (killed in a shoot-out with the police in July 1976) and Firmenich, the leaders of the ERP and the Montoneros, had met and co-ordinated the activities of their organizations which, since 1974, had spread to the countryside. While the Montoneros were by far the larger group, with the whole left wing of the Peronist movement as its base and (allegedly) some 25,000 armed members, it had little political cohesion or discipline and the smaller ERP, with a mere 5,000 members (but with better and heavier military equipment), was a more dangerous foe for the government. During 1975 and early 1976 there was an escalation of terrorist attacks and government repression, and Argentina became one of the very first cases in history of terrorism almost turning into urban guerrilla warfare.

In Brazil, where government repression was strongest, the character of the terrorist campaign was also the most cruel. The terrorists were accused, even by the extreme left wing, of 'militarist deviation' in trying to crush the enemy rather than win over the masses, and of neglecting 'armed propaganda'.[16] The Brazilian security forces, like those of Uruguay, were quite unprepared in the beginning to cope with urban terrorist tactics, but after a year or two they too gained experience. Carlos Marighella, the leader of the ALN, was killed in a police ambush in São Paulo in November 1969, as was Camara Ferreira, his successor, in October 1970. In December 1970, Fujimora, one of the leaders of the VPR, was shot. By that time the number of active terrorists had fallen to fifty, and Carlos Lamarca, a former army captain and the leader of the VPR, was hunted down in the countryside and shot in the state of Bahia in September 1971. Most of the terrorist operations took place in Rio de Janeiro and São Paulo and the number of victims, excluding terrorists, was relatively small – about one hundred killed over a period of five years. But the terrorists had an excellent flair for publicity and good connections with the media, and their exploits were extensively reported all over the globe. There is no reason to disbelieve the reports about systematic torture used against terrorists, but it is also true that the terrorists had few, if any, scruples; their victims included farm workers who had stumbled on terrorist hideouts, motorists killed by terrorists who needed their cars, and boatmen cut down after a getaway at gunpoint.[17]

Latin American urban terrorists developed a doctrine, but more by instinct than on the basis of socio-political analysis. They realized that a strategy that had worked in China (and in Cuba) would not be successful in countries in which the majority of the population lived in cities. Latin America, after all, had the fastest rate of urbanization in the world; to talk about the 'encirclement of the city by the village' in Uruguay or Argentina was to invite ridicule. The political as well as the military and economic centres of power were in the big conurbations; hence the decision to attack the enemy there, not on the periphery. True, all Latin American 'urban guerrillas' stressed the importance of building up rural guerrilla *foci*, but this resolution remained a dead letter in most cases and almost their entire effort was concentrated in the cities.

The two chief ideologists of urban terrorism in Latin America were Abraham Guillen (a refugee from Spain) and Carlos Marighella. Guillen's writings initially influenced both the Tupamaros and the Argentine ERP but he did not belong to either organization and criticized their strategy on various occasions; there is no reason to assume that he ever had any decisive influence on their strategy. Guillen advised the terrorists to engage in many small actions and thus to compel the security forces to cede terrain. His ideal cell consisted of five people who had to decide whether to launch an attack without referring the matter to the high command. Guillen explained the subsequent setbacks of the Tupamaros as the result of their decision to engage in big ('Homeric') battles as well as to establish 'fixed fronts' (supply depots, hospitals, 'people's prisons', etc.). Guillen advocated constant mobility and clandestine existence but at the same time insisted on the importance of political work to gain mass support. This was excellent advice but not very practical, since a movement observing strict rules of conspiracy could not possibly engage in political and propagandistic activity at the same time.

A similar contradiction pervades the writings of Carlos Marighella. Marighella had been a leading member of the Brazilian Communist Party but left in disgust because of its 'reformist' character. His reputation spread after his death in battle; the *Minimanual* was translated into many languages and almost as often banned by the authorities, even though it contained little that was not known. If Guillen was preoccupied with the politics of guerrilla warfare and condemned senseless murder, Marighella was predominantly interested in military (i.e. terrorist) action: the more radical and destructive the better. He advocated a scorched-earth strategy, the sabotage of transport and oil pipelines, and the destruction of food supplies. His assumption was that the masses would blame the government for the resulting calamities. He also wrote that 'urban guerrillas' should defend popular demonstrations, but this was hardly ever done. Typical of Marighella, and also of the Argentine terrorists, was the burning conviction that shooting was far more important than any other activity – especially intellectual discussion. There was contempt for ideology and 'politics'. The future society (Marighella wrote) would be built not by those who made long-winded speeches or signed resolutions, but by those steeled in the armed struggle. His writings are permeated with a fanatical belief in the justice of his cause and the single-minded advocacy of 'the revolution'; political details were of little importance.

For this anti-intellectual and even irrational attitude there were perhaps mitigating circumstances: the sterile and unending ideological debates of the Latin American left, which were usually a rehash of ideas imported from France. The Tupamaros, too, for years scrupulously refrained from issuing specific political statements, remaining deliberately vague about their aims, stressing that 'words divide us, actions unite us'. The contempt of the Argentine ERP for the doctrinal hairsplitting of their erstwhile Trots-kyite mentors has already been mentioned. Such ideological vagueness was partly tactical but, to a large degree, it was genuine, reflecting the prevailing state of ideological confusion: for many of these young men and women 'nationalist', 'socialist', 'revolutionary' and 'anti-American' were more or less synonymous. Erstwhile leading members of quasi-Fascist organizations or Peronist ideologists switched to the Castroite or Trotskyite camp with the greatest of ease.[18] When the Montoneros first appeared on the scene in 1970 with the murder of ex-President Aramburu, their political character genuinely puzzled outside observers: some commentators called them a movement of the extreme left, others wrote that they belonged to the far right.[19] Both, in a way, were right.

Like the early Russian Narodniki, Latin American terrorists assumed that the intelligentsia, especially the students, constituted the revolutionary vanguard, even though lip-service was paid to the central role of workers and peasants. Sabino Navarro, the chief of the Montoneros in 1970–1, was a worker, but he was the exception, not the rule. From other, earlier, terrorist movements they borrowed the concept of provocation; violence would produce repression, repression would result in more violence; by constantly harassing the government, they would compel it to apply ever more draconian measures. Thus the establishment would have to shed its liberal–democratic 'façade' (Venezuela, Uruguay) or quasi-populist front (Argentina) and antagonize large sections of the people. At the same time, attacks against the army would push the officers to the right and prevent a left-wing military takeover – such as in Peru – which the terrorists considered a major danger.

This theory of increasing polarization was based, as the Tupamaros and the Brazilians admitted after their defeat, on a serious overestimation of their own strength and an underestimation of the 'forces of repression'.

The Tupamaros had intimidated (and infiltrated) the police but the moment the army took over the combat against terrorism their strategy no longer succeeded. The Brazilian terrorists were also quite unprepared for the intensity of the government's backlash. Torture evoked much protest but it did not provide new recruits; the heroism of a Marighella was in vain, and, in the end, most came to consider the terrorist tactics quite pointless.

Conditions in Argentina were more promising inasmuch as the social basis of the terrorist movement was somewhat broader; the terrorists had the support of some trade unions, which were considerably stronger than those in Brazil or Uruguay. Furthermore, the terrorists benefited from the political vacuum caused by a succession of ineffective military juntas and the equally incompetent interlude provided by Peron and his widow. Thus the ERP and the Montoneros grew stronger but eventually all they achieved was the overthrow of a quasi-democratic regime and its replacement by another military dictatorship.

The innovations of Latin American urban terrorism lay in the practical field rather than in the production of any new concepts. Like the Palestinians, the Latin Americans realized that the mass media, domestic and foreign, were of paramount importance; on various occasions they seized radio and television stations and broadcast their propaganda. They were the first to engage in the systematic kidnapping of foreign diplomats and businessmen, correctly assuming that such operations would both embarrass the local government and attract worldwide publicity. It should be noted in passing that in the early phase of Latin American terrorism more foreigners than their own nationals were killed by Latin American terrorists. This may have been accidental; more probably it was part of their strategy, based on the assumption that acts of violence against foreigners would always be more popular. On a few occasions the Tupamaros engaged in major military operations (the seizing of public buildings in 1969, the occupation of police stations and airports in some provincial towns in 1971–2), as did the ERP and the Montoneros on a few occasions when they attempted to storm army camps. This was in line with their doctrine of escalating individual terror to mass action. But these operations were never quite successful; sooner or later the terrorists returned to the small-scale raids, kidnappings, bank robberies and hit-and-run attacks which were less risky and not necessarily less rewarding.

The most interesting innovation of the Latin American terrorists was the foundation of a 'Junta of Revolutionary Co-ordination', a terrorist international of sorts established by the Argentine ERP, the Tupamaros, the Chilean MIR and the Bolivian ELN. The ERP contributed an initial $5 million to the Junta's budget, which was used for arms production and procurement, operations in Europe (the assassination of Latin American diplomats), as well as the publication of a journal (*Che Guevara*). However, since among the four associates of the Junta only one was in a position to provide money and strength, the establishment of the new body meant only that the centre of gravity of Latin American urban terrorism moved for a few years to Buenos Aires.

The Last Decade

Left-wing political terror in the major Latin American countries declined in the late 1970s. In Brazil it had always been a marginal phenomenon, whereas in Argentina the Montoneros and the ERP had caused a considerable amount of disruption. Following the attack on police headquarters in June 1976 the state (federal) police was nearly paralysed. In the first five months of the year more than a hundred people in Argentina were killed. The ratio of left- and right-wing assassinations stood at about 2:1. Yet the terrorists, with their frontal attacks against army camps, had clearly overreached themselves. After Maria Estella Peron's regime was overthrown, four thousand terrorists or suspected terrorists were detained and many disappeared without a trace after being tortured. Within a short time both ERP and the Montoneros lost some nine-tenths of their strength, and those remaining at liberty either escaped abroad or continued to live deep within the underground. There had been 646 murders in 1976, but only 181 the year after, and in 1980 the statistics showed none. But as the ERP and the Montoneros were stamped out, they, their sympathizers, as well as many innocent people, had to pay a terrible price.

Political violence has not ceased in Latin America since, but it has assumed other forms. The conflicts in the Central American republics became more intense; among the prominent victims was the then chief of the National Guard in Nicaragua (March 1978) and the El Salvador foreign minister, not to mention the many thousands who were killed by right-wing terrorist squads in Guatemala between 1976 and 1984. However, the armed struggle in Nicaragua and El Salvador proceeded predominantly in the countryside with occasional forays into the big cities.

The same is true with regard to the Colombian M19, which first appeared in 1974, and the Peruvian Sendero Luminoso. M19 attracted much notoriety when it took hostage half the diplomatic corps in the capital during a diplomatic reception and again in 1985 when it seized the Supreme Court. Many perished in the subsequent shoot-out with the police. But just as the ideologies of these two groups are difficult to fathom, so are their motives, which do not seem to be entirely political. Links between narcotic producers and dealers and the terrorist groups in Peru and Colombia have been conclusively proven: for permission to operate freely in guerrilla-held territory such as the Upper Hualaga Valley in Peru, and for certain guard duties and attacks against American anti-narcotics observation stations, the terrorists were paid substantial sums. As President Belaunde has asked: 'From where do you think M 19 received so much money?'[20]

Peru

Of all the Latin American insurrectionist movements Sendero Luminoso has certainly been one of the strangest, but not the least effective. In the Indian villages of the Peruvian Andes there is a tradition of radical messianic ideas; all kinds of political parties, including the Trotskyites, have tried in the past to make inroads there without, however, any lasting success. Sendero came into being in Ayacucho, the capital of a department in southern Peru. It was headed by a philosophy professor at the local university and originally consisted almost entirely of university students and assistants. They were strongly influenced by the Cuban experience; most of them visited Havana, but ideologically the impact of Maoism in its pristine, most radical, form proved to be even stronger. They founded the Maoist Party of Peru and gradually established a foothold in the Indian villages of southern Peru. In this they succeeded partly as a result of the dedication of the militants, partly because of government neglect. The benefits of the land reform which had been carried out were not obvious; among the younger peasants there was a great deal of discontent about the lack of economic progress.

While the military junta was in power, prior to 1980, the guerrilla and terrorist activities of Sendero were on a limited scale, restricted to the burning of ballot boxes and bizarre symbolic deeds such as the hanging of dead dogs from lamp posts in Lima and Ayacucho. As the civilian–democratic government took over, Sendero became progressively more violent. A campaign of bombing government buildings was followed by terrorist activities on a wide front. This was in accordance with Mao's theory of the 'third stage of guerrilla struggle'.[21] Sendero Luminoso carried out more than 500 murders in 1983, attacking transport, communication, power plants and factories; among its victims was a fairly high number of policemen. In early 1986 President Garcia, following bomb attacks against the embassies of India, Spain, West Germany and China, had to call in the army to deal with a rapidly deteriorating situation. Garcia had been elected the previous summer as head of a left-wing coalition. He had channelled assistance to the neglected highland villages, revoked some of the emergency laws of the previous administrations, and tried to enter a dialogue with Sendero Luminoso. But all this was in vain. The attacks continued on an undiminished scale, and Lima became second only to Beirut in the number of robberies and abductions. Garcia sadly concluded that 'they are incapable of distinguishing between this government and previous ones'.[22] Whether the leaders of Sendero were indeed incapable is a moot question; it is equally possible that they disliked the new government as much as the former ones.

Where did their support come from to enable them to fight against a freely elected government and against the other political parties? It ought to be borne in mind that the Indians of the Peruvian highlands were politically as well as economically and socially isolated, outside the mainstream of Peruvian society. They probably did not even know that there were two dozen other Communist parties in Peru, that all the newspapers in Lima were free – and half of them were socialist or Communist. The rebellion drew its inspiration, at least in part, from the neglect of many decades, and it was helped by the stormy, altogether unplanned growth of Lima and other big cities. The capital had been a small town before the Second World War; in 1986 it counted six million inhabitants, with the inevitable slums housing the millions of recently arrived Indians. At the same time the police force was quite inadequate, with twenty-two patrol cars for the whole of Lima. Thus, inevitably, a breakdown in law and order ensued as Sendero Luminoso found some support not only among highland villagers but among the *Lumpenproletariat* of the big city.

Mention has been made of the fact that the founders and leaders of Sendero Luminoso were of European and mestizo stock. They had to study the Indian languages for years, since they were not even able to communicate with the masses they wanted to enlist.[23]

The name Sendero Luminoso is attributed to a speech by José Carlos Mariategui, who said that Marxism–Leninism will open the 'shining path to revolution'. But in many respects this was anything but a Marxist movement and it has never sought collaboration with other left-wing parties in Peru, nor – in contrast to most other guerrilla or terrorist groups – has it shown interest in publicity. The rise of Sendero Luminoso has been attributed by some observers to an acute agrarian subsistence crisis and the secluded character of the region. But Sendero emerged precisely at a time when new roads to the coast and the jungle were being built, telephones installed and inter-urban communication developed. A subsistence crisis existed all over the Andes; in fact the social (and national) problems were even more acute in Ecuador than in Peru or Colombia. But Ecuador was relatively free from guerrilla warfare and terrorism until attempts were made to import it from abroad in 1985 and 1986. In the final analysis accident did play a decisive role. An insurgency is unlikely to happen in a vacuum, but 'objective conditions' to some extent always exist without necessarily leading to a rebellion or terrorism. Mario Llerena, an early follower of Castro, has explained:

The one factor that gives the Cuban revolution its unique character [is] the Castro personality. Whatever way the political scientist or the historian may look at it, there is no escaping this fact. .... It can safely be asserted, without fear of indulging in fanciful speculation, that if Castro had been cut to the usual pattern of young Cuban revolutionaries, or if he had not existed at all, there would have been no Cuban revolution – not the kind it had turned out to be, at any rate. Castro's personality acted as the catalytic agent that transformed a popular protest of moderate democratic aspirations into a radical revolution, in a country where originally there was no desire, no expectation and no need for a radical revolution.[24]

Sendero Luminoso with its quaint and murderous antics will not succeed in encircling the cities and taking over power: Peru is not China and Maoism is quite inapplicable there. But it is still true that but for the leadership of Professor Abimael Guzman and the commitment of some of his fellows, the movement would not have become a major destabilizing factor in the history of contemporary Peru.[25]

Colombia

The Colombian case does not bear out the argument that violent action is most rampant where 'government oppression is most severe. Colombia's government was democratically elected; by Latin American standards it was one of the most liberal. Nor does economic development provide a clue, for Colombian economic growth exceeded the Latin American average; but neither economic crisis nor economic recovery seem to have had a significant correlation with the ups and downs of M 19 and the other guerrilla and terrorist groups.*

There is not much to be gained by a minute investigation of the ideology of these groups. There is in many Latin American countries always reason for legitimate discontent. There is also a strong tradition of political violence more deeply rooted in Colombia than in most other countries. This can be channelled by a handful of determined people into 'armed struggle'.

---

* FARC (Colombian Revolutionary Armed Forces), the other major insurgent group, is the armed wing of the Colombian Communist Party. It has also been active in narco-terrorism. According to the Colombian justice minister Lara, they received some $100 million for the purchase of weapons and equipment for guarding seven cocaine laboratories and an equal number of airstrips run by the drug dealers. M19 began its political career on the extreme right: it was the youth organization of the movement, headed by the dictator Rojas Pinilla, who ruled Colombia in the 1950s.

More frequently than not, 'armed resistance' has been based in the country-side, and this has dictated the strategy of these movements.

Central America

Terrorist attacks in Chile were mainly directed against businesses, both domestic and foreign; left to their own resources, Chilean terrorists did not constitute a serious threat to the Pinochet regime. The lessons from the failures of previous insurgencies were perhaps most acutely studied and absorbed in Central America; this refers above all to the importance of organizational and political support. If the Sandinistas (FSLN) overthrew Somoza in 1979, it was not mainly as the result of guerrilla campaigns or terrorist operations – though they did engage in both – but above all because they succeeded in gaining the political support of the urban middle class, of unions and sections of the clergy, and, last but not least, in obtaining foreign assistance.

Thus the FSLN became a model for the insurgents in other Central American countries and at the same time an invaluable source of support. This is true above all of El Salvador and Guatemala, countries plagued by internal war for many years. However, the insurgents were facing governments more popular or more determined than Somoza's, and if the rebels had learned from the Nicaraguan example, so had the rulers. The strategy of *guerra prolongada* – as distinct from terrorism on the one hand and guerrilla warfare (*focismo*) on the other – worked, up to a point; it was quite effective in harming the economy. But internal conflicts among the insurgents about tactics, and more effective counter-insurgency, took their toll; so did the social reforms carried out by the authorities in the rural areas. By 1982 the guerrillas had become a major military force in Guatemala; during the preceding four years they had killed more than a thousand policemen and soldiers. However, during the second half of 1982, in Operation Victoria, the guerrillas suffered heavy defeats. In the course of this operation the government armed the local population to fight the guerrillas, something which Somoza would never have dared.[26]

Sixteen years of military rule in Guatemala have resulted in many thousands of victims killed by the army and the death squads. When the Christian Democrat Cevezo Arevalo was elected in 1985, he faced a terrible heritage of murder, torture and hatred.[27]

A detailed review of the Central American insurgencies is outside our purview, and the same applies to the civil war in Lebanon, the Tamil insurgency in Sri Lanka, the popular resistance in Afghanistan or the struggle of the NPA in the Philippines. There were countless acts of terrorism in

Lebanon and in the other insurgencies, but they took place in the wider framework of a civil war.

The differences in political background, motives, purpose and strategy between these insurgencies, in which masses of people were involved, and the terrorist campaigns of small groups, are so pronounced that it is pointless to deal with them as if they all belonged in one category. Other examples are India and South Africa. Militant Sikhs killed Mrs Gandhi in 1984 and there were many other acts of communal violence in the Punjab.[28] But they were part of a wider struggle of a religious–ethnic minority, conscious of its distinct character and willing to fight to preserve it. Mass confrontations were an even more distinct feature of the struggle in South Africa. Since 1961 the African National Congress had a fighting organization, Umkhonto We Sizwe, which carried out some 150 terrorist attacks between 1977 and 1983. There were more such operations in 1984–6 including the attack against oil facilities in 1980 and the bombing near air force headquarters in 1983. But these acts of violence merely punctuated the political struggle. The demonstrations in the townships, the strikes and other mass action were infinitely more important. Given South African geography, there was no chance of launching guerrilla warfare.[29] Given the numerical superiority of the black population, there was no need to transform the mass struggle into a campaign of individual terror.

Iran

The Iranian terrorist campaign was one of the shortest, sharpest and most interesting in history. Terrorism had played only a minor role in the destabilization of the Shah's regime, which eventually led to his downfall. There were some political assassinations but the decisive factors were the mass protests in the streets of Tehran and other major cities, and the lethargic reaction of a ruler who was already suffering from an incurable disease.

The coalition which came to power after the Shah had left contained different and contradictory elements. It included extreme Shiite ayatollahs, radical university students and various kinds of moderates. Khomeini and his followers stood for the Islamization of public life, and they accused their former allies, the Fedayeen,[30] of corrupting Islam with Marxism and the Mujaheddin of fomenting strikes against the regime.

When Prime Minister Bani Sadr resigned in June 1981, the opposition declared armed struggle against the Islamic fundamentalists and their followers. The Mujaheddin and Fedayeen felt optimistic about the outcome. These were, after all, battle-tested organizations who had fought the Shah's regime throughout a decade. Furthermore they had the support of part of the officer corps. As one of them put it at the time:

With no more than a few hundred poorly armed members we made SAVAK and the Imperial Army desperate. Now with several thousand well armed Mojahed and hundreds of thousands of genuine supporters throughout the country we are a power to reckon with.[31]

The outcome of their first attack seemed to justify such optimism. It began with the bombing of the headquarters of the Islamic Republican Party (IRP), the leading political movement. The roof, quite literally, collapsed over the building and buried seventy-two of the leading figures of the IRP, including Beheshti, the party secretary, four cabinet ministers, six under-secretaries, twenty-seven members of parliament, and other leading figures. At the same time, all over Iran a systematic terrorist campaign got under way, aimed at eliminating the chief police officers, the main ideologues of the IRP, leaders of the Revolutionary Guard, Friday prayer leaders, revolutionary court judges, and other key figurers. This culminated in a second deadly bombing on 10 August, in the prime minister's office, when the National Defence Council was in session. The president of Iran, Ali Rajai, was among the victims as were the prime minister and the chief of police. Seldom if ever had a terrorist group succeeded in killing so many of its leading opponents in so short a period. They felt so confident that in the following month they began to come out in the open – organizing street demonstrations in Tehran and launching massive frontal attacks against the revolutionary guards, the main pillar of the regime. Nor were the attacks limited to the capital. Similar operations took place in Isfahan, Tabriz, Abadan, Bandar Abbas and the other major cities of the country.

Yet within a few weeks, the power of the anti-Khomeini terrorists was broken, and within a year they no longer existed. Their remnants could be found in exile in France – then in Baghdad – under Massoud Rajavi, the only surviving founder member of the Mujaheddin. The terrorists had committed a fatal mistake in their assessment of the political situation: for so many years they had claimed in their propaganda that the Shah was the cruellest despot in the world and that SAVAK, his secret police, was the most effective tool of repression, capable of committing any atrocity. In the end they came to believe their own propaganda. Yet in actual fact, compared with Khomeini and his followers, the Shah was a moderate who was subject to many restraints, and SAVAK, despite its notoriety, was neither particularly effective nor as brutal as its successor.

The Shiite fundamentalists could safely ignore Western public opinion. They had no compunction whatsoever about the number of people executed nor the choice of the victims, nor the bestiality of the torturers. Bodies were mutilated, teachers were shot in front of their pupils, some of those executed were thirteen-year-old girls, and the standing order was to deny medical help to the terrorists who had been wounded.

According to one estimate there were 800 executions following the two major attacks. Amnesty International reported that 2,946 were killed within one year (June 1981 to June 1982), and the Mujaheddin have given a figure of 7,746 for a two-year period (June 1981 to September 1983). It was a truly effective dictatorship. Unlike in Argentina, no mother in Iran dared to demonstrate against a regime which had murdered her son or daughter. Tens of thousands of Iranians escaped their country in this, the third emigration wave. Firmly entrenched, the Khomeini regime carried its terror abroad – to Iraq, Lebanon and even France.

It was the basic mistake of the Mujaheddin – supported perhaps by some of their well-wishers outside Iran – to believe that terrorism was invincible. They thought they were still fighting the Shah or perhaps some Western-style liberal regime. Facing a determined foe their weakness emerged only too clearly:

Despite heavy odds, Khomeini's personal magnetism, and the availability of scores of leaders willing to serve, despite clear threats to their safety, helped the regime to overcome the immediate crisis. Showing supreme confidence in his regime's survival, Khomeini expressed no anxiety. . . . We have a long line of committed people willing to become martyrs for the revolution. . . .[32]

The Iranian revolution brought about the rise to power of a new class, not the radical intellectuals but the clergy, representing the aspirations of the *mustazefin*, the poor and despised in the urban centres. While the ravages of an inconclusive war should have brought about a new crisis in Tehran, the internal splits among the Mujaheddin effectively paralysed the opposition.[33]

Right-wing Terrorism

In the media, in general debate and even in academic discourse, it is frequently taken for granted that terrorism is bound to be left-wing and revolutionary in character, that 'terrorist' is almost a synonym for these terms. Such beliefs are by no means limited to opponents of terrorism; they are equally found among those who wish to find mitigating circumstances for (left-wing) terror. In actual fact, much terrorism, past and present, is by no means left-wing in inspiration. Categories such as 'left' and 'right' frequently fail to shed light on terrorism. This is true even in Western Europe and North America, where the ideological orientation of the terrorists seems more clearly defined than in the Third World. It is pointless to define Abu Nidal or Shiite terrorists – and their sponsors – as men of the left or the right: they are both and neither. However, the use of these terms and the resulting confusion is deeply rooted, and the old concepts are likely to persist for a long time to come.

Most of the terrorist groups active in Europe between the two world wars gravitated to the right, and the same is true of terrorism outside Europe during the same period – for instance, in India and Japan. In the terrorism of the 1960s and 1970s, groups deriving their inspiration from Marxism or anarchism were predominant, but they by no means had the field all to themselves. The terroristic outrages which involved most victims in Europe, such as the bomb at the Munich Oktoberfest (1980) and the explosion at Bologna railway station (1980), as well as the bomb in the Naples-to-Milan express (December 1984), were not carried out by left-wing groups.[34] It could still be argued that right-wing terror was far less frequent and systematic, and the number of right-wing terrorists in Western Europe much less numerous than those of the left. But this would certainly be false with regard to Turkey and Central America.

Right-wing terrorism in Europe usually emanated from small groups which regarded themselves as successors to the Fascist and Nazi parties of the 1930s. There is a certain irony in this, for the historical Fascist movements, while not rejecting individual terrorism in principle, opted on the whole for mass violence, such as street fighting. The explanation is not difficult to find: the Fascist parties of the 1930s were mass movements, the neo-Fascists of the 1970s were not. Nor was there any hope that they would make major progress in democratic elections. In these circumstances, a terrorist strategy might have seemed the only viable political perspective: to create chaotic conditions, to bring about economic paralysis, in the hope that as a result more and more people would become disaffected with the state and the democratic order, so that eventually a new authoritarian regime would emerge by popular acclaim. The name of the leading Italian neo-Fascist group, New Order (Ordine Nuovo), was not chosen by accident. Seen in a European perspective, right-wing terrorism was most rampant in Italy, where in 1983 and 1984 almost half of those arrested as suspected terrorists were from the far right. There was less right-wing terrorism in West Germany – the Munich bomb had almost certainly exploded inadvertently. There was not much right-wing terrorism in France either. The right-wing terrorists appeared on the scene in both Germany and Italy after the main left-wing terrorist groups had been defeated. Their activities were therefore bound to attract more attention.

Right-wing terrorism in Germany and France was mainly directed against Jewish institutions, and even more against foreign workers; among those killed in Germany were Vietnamese and Turks. The Italian groups such as the Nuclei Armati Revoluzionari (NAR) engaged in indiscriminate bombings in public places, including schools and public conveyances. Subsequently they became more selective in their targets, attacking policemen, gypsies, prostitutes, discotheques – and, in two instances, porno shops in Amsterdam. Unlike the Red Brigades, the Italian terrorists of the right have never executed complicated operations such as the kidnapping of prominent politicians, for two reasons: they were numerically much weaker and probably lacked assistance from abroad. On the other hand, their leaders and members did not have the same sophistication as the Red Brigadists. Both Italian and German terrorists of the right came almost without exception from families which were proletarian or lower-middle-class – in contrast to the terrorists of the left, who usually came from a higher social background. Few right-wing terrorists had attended universities; they were not part of the intellectual milieu to which Baader–Meinhof and the Red Brigades belonged. They were not much interested in books and ideas, and they spoke a language different from that of a Feltrinelli or the German students of sociology.

In view of the very small size of the right-wing terrorist undergrounds in France, West Germany and Italy and their internal divisions, not much is known about them. According to some reports, there exists a link-up with criminal elements in Italy. According to other accounts, both French and Italian groups have been penetrated by numerous policemen – or by former members of the police force who sympathized with their aims. If this were true, right-wing terrorism would almost certainly have shown greater professionalism. Many of their operations have remained mysterious to this day. Thus no claim has ever been made to authorship of railway terrorism in northern Italy, very much in contrast to general terrorist practice. West German right-wing terrorists have attacked US soldiers and NATO installations in Germany. While the German extreme right is bitterly opposed to 'US occupation' and the Western Alliance, it is of some interest that despite their avowed anti-Communism, these terrorists never attacked Communist or Soviet targets.

This raises endless questions about possible hidden influences: Wehrsport Gruppe Hoffmann, the strongest paramilitary German group, received its training with Fatah in Beirut, as did the German terrorists from the left. They received financial help and weapons from Libyans and the Palestinians, again like their enemies from the left. It stands to reason that such assistance was not given for purely altruistic reasons.

The Turkish example shows that terrorism, like politics, makes for strange bedfellows. Much of the terrorist fighting in Turkey was between left and right, between 'progressives' and the extreme left on the one hand, and Pan-Turkists, Muslim fundamentalists and extreme rightists on the other. But it also true that a newspaper of the far left turned virtually overnight into a mouthpiece of the extreme right; and that Erbakan, leader of the right, on some decisive occasions made common cause in the parliament with Ecevit, the head of the left. While Turkish workers of the right were battling with the left in the streets of West Germany, terrorists of both the right and the left were welcome guests in Bulgaria, a country not otherwise known for its sympathies with Pan-Turkism or Muslim fundamentalism. Obviously, there was more to the terrorism of the Turkish right than met the eye, and the same seems to be true, albeit to a lesser degree, of right-wing terrorists in other European countries.

Right-wing terrorist groups have appeared in all Latin American internal countries under a variety of names – the AAA in Argentina, Mano Blanco in Guatemala and Honduras, Orden de la Muerte and Escadron de la Muerte in Colombia, Ejercito Secreto Anti Communista and Organisacion Democratica Nacional in El Salvador, and many others. Some of them came into being in response to left-wing terrorism; this was the case, for instance, in Argentina. But even during the heyday of the left-wing Argentine terror, right-wing assassinations seem to have claimed as many victims as the other side, and after the defeat of the Trotskyites and the Montoneros, suppression was massive and cruel. Unlike the terrorists of the left, those of the right concentrated their activities in the cities; the exception was Nicaragua, where sections of the opposition formed a guerrilla movement against the Sandinista government. In many cases right-wing terrorist groups were little more than vigilante groups under the protection of the army and the police or, to make the situation even more complicated, under the auspices of extreme sections of the army and police. However, it would be mistaken to regard the terrorist groups of the right only as police agents. Just as the forces of the extreme left sometimes had deep roots among certain sections of the population, so had their opponents on the right, who organized 'revenge' squads. If the terrorists of the left assassinated senior government leaders, army officers and policemen, terrorists of the right singled out union leaders, university teachers and priests supporting the rebels. The case of El Salvador was extreme but in some respects not atypical.

The government of El Salvador was under onslaught from a dozen groups of extreme-left guerrillas and terrorists who eventually united into the Farabundo Marti Frente Nacional (FMNL) and wanted to bring about a 'Nicaraguan situation' through systematic attacks against the army, police and government supporters in general. These attacks continued even after Napoleon Duarte's reform government had come to power, for in the eyes of his opponents no radical change had taken place.

If the assassinations of the left in Central America had often been quite indiscriminate, those of the right were even more so. Right-wing terrorists sometimes claimed that their aim was not to harm anyone, but simply to warn the enemies of the people and 'traitors' (meaning all those favouring a dialogue with the left-wing guerrillas). But the number of those killed counted many thousands, including high churchmen, Jesuit priests and American nuns. What happened in El Salvador was no longer individual terror but a civil war in which fifty thousand people perished.

Some obvious differences can be discerned between right-wing terrorism in Europe and Latin America, differences stemming mainly from the different political context. European right-wing terrorist groups were small and their operations were mainly directed against democratic governments. In South and Central America right-wing terror was far more substantial. It usually took place – again with the exception of Nicaragua – in defence of military dictatorship. In addition it presented a mixture of police repression and vigilante activities. While right-wing terrorism in Europe was never more than a marginal phenomenon, this was certainly not the case in Latin America.

Labels such as 'left' and 'right' help little to clarify the battle fronts in the Middle East, in Northern Ireland or even in the Basque country. These movements derived their inspiration from both right-wing and left-wing ideologies, but religious and ethnic motives usually played an even more crucial role. Terrorism, to repeat once again, can appear in many different guises, and it has never been the monopoly of any specific political movement or ideology.

8

Terrorism Today III: International Terrorism

The term international terrorism covers a number of different issues in the contemporary world, from state-sponsored terrorism against foreign countries to co-operation between various terrorist groups. It also frequently refers to attacks against foreign nationals or property in the terrorist's own country or anywhere else.[1] None of this is new: there have been conspiratorial ties between revolutionary (and counter-revolutionary) groups in Europe since the early part of the nineteenth century, with Mazzini's Young Europe as the precursor. But these relations were largely limited to oral or written expressions of sympathy and solidarity. There was a great deal of cross-fertilization: the example of the Russian terrorists of 1881 inspired the Fenians and above all the anarchists. The Russian Social Revolutionaries, the Italian terrorists of the nineteenth century and the early IRA found imitators in many parts of the world. It was certainly not true (as alleged at the time) that 'Russian gold and Russian craft' governed Armenian terrorism. But the leaders of the Armenian movement who came to Turkey in 1892 were certainly of Russian origin.[2] The Indian nationalist press, on the other hand, frequently stressed that the application of 'Russian methods' by the British administration was bound to lead to Russian methods of agitation.

A British committee of investigation into terrorism in India noted that, together with the emphasis on religious motives, Bengali terrorist propaganda dwelt heavily upon the 'Russian rules' of revolutionary violence.[3] There were a few cases of active international collaboration: Orsini had British friends who helped to pay for his bombs. Later there was a London group of British friends of the Russian Revolution which contributed to pro-terrorist publications. The Fenians consulted the French General Cluseret when planning a rising in 1867; at a later date the Clan-na-Gael played with the idea of enlisting Russian help against Britain, just as Pilsudski envisaged an anti-Russian alliance with the Japanese. Devoy suggested helping the Mahdi in the Sudan with 20,000 armed Irishmen; Sean MacBride and Arthur Lynch fought in the Boer War against the British.[4] Italian anarchists operated in France, Switzerland and Spain as well as in their own country; Indian terrorists received theoretical instruction from the Russian Social Revolutionaries. Sometimes active intervention by foreign powers was alleged. Thus Miguel Angiolilo, who killed the Spanish prime minister, Canovas, in August 1897, was said to have been paid by the Cuban rebels against the Spanish, but this has not been proved. Russian involvement with the Serbian Black Hand is well known, but whether the Russians actually knew about the preparations for the murder at Sarajevo is not at all certain; the Black Hand had in fact voted on 14 June 1914 against the assassination precisely because it feared that war would ensue. Whether 'Apis', who organized the assassination, informed his Russian contacts of the vote is doubtful. But the aims of the Black Hand certainly transcended Serbia; in 1911 they had planned the assassination of the King of Greece.

Neighbouring countries often provided a sanctuary for terrorists; the Social Revolutionaries escaped whenever they could to semi-autonomous Finland where the Okhrana could not operate with as much ease as in Russia proper. Early South Indian terrorism found a haven in Pondicherry, a French colony outside the reach of the British police.[5] One of the Sarajevo conspirators in 1914, Mehmedbasic, escaped to Montenegro. When the Austrians demanded his extradition, the government went through an elaborate charade of searching for him but, in fact, let him escape arrest. Later IMRO had such a base for its forays in Bulgaria, the Croatians in Italy and Hungary, the IRA in the Republic of Ireland, the ETA in France, the Palestinians first in Jordan and later in the Lebanon. But for the existence of these sanctuaries, many groups would have had to cease operations.

Mention has been made of the fact that the massive systematic involvement of governments in terrorist movements in foreign countries dates back to the 1920s. The Italians were most active in this respect; Balbo, Ciano and other Fascist luminaries met the leaders of the Croatian Ustacha, provided them with every possible help and after the murder at Marseilles, Kvaternik and Pavelic, the main wire-pullers, escaped to Italy. The Italians refused to extradite them and at the same time Mussolini bitterly attacked those who charged Italy with abetting terrorism: 'We do not give our hands to murderers. Those who want to implicate Italy are cowards and liars.' Italy also gave money and supplied arms to the Macedonian IMRO. Previously IMRO had gravitated towards the Soviet Union but opposition within the organization (and on the part of official Bulgarian circles) prevented a rapprochement with Moscow. The Italians also supported the French

CSAR, a right-wing terrorist group founded by Eugène Deloncle in 1936. These were the *cagoulards*, the hooded men, who assassinated, among others, the brothers Rosselli, leaders of the Italian anti-Fascist group Giustizia e Libertà, in their French exile. For these and other services rendered, the Italians sent the CSAR 12,000 hand grenades and 170 machine-guns ·and submachine-guns, as well as hundreds of pounds of explosives.[6] Right-wing terrorist groups in Germany after the First World War seem to have received only minimal help from abroad. The Rumanian legionnaires apparently obtained none at all.

Nationalist terrorist groups usually had no scruples in seeking and accepting aid from foreign powers. Thus LEHI sent emissaries to Beirut in 1940 to establish contact with Italian and German officials, and four years later they sought a link with Soviet representatives. IRA leaders collaborated with Nazi Germany during the Second World War, which did not prevent them from accepting help from Communist countries two decades later. Members of LEHI or the IRA were not necessarily either Fascist or Communist. Like the Croats, the IMRO, the Palestinian Arabs or the Indian terrorists, they acted according to the time-honoured principle that the enemy of their enemy was their friend. Some foreign aid was given without strings attached but this was not always so. The fact that Lenin accepted German money in 1917 did not make him a German agent, but not all terrorists had his strength of character and clarity of vision. Prolonged and substantial subventions by foreign governments usually had a demoralizing effect on both the leadership and the rank and file of terrorist movements, which became increasingly dependent on their sponsors. Sometimes, when the payments were stopped, the terrorists would turn against their paymasters – more often the movement would simply collapse, as happened to the IMRO after the Bulgarians withdrew their support.

Multinational terrorism reached a first climax in the early 1970s. It involved close co-operation between small terrorist groups in many countries, with the Libyans, Algerians, Syrians, North Koreans and Cubans acting as the paymasters and suppliers of weapons and other equipment. They were also co-ordinators of a fascinating amalgam of East European and Latin American-style Communism, North African and Near Eastern clerico-Fascism, Islamic fundamentalism, West European anarchism, unpolitical technicians of terror and probably also a few madmen and madwomen. The Soviet Union began to support a number of terrorist movements such as Palestinian and African groups; mostly assistance would be given through various intermediaries so that its origins would be difficult to prove and, if something went wrong, charges of complicity could be indignantly denied. Countries such as South Yemen, Somalia and Uganda co-operated for a time with the terrorists for both political and financial reasons, but this was represented as humanitarian action motivated by the desire to save human lives. In short, terrorism became almost respectable, and there was a substantial majority at the United Nations opposing any effective international action directed against it.[7] This new multinational terrorism was, however, for all practical purposes surrogate warfare between governments; it had little in common, except in name, with the movements of national and social protest that had engaged in terrorist activities in previous decades. Some terrorist groups, to be sure, retained a substantial measure of independence, but others became almost entirely subservient to outside interests. If the Syrians supported Saiqa, one of the factions of the Palestinian resistance, the Iraqis, Libyans and other Arab states would back other Palestinian groups and, as the Lebanese civil war was to show, would expect their protégés to represent their interests. In brief, a new species of terrorism emerged, an almost impenetrable maze of linkages, intrigues, common and conflicting interests, including open and covert collaboration with foreign governments who preferred to stay in the shadows.

International government-sponsored terrorism became a permanent feature in international politics in the 1970s. As for its intrinsic importance, opinions differ. According to US Department of State reports, '[terrorism] is becoming increasingly frequent, indiscriminate and state-sponsored'. Some authorities have claimed that international terrorism has increased over the last fifteen years by 10 per cent annually; others have maintained that the rate of increase has been twice as much. According to one source, property damage caused by terrorism over the last fifteen years should be estimated at over one billion dollars.[8] One billion dollars is much less than the cost of a single nuclear submarine; much more damage is caused by rodents each year, not to mention major natural catastrophes. However, terrorism has received infinitely more publicity than mice and rats.

The decisive issue is not, of course, the actual amount of damage caused, or even the number of people killed (which has been small by any reckoning), but the fact that state-sponsored terrorism has not been decisively resisted and that, for this reason, it will continue to exist and may even increase in future. The US secretary of state was correct when he noted that while violent or fanatical individuals and groups can exist in almost any society, terrorism would long since have withered away in many countries had it not been for significant support from outside.[9] State-sponsored terrorism existed, as has been shown, well before the Second World War, but it was on a minor scale, and it was not customary to brag about it. Such operations were carried out but no one would be eager to claim credit, irrespective of success or failure. The Soviet Union and some of her allies have been charged with responsibility for much of international terrorism by providing the infrastructure for this new kind of surrogate warfare. It remains therefore to be investigated what factual basis there is in these claims.

Soviet Attitudes to Terrorism

Official Soviet spokesmen have always condemned terrorism, denouncing it as adventurist, elitist and objectively serving the interests of imperialism and the forces of reaction. Yet, at the same time, the Soviet Union has provided arms, financial aid, military training and, on occasion, political support to various terrorist groups. In practice, as distinct from doctrine, the Soviet Union has given selective support to 'national liberation movements' employing terroristic means. It has also assisted some groups which even by stretching a vivid imagination cannot be classified as belonging to the 'national liberation' camp. Furthermore, it has closely co-operated with the countries which have been the main sponsors of international terrorism, Libya and Syria.

The ambiguity has a twofold source. It dates back to the days of Marx, Engels and Lenin; their opposition to Bakuninist, Blanquist and Mostian practices is well known. But there was always room for exceptions: special allowances were made for the Irish Fenians and for the Russian Narodnaya Volya. In a similar way, Soviet leaders denounce terrorism in principle but given the existence of such groups, and the fact that assisting them may be politically expedient, the Soviets will not hesitate to support them.* On the ideological level, the problem can easily be solved: groups receiving Soviet help are by definition not terrorist but rather national liberation movements, part of the 'world revolutionary process'. They weaken the West and thus 'objectively' promote world peace and progress. For a variety of reasons, the Soviet Union would no doubt prefer means other than terrorism to be used; such actions are usually difficult to control and, if they fail, are bound to have an adverse effect on Communist parties and the Soviet Union. The Soviet Union cannot openly support terrorist groups without harming its image of responsible statesmanship and complicating its relations with foreign states. In addition, terrorism is problematic from the Soviet point of view, for there is always the risk that the example

---

* 'Political terrorism is rampant in the world of capital. In its most varied forms it always accompanies the destabilization of undemocratic reactionary regimes. Terrorism has become a symptom of the invalidity of the capitalist system of rule' (Yu. Pankov (ed.), *Political Terrorism, an Indictment of Imperialism* (Moscow, 1983), p. 19). See Roberta Goren, *The Soviet Union and Terrorism* (London, 1984), *passim*.

may be emulated and that terrorist operations may be used against Soviet representatives abroad or inside the countries belonging to the socialist camp.

Marxism–Leninism teaches the 'unity of theory and practice', but as far as terrorism is concerned, theory and practice certainly diverge. Soviet publications give certain clues about Communist doctrine but they do not necessarily reflect Communist practice. Compared with the enormous literary output on terrorism in the West, Soviet writings on the subject are few.* While Soviet spokesmen do not belittle the significance of the subject, they do not see it as the greatest threat to world peace. Soviet experts differentiate between nationalist, neo-Fascist and ultra-leftist groups, and they emphasize that many terrorist groups in the contemporary world tend to use revolutionary and even Marxist–Leninist slogans. However, the use of such slogans, as they see it, is no more than a case of political and social mimicry. The ideology of these groups is a mixture of nationalist, religious and radical ingredients; in many cases the mimicry may well be not deliberate fraudulence but self-deception. Terrorists may be convinced that they fight for a just cause, for the liberation of their people and/or the radical transformation of society. They are romantics and willing to sacrifice their lives. However, the fact that the beliefs of the terrorists

---

* There are propagandistic writings blaming the CIA for state terrorism or apologetic books refuting Western claims concerning a Soviet-sponsored international terrorist network. An example for this genre is Georgi Vetchnadze, *Za Kulisami odnoi diversi* (*Behind the Scenes of One Provocation*) (Moscow, 1985), purporting to give the true account of the real wire-pullers behind the attempt to kill the Pope in Rome in 1981. Another example is Afanasi Veselitski, *Ubitsi. Strategia destabilisatsia i taktika terrora na Apeninakh* (*Murderers: The Strategy of Destabilization and the Tactics of Terror in the Appenines*) (Moscow, 1985), claiming that Aldo Moro was killed by the CIA, and also E. Kovalev and V. Malyshev, *Terror – vdokhno-viteli i ispolnitelni* (*Terror: The Inspirators and the Hatchetmen*) (Moscow, 1984). While the Veselitski book is introduced as a mixture of novel and documentation, Kovalev purports to be non-fiction. Books by Ernest Genri, a veteran Stalinist journalist, and a volume edited by Professor Y. Pankov were mainly for consumption abroad. Their thesis is that terrorism is both an indictment and a tool of imperialism. These and similar authors show little familiarity with the subject. On a somewhat higher level is A. S. Grachev, *Tupiki politicheskovo nasilia* (*The Blind Alleys of Political Violence*) (Moscow, 1982), issued by an academic publishing house, but the author seems not to have had access to the essential Western literature on the subject. The same is true of A. Asevski, *Kto organizuyet i napravlayet mezhdunarodni terrorism* (*Who Organizes and Directs International Terrorism*) (Moscow, 1982); V. Kassil and L. Kolosov, *Terrorism bez maski* (*Terrorism Without a Mask*) (Moscow, 1983); and A. M. Baichorov, *Neokolonialism i mezhdunarodni terrorism* (*Neocolonialism and International Terrorism*) (Moscow, 1985). A Soviet author who has obviously studied the subject in depth and who is familiar with both terrorist and anti-terrorist literature is Viktor Vladimirovich Vityuk, *Pod chuzhim znamenami. Litsemerie i samo-obman levovo terrorisma.* (*Under False Flags: Hypocrisy and Self-Deception of Leftwing Terrorism*) (Moscow, 1985). Another competent work is S. A. Efirov, *Pokushenie na Budushe* (*Attack on the Future*) (Moscow, 1984).

are genuine and sincere does not necessarily mean that the terrorists fight for a just cause. Even groups for which Soviet experts have sympathies in view of their 'progressive' character, such as the Spanish ETA and in particular the IRA, are in the final analysis nationalist and not socialist in inspiration.[10]

In contrast to many Western writers on the subject, Soviet experts are perfectly aware of the fundamental difference between terrorism and guerrilla warfare: 'Urban guerrilla is a fraudulent concept, scheduled to mask ordinary terrorism' (Vityuk). The Soviets note that Marighella, who raised the banner of urban guerrilla warfare, had the courage to admit that this was tantamount to practising terrorism, which is more than can be said of many of his Latin American and European followers, who fail to concede this obvious point. Soviet ideologists by no means oppose in principle the use of revolutionary violence; their aversion to terrorism carried out by marginal groups is based mainly on their recognition of the fact that it usually causes more harm than good.

Why not support terrorism if, as Soviet writers have written, 'it always accompanies the destabilization of undemocratic, reactionary regimes'? Soviet writers take, on the whole, a dimmer view of terrorism in Europe (and North America) than in South America, where the armed struggle may be not just a real, but sometimes the only possible means to overthrow a military dictatorship. Whereas the political views of European terrorists are wrong *ab initio*, the Latin Americans, as the Soviets see it, start from correct premises: they do not, in principle, hold the masses in contempt. However, the logic of urban terrorism 'sooner or later induces them to make an about-turn and they come to regard the masses as an object of political manipulation.'[11] Nevertheless, despite their grave political mistakes, the fate of Latin American 'urban guerrillas' is 'deeply tragical'. Soviet writers quote with approval Che Guevara, who opposed urban terrorism, in contrast to those of his successors who did not heed his advice.[12]

According to the Soviet party line, there is a fundamental difference between the national liberation movements and terrorism; but Soviet authors still get involved in contradictions when dealing with groups such as the Irish or the Palestinians. They accuse the British of using violence against the national liberation war of the PIRA and of calling the freedom fighters 'killers' and terrorists. At the same time, they approvingly quote the head of the Irish Communist Party denouncing the PIRA bombing campaign which 'objectively serves the interests of British Colonial rule . . .'.[13]

In a similar way, all but one Palestinian organization including the PFLP and PFLP–General Command are *bona fide* progressive national liberation movements; the exception is Black September, which according to the

Soviet version 'follows the instructions of the Israelis and ... Scotland Yard'.[14] (The author seems to believe that the London police and British Intelligence are housed under the same roof.)

Soviet attitudes are negative towards Japanese and West German 'Red Armies', as well as the (defunct) Spanish Grapo and the Italian Red Brigades. They are also scathing about Fanon's 'coloured nationalism' and note that certain postulates of left-wing terrorism 'smell of Fascism'.[15] Soviet observers fail to see in the operations of the European terrorists any mitigating factors; they blame intellectuals such as Heinrich Böll, Günther Grass and Alberto Moravia as well as Sartre and some progressive theologians for lending the terrorists moral respectability or even superiority; they have ridiculed churchmen (such as the British clergyman Paul Oestreicher) who called the German RAF 'new crusaders'. Soviet critics have gone as far as blaming the Italian government for not dealing with terrorism more harshly.[16] The assumption of left-wing terrorists that there is nothing to choose between democracy and Fascism strikes Soviet observers as a manifestation of political cretinism.

Soviet experts do not believe in the genetic base of terrorism: 'Terrorists are not born, terrorism is an acquired habit.'[17] However, there are certain psychological features typical of left-wing terrorists; there are certain prototypes such as the 'idealist', the 'condottiere' and the individual who has not found his or her place in society.[18] The idealists are driven by moral absolutes; they have constructed an ideal pattern for both society and human beings. As they realize that the world does not live up to their expectations, they conclude that society does not deserve to exist at all. This kind of frustration leads to 'pseudo-revolutionary impatience', to destruction, and quite frequently to self-destruction. If left-wing terrorism is a social phenomenon, what are its social roots? At this point Soviet authors face certain difficulties, for however strongly they may dissociate themselves from 'vulgar reductionism', sooner or later they have to put the blame on the capitalist social order, despite the obvious fact that the most highly developed capitalist countries have witnessed very little terrorism.

Thus some Soviet authors have commented intelligently and realistically on left-wing terrorism. It is only fair to add that they could not write with equal candour on the far more important species of nationalist–separatist terrorism.

If doctrinal writings were the only clue about Soviet attitudes to terrorism, the conclusion would be obvious: the Soviet Union rejects terrorism *tout court* as repugnant to Communist morality, politically inopportune and frequently counter-productive. Yet political reality is often more complicated. In actual fact the Soviet Union has engaged in individual terrorism:

it has assisted, directly and indirectly, not only 'movements of national liberation' such as the African National Congress, but also groups which have engaged exclusively in terrorism as distinct from guerrilla warfare. The most famous victim was, of course, Leon Trotsky; so far no Soviet author has claimed that he was killed by the CIA in his Mexican asylum in 1940. There were other such cases, concerning above all agents of the Soviet secret service who defected and leading members of émigré organizations.

Even if one leaves aside as 'not proven' the most notorious recent case – the attempted assassination of Pope John Paul II, where the extent of Bulgarian involvement cannot be proven in a court of law – it is easy to point to other examples of political terrorism by Communist parties in and out of power. Thus the Venezuelan Communist Party opted for urban terrorism in the early 1960s; there is reason to assume that this was their own decision, not Moscow's. On the other hand, the Soviet Union did nothing at the time to dissociate itself from the Venezuelans. Among other Latin American Communist parties which have engaged in terrorist operations are those of Colombia, Guatemala, Haiti and the Dominican Republic. Most of these were small parties and their attitudes were not representative of Latin American Communism. Even in Colombia, the FARC – one of the main terrorist groups led by Manuel Marulande, a member of the Central Committee of the Communist Party – did not use terrorism as the only form of political struggle. Some leading Latin American Communist spokesmen sharply condemned the 'desperate adventures of ultra-leftists who engaged in kidnappings and attacks which had no working-class support and which contributed nothing to the revolutionary cause'.[19]

Rodney Arismendi, leader of the Uruguayan Communists, said in an interview with the Italian *Unità* that his party considered the Tupamaros sincere, honest and courageous revolutionaries and that the Communists had defended them on occasion. But Tupamaros tactics did not correspond to the needs of Uruguay. To make the overall picture even more confused, it appears that some Soviet help has apparently been extended to the Tupamaros, the Argentine ERP (despite its one-time Trotskyite inclination) and other such groups by way of Cuba, without the knowledge of the local Communist parties.

The Cubans, on the other hand, gave more or less indiscriminate support to Latin American guerrilla and terrorist organizations up to about 1970. Doctrinally the Cubans should have helped only guerrilla movements. But in fact they also supported terrorists, especially after the collapse of most Latin American guerrilla movements.[20]

Cuban support became more selective after 1970, partly perhaps as a result of Soviet pressure, partly in view of the realization that the 'revolutionary wave' of the 1960s had passed and that it was desirable to normalize Cuba's relations with other Latin American governments. This led to bitter recriminations on the part of the more militant Latin American guerrilla and terrorist groups which claimed that Cuba had sacrificed (if not betrayed) the revolutionary cause. These charges were on the whole unjustified because Cuba continued, albeit somewhat more discreetly, to provide training, arms and money to Latin American terrorists as well as to other such groups in various parts of the world. This emerged quite clearly from the expulsion of several Cuban 'diplomats' from France in connection with the affair of the notorious Carlos in 1975. Cuban diplomats were expelled throughout the 1970s and early 1980s from various Latin American and West European countries as the Soviet Union gradually disengaged itself from direct involvement in Latin American terrorism. (Soviet diplomats had been expelled from Mexico in March 1971, from Bolivia in March 1972 and from Colombia in August 1972 as evidence of links with local terrorist groups was revealed.) After 1972 a new division of labour came into force with Cuba and North Korea taking over a large share of the Third World terrorist burden. Beginning in 1968–9 terrorist training centres were established in North Korea; the trainees have been traced to and, in some cases, apprehended in Latin America (Mexico, Brazil, Bolivia, Colombia and elsewhere), the Middle East and Asia (Sri Lanka, Malaya, Indonesia) and also Africa. While Vietnam since the end of the war has not engaged in terrorism, at least not outside its own borders, North Korea has done so with a vengeance, culminating in the assassination of several members of the South Korean government during a state visit to Burma.

Following the arrest of graduates of training centres in Soviet-bloc countries and the seizure of documents, a great many details have become known about the location of these centres, the curriculum and even the identity of the instructors. The courses have ranged from operating tanks and anti-aircraft guns to the handling of explosives and communication equipment. The participants in the courses have come from many countries; they include all Palestinian groups including those which have no conceivable use for tanks and anti-aircraft guns, Latin Americans, Africans and so on. The list of those who have *not* received training in Soviet-bloc countries is shorter. It includes most right-wing terrorists with, however, some notable exceptions. The Bulgarians took some right-wing Turkish terrorists under their wing, and the PLO has trained neo-Nazi terrorists from West Germany in their camps in Lebanon. The Soviet Union and the other eastern bloc countries have not, as a rule, trained West European and North American terrorists, again with a few exceptions.[21] The Soviet leaders correctly assumed that the political damage caused by a discovery would outweigh the possible benefits. It was therefore decided at an early date that if the European terrorists received any help at all, it would be channelled through Libya, Cuba, Syria and the PLO.

The PLO and the other Palestinian groups were for a long time the main transmission belt to various terrorist groups with which the Soviet Union did not want to deal directly. With the loss of their bases, first in Jordan and later in Lebanon, this function of the PLO has been substantially reduced.

Soviet attitudes towards the PLO were initially fairly cool; prior to 1968 the militant Palestinians were on occasion even denounced as reactionary, adventurist and ultra-revolutionary.[22] Afterwards Soviet attitudes became more friendly, partly because of the fear that the PLO could come under Chinese influence (Peking had recognized the Palestinians as early as 1964), partly as the result of Russia's loss of her foothold in Egypt after Nasser's death. However, the first official visit of PLO leaders to Moscow did not take place until as late as 1974. While the smaller Palestinian groups such as the PFLP were ideologically much closer to the Russians than Fatah, the Soviet leaders, realizing that these groups were bound to remain small, did not apparently give the self-styled Arab Marxist groups any preferential treatment.[23]

The high tide of Soviet–PLO relations was between 1979 and 1982.* The position of the PLO weakened following its involvement in the Lebanese civil war, the Israeli invasion and the internal splits among the Palestinians. As Syria and Libya, Russia's allies, turned against Arafat and tried to destroy the PLO as a semi-independent force, the Soviet Union faced a serious dilemma. There was no alternative force which could take the place of Fatah. The Soviet Union continued to support the PLO even during its most difficult period (1983–5), but it had clearly ceased to be a central factor in Soviet political thinking. As the Soviets realized that the radical camp would remain divided for the foreseeable future, there was an inevitable cooling off in relations between Moscow and the Palestinians.

Training camps apart, arms supplies to terrorists have included not only the standard Kalashnikov (AK-47) assault rifle, automatic pistols, sub-machine-guns and RG-3 hand grenades, but also relatively sophisticated

---

* According to the PLO representative in Moscow his organization enjoyed a special diplomatic status in the USSR. Members of the head office were permitted to travel freely all over the USSR while ambassadors accredited to the USSR may not move about without official permission beyond a distance of 110 kilometres. (Muhammed as Sha'r in *Al Safir*, 17 February 1981, as quoted in S. Elad and A. Merari, *The Soviet Bloc and World Terrorism* (Tel Aviv, 1984), p. 39.)

weapons such as the RPG-7 anti-tank missile launchers (used by the PFLP and the IRA) and the SA-7 surface-to-air missiles (used by the PFLP and ZAPU). These and other items have been widely documented and need not be enumerated; the same is true of arms shipments that were intercepted – from the Czechs and Fatah to the IRA, from Bulgaria to Turkey, from Libya to Colombia and Central America, from Iraq to Italy and so on.[24]

Less well known is the logistic support which has been given by Soviet-bloc countries, especially with regard to attack and escape routes. Several attacks against trains carrying Jewish emigrants from the Soviet Union were staged from Czechoslovakia; German terrorists have been hiding in Bulgaria, Rumania and even Yugoslavia. Hotels in Sofia have been used to prepare various terrorist attacks, including the massacre at the Munich Olympic Games in 1972. The role of South Yemen, Libya and Cuba in this context has frequently been documented.

Thus the available evidence suggests that the Soviet attitude towards the practice of terrorism has been more tolerant than its theory. Wherever possible, it prefers to work through surrogates, Communist and non-Communist alike. It is also true that on a few occasions, Soviet-bloc countries have co-operated with the West in the apprehension of terrorists; a number of West German terrorists were arrested in Bulgaria and extradited. On some occasions the Soviet bloc has even voted with the West in favour of anti-terrorist resolutions at the United Nations, usually after having been on the receiving end of a terrorist operation. Thus, following the hijacking of a Soviet plane in October 1970, the Soviet Union voted for a UN resolution calling for the punishment of the hijackers; after the murder of a Soviet diplomat in Lebanon in 1985, they voted for a strongly worded condemnation of terrorism. Furthermore, the Soviet Union has fairly consistently opposed attacks against diplomats and hijackings, as distinct from other targets of terrorist attacks.

If Soviet spokesmen could define their attitude towards terrorism openly and without inhibitions, they would probably argue that if they are giving support to terrorists, so are Western powers; if Nicaragua is sheltering Italian terrorists, so is France; if the Soviet bloc has done so on a much wider basis, this is not a question of principle.* Furthermore, Soviet spokesmen could argue that if it were true that Moscow is the *fons et origo* of international terrorism, the main wire-puller and co-ordinator, there would

---

* Given the compartmentalization of knowledge in the Soviet Union, it is likely that those who write articles and books about terrorism in the Soviet Union may claim in good faith that their country does not support acts of terror. Very likely, even the foreign minister is not always told the whole truth.

be a hundred times more of it, given the enormous potential resources of the Soviet Union and its allies in this respect. The truth is somewhere between the professions of innocence and the claims that all terrorist operations are somehow engineered by Moscow. In the overall Soviet strategy of increasing its influence in the Third World and weakening the NATO allies, terrorist activities play a certain, albeit minor role. The difficulty as seen from Moscow is that support for terrorism is a fine art, that it is effective only in certain conditions, and that, like certain medicines, it may have unpleasant side-effects.

In principle, terrorism provides a substitute for conventional warfare. It helps to destabilize political regimes considered hostile by the Soviet Union, and it increases tensions and adds to the general insecurity inside those countries. Terrorism may compel governments to adopt oppressive measures limiting individual freedom, thus alienating sections of the population and weakening the internal consensus. This was the original argument of the Tupamaros and other Latin American terrorists and, while it appears superficially persuasive, it has in fact not worked well in practice even in Latin America, let alone in other parts of the world. For while the anti-terrorist measures of the government have indeed provoked protest among some intellectuals and to a certain extent on university campuses, the great majority of the population, including the working class, the trade unions and in some cases even the Communist parties, have demanded even tougher measures against terrorism. In other words, anti-terrorist measures have frequently been quite popular.

Equally, the argument has been found defective according to which terrorism makes it necessary for Western governments to devote a higher share of their defence efforts to internal security, thus weakening external defence. This is because a major terrorist campaign creates the impression that the country in question is under siege, and thus makes it much easier for governments emphasize the need for greater defence spending. The terrorist campaignagainst NATO bases and personnel in Western Europe in 1983–5 did not prevent the stationing of the missiles nor weaken NATO to any significant degree. On the contrary, it helped to embarrass the peace movement which from the Soviet standpoint was a far more effective factor in the struggle against NATO.

International terrorism, it could be argued, is bound to deepen the conflicts between members of the Western Alliance.* America will usually

---

* The bickering between Washington and the West European allies after the American action in 1986 against Qadhafi was followed with evident relish in Moscow. But since Moscow still had no full control over Qadhafi, the situation was far from ideal from the Soviet point of view.

advocate a tougher line while European countries, as past experience has shown, will think of various reasons in favour of inaction. However, this is true only as long as such terrorist operations are relatively infrequent and of no major consequence. The moment terrorism becomes a real danger to the survival of a Western government, it will be only too eager to co-operate with the US.

Soviet ideologists have admitted after years of doctrinal hesitation that the experience of Cuba and Nicaragua has shown that military political fronts (or 'insurrectionary centres') are capable in certain conditions of acting as substitutes for the political parties of the proletariat (i.e. the Communist Party). This is tantamount to accepting the old Castroist–Guevarist approach, but it refers to guerrilla warfare; an urban terrorist group cannot normally act as a 'military political front' or even as an insur-rectionary centre.

All of which tends to prove that while terrorism is part of a general strategy of destabilization, it is a relatively unimportant component. The problem facing the sponsors of terrorism is that a little terrorism is no more than an irritant, whereas terrorism on a massive scale is bound to backfire, strengthening rather than weakening the national consensus and helping the government to consolidate its position – as happened in Italy and in other countries. Terrorism may still be of some use in certain conditions from the Soviet point of view, be it as a means of elimina-ting or threatening individuals considered particularly dangerous, or in cases in which society and the state are too weak to cope with the terrorist danger.

One could point to Lebanon in this connection, but it was a case *sui generis*, a civil war fought by small semi-regular armies or militias in which terrorism played a role, but not a decisive one. There is no reason to doubt the sincerity of the Soviet authors who argue that an energetic, deci-sive campaign will always defeat the terrorists within a short time:

Victory over terrorism is possible also in the framework of bourgeois–democratic regimes on the basis of the existing laws. There is no need for greater severity on the part of these governments nor have democratic principles to be jettisoned. All that is needed is the strict observation of the legal forms of reacting to political protest in contrast to terrorist activities, a consistent attitude towards terrorism and its threats, a struggle against all forms of terrorism, without exception, from both right and left and all those who inspire and protect it. . . .[25]

This is a fairly realistic appraisal of the prospects of terrorism in Western societies, and Western commentators can do little but say 'Amen'. Whether the Soviet leadership and its 'organs' will act according to this political analysis is yet another question. Support for terrorism will probably continue, albeit not on a massive scale, and Soviet denials will also continue.

The Rise of Qadhafi

Muamar al Qadhafi emerged in the 1970s as one of the most active, and certainly the loudest, supporter of international terrorism. The leader of a group of 'free officers' who overthrew the Senussi monarchy in Libya in September 1969, he became subsequently the head of the 'revolutionary council' which ruled the country and engaged in various eccentric political–social experiments. Qadhafi's idol was Gamal Abdul Nasser, the Egyptian leader; his aim was the unification of the Arab world, close collaboration with all Muslim countries and eventually the revolutionary transformation of the whole world, whatever that may have meant. His political ideas which he publicized in some detail in his 'Green Book', the first part of which appeared in 1975, were based on Islam which, as he saw it, was the embodiment of freedom, socialism and (Arab) unity. Islam in his view did not conflict with nationalism, it was a doctrine of permanent revolution: to understand and practise Islam correctly, one had to go back to its original roots. Qadhafi belonged to the generation of 'Sawt al Arab', the young listeners to the heady ideas of Nasserism broadcast in the 1960s by Cairo radio to many millions of frustrated young people looking for an ideological compass in a world of confusion.

Qadhafi's views were bound to collide with those of other leaders and thinkers in the Islamic world; like all the great world religions, Islam can be interpreted in many different ways. The idea of Islamic socialism, for instance, was first developed by the Muslim Brotherhood, a fundamentalist sect. But far from acknowledging this, Qadhafi treated the Brotherhood as a bitter enemy of his regime. Gradually, Qadhafi persuaded himself that he was the best, indeed the only, correct interpreter of Islam.

Libya is a small country. The number of its inhabitants is a mere three million of which a considerable part are Bedouins who have not yet been integrated into the political and social processes of a modern society. Normally the ideas of the leader of a small country, however forcefully stated, would be of limited interest to the outside world. But Libya came in the 1970s into a great deal of money, derived from oil royalties, and Qadhafi used a significant part of these funds to promote his views abroad. Political influence could be gained by means of propaganda, terrorism and direct payments to foreign political leaders.

Meanwhile, inside Libya a pronounced cult of personality had developed very much in contrast to the ideas of 'popular revolution' and 'direct democracy' – the official doctrine of the country. The leader strutted on the political scene in all kinds of fancy uniforms, accompanied by a detachment of female soldiers and, to be on the safe side, a group of East German bodyguards. He delivered bombastic speeches which made Mussolini in retrospect appear a restrained and moderate elder statesman. His behaviour was erratic by any standards; he resigned frequently from his official positions – only to withdraw his resignation after a few days. He announced the merger of his country first with Egypt, and later with the Sudan, Syria, Morocco, Tunisia and Malta, even though he must have known that these gestures would be of no practical consequence.

These and other exploits made many outside observers doubt his sanity. Yet the pattern of his behaviour was neither quite sane nor consistently insane. He was a devout Muslim and gave financial support to Muslims in many parts of the globe. However, when it suited him, he would support politically or materially non-Muslims fighting his own co-religionists – such as the rebels in southern Sudan or the ruling clique in Ethiopia, or indeed the Soviet leaders who had invaded Afghanistan. Hence the question of whether Islam was for him an article of faith or a tool to legitimize his own aspirations. His speeches and declarations to the press were replete with extreme threats. He would carry his propaganda war to America and other distant parts of the globe, claiming that any attack against Libya would trigger off a third world war. Yet when faced with a real challenge, such as the shooting down of a Libyan plane by the Israelis or American fighters, he would react with the utmost caution. Like a mischievous child he would instinctively know how far he could go in his transgressions, whether he could persevere without much risk or whether he had to retreat so as not to bring upon himself some real punishment.

Qadhafi's foreign political thoughts were first summarized in the so-called 'third international theory', a doctrine distinct from both capitalism and Communism. It was, however, by no means clear what the doctrine meant in practical terms. It seemed that while Qadhafi had strong likes and even stronger aversions, his strength was not really in the field of theory and ideology. His hatred of 'imperialism' (and especially of America) was real enough; as early as 1972 he announced that he would carry the war to America, enlisting in the struggle the five million Muslims living in the United States. He stood uncompromisingly for the destruction of the state of Israel and he attacked on many occasions the moderate Arab governments. But on other occasions he would co-operate with the conservatives and he did not get along too well with those who ideologically should be his friends, including the Palestinians, the Algerians and the Iraqis. Even relations with the Soviet Union, which provided enormous quantities of arms to Libya, were subject to fluctuations. There was a first crisis in relations in 1972–3, followed by a long rapprochement, fresh quarrels and more affirmations of friendship. Qadhafi remained a source of irritation to friends and foes alike.

Qadhafi's behaviour has been explained at times with reference to his origins – he was born in a Bedouin tent – to Islam and to Nasserism. But neither his initiatives nor his inconsistencies, neither his fanaticism nor his bombast, could be satisfactorily explained by the concept of the tribe, certain Islamic traditions or the idea of Arab unity. These and other components were part of his mental make-up but there was also a strong element of idiosyncratic behaviour, even of madness, which made him a phenomenon *sui generis* in contemporary politics. Some observers of international affairs found it difficult to understand how a political leader showing such irrational behaviour could last any length of time. But while there is no room for an eccentric in a bureaucracy, there are many examples in history illustrating that the rules at the top of the political ladder are quite different, provided only that the leader has a minimum of charisma. Qadhafi certainly seems to have had charisma as far as his fellow Libyans were concerned. Those who did not admire him, feared him and kept silent.[26]

It was Qadhafi's firm belief that, given his global mission, he had the right to interfere in the affairs of every foreign country. The accepted rules of international law and behaviour could be safely disregarded if they stood in the way of his fulfilling his mission. Since 1976 Qadhafi's henchmen have killed Libyan émigrés or tried to kidnap these 'stray dogs' in Britain, Italy, West Germany, Cyprus, Greece, Egypt and other countries. When it appeared that these forays encountered little resistance, they were intensified and became more frequent in 1984–5. The pattern was almost always the same. If a Libyan killer squad was apprehended abroad, Qadhafi would arrest a substantial number of the citizens of that country working in Libya, whereupon the British, German, Italian or Greek authorities would release the assassins before or after having put them on trial. This charade became so common that the authorities in Greece and elsewhere would no longer bother to arrest the Libyan hitmen but simply deported them.

Libyan forces engaged in military intervention in African countries such as Chad and Niger, but politically more significant was the support given (sometimes selectively, at other times quite indiscriminately) to terrorist movements from Northern Ireland to New Caledonia in the Pacific. Such support, including the provision of money, weapons, training, logistical help and asylum, was not, in principle, kept secret by Qadhafi.* Libya had a duty to support all groups fighting for national liberation and since almost every terrorist group claimed to fight for national liberation, they became almost by definition eligible for support, unless of course their activities were of no political interest to the Libyans. Among those who were helped were the Action Directe in France, as well as Italian, Irish and West German terrorists. On a few occasions Libyan assistance, direct or through mediators, would be given to more than one group in a country. Thus terrorists of both the extreme left and the far right in Turkey and Spain received assistance.

In principle, Libya's main target was, of course, Israel. According to the Baghdad agreement of 1978, Libya was to make a yearly contribution of almost $40 million to the PLO budget. Furthermore, very substantial quantities of arms were supplied to the Palestinian resistance during the Lebanese civil war including SA-9 surface-to-air missiles, BM-21 rocket launchers, GRAD missiles and 130 mm and 122 mm guns as well as patrol boats. Libya paid for most of the Black September operations (such as the attack in the Munich Olympic village) and the seizure of the OPEC headquarters in Vienna (December 1975). It paid not only Arafat; proportionally more was given to the 'rejectionist' groups such as the PFLP and subsequently also to Abu Nidal.

Two small groups which split away from Fatah in 1972 and 1984 respectively were taken over by Libyan Intelligence; they were the 'National Arab Youth Organization for the Liberation of Palestine' and the 'Revolutionary Arab–Palestinian Committees'. The former blew up a TWA plane over Athens, a British plane in Amsterdam, a Pan-Am plane in Rome, and there was another attack against TWA passengers in Athens. After 1974, this group ceased operations. The 'Revolutionary Committees' constituted of Palestinians and Lebanese were stationed in the Beka'a valley; they undertook a few abortive attempts to infiltrate Israel.

Far more significant was Libyan support for the Abu Nidal group, which had been for many years under the direct control of Iraqi Intelligence. However, during the Iraq–Iran war the presence of this group became an embarrassment for the hard-pressed Baghdad government and Syria,

---

* On some occasions such open admissions were thought to be inopportune. After the murder of Ezzedin Ghadamsi, a prominent exile living in Austria, the Libyan authorities professed to be shocked and put the blame on America. They wanted, no doubt, to spare the feelings of Chancellor Kreisky, one of Qadhafi's few admirers in Europe.

in co-operation with Qadhafi, took on the sponsorship. Abu Nidal offices were opened in Tripoli and in order to give the new relationship official sanction, Abu Nidal met Qadhafi and his deputy, Jalloud, in September 1985. According to press reports the Libyan government paid this group $12 million yearly as well as bonuses for specific operations. Abu Nidal operations were under the control of three Libyan Intelligence officers whose names were published in the Arab press.[27]

However, while in theory Israel was the great enemy against which all efforts ought to be directed, many more Arabs and citizens of third countries were killed by Qadhafi-sponsored terrorists than Israelis. The readiness of every Libyan boy and girl to engage in a suicide mission against the Zionist enemy was proclaimed in many speeches and articles. But in actual fact few Libyans participated in the fighting except a small contingent of soldiers stationed in Lebanon during the civil war, and some of the assassins hunting Libyan émigrés in Europe and the Middle East. But even for these purposes foreign mercenaries were frequently employed; advertisements to enlist mercenaries were periodically published in the press in various countries. In April 1986 the Libyan government advertised for volunteers in Indian newspapers offering wages many times that of the income of the average Indian worker. Apparently there was not sufficient man- and womanpower available inside Libya to engage in the 'suicide missions'. Attacks against Israeli targets were notoriously difficult and this may also explain the choice of 'softer' targets, especially in Europe, but also in other Arab countries.

Terrorist groups sponsored by Libya at one time or another tried to assassinate President Sadat, King Hussain of Jordan (by downing his plane with a SA-7 missile), Arafat and other 'moderate' PLO leaders, the King of Morocco; they hijacked an Egyptian plane in November 1985 and they put mines in Egyptian territorial waters in the Red Sea in 1984. PLO representatives killed by Libyan-sponsored terrorist groups include Said Hamami, Dr Sartawi and others in Jordan, Belgium, France and elsewhere. Other attempts were directed against American targets in Egypt; some of these operations were spectacular failures but this did not deter the sponsors.

Libyan assistance was first and foremost financial in character. According to Lebanese press reports in 1984 there was a more or less fixed scale ranging from throwing hand grenades to a fully fledged suicide mission – in which case a stipend of 300,000 Lebanese pounds was to be paid to the bereaved family.[28] 'Abu Musa', the head of the Fatah rebels who with Syrian help turned against Arafat during the fighting in Tripoli, Lebanon, in late 1983 received allegedly more than $30 million from Qadhafi.

According to Arab press reports, Qadhafi offered millions of dollars for a 'contract' to kill Mohammed Bakhush, a former Libyan prime minister and a political refugee in Cairo. While very considerable sums seem to have changed hands, it also appears that the Libyans frequently promised more than they delivered – to terrorists as well as to foreign governments – and this became a perennial weakness of Libyan strategy.

Libya has provided some twenty training bases for terrorists from many countries including Latin America. The basic courses in these camps reportedly took some six months; this was followed by special training in explosives, hand-held missiles and various forms of sabotage. Some of these bases were small, others were located inside military camps; the authorities usually kept the various nationalities apart. The general oversight was in the hands of three bodies – the 'Headquarters of the Revolution' (headed by Qadhafi), the 'Arab Office', focusing on acts of terror in the Arab world, and the 'foreign contacts office', which was in charge of co-ordination with terrorists from other countries. Among the instructors were some Libyans but mainly experts from East Germany and Cuba, as well as a few ex-CIA agents.[29]

Other assistance to terrorist groups included the smuggling of weapons to European and Middle Eastern countries through the Libyan diplomatic mail; forged or genuine passports have been provided,[30] and asylum has been given to terrorists on the run – among them the killers of the Israeli athletes (1972), the terrorists who seized the Saudi embassy in Paris (1973), the perpetrators of attacks in Kuala Lumpur (1973), Athens (1973), Vienna (the OPEC hijacking, 1975) and others.

The case of Libya is unique in the modern world, with regard to both the extent of support for terrorist groups given by a small and weak country, and the open admission that such help was indeed given. Syria, Iraq and Iran also used terrorist groups for their purposes but their assistance was more selective, and they usually have not admitted their sponsorship, let alone boasted about it. Thus the Libyan phenomenon ought to be explained first and foremost with reference to Qadhafi, his feeling of mission, his lack of restraint and his megalomania. There is every reason to assume that, but for his exploits, Libya would figure no more prominently than other countries of similar size. Qadhafi discovered that the sponsorship of worldwide terrorism gave his regime – and above all his own person – an importance which they would not have obtained in any other way. Having become accustomed to this role and all its concomitants, such as the incessant media exposure, Qadhafi persuaded himself that he was one of the great leaders of our time, perhaps of all time.

Western media and statesmen were certainly not free of blame. It was a unique case: never before had a person of so little consequence been built up into a demonic figure threatening all mankind, never had a little man who was obviously not quite stable been transformed into a superhuman figure and been taken so seriously. Future historians may find it inexplicable how television turned low comedy into high drama. While Gamal Nasser had been in some ways a tragic hero there was nothing either tragic or heroic in the man who ruled Libya for so many years, and who figured so prominently in the Western media.

Abu Nidal

The relationship between Qadhafi and Abu Nidal was comparable in some respects to that between the Soviet Union and Qadhafi; the junior acting as substitutes for the senior partners, who were by no means, however, in full control. Sabri al Banna (Abu Nidal) attained fame in the 1980s as the most radical and ruthless Palestinian leader, not shying away from any act of terror. At the same time it was widely accepted that the Abu Nidal group, unlike the PLO, was not a free agent but acted most of the time on behalf of certain Arab governments in their struggle against each other and also against the official PLO leadership. For Abu Nidal, Arafat was a traitor to the Arab cause, whereas Arafat regarded Abu Nidal as an agent (possibly in Israel's pay!) who had been condemned to death by a PLO tribunal.

The history of the Abu Nidal group is chequered and in some respects presents major riddles. Al Banna hails from a well-to-do merchant family in Jaffa, where he was born in the late 1930s. He originally belonged to the PLO; in contrast to the other PLO leaders, he had no academic training.[31] He worked for a while in Saudi Arabia and seems to have been a member of Black September: Abu Iyad, who masterminded Black September, was his patron in the early days. He was sent to Khartum in 1969 to open a PLO office but something went wrong with his mission and he was transferred to Baghdad as the organization's local representative. However, after a short time he left the organization, allegedly because it was not radical enough, and he began to work for Iraqi Intelligence. The fact that he was isolated in the Palestinian resistance seems not to have bothered him unduly: he had now a powerful protector – a country also isolated in the Arab world at the time, which liberally supported him and his followers. There were at the time some 200 of them, mainly young Palestinians resident in Iraq, some of them related to him through family ties, others students whose fees were paid by his organization.*

---

* Familiar and clannish ties are of basic importance in the constitution of the smaller Middle Eastern terrorist groups. This is true not only with regard to Abu Nidal but perhaps even

Most Abu Nidal operations in the 1970s were directed against other Arab leaders: they wanted to kill Arafat at a meeting in Morocco, but the plan failed. His men attacked PLO offices in Syria, Italy, Pakistan, France and Britain; among their victims was Said Hamami. Above all, some seventy operations were carried out against Syria, both inside that country and abroad. Syria was traditionally Iraq's main rival for hegemony in the Arab world. At one stage he seems to have contemplated the murder of Bruno Kreisky, the Austrian Chancellor, probably in view of his friendship with Arafat. But this plot too failed, and the same is true of certain operations in France, where Abu Nidal had established close co-operation with the left-wing Action Directe.

Other Abu Nidal operations were directed against Jordan, both in Amman and Greece; the Jordanian ambassadors to Italy and India were shot (both in 1983); the local PLO representative in Kuwait was shot in his home, and Kuwaiti representatives were attacked in countries such as Spain. There were also some attacks against Jewish and Israeli targets, including synagogues in Europe and the shooting of Shlomo Argov, the Israeli ambassador to London, which triggered off the Israeli invasion of Lebanon in 1982.

A list of the Abu Nidal operations shows that the place of this group is more in the fold of international terrorism than in the anti-Israeli struggle of the Palestinians. It was not, of course, the first time that a terrorist leader became the agent of interests alien to the cause to which he had originally devoted his life. But it was still remarkable with what ease Abu Nidal changed masters, and that his employers let him go without apparent rancour.

Having been for many years in Iraq's service, and having staged countless attacks against Syria, Abu Nidal almost overnight switched his allegiance. It is perhaps understandable that Iraq let him do so since he had become

---

more pronounced in the case of Georges Abdallah, the head of the Lebanese Armed Revolutionary Faction (FARL). The arrest of Abdallah caused a wave of terrorist attacks in France during the summer and autumn of 1986. The group had been responsible for various terrorist attacks in Italy and France. It was based on the Abdallah clan in two Northern Lebanese villages, Kobayat and Andakt. Abdallah's brothers were among the members of this group, the armed wing of the (Christian) Lebanese 'Syrian Popular Party'. Originally pro-Fascist, this group later gravitated towards a self-styled Marxist faction, the Popular Front for the Liberation of Palestine (PFLP). There is reason to believe that it was under the control of Syrian Intelligence. But while doctrines and ideological affiliations changed, internal cohesion provided by family and clan remained stable.

an embarrassment now that the war with Iran was not going well and Iraq desperately needed friends. It is more astonishing that the Syrians accepted him with open arms and even decided to 'share' his services with Libya: apparently, they did not want to become identified too closely with this group, whereas Qadhafi had no such scruples. The Middle East has always been the scene of rapidly changing allegiances; the fact that much blood has been spilled has seldom prevented subsequent reconciliations. Few would have assumed that after Black September, Arafat and the other PLO leaders would ever return to the Jordanian capital as honoured guests of King Hussain, and there have been many startling reversals in the Lebanese civil war. But the case of Abu Nidal still remains a puzzle. At one stage in its history the direction of the group seems to have been taken over by a group of Iraqi Intelligence officers; these were later replaced by Syrian and Libyan officers. To make the picture even more confused, there have been links between Abu Nidal and Iran as well as Bulgaria, where the group kept a base. Did the group have any independent character at all or was it a joint venture of a consortium of secret services?

In the early 1980s the group tried to acquire some respectability by enlisting a few well-known Arab intellectuals such as the Palestinian writer Naji Alush and some other prominent figures including Abu Musa, the chief rebel against Arafat in Fatah. But neither stayed very long; they seem to have had their doubts about the political *bona fides* of the Abu Nidal group,[32] which had become something of a latter-day collective successor to the elusive Carlos as terrorists of fortune. They acquired the reputation of killers willing to serve the highest bidder.

Euroterrorism and the fight against NATO

There has been no international terrorist brigade, as some have suspected, but there certainly has been close co-ordination and collaboration on many occasions. One obvious example was the campaign against NATO – an obvious target for terrorists of the extreme left and, in West Germany, also from the far right. The attempted assassination of General Haig when he was Secretary-General of NATO in Brussels and the kidnapping of US General Dozier in Italy were the precursors of this campaign. In 1984, several West European terrorist groups made common cause in a series of attacks against Western defence headquarters and installations. The groups involved were small: these were the remnants of the Italian Red Brigades, the French Action Directe which had come into being in 1979, the survivors of the German RAF, the Portuguese Forças Populares do 25 Abril (FP-25) whose most prominent supporter was allegedly Otelo

Carvalho, and above all the small but active Belgian Fighting Cells (ccc). These attacks included bombing of NATO fuel pipelines in Spain, Germany and Belgium, of military communication centres, air and naval bases, the NATO Iberian headquarters, US corporations such as Litton and Honeywell, the offices of the Western Union and the European Space Agency.

The Belgian terrorists had initially refrained from operations likely to result in loss of life, but in mid-1984 they announced that they had changed their approach and would kill from now on 'Yankee military and their accomplices'. The Belgian security forces had little experience in coping with violent men and women of this kind, but after a few months the leading figures of the ccc were apprehended and Belgian terror came to an end. The French police found it less easy to deal with Action Directe, for of all the West European countries France had been one of the most permissive, extending asylum to terrorists from many lands. France did not sign the European convention on terrorism. If the French government had assumed that such tolerance would result in gratitude on the part of the terrorists, this proved to be mistaken. Between 1968 and 1984, 157 diplomats were attacked in France; in 1982–3, 111 international terrorist incidents took place in which 45 people were killed and more than 400 were wounded. French official policy became tougher following this escalation. There was a further clampdown after the murder of General René Audrian, the overseer of France's arms exports, in January 1985. Following the arrest of a few dozen militants, the anti-NATO terror quickly abated and the formation of a 'political military front to fight NATO's new politics', solemnly announced by the terrorists, remained a dead letter. The deployment of the Euro-missiles was certainly not affected by the Euroterrorists.*

The anti-NATO campaign was a half-hearted affair. The cause did not prove to be popular and the number of those involved was small. Perhaps it was a mere rehearsal or a trial balloon. If sponsors were involved, they must have quickly realized that a campaign of this kind was playing with fire in more than one sense; it was dangerous to galvanize the Western European secret services into action. For once security forces began their investigations, mass searches and arrests, they were likely to interfere with all kinds of clandestine actions which they were not meant to know about.

---

* As in West Germany, there were in France some small terrorist groups of the extreme right, such as the Charles Martel club, and also separatist terrorists, above all in Corsica. Between 1982 and 1984 there were no less than 1,300 bomb attacks in Corsica. But most of them were not meant to kill, merely to cause material damage. See José Gil, *La Corse: Entre la liberté et le terreur* (Paris, 1984), *passim*. Corsica had a tradition of both banditism and clanism and these are two essential aspects for an understanding of Corse terrorism. Two foreign tourists were killed in a terrorist attack in May 1986.

A terrorist anti-NATO campaign made sense only if staged on a massive scale, but this was politically inopportune. In the circumstances, the wire-pullers – if indeed such were involved – probably decided to call off an action the purpose of which was apparently never entirely thought through to the end.

A new attempt was made in late 1985 to co-ordinate the operations of various West European terrorist groups. This expressed itself above all in manifestos and publications as well as an international terrorist congress which took place in Frankfurt in January 1986.* According to these proclamations the main enemy were the US armed forces in Europe. Since the terrorists could not possibly defeat US military power, the correct strategy was to kill individual soldiers to demoralize their colleagues and lower their capacity to fight. The murder of an individual American soldier, Pimental, had been widely condemned on the extreme left in 1985, but according to the manifesto of 1986 the killing had been perfectly justified: 'it is either them or us ...'. Among those represented in Frankfurt, or present as guests, were German, French, Belgian, Spanish and Portuguese terrorist groups as well as the PLO, the PFLP, the ANC, IRA and INLA, the Tupamaros, the Italian Red Brigades and ETA. The manifestos were strictly Marxist–Leninist in style but the greatest applause was received by a speaker of the Libyan People's Bureau; this was probably not unconnected with the financing of the congress and most of the organizations which participated in its proceedings. Another interesting new feature was the emergence of contacts between the terrorist scene and the Green parties in West Germany, Austria and Switzerland.[33] The Green parties had originally been pacifist in inspiration but since their ideology was never clearly defined, they eventually came to encompass advocates of violence. It is, of course, much too early to say whether the attempts to establish a terrorist 'popular front' will be lasting and successful. While it makes sense from the terrorist point of view to have a wide periphery of sympathizers, it also makes it easier for the security forces to trace the terrorist activists and to apprehend them. No less than 500 people reportedly attended the Frankfurt congress which took place under the slogan 'The armed struggle

---

* The spreading of periodicals expressing the views of terrorists or terrorist sympathizers was a new phenomenon. There were, for example, *Zusammenkämpfen*, published in Germany, the Dutch *De Knipselkrant*, the French (Belgian) *Ligne Rouge*, as well as local regional papers published in Hamburg, Hanover, Frankfurt, Munich, Stuttgart, etc. The report about the Frankfurt terrorist congress appeared in *Zusammenkämpfen*, January 1986. It was probably the first time that a terrorist group had applied for (and received) permission to have a conference in the building of an institution of higher learning. *Exclusivbericht*, Wiesbaden, 20 April 1986. See also *Frankfurter Allgemeine Zeitung*, 18 July 1986.

as a strategic and tactical necessity in the fight for revolution ...'.

Narco-terrorism

Ten years ago the drug trade did not yet figure in surveys of global terrorism. There were some rumours – and perhaps more than rumours – about links between the production of drugs in the 'golden triangle' in South-east Asia and various local warlords and insurgencies. Since then the international drug trade has expanded enormously; furthermore, in the words of one observer, there has been a tendency for insurgency, terrorism and the drug trade to be located in roughly the same areas.[34] This is as true of Lebanon and Turkey as it is of Colombia, Bolivia and Peru. The coincidence has been too striking to be ignored. Involved in the drug trade have been the Colombian FARC and the M19 as well as the Peruvian Sendero Luminoso, Palestinian and other Middle Eastern terrorist organizations, both the Turkish left and right, and the Armenians and Tamil separatists. There have been such charges even against the Red Brigades and ETA, and some Soviet-bloc countries, particularly Cuba and Bulgaria, have profited by providing logistic support to drug smugglers or, as in the case of Laos, by actually growing opium.

The profits made in the drug trade are immense; the value of illegal drugs sold in the United States alone has been estimated at between $45 and 110 billion annually. No one has suggested that more than a tiny portion of this has found its way into the pockets of guerrillas, terrorists and their patrons. Nor has it been claimed that the terrorists have sponsored the drug trade. The relationship has been 'symbiotic', a response to evolving opportunities, rather than based on a masterplan.[35] But if the involvement of certain corrupt – or very poor – governments, or international crime syndicates such as the Mafia did not come as a surprise, the terrorist link did. For in the common view, most terrorist groups were idealistic, burning with desire to abolish injustice and build a better world. How to explain the involvement of these pure people with very impure business?

The evidence is overwhelming. It has come to light in reports of many governments, in court cases from the US to Sweden and from Italy to Turkey. It has been mentioned even in United Nations documents.* Terror-

---

* See the various US government annual National Intelligence estimates published by the US National Narcotics and Consumers Committee; various congressional hearings on drugs and terrorism; the reports by the Drugs Enforcement Agency (DEA) and the Department of State; the Lara trial in Miami (November 1982); the revelations following the extradition to Turkey of Ugurlu, the godfather of the Turkish Mafia; the television interview of Carlos Lehder, a leading figure in the field, and other published material.

ist involvement has taken place not so much in the production of drugs as in the trafficking. Drugs are mainly grown in rural areas which are not easily accessible such as Colombia and South-East Asia; guerrilla groups are known to have defended the growers of opium and hashish against attacks by drug enforcement units and guarded access to private airports from which the drugs were shipped. They have also taken part in attacks against government agents engaged in anti-narcotic activities. Such operations seem not to have caused major ideological qualms to revolutionary groups, even though ideologically Peru's most prominent revolutionaries, the Sendero Luminoso, would angrily reject any common interest with the major *traficantes*. The drug dealers do not want to change a system under which they have become rich, whereas the Sendero Luminoso stands for a rural-based revolution and the ouster of non-Indian elites.[36]

But the guerrillas needed both money and arms, and there was no easier way to receive both than by helping with the drug traffic, most of which is scheduled for export, mainly to the United States.* It is not a marriage of love, but of convenience. It is also true that growing narcotics is genuinely popular in the countryside. The livelihood of many hundreds of thousands of Colombians, Bolivians and Peruvians depends on this cash crop; the government agent (let alone the foreigner) who wants to destroy the crops is naturally regarded as the enemy. And since a dedicated revolutionary should always be with the masses, a case could be made in favour of protecting the poor peasants.

There are good reasons why a country such as Bulgaria should have had a finger in this extremely profitable pie. Drug trafficking inside Communist countries is severely punished but since the smuggled goods are scheduled for the decadent West, and since Cuba and Bulgaria desperately need foreign currency, the temptation may be irresistible. The same seems to be true of Laos, the only Communist country in which opium is actually grown and manufactured on state farms.

The co-operation between *traficantes*, guerrillas and terrorists has been documented in greatest detail in Colombia where both major groups, the

---

* According to the testimony of a former drug dealer tried in Miami, the Cuban Vice-Admiral Santamaria-Cuadrando told the crew of a cargo ship smuggling $19 million of drugs into the US that 'we are going to fill Miami completely with drugs . . . so that more young Americans will die'. The evidence of drug dealers may not be entirely reliable, or the admiral's outspoken view may not faithfully express his government's views. It is also true that Miami-based anti-Castro groups have equally been involved in the drug trade. But the basic idea is plausible and it must have occurred to the Cuban rulers, who have also provided a safe haven for the flotilla of the notorious Robert Vesco.

FARC and M19, have co-operated with the leading drug traffickers, a fact which has been admitted in the media by the latter. An armistice between the government and the FARC came into force in 1984 and this had its repercussions also on the drug scene. On the other hand, the third Colombia terrorist group, the ELN, had also been involved in the narcotics trade. According to Colombian press reports, twenty-four ELN members were arrested in May 1984 in possession of 150 tons of marijuana. Co-operation with the drug barons was sanctioned on an official level by the Seventh National Conference of the Colombian Communist Party in 1982, and the material awards were quickly forthcoming.

It was not the only Communist Party to take a decision of this kind; the Burmese Communist Party and that of Thailand have adopted similar resolutions. While the FARC (the armed wing of the Colombian Communist Party) fought the government, it collected protection money from peasants growing coca and marijuana; on one front alone it is believed to have obtained $3.8 million per month in taxing the coca industry.[37] This is not to imply that the leading traffickers relied exclusively on protection by the guerrillas and terrorists; they have established private armies of their own which are sometimes better equipped than the regular forces in these countries. The murder of the Colombian minister of justice Rodrigo Lara-Bonilla, a thorn in the side of the *traficantes*, was carried out by criminals rather than terrorists.

The relationship between governments, *traficantes* and terrorists in Latin America is complicated and given to frequent change. Just as terrorists and *traficantes* have made common cause against the government, the fronts have been reversed at times. The Colombian government has concluded an armistice with the insurgents so as to have a free hand in the battle against the drug dealers, and the terrorists have abducted members of families of the richest drug dealers to extort money. The state of affairs resembles more the relations between the leading bootleggers in Chicago during prohibition, than the relations between fighters for a society in which justice and freedom will prevail.

What matters is that terrorists have benefited substantially from drugs; their share has been significant in terms of their needs. Instead of collecting a few hundred thousand dollars as a result of bank robberies and other such operations involving careful planning and sometimes even risks, they have earned many millions without much effort. Furthermore, the network of smugglers who took the heroin abroad could be used to supply them with weapons. Whereas the symbiosis has been well documented in Latin America and South-East Asia, it has been more murky elsewhere. The involvement of the Tamil separatists in the drug trade emerged as a result of arrests in Italy in March 1985. In the Beka valley in Lebanon, all warring parties derived part of their income from the drug industry. Armenian traffickers were arrested in Sweden, Greece, Cyprus, Switzerland and the US. It could not be proven in the courts that the smugglers passed part of their profits to ASALA, but there is much reason to assume that they did so. An investigation by Istanbul police in 1981 revealed that the left-wing Dev-Sol had engaged in heroin sales, and so had the right-wing 'Grey Wolves'.[38]

In Sicily, the Mafia has kept the Red Brigades out of the island, but elsewhere in Italy there has been some co-operation between the underworld, including drug dealers, and terrorist groups. The Basque ETA has vehemently denied any involvement in the drug trade, but it is generally believed that this is less than the truth; the bishops of northern Spain have issued a pastoral letter criticizing ETA for involvement in the drug traffic, adding that Spanish security services also used drugs as payment for information.[39]

For a long time the symbiotic relationship between *traficantes* and terrorists was doubted by the US administration. The DEA argued that with the possible exception of the FARC and the Shan United Army, there was no evidence of wholesale participation by terrorist groups in drug trafficking. They believed that while the connection was increasing, it had no significant impact on drug availability in the US. Terrorist groups (it was argued) were not in a position to compete with established drug smuggling organizations.[40] The DEA tended to play down the narco-terrorist connection, simply because its main interest was in the availability of drugs inside America, not the problems of terrorism, whereas the State Department was preoccupied with the foreign connections, the manner in which the drugs were smuggled into the United States and the links with terrorists. If there was still lack of evidence in 1983–4 about the terrorist connection and Cuban involvement in the drug traffic, two years later it was said in the senate hearings that it had been finally established that Castro's government had assisted the terrorists in Colombia by bartering arms for drug money, that they had 'money coming out of their ears now, that they had more arms than people to use them'.[41]

Several questions still remain open concerning the extent of the involvement of Communist governments, such as those in Cuba and Bulgaria, in the drug traffic. The governments concerned must be aware that, ideological reasons quite apart, these activities constitute a domestic danger. If the profits in this trade are enormous, so are the temptations. There is reason to believe that Communist officials as well as terrorist leaders are not immune from the corruption which always accompanies the drug trade.

Should the rulers not be afraid of contamination? The fact that they are, in principle, opposed to the consumption of drugs has not prevented them from participating in this sinister trade.

Conclusion

Libya has given more money and the Soviet Union more arms to terrorist groups, but the overall role of Syria and Iran in international terrorism in the 1980s has been at least equally important, even though, unlike Qadhafi, these two Middle Eastern countries have not heralded their activities from the roof tops.* The attacks sponsored by Syria and Iran have been distinguished by high professionalism: the result, most probably, of the direct involvement of regular army officers. These operations were directed mainly against Arab countries which took an anti-Iranian line in Tehran's war with Iraq, against Turkey on the part of Syria, against the United States and France. The Beirut attacks of 1984 caused the withdrawal of the multinational force from Beirut. Other targets were political émigrés from Iran and Syria who made their homes abroad. Israel, on the other hand, was only rarely affected by these attacks.

The involvement of some of the minor Communist states such as North Korea, South Yemen and Bulgaria is a matter of record; North Korean support was always erratic and South Yemen, in view of her distance and isolation, always served more as a 'safe house' than an active participant in international terrorism. In both cases there was a decline in involvement, caused by South Yemen's internal troubles and North Korea's attempt to normalize its relations with its neighbours, including South Korea. The same is true, within limits, of Cuba; since Castro's ambitions have increasingly been to become a Latin American elder statesman rather than a revolutionary firebrand, support for terrorism – as distinct from guerrilla insurgencies – had to be restricted in South and Central America; less caution has been applied in Africa and the Middle East. Cuba had always nursed certain misgivings about the Marighella approach, i.e. urban terrorism. The problem facing the Cubans was that their main clients in the

---

* The Iranians, however, have done little to impose secrecy on the training camps for their recruits, domestic and foreign, for instance at Vakilabad, or (for women only) at Beheshtia. The existence of these camps was mentioned in local broadcasts and the trainees were interviewed. Many of them apparently specialized in the hijacking of aeroplanes. On Iranian government involvement in terrorism see *International Terrorism, Insurgency, and Drug Trafficking: Present trends in terrorist activity*. Hearings on 13–15 May 1985. Joint Hearings before the Committee on Foreign Relations and Committee on the Judiciary, United States Senate (Washington, 1986), pp. 39–71.

late 1970s, such as the Colombians, practised both guerrilla warfare *and* terrorism, and the Cubans were not in a position to dictate their tactics.

If the Western governments have charged the Soviet bloc with much of the responsibility for international terrorism, the Soviet Union and its allies have argued that the Western governments, and above all the United States, have been the main inspirers of terrorism. Instances of Western involvement in various Third World insurgencies can be found without difficulty. The United States has supported the 'Contras' in Nicaragua and Unita in Angola (which also got help from South Africa), Israel has kept a militia in South Lebanon, the French have intervened in Chad, the British (indirectly) in some of the minor Persian Gulf principalities – not to mention the massive help given to the Afghan rebels by America via Pakistan.

However, a mere listing of the major cases of intervention shows the basic differences; Western nations have become involved in civil wars and insurgencies, supporting various guerrilla-type organizations. Such operations are now the accepted mode of conflict in some Third World countries in the absence of regular warfare. True, Western-supported guerrilla movements have also engaged in acts of terrorism. However, there has been no Western equivalent of terrorism of the kind practised by the various Abu Nidals and Carlos, the Red Brigades and the RAF. There has been counter-terrorism such as the Israeli efforts to eliminate the leaders of Black September responsible for the Munich massacre. There have been no attempts on the part of the Western powers to assassinate political émigrés.

The difference between Western and Soviet as well as Libyan, Syrian and Iranian involvement was both quantitative and qualitative in character. The Western countries are *status-quo* orientated. They want to prevent insurgencies and other forms of destabilization and, from a purely technical point of view, they are ill-equipped to deal with such contingencies. The Russians and their allies have had not only far greater experience and competence in this field, they also do not have to render account to their parliaments, and their media do not report the support given to terrorist allies. While the Soviet Union has its proxies such as Cuba or Bulgaria, America has no such substitutes. If, despite these handicaps, a terrorist plot is nevertheless hatched from time to time in the West, it is usually bungled, causing a major scandal and the downfall of those who ordered it. The French operation against the *Rainbow Warrior* ship in New Zealand was a perfect example. Moral and political inhibitions quite apart, the equation of Western and Eastern support for terrorism makes little sense; it is like equating the achievements of professionals with amateurs.

Western powers would have been incapable of conducting international terrorism even if they had tried; they have in most cases failed to react effectively against it, and this for a number of obvious reasons. International terrorism does not offer easy and obvious targets for retaliation; many innocent are bound to get killed and injured if retaliation is nevertheless tried. This in turn is bound to cause a humanitarian backlash at home. An attack against state-sponsored terrorists is bound to lead to violations of international law and to military escalation. The state which retaliates finds itself in the role of the aggressor.

Seen in this perspective, state-sponsored terrorism has undoubted advantages for use against democratic societies. It seems to offer the possibility of engaging in acts of violence at minimum risk. This has led some observers to predict that this strategic tool will be used increasingly often and with an ever greater impact. But this is to misjudge the nature and the inherent limits of the threat. International terror, like terror in general, can operate without fear of massive retaliation only if it is not too frequent and damaging. If it is used too often and causes too much damage, anger and frustration, the political calculus changes. The considerations which militate against retaliation in democratic societies no longer prevail; a process of escalation gets under way which, in turn, may lead to full-scale conflict. For this reason only gross miscalculation will induce the sponsors of international terrorism to carry their campaign beyond a point of no return. This may happen, but it is unlikely to occur; the limits of this strategic tool are obvious: up to a certain point it is helpful, beyond it the risks become too great as terrorism turns into war.*

---

* President Asad of Syria emerged in 1986 as one of the most active sponsors of international terrorism. Syrian agents engaged in operations in Britain, West Germany, France, Turkey and other countries. The ensuing publicity was not welcome in Damascus and there were the usual vehement denials. The Soviet Union defended Syria (or, to be precise, denied that any terrorist operations had taken place). At the same time a long programmatic article was published in *Pravda* warning Soviet allies to be careful that their 'struggles' should not escalate into full-scale war which could lead to a world conflagration. They should go on fighting, but the need for prudence and caution was impressed on them (E. Plimak in *Pravda*, 14 November 1986).

9

Conclusions

Reviewing the balance sheet of terrorism over two decades, the question arises: why should the terrorist phenomenon have dominated this age as much as it did? How to explain that in the speeches of the President of the United States mention was so often made of the ruler of a small and, on the whole, unimportant country – a ridiculous rather than a demonic figure? How to explain that the Western media reported incessantly and in minute detail on the exploits and the bombast of this soldier in his bemedalled tunic who had never fired a shot in anger? Compared with the truly important problems of our time – the potential dangers of modern technologies, global debt, hunger in the Third World, overpopulation, certain new and incurable diseases – terrorism was, after all, a side-show. True, a number of leading statesmen were assassinated, and not a few innocent bystanders were killed. Aircraft were hijacked and car-bombs exploded on the streets of various cities. But with all this, terrorism directly affected the lives of only a handful of people. It did not cause major political, economic, social or cultural upheaval. Men and women went on with their pursuits as they had done twenty years earlier. One bank was robbed, but all others continued to function; one plane was hijacked, but all others continued to fly, more or less acording to schedule. Future historians may well be intrigued not so much by the occurrence of terrorism as by the enormous attention it received.

Some of the reasons have been alluded to in the course of this study. International terrorism is an affront to civilization; the fact that its perpetrators so often went scot-free, and that some of its sponsors even bragged about their exploits, caused deep frustration and anger. When Thomas Jefferson was told that Barbary pirates had captured American ships, he warned congress not to appease the Moroccans because 'an insult unpunished is the parent of others'. But he also wrote to Nathaniel Green on a subsequent occasion that the outrage left the faculty of his mind absolutely suspended between indignation and impotence. This, by and large, has been the reaction of subsequent generations of Americans. Nevertheless, future historians will be intrigued and puzzled by the staggering disproportion between the enormous amount of talk about terrorism and the tiny effort made to combat it and the minute sums of money allocated for this purpose. The historians may well come to believe that terrorism could not possibly have been the great danger it was alleged to be, for otherwise a much greater effort would have been made to confront it.[1]

There has been in this age a lack of clarity about the origins of terrorism and what could be done about it. Above all, there was a tendency to use terrorism as a catch-all term for almost every form of violence short of full-scale war. Indiscriminate use of the language has led to loose thought on the subject.

Generalizations were made about terrorist groups: their constitution, their aims and the political context in which they operated. Much confusion has resulted from generalizing on movements such as Fascism while ignoring the major differences between Fascist regimes and parties. Greater yet were the differences between terrorist groups, simply because terrorism is neither a political regime nor a creed nor a party, but rather a specific manifestation of political violence. True, there were marked similarities between certain terrorist groups, but none at all between others. Too often it was forgotten that while there have been (and still are) terrorists and terrorist groups, terrorism *per se* has never existed except in the realm of concepts and abstractions. At the same time, various panaceas have been offered. If only a certain course of action were followed, terrorism would decline steeply or disappear altogether. There was a time in the history of mankind when pills were sold in the streets to prevent earthquakes. Today, on a slightly higher level of sophistication, it is still argued that if only one specific social or national problem were solved, terrorism would vanish. Injustice, to be sure, should always be removed and grievances redressed. But it should also have been clear that the connection between terrorism and 'objective factors' is far more tenuous than commonly believed: there is a great deal of terrorism without injustice and oppression, and a great deal of oppression without terrorism. Furthermore, a satisfactory solution for conflicts acceptable to all sides may often not exist, and a compromise solution will always have opponents.

The great shock caused by terrorism in our time was perhaps rooted in excessive expectations, and surprise that such things could occur at all. The shock of terrorism around the turn of the century was less palpable to our ancestors simply because their expectations about universal peace were lower. But after the Second World War, generations grew up in

Western Europe and North America believing that standards of democracy, freedom and humanism were equally high all over the globe. It was difficult to realize that violence was never far from the surface in many parts of the world – and perhaps even in their own society.

A review of political terrorism written before the First World War would have concentrated on Russian and Irish terrorism, as well as on the anarchists of the 1890s; perhaps some passing remarks would have been made about the national struggles of the Macedonians, Serbians and Armenians, too. It would have reached conclusions on terrorist motives and aims very different from those propounded by an author writing in the 1930s. By then Russian and anarchist terrorism already belonged to distant history, and the terrorism of the extreme right was of considerably greater importance.

A study of terrorism undertaken in 1970 would have focused on groups in Western Europe, Latin America and North America, many of which no longer exist. Today the terrorist scene is dominated by new trends such as narco-terrorism and terrorism as substitute warfare sponsored by certain states. At the same time, some of the old national separatist terrorism continues in various parts of the world. Contemporary terrorism can only be understood in its historical development, not through facts and figures fed more or less indiscriminately into computers. But it is also true that the terrorism of the 1980s is no longer that of the Narodnaya Volya. An overall assessment written today has to take account both of historical roots and of new manifestations.

During the last two decades terrorism has by and large superseded guerrilla warfare. As decolonization came to an end, there was a general decline in guerrilla activity. Rural guerrillas learned by bitter experience in the 1960s that the 'encirclement of the cities by the countryside' was not the universal remedy advocated at one time by the Chinese and the Cubans. There are exceptions, for instance in the Philippines and Sri Lanka, where guerrilla warfare of sorts continues as these lines are written. But by and large the scene of operations has moved from the countryside to the cities, where the strategy and tactics of rural guerrilla warfare are not applicable. There have been revolutions, civil wars, insurrections and *coups d'état* in the cities, but 'urban guerrilla warfare' can occur only when public order has completely collapsed and private armies or armed bands freely roam the streets. Such a state of affairs does happen – for instance, in Beirut in the 1970s and 1980s – but it is a rare exception. Usually, after a few days or weeks, the insurgents either overthrow the government in a frontal assault or they are defeated. The perpetuation of chaos is an exception in developed or even semi-developed countries.

While there is no such thing as 'pure' terrorism or 'pure' guerrilla warfare, mention has been made more than once in this study of the essential difference between guerrilla warfare and terrorism. Urban slums or wealthy quarters do not provide the sanctuary given by the jungle or distant mountain regions. For this reason terrorists have to operate in small units, frequently of three, four or five. Terrorist movements usually consist of a few hundred and sometimes only a few dozen members. Again, there have been notable exceptions of organizations numbering a thousand or even a few thousand members. The small number is the source of terrorist strength, but also their political weakness. For, while it is difficult to detect small groups and while they can inflict considerable damage, their political effect is bound to be limited. In the 1960s and 1970s, viewers and readers in the Western world were led to believe that the terrorist 'armies' and 'brigades' figuring so prominently in the news were substantial organizations to be taken seriously. Their 'communiqués' were published in the mass media, and earnest sociological and psychological studies were published about the motives and the ideology of their members. But quite frequently these were minute groups of between five and a hundred members, and their main victories were in the field of publicity. Even some of the more substantial groups such as the Tupamaros, the Brazilian ALN, the Argentine ERP and Montoneros, the Italian Red Brigades and the various Turkish groups had no significant public support – hence their sudden collapse and disappearance.

Some of the nationalist–separatist groups have been more successful, either because their ethnic–religious appeal guaranteed them wider popular support, or because they received massive support from foreign powers, or because the government of their country was in an advanced state of decay, no longer capable of mobilizing the vastly superior resources of the state against the terrorists. Broadly speaking, 'internal' terrorism, be it of the extreme left or right, has failed. Nationalists and separatists have been doing better, even though they have not been able to achieve any decisive victories. Terrorism continues, partly because on a small scale it has existed almost always throughout history, but mainly because foreign support ('international terrorism') has prolonged the life-span of terrorism which otherwise might well have been much shorter.

During the last two decades, a mythology of terrorism has emerged. Some of the misconceptions were mentioned at the beginning of this study but, at the cost of repetition, it is necessary to repeat some of the essential facts about terrorism in an attempt to disentangle truth from myth.

Contrary to widespread belief, terrorism is neither new nor unprecedented. It is sometimes argued that terrorism in the past was sporadic and without ideology. But the Russian Social Revolutionaries were as well organized as any contemporary group, and if their weapons were less advanced, their political and ideological sophistication was on a higher level. There is little in contemporary literature, technological guidance apart, that cannot be found in the Russian brochures of the last century, in the writings of Most and the columns of his *Freiheit*.

Terrorism, we are told, is a politically loaded term which should be discarded because one nation's terrorism is another's national liberation. Terrorism, in other words, can be a liberating force in certain circumstances, a proposition which is difficult to deny. But whereas the Russian terrorism of the last century was directed against a despotic regime, most of the contemporary terrorist movements fight either permissive liberal states or ineffectual authoritarian regimes. Having been the *ultima ratio* of the oppressed, terrorism has become far more often than not the *prima ratio* of a motley crowd. Terrorism nowadays is virtually never directed against the worst forms of dictatorship; there were no terrorist movements in Nazi Germany or Fascist Italy, and there are none within the Communist regimes. The nationalist terrorism of a bygone era aimed at liberation from foreign rule. In our time liberation movements still exist, but very often their aim is domination, not liberation; this kind of terrorism is simply one form of nationalist or religious strife.

Terrorism is widely believed to be left-wing and/or revolutionary in character, and it is perfectly true that terrorists always claim to act on behalf of the 'masses'. But they also believe that the liberation of the masses is the historical mission of a chosen few. If at the present time most terrorist manifestos are phrased in left-wing language, a past generation of terrorists gravitated towards Fascism. The ideology of terrorists usually encompassed elements of far-left ideology as well as that of the far right or Fascism. Slogans change with intellectual fashions; they should neither be ignored nor taken too seriously.*

The real inspiration of terrorism is usually a free-floating activism which can with equal ease turn left and right in orientation. Terrorism is not

---

* While Baader–Meinhof and the Red Brigades were in the beginning deeply involved in ideological discussions, the second and third generation of German terrorists and, *a fortiori*, the French terrorists of Action Directe or the Belgian ccc, showed little interest in political–theoretical questions and have hardly published any manifestos. See Alain Hamon and Jean Charles Marchand, *Action directe* (Paris 1986), p. 101 *et seq*. They lacked interest in the subject and wanted to put themselves in deliberate contrast to those intellectuals of the left who did nothing but debate politics and publish manifestos. ('*Les documents qui proposent DOCOM, sont des documents de combat, non des analyses de salon . . .* ': *Docom*, 1981 or 1982.)

a philosophy; it is always action that counts. Terrorism is believed to appear wherever people have legitimate grievances. Remove the grievances, poverty, injustice, inequality, lack of political participation, and terror will cease. It is perfectly true that in a world ideally constructed and consisting of perfect human beings, there would be no terrorism. It is also true that in wealthy societies, where there is no gross social injustice, a great deal of freedom, and a long history of democratic institutions and tolerance, there is little or no terrorism. These are usually small countries, a fact which also bears mentioning. But the great majority of mankind lives in other conditions and, as historical experience shows, societies with the least political participation are also free of terrorism. Given the imperfect character of human beings and social institutions, grievances can be reduced but not eradicated. Only in democratic societies can grievances be voiced openly. It is perception that counts: a major grievance can be fatalistically accepted, whereas at other times and in other places a minor grievance may produce the most violent reaction. Some grievances can be remedied without a great effort but others, especially those pertaining to national and religious conflict, cannot be easily solved because the demands are mutually exclusive. Acceding to the demands of one group may mean injustice to another; it may lead to the establishment of non-viable states and the crippling of society.

It is perfectly true that in some countries terrorists have been fighting dictatorships for greater political freedom and social justice. But whether there would be more freedom if they were to prevail is a moot question. It may well mean the replacement of one type of dictatorship by another, more effective or more charismatic but more severe; the case of Iran provides a great deal of food for thought, and there are many other such cases.

As for the terrorism directed against the democratic states of the West, the shortcomings of these political systems are well known. But to suggest that the terrorists are somehow qualified by character or intellect to lead the way to a better future is to invite ridicule. However democratic a society, however near to perfection the social institutions, there will always be alienated and disaffected people claiming that the present state of affairs is intolerable, and there will be aggressive people more interested in violence than in freedom and tolerance.

Terrorism, it is sometimes argued, is highly effective. Terrorism has on occasion caused political change, but it has had a lasting effect only in rare circumstances, usually when political mass movements used terror as one instrument within the framework of a wider strategy. There is no known case in modern history of a terrorist group seizing political power.

Society usually tolerates terrorism as long as it is a mere nuisance. Once insecurity spreads and terror becomes a real danger, the authorities are no longer blamed for disregarding human rights in their fight against terror. Violence triggers off counter-violence and greater repression.

The means of repression at the disposal of the state are infinitely more effective; the terrorists' only hope is somehow to prevent the state from using its powers. If the terrorist is the fish – to use Mao's illustration – the permissiveness of liberal society and the incompetence of some autocratic regimes are the water which the terrorist needs for survival. A government may be so weak and irresolute, a society in a state of such advanced decay that it may no longer be capable of defending itself against a terrorist challenge. But these are rare exceptions. It is unlikely that the Lebanese example will be widely copied. In any case, the Lebanese chaos was not the result of a terroristic campaign, but rather of a civil war followed by invasions by Syria and Israel. The basic question is not whether terrorism can be defeated; even third-rate dictatorships have shown that it can be put down with great ease. The real problem is the price to be paid by liberal societies cherishing their traditional democratic values. It is not difficult to destabilize a democratic regime outside Europe and North America so that it will turn into a dictatorship. But the road back from a dictatorship is long and difficult, as the Uruguayan and Argentine examples have shown. Not only the terrorists have suffered horribly in the process. Terrorism is not a threat to society, but it may become in certain conditions a threat to civil liberties.

Terrorists, it is said, are idealists. They are more humane and intelligent than ordinary criminals. Such statements, true or not, contribute little to the understanding of contemporary terrorism. The essential humanity of the early Russian terrorists is beyond question. But this is no longer true of most of the terrorist movements which have appeared on the scene in recent decades. In any case, some of the worst horrors in the annals of mankind have been perpetrated by those whose idealism was never doubted. The love of adventure is an important motive in a world devoid of much thrill and excitement. Many terrorists in Latin America and Europe have had a higher education; they may be well read and articulate. But this is not to say that they are more mature, or have greater common sense and humanity than their contemporaries who did not have the benefit of attending a university. With some notable exceptions, these terrorists have shown great political naivety. Larger issues and future perspectives are of little interest to them; frequently they have been manipulated, wittingly or unwittingly, by outside factors.

The early terrorists abstained from acts of deliberate cruelty. But with the change in the character of terrorism, decent and humane behaviour is no longer the norm. The terrorist of recent vintage may preach the brotherhood of man and sometimes even practise it. But more often than not, he has liberated himself from moral scruples and persuaded himself that all is permitted since everyone else is guilty. He will as easily turn against his compatriots and kill his comrades as he will terrorize his enemies, for human life is no longer his major value. It is the terrorists' aim not just to kill but to spread confusion and fear. They believe that the great aim justifies all means, however atrocious.

At the same time there has been a confluence of terrorism and the criminal underworld, be it within the framework of narco-terrorism or because the wealthy terrorist groups have hired killers to carry out some of their dangerous assignments. The ordinary criminal may torture a victim but this will be the exception rather than the rule. He is usually motivated by material gain, not fanaticism. He will not kill indiscriminately unless paid to do so. Seen in this light, the danger of criminal terrorism is perhaps less than it would appear to be at first sight. But it is also true that an alliance with gangsters would have been unthinkable among nineteenth-century terrorists, and this points to the changes that have taken place in the character of terrorism.[2]

The recent history of terrorism offers a number of lessons to terrorists and governments alike, which run counter to conventional wisdom. Terrorists have been slow in accepting the obvious fact that terror is almost always more popular against foreigners than against their own countrymen (or co-religionists). Most terrorists in our time who have had any success at all have had the support of a specific national or religious group; it was the sectarian appeal that counted, not the revolutionary slogans – a fact that the Irish, Basques, Arabs and others found out by trial and error.

Terrorists have been quicker in accepting the other chief lesson: that the media are of paramount importance in their campaigns; that the terrorist act by itself is next to nothing, whereas publicity is all. But the media, constantly in need of diversity and new angles, make fickle friends. Terrorists will always have to innovate. They are, in some respects, the super-entertainers of our time. The real danger facing the terrorist is that of being ignored, receiving insufficient publicity, losing the image of the desperate freedom fighter and, of course, having to face determined enemies who are unwilling to negotiate regardless of the cost. There are few such people in authority in democratic societies. Leaders who might not hesitate to sacrifice whole armies during wartime appear willing to make almost any concession to save a single human life in peacetime, even knowing that these concessions will lead to new outbreaks and fresh victims of terror.

When an anarchist tried to kill the Italian king around the turn of the century, Umberto noted that this was the professional risk facing kings. Such philosophical resignation (or sense of duty) is no longer universal. Diplomats, it is reported, have protested against the hard line vis-à-vis terrorism taken by their governments, because they fear for their lives if taken hostage by terrorists.

To succeed, terrorist demands have to be 'realistic' (i.e. limited in character). Democratic authorities instinctively give in to blackmail, but they can afford to do so only up to a certain point. Thus the demand for money or the release of some terrorist prisoners is usually a realistic demand. But there are limits beyond which no government can go, as terrorist groups have discovered to their detriment.

The lessons for governments are equally obvious. If political leaders had refused to give in to terrorist demands, terrorism in Europe would have been very much reduced in scale. The attitude of Bruno Kreisky, Austrian chancellor in the 1970s, and his minister of the interior, who shook hands with the terrorists after they had killed an Austrian policeman, was not only aesthetically displeasing, it was also counter-productive. For, as a result, Austria was not spared further terrorist acts; on the contrary, she became known as a soft target. The same has held true with regard to Greece under Papandreou, who also gave full recognition to terrorist groups. But it is only fair to add that all democratic governments have at one time or another acted in a similar way, by compromising with the terrorists. The British and the Germans have released imprisoned terrorists, Americans and Frenchmen paid ransoms.* Even the Israelis have freed terrorists who were in their hands.

The present study deals with terrorism and not the ways and means to prevent and combat it. But counter-terrorism has to be mentioned at least in passing. Which reactions to terrorism have been effective and which have failed? There is no all-comprehensive answer because of the great differences in character of terrorist movements. But it is still possible to point to some general lessons. Thus, to mention one example, it is not true that an improvement or deterioration in economic conditions has a marked influence on the level of terrorism.[3] Terrorism is about political, not economic power. It does not occur at a time of economic crisis, but, on the contrary, when economic conditions are relatively good.

---

* There has been little difference in this respect between French governments of the left and those of the right, except that the former were more lenient towards home-grown terrorism of the left (Action Directe) whereas the latter tried to appease Middle Eastern terrorism.

Do political reforms or concessions to terrorists have an effect? This depends on the kind of demands, and the whole political context. Turkey could belatedly apologize to the Armenians, but it could not give them a state inside Turkey; India could grant greater autonomy to the Sikhs but not accept secession; the Israelis could make all kinds of concessions to the Palestinians, but they will not dismantle their state. Sometimes the deals made with national minorities have worked, as in the case of Alto Adige (South Tyrol), where violence was always small-scale. It is not certain as yet to what extent it has worked in Spain. The fact that most of Ireland became independent in 1921 did not prevent the civil war in the north sixty years later. If the terrorists' demand is all or nothing – as it often is – concessions based on a compromise will not put an end to bloodshed. The terrorist mentality is opposed to concessions. True, political concessions may still to a certain extent dry up the water in which the terrorist fish swim; if it were a question of popular elections in order to win over the 'silent majority', concessions could work. But unlike political parties, terrorists do not care about parliamentary majorities. A few hundred extremists based on a relatively small part of the population stand a good chance of preventing a policy of reconciliation – by their acts of provocation, assassinating moderate leaders, shouting 'betrayal' and so on. If appeasing the terrorists seldom works – unless their demands are limited and realistic – what in the light of historical experience is the efficacy of an uncompromising policy?*

Harsh, violent measures always cause the defeat of terrorists except perhaps in the case of a broadly based national movement using terrorism as one of several strategies in its political–military struggle. This is a fundamental fact which many observers of the terrorist scene find difficult to

---

* Whether a government should negotiate with terrorists in an acute crisis, such as the hijacking of an aircraft, is not a question of principle. Rescue missions frequently succeeded; the most famous were at Entebbe and Mogadishu (1977). But there were others, such as the successful stormings of an Indonesian airliner in Bangkok and an Egyptian Boeing 737 at Luxor, several Israeli successes in releasing hostages, the freeing of the Iranian embassy in London by the SAS, and so on. On the other side of the ledger are failures such as the disaster at Malta in November 1985, when fifty-nine hostages of a plane hijacked by the Abu Nidal gang were killed during an Egyptian commando attempt to release them. In the same month there were some 100 victims at the Palace of Justice in Bogota, when government troops tried to free the hostages kept by M 19. Each situation, needless to say, is different and has to be judged on its merits. Unless the units employed in rescue attempts are well trained and unless there is full co-operation on the part of the local authorities (which was not the case in Malta, or earlier in Cyprus) prospects of success are not good. But even in ideal conditions, an element of luck is involved.

accept.* But it has emerged time and time again that the terrorist reservoir is not unlimited, and that imprisoning or executing terrorists does not automatically bring new recruits. On the contrary, such actions weaken the terrorists. The more violence is applied, the more brutal and sweeping the anti-terrorist measures, the quicker and more complete is the defeat of the terrorists. The blood of the martyrs may be the seed of the church, but this is not usually true of terrorism. Obvious examples are Iran under Khomeini and the Argentine junta in the late 1970s. Such measures are applied by dictatorships; they are, of course, repugnant to democratic regimes. Some democrats have been uneasy even about the limited application of force shown by the Turkish military, while suppressing terrorism in their country. It has also been shown that half-hearted repressive measures frequently do not work: a state of emergency is lifted after a short while, mass arrests are followed by mass escapes from prison or amnesties. Such signals have the opposite effect. They create the impression that the authorities are weak and that only one more determined push on the part of the terrorists is needed to overthrow the system.

The 'correct' strategy of a democratic regime depends entirely on the specific challenge it confronts. If it faces an attempt by a small, disaffected minority to impose its demands on the great majority, political concessions are *a priori* ruled out, and there is no alternative to eliminating those who challenge the democratic order. If the terrorism is a manifestation of grievances, national or social, which are at least in part legitimate, the ideal approach is a mixture of political reforms and counter-terrorist means, acceding to those demands that are justified and realistic. In some cases this may lead to an armistice and eventually to the terrorists desisting from the 'armed struggle'. Elsewhere there is no alternative but to fight terrorism until it is defeated.

As 'internal terrorism' has declined over the last decade, and as international terrorism has taken a more central place, international co-operation against terrorism has been invoked a great many times. It is a hopeless undertaking as long as some states sponsor, finance, equip, train and provide sanctuaries to terrorist groups. Spokesmen for democratic societies will continue to proclaim that terrorism is abhorred and condemned by 'the whole civilized world'. But these days this covers not even half of mankind. Proceedings in the UN show that it is very difficult to have terror-

---

* 'The more terrorists in prison, the lower the violence level': Christopher Hewitt, *The Effectiveness of Anti-Terrorist Policies* (Lanham, 1984), p. 89. This is the conclusion of a detailed statistical investigation (and also a matter of common sense). Those who regard terrorism as the inevitable consequence of legitimate grievance may find this proposition impossible to accept.

ism condemned even on paper, unless some of the leading Communist or Third World countries happen to be on the receiving end of terrorist operations. Debates on how to counteract terrorist activities began in the League of Nations after the murder of King Alexander of Yugoslavia in 1934. They have continued in the United Nations for many years, preoccupying the General Assembly since 1972 and the US Sixth Committee (on legal affairs) even longer. An *ad hoc* UN Committee on International Terrorism, invited in 1977 to study the underlying causes of terrorism, condemned in 1979 acts of terrorism, and in 1985 'unequivocally condemned' such acts. All these resolutions were, however, of no consequence. Different countries have different notions about the legitimacy of terrorism, which became manifest in the many stipulations attached. International law is not only inadequate to deal with terrorism, it has also been used to legitimize terrorism.[4]

These debates will no doubt go on for many years, and it would clearly be wrong to pay too much attention to them. International terrorism is an extra-legal activity and for this reason the contributions of legal experts are bound to be limited.*

Specific bilateral agreements or pacts between groups of countries may on occasion be more effective. This was true, for instance, of the US–Cuban pact concerning the hijacking of aeroplanes; as a result the incidence of hijacking sharply declined. Also effective was the 1973 Convention on the Prevention and Punishment of Crimes Against Internationally Protected Persons Including Diplomatic Agents. Whatever the policy advocated by their governments, diplomats clearly do not wish to be on the receiving end of terrorist acts. But even in this seemingly clear-cut case, there could be no full agreement that it was wrong to attack, kidnap or kill diplomats; a provision had to be inserted to the effect that on certain occasions it would be right to do so.

The exchange of information about terrorism between NATO countries and some others has somewhat improved during the last decade. As a result some terrorist attacks have been prevented. Active collaboration in counteracting terrorism has not made much progress. The US has complained about Italian reluctance to hand over terrorists who engaged in attacks against US targets, yet American courts have not always been

---

* In June 1986 Andreas Papandreou, Prime Minister of Greece, proposed a conference under the auspices of the UN to find a definition of terrorism. To facilitate this, he provided a definition of his own, according to which the actions of small terrorist groups, such as the 17 November gang in Greece, were reprehensible. He also denounced the attempts to destabilize regimes in such countries as Libya, Afghanistan and Nicaragua. (*Washington Post*, 14 June 1986.)

forthcoming in extraditing IRA gunmen. France was for a long time a haven for terrorists not only from Latin America and the Middle East, but also from neighbouring European countries such as Italy and Spain. More stringent measures were taken only after terrorist operations in France became more frequent, and after it emerged that French terrorists had close connections with foreign comrades.

In certain conditions quiet diplomacy has been of some help in issuing warnings that have pre-empted terrorist actions. Most sponsors of state terrorism do not want their involvement to become known. At the very least they will temporarily scale down their involvement once it appears that high-value, low-risk undeclared war might turn into a declared war in which the risks are high and the value at best uncertain.

A truly effective concerted action against terrorism is possible, but only on the basis of the strategy first advocated by the nineteenth-century Russian terrorists of 'hitting the centre', meaning the main sponsors of international terrorism.

But 'hitting the centre' may not be easy for a variety of reasons. Unlike the terrorists, their sponsors frequently do not admit their responsibility for a certain terrorist operation or campaign, and the aggrieved party may find it difficult to provide evidence that would stand up in a court of law. In this business smoking guns are seldom left at the scene of a crime. Even if there is such evidence, to reveal it would usually mean to give away the identity of a well-placed intelligence source in the terrorist leadership, of which there are probably not that many.

For a country or a group of countries subject to attacks by international terrorism, there are broadly speaking three ways to react. Given the inertia of democratic governments and the difficulties involved, the natural reaction is to condemn the attacks but to refrain from any physical act of retaliation. As long as attacks occur relatively rarely, and do not involve many victims, this is a feasible policy. But lack of reaction may well be interpreted as a sign of weakness, in which case the attacks may become more frequent and murderous. The sponsors of international terrorism resemble in some respects naughty children trying to find out by trial and error how far they can go in provoking the adults without incurring punishment.

If an escalation in international terrorism does take place, the obvious way to retaliate is, of course, to pay the sponsors back in their own coin. As Colonel Grivas, head of EOKA in Cyprus, put it: to catch a mouse, one uses a cat, not a tank or an aircraft carrier. But democratic countries may not have 'cats', meaning a covert action capacity (or 'active measures' to use the Russian term). Even if they have a capability of this kind, they may find it difficult to use it, either because terrorist acts are much easier to carry out in open societies than in dictatorships, or because those who engage in covert action on behalf of a democratic country are not normally permitted to kill enemy leaders. In the United States there is an absolute prohibition by presidential order.

Thus, in the absence of 'cats', retaliation will take the form of military action. This means escalation and it is undesirable for a number of reasons. Innocent people are likely to get killed and those who retaliate will be blamed for creating a new and dangerous situation. This has been the fate of the Israelis, who for a long time preferred to react by way of surgical air strikes (which on occasion hit the wrong target) rather than to employ more complicated methods of retaliating. It was also the fate of the United States after the strike against Libya in April 1986. Those who retaliate become attackers and earn the opprobrium of the international community. No government will lightly take such a course of action; it will adopt it only if it has reason to assume that the alternative – refraining from counter-action – would have fateful consequences, or if public opinion is so strongly in favour of retaliation that it cannot safely be ignored.

In some instances terrorism may not outgrow the nuisance stage, in which case no further drastic action will be necessary. There is an inclination to magnify the importance of terrorism in modern society: society is vulnerable to attack, but it is also quite resilient. Oil ministers are abducted, but not a single drop of oil is lost. Describing the military exploits of his Bedouin warriors, Lawrence of Arabia once noted that they were on the whole good soldiers but for their unfortunate belief that weapons were dangerous and destructive in proportion to the noise they created. Present-day attitudes towards terrorism in the Western world, especially among the media, are strikingly similar. Terrorism makes a tremendous noise, but compared to some other dangers facing mankind, it seems almost irrelevant.

What is true for the US does not necessarily apply to other countries. The governments of Italy and Turkey in the 1970s faced a real threat of breakdown in public order which could not be belittled or ignored. The terrorist threat to the United States does not affect her national existence, whereas the antagonists of Israel have made no secret of the fact that they want ultimately to destroy the Jewish state. The counter-terrorism policy of a country whose physical existence is at stake is bound to be different from one that is not. A country under direct attack will prefer to err on the side of overreaction. It will not be unduly concerned by condemnations from international bodies such as the UN. Everyone wants to be a member of good standing in the international community, but not at the cost of committing suicide.

The virtual impossibility of outlining a counter-terrorism policy of universal validity was pointed out by the US Vice-President's Task Force on combating terrorism after lengthy deliberations in 1985: 'Because acts of terrorism vary so much in time and location, jurisdiction and motivation, consistent response is virtually impossible.' One can always outline certain general guidelines: the strengthening of international co-operation and Intelligence-gathering, the strengthening of security at airports and US installations abroad, and the imposition of sanctions on countries violating the Viennese Convention on diplomatic privileges. One could make the murder of a US citizen a federal crime, and so on. For the US, a no-concessions policy is probably the best way of ensuring the safety of the greatest number of people. The Bush task force did not rule out the right of the US government to retaliate by way of the 'judicious employment of military force', alone or in concert with other nations. But if, as is stated, the resistance to terrorism has to be carried out by legal means only, it remains to be asked how military force can be used without a declaration of war and still comply with the legal world order. There are certain provisions in international law referring to the right of self-defence and hot pursuit, but they are necessarily controversial. Terrorists do not bother unduly about international law, and they compel their victims to act likewise. But there is a difference in kind between the freedom of action of a global power like the United States and that of a small nation. It is much easier for a small country to react, especially if its existence happens to be at stake. The more powerful a country, the stronger the constraints on it to act cautiously. Everything a major power does is important, for its action may lead to a major international conflict, whereas small countries enjoy the benefits of less responsibility.

In most speeches and publications on international terrorism, reference is made to its steady and inexorable growth. In fact, the number of terrorist operations has fluctuated considerably.*[5] The perception of a steady

---

* To return once again to the question of statistics: an official US survey on patterns of global terrorism in 1984 noted that 'our tallies of terrorist incidents are not comprehensive and in some ways represent only the tip of the iceberg'. It could not possibly be different. But in these circumstances – in view of the impossibility of measuring the size of the iceberg – statements about the increase in global terrorism should be made only on the basis of unassailable evidence. The survey just mentioned states *expressis verbis* that 'the apparent increase in the number of international terrorist incidents in 1984 is at least partly the result of these [statistical] refinements'. In other words, terrorist acts by rural insurgent groups in Asia, Africa and Latin America, which were not counted in previous years, were included in 1984. This was, of course, bound to inflate the figures. (US Department of State, *Patterns of Global Terrorism 1984* (November 1985), pp. 1–2.

increase in terrorism has been caused by its dramatic character, the enormous publicity given to individual terrorist operations, and the loose use of the term 'terrorist'. Many forms of political violence ranging from government repression to civil war, insurrection and rural guerrilla war are lumped together under the heading 'terrorism' in speeches, research programmes and statistics, as if terrorism were a synonym for political violence in general.

That there has been a great deal of political turbulence in many parts of the world is not in doubt; nor is there any reason to assume that there will be fewer *coups d'état*, insurrections, civil wars or local wars in coming years. Not a global threat now, terrorism could become one as a result of technological developments. Alternatively, state-sponsored terrorism could lead to escalation and, ultimately, to full-scale war.

Professor Bernard Feld, a leading American physicist, once discussed the nightmarish consequences of the disappearance of twenty pounds of plutonium from government stocks. What if the mayor of Boston received a note to the effect that a terrorist group had planted a nuclear bomb somewhere in central Boston – accompanied by a crude diagram, which showed that the bomb would work? Professor Feld stated that he would advise surrender to blackmail rather than risk the destruction of his home town. Mr Clint Eastwood's attitude has been different, and the subject has since come up in many dozens of thrillers and films. Such fears in one form or another have been expressed for almost a century, albeit with less justification. If Most and some of his anarchist contemporaries hailed dynamite as the ultimate weapon – a panacea for all political and social problems – such joy was not universally shared. Thus a British police officer in the 1890s said:

> Murderous organizations have increased in size and scope; they are more daring, they are served by the more terrible weapons offered by modern science, and the world is nowadays threatened by new forces which, if recklessly unchained, may some day wreak universal destruction. The Orsini bombs were children's toys compared with the later developments of infernal machines. Between 1858 and 1898 the dastardly science of destruction has made rapid and alarming strides. ...[6]

With the use of poison gas in the First World War, fears were voiced that millions of people would die in gas-bomb attacks. Musprath wrote in the 1920s that, with the help of certain chemicals, unlimited areas could be destroyed in a very short time. Lord Halsbury, former chief of the explosives department of the British Ministry of War, told the House of Lords in 1928 that forty tons of diphencyclanarsin (a poison gas of the Blue Cross type) were sufficient to destroy the whole population of London.

But the quantity of the poisonous material needed was so large that it was generally assumed that only a modern army would be capable of using these lethal weapons. There had been talk in Irish extremist circles in the United States in the 1880s about the use of poison gas, but this was sheer fantasy at the time. Bacteriological warfare, including the poisoning of water reservoirs, was first discussed as a practical possibility during the First World War. According to one report, 'Anarchist elements' had been hired towards the end of the war to carry cholera bacilli from a neutral state to the territory of a belligerent.[7] The neutral country was apparently Switzerland, and the 'Anarchist elements' were to smuggle the bacilli in fountain pens to Russia.

There is reason to doubt the authenticity of the report, and it is not certain that the scheme would have been practical. But in the 1920s the danger was taken seriously, and a study commission on bacteriological warfare was established by the League of Nations. In 1936 a first nerve gas (GA-Tabun) was synthesized in Germany, to be followed by the discovery of even more toxic agents: Sarin (Great Britain) in 1938, and Soman in 1944, both fatal within minutes. They all belong to the organo-phosphates (OPA), a group of substances first discovered in 1854, although their toxic properties were then unknown. Considerable quantities of these and other gases were produced but not used by the belligerents in the Second World War. In 1944 a germ warfare centre was established in the United States. There were similar establishments in other countries.

Even before the first nuclear device had been exploded, scientists and statesmen in the United States voiced the fear that some insane people or agents of a hostile power could smuggle a bomb wherever they wanted: 'twenty thousand tons of TNT can be kept under the counter of a candy store'.[8] The plausibility of such a threat has been discussed and investigated ever since. During the 1970s there were 175 cases of threatened violence at nuclear plant facilities. In 1973 a group of ERP terrorists attacked a nuclear plant near Buenos Aires which was not yet operating. A fire was started in 1975 at a nuclear plant at Fessenheim, France, allegedly by the Meinhof–Puig–Antich group. With the growth of the civil nuclear industry, the establishment of new reactors all over the world and the declassification of technical information, the danger has grown that technically competent people, having stolen a sufficient quantity of plutonium, could build a primitive nuclear device. The plutonium needed could either be stolen while in transit or smuggled out from a plant. Nor were the theft of a nuclear device or the emergence of a black market in plutonium ruled out.

However stringent the means of control employed, it was assumed that they could not possibly be totally effective. Various official and private reports concluded that a sufficiently determined and able group could perform acts of sabotage endangering not only nuclear plants, but also the safety of the public living in their vicinity. Another study stated that the acquisition of special nuclear materials by a terrorist group was a threat to be taken very seriously.[9]

If the United States faced such dangers, they existed, *a fortiori*, in other countries where supervision was less effective and terrorism more active. Yet another study argued that while INW (illicit nuclear weapon) production was both plausible and feasible, the probability of success was low. Assuming that SNM (special nuclear material) had been acquired in sufficient quantity, an effort by a sizeable group of people would be needed over a lengthy period. There was low probability that such a group would have the skills, motivation, resources and opportunities to make the venture a success.[10] The fuel delivered to atomic plants has characteristics which make it nearly impossible to convert to nuclear weapons. The terrorist group would have to steal a number of centrifuges to produce high-enriched uranium stolen from low-enriched or natural uranium. The popular idea of a nuclear device produced in a garage and transported on a tricycle seems to belong for the time being to the realms of fantasy. Various other means of nuclear sabotage have been mentioned, such as the deployment of plutonium powder. All these possibilities have to be taken seriously, and the danger will undoubtedly increase in the future, even though the risks involved for nuclear terrorists are formidable. According to some estimates there is a 50 per cent death risk on stealing nuclear material, and about 30 per cent in bomb manufacture. But terrorist groups ready to make use of nuclear devices or poisonous substances cannot be measured by rational standards in any case. It is also true that the technical obstacles would be greatly reduced if the terrorists could count on the help of a friendly government which had nuclear reactors and the facilities to produce plutonium or uranium-235. All this may take longer than some experts assume, but there is little reason to doubt that 'if present trends continue, it seems only a question of time before some terrorist organization exploits the possibilities for coercion which are latent in nuclear fuel'.[11] In the meantime certain safeguards – sensors, for instance – may be created and developed. But there is no reason to assume that there will ever be totally effective safeguards.

In 1985–6, an international working group assessing the dangers of international nuclear terrorism noted that while some 155 bombings or other attacks had taken place during the preceding two decades at the sites of nuclear reactors in Europe and America, none had caused a serious accident. Most of these had been the work of nuclear protesters rather than terrorists. According to the same source, the nuclear weapons sector was considered less vulnerable to attack, because substantial resources had been allocated to protective measures such as the PAL systems (permissive action links) with commandable features which rendered stolen weapons useless. However, not all tactical nuclear weapons have as yet been fitted with advanced self-protecting systems, including those on board ships. More vulnerable to both sabotage and theft are civilian nuclear facilities, such as power reactors and research reactors. Experts tend to believe that while crude nuclear bomb-making may not be as simple as previously believed, it is still feasible with a sufficient quantity of reactor-grade plutonium or highly enriched uranium.[12]

Nuclear terrorism could not only pose a major threat to individual nations, it could also lead to a major international crisis. With these dangers in mind US Senators Nunn and Warner suggested in 1985 the establishment of US–USSR Nuclear Risk Reduction Centres, to co-ordinate the responses of the superpowers to nuclear terrorist threats, with a view to exchanging information through existing hot-line arrangements and to arranging possible common action. In pursuance of this initiative, American and Soviet representatives met in Geneva in May 1986 to consider steps relating to the establishment of such centres.

Most attention has focused on the potential of nuclear blackmail because it is the most dramatic threat. But modern technology has provided other, equally lethal weapons that are more frequently discussed in scientific literature than in popular writing.[13] There are the various poisons such as the OPAS, which include the nerve gases mentioned above and the monofluoroalipathic compounds as well as BTX (Botulinum toxin), which is physiologically effective however it enters the body. In addition there are a great many other potential biological weapons capable of spreading contagious diseases ranging from anthrax to bubonic plague, from certain forms of encephalitis to psittacosis.[14] Some bacteria are difficult to cultivate or to disseminate, but the list of those that could possibly be used is still uncomfortably long. Most of the biological pathogens (like most of the highly poisonous substances) have been available for many decades but there have been several important technological developments since the Second World War. These include the continuous culture of micro-organisms, the production of monodisperse aerosols and the stabilization of organisms to maintain their viability in aerosol dissemination.[15] At the same time modern society has become more vulnerable as the result of rapid communication, central ventilation, central water storage systems and many other factors.[16] Biological pathogens are more easily available than SNM; transport and dissemination might be undertaken by very small groups of people, and possibly even individuals. On the other hand, it is precisely the almost unlimited destructive character of biological pathogens which makes them less suitable as a terrorist weapon, not only because nuclear terrorism has the greater publicity value, but mainly because a threat to use biological pathogens would be less credible. A terrorist group could prove that it is capable of carrying out a nuclear threat by exploding a device in a sparsely inhabited area, whereas a 'trial epidemic' would be impossible to launch. A crude fission bomb of around 0.1 kiloton would have a limited effect – that of a bomb of 100 tons of high explosives or more. It would destroy a big factory, or several blocks of buildings. An epidemic, on the other hand, could spread to all parts of the globe, which makes it impractical for international terrorism. A weapon of this kind is more likely to be used by a madman than a political terrorist.* For these and other reasons the use of biological weapons, despite their greater availability, seems less likely than the use of chemical agents like the OPAS. Some OPAS are commercially available in any case. But like home-made nuclear devices chemical agents involve high risks for those who prepare them, and their effectiveness is not guaranteed. In the mid-1970s there were reports that mustard gas was stolen from German ammunition bunkers, allegedly by the Baader–Meinhof gang; a quantity of nerve gas stolen by criminals had been recovered by the Austrian police. There were also unconfirmed reports that the Baader–Meinhof gang and a Spanish terrorist group had enlisted the services of chemists and microbiologists, and that an Arab pharmaceutical congress had pledged support to the PLO, urging training in biological warfare.[17] An amateurish attempt was made to inject poison into Israeli oranges scheduled for export. But there has not been as yet a single attempt at terror on the grand scale.

Terrorists could obtain nuclear material – or a bomb or two – by theft or as a gift, but there are also other possibilities: for instance, as the result of a revolution or a coup in a country which has a nuclear weapons programme, either open or clandestine. Yet another possibility is the manufacture of nuclear devices. According to calculations made by Hans Bethe, a minimum of six qualified scientists and engineers with the right specializations are needed, and at least one of them would have to know about

---

* Even in dictatorships, attempted assassinations by individuals have been far more difficult to detect than those undertaken by groups. The attempt against Hitler's life, which came nearest to success before the conspiracy of 1944, was made by George Elser, a carpenter who put the bomb in the Munich Hofbräuhaus in November 1939. He acted entirely on his own and would probably never have been caught but for his foolish attempt to cross the border into Switzerland. See Peter Hoffman, *Die Sicherheit des Diktators* (Munich, 1975), p. 119 *et seq.*

weapons design. Other estimates claim that ten to twenty qualified people would be needed for working under minimum safety precautions, and their equipment would not be cheap.[18] However, according to the 1986 task-force report, a smaller group might be sufficient, without previous experience in weapon design.

It might not be too difficult to obtain the money; to get suitable facilities and enlist the right people would be less easy. Assuming that the work has been accomplished, there remains the task of authenticating it, either by exploding it over a live target or by way of a secret or open ultimatum. Obviously, the origin of a weapon of this kind would have to be hidden, for if it were to appear that a government was behind the threat of nuclear terrorism, all the advantages of anonymity would be lost and the government in question would be open to nuclear reprisal. Nuclear terrorism, in other words, would turn into nuclear war; its basic advantage – the absence of a target for retaliation – would be lost. This, then, is the basic weakness of nuclear terrorism, but there are still other problems:

Having demonstrated that it possessed atomic weapons, the group would presumably be in a position to demand special treatment. Would possession of nuclear weapons enable a terrorist group to demand greater concessions than terrorists in the past have demanded? To achieve permanent policy changes, the terrorist threat would have to be maintained indefinitely. How long could a terrorist nuclear group expect to maintain a threat before its weapon was captured?[19]

If the nuclear terrorist group demanded, for instance, a territory of its own, and if its demand were fulfilled, it would immediately become hostage to nuclear (or other) retaliation. It is no doubt still true, as Thomas Schelling wrote several years ago, that the production of nuclear weapons requires a group of significant size, high professional quality and excellent organization and discipline to convert illicitly obtained nuclear material into usable weapons.[20]

The technical difficulties might be overcome, thanks to proliferation and miniaturization in the nuclear field, and to the presence of so many such weapons, which are not all guarded perfectly. The political problems of nuclear terrorism are more difficult, and this refers also to chemical as well as to biological agents, which are older than nuclear arms. Mention has already been made in passing of the fact that toxic chemicals are easily accessible, whereas for the potentially far more lethal biological agents – toxins and living organisms – a higher degree of scientific knowledge is needed, and access and dissemination are also more difficult.[21]

Groups such as the German, Italian, French, Turkish or Latin American terrorists are unlikely to use nuclear, chemical or bacteriological weapons, assuming that they have any political sense at all – an assumption that cannot always be taken for granted. They claim to act on behalf of the people, they aspire to popular support, and clearly the use of arms of mass destruction would not add to their popularity. Nor is it likely that the PIRA or the ETA would use such weapons in Northern Ireland or Euzkadi; the number of Catholics and Basques respectively who would be killed would probably equal that of murdered 'enemies'. One cannot rule out, at least in theory, the use of such weapons in mainland Britain or in Spain. Arab terrorists might deploy them against Tel Aviv residents rather than against Jerusalem with its many Arabs. These weapons are more likely to be used – if at all – by individual madmen or nationalist–separatist groups against heavy concentrations of 'enemy' population.

Terrorism using arms of mass destruction is certainly feasible now, and it will be even easier to accomplish in the future. But how likely is it to occur? For a variety of reasons these are not rational weapons for non-state actors. If Libya, for example, obtained nuclear weapons, it would probably use them itself at a time and place of its choice rather than leave them to Abu Nidal and his ilk, thus inviting nuclear (or biological or chemical) retaliation at some unknown date. Precisely because these weapons are so deadly, retaliation will be equally deadly, unless it is assumed that the capacity of the victim of a nuclear strike will be wiped out at the first strike, which is highly unlikely.

This still leaves the 'crazies', terrorists with no constituency, who have nothing to lose and who might contemplate any course of action, however mad. But they are the least likely to obtain weapons of this kind, and it does not affect our conclusion that while the use of these weapons can never be entirely ruled out, the probability still remains low.*

Most of the speculation on future terrorist threats has focused on nuclear and bacteriological–biological weapons. Comparatively little attention has been paid to possible attacks on the technological infrastructure of modern society. In 1985 Japanese terrorist groups simultaneously attacked twenty-

---

* It has been argued that with their sense of the dramatic, terrorists would always prefer the 'big bang' of a nuclear explosion to the far less impressive effects of chemical or biological toxins, even if the latter might be as deadly in the end. But much will depend on the availability of means of mass destruction to terrorists and their sponsors. While the origin of nuclear weapons can be easily traced, this could be more complicated in the case of chemical and biological agents, which makes retaliation more difficult.

three nodes on the Tokyo metro system. In the same way other critical checkpoints of the system are vulnerable: electrical power, food-supply chains, transportation, and the sanitary and water systems. Modern communications systems are vulnerable to physical disruption and passive tampering as with the introduction of a 'virus' – a Trojan horse which could destroy major data and control systems, while defeating carefully designed security barriers.[22] Such actions might be very effective in paralysing normal life in a country; it would keep a society hostage. But it is quite remote from original terrorist strategy. What useful purpose would it serve to attain certain specific demands? Sabotage operations of this kind would probably be of greater interest to an enemy nation in time of war than to a terrorist group.

Nor should it be forgotten that anti-terrorist technology and tactics are also bound to make progress in the years to come. This applies to 'active measures': the whole field of 'black programmes', including the capacity to shut down internal-combustion engines within a certain perimeter and neutralize individual terrorists from a considerable distance. It also pertains to defensive measures such as remote-sensing capacities that distinguish terrorists from their victims, high-explosives detection techniques, high-speed discovery techniques that detect the presence of a single molecule of a toxin and so on. So far anti-terrorist technology has always been reactive, lagging behind the terrorist threat. But if the terrorist threat should grow, higher priority will be given to the funding not only of deterrents to attacks but also of means capable of paralysing terrorist efforts altogether.[23]

The main task of counter-terrorist strategy is to identify the future major threats. While this is impossible with total accuracy, there are still various degrees of probability. The main danger today is not the unlimited spread of terrorism, in terms of both numbers and efficiency, nor the use of some exotic weapons. The real danger is escalation into something more destructive than mere terrorism. There is a self-regulating mechanism for internal terrorism; the more massive its onslaught, the more severe its repression. But the victims of terrorism instigated and controlled from abroad may not have the capacity to retaliate on the same level of low-intensity warfare. They may have to hit back with full military means in order to compel the sponsors of terrorism to desist. This may lead to military actions such as the invasion of Lebanon following the attempted murder of Shlomo Argov, the Israeli ambassador in London.

It could be argued that the Israeli invasion took place only because a faction in the Israeli leadership favouring this course of action was waiting for a suitable occasion. Equally, it might be argued that Syria wanted war in early 1986 when it commissioned one of its agents to smuggle a time-bomb aboard an El Al jumbo jet. For it is difficult to believe that those who instigated this action did not anticipate its consequences.

But this is to overrate the degree of rational thinking in politics. The state sponsors of international terrorism frequently do not have full control over their terrorists, their timing and the extent of damage the terrorist act might inflict. A bomb meant to kill a few may instead kill several hundred, and this could have consequences which were not calculated. And even if the terrorists want war, they may have second thoughts after the immediate occasion passes, if only because their patron will refuse to give full backing in case of war.

The danger of international terrorism, in other words, is not in terrorist acts *per se*, but in triggering off a wider and more dangerous armed conflict. For this reason, it is important to prevent an escalation, to resist state-sponsored terrorism from the beginning, not to lead its sponsors into temptation. It is equally important to have full understanding with the Soviet Union and the Soviet-bloc countries in this respect. They regard terrorism on the whole as a minor weapon in their strategy vis-à-vis the West. But it ought to be made clear that there is no scope for terrorist operations in relations between East and West, even on a low level. True, the Soviet Union may not have full control over its proxies, but since it is unlikely that countries such as Libya or Syria will accept the risk of becoming involved in a major war unless they are reasonably certain to have full Soviet support, the Soviet Union is in a position to prevent escalation. If the Soviet leaders will use this leverage, international terrorism will be contained in the future without too much difficulty. There is some reason for optimism that caution will prevail, for Soviet leaders, unlike some of their subcontractors, are neither fanatics nor irresponsible gamblers. They want to make gains but not at high risks. Terrorism may be a low-risk venture from a Middle Eastern point of view, but this perspective is not necessarily shared by a global power. Since the Soviet Union quite frequently benefits from the destabilizing effects of terrorism, it would be unrealistic to expect full Soviet co-operation in the battle against terrorist movements towards which it feels a political affinity. However, the decisive issue is not whether the Soviet Union will publicly dissociate itself but whether active help and guarantees will be given to terrorists.

Contemporary terrorism has moved far from its origins, which were rooted in the struggle against despotism. Terrorism appeared in the secret societies and revolutionary organizations of the nineteenth century, fighting tyranny against which there was no legal redress. It was adopted by national movements against foreign oppressors and by sections of the extreme left and right. Circumstances still vary today from country to country and what is said about one is not necessarily true of another. Violent resistance against the authority of the state is still justified in non-democratic regimes, against severe oppression and in defence of a just cause. By and large, however, there has been an essential change in the character of terrorism over the last hundred years with the shedding of restraints, the deliberate choice of innocent victims, the growth of multinational, remote-controlled terrorism usually sponsored by tyrannical regimes, and, above all, the failure or the unwillingness of terrorists to challenge effective dictatorships. Once it was the strategy that the poor and weak used against ruthless tyrants. Today its more typical representatives are no longer poor, and modern technology is giving them powerful weapons. Some present-day terrorist groups have quite clearly acquired the characteristics once attributed to tyranny, *atrox et notoria injuria*. The tyrant wants to impose his will on society and to keep it at ransom, and so do terrorists. Others genuinely believe in their 'liberating' mission, yet if their actions have any effect at all it is that of unwitting pacemakers of a new breed of tyrants. The wheel has come full circle.

Bibliography

The literature on terrorism has grown enormously during the last decade. Of the existing bibliographies and guidebooks the most recent and comprehensive is Alex P.Schmid, *Political Terrorism* (Amsterdam, 1983; New Brunswick, 1986). The following should also be mentioned: Augustus R.Norton and Martin H.Greenberg, *International Terrorism: An Annotated Bibliography and Research Guide* (Boulder, Colorado, 1980); and Edward Mickolus, *The Literature of Terrorism* (Westport, Conn., 1980). Another useful handbook is Peter Janke, *Guerrilla and Terrorist Organizations* (New York, 1983). Also L.Bonanate, *La violenza politica nel mundo contemporaneo* (Milan, 1979); M.J.Smith, Jr, *The Secret Wars*, vol. III: *Terrorism 1968–80* (Santa Barbara, 1980); V.Tutenberg and Ch.Pollak, *Terrorismus, Gestern, Heute, Morgen* (Munich, 1978); Uwe Backes (ed.), *Totalitarismus, Extremismus, Terrorismus* (Düsseldorf, 1984). Unfortunately there is no truly international guide in this respect. The quarterly journal *Terrorism* has published over the years many articles, documents and reports on conferences. Documents concerning the history of terrorism can be found in the *Terrorism Reader* (New York, 1978; new revised edn 1987), edited by the present writer.

General Literature on Terrorism

Y.Alexander (ed.), *International Terrorism* (New York, 1976).

M.C.Bassiouni (ed.), *International Terrorism and Political Crimes* (Springfield, 1975).

B.J.Bell, *Transnational Terror* (Washington, DC, 1975).

Anthony Burton, *Urban Terrorism* (London, 1975).

R.Clutterbuck, *Protest and the Urban Guerrilla* (London, 1973).

R.Clutterbuck, *Living with Terrorism* (London, 1975).

Roland Gaucher, *The Terrorists* (London, 1968).

F.Hacker, *Terror, Mythos, Realität, Analyse* (Vienna, 1973).

International Terrorism, US House Committee on Foreign Affairs, Washington, DC, 1974.

Hans Langemann, *Das Attentat* (Hamburg, 1957).

J.Malin (ed.), *Terror and Urban Guerrillas* (Coral Gables, 1971).

W.Middendorff, *Der politische Mord* (Wiesbaden, 1968).

Robert Moss, *Urban Guerrillas* (London, 1972).
Political Kidnappings, Committee on Internal Security, House of Representatives, Washington, DC, 1973.
David C. Rapoport, *Assassination and Terrorism* (Toronto, 1971).
Lester Sobel, *Political Terrorism* (New York, 1975).
Terrorism, Parts 1–4, Committee on Internal Security, House of Representatives, Washington, DC, 1974.
Terrorism, Staff study, Committee on Internal Security, House of Representatives, Washington, DC, 1974.
Terrorist Activity, Parts 1–8, Committee of the Judiciary, House of Representatives, Washington, DC, 1974–5.
Jerzy Waciorski, *Le Terrorisme politique* (Paris, 1939).
Paul Wilkinson, *Political Terrorism* (London, 1974).

Tyrannicide, Secret Societies

J. Althusius, *Politica metodice digesta* (1603).
M. Ballestreos-Gaibrois, *Juan de Mariana, cantor de España*, 2 vols. (Madrid, 1938–9).
A. Blanqui, *Textes Choisis* (Paris, 1955).
J. Boucher, *De iusta Henrici III* ... (1589).
G. Buchanan, *De Jure Regni apud Scotos* ... (1579).
P. Buonarroti, *Conspiration pour l'égalité dite de Babeuf* (1828).
L. Daneau, *Politicae Christianae libri VII* (1596).
M. Dommanget, *Pages Choisies de Babeuf* (Paris, 1935).
Duplessis-Mornay, *Vindiciae contra Tyrannos* (1579).
T. Frost, *The Secret Societies of European Revolution*, 2 vols. (London, 1876).
O. Jaszi and D. Lewis, *Against the Tyrant* (New York, 1957).
R. M. Johnston, *Napoleonic Empire in Southern Italy*, 2 vols. (London, 1904).
M. I. Kovalskaia, *Dvizhenie Karbonartsev v Italii 1808–1821* (Moscow, 1971).
La Boetie, *De la Servitude volontaire au contru'un'* (1578).
P. Liman, *Der politische Mord im Wandel der Geschichte* (1912).
O. Lutaud, *Des Révolutions d'Angleterre à la révolution française* (Paris, 1973).
J. de Mariana, *De rege et regis institutione* (1599).
R. Mousnier, *Assassinat d'Henri IV* (Paris, 1964).
W. Platzhoff, *Die Theorie von der Mordbefugnis der Obrigkeit im 16. Jahrhundert* (1906).
C. Rossaeus, *De justa Rei publicae Christianae* (1590).
John of Salisbury, *Policraticus* (1595).
F. Schoenstedt, *Der Tyrannenmord im Spätmittelalter* (1938).
G. Sencier, *Le Babouvisme après Babeuf* (Paris, 1912).
E. Sexby, *Killing No Murder* ... (1657).
D. Spadoni, *Sette cospirationi e cospiratori* (Turin, 1904).
G. Weill, *Le Parti Républicain en France 1814–1870* (Paris, 1900).

Bakunin and Nechaev

M. Bakunin, *Izbrannie Sochineniia*, 5 vols. (Petrograd, 1919–21).
M. Bakunin, *Gesammelte Werke*, 3 vols. (Berlin, 1921–4).
E. H. Carr, *Michael Bakunin* (London, 1937).
M. Confino, *La Violence dans la violence* (Paris, 1973).
H. E. Kaminski, *Bakounine: La vie d'un révolutionnaire* (Paris, 1938).
A. Lehning, *Michel Bakounine et ses relations avec Sergej Necaev* (Leiden, 1971).
M. Nettlau, *Michael Bakunin eine Biographie*, 3 vols. (London, 1896–1900).
Y. M. Steklov, *M. A. Bakunin, yevo zhizn i deatelnost, 1814–76*, 4 vols. (Moscow, 1926–7).

Terrorism in Russia (1870–1920)

The most important sources for the study of Russian terorrism are the journals of Narodnaya Volya and the Social Revolutionaries as well as Burtsev's *Byloe* and the periodicals of the early Soviet period such as *Katorga i Sylka*.

Paul Avrich, *The Russian Anarchists* (Princeton, 1971).
V. Bogucharski, *Aktivnoe Narodnichestvo* (Moscow, 1912).
V. Burtsev, *Za sto let* (London, 1897).
V. Burtsev, *Doloi Tsarya* (London, 1901).
V. Burtsev, *Borba za svobodnuyu Rossiu* (Berlin, 1924).
V. M. Chernov, *Pered Burei* (New York, 1953).
M. Confino, *La Violence dans la violence* (Paris, 1973).
Da zdravstvuyet Narodnaya Volya (Paris, 1907).
V. I. Debogori-Mokrievich, *Vospominania* (St Petersburg, 1906).
Vera Figner, *Memoirs of a Revolutionist* (New York, 1927).
David Footman, *Red Prelude* (London, 1943).
B. S. Itenberg, *Dvizhenie Revoliutsonovo Narodnichestva* (Moscow, 1965).
A. I. Ivianski (ed.), *Zhizn kak Fakel* (Moscow, 1966).
Jan Kucharzewski, *Od Bialego Caratu do Czerwonego*, 7 vols. (Warsaw, 1926–35).
T. G. Masaryk, *Zur russischen Geschichts- und Religionsphilosophie* (Jena, 1913).
N. Morozov, *Povest moei Zhizni* (Moscow, 1947).
'Narodovoltsi' (Moscow, 1931).
G. Nestroev, *Iz dnevnika Maksimalista* (Paris, 1910).
B. Nikolajewski, *Asew* (Berlin, 1932).
Padenie tsarskovo rezhima, 3 vols. (Moscow, 1920–25).
B. Savinkov, *Erinnerungen eines Terroristen* (Berlin, 1927).
A. Spiridovich, *Histoire du terrorisme russe* (Paris, 1930).
I. Steinberg, *Spiridonowa* (London, 1935).
S. Stepniak-Kravchinski, *Podpolnaya Russia* (Moscow, 1960).
L. Tikhomirov, *Vospominania* (Moscow, 1927).
L. Venturi, *Roots of Revolution* (London, 1966).

L. Volin, *Nineteen Seventeen* (London, 1954).
S. S. Volk, *Narodnaya Volya* (Moscow, 1966).

Ireland and Ulster

Tom Barry, *Guerrilla Days in Ireland* (New York, 1956).
P. S. Beaslei, *Michael Collins and the Making of a New Ireland* (London, 1926).
R. Bennet, *The Black and Tans* (London, 1959).
D. Boulton, *The UVF 1966–1973* (Dublin, 1973).
J. Bowyer Bell, *The Secret Army* (London, 1970).
Andrew Boyd, *Holy War in Belfast* (London, 1969).
D. Breen, *My Fight for Irish Freedom* (Kerry, 1964).
Thomas N. Brown, *Irish–American Nationalism* (New York, 1966).
Tim Pat Coogan, *The IRA* (London, 1970).
Tom Corfe, *The Phoenix Park Murders* (London, 1968).
Devoy's Post Bag, ed. W. O'Brien and D. Ryan, 2 vols. (Dublin, 1953).
J. Devoy, *Recollections of an Irish Rebel* (Shannon, 1969).
O. D. Edwards and F. Pyle (eds.), *The Easter Rising* (London, 1968).
M. Harmon, *Fenians and Fenianism* (Dublin, 1968).
Ireland and the Irish Question. A collection of writings by Karl Marx and Friedrich
    Engels (New York, 1972).
F. X. Martin (ed.), *Leaders and Men of the Easter Rising* (New York, 1967).
Jeremy O'Donovan Rossa, *My Years in English Jails* (New York, 1967).
Desmond Ryan, *The Phoenix Flame* (London, 1937).
Desmond Ryan, *The Rising* (Dublin, 1957).
Desmond Ryan, *James Connolly* (Dublin, 1924).
M. F. Ryan, *Fenian Memoirs* (Dublin, 1945).
Mac Stiofain, *Revolutionary in Ireland* (London, 1975).
C. Tansill, *America and the Fight for Irish Freedom* (New York, 1957).
P. J. P. Tynan, *The Irish Invincibles* (New York, 1894).
T. D. Williams, *Secret Societies in Ireland* (Dublin, 1973).

Terrorism and the Police Counter-terror

Sir Robert Anderson, *Sidelights on the Home Rule Movement* (London, 1907).
L. Andrieux, *Souvenir d'un préfet de police* (Paris, 1885).
A. Bekzadian, *Der Agent Provocateur* (Zurich, 1913).
H. Le Caron, *Twenty Five Years in the Secret Service* (London, 1892).
R. Garraud, *L'Anarchie et la répression* (Paris, 1885).
A. Gerassimoff, *Der Kampf gegen die erste russische Revolution* (Berlin, 1933).
Lucien de la Hodde, *Histoire de sociétés secrètes* (Paris, 1850).
Maurice Laporte, *Histoire de l'Okhrana* (Paris, 1935).
Jean Longuet et G. Zilber, *Les Dessous de la police russe* (Paris, 1909).
A. P. Vasilief, *Police russe et révolution* (Paris, 1936).

India

U.S.Anand, *Savarkar* (London, 1967).
Anon, *The Philosophy of the Bomb* (n.p., 1930).
V.Chirol, *Indian Unrest* (London, 1910).
Manmathnat Gupta, *History of the Revolutionary Movement in India* (Delhi, 1960).
Dhananjang Keer, *Veer Savarkar* (Bombay, 1966).
R.C.Majumdar, *History of the Freedom Movement in India*, 3 vols. (Calcutta, n.d.).
B.R.Nanda, *Socialism in India* (New Delhi, 1972).
Report of the Commission of Inquiry into the Conspiracy to Murder Mahatma Gandhi, 6 vols. (New Delhi, 1970).
J.N.Vajpeyi, *The Extremist Movement in India* (Allahabad, 1974).
Yashpal, *Singhavalokan*, 3 vols. (Lucknow, 1951–2).

Doctrine and Sociology

E.H.Carr, *Michael Bakunin* (New York, 1961).
David Caute, *Fanon* (London, 1970).
Gérard Chaliand, *Mythes révolutionnaires du Tiers Monde* (Paris, 1976).
James Connolly, *Revolutionary Warfare* (Dublin, 1968).
H.Eckstein (ed.), *Internal Wars* (New York, 1964).
Frantz Fanon, *The Wretched of the Earth* (New York, 1963).
Emma Goldman, *Anarchism and Other Essays* (New York, 1910).
Feliks Gross, *Violence in Politics* (The Hague, 1972).
Abraham Guillen, *Philosophy of the Urban Guerrilla* (New York, 1973).
P.A.Kropotkin, *Selected Writings* (Cambridge, Mass., 1973).
A.Lehning, *Bakunin et ses relations avec S.Nechaev* (Leiden, 1971).
Emilio Lussu, *Théorie de l'insurrection* (Paris, 1971).
C.Marighella, *Mini Manual of the Urban Guerrilla* (London, 1971).
Johann Most, *The Beast of Property* (New Haven, Conn., c. 1885).
Johann Most, *Revolutionäre Kriegswissenschaft* (New York, c. 1884).
N. Morozov, *Terroristicheskaya Borba* (London, 1880).
George Plekhanov, *Anarchism and Socialism* (Minneapolis, n.d.).
D.C.Rapoport, *Assassination and Terrorism* (Toronto, 1971).
V.Tarnovski, *Terrorism i routina* (Geneva, 1880).

Middle East
(see also notes to Chapter 6)

1. Palestine 1938–48
J.Banai, *Hayalim Almonim* (Tel Aviv, 1958).

Y.Bauer, *Diplomacy and Resistance* (New York, 1970).
M.Begin, *The Revolt* (London, 1964).
Lohame Herut Israel, 2 vols. (Tel Aviv, 1959).
D.Niv, *Ma'arakhot ha'irgun hazvai haleumi*, 5 vols. (Tel Aviv, 1977).
N.Yalin-Mor, *Lohamei Herut Israel* (Tel Aviv, n.d.).

2. Terror and the Arab–Israeli Conflict

N.Aloush, *Al thawra al filistiniya* (Beirut, 1970).
G.Chaliand, *The Palestine Resistance* (London, 1972).
J.Cooley, *Green March, Black September* (London, 1973).
G.Denoyan, *El Fath parle* (Paris, 1970).
Y.Harkabi, *Fedayeen Action and Arab Strategy* (London, 1968).
Y.Harkabi, *Palestinians and Israel* (Jerusalem, 1974).
L.Kadi, *Basic Political Documents of the Armed Palestinian Resistance Movement* (Beirut, 1969).
W.Kazziha, *Revolutionary Transformation in the Arab World* (London, 1975).
L.Khaled, *My People Shall Live* (London, 1973).
G.Khorshid, *Dalil Harakat al muqawama al filistiniya* (Beirut, 1971).
J.Laffin, *Fedayeen.* (London, 1973).
Z.Schiff and R.Rothstein, *Fedayeen* (London, 1972).
R.Tophoven, *Fedayin, Guerilla ohne Grenzen* (Munich, 1975).
E.Yaari, *Strike Terror* (Jerusalem, 1970).

Anarchism

David Apter and James Joll (eds.), *Anarchism* (London, 1971).
Alexander Berkman, *Prison Memoirs of an Anarchist* (New York, 1912).
Andrew Carlson, *Anarchism in Germany* (New York, 1972).
April Carter, *The Political Theory of Anarchism* (London, 1971).
Richard Drinnon, *Rebel in Paradise* (Chicago, 1961).
Felix Dubois, *Le Péril anarchiste* (Paris, 1894).
Emma Goldman, *Living My Life* (New York, 1931).
Daniel Guérin, *L'Anarchisme* (Paris, 1965).
J.Guillaume, *L'Internationale* (Paris, 1910).
I.L.Horowitz (ed.), *The Anarchists* (New York, 1964).
Richard Hostetter, *The Italian Socialist Movement* (Princeton, 1958).
James Joll, *The Anarchists* (London, 1964).
P.A.Kropotkin, *Selected Writings* (Cambridge, Mass., 1973).
Cesare Lombroso, *Les Anarchistes* (Paris, 1894).
Jean Maitron, *Histoire du mouvement anarchiste en France 1880–1914* (Paris, 1955).
M.A.Miller, *Kropotkin* (Chicago, 1976).
Max Nettlau, *Anarchisten und Sozialrevolutionäre* (Berlin, 1914).
Max Nomad, *Aspects of Revolt* (New York, 1959).
Max Nomad, *Rebels and Renegades* (New York, 1932).
Vernon Richards (ed.), *Enrico Malatesta* (London, 1965).

Rudolf Rocker, *Johann Most* (Berlin, 1924).
Rudolf Rocker, *The London Years* (London, 1956).
Victor Serge, *Memoirs of a Revolutionary* (London, 1963).
E. Sernicoli, *L'Anarchia*, 2 vols. (Milan, 1894).
E. A. Vizetelly, *The Anarchists* (New York, 1912).
George Woodcock, *Anarchism* (London, 1962).
E. V. Zenker, *Anarchism* (London, 1895).
Hector Zoccoli, *Die Anarchie und die Anarchisten* (Leipzig, 1909).

Terrorist Groups in Various Countries, 1870–1939

Louis Adamic, *Dynamite* (New York, 1934).
Wayne G. Broehl, *The Molly Maguires* (New York, 1966).
C. Christowe, *Heroes and Assassins* (New York, 1935).
C. Z. Codreanu, *Pentru Legionari* (Bucharest, 1937).
V. Dedijer, *The Road to Sarajevo* (New York, 1966).
Den Doolard, *Quatre mois chez les Comitadjis* (Paris, 1932).
M. Fatu and Ion Spalatelu, *Garda de Fier* (Bucharest, 1971).
E. Gumbel, *Vier Jahre politischer Mord* (Berlin, 1922).
R. Hunter, *Violence and the Labor Movement* (New York, 1914).
H. Karasek (ed.), *Haymarket, 1886, die deutschen Anarchisten in Chicago* (Berlin, 1975).
M. Lacko, *Arrow-Cross Men* (Budapest, 1969).
L. Nalbandian, *The Armenian Revolutionary Movement* (Berkeley, 1963).
A. Nazabek, *Through the Storm* (London, 1899).
M. S. Packe, *The Bombs of Orsini* (London, 1957).
C. Papanace, *La genesi ed il martirio del Movimento Legionario Rumeno* (n.p., 1959).
J. Perrigault, *Bandits de l'Orient* (Paris, 1931).
E. von Salomon, *Die Geächteten* (Berlin, 1932).
C. Sburlati, *Codreanu, il Capitano* (Rome, 1970).
R. Storry, *The Double Patriots* (London, 1957).
J. et J. Tharaud, *L'Envoyé de l'archange* (Paris, 1939).

Latin America
(see also footnotes to Chapter 7)

Actas Tupamaros (Buenos Aires, 1971).
F. R. Allemann, *Macht und Ohnmacht der Guerilla* (Munich, 1974).
V. Bambira *et al.*, *Diez años de insurrección en America Latina*, 2 vols. (Santiago, 1971).
R. Debray, *La Critique des armes,* 2 vols. (Paris, 1973–4).
R. Debray, *Revolution in the Revolution* (New York, 1967).
C. Detrez, *Les Mouvements révolutionnaires en Amérique Latine* (Brussels, 1972).

F.Gèze and Alain Labrousse, *Argentine, révolution et contrerévolution* (Paris, 1975).
M.E.Gilio, *The Tupamaro Guerrillas* (New York, 1972).
Boris Goldenberg, *Kommunismus in Latein Amerika* (Stuttgart, 1971).
Ernesto Ché Guevara, *Guerrilla Warfare* (London, 1969).
E.Halperin, *Terrorism in Latin America* (Washington, DC, 1976).
Donald C.Hodges, *The Latin American Revolution* (New York, 1974).
INDAL, *Movimientos Revolucionarios en America Latina* (Louvain, 1973).
James Kohl and John Litt, *Urban Guerrilla Warfare in Latin America* (Cambridge, 1974).
Alan Labrousse, *Les Tupamaros* (Paris, 1970).
Robert Lamberg, *Die Guerilla in Lateinamerika* (Stuttgart, 1972).
C.Marighella, *For the Liberation of Brazil* (London, 1971).
Ernesto Mayans, *Tupamaros, antologia documental* (Mexico, 1971).
A.C.Porzecanski, *Uruguay's Tupamaros* (New York, 1973).
Joãs Quartim, *Dictatorship and Armed Struggle in Brazil* (New York, 1973).
Hugh Thomas, *Cuba* (London, 1970).
Luigi Valsalice, *Guerriglia e Politica, l'esemplo del Venezuela* (Florence, 1973).
Luis Mercier Vega, *Guerrillas in Latin America* (London, 1969).

Spain

B.Bolotten, *The Grand Camouflage* (New York, 1961).
Gerald Brenan, *The Spanish Labyrinth* (Cambridge, 1943).
H.M.Enzensberger, *Der kurze Sommer der Anarchie* (Frankfurt, 1972).
Clara E.Lida, *Anarquismo y revolucion en la España del XIX siglo* (Madrid, 1972).
Cesar M.Lorenzo, *Les Anarchistes espagnols* (Paris, 1969).
G.H.Meaker, *The Revolutionary Left in Spain 1914–1923* (Stanford, 1974).
Angel Pestaña, *Lo que apprendi en la vida* (Madrid, 1933).

Terrorist Groups in Various Countries Since 1945

A.Adelson, *S.D.S.: A profile* (New York, 1972).
'Avner', *Memoirs of an Assassin* (New York, 1959).
E.Bacciocco, *The New Left in America* (Stanford, 1974).
Günter Bartsch, *Anarchismus in Deutschland*, vol. II (Hanover, 1973).
B.J.Bell, *Transnational Terror* (Washington, 1975).
R.Clutterbuck, *Protest and the Urban Guerrilla* (London, 1974).
R.Clutterbuck, *Living with Terrorism* (London, 1975).
Regis Debray, *Revolution in the Revolution* (New York, 1967).
Jacques Duchemin, *Histoire du FLN* (Paris, 1962).
Geoffrey Fairbarn, *Revolutionary and Communist Strategy* (London, 1968).
M.Feraoun, *Journal 1955–1962* (Paris, 1962).
C.Foley and W.Scobie, *The Struggle for Cyprus* (Stanford, 1973).

G.Grivas-Dighenis, *Guerrilla Warfare and 'EOKA' Struggle* (London, 1964).
G.Jackson, *Blood in My Eye* (London, 1975).
Harold Jacobs (ed.), *Weatherman* (New York, 1970).
Kollektiv RAF, *Über den bewaffneten Kampf in Westeuropa* (Berlin, 1971).
Jay Mallin (ed.), *Terror and Urban Guerrillas* (Coral Gables, 1971).
J.Massu, *La Vraie Bataille d'Alger* (Paris, 1971).
K.Mehnert, *Jugend im Zeitbruch* (Stuttgart, 1976).
G.Morf, *Terror in Quebec* (Toronto, 1970).
Robert Moss, *The War of the Cities* (New York, 1972).
M.Müller-Borchert, *Guerilla im Industriestaat* (Hamburg, 1973).
Julian Paget, *Last Post: Aden 1964–67* (London, 1969).
L.Payne and T.Findley, *The Life and Death of the SLA* (New York, 1976).
Prairiefire (n.p., 1974).
J.Raskin, *The Weathereye* (New York, 1974).
R.Rauball (ed.), *Die Baader–Meinhof Gruppe* (Berlin, 1973).
Kirkpatrick Sale, *S.D.S.* (New York, 1974).
Sasho Henshu (ed.), *Sekigun* (Tokyo, 1975).
Alex Schubert, *Stadtguerilla* (Berlin, 1974).
Stadtguerilla und soziale Revolution (Haarlem, 1974).
S.Stern, *With the Weathermen* (New York, 1975).
T.Tachibara, *Chukaku us Kakumaru*, 2 vols. (Tokyo, 1975).
R.Tophoven (ed.), *Politik durch Gewalt* (Bonn, 1976).
Pierre Vallières, *Nègres Blancs de l'Amérique* (Montreal, 1969).
R.Wassermann (ed.), *Terrorismus contra Rechtsstaat* (Darmstadt, 1976).

The Last Decade

Fuad Ajami, *The Vanishing Imam: Musa al Sadr and the Shia of Lebanon* (Ithaca, 1986).
Y.Alexander, D.Carlton and P.Wilkinson (eds), *Terrorism, Theory and Practice* (Boulder, Colorado, 1979).
Y.Alexander and S.M.Finger (eds), *Terrorism, Interdisciplinary Perspectives* (New York, 1977).
Y.Alexander and John Gleason, *Behavioral and Quantitative Perspectives on Terrorism* (New York, 1981).
Y.Alexander and Kenneth Myers (eds), *Terrorism in Europe* (New York, 1982).
John W.Amos, *Palestinian Resistance* (New York, 1980).
Anon., *Narcotrafico y Politica*, 2 vols. (La Paz, 1982–5).
Stefan Aust, *Der Baader Meinhof Komplex* (Hamburg, 1985).
Shaul Bakhash, *The Reign of the Ayatollahs* (New York, 1985).
Tullio Barbato, *Il terrorismo in Italia* (Milan, 1980).
Jillian Becker, *Hitler's Children* (London, 1977).
L.R.Beres, *Terrorism and Global Security* (Boulder, Colorado, 1979).
Giorgio Bocca, *Il terrorismo italiano* (Milan, 1981).

L.Bonanate and P.Gastaldo (eds), *Il terrorismo nell'età contemporanea* (Florence, 1981).

J.Bowyer Bell, *A Time of Terror* (New York, 1978).

J.Bowyer Bell, *Terror Out of Zion* (New York, 1977).

Bundesministerium des Inneren, *Analysen zum Terrorismus*, 5 vols. (Opladen, 1981–4).

Anthony Burton, *Revolutionary Violence* (London, 1977).

Peter Calvert, *Guatemala* (Boulder, Colorado, 1985).

David Carlton and Carlo Schaerf (eds), *Contemporary Terror* (London, 1981).

Olivier Carre, *Septembre Noir* (Brussels, 1980).

Jean Paul Charnay, *Terrorisme et culture* (Paris, 1981).

Robert R.Clark, *The Basque Insurgents, ETA 1952–80* (Madison, Wisconsin, 1984).

Thurston Clark, *By Blood and Fire* (New York, 1981).

Ray S.Cline and Yonah Alexander, *Terrorism as State Sponsored Covert Warfare* (Fairfax, Virginia, 1986).

Ray S. Cline and Yonah Alexander, *Terrorism: The Soviet Connection* (New York, 1984).

R.Clutterbuck, *Britain in Agony* (London, 1978).

R.Clutterbuck, *Guerrillas and Terrorists* (London, 1977).

R.Clutterbuck, *Kidnap and Ransom – The Response* (London, 1978).

Helen Cobban, *The Palestinian Liberation Organization* (London, 1984).

Tim Pat Coogan, *The IRA* (new edn, London, 1980).

Nancy Crawshaw, *The Cyprus Revolt* (London, 1978).

Martha Crenshaw (ed.), *Terrorism, Legitimacy and Power* (Wesleyan University Press, 1983).

C.Dobson and R.Payne, *The Weapons of Terror* (London, 1979).

C.Dobson and R.Payne, *War Without End* (London, 1986).

S.A.Efirov, *Pokushenie na budushe* (Moscow, 1984).

S.Elad and A.Merari, *The Soviet Bloc and World Terrorism* (Tel Aviv, 1984).

Riad el Rayyes and Dunia Nahas, *Guerrillas for Palestine* (Beirut, 1974).

G.Fauriol, *Latin American Insurgencies* (Washington, DC, 1986).

Franklin Ford, *Political Murder* (Cambridge, Mass., 1985).

R.Friedlaender, *Terrorism and the Law* (London, 1979).

H.Geisler (ed.), *Der Weg in die Gewalt* (Munich, 1978).

Jose Gil, *La Corse entre la liberté et le terreur* (Paris, 1984).

Richard Gillespie, *Soldiers of Peron* (Oxford, 1982).

Galia Golan, *The Soviet Union and the PLO* (London, 1980).

A.S.Grachev, *Tupiki politicheskovo nasilia* (Moscow, 1982).

Alain Gresh, *The PLO: The Struggle Within* (London, 1983).

Desmond Hamill, *Pig in the Middle* (London, 1985).

Alain Hamon and Jean Charles Marchand, *Action Directe* (Paris, 1986).

Paul Henze, *The Plot to Kill the Pope* (New York, 1983).

Christopher Hewitt, *The Effectiveness of Anti-Terrorist Policies* (Lanham, 1984).

Michael Horn, *Sozialpsychologie des Terrorismus* (Frankfurt, 1982).

A.Horne, *A Savage War of Peace* (London, 1979).

Herbert Jaeger (ed.), *Lebenslaufanalysen* (Opladen, 1982).

K. Jeffery, *The Divided Province* (London, 1985).

Brian M. Jenkins, *Combating International Terrorism* (Santa Monica, 1977).

J. Kaufmann, *L'Internationale Terroriste* (Paris, 1977).

Kevin Kelly, *The Longest War* (London, 1982).

Hans Joachim Klein, *Rückkehr in die Menschlichkeit* (Reinbek, 1979).

Robert Kuppermann and Darrel Trent, *Terrorism: Threat, Reality and Response* (Stanford, 1979).

A. Kurz and A. Merari, *Asala* (Boulder, Colorado, 1986).

J. Laffin, *The PLO Connection* (London, 1982).

Paul Leventhal and Yonah Alexander (eds), *Nuclear Terrorism* (Washington, DC, 1986).

Marius Livingstone, *The War Against Terrorism* (Lexington, 1982).

Neil C. Livingstone (ed.), *Fighting Back* (Boston, 1986).

Juliet Lodge (ed.), *Terrorism: A Challenge to the State* (New York, 1981).

Y. Melman, *Abu Nidal* (New York, 1986).

Thomas Meyer, *Am Ende der Gewalt* (Berlin, 1980).

Abraham H. Miller, *Terrorism and Hostage Negotiation* (Boulder, Colorado, 1980).

Abraham H. Miller (ed.), *Terrorism, the Media and the Law* (New York, 1982).

W. Mommsen and G. Hirschfeld, *Social Protest, Violence and Terror* (London, 1982).

S. Nath, *Terrorism in India* (New Delhi, 1980).

Bard E. O'Neil, *Armed Struggle in Palestine* (Boulder, Colorado, 1978).

S. von Paczenski (ed.), *Frauen und Terror* (Reinbek, 1978).

Daniel Pipes, *In the Path of God* (New York, 1983).

Vitofranco Pisano, *Contemporary Italian Terrorism* (Washington, DC, 1979).

Vitofranco Pisano, *Terrorism in Italy, 1983–1985* (Washington, DC, 1985).

U. Ra'anan *et al.* (eds), *Hydra of Carnage* (Lexington, 1986).

J. Randal, *The Tragedy of Lebanon* (London, 1983).

Luciano Rincon, *ETA* (Barcelona, 1985).

Alex P. Schmid and J. de Graaf, *Violence as Communication* (London, 1982).

J. Servier, *Le Terrorisme* (Paris, 1981).

Jennifer Shaw (ed.), *Ten Years of Terrorism* (London, 1979).

A. Silj, *Mai più senza fucile* (Florence, 1977).

R. Solé, *Le défi terroriste* (Paris, 1979).

C. Sterling, *The Terror Network* (New York, 1981).

C. Sterling, *The Time of Assassins* (New York, 1983).

Michael Stohl (ed.), *The Politics of Terrorism* (New York, 1979).

N. O. Sullivan, *Terrorism, Ideology and Revolution* (Boulder, Colorado, 1986).

V. V. Vityuk, *Pod chuzhimi snamenami* (Moscow, 1985).

G. Wardlaw, *Political Terrorism* (Cambridge, 1983).

Paul Wilkinson, *Terrorism and the Liberal State* (London, 1986).

R. Wright, *Sacred Rage* (New York, 1985).

A. Yodfat and Arnon Ohanna, *PLO, Strategy and Tactics* (London, 1981).

Zengakuren to Zenkuoto (Kodansha, 1985).

Notes

Introduction

1. Alex Schmid, *Political Terrorism* (Amsterdam, 1983).
2. Michael Stohl and George A. Lopez, *International Dimensions of State Terrorism* (New York, 1984), p. 55. These remarks refer predominantly to the United States.
3. Paul Johnson, 'The Cancer of Terrorism', in Benjamin Netanyahu (ed.), *Terrorism* (New York, 1986), p. 31.
4. The figures refer to the period from 1980 to 1985, based on State Department statistics.

A Note on Terrorist Statistics

Most terrorist operations since 1945 have taken place far away from diplomats, journalists and television cameras, and therefore they are not listed in the official statistics. There were hundreds of thousands of victims during the Colombian *violencia* (1948–62), in the wake of the partition of India (1947–9), during the 1970s in several Central American countries, such as El Salvador and Guatemala, and, during the same period, in the Lebanese civil war. There are no accurate statistics, not even reliable estimates, with regard to the number of victims of terrorist operations during the Vietnam war, the Algerian war of liberation, the Afghan resistance against Soviet occupation, and similar insurgencies. If all these operations were taken into account in the statistics on terrorism, it would appear that there has been more or less continuous violence since the end of the Second World War, with peaks in the late 1940s, and again in the 1960s and the late 1970s, a decline in the early 1980s, and a resurgence in the middle 1980s, mainly as the result of ethnic strife in Sri Lanka and the conflict between Sikhs and Hindus, as well as acts of violence in South Africa.

Statistics on terrorism concentrate on international terrorism, which can also be interpreted in various ways. Some statistics, for example, include terrorist operations in Northern Ireland, Italy and Turkey while others do not; the results therefore diverge widely. Some statistics concentrate on state-sponsored terrorism, but even in this context there is room for different interpretations; Turkish terrorism in the 1970s, and some of the terrorism in the wake of the Lebanese civil war, were undoubtedly instigated and supported by foreign powers.

This is not to argue that statistics on terrorism are altogether useless. Certain trends emerge, such as the fact that the hijacking of aeroplanes and the sending of letter bombs have markedly declined over the last fifteen years, while certain other forms of terrorist attacks have increased. It is also true that these statistics convey a more or less accurate picture with regard to the ups and downs of terrorist operations in certain countries – usually in Europe and North America. However, attempts to present *global* figures on terrorist activities usually create a distorted picture, inevitable in the circumstances, and lead to unwarranted generalizations.

See *Lethal Terrorist Actions Against Americans 1973–1985*, published by DC/TAD, Department of State, 1986; *Terrorist Attacks on U.S. Businessmen Abroad*, Department of State, 1986; *Patterns of Global Terrorism 1984*, Department of State, 1985; *International Terrorism*, Selected Documents, 25, Department of State, 1986.

1 The Origins

1. *Dictionnaire, Supplément* (Paris, an VII (1798)), p. 775.
2. *Le Néologiste Français*, quoted in A. Aulard, *Paris pendant la réaction thermidorienne et sous le Directoire* (Paris, 1902), v, p. 490. See also F. Brunot, *Histoire de la langue française des origines à 1900* (Paris, 1937), IX, p. 871.
3. James Murray, *A New English Dictionary on Historical Principles* (Oxford, 1919). It also had a different meaning for a while – an alarmist or scaremonger.
4. Thomas de Quincey, 'On Murder Considered as One of the Fine Arts', in *The English Mail Coach and Other Writings* (Edinburgh, 1862), p. 52.
5. The main sources are M. Hengel, *Die Zeloten* (Leiden, 1961), pp. 47–51; Cecil Roth in *Journal of Semitic Studies* (1959), pp. 332–55; S. Kleinfelder, 'Sicarius', in Pauly-Wissowa, *Real Lexicon*; S. G. E. Brandon, *Jesus and the Zealots* (Manchester, 1967), pp. 56–7; Josephus Flavius, ed. Thackeray, 2 vols. (London, 1956); Y. Yadin, *Megilat Bne Or ubne Khoshekh* (Jerusalem, 1957); R. Laqueur, *Der Jüdische Historiker Flavius Josephus* (Giessen, 1920).
6. B. Lewis, *The Assassins* (London, 1967), p. 47; see also M. G. S. Hodgson, *The Order of Assassins* (The Hague, 1955), and the articles in *Speculum*, 27 (1952), by B. Lewis and Y. Prawer.
7. Both *sicarii* and Assassins have made a contribution to the terminology of modern terrorist groups. The *Sikarikin* (and the *Biryonim*) were precursors of the 'dissident terrorists' in mandatory Palestine and the term *fida'i* was, of course, adopted by the Palestinian Arab terrorists. Abba Achimeir, a Revisionist ideologist, asserted in a pamphlet on the *sicarii* in the 1930s that they were unknown heroes who chose as victims central figures of the establishment: 'what mattered was not the action but the purpose behind it.' Avraham Stern in one of his poems called Jerusalem 'the city of prophets and biryonim' (*ir nevi'im vebiryonim*).
8. The main sources are Sleeman's writings, and most recently George Bruse,

The Stranglers (London, 1968), p. 111.

9. The most recent survey of Chinese secret societies is Jean Chesneaux (ed.), *Popular Movements and Secret Societies in China 1840–1950* (Stanford, 1972).

10. On the Mafia in politics see V. Frosini, *Mitologia e sociologia della Mafia* (Milan, 1969); G.C. Maino, *L'opposizione mafiosa 1870–1882* (Palermo, 1964); M. Pantelone, *The Mafia and Politics* (New York, 1966).

11. Charles C. Alexander, *The Ku Klux Klan in the Southwest* (University of Kentucky Press, 1965), p. 254.

12. *Pamiatnaya Knizhka Sotsialista-Revolutsionera* (Paris, 1914), p. 8 *et seq*. These figures do not include terrorist operations carried out by other political groups but they accurately reflect the general trend.

13. St Christowe, *Heroes and Assassins* (New York, 1935), p. 50 *et seq*. There is no history of the IMRO, but see D. Kosev, *Istorija na makedonskoto natsionalno-revoliutsonno dvizhenie* (Sofia, 1954), and *Makedonia, minalo i novi borbi* (Sofia, 1932).

14. On the terrorist operations among Polish socialists see T. Jablonski, *Zarys Historii PPS* (Warsaw, 1945), and Kwapinski, *Organizacia Bojowa* (London, 1943); also Georg W. Strobel, *Die Partei Rosa Luxemburgs* (Wiesbaden, 1974), pp. 288–94; for a local survey on Lodz, where terrorist operations were very frequent, *Zrodla do dziejow rewolucii 1905–1907 wokregu Lodzkim* (Warsaw, 1957), *passim*. For the history of Indian terrorism see Nirajan Sen, *Bengal's Forgotten Warriors* (Bombay, 1945); B. Hardass, *Armed Struggle for Freedom* (Poona, 1958); H. Mukerjee, *India's Struggle for Freedom*, 3 vols. (Bombay, 1962), and other literature quoted below.

15. E. A. Vizetelly, *The Anarchists* (New York, 1912), p. 293.

16. Wayne G. Broehl, Jr, *The Molly Maguires* (New York, 1966), p. 350.

17. For an excellent bibliography on Spanish anarchism see J. Romero Maura, 'The Spanish Case', in David E. Apter and James Joll (eds), *Anarchism Today* (London, 1971). The most important recent studies are those by John Brademas and Gerald H. Meaker; see below.

18. David Rock, *Politics in Argentina 1830–1930: The Rise and Fall of Radicalism* (Cambridge, 1975), p. 163 *et seq*.

19. P. Wurth, *La Répression internationale du terrorisme* (Lausanne, 1941); see also the *Journal Officiel de la SDN*, 1934–5.

20. Jawaharlal Nehru, *An Autobiography* (London, 1936), p. 175.

21. *Ibid.*, p. 482.

22. Abdel Fatah Ismail, 'How We Liberated Aden', *Gulf Studies* (April 1976), p. 9.

23. Urban terrorism had in fact played a part of some significance in Castro's campaigns, but its importance has always been played down in official Cuban historiography.

2 The Philosophy of the Bomb

1. For a recent summary of ancient and medieval writings on tyrannicide, see

Roland Mousnier, *L'Assassinat d'Henri IV* (Paris, 1964), pp. 47–90. Oliver Lutaud traces the discussions on tyrannicide throughout the seventeenth and eighteenth centuries, *Des Révolution d'Angleterre à la révolution Française* (The Hague, 1973).

2. J.W.Allen, *A History of Political Thought in the Sixteenth Century* (London, 1960), p. 320.

3. N.A.Morozov, *Povest moei zhizni* (Moscow, 1965), p. 420. N.A.Morozov, *Terroristicheskaya Borba* (London, 1880), *passim*.

4. *Della Tirannide, Opere di Vittorio Alfieri* (Piacenza, 1811), xx, p. 252. Paul Sirven, *Vittorio Alfieri* (Paris, 1938), iii, p. 257 *et seq*.

5. P.Buonarroti, *History of Baboeuf's Conspiracy for Equality* (London, 1836), p. 244; Richard Cobb, *The Police and the People* (London, 1970), p. 195.

6. A.Spitzer, *Old Hatreds and Young Hopes* (Cambridge, Mass., 1971), p. 292; Pierre Mariel, *Les Carbonari: idéalisme et la révolution* (Paris, 1971), *passim*.

7. Bartoldi, *Memoirs of the Secret Societies of the South of Italy* (London, 1821), pp. 176–7.

8. Vicomte d'Arlincourt, *L'Italie rouge* (Paris, 1850), p. 4 *et seq*.

9. Bartoldi, *op. cit.*, p. 30.

10. A.Ottolini, *La Carboneria dalle origini ai primi tentativi insurrezionali* (Modena, 1946); A.Falcionelli, *Les Sociétés secrètes italiennes* (Paris, 1969); P.Mariel, *Les Carbonari* (Paris, 1971).

11. *Della guerra nazionale d'insurrezione per bande* (Italy, 1830), i, p. 235. See W.Laqueur, *Guerrilla* (Boston, 1976), ch. 3, *passim*.

12. G.Mazzini, *Scritti editi ed inediti* (Imola, 1931), lix, pp. 331–2.

13. J.K.Bluntschli, *Die Kommunisten in der Schweiz* (Zurich, 1843), pp. 106–13.

14. Wilhelm Weitling, *Garantien der Harmonie und Freiheit* (Hamburg, 1849), pp. 221, 225, 236.

15. The article was first published in the monthly *Die Evolution* in Biel, Switzerland. See C.F.Wittke's Heinzen biography, *Against the Current* (Chicago, 1945), pp. 74–5. The article was reprinted many times, for instance in Most's *Die Freiheit*, about which more below. As a result of yet another publication, after the assassination of President McKinley, Most got a year's prison sentence on Blackwell's Island, even though Most's attorney, Morris Hillquit, drew the attention of the court to the fact that the author of the article had been dead for a long time and that, in any case, it had been directed against European kings, not American presidents. In actual fact, Most's article was a paraphrase of the Heinzen essay, not a reprint.

16. *Perezhitoe i Peredumannoe* (Berlin, 1923).

17. E.H.Carr, *Michael Bakunin* (London, 1961), p. 128.

18. Quoted from a pamphlet published in Geneva in 1869. The theme also occurred in Bakunin's letters to his friends and it appears in M.Confino's and Arthur Lehning's studies.

19. M.Bakunin, *Sobranie sochinenii i pisem* (Moscow, 1935), iv, pp. 172–3.

20. Originally published in *Pravitelstvenni Vestnik*, July 1871, it has been translated and republished, usually incomplete, many times since. It is quoted here from M.Confino, *Violence dans la violence* (Paris, 1973), p. 97 *et seq*.

21. V.I.Burtsev, *Za sto let* (London, 1897), pp. 40–6; for the literature on the Zaichnevski circle see F.Venturi, *Roots of Revolution* (London, 1960), p. 763.

22. Venturi, *op. cit.*, pp. 336–7; for the literature on the Ishutin 'organization' see *ibid.*, pp. 768–9.

23. N.I.Sheveko, *Khronika sotsialisticheskovo dvizheniya v Rossii, 1878–1887* (Moscow, 1906), p. 19; these are the internal annual reports of the Ministry of the Interior.

24. G.V.Plekhanov, *Sochineniya* (n.d.), IX, p. 20.

25. On p. 19. The brochure is quoted here from the 1920 Petrograd reprint. Kravchinski–Stepniak subsequently became the best-known chronicler of the Narodnaya Volya. His *Podpolnaya Rossia* (*Underground Russia*) appeared in many languages.

26. N.A.Morozov, *Povest moei Zhizni* (Moscow, 1965), II, p. 48.

27. S.S.Volk, *Narodnaya Volya* (Moscow, 1966), p. 89.

28. O.V.Aptekman, *Obshestvo Zemlya i Volya* (Moscow, 1966), p. 89.

29. Burtsev, *op. cit.*, pp. 149, 154.

30. Felix Kon quoted in Volk, *op. cit.*, p. 234.

31. Plekhanov, *op. cit.*, II, p. 350.

32. Nikolai Morozov, *Terroristicheskaya Borba* (London, 1880); Romanenko's pamphlet was published under the pen name V.Tarnovski – *Terrorism i rutina* – in Geneva in the same year. Articles in favour of terrorism had appeared in the Russian émigré press even before, notably by Kaspar Turski in Tkachev's *Nabat*. But Tkachev was a Blanquist who would not accept a single-minded concentration on terrorist acts.

33. Morozov, *Povest*, II, p. 418.

34. Morozov, *Terroristicheskaya Borba*, p. 7 *et seq*.

35. V.Tarnovski (G.Romanenko), *Terrorism i rutina* (Geneva, 1880), p. 18 *et seq*.

36. This pamphlet appeared in 1884; it was hectographed, not printed. It was not accessible to me and I have quoted from Z.Ivianski, 'Individual Terror as a Phase in Revolutionary Violence in the Late Nineteenth and the Beginning of the Twentieth Century' (in Hebrew), doctoral dissertation (Jerusalem, 1973).

37. M.P.Dragomanov, *Terrorism i Svoboda* (Geneva, 1880), *passim*; see also his subsequent *La Tyrannicide en Russie et l'action de l'Europe Occidentale* (Geneva, 1883).

38. *Literatura partii Narodnoi Voly* (Moscow, 1907), p. 451 *et seq*.

39. L.Deitch, *Delo Pervovo Marta 1881 goda* (Moscow, 1906), p. 412.

40. Venturi, *op. cit.*, p. 597.

41. *Sotsial Demokrat*, I, p. 1.

42. *Podpolnaya Rossiya*, quoted from the most recent edition (Moscow, 1960), p. 201.

43. *Podgotovitelniya Raboti Partii Narodnoi Volny* (St Petersburg, 1892).

44. A.I.Ulianova-Elizarova, *A.I.Ulianov i Delo I Marta 1887* (Leningrad, 1927); A.I.Ivianski (ed.), *Zhizn kak Fakel* (Moscow, 1966); B.C.Henberg and A.Y.Cherniak, *Zhizn A.Ulianova* (Moscow, 1966).

45. An even earlier brochure by Alisov on terrorism (1893) was not accessible to me.

46. V.I.Burtsev, *Doloi Tsaria* (London, 1901), p. 22.

47. *Nasha zadacha* (1902).

48. 'Terroristicheskii element v nashei programme', *Revoliutsionnaya Rossia*, 7 June 1902.

49. *Iskra*, 1 May 1902.

50. Alexander Gerassimov, *Der Kampf gegen die erste russische Revolution* (Berlin, 1933), p. 205.

51. L. Tikhomirov, *Vospominaniya* (Sofia, n.d.), pp. 104–5.

52. Manfred Hildermeier, 'Sozialstruktur und Kampfmethode der Sozial-Revolutionären Partei', in *Jahrbücher für Geschichte Osteuropas* (December 1972), pp. 539–40.

53. *Protokoly Pervovo sezda partii Sotsialistov-Revoliutsionerov* (n.p., n.d.), p. 314.

54. G. Nestroev, *Iz dnevnika Maksimalista* (Paris, 1910), p. 153.

55. 'Vopros o Terrore', *Sotsial Revoliutsioner* (Paris, 1910), ii, pp. 1–52. This is an abridged version of the main speeches and the discussion at the May 1909 meeting. Further contributions in the journal *Znamya Truda* throughout 1909–12.

56. P. Avrich (ed.), *The Russian Anarchists* (Princeton, 1971), p. 48 *et seq.*

57. *Ibid.*

58. Boris Savinkov, *Erinnerungen eines Terroristen* (Berlin, 1929), p. 29.

59. V. Dedijer, *The Road to Sarajevo* (New York, 1966), pp. 178, 205.

60. William L. Langer, *The Diplomacy of Imperialism 1830–1902* (New York, 1956), p. 156 *et seq.*

61. Louise Nalbadian, *The Armenian Revolutionary Movement* (Berkeley, 1963), pp. 168–73.

62. Avetis Nazarbeck, *Through the Storm* (London, 1899), p. 212.

63. *St James Gazette*, 29 August 1896; *Foreign Relations of the United States 1895* (Washington, 1896), p. 1416.

64. *La Vérité sur les massacres d'Arménie*, Par un Philarmene (Paris, 1896), *passim.*

65. *Bal Ganjadhar Tilak, His Writings and Speeches* (Madras, n.d.).

66. Dhanonjay Keer, *Veer Savarkar* (Bombay, 1950), p. 41.

67. S. Wolpert, *Tilak and Gokhale: Revolution and Reform in the Making of Modern India* (Berkeley, 1962), p. 81.

68. *Source Material for a History of the Freedom Movement in India* (Bombay, 1958), ii, p. 978 *et seq.*

69. Valentine Chirol, *Indian Unrest* (London, 1901), p. 71.

70. The book was first published in Holland in 1909: a French edition came out a year later.

71. Keer, *op. cit.*, p. 401; J. C. Jain, *The Murder of Mahatma Gandhi: Prelude and Aftermath* (Bombay, 1961), *passim.*

72. Bipan Chanda, 'The Revolutionary Terrorists in Northern India in the 1920s', in B. R. Nanda (ed.), *Socialism in India* (Delhi, 1972), p. 165 *et seq.*

73. *Peaceful and Legitimate*, quoted in Chanda, *op. cit.*, p. 181.

74. Chanda, *op. cit.*, p. 183.

75. The document was clandestinely distributed in various parts of India in late January of 1930 and is now exceedingly rare. I am grateful to Professor Bipan Chanda of Jawaharlal Nehru University of New Delhi who obtained a copy for me.

76. *Young India*, 2 January 1930.

77. *Speeches and Writings of M. K. Gandhi* (Madras, n.d.), p. 231.

78. *The Philosophy of the Bomb, passim.*

79. *Ibid.*

80. *Ibid.*

81. Virendra Sandhu, *Yugdrastha Bhagat Singh* (Delhi, 1968); Gopal Thakur, *Bhagat Singh* (New Delhi, 1957); *Lahore Conspiracy Case* (exhibits).

82. Secretary of State for India, *Terrorism in India* (HMSO, London, 1933), p. 328.

83. R.C.Majumdar, *History of the Freedom Movement in India* (Calcutta, 1963), II, p. 529.

84. George Woodcock, *Anarchism* (London, 1962), p. 308.

85. *Bulletin de la Fédération Jurassiene*, 3 December 1876.

86. David Stafford, *From Anarchism to Reformism: A Study of the Political Activities of Paul Brousse 1870–1890* (London, 1971), p. 76 *et seq.*

87. *Bulletin*, 31, 5 August 1877, in J.Guillaume (ed.), *L'Internationale, documents et souvenirs 1864–1878* (Paris, 1910), II, p. 224; according to Guillaume, *op. cit.*, IV, p. 206, the expression was first used in a speech in Geneva by Andrea Costa on 9 June of that year. The era of 'propaganda by deed' is exceedingly well documented. The following are of particular interest: R.Hunter, *Violence and the Labor Movement* (New York, 1914), ch. 3; Andrew R.Carlson, *Anarchism in Germany* (New York, 1972), ch. 8; Richard Hostetter, *The Italian Socialist Movement* (New York, 1958), chs. 14 and 15; E.Semincoli, *L'Anarchia*, vol. I: *La propaganda di fatto* (Milan, 1894), H.Zoccoli, *L'Anarchia* (Torino, 1907), p. 43 *et seq.*, as well as the histories of anarchism by Nettlau, Maitron *et al.*, mentioned below.

88. *Le Révolte*, 25 December 1880; Guillaume, *op. cit.*, II, p. 96.

89. *Le Révolte*, 18 October 1879.

90. Kropotkin to Georg Brandes, *Freedom*, October 1898; P.A.Kropotkin, *Selected Writings on Anarchism and Revolution* (London, 1973), pp. 20–3.

91. Max Nettlau, *Anarchisten und Sozialrevolutionäre* (Berlin, 1919), pp. 217–18.

92. *Le Révolte*, 23 July 1881.

93. *L'Internationale* (London), May 1890.

94. *La Dynamite et l'anarchie* (Geneva, n.d.); many quotations, some of doubtful provenance, appear in Felix Dubois, *Le Péril anarchiste* (Paris, 1894), *passim.*

95. J.Maitron, *Histoire du mouvement anarchiste en France (1880–1914)* (Paris, 1955), p. 211; E.V.Zenker, *Anarchism* (London, 1895), p. 262.

96. Maitron, *op. cit.*, p. 196; similar suggestions had been made by Colonel de Wust and other eighteenth-century theoreticians of the *petite guerre* – but had been rejected as outdated at the time. Laqueur, *op. cit.*, ch. 3, *passim.*

97. Maitron, *op. cit.*, p. 197.

98. Woodcock, *op. cit.*, p. 326.

99. Prolo, *Les Anarchistes* (Paris, 1912), p. 55.

100. *Le Révolte*, September 1886, quoted in Maitron, *op. cit.*, p. 245.

101. *Le Révolte*, 18 March 1891.

102. Gerald Brenan, *The Spanish Labyrinth* (Cambridge, 1960), p. 251.

103. Romero Maura, 'Terrorism in Barcelona and its Impact on Spanish Politics 1904–19', *Past and Present* (December 1968); Gerald H.Meaker, *The Revolutionary Left in Spain, 1914–1923* (Stanford, 1973), pp. 173–5.

104. Quoted in H. David, *History of the Haymarket Affair* (New York, 1936), p. 121; Samuel Yellen, *American Labor Struggles* (New York, 1936), *passim*.

105. David, *op. cit.*, p. 122.

106. *Ibid.*, p. 343. See also H. Karasek (ed.), *1886, Haymarket. Die deutschen Anarchisten von Chicago* (Berlin, 1975), p. 65 *et seq.*

107. A. Berkman, *Prison Memoirs of an Anarchist* (New York, 1970), p. 5.

108. *Ibid.*, p. 7.

109. Emma Goldman, *Living My Life* (New York, 1970), I, p. 97.

110. *Freiheit*, 17 May 1879.

111. *Freiheit*, 18 September 1880.

112. *Freiheit*, 19 March 1881, 4 March, 11 March 1882.

113. *Freiheit*, 8 March 1884, 15 November 1884.

114. *Freiheit*, 8 March 1884.

115. *Freiheit*, 14 March 1885.

116. Ragnar Redbeard, *Might is Right* (1921), p. 70 (first published in Chicago, 1930). An earlier edition of the same work was published under the title *Survival of the Fittest* (1896). The idea that might is right has occurred in terrorist manifestos with surprising frequency. Thus Black September after the Munich massacre in 1972: *Le monde ne respecte que les forts. . . . Problèmes politiques et sociaux*, 30 May 1975. A reprint of Redbeard's book was published in New York in 1972.

117. Redbeard, *op. cit.*, p. 60.

118. *Ibid.*, p. 39.

119. *Freiheit*, 7 June 1884.

120. *Freiheit*, 16 February 1884.

121. *Freiheit*, 5 May, 26 May 1883.

122. Andrew R. Carlson, *Anarchism in Germany* (New York, 1972), p. 255.

123. *Freiheit*, 5 May 1883; J. Most, *Revolutionäre Kriegswissenschaft* (n.p., n.d.), pp. 69–71.

124. *Freiheit*, 13 September 1884.

125. *Freiheit*, 16 April 1887.

126. *Freiheit*, 30 October 1886.

127. *Freiheit*, 12 January 1884, 13 September 1884.

128. Carlson, *op. cit.*, p. 279; Rudolf Rocker, *Johann Most, das Leben eines Rebellen* (Berlin, 1924), p. 162.

129. *Freiheit*, 11 October 1890.

130. *Freiheit*, 30 July 1887.

131. *Freiheit*, 24 April 1886.

132. Wisnitzer, 'Marx und Engels und die irische Frage', *Archiv für Geschichte des Sozialismus*, X (1922); Eduard Bernstein, 'Fr. Engels und das heutige Irland', *Neue Zeit* (1916).

133. Gustav Mayer, *Friedrich Engels* (Haag, 1934), II, p. 256.

134. *Karl Marx, Friedrich Engels i revoliutsionnaya Rossiya* (Moscow, 1967), *passim; Perepiska K. Marksa i. F. Engelsa s russkimi politicheskimi deyatelami* (Moscow, 1951).

135. *Perepiska*, p. 294; Volk, *op. cit.*, pp. 436–7; Mayer, *op. cit.*, p. 423.

136. *Ireland and the Irish Question: A Collection of Writings by Karl Marx and*

Friedrich Engels (New York, 1972), p. 149.

137. *Ibid.*, p. 230.

138. V.I.Lenin, *Polnoe sobranie sochineniya*, IX, p. 130.

139. *Ibid.*, XLIX, p. 312.

140. *Ibid.*, V, p. 7.

141. Bolshevik expropriations are described in detail in Boris Souvarine's *Stalin* (Paris, 1939).

142. *Der Kampf*, November 1911.

143. *Przeglad Socyal-demokratyczny*, May 1909.

144. Hsi-huey Liang, *The Berlin Police in the Weimar Republic* (Berkeley, 1970), *passim*.

145. Thomas N.Brown, *Irish American Nationalism* (New York, 1966), p. 67.

146. P.J.P.Tynan, *The Irish Invincibles* (New York, 1894), p. 488.

147. Tynan, *op. cit.*, p. 490.

148. *Devoy's Post Bag*, ed. W.O'Brien and D.Ryan (Dublin, 1953), II, p. 41.

149. *Irish World*, 3 March 1876.

150. Tom Corfe, *The Phoenix Park Murders* (London, 1968), pp. 31, 138.

151. *Frankfurter Zeitung*, 9 May 1931.

152. W.Kube (ed.), *Almanach der nationalsozialistischen Revolution* (Berlin, 1933), p. 107.

153. J.Goebbels, *Knorke, Ein neues Buch Isidor* (Munich, 1929), p. 18; J.Goebbels, *Kampf um Berlin* (Munich, 1941), pp. 62–3.

154. Renzo de Felice, *Mussolini, il rivoluzionario* (Turin, 1965), p. 120.

155. Hermann Okrass, *Hamburg bleibt rot* (Hamburg, 1934), p. 198; Wilfrid Bade, *Die SA erobert Berlin* (Munich, 1937), p. 88.

156. Goebbels, *Kampf um Berlin*, pp. 62–3: 'there were 85 injured; everything went as planned, before we were a small *Verein*, now we got publicity . . .'.

157. Thor Goote, *Kameraden die Rotfront und Reaktion erschossen* (Berlin, 1934), p. 231.

158. *Abwehrblätter* (October 1931), p. 182.

159. Gabriele Krüger, *Die Brigade Ehrhardt* (Berlin, 1932), *passim*.

160. Ernst von Salomon, *Die Geächteten* (Berlin, 1932), *passim*.

161. M.Lacko, *Arrow-Cross Men, National Socialists* (Budapest, 1969), p. 43.

162. Eugen Weber, in H.Rogger and E.Weber, *The European Right* (Berkeley, 1963), p. 531.

163. Weber, *ibid.*, p. 537; see also Corneliu Zelea Codreanu, *Pentru Legionari* (Bucharest, 1936), *passim*.

164. O.Tanin and E.Yohan, *Militarism and Fascism in Japan* (London, 1934), pp. 125, 219.

165. R.Storry, *The Double Patriots* (London, 1957), pp. 70, 192.

166. Friedrich Berg, *Die weisse Pest* (Vienna, 1926), p. 32.

167. Carl Schmitt, *Der Begriff des Politischen* (Munich, 1932), *passim*.

168. On the *Landvolk*: Herbert Volck, *Rebellen um Ehre* (Berlin, 1932), p. 278 *et seq.*; Rudolf Heberle, *Landbevölkerung und Nationalsozialismus* (Stuttgart, 1965), *passim*.

3 The Sociology of Terrorism

1. Of the fifty-odd heads of state or prime ministers killed since 1945, a majority were murdered not by terrorists but during a *coup d'état*. Details are discussed in Franklin L.Ford, *Political Murder* (Cambridge, 1985), *passim*.

2. *United Irishman*, 14 February 1885.

3. Jim Devoy, *Recollections of an Irish Rebel* (Shannon, 1969), pp. 211–12.

4. J.Remak, *Sarajevo* (London, 1959), p. 56.

5. Michael St John Paeke, *The Bombs of Orsini* (London, 1957), p. 293.

6. Louis Adamic, *Dynamite* (New York, 1935), p. 196.

7. Gerald W.Meaker, *The Revolutionary Left in Spain, 1914–23* (Stanford, 1974), p. 173. But on other occasions terrorism has had no effect on the social policy of big corporations. See for an illustration: David W.Barkey and Stanley Eltzen, 'Towards an Assessment of Multi-National Corporate Social Expenditures in Relation to Political Stability and Terrorist Activity. The Argentine Case', *Inter-American Economic Affairs* (1981), pp. 77–90.

8. Bernard B.Fall, *Last Reflections on a War* (New York, 1967), p. 219.

9. This was true even in Argentina where the Montoneros showed a great deal of competence and daring in their military actions. See Richard Gillespie, *Soldiers of Peron* (Oxford, 1982), p. 197 *et seq*.

10. Adrian Lyttleton, *The Seizure of Power* (London, 1973), p. 61.

11. F.Venturi, *Roots of Revolution* (London, 1960), p. 563.

12. F.Ferracuti and F.Bruno, 'Psychiatric Aspects of Terrorism in Italy', in I.L. Barak-Glantz and C.R.Glantz (eds), *The Mad, the Bad and the Different* (Lexington, 1981), p. 199 *et seq*. See also F.Ferrarotti, *Alle Radici della Violenza* (Milan, 1979) and *L'ipnosi della Violenza* (Milan, 1980).

13. Karl Heinz Janssen, 'Wieviele Jahre sind genug?', *Die Zeit*, 26 May 1986. Hans Josef Horchem, 'Terrorismus in der Bundesrepublik Deutschland', *Beiträge zur Konflikt-Forschung*, 1 (1986), pp. 5–24.

14. Horst Herold, *Der Spiegel*, 11 May 1981.

15. Lucien de la Hodde, *Histoire de sociétés secrètes* (Paris, 1850), p. 14.

16. Ivan Avacumovic, 'A Statistical Approach to the Revolutionary Movement in Russia', *American Slavic and East European Review* (April 1959), p. 183.

17. A.C.Porzecanski, *Uruguay's Tupamaros* (New York, 1973), p. 30 *et seq*. Ernst Halperin, *Terrorism in Latin America* (Beverly Hills, 1976), p. 37 *et seq*.

18. But it was still a relatively small minority; workers were interested in social and political action, not in terrorism.

19. E.Wasiolik, *The Notebook for the 'Possessed'* (Chicago, 1968), *passim*; A.Volynski, *Kniga Velikovo Gneva* (St Petersburg, 1904), *passim*.

20. Boris Savinkov, *Erinnerungen eines Terroristen* (Berlin, 1929), p. 73.

21. Manfred von Killinger, *Ernstes und Heiteres aus dem Putschleben* (Munich, 1934), p. 15.

22. Wayne G.Broehl, Jr, *The Molly Maguires* (New York, 1966), p. 20.

23. See, for instance, Hermann Reisse, *Sieg Heil SA* (Berlin, 1933), p. 100; W.Kube (ed.), *Almanach der nationalsozialistischen Revolution* (Berlin, 1933), p. 117 *et seq*.

24. *Rote Fahne*, 26 June 1923.
25. André Haynal *et al.*, *Fanaticism* (New York, 1982), p. 28.
26. S. Kravchinski, *Podpolnaya Rossiya* (Moscow, 1960 edn), p. 42 *et seq.*
27. Emma Goldman, 'The Psychology of Political Violence', in *Anarchism and Other Essays* (New York, 1910), p. 113.
28. G. Nestroev on Sokolov, *Iz dnevnika Maksimalista* (Paris, 1910), pp. 64, 75.
29. S. S. Volk, *Narodnaya Volya* (Moscow, 1966), p. 468.
30. The Israeli authorities carried out a series of psychological tests in the Al Ansar camp in 1982–3 among Palestinians and other detainees, but found no consistent pattern of psychological imbalance among those interviewed.
31. *Lebensläufe ... passim (Analysen zum Terrorismus*, Opladen, 1982).
32. The Irgun old-timers within the Israeli Likud Party call themselves to this day '*mishpakha lohemet*' – i.e. the fighting family.
33. Kent Layne Oots and Thomas C. Wiegele, 'Terrorist and Victim: Psychiatric and Psychological Approaches from a Social Science Perspective', in *Terrorism*; J. A. Stegenga, 'The Physiology of Aggression (and of Warfare)', *International Journal of Group Tensions* (1978), nos. 3–4, pp. 51–67. There seem to be no systematic studies so far in this field concerning, for instance, the hormone profile of terrorists and other aspects of stress physiology.
34. It could be argued, for instance, that while there are bound to be unbalanced, highly aggressive individuals in every society, this could manifest itself in single political assassinations rather than systematic terrorist campaigns.
35. James Q. Wilson, *Political Organization* (New York, 1973); S. Verba, *Small Groups and Political Behavior* (Princeton, 1961); Martha Crenshaw, 'An Organizational Approach to the Analysis of Political Terrorism', *Orbis* (Fall 1985), pp. 465–89.
36. Crenshaw, *op. cit.*, p. 480.
37. R. C. Majumdar, *History of the Freedom Movement in India* (Calcutta, 1963), p. 480.
38. Vladeta Milicevic, *Der Königsmord von Marseille* (Bad Godesberg, 1959), p. 44.
39. Wilhelm Herzog, *Barthou* (Zurich, 1938), p. 256.
40. Whether Graiver was killed at the time of this accident remains a matter of dispute to this day.
41. *Economist*, 1 August 1986.
42. Michael Baumann, *Wie alles anfing* (Munich, 1975), pp. 117–18.
43. *Sunday Press* (Dublin), 15 February 1976.
44. Major Arthur Griffith, *Mysteries of Police and Crime* (London, 1898), ii, p. 459.
45. *New York Sun*, 29 November 1895.
46. D. Kantor, 'Dynamit Narodnoi Volyi', *Katorga i Sylka* (1929), pp. 8–9, 119–28. Nobel was a radical in both religious and political matters and his biographers note that there can be no doubt that his attitude was affected by the Russian milieu in which he grew up. H. Schueck and R. Sohlma, *The Life of Alfred Nobel* (London, 1929), p. 217. See also the most recent biography, St Tjerneld, *Nobel – En biografi* (Stockholm, 1972), *passim*.

47. J.Most, *Revolutionäre Kriegswissenschaft* (n.p., n.d.), p. 39.

48. Jack London, *The Assassination Bureau Ltd* (London, 1964), p. 6.

49. W.d'Arcy, *The Fenian Movement in the United States 1858–1866* (Washington, 1947), p. 406.

50. Victor Drummond, British chargé d'affaires in Washington to James G.Blaine, secretary of state, 28 July 1881. In the *Annual Report of the American Historical Association for the Year 1941* (Washington, 1942), p. 146.

51. Z.Ivianski, 'Individual Terror as a Phase in Revolutionary Violence in the Late Nineteenth and the Beginning of the Twentieth Century' (in Hebrew), doctoral dissertation (Jerusalem, 1973), p. 190.

52. Nikolajewski, *Asew*, p. 177.

53. J.Bowyer Bell, 'The Thompson Submachine Gun in Ireland, 1921', *Irish Sword*, VIII, p. 38.

54. SOE brochure *c.* 1943 quoted in Pierre Lorain, *Secret Warfare* (London, 1983), p. 154.

55. For a general survey of the armoury see Harvey McGeorge II, 'Kinetics of Terrorism', *World Affairs* (Summer 1983), pp. 24–41.

56. Beth A.Salamanca, 'Vehicle Bombs: Death on Wheels', in N.Livingston (ed.), *Fighting Back* (Boston, 1986), pp. 35–47.

57. Alexander Gerassimov, *Der Kampf gegen die erste russische Revolution* (Berlin, 1933), p. 211.

58. F.J.Klein, *Sturm 138* (Leipzig, 1937), p. 89.

59. David C.Rapaport, *Assassination and Terrorism* (Toronto, 1971), *passim*.

60. Adamic, *op. cit.*, p. 147.

61. Carl E.Baumann, *The Diplomatic Kidnappings: A Revolutionary Tactic of Urban Terrorism* (The Hague, 1973), *passim*.

62. Clara E.Lida, *Anarquismo y Revolucion en España del XIX siglo* (Madrid, 1972), p. 254; *idem*, 'Agrarian Anarchism in Andalusia', Documents on the Mano Negro, *JRSH* (1969), p. 315 *et seq*.

63. *Der Weg zum Nationalsozialismus* (Gaupresseamt Berlin-Fürstenwalde, n.d.), p. 329.

64. Major Carlos Wilson, *The Tupamaros* (Boston, 1974), p. 147.

65. E.Faller, *Gewaltsame Flugzeugentführungen* (Berlin, 1972); James A.Arey, *The Sky Pirates* (New York, 1972), *passim*; *La Documentation Française, problèmes politiques et sociaux; 'La Piraterie Aérienne'*, 22 March 1974; S.K.Agrawala, *Aircraft Hijacking and International Law* (Dobbs Ferry, 1973); Nancy D.Joyner, *Aerial Hijacking as an International Crime* (Dobbs Ferry, 1974); Edward McWhinney *The Illegal Diversion of Aircraft and International Law* (Leiden, 1975). There were thirty-five successful hijackings throughout the world in 1968; the figure rose to eighty-seven in 1969 and eighty-three in 1970; there were fifty-eight such cases in 1971, sixty-two in 1972, followed by a sharp decrease to twenty-two in 1973. Between 1980 and 1984 there was a total of thirty-four sky-jackings.

66. RPGs have been used on a few other occasions such as the killing of Somoza in Asunción, by the ERP in Paraguay in September 1980, and against the US embassy in Lisbon.

67. Quoted in D.D.Egbert, *Social Radicalism and the Arts* (New York, 1970), p. 254.

68. *Le Monde*, 12 May 1976.

69. Jürg Altwegg, *Die Republik des Geistes* (Munich, 1986). See p. 271 for examples of right-wing enthusiasm about left-wing terrorism.

70. In a film based on Sciascia's book *Todo modo*, Moro was 'executed' several months before his actual murder. For a literary description of Olof Palme's murder ten years before the event see Chapter 5.

71. For a discussion on these points see H.Böll *et al.* (eds), *Briefe zur Verteidigung der Republik* (Reinbek, 1977). K.Sontheimer and J.Habermas, 'Linke, Terroristen, Sympathisanten', *Sueddeutsche Zeitung*, 273, 1977.

72. I first used this formulation in an article written in 1976: 'The Futility of Terrorism', *Harper's* (March 1976), p. 104. It has been frequently quoted since, sometimes with disapproval. I see no reason in retrospect to modify it.

73. Quoted in R.Clutterbuck, *The Media and Political Violence* (London, 1984), p. 89.

74. Camilo Catano, 'Avec les guerrillas de Guatemala', *Partisans* (July 1967), p. 150.

75. Jacques Duchêne, *Histoire du FLN* (Paris, 1962), p. 263.

76. Abdul Fatah Ismail, 'How We Liberated Aden', *Gulf Studies* (April 1976), p. 6.

77. In March 1986, one hundred people were killed in the Punjab mainly through extremist Sikh violence. Coverage was minimal because the networks were not interested in the Punjab.

78. William C.Adams, 'The Beirut Hostages: ABC and CBS Seize an Opportunity', *Public Opinion* (August–September 1985), pp. 43–4.

79. For a fuller list of examples on how terrorists induce the media to adopt their language see Alex P.Schmid and Jenny de Graaf, *Insurgent Terrorism and the Western News Media*, p. 95.

80. Robert Kleiman, *Terrorism*, 2: 1/2, p. 116. The vested interest of the media in the terrorists as 'newsmakers' perhaps never appeared more clearly than when the (British) National Union of Journalists sent a cable of condolence to Qadhafi (April 1986) after the US air attack.

81. Marvin Maurer, 'The TWA Hijack', *Midstream* (November 1985), p. 10.

82. John Bullock, 'Manipulation – The Beirut Syndrome', and Michael Cockerell, 'Amal – Masters of Propaganda', *IPI Report* (September 1985), pp. 17–18.

83. Alex P.Schmid, *Political Terrorism* (Amsterdam, 1983), 115.

84. *Ibid.*, p. 163.

85. The literature about terrorism and the media has grown enormously in recent years. See *ibid.*, Bibliography, pp. 2720–2878, as well as a special issue of *Terrorism* ('Terrorism and the Media', 1979), a publication with the same title published by the International Press Institute in 1980, and Herb Greer, 'Terrorism and the Media', *Encounter* (August 1982).

86. An excellent account of the informer's psychology is given in Liam O'Flaherty's famous novel, *The Informer*.

87. Sir Robert Anderson, *Sidelights on the Home Rule Movement* (London, 1907), p. 89.

88. 'Degayevshina', *Byloe* (April 1906).
89. Alexander Bekradian, *Der Agent Provocateur* (Zurich, 1913); Gary T.Marx, 'Thoughts on a Neglected Category of Social Movement Participant: The Agent Provocateur and the Informant', *American Journal of Sociology* (September 1974), pp. 402–42.
90. Christo Salianoff, 'Briefe und Beichten', *Deutsche Rundschau* (September 1928), p. 173.
91. Gillespie, *op. cit.*, pp. 218–23.
92. Interview in *New York Herald*, 10 February 1889; the exploits of Le Caron are described in his autobiography and in Anderson, *op. cit.*, *passim*.
93. De la Hodde, *op. cit.*
94. Many revealing facts about the activities of the West European police forces were listed in a speech by August Bebel, delivered in Berlin in 1898, later published as a brochure, *Attentate und Socialdemokratie* (Berlin, 1905), *passim*.
95. A.T.Vasilyev, *The Okhrana* (London, 1930), p. 53.
96. For Azew and similar cases see: Jean Longuet and Georges Silber, *Terroristes et policiers* (Paris, 1909); Nikolayevski, *op. cit.*; and the memoirs by high Okhrana officials such as Spiridovich, Vasilyev, Gerassimov *et al.*
97. Stephen Lukashevich, 'The Holy Brotherhood', in *American Slavonic and East European Review* (1959), p. 502 *et seq.*
98. T.D.Williams, *Secret Societies in Ireland* (Dublin, 1973), p. 105.
99. Max Nomad, *Apostles of Revolution* (New York, 1909), p. 207.
100. 'The bombs exploding in Havana gave Washington the impression that the Machado regime was in a permanent crisis. It was only when President Roosevelt's decision to ease him out of office became known in Cuba that the internal opposition against Machado grew strong enough to overthrow him': Halperin, *op. cit.*, pp. 7–8.

4 Interpretations of Terrorism

1. Alex P.Schmid, *Political Terrorism* (Amsterdam, 1983), pp. 119–58.
2. Perhaps the first to propose this thesis was Th.P.Thornton, 'Terror as a Weapon of Political Agitation', in H.Eckstein (ed.), *Internal War* (New York, 1964), p. 73 *et seq.*
3. This proposition is endlessly repeated in the media.
4. In some places leaders of warring factions have enjoyed relative immunity, but this has less to do with a gentleman's agreement than with the fact that they are better guarded and therefore more difficult targets.
5. N.Chomsky and E.S.Hermann, *The Political Economy of Human Rights*, vol. i: *The Washington Connection and Third World Fascism* (Nottingham, 1979), p. 19.
6. Edward F.Mickolus, 'An Events Data Base for Analysis of Transnational Terrorism', in Richard J.Heuer, Jr. (ed.), *Quantitative Approaches to Political Intelligence: The CIA Experience* (Boulder, Colorado, 1978), pp. 128–9.

7. Martha Crenshaw, in M.Crenshaw (ed.), *Terrorism, Legitimacy and Power* (Middletown, Conn., 1983), pp. 2–4.

8. 'For the purpose of the present report, no such universality of consensus is needed in order to arrive at working definitions': US National Advisory Committee on Criminal Justice, Standards and Goals, *Report of the Task Force on Disorders and Terrorism* (Washington, DC, 1976), p. 3.

9. Emma Goldman, 'The Psychology of Political Violence', in *Anarchism and Other Essays* (reprinted Port Washington, 1960), p. 113.

10. C.Lombroso and R.Laschi, *Le Crime politique et les révolutions* (Paris, 1982), *passim*.

11. R.Garraud, *L'Anarchie et la répression* (Paris, 1895), *passim*.

12. C.Lombroso, *Les Anarchistes* (Paris, 1896), p.184 *et seq*.

13. E.V.Zenker, *Anarchism* (London, 1895), p. 262.

14. Lucian Pye, in Eckstein, *op. cit.*, p. 162.

15. *Encyclopaedia of the Social Sciences* (New York, 1934), vol. 14.

16. Edward E.Gude, in J.C.Davies (ed.), *When Men Revolt and Why?* (New York, 1971), p. 252.

17. Samuel P.Huntington, *Political Order in Changing Societies* (New Haven, Conn., 1968), *passim*.

18. Barrington Moore, Jr, *Social Origins of Dictatorship and Democracy* (Boston, 1968); Theda Skocpol, *States and Social Revolutions* (Cambridge, 1979). A detailed critical survey of these and many other theories and hypotheses can be found in Ekkart Zimmermann, *Krisen, Staatsstreiche und Revolutionen* (Opladen, 1981).

19. Douglas P.Bwy, 'Political Instability in Latin America: The Cross-Culture Test of a Causal Model', *Latin American Research Review* (Spring 1968).

20. See for instance Todd Sandler *et al.*, 'A Theoretical Analysis of Transnational Terrorism', *American Political Science Review* (March 1983), pp. 36–54. Todd Sandler *et al.*, 'Economic Methods and the Study of Terrorism', paper presented at the Conference on Research and Terrorism, University of Aberdeen, April 1986.

21. Lloyd A.Free, in Davies, *op. cit.*, p. 258.

22. Ivo K.Feierabend and Rosalind Feierabend, 'Aggressive Behaviors within Politics, 1948–1962', *Journal of Conflict Resolution*, x: 3, p. 269.

23. Betty Nesvold, 'A Scalogram Analysis of Political Violence', in J.V.Gillespie and B.A.Nesvold, *Macro-Quantitative Analysis Conflict, Development and Democratization* (Beverly Hills, 1971).

24. T.R.Gurr, 'The Calculus of Civil Conflict', *Journal of Social Issues*, I (1972), p. 29.

25. *Ibid*.

26. Feierabend and Feierabend, *op. cit.*, p. 269.

27. Gurr, *op. cit.*, p. 44.

28. Harry Eckstein, 'On the Etiology of Internal Wars', *History and Theory* 2 (1965); *idem.*, *The Study of Internal Wars* (Princeton, 1969); Erich Weede, 'Unzufriedenheit, Protest und Gewalt, Kritik an einem makropolitischen Forschungsprogramm', *Politische Vierteljahresschrift* (September 1975).

29. T.Gurr and Duval, 'Civil Conflict in the 1960s', *Comparative Political Studies*, 6 (1973), *passim*.

30. D.A.Hibbs, *Mass Political Violence* (New York, 1973), *passim*.

31. Lodhi and C.Tilly, 'Urbanization, Crime, and Collective Violence in 19th-century France', *Journal of Sociology*, 2 (1972), p. 297; Snyder and C.Tilly, 'Hardship and Collective Violence in France 1830–1960', *American Sociological Review* (October 1972), p. 520.

32. Peter Calvert, *A Study of Revolution* (London, 1970).

33. Egbal Ahmad, in N.Miller and R.Aya (eds), *National Liberation* (New York, 1971), p. 137 *et seq*.

34. In David E.Apter and James Joll, *Anarchism Today* (London, 1971), p. 65.

35. P.Wilkinson, *Political Terrorism* (London, 1974), p. 129.

36. P.M.Cobbs and H.Grier, Foreword to Jerome H.Skolnik, *The Politics of Protest* (New York, 1969), xii.

37. John Dollard *et al.*, *Frustration and Aggression* (New Haven, Conn., 1939).

38. E.F.Durbin and John Bowlby, *Personal Aggressiveness and War* (London, 1938), p. 28.

39. Gurr, *op. cit.*

40. Leo Seechrest and J.M.G. van der Dennen quoted in Schmid, *op. cit.*, p. 162.

41. Lawrence C.Hamilton quoted in Schmid, *op. cit.*

42. Ted Robert Gurr, 'Some Characteristics of Political Terrorism in the 1960's', in M.Stohl (ed.), *The Politics of Terrorism* (New York, 1979), pp. 24–5.

43. This found its best-known popular expression in *Das Sogenannte Böse, Zur Naturgeschichte der Aggression* (Vienna, 1963). The classic work on instincts is N.Tinbergen, *The Study of Instincts* (Oxford, 1953).

44. For a collection of critical views see Ashley Montague (ed.), *Man of Aggression* (New York, 1968).

45. C.Lombroso, *L'uomo delinquente* (1876). On other occasions, as already mentioned, he believed that he had detected a connection between nutrition and terrorism.

46. The debate was triggered off by a short paper by P.A.Jacobs, M.Brunton and others in *Nature* (1965), p. 135.

47. Martha Crenshaw, 'The Psychology of Political Terrorism', in G.Hermann (ed.), *Political Psychology* (San Francisco, 1986), pp. 379–413.

48. Schmid, *op. cit.*, p. 225.

49. *Analysen zum Terrorismus*, in four volumes; vol. I: *Ideologien und Strategien*, vol. II: *Lebenslaufanalysen*, vol. III: *Prozesse und Reaktionen in Staat und Gesellschaft* (part I), vol. IV: *Prozesse und Reaktionen in Staat und Gesellschaft* (Part II) (Opladen, 1984).

50. *Analysen zum Terrorismus*, 3, Gruppenprozesse (Opladen, 1982), p. 174.

51. According to the Annual CIA Research Paper (June 1981) on international terrorism, some 30 per cent of all international terrorist incidents were telephone or letter threats.

52. E.V.Walter, *Terror and Resistance* (London, 1969).

53. Feliks Gross, 'Political Violence and Terror in 19th and 20th Century Russia and Eastern Europe', in J.F.Kirkham *et al.*, *Report to the National Commission on the Causes and Prevention of Violence* (Washington, DC, 1969).

54. Eckstein, 'On the Etiology of Internal Wars', p. 153.

5 The Image of the Terrorist: Literature and the Cinema

1. Richard Blackmur, *The Art of the Novel: Critical Prefaces by Henry James* (New York, 1946), p. 59.
2. Malcolm Brown, *The Politics of Irish Literature* (London, 1972), p. 278.
3. J.L.Borges, *Labyrinths, Selected Short Stories and Other Writings* (New York, 1964), pp. 72–5.
4. *The Works of R.L.Stevenson* (London, 1911), v, p. 130.
5. G.K.Chesterton, *The Man who was Thursday* (London, 1908).
6. *The Times* (London), 17 March 1881, quoted in W.H.Trilley, *The Background of the Princess Casamassima* (Gainesville, Florida, 1960), p. 19.
7. Émile Zola, *Les Trois Villes, Paris* (Paris, 1898).
8. John Henry Mackay, *Die Anarchisten* (Berlin, 1893), pp. 240–4.
9. Pio Baroja y Nessi, *Aurora Roja*, part 3 of *La lucha por la vida* (Madrid, 1904).
10. *Ibid.*, p. 358.
11. Published first in Prague in 1911 in the journal *Kvety*.
12. On Libertad and his group: Jean Maitron, *Histoire du mouvement anarchiste en France (1880–1914)* (Paris, 1955), p. 420 *et seq.*, and Victor Serge's autobiography, *Memoirs of a Revolutionary 1901–1941* (London, 1963); *Namesti Republiky* was republished in Czechoslovakia under the Communist regime with some major ideological adjustments.
13. The play was performed in Paris in 1897; its première in the original Norwegian did not take place until two years later.
14. Bertold Brecht, *Die Massnahme*, first performed in Berlin in December 1930; see also B.Brecht, *Anmerkungen zur Massnahme*, in *Schriften zum Theater*, vol. 2 (Frankfurt, 1963).
15. First performed in Paris in December 1949; see also Camus, *L'Homme revolté* (Paris, 1951).
16. See V.Gebel, *Shestidesyatye Gody* (Moscow, n.d.), and the biographical studies by P.Kowalowski, Leonid Grossman, B.M.Drugov and V.Setschkareff.
17. *Podpolnaya Rossiya*. The book was published in Italian in Milan (1882); a recent Russian edition of 1960 is quoted here.
18. Sophia Kovalevski, *Vera Barantzova* (London, 1895), p. 281; the author is better remembered as a distinguished mathematician.
19. Stepniak, *The Career of a Nihilist (Andrei Kozhukhov)* (London, 1889), p. 320: the Russian version was published in Geneva in 1898.
20. The book was first published in two parts in 1908. It is now exceedingly rare; the Library of Congress, for instance, has only the Hebrew translation. *Lehavot*, 2 vols. (Naharia, 1939–40). The book exercised a powerful influence on the left-wing Jewish youth movement in Poland – *Habent sua fata libeli*. I have used a more recent Polish edition (2 vols., Cracow, 1946–7). A French translation exists.
21. V.L.Burtsev, *Borba za svobodnuyu Rossiu* (Berlin, 1923), I, p. 183 *et seq.*; see also Cz.Milosz, *Czlowiek wsrod skorpionow* (Paris, 1962), pp. 84–107.

22. V. Ropshin, *Kon Blednyi (The Pale Horse)* (St Petersburg, 1909), p. 124; first published in the journal *Russkaya Mysl*. (January 1909).

23. First published in instalments in the journal *Zavety*, 1912; there was an English edition in 1916 or 1917: *What Ever Happened*. Cf. G. Plekhanov, in *Sovremennyi Mir*, 2 (1913); Chonov in *Zavety*, 8 (1912); and A. Amfiteatrov in *Zavety Serdtsa* (Moscow, 1909).

24. There is yet another Azev novel by Roman Gul, *General B.O.* (London, 1930) and Rebecca West has also written about the subject (*The Birds Fall Down* (London, 1966)).

25. *Borstal Boy* (London, 1958), p. 11.

26. Donald Davie, 'The Young Yeats', in Conor Cruise O'Brien, *The Shaping of Modern Ireland* (London, 1960), p. 143.

27. Sean O'Casey, *Drums Under the Windows* (New York, 1960), p. 423.

28. Liam O'Flaherty, *Civil War*; Sean O'Casey, *The Plough and the Stars* (London, 1926).

29. O'Casey, *Collected Plays* (London, 1949), I, p. 156.

30. Conor Cruise O'Brien, 'An Unhealthy Intersection', *New Review* (July 1975); see also W. A. Armstrong, 'History, Autobiography and "The Shadow of a Gunman"', *Modern Drama*, 2 (1960).

31. Liam O'Flaherty, *The Martyr* (London, 1933); see also Liam O'Flaherty, *The Assassin* (London, 1928), *passim*.

32. Regis Debray, *L'Indésirable* (Paris, 1976), p. 77.

33. *Izbrani Proizvedeniya* (Sofia, 1953), p. 156.

34. A. Stern, *Bedamai lead tikhi* (Tel Aviv, 1976), p. 18; his friend Y. Ratosh dedicated an untranslated (and perhaps untranslatable) poem *Argaman (Purple)* to the solitude of Yair's life and the ultimate futility of his death.

35. Gyorgy Kardos, *Avraham's Good Week* (New York, 1975).

36. E. von Salomon, *Die Geächteten* (Berlin, 1935).

37. *Ibid.*, p. 302.

38. Hanns Johst, *Schlageter*, in Günther Rühle, *Zeit und Theater* (Berlin, 1975), III, p. 28. The play was first performed on Hitler's birthday, 20 April 1933.

39. Arnolt Bronnen, *O/S* (1929); *Rossbach* (1930); Hans Fallada, *Bauern, Bonzen, Bomben* (1931).

40. M. Djilas, *Memoirs of a Revolutionary* (London, 1973), p. 132 *et seq.*

41. Michael Baumann, *Wie alles anfing* (Munich, 1975), p. 130.

42. Two of Khanafani's novels were made into films, *Les Dupes* and *Le Couteau*, both produced in Syria; the Algerians produced a terrorist 'action' film (*Sana'ud (We Shall Return)*) which was, however, criticized for lack of political content and for making too many concessions to Wild West style.

43. Alfred Faraj's play *Al nar valseitun (The Fire and the Olive Tree)*; Suheil Idris's *Sahra min Dam (Flower of Blood)*; Abdul Rahman al Sharqawi's *Watani Akka (Acre, My Homeland)*; Moen Basisu's *Shamshun va Dalila*. See Sasson Somekh in *New Outlook* (January 1972), and Shimon Ballas, 'The Ugly Israeli in Arab Literature', *New Outlook* (November 1974), as well as the same writer's series of articles in *Ha'olam Haseh* (9, 16 and 23 July 1975).

44. Meri Franco-Lao, *Basta* (Paris, 1967).

45. *No znaem, kak znal ty rodymyi, chto skoro iz nazhikh kostei, rodymetsya mstitel surovy I budet on nas posilnei.*

46. *Terrorism Part 2*, Hearing before the Committee on Internal Security, House of Representatives (Washington, DC, 1974), p. 3208.

47. Graham Greene, *The Honorary Consul* (New York, 1973), Heinrich Böll, *Under the Net* (New York, 1979), Mary McCarthy, *Cannibals and Missionaries* (New York, 1979), Doris Lessing, *The Good Terrorist* (London, 1985).

48. *Under the Net* (New York, 1979).

49. From a speech on the occasion of the W. H. Smith Award for Literature, *Hampstead and Highgate Gazette*, 2 February 1986.

50. John Le Carré, *The Little Drummer Girl* (London, 1984).

51. James N. Rowe, *The Judas Squad* (Boston, 1977); Laurence Delaney, *The Triton Ultimatum* (New York, 1977); Geoffrey Household, *Hostage London* (Boston, 1976); Anthony Trew, *Ultimatum* (London, 1975), Larry Collins and Dominique Lapierre, *The Fifth Horseman* (New York, 1980); William Katz, *North Star Crusade* (New York, 1976); Joseph di Mona, *The Benedict Arnold Connection* (New York, 1976); James Mills, *The Seventh Power* (New York, 1975); Tom Harris, *The Black Sunday* (New York, 1975).

52. Alastair MacLean, *The Satan Bug* (New York, 1978).

53. Eric Ambler, *The Levanter* (London, 1972); Sandor Frankel and Webster Mews, *The Aleph Solution* (New York, 1978); Robert Katz, *The Tripoli Documents* (New York, 1976); Marvin Kalb and Ted Koppel, *In the National Interest* (New York, 1976); Anthony Price, *The Alamut Bomb* (London, 1972); Marvin Albert, *The Gargoyle Conspiracy* (New York, 1975).

54. Robert Ludlum, *The Matarese Circle* (New York, 1979); Frederick Forsyth, *The Day of the Jackal* (New York, 1971); Colin Forbes, *The Stone Leopard* (New York, 1975); Douglas Fairbairn, *Street 8* (New York, 1977).

55. James Atwater, *Time Bomb* (London, 1977); Bartholomew Gill, *McGarr and the Politician's Wife* (London, 1977); H.K.Fleming, *The Day They Kidnapped Queen Victoria* (New York, 1978); James Reid, *The Offering* (New York, 1977); Gerald Seymour, *Harry's Game* (London, 1975); N.Stahl, *The Savage Day* (London, 1972).

56. Michael Wolfe, *The Panama Paradox* (New York, 1977); Brock Yates, *Dead in the Water* (New York, 1975); Richard Condon, *The Whisper of the Axe* (New York, 1976).

57. Per Wahlöö and J.Sjöwall, *The Terrorists* (New York, 1976); Warren Kiefer, *The Kidnappers* (New York, 1977); David Chandler, *Casablanca Opening* (New York, 1977); Philip Atles, *The Underground Cities Contract* (New York, 1974); Derek Lambert, *The Yermakhov Transfer* (New York, 1974); Kenneth Royce and Oliver Jacks, *Assassination Day* (New York, 1976); David Lippincott, *Salt Mine* (New York, 1979).

58. Peter Ritner, *The Passion of Richard Thynne* (New York, 1976); William Marshall, *Gelignite* (New York, 1977); Gerald Seymour, *The Glory Boys* (London, 1976); Norman Hartley, *The Viking Process* (New York, 1975); Adrian Hall, *The Kobra Manifesto* (New York, 1976); Frederick Forsyth, *The Devil's Alternative* (New York, 1980).

59. Alan Burns, *The Angry Brigade* (London, 1973); James McClure, *Rogue Eagle* (New York, 1976).

60. Angel Amigo, *Operacion Poncho* (San Sebastian, 1978); Martin Ugalde, *Las Brujas de Sorjin* (Saint Jean de Luz, 1978).

61. K. C. Tessendorf, *Kill the Tsar* (New York, 1986).

62. Corinne Lucas, 'Political Terrorism' in *Ogro*, an interview with Gillo Pontecorvo, *Cineastic* (Fall 1980), pp. 2–15.

63. Dan Yakir, *New York Times*, 7 September 1980.

6 Terrorism Today I: Nationalism and Separatism

1. Alex Schubert, *Stadtguerilla* (Berlin, 1974), pp. 3–22.

2. This is not true of the South Moluccans, the Croatians, the extremists in Alto Adige (South Tyrol) or the Shiites.

3. So much so that in this specific incident no Irish group wanted to accept responsibility.

4. The PIRA certainly had the capacity to engage in such operations. To give but one example: Seamus Twomey, one of its leaders, escaped from a Dublin prison with the help of a helicopter.

5. Patrick O'Donnell, *The Irish Faction Fighters of the Nineteenth Century* (Dublin, 1975), p. 63.

6. It was in the tradition, for instance, of Thomas Ashe, president of the Irish Republican Brotherhood, who fasted to death in Mountjoy prison, Dublin, in 1917.

7. *Guardian*, 11 January 1986.

8. This included support for Arab institutions in the Israeli-occupied Left Bank, but it did not include the sums given by individual Arab rulers to their favourite groups such as Abu Nidal.

9. *Al Ahram*, 28 June 1976. Less than two years later the editor of *Al Ahram* was killed by Arab terrorists in Cyprus while attending an international Communist front meeting.

10. Quoted in John Gerassi, *Towards Revolution* (London, 1971), I, p. 231.

11. Interview in *Palestine Studies* (Fall 1985).

12. The literature of and on the Palestinian groups is enormous. The *Journal of Palestinian Studies* provides substantial current coverage and has published most relevant documents. Of the recent works John W. Amos, *The Palestinian Resistance* (New York, 1980), Helena Cobban, *The Palestinian Liberation Organization* (Cambridge, 1984) and Y. Arnon Ohanna and A. Yodfat, *PLO, Strategy and Tactics* (London, 1981), provide both a general survey and further bibliographies.

13. This could explain the fact that there has been no terrorism in Catalonia, though complaints similar to those of the Basques have been voiced in Barcelona. But the Catalonians are far more numerous than the Basques and are not afraid of being 'swamped' by the Spanish.

14. Robert P. Clark, *The Basque Insurgents* (Madison, Wisconsin, 1984), p. 144.

15. By 1986, Basque (together with Spanish Catalan and Galician) had achieved equal status as official languages.

16. G. Chaliand and Yves Ternon, *The Armenians* (London, 1983).

17. The most detailed description so far of the ASALA is by Anat Kurz and Ariel Merari, *Asala* (Boulder, Colorado, 1985), which deals with the escalation of terror (p. 24) and the leader of the group, the elusive Mr Hagopian (pp. 35–6).
18. Marvin Zonis, quoted in Robin Wright, *Sacred Rage* (New York, 1985), p. 31.
19. Other suicide missions happened elsewhere, including the Japanese Red Army attack at Lod airport, and the ASALA attack in Ankara (1982).
20. Ariel Merari and Yosefa Braunstein, *Special Report: Shi'ite Terrorism*, Jaffee Centre for Strategic Studies (Tel Aviv University, 1984).
21. Twenty-five years ago the Shiites were not a significant factor among the population of Beirut, but today they are the most numerous group.
22. For the general background to radical Islam see A.R.Norton, *Harakat al Amal* in *Political Anthropology* (1984), p. 3; Em. Sivan, *Radical Islam*; O.Carre (ed.), *Radicalisme islamique d'aujourdhui* (Paris, 1984); Martin Kramer (ed.), *Protest and Revolution in Shi'i Islam* (Tel Aviv, 1985), as well as the literature mentioned in these books.
23. Daniel Pipes, *In the Path of God: Islam and Political Power* (New York, 1983), pp. 135–8. Following the emergence of the Shiite fighting groups a great deal of literature has appeared. The most important was the pioneering study of Fouad Ajami, *The Vanished Imam: Musa al Sadr and the Shia of Lebanon* (Ithaca, 1986). About other Shia organizations outside Iran see Juan R.I.Cole and Nikki R.Keddie (eds), *Shi'ism and Social Protest* (New Haven, Conn., 1986).
24. Khuswant Singh, *History of the Sikhs* (Princeton, 1963), II, p. 153.
25. Richard F.Fox, *Lions of the Punjab* (Berkeley, 1985), pp. 160–84.

7 Terrorism Today II: Left and Right

1. Frantz Fanon, *The Wretched of the Earth* (London,1967), p. 74.
2. Hans Joachim Klein, *Rückkehr in die Menschlichkeit. Appell eines ausgestiegenen Terroristen* (Hamburg, 1979), *passim*.
3. St Aust, *Der Baader Meinhof Complex* (Hamburg, 1985), *passim*.
4. Alex Schubert, *Stadtguerilla* (Berlin, 1974), *passim*. See also Thomas Meyer, *Am Ende der Gewalt* (Berlin, 1980); Kollektiv RAF, *Über den bewaffneten Kampf in Westeuropa* (Berlin, 1971); M.Müller-Borchert, *Guerilla im Industriestaat* (Hamburg, 1973); M.Baumann, *Wie alles anfing* (Munich, 1974); N.A. *Stadtguerilla und Soziale Revolution* (Haarlem, 1974); *Holger, der Kampf geht weiter* (n.p., 1974); *Bewaffneter Kampf, Texte der RAF* (n.p., 1974); F.Woerdemann, *Terrorismus* (Berlin, 1976); Bernhard Vesper, *Die Reise* (Frankfurt, 1977); *Dokumentation zum Sozialistischen Patienten-Kollektiv, Heidelberg*, ed. Basisgruppe Medizin, University of Giessen (n.d.). The most ambitious survey is the four-volume, semi-official *Terrorismus Analysen* (Opladen, 1980–4).
5. The doctrinal differences between the Brigate Rosse and the smaller groups such as Prima Linea (Front Line), Potere Operaio (later Autonomia Operaia) and the NAP were insignificant.

6. Vitofranco Pisano, 'Terrorism and Security: The Italian Experience' (November 1984) and 'Terrorism in Italy: Update Report' (1983–5) – both written for the Subcommittee on Security and Terrorism of the Committee on the Judiciary, US Senate. Tullio Barbato, *Il terrorismo in Italia* (Milan, 1980); G.Bocca, *Il terrorismo italiano* (Milan, 1978); Em. Papa, *Il processo alle Brigate Rosse* (Torino, 1979).

7. George Harris, 'The Left in Turkey', *Problems of Communism* (July/August 1980); Gerif Mardin, 'Youth and Violence in Turkey', *Archives Européenes de Sociologie* (1979), pp. 229.

8. Literature on the United Red Army and other Japanese terrorist groups is not available in languages other than Japanese. On its origins see Takashi Tachibara, *Chukaku us kakumaru*, 2 vols. (Tokyo, 1975); on its ideology, *Uchi Geba no Ronri* (*The Logic of the Inner Struggle*, Geba = Gewalt) (Tokyo, 1974); of particular interest are the essays on the aesthetics of assassination (p. 57 *et seq.*), the philosophy of murder (p. 77) and the philosophy of hatred (p. 147); a documentary record is *Sekigun* by the Sasho Henshu committee (Tokyo, 1975), with a detailed bibliography (pp. 361–484).

9. Literature on the Weathermen and the Black Panther party is abundant: *Prairie Fire* (n.p., 1974); Harold Jacobs (ed.), *Weatherman* (Berkeley, 1970); J.Raskin (ed.), *The Weather Eye* (New York, 1974); Kirkpatrick Sale, *S.D.S.* (New York, 1974); as well as *Liberation News Service*, *The Guardian*, *The Berkeley Barb* and congressional publications such as *The Weatherman Underground* (January 1975). On black terrorism: Philip S.Foner, *The Black Panther Speaks* (New York, 1970); the writings by Eldridge Cleaver, Stokely Carmichael, David Hilliard, George Jackson, Huey Newton, Bobby Seale (*Seize the Time*) and others; the periodical *Black Panther* and the periodicals of the Cleaver faction.

10. George Jackson, *Blood in My Eye* (London, 1975), p. 65.

11. Fritz René Allemann, *Macht und Ohnmacht der Guerilla* (Munich, 1974), p. 133; Luigi Valsalice, *Guerriglia e Politica, L'Esemplo di Venezuela 1962–69* (Florence, 1969); Robert J.Alexander, *The Communist Party of Venezuela* (Stanford, 1969); Norman Gall, *Teodoro Petkoff, Field Staff Reports*, 1972.

12. For a short summary of Latin American guerrilla doctrine in the early 1960s and bibliographical references see W.Laqueur, *Guerrilla* (Boston, 1976), ch. 8.

13. The literature on the subject is so large that a stage has been reached in which bibliographies of bibliographies are needed. See A.Thomas Ferguson's valuable essay in Sam C.Sarkesian (ed.), *Revolutionary Guerrilla Warfare* (Chicago, 1975), pp. 617–23. To this the following two bibliographies should be added: Russell, Miller and Hildner, 'The Urban Guerrilla in Latin America', *Latin American Research Review* (Spring 1974); *Bibliografia: Guerra Revolucionaria y Subversion en el Continente* (Washington, DC, 1973).

14. The literature on the Tupamaros is vast. Among the most important the following should be mentioned: *Actas Tupamaros* (Buenos Aires, 1971); M.E.Gilio, *The Tupamaro Guerrillas* (New York, 1970); A.Mercader and J. de Vera, *Tupamaros, Estrategia y Accion* (Montevideo, 1969); A.Porzecanski, *Uruguay's Tupamaros* (New York, 1973); Alain Labrousse, *The Tupamaros* (London, 1973); *Generals and Tupamaros*, Latin American Review of Books (London, 1974); Regis Debray, *La Critique des armes*, vol. I (Paris, 1974); Major Carlos Wilson, *The Tupamaros*

(Boston, 1974); Carlos Suarez and Ruben Anaya Sarmiento, *Los Tupamaros* (Mexico, 1981); Angel Guttierez (ed.), *Los Tupamaros*, etc. (Mexico, 1978); Ernesto Mayans (ed.), *Tupamaros, Antologia documental* (Cuernavaca, 1971); and a source book, J.Kohl and J.Litt (eds), *Urban Guerrilla Warfare in Latin America* (Cambridge, Mass., 1974).

15. Primary sources on urban terror in Brazil and Argentina are difficult to come by. Most of the earlier literature on Argentina has been overtaken by Richard Gillespie, *Soldiers of Peron* (London, 1982). But see also Vannia Bambirra (ed.), *Diez Anos de Insureccion en America Latina*, 2 vols. (Santiago, 1971). The best descriptive account is Allemann, *op. cit.* On the early phase, the articles by Hector Suarez in *Granma* (Havana) should be mentioned, 13 and 27 December 1970, 3 and 17 January 1971, and in *Punto Final*, pp. 122–5. The main sources are *Punto Final* (Chile under Allende), *Tricontinental Bulletin*, *Bohemia* and *Granma* (Havana), *Prensa Latina, Latin America*. The Montoneros published a (legal) newspaper, *La Causa Peronista*, which was shut down in 1974; the ERP issued various illegal newsheets such as *Estella Roja, El Combatiente, Liberacion*. On the ERP: *Resoluciones del V Congreso y de los comite central y comite ejecutivo posteriores* (the resolutions of the PRT congress in which the creation of an armed organization was officially decided; there is reason to believe that the organization existed well before). Marighella's writings have been translated – *For the Liberation of Brazil* (London, 1973); see also Joao Quartin, *Dictatorship and Armed Struggle in Brazil* (New York, 1971); and *Pan de Arara, La Violencia Militar en el Brasil* (Mexico, 1975).

16. Joao Quartin, *Dictatorship and Armed Struggle in Brazil* (New York, 1971), *passim*. Fernando Gabeira, *O que e isso, companheiro* (Rio de Janeiro, 1980); Alfredo Surkis, *Os Carbonarios* (São Paulo, 1980).

17. R.D.Evans, *Brazil, the Road back from Terrorism*, Conflict Studies, 47 (July 1974).

18. John William Cooke, *La lucha por la liberacion nacional* (Buenos Aires, 1973); Donald C.Hodges, *Philosophy of the Urban Guerrilla* (New York, 1973), pp. 9–12.

19. R.Lamberg, *Die Guerilla in Lateinamerika* (Stuttgart, 1972), p. 217.

20. *DEA Oversight and Budget Allocation for Fiscal Year 1986*. Subcommittee on security and terrorism of the committee on the judiciary, US Senate, 19 March 1985, pp. 32, 33. See also Rensselaer W.Lee, 'The Latin American Drug Connection', *Foreign Policy* (Winter 1985–6), p. 153.

21. The most detailed review of Sendero Luminoso is Cynthia McClintock, 'Why Peasants Rebel: The Case of Peru's Sendero Luminoso', *World Politics* (October 1984); of great interest is David Scott Palmer (who taught at Ayacucho), 'The Sendero Luminoso Rebellion in Rural Peru', in G.Fauriol (ed.), *Latin American Insurgencies* (Washington, DC, 1985), pp. 67–9; for the early years, Piedad Pareja Pflucker, *Terrorismo y sindicalismo en Ayacucho* (Lima, 1980).

22. *Washington Post*, 19 February 1986. Some two hundred members of Sendero Luminoso were killed following a prison revolt in June 1986, a massacre denounced by President Garcia. It was yet another example of the consequences of the strategy of provocation.

23. The demographic composition of Peru is about 45 per cent Indian, 45 per

cent mestizo and 10 per cent European.

24. Mario Llerena, *The Unsuspected Revolution* (Ithaca, 1978), p. 198.

25. On the Chinese model, some of the leading cadres provided tuition (in Quechua) as well as paramedical services. In some cases they even married into the local population.

26. Cesar D. Sereseres, 'The Highland War in Guatemala', Fauriol, *op. cit.*, pp. 97–130.

27. On El Salvador, Mario Menendez Rodriguez, *El Salvador, Una Autentica Guerra Civil* (San José, 1981). On Guatemala, Peter Calvert, *Guatemala* (Boulder, Colorado, 1985); on Nicaragua, Michael Rediske, *Umbruch in Nicaragua* (Berlin, 1984), and David Nolan, *The Ideology of the Sandinistas and the Nicaraguan Revolution* (Coral Gables, 1984).

28. On Sikh political violence in 1984–5 see Murray J. Lead, 'The Punjab Crisis', *Asian Survey* (May 1985), pp. 475–98; Sayamurthy, 'India's Punjab Problem', *World Today* (March 1986).

29. In contrast to Namibia, where SWAPO operated in guerrilla units of up to sixty people using mortars and rockets.

30. The Fedayeen were split at the time, with a majority willing to make concessions to the clergy.

31. Musa Khiyabani, 'Mojahed', 31 July 1981, quoted in Sepehr Zabih, *Iran Since the Revolution* (Baltimore, 1982), p. 146. See also Shaul Bakhash, *Iran under the Ayatollahs* (New York, 1985), p. 219 *et seq*.

32. Zabih, *op. cit.*, p. 150.

33. Massoud Ragavi decided to share the leadership of his organization with a woman who happened to be his third wife. This exposed the Mujaheddin to much criticism.

34. The number killed in Munich was thirteen; eighty-five perished in Bologna, and fifteen in Naples.

8 Terrorism Today III: International Terrorism

1. The term 'transnational terrorism' was introduced in this connection at one stage, but has not caught on in general usage.

2. *Parliamentary Papers, Turkey, No. 6* (1898), pp. 103, 171.

3. (Rowlett), *Report of the Committee appointed to investigate revolutionary conspirators in India* (1918), Cmd 9190, p. 14.

4. Dr Mark F. Royal, *Fenian Memoirs* (Dublin, 1949), p. 40 *et seq*.

5. M. G. Indira Devi, *Terrorist Movement in South India: A Case Study* (Kerala, 1977), p. 14.

6. J. Plumyène and R. Lassiera, *Les Fascismes français* (Paris, 1963), pp. 84–6; G. Warner, 'France', in S. J. Woolf (ed.), *European Fascism* (London, 1968), p. 270.

7. 'La Lutte Internationale contre le Terrorisme', *La Documentation française*, 30 May 1973, pp. 31–66.

8. *Terrorism*, 8: 3 (1986), p. 273.

9. George Schultz in New York, 25 October 1984.

10. Viktor Vladimorovich Vityuk, *Pod chuzhim znamenami. Litsemerie i samo-obman levovo terrorisma* (Moscow, 1985), p. 4. The following description of Soviet views is based predominantly on Vityuk's study, and to a lesser extent on Efirov's and Grachev's books, which is to say at their most informed rather than their most primitive level.

11. Vityuk, *op. cit.*, p. 25.

12. Vityuk, *op. cit.*, p. 22; A.S.Grachev, *Tupiki politicheskovo nasiliia* (Moscow, 1982), p. 85 *et seq.*

13. Lidia Modzorian, *Terrorizm, pravda i vymysel* (*Terrorism, Truth and Invention*) (Moscow, 1983), pp. 186–7.

14. *Ibid.*, p. 191.

15. Vityuk, *op. cit.*, p. 71.

16. *Ibid.*, p. 195.

17. *Ibid.*, p. 125.

18. *Ibid.*, p. 129.

19. Luis Carlos Prestes, the Communist leader, in *Tribuna Popular*, 12 and 13 January 1973.

20. This shift in strategy is reflected in many articles published in *Tricontinental* in 1969 and 1970.

21. The Italian Red Brigades received some help from Czechoslovakia and Bulgaria; members of ETA were apparently trained in Cuba in the early days. ETA also trained in Algeria and since 1976 in Libya.

22. G.Mirski, 'Arabski narodi prodolzhaiut Borbu', *IMEMO* (March 1968), and other writings of the same author; see also L.Steidin, 'Imperialisticheski Zagovor', *Kommunist* (July 1967), p. 107 *et seq.*

23. This subject is treated in some detail in Galia Golan, *The Soviet Union and the PLO* (London, 1977), and Y.Arnon Ohanna and Arye Yodfat, *PLO, Strategy and Tactics* (London, 1981).

24. For a fairly extensive list see S.Elad and A.Merari, *The Soviet Bloc and World Terrorism* (Tel Aviv, 1984), pp. 20–4.

25. Vityuk, *op. cit.*, pp. 189–90.

26. The Qadhafi phenomenon has not yet been explored in any depth. The most useful study so far is a dissertation, subsequently published as a book: Gideon Gera, *Libya under Qadhafi* (in Hebrew) (Tel Aviv, 1983). See also Lisa Anderson, 'Qadhafi and his Opposition', *Middle East Journal* (Spring 1986).

27. *Al Taliya al Arabia*, 2 December 1985. But supervision and guidance was apparently shared with the Syrians. Fatah as well as the PFLP and PDFLP wanted to receive money *and* to remain independent; the Abu Nidal group presented fewer problems for the Libyans.

28. Not all the money came from the Libyan treasury; 6 per cent of the monthly income of all Palestinians working in Libya was deducted for contribution to a 'military fund'.

29. Many details about training in Libya have come to light in the wake of trials against terrorists, for instance following the arrest of members of a PFLP unit in Istanbul.

30. The Tunisian passports used by the Abu Nidal units in Italy and Austria in December 1985 originally belonged to 'guest workers' who were deported from Libya earlier that year.

31. Arafat studied engineering, Abu Iyad and Abu Jihad studied humanities. Sartawi was a surgeon. Both Habash and Hadad of the PFLP were physicians.

32. The only serious study so far on the Abu Nidal group is Yossi Melman, *Profile of a Terrorist Organization* (in Hebrew) (Tel Aviv, 1984; US edn, New York, 1986). The author covered the London trial of the members of the gang who shot the Israeli ambassador in 1983.

33. One example should suffice: two editors of a Berlin regional paper (*Radikal*) were sentenced to a prison term for having promoted a terrorist organization. The Green Party made them candidates for the European parliament and as a result they did not have to go to prison.

34. Mark S. Steinitz, 'Insurgents, Terrorists and the Drug Trade', *Washington Quarterly* (Fall 1985).

35. The phrase is Paul Henze's: 'Organized Crime and Drug Linkage', in U. Ra'anan (ed.), *Hydra of Carnage* (Lexington, 1986), p. 184.

36. Richard B. Craig, 'Illicit Drug Traffic and U.S.–Latin American Relations', *Washington Quarterly* (Fall 1985), p. 109.

37. Steinitz, *op. cit.*, p. 142. German Caycedo, *El Karina* (Bogota, 1984), includes interviews with members of M19 about drug and arms smuggling. On politics and drug trafficking in Bolivia, see Anon. *Narcotrafico y Politica*, tomo I (La Paz, 1982); Anon. *Narcotrafico y Politica*, tomo II (La Paz, 1985); Canelas, *Bolivia: Coca Cocaina* (Cochabamba, 1985).

38. Steinitz, *op. cit.*, p. 146. There are indications that the Afghan Mujaheddin have also derived part of their war chest from the production and sale of drugs. So has the El Salvador right-wing ARENA.

39. Reuters, 20 November 1984, quoted in Steinitz, *op. cit.*, p. 146.

40. Testimony of Francis A. Muller of DEA, in *Drugs and Terrorism* (1984), pp. 14–23.

41. DEA Oversight and Budget, Authorization for Fiscal Year 1986. Subcommittee on Security and Terrorism of the Committee of the Judiciary, US Senate, 19 March 1985 (Washington, DC, 1985), pp. 32–3.

9 Conclusions

1. About $20–30 million were invested annually in counter-terrorist R and D, much less than the corresponding budget of a major pharmaceutical company.

2. When M19, the Colombian terrorist organization, stormed the Palace of Justice in Bogota on 6 November 1985, one of their first acts was to destroy the files relating to drug cases.

3. For a statistical investigation, see Christopher Hewitt, *The Effectiveness of Anti-Terrorist Policies* (Lanham, 1984), p. 47.

4. For a review of how the United Nations has been coping with terrorism, see Abraham D. Sofaer, 'Terrorism and the Law', *Foreign Affairs* (July 1986).

5. CSIS, *Combating Terrorism: A Matter of Leverage* (Washington, DC, 1986), p. 38.

6. Major Arthur Griffith, *Mysteries of Police and Crime* (London, 1898), II, p. 469.

7. Norman Angell (ed.), *What Would be the Character of a New War?* (New York, 1933), p. 388.

8. Edward Condon, quoted in Dexter Masters and Katherine Way (eds), *One World or None* (New York, 1946), p. 40.

9. Reports by the Sandia and Mitre Corporations, 1976.

10. S.J.Berkowitz *et al.*, *Superviolence*, Acton Report, 1972.

11. M.Willrich and Theodore Taylor, *Nuclear Theft Risks and Safeguards* (Cambridge, Mass., 1974), p. 115. See also V.Gilinsky, in B.Boskey and M. Willrich (eds), *Nuclear Proliferation* (New York, 1970); E.M.Kinderman *et al.*, *The Unconventional Nuclear Threat* (Stanford Research Institute, Menlo Park, 1969); and many other studies.

12. *International Task Force on Prevention of Nuclear Terrorism* (Washington, DC, 1986), p. 1 *et seq.*

13. For a short survey on chemical and biological weapons see SIPI, *Arms Uncontrolled* (Cambridge, Mass., 1975), and a more detailed report in Berkowitz, *op. cit.*

14. J.H.Rothschild, *Tomorrow's Weapons* (New York, 1964).

15. Berkowitz, *op. cit.*, chs 8 and 9, *passim*.

16. C.G.Hedden, 'Defense Against Biological Warfare', *Annual Review of Microbiology* (1967), p. 639.

17. Roberta Wohlstetter, 'Terror on a Grand Scale', *Survival* (May–June 1976), p. 102. See also Brian Jenkins, *High Technology Terrorism and Surrogate War*, Rand Paper (Santa Monica, 1975), p. 559; *idem.*, 'Nuclear Terrorism and Its Consequences', *Social Science and Modern Society* (July–August 1980); David Rosenbaum, 'Nuclear Terror', *International Security* (Winter 1977), p. 140 *et seq.*

18. R.W.Mengel, 'Terrorism and New Technologies of Destruction', in Martin H.Greenberg and Augustus R.Norton (eds), *Studies in Nuclear Terrorism* (Boston, 1979), pp. 214–15.

19. Stanley P.Bernard, 'Nuclear Terrorism, More Myth than Reality', *Air University Review* (July–August 1985), p. 30 *et seq.* See also 'If Terrorists Go Nuclear', *Science*, 11 July 1986.

20. Thomas Schelling, 'Thinking About Nuclear Terrorism', *International Security* (Spring 1982), p. 65.

21. 'Potential for Use by Terrorists of Binary Weapons', in *Binary Weapons: Implications of the U.S. Chemical Stockpile Modernization Program for Chemical Weapons Proliferation*, Congressional Report, 24 April 1984.

22. CSIS, *Combating Terrorism: A Matter of Leverage* (Washington, DC, 1986).

23. *Ibid.*, p. 19 *et seq.*

Abbreviations

AAA: Argentine Anticommunist Alliance
Al Amal: Islamic Hope, Shiite, Lebanon
Abu Abbas: Palestine Liberation Front–Fatah faction, Syria
Al Daawa: (The Call), Iraq
Abu Musa: Fatah faction, Syria
Abu Nidal: Also known as Fatah Revolutionary Council, Syria, Libya
AD: Action Directe, France
ALN: Acao Libertadora Nacional, Brazil
ANC: African National Congress, South Africa
Asala: Armenian Secret Army
AUTOP: Workers Autonomy, Italy
Black September: Palestinian
Brigate Rosse: Red Brigades, Italy
CAL: Commandos Armados de Liberacion, Puerto Rico
CCC: Cellules Communistes Combatants, Belgium
Chukaku-Ha: Middle Core Faction, Japan
DEVSOL: Revolutionary Left, Turkey
ELF: Eritrean Liberation Front
ELN: Ejercito de Liberacion National, Peru
ELS: Southern Liberation Army, Mexico
EOKA: Ethniki Organosis Kyprion Agoniston (National Organization of Cypriot
    Fighters), Cyprus
EPL: Ejercito Popular de Liberacion, Colombia
Eros: Eelam Revolutionary Organization of Students, Sri Lanka

ERP: Ejercito Revolucionario del Pueblo Argentina, also El Salvador
ETA: Euzkadi ta Azkatazuna, Basque, Spain
FALN: Fuerzas Armadas de Liberacion Nacional, Venezuela
FAR: Fuerzas Armadas Rebeldes, Guatemala
FARC: Fuerzas Armadas Revolucionarias de Colombia, Colombia
FARL: Lebanese Armed Revolutionary Faction
FARN: Armed Forces of National Resistance, El Salvador
Fatah: Harakat Tahrir Falistin, Palestinian
Fedaj Khalq: Fedaj Struggle, Iran
FLNC: Corsican National Liberation Front
FLO: Front de Libération du Québec, Canada
FMLN: Frente Farabundo Marti, San Salvador
FMPR: Manuel Rodriguez Patriotic Front, Chile
FP 25: Forças Populares do 25 Abril, Portugal
FRAP: Fuerzas Revolucionarias Armadas del Pueblo, Mexico
FRAP: Frente Revolucionario Anti Fascista y Patriotico, Spain
FSLN: Frente Sandinista de Liberacion Nacional, Nicaragua
GRAPO: First of October Anti-Fascist Resistance Group, Spain
Grey Wolves: (Bozkurtlar), Turkey
Hizb Allah: Shiite, Lebanon
HRB: Croatian Revolutionary Brotherhood, Yugoslavia
IMRO: Inner Macedonian Revolutionary Organization
INLA: Irish National Liberation Army
IRA: Irish Revolutionary Army
Irgun: IZL, Irgun Zvai Leumi, Palestine
Islamic Jihad: Shiite, Lebanon
JCAG: Justice Commando of the Armenian Genocide
LEHI: Lohame Herut Israel, (Stern Gang) Palestine
LTTE: Liberation Tigers of Tamil Eelam, Sri Lanka
M 19:   Movimiento 19 Abril, Colombia
MANO: Movimiento Argentino Nacional Organisacion, Argentina
MANO: Mano Blanca, Guatemala
MIR: Movimiento de la Izquierda Revolucionaria, Venezuela, Chile, also Peru
MIRA: Movimiento Independista Revolucionario Armada, Puerto Rico
MLN: Movimiento de Liberacion Nacional, (Tupamaros) Uruguay, also in Chile
   and Guatemala
Mohamed Boudia Commando (Carlos Gang)
Montoneros (Juan Jose Valle Montoneros):   Argentina
MR-8:   Movimiento Revolucionario do Octobre 8, Brazil
MR-13: Movimiento Revolucionario Alejandro de Leon 13 Noviembre, Guate-
   mala
MRTA: Tupac Amaru Revolutionary Movement, Peru
Mujaheddin, Iran
NAP: Armed Proletarian Nuclei, Italy
NAPAP: Armed Nuclei for Popular Autonomy, France
NOA: Nueva Organisacion Anticommunista, Guatemala

PDFLP: Popular Democratic Front for the Liberation of Palestine
PFLP: Popular Front for the Liberation of Palestine (Dr G. Habash)
PFLP–GC: Popular Front–General Command (Syrian controlled)
PIRA: Provisional Irish Republican Army
PRD: Partido Revolucionario Dominican, Dominican Republic
RAF: Rote Armee Fraktion (Baader–Meinhof), West Germany
RZ: Revolutionare Zellen, West Germany
2nd of June: Second of June Movement, West Germany
Sendero Luminoso: Shining Path, Peru
SLA: Symbionese Liberation Army, United States
TELO: Tamil Eelam Liberation Organization, Sri Lanka
TPLA: Turkish People's Liberation Army
TPLF: Turkish People's Liberation Front
UDA: Ulster Defence Association, Northern Ireland
UFF: Ulster Freedom Fighters, Northern Ireland
UVF: Ulster Volunteer Forces, Northern Ireland
VPR: Vanguarda Popular Revolucionaria, Brazil
Weatherman: United States
Wehrsportgruppe Hoffmann: West Germany
Zapatista: Frente Urbana Zapatista, Mexico

Index

AAA (Argentine), 264
Abdallah, Georges, 287*n*
Abu Abbas, 219
Abu Iyad, 286
Abu Mahmoud, 221
Abu Musa, 100, 284, 288
Abu Nidal (Sabri al Banna), 4, 76, 78, 100, 111, 146, 207, 218, 221–2, 261, 283–4, 296; activities and character, 286–8
Acción Democrática, 247
Achille Lauro (ship), 116, 222
Action Directe (France), 5*n*, 236, 283, 287–9, 302*n*, 306*n*
Adam, Paul, 117
Adams, James, 103*n*
Aden, 21–2, 123
Adler, Friedrich, 63
Adorno, Theodore W., 119
Afghanistan, 296
Africa, *see* ANC, and individual countries
Afzal Khan, 44
Agca, Mehmet Ali, 242
Akselrod, Pavel, 29, 41
Alamat Ambush, The (Price), 198
Alarm, 52–3
al Banna, Sabri, *see* Abu Nidal
Albert, M., 198
Alexander, King of Yugoslavia, 20, 99, 145, 170, 309
Alexander II, Tsar of Russia, 16, 49, 54, 60–1, 77

Alexander III, Tsar of Russia, 38
Alexandrov, Todor, 77
Alexei, Grand Duke of Russia, 105
ALF, 221
Alfieri, Vittorio, 25
Alfonso XIII, King of Spain, 52
Algeria, 22, 75, 122, 124, 148, 204, 268
Algiers, 246
Al Hadaf, 190
Ali, Hassan Nasser, 147*n*
Al Iqab, 221
Allbeury, Ted, 198
al Masri, Zafer, 140
ALN (Brazil), 120, 246, 248, 301
Alto Adige (South Tyrol), 170, 307
Alush, Naji, 288
Amal, Al, 124, 231
Ambler, Eric, 198, 200
Amigo, Angel, 200
Amnesty International, 261
Ananias (high priest), 12
Anarchist, 53
Anarchists, 49–51; and assassinations, 15; Austrian, 134; and dynamite, 104, 313; German, 134; international, 51; Italian, 51, 267; and Most, 53–9; motives, 87; novels on, 176–8, 192, 197; and police informers, 134; and propaganda by deed, 18, 49–51; public reaction to, 117–18; Spanish, 85, 137, 157; violence of, 150–1; women among, 79

Anarchists, The (Mackay), 177
ANC (African National Congress), 107,
   140, 207, 259, 274
Anderson, Sir Robert, 129
Andrei Kozhukov (film), 189*n*
Andreyev, Leonid, 129, 182, 189*n*
Andrieux, Louis, 50, 134
Angiolilo, Miguel, 83, 267
Angola, 296
Angry Brigade, 236
Angry Brigade, The (Burn), 200
Antonio, Émile de, 202
'Apis', Colonel (Dragutin
   Dimitrijević), 267
Aptekman, O.V., 34
Aquinas, St. Thomas, 24
Arab Office (Libya), 285
Arab terrorists, Palestinian, 74, 76,
   140, 207; activities and character,
   215–22; anti-permissiveness, 161;
   brutality, 92; finances, 98, 113, 283;
   hijacks by, 115; international links,
   139, 204, 267, 269, 275, 283; novels
   on, 190–1; popular support for, 116;
   size of, 94; and Soviet Union,
   275–6; splits in, 96
Arafat is Next (Black), 198
Arafat, Yasser, 217, 219–21, 223, 276,
   283–4, 296–8
Aramburu, Pedro Eugenio, 114, 199,
   248–9, 252
Arciszewski, Tomasz, 88
Arendt, Hannah, 168
Arevalo, Cevezo, 258
Argentinian terrorists, 20, 248–54;
   eliminated, 139; recent, 308; right-
   wing, 264; *see also* ERP; Montoneros
Argov, Shlomo, 222, 287, 320
Arismendi, Rodney, 274
Aristotle, 24
Armenian terrorists, 7, 15, 17, 93–4,
   140, 207, 307; activities and
   character, 227–30; influences on,
   43, 266; personality of, 78, 161;
   popular support for, 117; strategy
   of, 74–5; weapons, 106; *see also* ASALA

arms and weapons, 101–9
Arrow Cross (Hungary), 68, 81
Artal, 77
Arturo Ui (Brecht), 84
Asad, Lieutenant-General Hafez el,
   297*n*
ASALA (Armenian Secret Army for the
   Liberation of Armenia), 115, 206–7,
   228–9, 294
Ashes and Diamonds (film), 189*n*
Assassins (Order of), 13, 15
Assault on Maris A, The (Stahl), 199
At Daggers Drawn (Leskov), 179
atentados sociales, 52
Atlas, Philip, 199
Audrian, General René, 289
Aurora Roja (Baroja), 177
Austria, 69, 163–4, 306
Azarika (684–700), 230
Azev, Evno F., 41–2, 81, 106, 110,
   134–5, 181, 194

Baader, Andreas, 78, 161, 237
Baader–Meinhof gang (RAF), 146, 206,
   236–8; activities, 296; bank robbery,
   97; and biological warfare, 317; and
   Euroterrorism, 288; film on, 201;
   ideology, 302*n*; in prison, 118, 237;
   psychology of, 161; public support
   for, 118–19; size of, 94; steal poison
   gas, 317; suicides, 231; women in,
   80
Ba'ath (Iraq), 221
Babeuf, François N., 26, 32, 134
Bach, A. N., 88
bacteriological and chemical warfare,
   313–14, 316–20
Baghdad agreement, 1978, 216
Bagrov (Stolypin's assassin), 81*n*, 130
Bakaj (Okhrana official), 181
Bakhush, Mohammed, 285
Bakunin, Mikhail, 29–32, 43; escapes,
   133; family origins, 79, 82; and
   Marx and Engels, 60; and
   Narodnaya Volya, 38, 82;

Bakunin, Mikhail—*cont.*
  'Revolutionary Catechism', 30–1, 54
Balbo, Italo, 267
Balkans, 42; *see also* individual countries
Balmashev, Stepan, 16, 40, 77, 90
Bande Mataram, 45
Bapat, Senapati, 44
Barbie, Klaus, 5*n*
Baroja y Nessi, Pio, 177
Barrault, Jean-Louis, 188
Barthou, Louis, 20, 170
Basisu, Moen, 190
Basque terrorists, 7, 20, 92, 116, 139, 169–70, 207, 215; *see also* ETA
Batista y Zaldiva, Fulgencio, 247
Battle of Algiers (film), 189*n*
Baumann, Michael, 188
Bazarov, 53
Beast of Property, The (Most), 54
Beauvoir, Simone de, 196*n*
Beckurts, 237
Begin, Menachem, 121
Behan, Brendan, 183
Beheshti, 260
Beirut: attacks in, 109, 123–5, 140, 231–2, 295; disorder in, 300
Bekolar ehad (Hazaz), 191*n*
Belaunde, Terry Fernando, 255
Belfast, 208–11, 213
Belgian terrorists, *see* CCC
Bell, Bowyer, 168
Belpaese, Il (film), 201
Belshazzar's Feast (Way), 198
Ben Bella, Ahmed, 189*n*
Benedict Arnold Connection, The (di Mona), 198
Benevskaya (Social Revolutionary), 85
Bengali terrorists, *see* Indian terrorists
Ben Ner, Yizhak, 191*n*
Berkman, Alexander, 53, 58, 77, 87
Berkowitz, Leonard, 158*n*
Berri, Nabih, 125, 231–2
Besy (The Possessed) (Dostoevski), 83–4, 179, 189*n*

Betancourt, Romulo, 247
Bethe, Hans, 317
Bewegung 2. Juni, 118, 161, 164, 236–7
Beyond Human Power (Bjørnson), 178
Bezmotivniki, 42
Bianco, Carlo, conte de Saint Jorioz, 27
Bible, Holy, 164, 186
biological warfare, *see* bacteriological and chemical warfare
Bismarck, Prince Otto von, 36, 54, 134
Bjørnson, Bjørnsterne, 86, 178
Black Brood (film), 202
Black Hand (Serbia), 267
Black Hundred, 20, 37, 41, 66, 74
Black, Lionel, 198
Black Panthers (USA), 244–5
Black September, 100, 217, 221, 272, 283, 288, 296
Black Sunday, The (Harris), 198, 201
Blanqui, Louis Auguste, 32
Blanquism, 61–2
Bloody Sunday (Londonderry, 1972), 210
BO, *see* Fighting Organization
Boer War, 267
Boevaya Organisatsia, *see* Fighting Organization
Bogdanovich (Governor of Ufa), 16
Bogolepov (Minister of Education), 16
Bogoraz-Tan, Vladimir G., 88
Bogota, 124, 307*n*
Bolivia, 246
Böll, Heinrich, 119, 196–7, 273
Bologna: railway station bomb, 1980, 262
Bolsheviks, 16, 41, 62–3
Bomb, The (Harris), 177–8
Bomba (Seyfeddin), 190*n*
Bonnot (gang leader), 87
Bonnot gang, 19, 106, 130, 189*n*
Borges, Jorge Luis, 175

Born, Jorge and Juan, 97
Bosnia, 74
Bourdet, Claude, 118
Bourne Identity, The (Ludlum), 198
Boutros Pasha, 21
Boxer Rebellion, 14
Brackenbury, 135
Brazilian terrorists, 148, 248–50, 253;
  eliminated, 139; *see also*
  Vanguardia Popular Revolucionaria
Brecht, Bertolt, 84, 178–9
Bresci, Gaetano, 51
Breshkovskaya, Catherine, 29
Brigate Rosse, *see* Red Brigades
Brighton: IRA bomb, 212
British terrorism, 135, 212; *see also*
  London
Bronnen, Arnolt, 187
Brousse, Paul, 48, 88
Brujas de Sorjin, Las (Ugalde), 200
Brzozowski, Leopold Stanislav, 180–1
Buchalo (Anarchist engineer), 106
Buchanan, George, 25
Bulgaria, 17, 64, 264, 267–8, 275, 288,
  291–2, 295
Buonarroti, P., 26, 134
Burke, Edmond, 4, 11
Burmese Communist Party, 293
Burn, Alan, 200
Burns, Lizzy, 59
Burtsev, Vladimir, 38–9, 113, 181
Bush Committee, *see* Vice-President's
  Task Force
Bwy, Douglas, P., 153

Cabrinovic, Vulkosava, 77
Cadoudal, Georges, 137
Caesar, Julius, 90, 191
Caesar's Column (Donnelly), 178
Cafiero, Carlo, 48
Cagney, James, 189*n*
Cagol, Maria, 80*n*, 85
cagoulards, 268
Calinescu, Armand, 68
Calvert, Peter, 156
Cambodia, 145

Camp David Agreement, 219
Camus, Albert, 133, 178
Canada: victims in, 166
Canadian terrorists, 81*n*, 139, 206,
  233; *see also* FLQ
cancones de protesta (songs), 191
Canovas, Antonio, 18, 83, 137, 267
Capone, Al, 109
Caracas, Venezuela, 246–7
Carbonari, 26–7
Cardozo, Cesareo and Graciela, 176*n*
Carey, James, 130
Carlist wars, 19
Carlos (Illich Ramirez Sánchez), 4,
  86, 198, 217, 275, 288, 296
Carmichael, Stokely, 244
Carnot, Sadi, 18, 73, 91, 104
Caro Papa (film), 201
Carpio, Caetano, 78, 133*n*
Carrero Blanco, Admiral Luis, 110,
  201, 225
Carvalho, Otelo, 289
Casablanca Opening, The (Chandler),
  199
Caserio, Santo Jeronimo, 91
Casey, Joseph, 87
Castro, Fidel, 22–3, 237, 247, 257, 295
Cathleen ni Houlihan (Yeats), 184
Caucasus, 42
Cavour, Camillo Benso, 27
CCC (Belgium), 236, 289, 302*n*
Central America, 258–9, 262, 265; *see
  also* Latin America, and individual
  countries
Central Intelligence Agency, *see* CIA
Chabrol, Claude, 189*n*
Chad, 282, 296
Chandler, David, 199
Charan Bhagwati, 110*n*
Charles Martel club, 289*n*
Ché Guevara (journal), 254
chemical warfare, *see* bacteriological
  and chemical warfare
Chernishevski, N. G., 53
Chernov, Viktor, 42
Chesterton, G. K., 175

Chevalier (inventor of first time-bomb), 101*n*

Chicagoer Arbeiterzeitung, 52

Chichester-Clark, Sir Robert, 208

Chile, 258; *see also* MIR

China, 64, 147, 250

CIA (Central Intelligence Agency, USA), 146, 165–6

Ciano, Count Galeazzo, 267

Cicero, 24

Cinema Militant (Hennebelle), 189*n*

Civil Disobedience movement (India), 47

Clan na-Gael (Ireland), 64, 266

Clark, Robert R., 224*n*, 227

Cleaver, Eldridge, 186*n*, 244

Clemenceau, Georges, 117

Cluseret, General Gustave Paul, 266

Cohen, Geula, 180*n*

Cole, G. D. H., 172

Collins, Larry, 198

Collins, Michael, 79, 110, 173

Colombia, 6, 98, 139, 147*n*, 248, 254–5, 257–8, 264, 274, 292, 296

Communism: attitude to terrorism, 64; and drugs, 292–3; founded, 27–8; Italian, 239–41; in Soviet Union, 89

Communist League, 27

Condition humaine, La (Malraux), 186

Condon, Richard, 199

Congress Party (India), 44

Connery, Sean, 189*n*

Conrad, Joseph, 3, 51, 129, 175, 180–1, 195

Conrad of Montferrat, King of Jerusalem, 13

Constance, Council of, 24

Constant, Marie, 50

Contras (Nicaragua), 296

Convention on the Prevention and Punishment of Crimes Against Internationally Protected Persons, 309

Corday, Charlotte, 79, 191–2

Corsica, 7, 169–70, 289*n*

Corydon, John Joseph, 134

Costa, Andrea, 88

Costa-Gavras, 189*n*

Costello (INLA leader), 215

counter-terrorism, 133–6, 304–12

Craxi, Bettino, 162–3

Croatian terrorists, *see* Ustasha

Cronin, Patrick, 132

Crozier, Brian, 168

CSAR (France), 69, 268

Cuba: and drug trade, 291, 294; and hijacked planes, 115, 309; international links, 268, 274–7, 279, 285, 295–6; terrorists in, 141, 165; *see also* Castro, Fidel

'Cult of Violence, The' (Gandhi), 46

Curcio, Renato, 80*n*, 85

Curley, Daniel, 77

Cypriot terrorists, 21–2, 138–9, 170, 246

Cyprus, 307*n*

Czechoslovakia, 277

Damour, 218

Dante Alighieri, 24

Dashnak party (Armenia), 43, 228

Datta, Batukeswar, 47

Davies, 152

Dawson Field hijacking, 115, 217

Day of the Dolphin, The (film), 202*n*

Day of the Jackal (Forsyth), 198; (film), 200

Dayan, Moshe, 198

Dead in the Water (Yates), 198

'Death for a death, A' (Stepniak), 33

Debray, Regis, 138, 147*n*, 185–6, 247–8

Debs, Eugene, 113

Decembrist Plot, 134

De droit des magistrats, 25

Degayev (later 'Dr Pell'), 130

Deitch, Lev, 38, 133

De Jure Regnis apud Scotos (Buchanan), 25

Delameter & Co., 105

Delaney, Lawrence, 198
Deloncle, Eugene, 268
Dembov (killed by own bomb), 104
De Officiis (Cicero), 24
De Quincey, Thomas, 12
Derekh Gever (Mossenson), 191*n*
Devil's Alternative, The (Forsyth), 199
Devoy, Jim, 74
Devoy, John, 65–6, 84, 266
Dev-Sol (Turkey), 294
Dimitrov, 238
di Mona, Joseph, 198
Dirty Hands (Sartre), *see Mains sales,
  Les*
di Stefano, Alfredo, 246
Djilas, Milovan, 188
Dohrn, Bernardine, 84, 245
Dollard, John, 158
Dollfuss, Engelbert, 69
Dominican Republic, 248, 274
Donnelly, Ignatius, 178
Dostoevski, Fedor M., 3, 51, 83–4,
  117, 150, 174–5, 179, 189*n*, 193
Dozier, Brigadier-General James,
  114, 120, 131, 240, 288
Dragomanov, M. P., 37
Drenkmann, Günter von, 114, 237
Drenteln (tsarist political police
  chief), 34, 191
drugs (narcotic), 291–5
Druze people, 218, 231
Duarte, Napoleon, 264
Duca (Rumanian Prime Minister), 68
Durnovo, P. N., 40
Durruti, Buenaventura, 19–20, 87
dynamiters (Ireland), 17, 92, 184
Dynamiters, The (Stevenson), 175

Eagles of the Palestinian Revolution,
  221
Eastwood, Clint, 202*n*, 313
Ecevit, Bülent, 264
Eckstein, Harry, 155, 171
Eco, Umberto, 119
Edward, Prince of Wales (*later* King
  Edward VII), 113

Egypt, 21
Eire (Republic of Ireland), 209–10,
  212–14
Ejercito Secreto Anti Communista (El
  Salvador), 264
ELN (Bolivia), 253, 293
El Salvador, 78, 139, 166, 254, 258,
  264–5
Elizabeth (Zita), Empress of Austria,
  18, 104
Elser, George, 317*n*
Emelianov (assassin of Alexander II),
  77
Encyclopaedia of the Social Sciences,
  152
Enforcer, The (film), 202*n*
Engels, Friedrich, 27, 35, 59–62, 234,
  270
Ensslin, Gudrun, 78, 237–8
Entebbe, 220, 307
EOKA (Cyprus), 22, 139
Erbakan, Necmettin, 264
ERP (Argentina); activities and
  character, 249–54; assassinations
  by, 250; class composition, 82;
  finances, 97; and Montoneros, 132;
  and nuclear plant, 314–15; size of,
  94; support for, 301; and Soviet
  Union, 274
Erzberger, Matthias, 69, 110, 118
Escadron de la Muerte (Colombia),
  264
ETA (Euzkadi ta Azkazatuna; Basque
  organization), 7, 83, 94–5, 97, 120;
  activities and character, 223–7; anti-
  permissiveness, 161; and drug
  trade, 291, 294; in elections, 120;
  informers in, 132; international
  links, 226, 267; legal and military
  arms, 147; motivations, 159; social
  composition, 168–9, 225–6; Soviet
  Union and, 272
Eura Nuva (Northern Ireland), 209
European Revolutionary Committee,
  32
Euroterrorism, 288–91

Evolution, Die (Heinzen), 28–9
Exposed (film), 202*n*

Fadlallah, Sheikh, 232
FAI Spain), 19
Fairbairn, Douglas, 198
Falange (Lebanon), 218
Fallada, Hans, 187
Fanon, Frantz, 118, 235, 236*n*, 273
FAR (Argentina), 248
FARC (Colombia), 120, 257*n*, 291,
    293–4
Farina, Homero, 114
Fascists, 67–70, 150, 164–5, 204, 262,
    302; ethics, 85, 92*n*
Fassbinder, Rainer Werner, 201
Fatah, al (Palestine), 83, 99–100,
    103*n*, 203, 208, 215–23, 263, 276
Feierabend, Ivo K. and Rosalind, 155
Feld, Bernard, 313
Feltrinelli (Italian publisher), 240
Fénelon, Felix, 117
Fenian terrorists: actions, 104; aims,
    74; finances, 100; influences on,
    266; and Marx and Engels, 59–61;
    and Soviet Union, 270; tactics, 113
Feranda, Adriana, 131
Ferreira, Camara, 250
Ferrer, Francisco, 96
Fetscher, Iring, 196*n*
Feuerbach, Ludwig Andreas, 32
FGCI (Italian Communist Youth), 239
fidaiin, 13
Field of Blood (Seymour), 199*n*
Fighters for the Freedom of Israel, *see*
    LEHI
Fighting Organization (Boevaya
    Organisatsia, Social
    Revolutionaries), 39–42; Azev
    heads, 81, 106, 135; Gershuni
    heads, 81, 127; Maximalists oppose,
    41–2; size of, 94
Figner, Vera, 87, 180*n*
Financial Times (London), 146
Finland, 69
Finnegan's Wake (Joyce), 183

Firmenich (Montoneros leader), 50
Fischer, Adolf, 85
Five from Barska Street, The (film),
    189*n*
Flames (Brzozowski), 180–1
FLN (Algeria), 22, 75
FLQ (Quebec, Canada), 81*n*, 170, 206,
    233
FMNL (El Salvador), 133*n*, 264
Ford, Aleksander, 189*n*
Ford, John, 188*n*
Forsyth, Frederick, 198–9
40 Days of Musa Dagh (Werfel), 227
FP-25 (Portugal), 288
France: Algerians attacked in, 143;
    Anarchists in, 15, 95; and ETA, 226;
    right-wing groups in, 69, 262–3;
    terrorists in, 163, 287*n*, 289, 306,
    310; *see also* CSAR
Franco, Francisco, 6
Frankel, Sandor, 198
Frankfurt Congress, January 1986, 290
Franz I, Emperor of Austria, 113
Franz Ferdinand, Archduke of
    Austria, 74, 77
Free India Society, 44
Freeling, Nicholas, 197
Freiheit, 50, 53–4, 56, 59, 134
Freikorps, 20, 67–8, 302; books on,
    187; cruelty of, 83; internal
    discipline, 132; and Nazis, 88;
    strategy of, 74
French Revolution, 11, 15, 26, 204
Frente Amplio (Uruguay), 121*n*, 249
Fresingea (thug), 14
Freud, Sigmund, 160
Frick, Henry C., 53, 77
Frolenko (Russian terrorist), 180*n*
Fromm, Erich, 188
FSLN, 139, 258
Fuchs von Glenarvon, Der (film),
    189*n*
Fujimora, Yoshitama, 250
Furaya, Yutaka, 243
Fusako, Shigenobu, 80
Futurist manifesto, 1909, 42

GAL (anti-ETA group), 225
Gandhi, M. K. (Mahatma), 44–7, 73
Gandhi, Indira, 111, 137, 144, 259
Ganz (Anarchist), 49
Garantien der Harmonie und Freiheit
  (Weitling), 28
Garcia Perez, Alan, 255–6
Garfield, James Abram, 18, 70
gas (poison), 314, 316
Gaulle, Charles de, 200
Gelignite (Marshall), 199
Genet, Jean, 118
Genossin, Die (Röhl), 196n
Gerassimov, Alexander, 40
German terrorists: ages, 77–8;
  Communism in, 64; finances, 101;
  international links, 204; personality
  of, 78n, 80, 82, 161; public reaction
  to, 119; *see also* Baader–Meinhof
  Gang; Freikorps; Nazis
Germany in Autumn (film), 201
Germany, West, 6, 88–9, 95, 143, 163,
  165, 169, 203; and New Left, 235–7;
  right-wing groups, 262; *see also*
  Baader–Meinhof Gang
Gershuni, Grigori, 41, 79, 81, 127,
  180n
Gestapo, 146
Ghadamsi, Ezzedin, 283n
Giogni, Professor, 240
Giustizia e Libertà, 268
Gladstone, William Ewart, 135
Glory Boys, The (Seymour), 199
Godse, Nathuram, 45
Goebbels, Joseph, 66–7
Goldenberg (of Narodnaya Volya),
  129, 181
Goldman, Emma, 53, 58, 79, 86, 87,
  92, 150
Goldwater, Barry, 200
González, Ana Maria, 176n
Gorky, Maxim, 182
Gots, Mikhail, 39
GPU (Russia), 64
Graiver, David, 99
Gramsci, Antonio, 235

Granger, Bill, 199
Granjo, Antonio, 138
Grass, Günter, 119, 196n, 273
Greece, 309n
Green, Nathaniel, 298
Green parties, 80, 226, 236, 290
Greene, Graham, 196
Greifenhagen, M., 196n
Grey Wolves (Turkey), 294
Griffin, C. S., 52
Grigorovich, Dmitri V. (*i.e.*
  Zhitlovski), 39
Grinevetski (assassin of Alexander II),
  104
Grisel, Georges, 134
Grivas, Colonel George, 310
Gross, Feliks, 168
Gruev, Damien, 17
Grupo des Treze, O (Portugal), 137
Guardian (newspaper), 146
Guatemala, 139, 248, 254, 258, 264,
  274
Guerre est fini, La (film), 189n
guerrilla warfare: distinguished from
  terrorism, 5, 146–8, 300–1
Guevara, Ernesto (Ché), 22–3, 147n,
  241, 244, 246–8, 272
Guide des films anti-imperialistes, 189n
Guillen, Abraham, 251
Gurney, Sir Henry, 21
Gurr, Ted R., 155, 159
Guzman, Abimael, 257

Habash, George, 78, 81, 215, 218–21
Habermas, Jürgen, 119
Hadad, Wadi, 221
Haganah, 81, 117
Haig, General Alexander, 116, 288
Haiti, 274
Halbgespräche (Jean Paul), 192
Hall, Adam, 199
Halperin, Ernst, 82–3
Halsbury, 2nd Earl of, 313
Hamami, Said, 219, 284, 287
Hangmen Also Die (Lang), 189n

Harakat Tahrir Falestin, *see* Fatah, al-
Hardman, J. B. S., 152
Harris, Frank, 177–8
Harris, Richard, 189*n*
Harris, Tom, 198
Harry's Game (Seymour), 199
Harting-Landesen (Okhrana agent), 134
Hartley, Norman, 199
Hawatme, Na'if, 78, 81, 215, 219, 221
Haymarket Square bombing, 19, 52–3, 118
Haywood, Bill, 52
Hazaz, Haim, 191*n*
Headquarters of the Revolution (Libya), 285
Hearst, Patty, 4, 87, 154, 244
Hecht, Ben, 96
Hegel, G. W. F., 53
Heinzen, Karl, 28–9
'Hell' (Russian terrorist organization), 32
Helldorf, Count, 67
Hennebelle, Guy, 189*n*
Henry, Émile, 18, 51, 70, 77, 90–1, 117
Herri Batasuna (Basque group), 224
Herzegovina, 42
Herzen, Natalie, 189*n*
Heydrich, Reinhard, 21, 127, 189*n*
Hidden Target, The (MacInnes), 198
Higgins, Jack, 198–9
History of Babeuf's Conspiracy for Equality (Buonarroti), 26
Hitchcock, Alfred, 188*n*, 202
Hitler, Adolf, 7, 66, 107*n*, 137, 143, 149, 170, 317*n*
Hizb Allah group, 231
Ho Chi Minh, 244
Hodde, Lucien de la, 81–2, 134
Holy Alliance, 26
Honduras, 264
Horkheimer, Max, 2
Household, Geoffrey, 198
HSRA (India), 45–6, 110*n*
Huch, Ricarda, 176

Hughes (IRA thief), 101
Human Factor, The (film), 202*n*
Hungary, 20, 75
Hunt, Leamon, 240
Huntington, Samuel, 152
Husayn, Imam, 230
Hussein, King of Jordan, 284, 288

IMRO (Macedonia), 17, 68, 70; changes in, 131; cruelties of, 84; finances of, 97, 113; international links, 267–8; novels on, 190*n*; strategy of, 76; studies of, 152
India Sociologist, 45
Indian terrorists, 17, 21, 44–8, 64, 233; book bombs, 106; finances, 96; international links, 266–8; mysticism among, 85; popular support for, 117; revival, 139; right-wing, 262; *see also* HSRA; Thugs
Informer, The (films), 188*n*
Informer, The (O'Flaherty), 184
informers, 127–36
INLA (Ireland), 209, 214–15
Inquisition, Holy, 146
intelligence operations, terrorist, 109–11
International Anarchist Congress, London, 1881, 49, 51
International Working People's Association, 52
Invincibles (Ireland), 65
Iqab, Al, *see* Al Iqab
IRA, 89, 147, 207; activities and character, 208–15; analysis of, 168–9; anti-permissiveness, 161; brutality, 92; class composition, 83; effectiveness of, 139; films and books about, 189*n*; finances, 96–8, 102; and ideologists, 120; and informers, 128; internal killings, 96; international links, 266–8; motivations, 159; and Nazis, 268; political activities, 147–8; size of, 94; and Soviet Union, 272; strategy, 211–12; suicides, 231; survival, 95;

IRA—*cont.*
weapons, 104–6; *see also* Northern Ireland; Provisional IRA
Iran: London Embassy incident, 307*n*; revolution (1978), 166; terrorists killed, 7; war with Iraq, 288, 295; *see also* Iranian terrorists
Iran, Shah of (Muhammad Reza Shah Pahlavi), 157, 259–60
Iranian terrorists, 104–6, 115, 139, 259–61, 285; *see also* Shiites
Iraq, 269, 283, 285, 287–8, 295
Ireland's Liberator and Dynamite Monthly (Rallihin), 104
Irgun Zvai Leumi (IZL; Israel), 21; aims, 74; effectiveness of, 139; finances, 96, 102; intelligence, 110; in Knesset, 88, 120; and LEHI, 132; letter bombs, 106; and media, 122; popular support for, 117, 120; prison escapes, 133; size of, 94; strategy of, 76; tactics of, 112
Irish Revolutionary Brotherhood, 96
Irish terrorists, 15,17, 64–5; ethics among,84; literature on, 164–5, 189*n*; and martyrdom, 86; mysticism among, 85; popular support for, 116; prison escapes, 133; tactics of, 76, 111; in USA, 65, 309–10; *see also* Fenians; IRA; Northern Ireland
Iron Guard (Rumania), 20, 68, 74; ethnic groups in, 81; finances, 97; international links, 268; mysticism among, 68, 85–6; splits in, 132
IRP (Islamic Republican Party), 260
Ishutin (founder of 'Hell'), 32–3, 69
Isidore, Saint, 24
Iskra, 39–40, 62
Islamic Amal, 231–2
Ismail, Abdul Fatah, 122
Ismailis, 13
Israel, 123, 139–40, 306–7; athletes murdered, 100, 216, 277, 283, 285, 296; destruction threat, 311; and Lebanon, 296, 304, 321; retaliation by, 311; *see also* Arab terrorists, Palestinian
Israeli zealots, 206*n*
Italian terrorists, 15; character of, 161–2; international links, 267–8; and New Left, 235, 239; right-wing, 262–3; *see also* Fascists; Red Brigades
Italy, 7, 309, 311
Ivanov, Ivan Ivanovich, 32
Ivianski, Z., 168
IWW (Industrial Workers of the World, USA), 19, 52
IZL, *see* Irgun Zvai Leumi

Jabotinsky, Vladimir, 185*n*
Jacks, Oliver, 199
Jackson, George, 244
Jacobins, 11, 26, 38, 191
Jalafe, Manuel, 147*n*
Jalloud, Major Abdul Salam Ahmad, 284
James, Henry, 51, 174–6
Japanese terrorists, 21, 68–9, 74, 82, 85, 204, 262, 319–20; *see also* Red Army, United
Javorov, Pejo, 185
JCAG (Armenian), 228
Jean Paul (*i.e.* J. P. F. Richter), 192
Jefferson, Thomas, 298
Jens, Walter, 119
Jewish terrorism, 22; *see also* Irgun Zvai Leumi; Israel; LEHI
Jews: in Narodnaya Volya, 81; and Nazis, 67
Jihad al Islami, Al, 230–2
John Paul II, Pope, 144, 242, 271*n*, 274
John of Salisbury, 24
Johst, Hanns, 187
Jordan, 154, 267, 276, 287
Josephus, Flavius, 12
Joyce, James, 87, 175, 183
Judas Goat, The (Parker), 198
Judith, 24, 27, 79, 191
June 2 Movement, *see* Bewegung 2. Juni

Juno and the Paycock (O'Casey), 184
Junta of Revolutionary Coordination, 253
Justes, Les (Camus), 178

Kadets (Russia), 37
Kalb, Marvin, 198
Kalyayev, Ivan P., 16, 40, 43, 83
Kamo (S.A. Ter-Petrosyan), 63, 113
Kanal (Wajda), 189*n*
Kapital, Das (Marx), 45
Karakozov, D. V., 33, 44
Karame, 208
Kardos, György, 186
Karmatis, 230
Karpovich (assassin of Boglyepov), 16, 40
Katz, Robert, 198
Katz, William, 198
Kautsky, Karl Johann, 64
Kennan, George, Sr., 83
Kennedy, John F., 73, 170
Kerensky, Aleksandr F., 182
Kern (assassin of Rathenau), 187
Khaled, Leila, 217
Khalturin, Stepan, 104, 189*n*
Khanafani, Ghassen, 190
Kharkin, 88
Khartoum: Saudi Embassy murder, 1972, 220
Khomeini, Ayatollah, 7, 230–2, 243, 259–61, 308
Kibalchich, Serge, 38, 76, 104
Kidnappers, The (Kiefer), 199
Kidnapping of the President, The (Tempelton), 201
Kiefer, Warren, 199
Killer Elite, The (film), 202*n*
Killing of Yesterday's Children (Power), 199
Killinger, Manfred von, 83
Kill the Tsar (Tessendorf), 200
Kinski, Nastassia, 202*n*
Kirov, Serge Mironovich, 64
Klein, Hans Joachim, 79, 98

Klements (of Narodnaya Volya), 191
Kletochnikov, Nikolai, 110
Kluge, Alexander, 201
Klyushnikov, Yu. V., 180
Knipselkrant, De (Dutch journal), 290*n*
Koestler, Arthur, 185–6
Koppel, Ted, 198
Korea, North, 268, 275, 295
Koschemann, Paul, 106*n*
Kovalevsky, Sophia, 180
Kovalski, I. M., 16
Krassin, L. B., 63
Kravchinski, *see* Stepniak, Serge Kravchinski-
Kreisky, Bruno, 283*n*, 287, 306
Krichevski (moderate socialist), 39
Kroesen, General Frederick James, 116
Krol, L. A., 88
Kropotkin, Peter A., 43, 79, 82, 87–8; and propaganda by deed, 49, 51
Kube, Wilhelm, 21
Kugelmann, L., 59
Ku Klux Klan, 14, 111
Kurds, 242
Kutuzov, Mikhail I., 189*n*
Kuwait, 109, 232, 287
Kvaternik (of Ustasha), 267

Lacraus, Os (Portugal), 137
Lamarca, Carlos, 250
Lambert, Derek, 199
Lang, Fritz, 189*n*
Laos, 291–2
Lapierre, Dominique, 198
Laporte, Pierre, 113
Lapua (Finland), 69
Lara, 291*n*
Lara-Bonilla, Rodrigo, 257, 293
Last Summer, The (Huch), 176
Latin America: drug trade in, 291–4; *see also* individual countries
Latin American terrorists, 94, 137–8, 172, 304; activities and character, 245–54; and the army, 76; Catholics

Latin American terrorists—*cont.*
among, 85; class composition, 82–3;
and Communist Party, 64; and New
Left, 203; and press, 122; popular
support for, 120; rural guerrillas,
23; right-wing, 264–5; songs of, 191;
Soviet Union and, 272, 274–5; *see
also* individual countries;
Montoneros; Tupamaros
Lavrov, Peter, 35
Lawrence, T. E., 311
League of Nations, 21, 309, 314
League of the Just, 27
Lebanon, 141, 144, 148, 166, 215, 218,
259, 267, 269, 279, 294, 296, 304,
320
Le Caron, H., 134
Le Carré, John, 197, 201
Legião Vermelha (Portugal), 138
Legionnaires *see* Iron Guard
Lehder, Carlos, 291*n*
LEHI (Stern Gang), 21; aims, 74;
effectiveness of, 139; ferocity, 91;
finances, 97, 102; international
links, 268; and Irgun, 132; in
Knesset, 88; novels on, 180*n*, 186;
Oriental Jews in, 81; and press, 122;
prison escapes, 133; public support
for, 117; size, of, 94; survival, 95;
tactics of, 112
Le Mouel, François, 136*n*
Lenin, Vladimir I., 16, 62, 137, 204,
268, 270
Leskov, Ivan, 117, 179, 193
Lessing, Doris, 196–7
Letelier, Orlando, 109
Letzte Sommer, Der (Huch), 176
Levanter, The (Ambler), 200
Libya, 268–70, 277, 280–6, 295, 311,
319, 321; *see also* Qadhafi, Muamar
al
Libyan People's Bureau, 290
Liebknecht, Wilhelm, 20, 54
Lierena, Mario, 257
Liga Communista Revolucionar, *see*
ETA

Ligne Rouge (journal), 290*n*
Lingg, Louis, 178
Lippincott, David, 199
Lisogub (of Narodnaya Volya), 180
listai, 13
Listok Narodnoi Voli, 35
Lithuanians, 217
Little Drummer Girl (Le Carré), 201
Litvinov, Maxim M., 63
Lockwood, Charles, 97
Lod airport massacre, 220
Lohame Herut Israel, *see* LEHI
Lomasney, Captain William Mackey,
74, 77, 104
Lombroso, Cesare, 68, 87, 151, 160
London terrorism, 18–19, 104
London, Jack, 105
Londonderry, 210–11
Lopatin (Russian emigrant), 60
Lorenz, Konrad, 160
Lorenz, Peter, 124*n*
Lost Honour of Katherine Blum, The
(film), 201
Ludlum, Robert, 198
Lukács, György, 235
Lumumba, Patrice, 244
Lutte Sociale, La, 50
Luxemburg, Rosa, 20, 63, 238
Lynch, Arthur, 267

M 19 (Columbia), 205, 254, 257, 291,
293, 307*n*
Ma'amar, Habib, 101*n*
MacBride, Sean, 88, 90, 267
McCafferty, Captain John, 105
McCartan, Dominic, 199
McCarthy, Joseph, 127
McCarthy, Mary, 196
McClive, James, 200
MacDermott, 'Red' Jim, 134
Macedonian terrorists, 15, 17, 42, 84;
see also IMRO
McGuinness, Martin, 215
Machado, Gerardo, 141
MacInnes, Helen, 198
Mackay, John Henry, 177, 192

McKinley, William, 18, 73
McLaglen, Victor, 188*n*
MacLean, Alastair, 198
MacNally, Leonard, 134
McNamara brothers (Los Angeles
  Times bombers), 19, 118
McParlan, James, 136
MacStiofain, Sean, 209
McWhirter, Ross, 129
Mafia, 14, 291, 294
Mahasabha (Hindu), 47
Mahdi, 267
Mahler, Horst, 78, 238
Mains sales, Les (Sartre), 178–9, 188*n*
Majerova, Marie, 177
Malatesta, Enrico, 48, 188
Malcolm X, 244
Mallarmé, Stéphane, 117
Malraux, André, 186
Malta, 307*n*
MANO (Guatemala), 92
Mano Blanco (C. America), 264
Maño Negra, 52, 114
Manson (Charles) family, 244
Man Who Was Thursday, The
  (Chesterton), 175
Mao Tse-tung, 22, 70, 93, 127, 237,
  244, 255, 304
Marat, Jean Paul, 192
Marcuse, Herbert, 119
Mariana, Juan de, 25
Mariategui, José Carlos, 256
Marighella, Carlos, 77, 87, 148, 241,
  250–3, 272, 295
Markevich, 180
Marshall, William, 199
Martov, Yuri O., 63
Marulande, Manuel, 274
Marx, Jenny, 61
Marx, Karl, 27, 35, 59–62, 152, 156,
  204, 234, 270
Marxism, 29, 59–60, 207, 271
Masaryk, Thomas G., 83, 86
Mason, James, 189*n*
Massey, Gordon (*otherwise* Patrick
  Gordon), 134

Massnahme, Die (Brecht), 178
Massu, General Jacques, 22
Matarese Circle, The (Ludlum), 198
Matteoti, Giacomo, 69
Maura, Romero, 157
Mauriac, Claude, 118
Maximalists, 63, 100, 112, 132
Mazzini, Giuseppe, 27, 43, 45, 236*n*,
  266
media: terrorists and, 121–7, 305
Mehmedbasic (assassin of Franz
  Ferdinand), 267
Meinhof, Ulrike, 4, 78, 87, 118,
  160–1, 196*n*, 237–8; *see also*
  Baader–Meinhof gang
Meinhof–Puig–Antich group, 314
Mein Kampf (Hitler), 55
Mein Leben für Irland (film), 189*n*
Meins, Holger, 237–8
Mensheviks, 63
Merari, Ariel, 231
Meriam, 167
Merkulov (terrorist turned police
  official), 129
Meshcherski, Prince V. P., 180
Metternich, Clemens, Count, 113
Mews, Webster, 198
Mexico, 162, 248
Mezentsev, N. V., 16, 33
Middle East, 8; *see also* individual
  countries
Mikhailov, Alexander, 77–8
Mikhailov, Ivan, 77
Mikhailov, Timofei, 83, 181
Mikhailovists, 132
Mikhailovski, Nikolai, 35
Mills, James, 198
Minimanual (Marighella), 251
MIR (Chile), 247, 253
Mirbeau, Octave, 117
Mirski (terrorist-informer), 129
Mischakim bechoref (Ben Ner), 191*n*
Mitrione, Dan, 189*n*, 249
MLN, *see* Tupamaros
Mogadishu, 307*n*
Mohtashami, Ali Akhbar, 232

Molière, Jean-Baptiste Poquelin, 12
Molly Maguires, 15, 19, 52, 136
Molly Maguires (film), 189*n*
Moluccans, South, 139, 206
Mommsen, Wolfgang, 206*n*
Monarchomachs, 25
Moniteur, 75
Montaldo, Giuliano, 201
Montand, Yves, 189*n*
Montes, Melida, 78, 133*n*
Montoneros (Argentina): class
    composition, 82; and ERP, 132;
    finances, 97, 99; ideology, 205;
    informers in, 132; intelligence,
    111*n*; nature and activities, 248–50,
    252–3; numbers of, 94; repressed,
    254, 264; support for, 301
Moore, Brian, 196*n*
Moravia, Alberto, 118, 196*n*, 273
Mord, Der (*Murder*; Heinzen), 28
Moro, Aldo: abduction and death, 74,
    108, 110, 116, 119, 131, 144, 163,
    200–1, 240, 271
Morozov, Nikolai A., 34–5, 88; and
    systematic terror, 236; and
    tyrannicide, 25; writings, 180*n*, 191
Morucci, Valerio, 131, 240
Moshukhin (Mosjoukine), Ivan, 189*n*
Mossenson, Yigal, 191*n*
Most, Johann, 53–9, 302; drinking, 90;
    and explosives, 50, 53, 104, 313;
    mellows, 87; in prison, 134
Motorman, Operation (Northern
    Ireland), 211
Mountbatten, Louis, 1st Earl, 212
Moyne, Walter E. Guinness, 1st
    Baron, 21
Mujaheddin (Iran), 259–61
Munich: Oktoberfest bomb (1980),
    262; Olympic village murders, 100,
    216, 277, 283, 285, 296
Murder (Heinzen), *see Mord, Der*
Muslim Brotherhood, 21, 120, 280
Musprath (on chemical warfare), 313
Mussawi, Husain, 232
Mussolini, Benito, 66–7, 267

Nada (film), 189*n*
Nagle (Irish informer), 134
Nakanune, 39
Namesti Republiky (Majerova), 177
Na Nozhakh (Leskov), 179
Naples–Milan express train: 1984
    bomb, 262
Napoleon Bonaparte, Emperor, 18,
    36, 101, 104, 109, 137
Napoleon III, Emperor of the French,
    18, 27, 75, 91*n*, 137
NAR (Italy), 262
Narodnaya Rasprava, 31
Narodnaya Volya, 16, 29, 34–40, 74;
    class composition, 82; and Degayev,
    130; dynamite activities, 104; ethics,
    84, 87, 92; finances, 96, 102;
    Marxists and, 60; and Nazis, 68;
    novels about, 180; organization,
    93–4; popular support for, 117;
    programme, 25; size of, 94; and
    Soviet Union, 270; tactics, 75
Narodovoltsy (Russia), 34–9, 62, 70
Nashe Raznoglasiya (*Our Differences*;
    Plekhanov), 60
Nasser, Gamal Abdel, 276, 280, 286
National Arab Youth Organization
    for the Liberation of Palestine, 283
Nationalist Action Party (Turkey),
    242
National Organization of Cypriot
    Fighters, *see* EOKA
Navarro, Sabino, 252
Nazarbeck, Avetis, 43
Nazis, Austrian, 69
Nazis, German, 66–7, 70, 163;
    intelligence, 110; and Nietzsche,
    119
Nechaev, Serge, 30–2, 38, 69; ethics
    of, 90; films on, 189*n*; Jackson on,
    244; Marx and Engels and, 60; and
    Narodnaya Rasprava, 31; in novels,
    181; personality, 79; in prison, 113
Nehru, Jawaharlal, 18, 21
Nekuda (Leskov), 179
'Nero' (Irish informer), 134

Netherlands, 163
Nevski, Alexander, 189*n*
New Left, 203, 206, 235–46
New Order (Ordine Nuovo, Italy), 262
Newton, Huey, 244
New York Times, 154
Nicaragua, 139, 254, 258, 265, 279, 296
Nicosia, 22
Nietzsche, Friedrich, 119
Niger, 282
Nippon Sekigun, *see* Red Army, United
NOA (Guatemala), 92
Nobel, Alfred, 104
Northern Ireland: bribes in, 128; casualties and victims in, 210–12; informers in, 132; and Irish independence, 307; media in, 123, 126; nature of terrorism in, 208–15; terrorist decline, 139; *see also* IRA; Irish terrorists; Provisional IRA
November Man (Granger), 199
Nowhere to go (Leskov), 179
NPA (Philippines), 258
nuclear weapons and installations, 314–20
Nunn, Senator Sam, 316
Nureyev, Rudolf, 202*n*

Oblomov (fictional figure), 193
Obolenski, Count (assassinated), 16
O'Casey, Sean, 183–4, 189*n*
O'Connor, Frank, 184
Odd Man Out (film), 189*n*
Oestreicher, Paul, 273
O'Faolain, Sean, 184
Offering, The (Reid), 199
O'Flaherty, Liam, 174, 184, 188*n*
Ogro (film), 201
Okhrana (Russia), 134–5, 267
Okladski, Ivan, 129
Old Man from the Mountain, 13
Oliveira Marques, A. H. de, 138

'Olson theory', 89
O'Neill, Terence, 208
Only Good German, The (Allbeury), 198
OPEC kidnapping, 1975, 87, 98, 113, 220, 283, 285
Operacion Poncho (Amigo), 200
Operation Emerald (McCartan), 199
Orden de la Muerte (Colombia), 264
Ordine Nuovo, *see* New Order
Organisacion Democratica Nacional (El Salvador), 264
organization, terrorist, 93–6
Organization Consul (Germany), 67, 314
Orly killings (ASALA, 1981), 229
Orsini, Felice, 27, 75, 91*n*, 104, 137, 314
Ossinski, V. V., 180
Our Differences (Plekhanov), 60
Ourselves Alone (film), 189*n*
Over Aevne (Bjørnson), 178

Paeschke (German newspaper editor), 114
Pais, Major Sidonio, 137
Paisley, Ian, 208
Pale Horse, The (Savinkov), 182
Palestine (ancient), 12–13
Palestinian terrorists *see* Arab terrorists, Palestinian; Irgun Zvai Leumi; LEHI; PLO; sicarii
Pallas, Paulino, 91
Palme, Olof, 8, 111, 128, 137, 200
Panama, 154
Panama Paradox (Wolfe), 199
Papandreou, Andreas, 306, 309*n*
Paris (Zola), 176
Paris Commune, 48
Parker, Robert P., 198
Parnell, Charles Stewart, 65
Parsons, Albert, 53
Passion of Richard Thyme, The (Ritner), 199
Paul, Jean, *see* Jean Paul

Pavelic, Ante, 88, 267
PDFLP (Palestine), 81, 83, 215–17,
   219–21
Pearse, Patrick, 236*n*
Peci, Fabrico, 131
Pepe, Guglielmo, 113
Perez, Hector Amodio, 132
Perón, Isabel, 253
Perón, Juan Domingo, 249, 253
Perón, Maria Estella, 254
Perovskaya, Sofia, 4, 35, 76, 82, 87,
   180
personality, terrorist, 76–93
Peru, 6, 139, 147*n*, 248, 252, 255–7
Pestaña, Angel, 52
Peter the Painter, 19
PFLP (Palestine), 81, 83, 101*n*, 205,
   215–17, 219–21, 272, 276–7, 283,
   287*n*
Philippines, 154, 207, 258, 300
Philosophy of the Bomb, The, 45–7
Phoenix (Aricha–Landau), 198
Phoenix Park murders, 17, 61, 65, 77,
   127, 130, 135
Piatka z ulicy Barskiej (A. Ford), *see
   Five from Barska Street, The*
Pichegru (attempted assassin of
   Napoleon), 137
Pigott, Richard, 134
Pilsudski, Joseph, 88, 266
Pimental (murdered US soldier), 290
Pinilla, General Gustavo Rojas, 257*n*
Pinkerton Agency, 135
Pisacane, Camille, 117
Pissarro, Camille, 117
pistoleros, 52
Plato, 24
Plehve, Vyacheslav K., 16, 41, 77,
   105, 135, 137
Plekhanov, Georgi V., 33–5, 41, 60, 62
PLO, 99–100, 103*n*, 120, 210; activities
   and character, 215–22
Plomienie (Brzozowski), 180
Plough and the Stars, The (film), 188*n*
Plough and the Stars, The (O'Casey),
   183

police informers, *see* informers
Polish terrorists, 17–18, 42, 71, 112
Pol Pot, 145–6
Politicheski Terror v Rossi
   (Sternberg), 37
Pontecorvo, Gillo, 189*n*, 201
*Popiol i Diament, see Ashes and
   Diamonds*
Popolo d'Italia, 66
Popovic, Cvetko, 77
popular support (for terrorists),
   116–21
Portell, José Maria, 121*n*
Portuguese terrorists, 137
Possessed, The (Dostoevski), *see Besy*
Power, M., 199
Prevention of Terrorism Act, 1974
   (UK), 145
Price, Anthony, 198
Princess Casamassima (James), 174,
   176
Princip, Gabriel, 77
Principles of Revolution (Bakunin), 30
Proll, Astrid, 78
propaganda by deed, 48–51, 58, 70, 88
Protazanov, Yacov, 189*n*
Protogerov (in IMRO), 77
Protogerovists, 132
Proudhon, Pierre Joseph, 48
Provisional IRA (PIRA), 76, 92, 95, 115,
   132, 140, 162, 209–15, 272; *see also*
   IRA
Przedswit, 39
Pugachov, Yemelyan I., 29

Qadhafi, Muamar al: and Abu Nidal,
   288; advertises for terrorists, 8; and
   Fatah, 221; murder squads, 145;
   and Musa Sadr, 231; payments by,
   98; popular acclaim for, 125*n*; rise
   and activities of, 280–6, 295; and
   Soviet Union, 279*n*
Quebec terrorists, *see* FLQ
Queen of the Nihilists (film), 189*n*

Radek, Karl, 85
Radowitsky, Simon, 20

RAF, *see* Baader–Meinhof gang
Rainbow Warrior (ship), 296
Rajar, Ali, 260
Rajavi, Massoud, 260
Rallihan, Patrick, 104
Rasin, Stenka, 29
Raspe (German terrorist), 78
Rasputina (Social Revolutionary), 85
Rathenau, Walther, 20, 67, 69, 74, 118, 127, 186
Ravachol (François Königstein), 18, 50, 90, 117
'Ravachole' (song), 50
Rawson jail escape (Patagonia), 249
Red Army (Germany), *see* Baader–Meinhof gang
Red Army, United (Japan), 220, 236, 243; cruelty of, 83–4, 95; size of, 94
Redbeard, Ragnar, 55–6
Red Brigades (Brigate Rosse, Italy), 74, 85, 206, 236; confessions in, 131; and criminals, 131; and drug trade, 291, 294; and Euroterrorism, 288, 290; ideology, 302*n*; ineffectiveness, 140; nature and activities, 239–41, 296; and popular support, 118–19, 240, 301; revulsion towards, 163; social background, 263; urban bases, 95
Red Fox (Seymour), 198
Red Legion (Portugal), 138
Red Spears (China), 14–15
Red Weekly, 201
Reed, Carol, 189*n*
Reid, James, 199
Reinstein (tsarist spy), 110
'Rejection Front' (Palestinians), 103*n*, 219
Resnais, Alain, 189*n*
Return to Haifa (Khanafani), 190
Revoliutsionnaya Rossiia, 39
Revolutionary Science of War, The (Most), 54
Revolution Script, The (Moore), 196*n*
Révolution Sociale, La, 50

Revolutionary Arab Palestinian Committees, 283
Rhodes, Cecil, 55
right-wing terrorism, 261–5
Rigi, Dino, 201
Risorgimento, 48
Ritner, Peter, 199
River of Unrest (film), 189*n*
Road of a Nihilist, The (Stepniak), 189*n*
Robespierre, Maximilien M. I., 25, 38
Robinson, Arthur, 188*n*
Rogue Eagle (McClive), 200
Röhl, Klaus Rainer, 196*n*
Rokotilov (Russian terrorist), 104
Roller coaster (film), 202*n*
Romanenko, Gerasim, 35–7
Rome: 1985 airport attack, 145
Roosevelt, Theodore, 55
Ropshin, V., *see* Savinkov, Boris
Rosenberg, Alfred, 55
Rosselli brothers (Italian anti-Fascists), 268
Rossa, Jeremy O'Donovan, 65, 87, 90, 105
Rote Armee Fraktion, *see* Baader–Meinhof gang
Rousseau, Jean-Jacques, 248
Rowe, James, 197
Royce, Kenneth, 199
RSSS (India), 45
Rubanovich (Social Revolutionary), 41
Rubin, Jerry, 186*n*
RUC (Royal Ulster Constabulary), 212
Rudé, George, 156
Rull, Juan, 130
Rumanian terrorists, 75, 85, 106; *see also* Iron Guard
Rummel, R. J., 153
Rusanov (of Narodnaya Volya), 39
Russian Revolution, First, 1905, 63, 111, 137
Russian Revolution, 1917, 165
Russian terrorists, 33, 74; and Lenin, 62; nationalist, 29–30, 33–42;

Russian terrorists—*cont.*
political nationalism, 15;
personalities of, 79, 83; right-wing,
20; *see also* Maximalists; Narodnaya
Volya; Social Revolutionaries;
Soviet Union
Rutenberg, Pinchas, 88
Rysakov (attempted assassin of
Alexander II), 77, 129
Ryss, Solomon ('Mortimer'), 130

Sadat, Anwar, 137, 144, 284
Sadr, Beni, 259
Sadr, Musa, 231
Sahra min Dam (Basisu), 190
Saint-Just, Louis de, 25
Saint Regent (attempted assassin of
Napoleon), 101, 104, 108
Saiqa, As- (Palestine), 215, 269
Saladin, 13
Salengro, Roger, 69
Sallustro, Oberdan, 249
Salomon, Ernst von, 67, 186, 188
Samperi, Salvatore, 201
Samuelson, Victor, 97
samurai, 68
Sandinistas (FSLN), 139, 258
San Michele (film), 189n
Sands, Bobby, 214
Santamaria-Cuadrando, Vice-
Admiral, 292n
Santucho, Mario, 250
Sarajevo assassinations, 1914, 72n, 77,
267
Sartawi, Isham, 219, 284
Sartre, Jean-Paul, 118, 178–9, 188n,
196n, 237, 273
Saudi Arabia, 99–100
Savage Day, The (Higgins), 199
Savarkar, Vinayak D., 44–5
Savasto, Antonio, 131, 137
Savinkov, Boris (V. Ropshin), 38, 40;
and Communists, 88; on killing,
133; prison escape, 133; writings,
174, 180n, 182–3, 193–4
Sawt al Arab, 280

Sazonov, Sergei D., 77, 137
Scascia, Leonardo, 119, 200
Schelling, Thomas, 318
Schiller, Friedrich von, 4, 24, 32
Schlageter, Leo Albert, 85, 187
Schleswig-Holstein, 71
Schleyer, Hans Martin, 110, 114
Schlöndorff, Volker, 201
Schmitt, Carl, 69–70
Schoeters, George, 81n
Schroeder (police agent), 134
Schulze (assassin of Erzberger), 110
Schumann, Jürgen, 126
Schweitzer (Social Revolutionary
weapons expert), 38, 104
Scorpions (Os Lacraus, Portugal), 138
Scrichio, Luigi, 131
Seale, Bobby, 244
Secret Agent, The (Conrad), 129, 175,
195
Secret Agent, The (film), 188n
secret societies, 25–7
Seeckt, Hans von, 68
Segal, George, 202n
Seljuqs, 13
Semashko, N. A., 63
Sempau, Ramón, 196n
Sender, Ramón, 177n
Sendero Luminoso (Peru), 95, 140,
161, 254–7, 291–2
Seneca, 24
Serbian terrorists, 15, 20
Serge Alexandrovich, Grand Duke of
Russia, 16, 83, 135
Serreaux (police spy), 50
Seurat, Georges, 117
Seven Red Sundays (Sender), 177n
Seven Who Were Hanged, The
(Andreyev), 129
17 November Gang (Greece), 309n
Seventh Power, The (Mills), 198
Sexby, E., 3
Seyfeddin, Omar, 190n
Seymour, Gerald, 198–9
Shadow of a Gunman, The (O'Casey),
183

Shah of Iran, *see* Iran, Shah of
Shake Hands with the Devil (film),
189n
Shan United Army, 294
Sharqawi, A., 190
'Shaul' (of LEHI), 132
Shell refinery, Singapore, 243
Shelley, Percy Bysshe, 3
Sherwood (denounces Decembrist
plot), 134
Shiite terrorists, 85, 206n, 219, 230–2,
260–1
Shivaji (seventeenth-century Hindu
rebel), 44
Sibai, Hassan, 13
sicarii, 12, 15
Siete Domingos Rojos (Sender), 177n
Signac, Paul, 117
Sikhs, 7, 133n, 206, 233, 259, 307
Singapore Shell refinery, 243
Singh, Bhagat, 21, 47
Sinn Fein, 120, 122, 215, 224; *see also*
IRA
Sipyagin, D. S., 16, 39
situationisme, 236
Six Day War, 1967, 216
Sjöwall, Maj, 200
Sleeman, William, 13
Social Democrats (Austria), 63
Social Democrats (Germany), 53–4,
61
Social Democrats (Russia), 39, 41
Social Revolutionary Party (Russia),
16, 39–42, 302; and dynamite,
104–5; emigrants, 88; ethics, 83;
finances , 96, 102; intelligence, 110;
international links, 266–7; and
Maximalists, 132; tactics, 76, 113;
see also Fighting Organization
Solinas, Franco, 201
Solovev, V. K., 16
Solzhenitsyn, Alexander, 81n
Somalia, 268
Somoza, Anastasio, 139, 258
Sorel, Georges, 68
Soul on Ice (Cleaver), 244

Sous les yeux de l'Occident (Conrad),
see Under Western Eyes
South Africa, 140, 259
Soviet Union, 227–9, 269; attitude to
terrorism, 270–80, 295–6, 321; and
Libya, 282; *see also* Russian
terrorists
Spanish terrorists, 6, 15; Anarchist,
19–20, 52; in unions, 75; working-
class, 73; *see also* Basque terrorists;
ETA
Spiridonova, Maria, 88
Sri Lanka, 140, 170, 207, 300
ss (Germany), 70
Stack, Sir Lee, 21
Stahl, N., 199
Stalin, Joseph V., 145, 149
Stammheim (film), 201
State of Siege (film), 189n
Stefanovich (of Narodnaya Volya),
180
Steinlen, T. A., 117
Stepniak, Serge Kravchinski-: age of,
77; and Bible, 86; in Herzegovina,
42; Kropotkin and, 49; writings,
32–4, 38, 180, 189n
Stern, Abraham ('Yair'), 91, 186
Sternberg, Lev, 37, 88
Stern Gang, *see* LEHI
Steunenberg, Frank, 19
Stevenson, Robert Louis, 175
'Stockholm syndrome', 125
Stolypin, Piotr Arkadevich, 16, 73,
81n, 130
Storr, Anthony, 158
Story of Seven Who Were Hanged
(film), 189n
Street 8 (Fairbarn), 198
Students for a Democratic Society
(SDS), 236
Stürgkh (Austrian Prime Minister), 63
substate actors, 2
Sudykin (Russian police official), 130
Sunni Muslims, 218
Sun Yat-sen, 14
Sweden, 8

Switzerland, 154
Symbionese Liberation Army (SLA), 94, 131, 171, 244
Syria, 215, 268–70, 275, 283, 285, 287–8, 295, 304, 321
Syrian Popular Party (Lebanon), 287*n*
Szalasi Ferenc, (Führer of Arrow Cross), 81

Tacitus, Cornelius, 12
tactics, terrorist, 112–16
Tailhade, Laurent, 117
Talaat, Pasher Mehmed, 228
Tal, Wasfi, 84, 219–20
Talvar, 46
Tamils (Sri Lanka), 96, 133*n*, 140, 170, 206
Tanter, Raymond, 153
Tate, Sharon, 84
Taviani (film director), 189*n*
Tehran: US Embassy occupied, 115, 124
Tel Aviv, 22
Tel al Za'atar, 218
Tell, Wilhelm, 4, 15, 25, 27, 191
Tempelton, C., 201
terrorism: causes of, 157–60; characteristics of, 5–10, 143–4, 150; definitions, 11, 144–5, 149–50, 152; and guerrilla warfare, 146–8; left- and right-wing, 143, 152; state-sponsored, 145–6, 269–70, 296–7; statistics on, 165–6
Terroristerna (Sjöwall and Wahlöö), 200
Terrorist League of Blood, 69
Tessendorf, K. C., 200
Thailand, 293
Thatcher, Margaret, 212
Theresa, Mother, 143
Thieves in the Night (Koestler), 185
Third Generation, The (film), 201
'third international theory', 281
Thirteen, The (Portugal), 138
Thompson, John T., 97, 106
Thornton, Thomas P., 168

Thugs, 13–15
Tikhomirov, L., 35–7, 40, 181
Tilak, Bal Ganjhadhar, 44–5
Tillesen (assassin of Erzberger), 110
Tilly, C., 156
time bombs, 101, 104
Tito, Josip Broz, 127
To chevo ne bylo (Savinkov), 182
Tocqueville, Alexis de, 152
Todd, Ian, 198
Tolstoy, Leo, Count, 68, 84
TPLA (Turkey), 242
Trepov, Dmitry, F., 33
Trew, Anthony, 198
Trilling, Lionel, 176
Trotsky, Leon, 63–4, 133, 145, 170, 274
TTA, 116
Tunisia, 154
Tupamaros (MLN, Uruguay): class composition, 82; effectiveness of, 138, 141; film on, 189*n*; and ideology, 138; informers in, 132; nature and activities, 248–53; numbers of, 94; as political party, 120*n*; popular support for, 120, 301; psychology of, 162; and Soviet Union, 274, 278; tactics of, 111, 114, 138; West German terrorists and, 203
Turgenev, Ivan S., 180
Türkes, Alpaslan, 242
Turkey, 6, 43, 103*n*, 139, 144, 161, 206, 241–3, 262–3, 275, 308, 311; *see also* Armenian terrorists; TPLA

Ugalde, Martin, 200
Uganda, 268
Ugurlu, 291*n*
Ukrainians, 18, 71, 74
Ulianov, Alexander, 38, 77
Ulysses (Joyce), 175, 183
Umberto I, King of Italy, 18, 21, 137, 306
Umhonto We Sizwe (of ANC), 259
Underground (film), 201

Underground Cities Contract, The (Atlas), 199
Underground Russia (Stepniak), 180
Under Siege (film), 201
Under Western Eyes (*Sous les yeux de l'Occident*; Conrad), 175, 188*n*
Union of Soviet Socialist Republics, *see* Soviet Union
Unita (Angola), 296
United Irishmen, 17
United Nations, 21, 269, 309
United Red Army, *see* Red Army, United
United States of America: attacked in Europe, 289–90; and drug trade, 291–2, 294; and IRA, 210, 309–10; numbers of terrorist victims, 6 and *n*, 8, 166; prohibition on killing enemy leaders, 311; reactions to international terrorism, 298–9; supports counter-insurgents, 296
United States terrorists, 52–3; activities and character of, 243–5; Anarchist, 15, 19; class composition, 82; financing, 98; Most and, 59; and government rewards, 128*n*; public reaction to, 118; in unions, 75; working-class, 73; *see also* Weathermen
URA, *see* Red Army, United
Uritski, Moise S., 16
Uruguayan terrorists, *see* Tupamaros
Ustasha (Croatia), 70; book about, 188; cruelties of, 84; effectiveness of, 139; finances, 97, 102; international links, 20, 139, 267
Ustryalov, G., 180

Vaillant, Auguste, 18, 91, 117
Van Donghen, Kees, 117
Vanguarda Armada Revolucionaria (VAR-Palmares), 248
Vanguardia Popular Revolucionaria (VPR, Brazil), 248
Varma, Krishna, 45
Vasoula (ship), 242

Venezuelan terrorists, 64, 246–8, 252, 274
Venturi, Franco, 38
Vergès, Jacques, 5*n*
Vesco, Robert, 292*n*
Vestnik Russkoi Revoliutsii, 39
Victor Emmanuel II, King of Italy, 27
Vice-President's Task Force on combating terrorism (USA), 144, 312
Victimarios, Los (Sempau), 196*n*
Vienna: 1985 airport attack, 145; *see also* OPEC kidnapping
Vietcong, 75, 141, 143
Vietnam, 21–2, 64, 148, 157
Volodarski, V., 16
Voltaire, François Arouet de, 86

Wahlöö, Per, 200
Wajda, Andrzej, 189*n*
Warner, Senator John William, 316
Way, Peter, 198
weapons, *see* arms and weapons
Weathermen (USA), 80, 84, 98, 202, 236, 243–5
Weede, Erich, 155
Wehrsport Gruppe Hoffmann (W. Germany), 263
Weitling, Wilhelm, 27–8, 79
Werfel, Franz, 227
Wessel, Horst, 84
Western Union of Mineworkers (Federation of Miners, USA), 15, 52, 106
Whisper of the Axe, The (Condon), 199
Wilhelm I, Emperor of Germany, 49
Wilkinson, Paul, 147
Wolfe, Michael, 199
women: as terrorists, 78*n*, 79–80, 225–6
World Revolutionary Union, 31
Wrath of the Lion (Higgins), 198
Wyllie, William Curzon, 45

'Yair', *see* Stern, A.
Yalin-Mor, Natan, 180*n*
Yates, Brock, 198
Yeats, William Butler, 183–4, 194, 236
Yemen, South, 268, 277, 295
Yokhelson, 88
Young Bosnians, 43
Young Egypt, 21
Young Europe, 266
Young India, 46
'Young Russia' group, 32
Yugantar, 44
Yugantar Party (India), 47
Yugoslavia, 17, 147; *see also* Ustasha

Zaichnevski, P. G., 32
ZAPU, 277
Zasulich, Vera, 16, 33, 38, 60, 87*n*, 180
Zealots, 12, 206*n*
Zemlya i Volya, 34
Zenga Kuren (student organization),
  236
Zenker, E. V., 151, 168
Zhelyabov, A. I., 34, 37, 77, 82, 181
Zimmermann, 237
Zinnemann, Fred, 200
Zola, Emile, 51, 117, 176
Zusammenkämpfen (journal), 290*n*